"Tussawehee, Bigfoot, Red Wolf. It is gratifying to see in print the names of people, stories and events that have been part of our oral history. Mr. Ontko's first two volumes of *Thunder Over the Ochoco* have been informative and exciting reading. The Western Shoshone look forward to Volume III, *Lightning Strikes!*"

**Western Shoshone National Council**

"The most factual writing by any author on the Shoshone Nation."

**Raymond D. Yowell**
Western Shoshone Citizen

"I wholeheartedly support the truth as written in Mr. Gale Ontko's series, *Thunder Over the Ochoco*. This writing is most exciting, factual and represents the Shoshone oral history as close as could be expected. He represents our heroes as no other could—dog soldiers such as Red Wolf, Wolf Dog and Has No Horse, men who played such important roles in our history and culture.

**Jack C. Orr (Dogowa)** ● ● ●
Citizen of the Western Shoshone Nation

## THUNDER OVER THE OCHOCO

# LIGHTNING STRIKES!

### Volume III

## GALE ONTKO

**Illustrations by Gale Ontko**

— *A Maverick Publication* —

ISBN 0-89288-265-4

Library of Congress Catalog Card Number: 93-18698

*On the cover:*
Watching the Wagons by Frank C. McCarthy
©1984, The Greenwich Workshop, Inc.
Courtesy of The Greenwich Workshop, Inc.
One Greenwich Place
Shelton, CT 06484-4675
For more information on limited edition prints and books by
Frank C. McCarthy, please call 1-800-577-0666

For additional copies of Gale Ontko's books, contact:
Maverick Distributors
P.O. Drawer 7289
Bend, Oregon 97708
541-382-2728

Published and printed by Maverick Publications, Inc.
P.O. Box 5007 • Bend, Oregon 97708

# DEDICATION

*To Beth, Greg, John and Steve:*
*the present dog soldiers of the Ochoco.*

# TABLE OF CONTENTS

## PART IV—Lightning Strikes!

## PART V — Dying Embers

## APPENDICES

# ACKNOWLEDGMENTS

*The hills on which the cattle graze*
*were once the battle-ground where men,*
*Far from the haunts of womankind,*
*won or were beaten—life throbbed then*
*With meanings all unknown to-day.*

**Arthur Chapman**
*The Changed Hills*

The author-historian, Paul Bailey, once observed that no man builds a book entirely alone and that statement fits this volume like a well-worn glove. *Lightning Strikes!* is the account of some Indians who drew a life sentence for the unpardonable sin of blocking the economic progress of the United States and specifically the commercial expansion of the state of Oregon. Although I gained valuable information from descendants of Snake warriors; regular and volunteer army personnel; civilian army scouts; and the first white settlers in the Ochoco Valley; to get the full story I had to rely heavily on other sources of information. These would include Oregon Legislative Documents, county records, U.S. House and Senate Executive Documents, Bureau of Indian Affairs reports, War Department reports, military correspondence, and soldier's personal diaries. I am also deeply grateful for all the help received from staff members of the State Archives, Salem, Oregon; the National Archives, Washington, D.C.; the Library of Congress; the Bancroft Library, Berkeley, California; and the various county libraries I visited throughout the western states.

Many people helped in finding and providing the photographs that appear in this volume of *Thunder Over the Ochoco*. I would especially like to thank: Keith McCoy, Carrol Howe, Jon & Donna Skovlin, John Griffin, Katherine Ferl (Lake County Historical Society), Kay Fossey (Wind River Reservation), Sara Gooch (Modoc County Historical Society), U.S. Senate Historian Matthew Cook, William Alley (Southern Oregon Historical Society), Jim and Peg Iler, Wayne Rich (Shasta Historical Society), Weslie Welcome (Harney County Historical Society), Lee Brumbaugh (Nevada Historical Society), William Kooiman (San Francisco Maritime Museum), Joyce Justice (Seattle Regional Office, National Archives), Jo Anne Cordis (Central Oregon Community College), Judy

Gage (Oregon Sheriffs' Association), Mary Stillwell (Cascade Locks Museum), Marcus Robins (Portland city archivist), Tom Robinson (Portland Photo Research Group), Pat May (Old Wasco County Pioneers), Paula Knuttner (Fort Dalles Museum), Gene Luckey, David Wendell (Oregon State Archives), Melissa Minthorn (Tamustalik Cultural Institute, Umatilla Tribe), Gloria Meyer, and Ellen Kuniyuki Brown (archivist, Texas Collection, Baylor University).

*Gale Ontko*
March 1997

# INTRODUCTION

*What tall and tawny men were these,*
*As somber silent as the trees*
*They moved among!*
*And sad some way,*
*Yet not with sorrow borne of fear,*
*As the shadows of their destinies*
*They saw approaching year by year.*

**Joaquin Miller**
Canyon City Indian Fighter, 1864

With the signing of the 1855 treaties, Oregon Territory knew it had solved its Indian problems and by 1858 the native population, with or without its consent, was being herded like sheep onto government reserves. It was, said the white shepherds, for their own good. Some—specifically the obstinate Shoshoni—failed to see it in that light. No problem. The white chiefs in Salem could foresee no pressing need to occupy the land they inhabited and should the need arise, the Shoshoni could be dispatched in a moment of small consequent. Then accompanied by the symphonic boom of civil war guns, gold—ton upon ton of the precious metal—was discovered in eastern Oregon. . . the heart of Shoshoni land. The moment of small consequence had arrived. Regular army troops who had been half-heartedly irritating eastern Oregon since 1858 were called to a higher cause and Oregon—eager to capitalize on the gold strikes—joyfully threw her home guard into the field of honor. The Oregon Volunteers charged into the Shoshoni front fearful only that the campaign would be so short-lived that they wouldn't receive the glory and recognition that they thought they so richly deserved. Years of privation, heartache and death would pass. The Civil War would come and go but the Shoshoni still held on. For a bankrupt nation it was a burden they didn't need. The War Department with thousands of Civil War veterans looking for new opponents to conquer threw its muscle into the Oregon cause and the battle cry of freedom echoed across the land.

# THUNDER OVER THE OCHOCO

# LIGHTNING STRIKES!

## Volume III

# Part IV

## LIGHTNING STRIKES!

# LIGHTNING STRIKES!

## THE SHOSHONI WAR AND ITS EFFECT
## ON THE SETTLEMENT OF EASTERN OREGON

*This is one of the blackest councils ever held on the Pacific
coast. The scalp and war dance go on the night through. . . .*

**Major John Owen**
Snake War Council, 1858

Roaming the lush foothills and timbered ridges of eastern Oregon were
numerous bands of Shoshoni Indians known and feared as the Snake war tribes.
These proud mountain people were uniting under the leadership of the war chief
Has No Horse, and backed by such men as Broken Knife, Big Man, Pony Blanket
and War Spirit. Soon Has No Horse's dog soldiers would be recognized as the best
light cavalry the United States army had yet encountered. Oregon Territory had
been studiously but ineffectively trying to ignore this grim reality since 1857, the
year the Shoshoni formed the Paviotso Confederacy and graduated from sporadic,
uncoordinated raids into concentrated hostility. The Shoshoni who came forward
with proposals for action were followed by those who did not know which way to
turn. These followers believed that their chosen leaders possessed supernatural
powers which made them indestructible. Bullet proof or not, the war chiefs would
stall settlement of the Ochoco for another decade. In 1858, Wolf Dog, head chief
of the Snake war tribes and his military commanders declared full scale war against
the American invaders with every intention of winning . . . or dying.
They died.

*He and his warriors were certainly as fine-looking a lot of
pirates as ever cut a throat or scuttled a ship. . . .*

**Captain John Gregory Burke**
Third U.S. Cavalry, June 1876
In reference to Has No Horse

3

# SHOSHONI DECLINE OF INFLUENCE

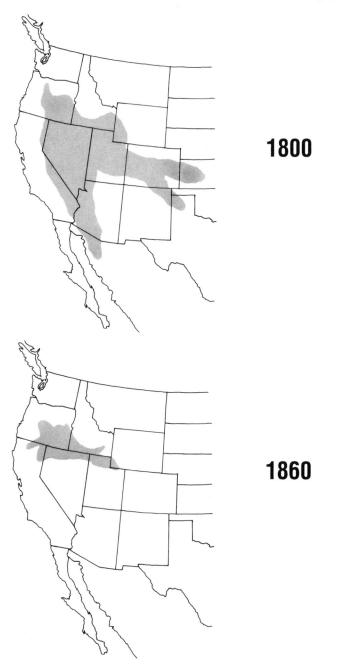

1800

1860

# CHAPTER 88

# GHOST PEOPLE

*The mass of mankind has not been born with saddles on their backs, nor a favored few booted and spurred, ready to ride them legitimately by the grace of God.*

**Thomas Jefferson**
President of the United States

By 1850, Oregon was experiencing the uneasy feeling that all was not well with her squalid native population. All Indian tribes were reacting in a surly manner but the least cooperative were . . . "those damn murderous Snakes!"

Shoshoni outriders had all but stopped wagon movement along the Oregon Trail. At the same time other Shoshoni hostiles had swung into northern Nevada and Utah where they were sniping at both Oregon and California emigration. These mountain bandits were operating out of the *Ochiho Gaiya*, Land of the Red Willow . . . legendary and descriptive Shoshoni name for interior Oregon, a territory where no white man had dared to settle.

In shape, the Ochoco resembled a gauntlet tossed across the heart of Oregon. Bordered on the west by the Deschutes River; on the north by the John Day and Powder Rivers; on the east by the Snake River; and on the south by the Great Basin, the Ochoco encompassed the southern Blue Mountains. Its outer perimeter—flanked by snow-capped peaks, waterless plateaus and awesome river gorges—promised hell to weary travelers. Its beautiful interior—crisscrossed with clear mountain streams, carpeted with grass and teaming with wildlife—was a storehouse unequaled in the Pacific northwest. Here, was the last stronghold of the Shoshoni nation . . . an inland empire ruled by the powerful Snake war tribes whose hunting grounds straddled the transition zone between plains hunter, coastal fisherman and desert seed gather.

Their predatory raids from the Dakota plains to the Pacific coast had gained the Shoshoni an unsavory reputation, for, with the acquisition of the horse, these mountain people transformed from timid, down-trodden farmers into a wild and dangerous group constantly in search of bloody conquests. By 1620, the Shoshoni controlled a 240,000 square mile area known to them as *Oyerungun*, Land of Peace and Plenty . . . a vast territory larger than most European countries. They were brutal warriors known in their own language as *Saydocarah*, The Conquerors and

5

feared by all western tribes as *Shoshonee*, the Enemy. At the close of the 17th century, the Shoshoni were confronted by an equally barbaric foe . . . the European. Through these people, the Shoshoni became known and hated as Snakes . . . the Killers.

Most Europeans were referred to as *tavibo* by the Shoshoni which simply meant "white man." But the Americans—now on a collision course with a Shoshoni war lance—were called *soo yawpi* . . . the Ghost People. This name had nothing to do with the coloring of the yankees' skin. When American first met Shoshoni, he always wanted to "swap" for furs, for horses, for women, for anything of value which Shoshoni might possess. Since the word "swap" in the Shoshoni language means "ghost," it soon evolved that Americans were Ghost People.

Some of the first Europeans to be visited by the Shoshoni on their far-reaching raids were the British. These Hudson's Bay employees believed—and rightly so—that the Shoshoni could present a problem to future expansion into the Pacific northwest. Therefore, they must be exterminated. Having formulated a plan for Shoshoni annihilation, the British armed other Indian nations with firearms and gave detailed instructions on how "to wipe out the Snakes." The red collaborators didn't succeed, but not for lack of trying.

In a 25 year span of dispassionate destruction, the Shoshoni nation was split to the core and bleeding like a wounded buffalo. According to David Thompson's *Narrative*, this slaughter began as early as 1787. Hodge, in his *Handbook of American Indians*, confirms this mass homicide, stating that when Lewis and Clark arrived in the Pacific northwest . . . "the Shoshoni had been driven into the mountains (Blues) to escape the Siksika (Blackfeet) who possessed firearms."

Many Shoshonean tribes—notably the Great Basin family groups—were so badly demoralized that by 1812, they had degenerated into pitiful, horseless wanderers known as Maggot Eaters, People Without Meat and Earth Eaters . . . descriptive names sadly bestowed by their own kinsmen. Because of the advancing Americans, these unfortunates would never recover from the British inspired Blackfoot-Sahaptin invasion. As the Paiutes or Digger Indians (a collective name given them by their white brothers), they so confused early explorer-historians that it is almost impossible through present research to separate these pathetic Paiute outcasts from the undefeated members of the Shoshoni nation. The Shoshoni had a better way of identifying them. If mounted and hostile they were Shoshoni; if afoot and starving they were *Shoshokos*, "walking people," and as such were called Earth Eaters because they couldn't hunt big game.

They—the Shoshoni proper—were composed of a tough segment who survived the death plot. Under the leadership of Owitze, Man With a Twisted Hand and a gaunt young brave called Gotia, The Red Wolf, they emerged as the dreaded Snake war tribes. These people—forged in the smoke and flames of a smooth-bore musket—were more cautious, more aloof, more vindictive, more deadly than before.

For the next 30 years, European and Shoshoni attempted to ignore each other with varying degrees of success. To further intensify an already explosive situation, sensuous Shoshoni maids presented irresistible temptation to that breed of American called "Mountain Man." If caught in the act of love, he died. So did his French and Canadian counterparts. During the peak of the fur trade era, the Snake country expeditions became the most hazardous undertaking in the 150 year history of the fur trade . . . a suicide mission offset only by the knowledge that the sorties into Shoshoni hunting grounds were by far the most profitable to the fur companies. And more white men would die to bolster the economy of Great Britain, Russia and the United States.

In the fall of 1837, Twisted Hand fell victim to a trapper's bullet and Red Wolf—father-in-law to Milton Sublette, Joe Meek and Robert Newell—inherited the shaky position of head chief of the Snake war tribes. Shortly thereafter, the world fur market collapsed but in passing it saw the advent of the American settler.

By topographic necessity, the American trail to the Willamette Valley entered the outer limits of Red Wolf's domain at Hell's Gate rock on the Snake River. Ironically, it left Shoshoni territory at Hell Gate Canyon on the Columbia. In the beginning, the Shoshoni interfered with traffic along this route only when errant wagon trains approached the inner Ochoco; and the early migration honored this arrangement by staying clear of interior Oregon.

This tacit agreement went into effect at the start of emigration, for the natural wagon road between the Snake River Crossing and the Willamette Valley settlements lay within the boundaries of the Ochoco. However, at the Ochoco's eastern border, the Oregon Trail swerved sharply to the north and inched its tortured course over the northern shoulder of the massive Blue Mountains carefully maintaining a wide interval between the rutted wheel tracks and Shoshoni land to the south. The southern emigrant route known as the Applegate Trail maintained an equal distance passing some 130 miles south of the Blues across the barren Black Rock Desert and slipping into the Cascade Range in the vicinity of Klamath Lake. As the years rolled by so did the wagon trains in ever-increasing numbers. With the passage of each homestead party bearing ever closer to the Ochoco, the Shoshoni became more aware of their uncertain tenure as property holders.

In the spring of 1852, Red Wolf was struck down by cholera. In an internal power struggle which split the Shoshoni nation from chest to pelvis, the tough Hoonebooey warrior, Weahwewa—Wolf Dog—seized the reins of command from the popular Tussawehee brave Washakie—Gourd Rattler. In a huff, Gourd Rattler—taking half of the fighting men of the Snake war tribes with him—galloped into the Wyoming country where he joined forces with the Ghost People.

In a swift move to counteract this loss, Wolf Dog—finalizing an agreement initiated by Red Wolf—united the mounted Paiutes and Utes with the Snakes forming the Paviotso Confederacy. For his war chiefs, he chose three of the toughest dog soldiers in the Shoshoni alliance; Has No Horse, War Spirit and Bad Face soon to be recognized by the Americans as Ochiho, Paulina and Winnemucca. These warriors would lay siege to portions of four western states. With the change of command, anyone—white or red—who ventured across Wolf Dog's established deadline was subject to punishment. Nevertheless, the Americans—oblivious to the mounting danger and flaunting their constitutional rights like a banner—kept pushing nearer and nearer to Shoshoni hunting grounds clamoring for more Indian land as their just reward. No more did the Ghost People wish to swap. They were taking.

Territorial administrators cast integrity aside to satisfy this growing demand. Indians once friendly to Oregonians suddenly found themselves classified in the same unwanted category as the Snakes. The Snakes emerged as bone-crushing wolves. Farmers and merchants were forced into the unskilled role of mountain riflemen. This was the situation in Indian infested Oregon Territory at the dawn of the Civil War.

# CHAPTER 89

# WHITE BEARD

*Death is on our trail!*

**Pile of Clouds**
Shoshoni medicine man

Prior to his death, Yellow Serpent—in a deft political move never fully understood even by the men involved—united the Walla Wallas with the Snake war tribes. It was an alliance in name only for the Walla Wallas, although backed by the dog soldiers during the Yakima War, never took up arms to aid their Shoshoni allies. In fact, just the opposite would happen, Now, in the summer of 1858, the Walla Wallas were being herded onto the Warm Springs Reserve like a flock of sage hens where they appeared eager to join forces with the Klickitats and Wascos in their acceptance of white domination. Old enmities were quickly rekindled between the former partners, for the Snakes loathed the Confederated Tribes of Warm Springs as much as they hated the Americans. Has No Horse swore that Woman's Shirt—tough old war chief of the John Day Walla Wallas—would regret this change of allegiance to his dying day. Unknown to either man, this would not be long in coming.

Adding to the Snakes' poor humor, Col. Lawrence Kip with 240 artillerymen, 16 wagon-mounted howitzers and 60 mounted infantrymen armed with .54 caliber Sharps rifles moved east of the Cascades in early August on orders from Gen. Newman Clarke to keep the Applegate Trail open to emigration "no matter what it may cost." [1] Pushing deep into Snake hunting grounds, Col. Kip set up a security guard the entire length of the trail from Raft River in Idaho to Klamath Lake in south central Oregon.

Bad Face and Little Rattlesnake quickly voiced their disapproval to Wolf Dog, demanding immediate action. As badly as Wolf Dog needed supplies, he was not foolish enough to send his warriors against army howitzers. And so, for the first time since its opening in 1846, the southern emigrant route was immune to

---

1    The *Sacramento Union* was the first to leak this information on August 23, 1858. It was later confirmed by Col. Kip in his *Army Life on the Pacific*, pp. 16-18. For this push on Wolf Dog, he had three batteries of artillery from San Francisco; one battery from Fort Umpqua, Oregon; and one company of infantry detached from Fort Jones, California.

Shoshoni attack. There were easier targets for the Shoshoni to concentrate on and they would be equally as lucrative as the southern traffic.

Rumor trickled in from the Mountain Gap People that Col. Wright was busily engaged chasing Yakima, Coeur d'Alene and Nez Perce fugitives around Washington Territory leaving his main charge, the Oregon Trail, virtually unguarded. A tactical error on his part. Has No Horse and Big Man swung eastward to pick up provisions while Paulina—the War Spirit—readied his braves for a surprise raid to the west.

During this period, hunting parties coming in from the Dakota plains reported that things were going poorly for all the Shoshoni related tribes. On September 11, 1858, just four days after Col. Wright had broken the back of the Confederated Tribes of Middle Oregon, Gen. William Harney—in his last official act as Commander of the Military Department of the Platte—ordered the Wichita Expedition into the wind-swept plains. Their mission was to insure that the grand opening of the Butterfield stage route would happen without Indian interference. On October 10, the first overland link between St. Louis and San Francisco occurred as scheduled and in so doing, announced the beginning of the end of the Comanche tribes.[2]

North of the Canadian River, the Wichita Expedition launched its first murderous attack. In the bleak depression of Little Robe Creek, 76 Comanche warriors took their last look at the Kansas prairies including the invincible Iron Jacket whose coat of Spanish armor was said to be impervious to rifle bullets. Another white man's lie! By December 1859, the Children of the South Wind were unwilling residents of the Great White Father's reservation.

Brig. Gen. William Selby Harney—southern aristocrat, flamboyant red-haired veteran of the Black Hawk and Mexican wars—was a man's man. Darling of the American public, he knew how to handle Indians although in the process his hair would turn white as Strawberry Mountain in mid-winter. Less than three years before his destruction of the Comanches, he had "crushed the Sioux uprising on the Platte." At the time, President Pierce—a compassionate man who had the best interests of his native population at heart—wanted nothing more than to restore some semblance of order when he recalled Harney from leave in Paris and sent him west with 1,200 soldiers to awe the Indians. And awe them he did, at Little Thunder's Sioux village near Ash Hollow on the Oregon Trail.

Little Thunder had not received word of Harney's order instructing friendly tribes to cross the south fork of the North Platte if they didn't want to be annihilated. Impatiently, Harney sent his cavalry around to the rear of the encampment. He himself approached the village under a flag of truce, parlayed until he felt the

---

2    The Overland Stage Co. was now boasting the longest stage route in the world. The official distance between St. Louis and San Francisco was 2,757.5 miles with an average travel time of 23 days, 20 hours.

cavalrymen were in place and then told the Indians "to fight!" It was quick and vicious . . . five dead soldiers to 86 Sioux killed, 70 women and children captured.

Harney's Department of the Platte—both solvent and the terror of the plains Indians—received national acclaim, bordering on adulation for sweeping the eastern Oregon Trail clear of unnecessary road-blocks. Clarke's Department of the Pacific—debt-ridden and ineffectual because of political opposition in the Willamette Valley—reeled under the blast of public criticism because of Wolf Dog's repeated attacks on western emigration.

Two days after Harney launched his attack on the Comanches, the Secretary of War—goaded into action by a hostile press—gave the order to sub-divide the Department of the Pacific into the military districts of Oregon and California: a grim admission that the Shoshoni were worthy opponents deserving of a concentrated military offensive. It was now up to the army to select a man tough enough to handle the Oregon command.

On October 29, 1858, "White Beard" Harney, scourge of the Platte, rode in from the  high plains to relieve Brig. Gen. Newman Clarke of his western command. Riding with him was the portly Father Jean Pierre DeSmet, who had been appointed a U.S. army chaplain to aid Harney in quelling the Shoshoni. Father DeSmet was no newcomer to Oregon, having started his first work here in 1840. Presumably, the good father was to prepare the heathen for a face to face encounter with the Sky Father before Harney directed them onto the Sundown Trail—although it was said that DeSmet was "not always tolerant to those of a different faith." Neither was he well-versed in dealing with the Shoshoni, who adamantly refused to seek his services during his earlier tenure in Oregon Territory; a slight which caused DeSmet to sarcastically comment, "they are called Snakes because in their poverty they are reduced like reptiles to the condition of digging in the ground and seeking nourishment from roots." Apparently, camas roots were not as appetizing as potatoes to the roly-poly priest.

On his trek into Oregon, Harney made a thorough inventory of men and equipment stationed at the three fortresses east of the Cascade Mountains. He was favorably impressed with what he found—leaving no doubt that Gen. Clarke was a much better strategist than the Oregonians, press and bureaucrats had lead the public to believe.

Harney's first stop was at Fort Walla Walla—the easternmost bastion of the Oregon Military District—and he was elated. Post Commander Col. George Wright—West Point, Class of '22—was a man of Harney's temperament. Wright permitted no foolishness from the native Oregonians and they "damn well better believe it." Less than three weeks before Harney's arrival, he had given them a lesson in the meaning of loyalty. When rounding up the Columbia tribes for placement on the reservation, Wright was well aware that the Walla Wallas had made a clandestine arrangement of sorts with the Snakes. The fact that they were being herded onto the Warm Springs Reserve and pledging support to the United

States government was not enough. They had made the fatal mistake of condoning hostile acts by virtue of Yellow Serpent's attempted collusion with Wolf Dog. Yellow Serpent had already paid the supreme penalty but to insure his tribesmen didn't entertain like thoughts, Wright ordered them to appear at Fort Walla Walla for further counseling. Still under suspicion was the old war chief, Woman's Shirt, now leader of the Walla Wallas.

Upon arrival at the fort, Wright asked those who had been involved in past hostilities to stand. Finally, 35 warriors stoically rose to their feet. Wright scanned them for perhaps a minute, then pointed his finger in a random selection. Woman's Shirt's luck had run out. As Wright pointed, armed guards seized the four men indicated and escorted them to the main stockade gate. There, in full view of their comrades-in-arms, they were "hanged by the neck until dead!" It was the Sabbath, October 10, 1858 . . . the same day the Butterfield Stage thundered into San Francisco on its maiden voyage.[3]

Wright had little fear of retaliation from the Indians because Fort Walla Walla, guardian of the Oregon Trail, was well fortified with four wagon-mounted-howitzers ready to roll, backed by 80 cavalrymen and 130 mounted infantrymen armed with Sharps rifles and 65 artillerymen packing frontier model .44 Colts with an effective range of 75 yards.

Northwest of Fort Walla Walla sat Fort Simcoe under command of the hot-headed southerner, Major Robert Garnett. His troops consisted of 195 mounted riflemen of the 4th U.S. Infantry Regiment who were guarding the Yakima Reservation. On a side note, one company under the command of Lt. George Crook was manning a "20-canoe navy" exploring the Columbia River.[4] Fort Simcoe was an easy ride from Fort Walla Walla so this force was sufficient to protect that area in view of the fact that no major emigration routes were involved and the Shoshoni had never been known to operate north of the Columbia River. This, coupled with the knowledge that all Washington Territory tribes were firmly ensconced on reservations left little room for fear.

Some 130 miles down river on the south bank of the Columbia, Capt. Thomas Jordan—operating out of Fort Dalles—covered both the extreme western end of the Oregon Trail and the Applegate Trail. Under his command were 200 riflemen of the 9th U.S. Infantry Regiment; one battery of 3rd U.S. Field Artillery and one troop of 1st U.S. Cavalry. In the field, under the command of Col. Kip were four batteries of 3rd U.S. Artillery and a company of 4th U.S. Infantry patrolling the Applegate Trail. Because of his positioning, Captain Jordan could serve as quick backup for either Forts Simcoe or Walla Walla.[5]

---

3     Glassley, *Pacific Northwest Indian Wars*, p. 150; Lewis, "Treasures of the American West," *The Book of the American West*, pp. 121-23.

4     Hart, *Old Forts of the Northwest*, p. 141.

5     U.S. House Executive Document 2, Vol. II, Pt. II, p. 78, 35th Congress, 1st Session.

Harney was confident these troops could handle any possible Shoshoni disturbance. However, in the back of his mind, he resolved to establish another outpost. In 1857, Harney had petitioned his superiors to establish a garrison at or near the Hudson's Bay fort on the Boise River which was inadequately protected from either Fort Walla Walla or Fort Laramie and this pocket was Wolf Dog's main area of attack. Then it had been a thorn on his extreme western flank—now it was a hole on his eastern perimeter.[6]

When Harney was detailed to Oregon, he felt he had a reputation to uphold and he was a very shrewd politician. His first official act as Department Commander, endearing him to the public, was the re-opening of eastern Oregon territory to settlement. This order went into effect October 31, 1858, two days after his arrival at Fort Vancouver. This reversal of Gen. Wool's closure occurred simultaneously with the rumor that Oregon was to be admitted into the Union and granted the full rights of statehood.

The Snakes, their savage distrust stirred by this retraction, surmised that the years of waiting for the white invasion were about to be over. In anticipation of new aggression, they deemed it prudent to jog the Oregonian's memory one more time that Wolf Dog meant business when he ordered the Ghost People to stay out of the Ochoco. In the minds of the Shoshoni, the most effective warning was a violent one. This would also come at a time when Oregon was struggling with the issue of slavery—a matter of grave political concern should the territory be granted statehood.

---

6     U.S. House Executive Document, 1, 34th Congress, 3rd Session.

# THE INNER OCHOCO

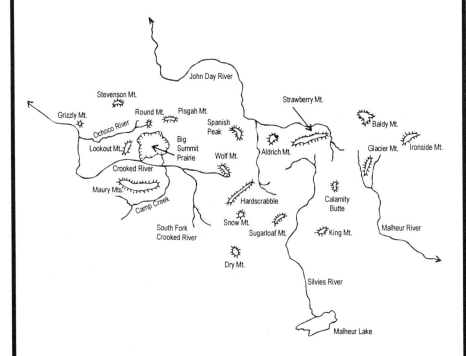

John Day River

Stevenson Mt.

Strawberry Mt.

Grizzly Mt.

Round Mt. Pisgah Mt.

Baldy Mt.

Ochoco River

Spanish Peak

Lookout Mt.

Big Summit Prairie

Aldrich Mt.

Glacier Mt. Ironside Mt.

Wolf Mt.

Crooked River

Maury Mts.

Hardscrabble

Calamity Butte

Malheur River

Camp Creek

Snow Mt.

South Fork Crooked River

Sugarloaf Mt.

King Mt.

Dry Mt.

Silvies River

Malheur Lake

# THE OCHOCO IN RELATION TO OREGON

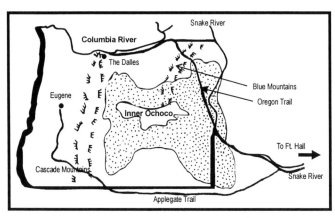

Snake River

Columbia River

The Dalles

Blue Mountains

Eugene

Oregon Trail

Inner Ochoco

To Ft. Hall

Cascade Mountains

Snake River

Applegate Trail

# CHAPTER 90

# SOLD . . . FOR THREE HORSES!

> . . . the long hot march by ashen plain,
> The burning trail by lava bed,
> But on and on their mothers led,
> If but to find a place to die. . . .

**Joaquin Miller**
Editor, *Democratic Herald*, Eugene City
(a pro-slavery newspaper)

The sun—a blazing ember in the cloudless sky—scorched the barren surface of the high desert plateau. A searing wind shuffled the ashen dust in choking protest. Circling buzzards watched in anticipation as the staggering line of men, women and children forced their way through the clawing sage. Their captives beat them unmercifully in an effort to hasten the pace for they were deep in Shoshoni country and they had no desire to be seen by a mounted patrol. Their goal at this point in time was Klamath Lake, some 75 miles to the southwest. Once they reached this sanctuary, the slavers had to make a difficult decision.

They could travel the ancient trade route up the eastern face of the Cascade Range to the Columbia River . . . a distance of 240 miles and take the risk of running head-on into a Snake hunting party; or they could prod their captives over the twisted lava fields of the southern Cascades and travel down the Willamette River to Oregon City, a trek of 250 miles. Odds were, they could make a much better profit on their merchandise on the Columbia but the chances of reaching Oregon City with their catch was infinitely better, though technically, they would be hawking their wares in the free Territory of Oregon. Either way, the Paiute captives had little to gain for they would end up in the valley settlements or a Wasco village where they would become unwilling servants for whatever drudgery their newly acquired masters might desire.

The Shoshoni raided, they plundered, they fought to the death but they never lowered themselves to the base position of slavers. Five hundred years of living in shackles obedient to the Columbia and Missouri tribes had instilled in their minds an intense hatred toward human bondage. Had anyone told the Snakes that Oregonians supported the Union on the slavery issue, they would have laughed in their face. Since 1850, they had to be on constant alert to protect their destitute relatives from capture and enslavement. The Americans along with the Wasco, Klickitat and Walla Walla had made traffic in human merchandise a very profitable business. So lucrative that Modoc and Klamath slavers would risk death to sneak onto Shoshoni soil to hunt Paiutes.

By 1858, it was a sure bet that any Paiute had a sister, brother, wife, husband, son, or daughter sold into slavery, for the two largest slave markets west of the Mississippi River were located in Oregon. One on a rocky shelf above the Willamette River in Oregon City and the other on a wind-swept bluff east of The Dalles City overlooking the Columbia River.[1] At either location an auctioneer had to bellow to make himself heard over the roar of the rushing water ". . . I have a young brave and his woman," goes an old report of a slave sale. "There are four kids, too, but you can take 'em all or buy 'em separate. . . ."

The markets flourished between 1840 and 1860. Here Modoc and Klamath slavers rubbed shoulders with American, Chinook and French buyers. An Oregon missionary wrote to an eastern friend . . . "today, a large party of Klamath Indians, fierce and war-like, from the south, came in with about 20 slaves and sold most of them. Some, I am informed, were sold for three horses each. . . ."

Apparently these were prime laborers for the common payment for a Paiute slave was either a horse, six beaver skins or two blankets. Buyers at the Celilo market were mainly Wascos, Klickitats and Walla Wallas. At the 11th Street market in Oregon City, they were primarily American and Canadian. The Paiutes sold into slavery received very cruel treatment, poor food, miserable quarters and did the most menial labor.[2] When hurt or sick, they received no treatment and frequently died in agony.

Aside from the fact that Paiutes were a convenient supply for the slave markets, there were several reasons for using them instead of Negroes. The most important was economics. Judge George Williams—a loyal southerner but also a strong anti-slavery advocate—in his "Free State Letter" to the editor of the *Oregon Statesman*, July 28, 1857, reminded the settlers that "a good slave (Negro) in Oregon would be worth $2,000. Now the interest on this sum at 20% would be $400 per annum which would hire a white man for 10 months at $40 a month and you wouldn't be bothered with taking care of him. Besides," he argued, "with a Negro slave you must tell him what to do and whip him if he fails to do so."

---

1    For more details see Peter Thompson's "Slave Trade Once Flourished," *The Oregon Journal*, files of 1961.

2    The Ford House in the old town of Ellendale, Polk County, Oregon, with slave quarters in the rear was still standing in 1979. Colonel Nathaniel Ford, who came to Oregon in 1844, brought with him three Negro slaves. Two of the slaves were married and had children. They apparently won their freedom in 1852 and went to live near Jim Nesmith, commander of the volunteer force during the Yakima War and a strong abolitionist. Ford refused to give up the Negro couples children until finally forced to do so when the parents (most likely through the help of Nesmith) fought their case before Federal Judge George H. Williams in 1853.

Another problem with importing Negroes was the provision set by law that slaves had to be manacled to be taken by the trader from one slave state to another. It was rather difficult to safely transport them thousands of miles across the wilderness with . . . "feelings of hatred and revenge rankling in their dark bosoms." Obviously, they wouldn't be too friendly towards a man who bought them on speculation for resale in Oregon Country. And finally, there was always the possibility of escape once in Oregon. As Judge Williams warned . . . "eastward dwell numerous Indian tribes [Shoshoni] to whose welcome embrace a slave might fly and be safe. No fugitive slave law would avail them or friends of the master be found to assist in his [the slave's] recapture."

In view of this, Paiutes were a good investment. Transportation costs were non-existent. No risks need be incurred by white traders for they could hoodwink local natives into doing the dangerous work and the purchase price was right. Also, should one escape there was an unlimited supply east of the southern Cascade mountains.

One could certainly question, as did an Oregon missionary in the 1850s, that "French and American settlers openly buy and sell slaves. Are not the laws of the Union strict on the subject of enslaving Indians?" They were not. Technically, a Negro was covered by law. The Indian had no rights, whatsoever. The plight of the red man left the abolitionist cold though they were willing to pull down the whole fabric of America, if need be, to free the black man.

In 1776 the English colonies in North America asserted their claim to self-government. Their famed Declaration of Independence proclaimed among "truths to be self-evident" that "all men are created equal." They further declared that it was the right of all citizens to enjoy "life, liberty, and the pursuit of happiness." The aims of that Declaration were noble, yet at the time the 13 colonies broke from Britain, their population was about three million. Of these, more than half a million were slaves. Thomas Jefferson, a prime mover behind the Declaration remained a slave owner throughout his life.

The black slave had become a domestic animal, occasionally ill-treated, but more often kindly and sometimes even affectionately used. The Indian had remained, in the view of the white man, a wild beast of the forest to be exploited or exterminated. Two centuries of almost yearly conquest over a weak foe had implanted in the Americans a feeling that nothing could block their way. As one historian would put it, "Almost the only foreigners we had known had been poverty-stricken European and American savages. Both fed our sense of superiority."[3]

In a debate in the U.S. Senate, February 14, 1857, Stephen A. Douglas would answer the missionary's question when he shouted . . . "I am aware sir, that the act of Congress was passed prohibiting slavery in Oregon but it was never passed here

---

3    James Adams, *The Epic of America*, p. 161.

until six years after the people of that territory had excluded it by their own law." However, "their own law was a two-edged sword."

Slavery was a matter very much on the minds of Oregonians for many years before the Civil War. It became an issue during the formation of Oregon's first government. The subject was obviously a political hot-potato for on June 26, 1844, the Provisional Legislature decided on one hand to outlaw slavery and in the same enactment ruled that Negroes could not reside in the territory as free men. The Indians were not even acknowledged with a decision. The 1844 statute, as ratified in 1845 (the same year Col. James "Nigger Jim" Taylor introduced several wagon loads of Negro families to the Oregon Trail), further stipulated that a Negro, now that he had been granted freedom under the law, had to leave Oregon within two years (male) and three years (female) . . . "or he or she shall receive upon his or her bare back not less than 20 or more than 30 stripes to be inflicted by the county constable."

So, legally, Oregon was free territory. In reality, it was aligned with the slave states.[4] Politically, Oregon supported the Democratic Party and almost without exception, the Democrats favored slavery . . . or at least did not actively oppose it. On the other hand, the Republican Party arising as it did from the ashes of the Whig Party and the Free Soil Debate was strong for abolition. The Republicans would nominate Abraham Lincoln as their candidate for president.

In the 1850s, while the Shoshoni schism was in progress, a split between the Northern states and the Southern states seemed imminent. Sectionalism became increasingly bitter throughout the land and Oregon was no exception. Heated debates over the slavery issue raged the length and breadth of the Willamette Valley. Impassioned as this issue became, an even more controversial subject was a new creation called the hoopskirt.

*Harper's Weekly* in defense of this strange fashion stated without qualms that "rightly or wrongly, the aesthetic eye requires that the female figure shall be broader at the base than at any other point. Certainly a woman without hoops, with garments clinging to her person and exposing in the wind, the contour of every limb is neither gracefully nor delicately attired."[5] This editorial view was not whole-heatedly accepted by Oregon's male population. Perhaps because they lacked the "aesthetic eye," these uncouth gentlemen preferred the revealing buckskins and flimsy gingham dresses of Paiute and Negro slave women. Most likely they would have endorsed a modern philosopher's observation on the trouser craze when she commented with some accuracy. . . . "the girl whose tailored

---

4  For a full discussion of the slavery issue see T.W. Davenport, "Slavery Question in Oregon," *Oregon Historical Quarterly*, Vol. IX, No. 3, September 1908.

5  *Harper's Weekly*, February 12, 1859, p. 99. In defense of *Harper's*, the *North American Review* considered the *Weekly* as a reliable source, to be one of the most powerful organs of public opinion in the United States "read in city parlor, in the log hut of the pioneer, by every campfire. . . ." This endorsement was made in the April 1865 issue of the *Review*.

jeans reveal her ultimate dimension is basically, one can't but feel, just panting for attention."

Whatever, high fashion had to give way when it was rumored that Jo Lane—Oregon's Congressional Delegate—was master-minding a plot to hand over the Pacific territories to the Southern pro-slavery cause. In an effort to stave this off, Congress, in sudden action uncommon for them, began beefing up military strength in Oregon. On September 13, 1858, by order of the Secretary of War, the Military Department of the Pacific was sub-divided into the Military Districts of Oregon and California. Under this arrangement, the Departmental Commander would be headquartered in San Francisco with a District Commander in charge of Oregon stationed at Fort Vancouver. Immediately, Brig. Gen. William Harney, the man who crushed the Sioux Rebellion of 1855, was transferred to the West Coast. Not only did he command the Department but he also took personal charge of the Oregon front and delayed the expected division of the Military Department for two years. This would not happen until the late fall of 1860.

Unfortunately, Harney was a poor choice for this mission. Although he was one of the best military strategists of his time and was successful in holding the Paviotso Confederacy in check, Harney was not the man for the Oregon situation. In 1860, he was recalled to Washington, D.C. and relieved of duty. His loyalties lay with the South no matter how hard he tried to keep that feeling from interfering with his military career.

While this political in-fighting was going on, the Snakes—fed-up with the Wasco-Walla Walla slave trade and other grievances—geared for battle. In spite of White Beard Harney and the U.S. Army, they were going to lay waste to the Warm Springs Reservation and a few Confederated tribesmen in the process. The seeds for retaliation were planted in the dying hours of 1858. They would germinate during the Moon of Small Tracks (January) 1859.

# MILITARY FORTS AND ROADS

## EASTERN OREGON—1864-1880

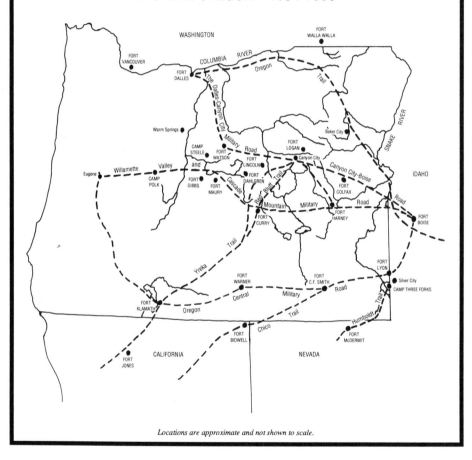

*Locations are approximate and not shown to scale.*

# CHAPTER 91

# THIS IS WARFARE?

*The harder you're thrown, why the higher you bounce;*
*Be proud of your blackened eye!*
*It isn't the fact that you're licked that counts;*
*It's how did you fight and why?*

**Edmund Vance Cooke**
*How Did You Die?*

To better understand what the army had to face in the coming battle of the Ochoco, it is necessary to digress for a moment and take a look at Shoshoni military tactics. The Snake warrior with no weapons save his bow and arrows, lance, war club, knife and shield roamed over a vast empire . . . the lord of the land, fiercer than the grizzly he hunted; wilder than the coyote he called brother. He could be a good friend—but no mercy need be expected from him as an enemy. Although now armed with the latest in modern firearms, he would rely heavily on the time-proven weaponry of the dog soldier to deal misery and death to the invaders.

Engaged in conflict with Europeans for nearly 200 years, the dog soldier developed a style of warfare completely different from other North American Indians. He knew his limitations and he worked the odds to his best advantage. With the stress caused by the endless advance of white civilization the men who came forward with proposals for action were followed by those who did not know which way to turn. These followers seriously believed that their leaders possessed supernatural powers which made them indestructible.[1] The war lords were smart enough to know better but they let the partisans believe whatever they wanted to.

Shoshoni boys were taught from birth that men hunted to live but lived to win honors and booty in war. The Snakes believed that anyone who did not fight was not truly a man. Because of this, many aging warriors felt that life had become purposeless and would bitterly quote the Shoshoni idiom . . . "a brave man dies young." More than a few elderly warriors, realizing that their skills and strength were fading, chose to commit suicide by battle. One such glorious death was

---

[1]    Most historians list the men who emerged as bulletproof leaders in the 1860s as Weahwewa (Wolf Dog), Ochiho (Has No Horse), Oitz (Left Hand), Egan (Pony Blanket), Winnemucca (Bad Face), and Oulux (Big Man). Whiting, *Paiute Sorcery*, p. 22.

witnessed by a troop of 1st Oregon Cavalry while pursuing a Snake raiding party. An aged warrior reined in his mount, dismounted and calmly removed his moccasins—a sure sign that he didn't intend to leave the spot alive. The old man fought hard, wounding three soldiers before he died with more than 20 bullets in his body. But while he made his stand, his friends got away.

The difference between a Snake warrior and an American soldier would soon become apparent. The soldier—a paid combatant—would keep risks proportional to the objective at hand. The warrior—a natural-born fighter—regarded daring itself as a high value. To him, there was nothing so thrilling as being shot at and missed. The Shoshoni was in no sense a coward. He knew his business and played his cards to suit himself. He never wasted a shot and never lost in a fight where a brisk run across the nearest ridge would save his life and exhaust the heavily clad American soldier who endeavored to catch him. In a long pursuit, he would jump off his pony and run along side to keep his mount fresh while the American drove his horse into the ground.

The U.S. Indian fighting army—flush with victory after slaughtering amassed forces of Cayuse, Rogue and Yakima warriors—would now march toward a tactical awakening. It was one thing to make a sabre charge backed by artillery into a crowd of bunched-up Indians, and quite another to conduct military operations on Wolf Dog's terms. In most cases when the regular or volunteer army troops rode out to engage the Snakes, they found nothing. Then, an unwary lone soldier might wander past a sage bush or down log and a dog soldier lurking in ambush would pierce him with a lance. To attempt pursuit was worse than useless. All that could be done was to bury the dead. It was this method of attack that unnerved army personnel and made the dog soldiers such a terror to those unlucky enough to make contact with them.

The dog soldiers knew that they were by far more formidable when dispersed than when moving in large groups. Over the years, Shoshoni military policy was designed to wear out the enemy by vexation tactics in which any pursuit degenerated into a will-o-the-wisp chase. When trailed, they never stayed together or even in single file, always doubling back, changing directions, perhaps not uniting for miles . . . even hundreds of miles. It was not uncommon for a Snake raiding party to rendezvous as far away as Walker Lake in Nevada; the Uinta Mountains in Utah; or the Wind River Range in Wyoming and then plunder their way back into the Ochoco. In this manner, not only was pursuit retarded but most generally lost or given up.

On these diversionary maneuvers, they would leave one or two men in select spots watching the back-trail and waiting for the approach of the pursuers where they would shoot, causing them to bunch up and lose more precious time; or they would sneak into the enemy's camp at night and stampede their horses. The advance party would mark their trail by cutting a small incision in the bark of a tree, by tracing a pictograph on a smooth-faced rock under a ledge to protect it from the elements, or perhaps a rock was placed in the crotch of a tree or a sapling laid against another tree, or an oily pitch smoke would appear from a mountain top. In this way, the rear guard always knew the progress of the advance party.

When on these forays, the dog soldier was usually near-naked packing a blanket thrown over the shoulder, a water-tight jug to serve as a canteen, a small amount of jerked meat and his sacred relics or medicine. The well-equipped warrior had a mirror tied to his hair for signaling and carried good binoculars. Although an expert long-distance rifle shot, he much preferred to pack a shot-gun or revolver for close quarters fighting. However, his primary battle gear consisted of the weapons used to hunt big game.

Popular opinion has regarded the Indian bow and arrow as a primitive weapon, and quite useless in warfare against the U.S. Army. Try telling that to a veteran of the Shoshoni Wars! At 50 yards, a well-shaped obsidian tipped arrow was lethal and accurate. A handful drawn from quiver and discharged would make more rapid fire than a revolver and at short range would penetrate a piece of wood farther than the ball of a Colt navy pistol. Over 4,000 years ago, the Mayans—in their blood rituals—used the sharpest knives yet known to man. They were sharper than today's best boning cutlery, sharper than diamond scalpels and as much as 500 times sharper than modern razor blades. They were made from volcanic glass, a material found in abundance at Glass Butte in central Oregon. . . better known as obsidian! In fact, the army maps of the 1860s designated Glass Butte as a prime military target marked as an "ammunition factory."

Warheads from two to three and a half inches long—often barbed and always chipped to a double edge—were attached by sinew to wooden shafts. Running the length of these shafts were three carved blood grooves which also served a deadly function. When the flesh of man or beast closed around the arrow these seams would act as conduits and gradually bleed the victim to death. This was the reason for attempting to remove the arrow as quickly as possible even though the warhead may remain in the victims body. Adding to the effectiveness of the arrow, quite often the warhead itself was impregnated with poison. Warriors, women and children alike used the bow and arrow but the women—as claimed by those who knew—were peculiarly adept with knife and hatchet.

The short 30-inch war bow used by the Snakes (the plains tribes used 32 to 40 inch war bows) to propel these projectiles was made of laminated horn and of such great elasticity and tension that a warrior could easily drive an arrow through a two-inch thick plank, a man or a buffalo. These highly prized bows—known to the Snakes as *awatas*—were often made by Mountain Snake craftsmen in whose hands the manufacture of horn bows had reached perfection.[2]

---

2    For detailed information on these bows wrought from sheep, buffalo and elk bones which were secured with deer and elk sinew see, *The Wind River Rendezvous*, Vol. XXI, No. 2, pp. 3-15.

The two to three pound war club head was made of solid rock, grooved to attach a handle and tapered to a blunt edge; whereas, the war hatchet—generally a Hudson's Bay axe—often had a hollow head and handle which could serve as a medicine pipe. Both of these weapons were capable of crushing a man's skull. The war shield made from several thicknesses of hide could turn a sabre thrust and to some extent deflect bullets. The five to seven foot long war lance packed an obsidian head nearly 18 inches long and was balanced with eagle feathers the full length of the shaft to give it steadiness in flight.

Another advantage the dog soldier held over his American counterpart was that he didn't require a supply train to survive. Snake warriors could find food on every hillside and were well acquainted with the water holes and springs. On the other hand, the whites could wander about half-crazed with thirst, maddened by the heat of a desert day or chilled by cold mountain winds at night unable to tell which plants were of food value and which were not.

Shoshoni in groups of two or three and even individually would steal in close to major wagon roads, military posts or ranch houses, hide behind whatever cover was available and remain for days scanning movements of the Americans waiting for a chance to stampede a herd, kill a man or loot a supply train. They knew how to disguise themselves so thoroughly that one might almost step on a warrior before seeing him. They could and did approach within earshot and even entered the enclosure of military outposts undiscovered until footprints were found. On such occasions, the warrior preferred the lance over the bow and hours may pass before a corpse was discovered.

Armed struggle with the Shoshoni was not going to be marked by glorious cavalry charges nor would it be distinguished by large groups clashing in hand to hand combat. This was a war of attrition. It would take thousands of soldiers to hold these invisible killers in check; warriors who refused to fight when pursued but instead scattered like quail, only to hover on the flanks of the advancing enemy . . . waiting . . . waiting . . . always waiting for an opportune time to strike.

# CHAPTER 92

# WARM SPRINGS UNDER FIRE

*The time to stop talking is when the other person nods his head affirmatively but says nothing.*

**Henry S. Haskins**
*Meditations in Wall Street*

As the winter of 1858-59 howled across the frozen Cascades, Oregon lawmakers snug in their winter quarters thought it may be wise, now that Harney had reopened eastern Oregon to settlement, to make peace with the Shoshoni. For some reason—maybe to overrun interior Oregon come spring—territorial officials voted to act with haste. Indian Agent A.P. Dennison, stationed at The Dalles City, had barely digested Christmas dinner when Indian Superintendent James Nesmith ordered him into the Ochoco to make contact with Wolf Dog.

The first week in January, Dennison—guided by the Umatilla army scout, Cut Mouth John—found Wolf Dog camped in the lower Crooked River Valley with 30 lodges of Bear Killer and Mountain Snakes.[1] After all the bad publicity given the Snakes, much to Dennison's surprise, they treated him "very kindly." He would soon find out why. Wolf Dog couldn't believe his good fortune. The Indian agent was inviting him to visit the Warm Springs Agency—giving him an opportunity to check out fortifications, troop strength and other vital military information at no risk. Of course he would accept the offer.

In a letter to Nesmith, Dennison—elated over his initial success—wrote that "Chief We-ah-we-ah (Wolf Dog) and eight of his headmen came to the Agency and I made them a few presents." He was certain that Wolf Dog would be "very glad to treat with the government." Dennison was basing this happy conclusion on the belief that the Snakes were "out of provisions and near

---

1    Dennison called the Mountain (Walpapi) Snakes the "wah push pel." Modern scholars refer to the Bear Killers (Hoonebooey) as Hunipui and have merged the Walpapi with the Bear Killers under the name of Hunipuitokas. The blending of identities may stem from the fact that Wolf Dog, head chief of the Snake war tribes, was a Hoonebooey (Bear Killer) by birth while his half-brothers, Paulina and Black Eagle were Walpapi (Mountain) by birth. Black Eagle—Wahweveh—because of a similarity in name to his half-brother, Wolf Dog—Weahwewa—has caused much confusion in identity in the various journals and military records of the period covering 1860 to 1880.

naked."[2] Others, including Gen. Harney were not so fully convinced of Wolf Dog's peaceful intentions. Among the eight headmen who accompanied Wolf Dog were Has No Horse, Paulina, Broken Knife, Yellow Jacket and Black Buffalo.[3]

As Dennison conferred with Wolf Dog, heavy troop movements were taking place on the Columbia River. *The Mountain Buck, Senorita* and *Multnomah* plied the lower river moving military personnel from Fort Vancouver to the portage at Cascade Locks. On the middle Columbia, the *Wright* and *Belle* were busily transporting troops and military supplies to Umatilla Landing and Fort Walla Walla. Capt. Henry Black brought in another company of 9th U.S. Infantry to bolster forces at Fort Dalles and Sheriff A.J. Crabb added a new cell block to the Wasco County jail in anticipation of housing more Indian war criminals. Up on Fifteenmile Creek between Fort Dalles and the Warm Springs stockade, ranchers were constructing a fort to ward off a Shoshoni attack.

During this frenzied activity, Oregon—on February 14, 1859—became the 33rd star on the flag of the United States and the Snakes were preparing a valentine message for the new addition to the Union. Fort Warm Springs nestled in a valley north of Quartz Creek at a spot called Simnasho would be the recipient.

Capt. Hiram Wilber, in command of two companies of Oregon Rangers, had been assigned to the Warm Springs Agency in the fall of 1858 to protect the reservation Indians from a suspected Shoshoni attack.[4] Contrary to Agent Dennison's recent discussions, Wolf Dog and his war chiefs planned to do just exactly that. Never on the best of terms with the Confederated Tribes of Middle Oregon, the Shoshoni believed that members of those tribes had betrayed their own leaders into the hands of the Americans on the promise of some farming equipment and government housing. Has No Horse, in a savage tribute to Black Ice, Muskrat Man, Kamiakin and Yellow Serpent, would vent his displeasure on their weak-willed followers.[5]

Under cover of a March snow storm, Snake dog soldiers forded the Deschutes River and without interference from the Oregon Rangers, rode up the Warm Springs River onto Schoolie Flat and slipped into Quartz Valley. Swift and efficient, they swept through the Agency compound leaving death and destruction in their wake. By the time the Oregon Rangers could boot-up and mount, the Snakes were pounding toward Crooked River herding 200 of the best war horses of the Confederated Tribes before them.

---

2     A.P. Dennison to J.W. Nesmith, Dallas, Oregon, January 17, 1859. National Archives, Bureau of Indian Affairs, Oregon Superintendency, Letters Received; U.S. Statutes at Large, Vol. 14, p. 683.

3     Information from Dave Chocktote, son of Black Buffalo.

4     *The Illustrated History of Central Oregon*, p. 308.

5     Black Ice, Muskrat man, Kamiakin and Yellow Serpent were leaders during the Cayuse and Yakima wars. For more details, see *Thunder Over the Ochoco, Vol. II, Distant Thunder.*

Splitting his command east of the Deschutes, Capt. Wilber headed for the John Day Valley while Lt. John Marden swung south toward Crooked River. Within two days, Sgt. John Wooley—tracker in charge of a small advance party—determined that they were chasing shadows. In the vicinity of Grizzly Mountain, the Snakes had split off in groups of two to four persons and there weren't enough Rangers to safely pursue each group without risking an ambush so the chase was abandoned.

Capt. Thomas Fitch, medical officer left in command at the Agency, dispatched Sgt. Ben McAtee to Fort Dalles requesting regular army reinforcements. This plea fell on deaf ears for it was felt by all concerned that it was more important to protect the Oregon Trail for the coming emigration than it was to prevent the Snakes from killing a few reservation Indians. Besides that, Gen. Harney had a greater objective in mind. Adding support to his decision of non-interference was a statement made by Robert Newell . . . mountain man, Indian fighter, politician who was once married to a Shoshoni woman. It was later determined that Newell was under the impression that the Rangers were concerned about the Digger Indians . . . the Shoshokos or horseless Paiutes.

In 1840, "Doc" Newell and his brother-in-law Joe Meek, were the first men to traverse the western Oregon Trail by wagon; Newell was a member of the new state legislature and was campaigning for the position of speaker of the house of representatives. It would not be prudent to advertise an Indian uprising with Oregon less than a month into statehood and courting more settlers. Any opinion voiced by the Hon. Robert Newell would be given much consideration. Therefore when he heard the complaint from Warm Springs that the Snakes were causing trouble, he calmly stated "Three or four men should be able to defend the Agency against a hundred of those pitiful creatures." Temporally, Dr. Fitch would become a firm believer in the Newell theory.

Indian Agent Dennison, having personally met Wolf Dog, Has No Horse and Paulina on their home ground, was not so certain about the accuracy of that comment. He hurriedly recruited a company of volunteers and requisitioned enough weapons and ammunition from the Fort Dalles arsenal to arm all civilian employees and trusted Agency Indians for a retaliatory raid into the Ochoco to recover the stolen livestock and punish the offenders.

Back on the Agency plains—while Dennison pleaded for assistance—Wolf Dog and Paulina split from the horse round-up and went off on some mischief of their own. It wasn't long thereafter that Capt. Alfred Pleasanton with a detachment of 2nd U.S. Dragoons surprised two Indian vagrants lurking on the outskirts of Fort Dalles. Since they appeared to be up to no good, he escorted them into The Dalles City where he lodged them in Sheriff Crabb's new addition to the county jail. They were booked on April 18, 1859. On his return from the arms delivery to Warm Springs, Dennison was somewhat startled when he recognized the cell-mates as being Wolf Dog and Paulina. He was now more than ever convinced that Wolf Dog—being lodged in jail—could not have taken part in the recent raids on Warm Springs. His vote of confidence didn't help much. They remained in prison.

Dennison was right on one count. Wolf Dog was innocent of any current wrong-doing. In his absence, Has No Horse was not idle. In early April, he struck the reservation again, killing four Agency Indians and capturing another 150 horses. In fact, the dog soldiers had barely crossed the Deschutes River when Dennison rode into the Agency headquarters with 40 rifles and a pack train loaded with ammunition led by army scout Charlie McKay and escorted by a company of volunteer rangers under the command of Sgt. McAtee.

Ben McAtee, a dedicated soldier, was becoming quite a celebrity in the Oregon Volunteers. In his off-duty hours, he was courting a mysterious Greek girl who traced her ancestry back to Eusebius Sophronius Hieronynus, the man who translated the Bible from ancient Hebrew into the common usage of today. An ordained priest in the Roman Catholic Church, he became private secretary to Pope Damascus I and is now venerated as St. Jerome. The sergeant would marry Alvira Hieronynus when he mustered out of the service in 1867.[6]

As soon as the reinforcements arrived, Capt. Fitch organized 53 Agency Indians into a rifle squad, placing them under the leadership of Pipsher Simtustus, a Walla Walla warrior whose brother was killed in the April raid. On April 12, leaving Warm Springs under the guard of Capt. Wilber, Fitch and his Indian riflemen, accompanied by a troop of Oregon Rangers under the command of Lt. Marden, galloped into the Ochoco seeking revenge.[7]

Sixteen days after Fitch forded the Deschutes on his punitive raid into Snake country, and 10 days after the imprisonment of Wolf Dog and Paulina, a potentially dangerous plan was gaining momentum. On April 28, army headquarters in New York City received a copy of Gen. Harney's Special Order No. 40 instructing Capt. H.D. Wallen, 4th U.S. Infantry Regiment, to conduct a military road survey from The Dalles City, Oregon to Salt Lake City, Utah through the heart of the Ochoco. Within days, Capt. Pleasanton relieved Wallen from his command of Fort Cascade, Washington Territory. On May 26, Wallen reported to Col. Wright at Fort Dalles for further instructions. Thanks to Capt. Fitch of the Oregon Volunteers, his new assignment would not be easy.

During the shuffle of regular army personnel, Fitch—cutting around the northern base of Stephenson Mountain—located the winter camp of Tall Man (Odukeo) on the John Day River. Tall Man and his warriors, who had not participated in the Warm Springs raids, were several miles upstream in pursuit of an elk herd when the volunteers arrived. Scouting the area and finding the camp

---

6    *The Illustrated History of Central Oregon*, p. 383.

7    Dennison to Nesmith, April 12, 1859; National Archives, Bureau of Indian Affairs, Oregon Superintendency, Letters Received.

unguarded, Fitch attacked at daybreak killing every man in camp and capturing most of the women and children.[8] A few of the women eluded their captors by plunging into the river which was so badly swollen with the spring run-off that the Rangers were unable to cross and continue the chase. One of these women had Tall Man's infant daughter with her.

The volunteers then torched the village and slaughtered all of the Indian ponies. In high good spirits, the Warm Springs militia prodded the Snake captives into the Agency compound on May 3, proclaiming victory. On the return march to the reservation, Tall Man's wife had been raped and beaten to death. She was one of the lucky ones. The Confederated tribesmen were notorious in their treatment of slaves, a fact well known throughout the Shoshonean tribes. Capt. Wallen would arrive at Fort Warm Springs with two companies of cavalry too late to prevent new acts of Shoshoni hostility.[9]

When word reached Dennison of Fitch's destruction of Tall Man's peaceful camp, he realized—even with Wolf Dog and Paulina locked behind bars—that a fight with the Shoshoni was imminent. He was right. With the capture of Wolf Dog, Has No Horse was in full command, not only of the Paviotso Confederacy, but the western Shoshoni nation as well and he was ready to even the score. The loss of Tall Man's village would be avenged quickly and violently. As the word went out for fighting men, a heavily armed prospecting party rode out of Lane County in search of the Blue Bucket gold strike. By June, they had penetrated as far as the headwaters of the Malheur River when they were overtaken by a Snake war party. In a running battle, they managed to escape to Fort Walla Walla with two men seriously wounded and a loss of $8,000 in property.[10]

Still believing Wolf Dog wished to be on friendly terms with the Americans, Dennison convinced Col. Wright that the chief could be of assistance in a peaceful settlement of the eastern Oregon conflicts. Since both captives "appeared to be well disposed," Dennison believed they would make excellent guides for Capt. Wallen's road expedition due to enter central Oregon within the week.[11] Thus, the head chief of the Snake war tribes and his number two war chief joined the United States Army. In the interim, they were held in the Wasco County jail. Guided by the enemy into a land already echoing with Shoshoni gunfire, Capt. Wallen was expected to mark a military route the full width of Oregon and halfway across the territory of Utah on lands under the complete control of the Paviotso Confederacy.

---

8     Dennison to Harney, May 13, 1859. National Archives, Bureau of Indian Affairs, Oregon Superintendency, Letters Received.

9     *U.S. Messages and Documents 1859-60*, p. 113.

10     *The Sacramento Union*, July 7, 1859.

11     Comments on the captives' good conduct can be found in letters from Dennison to Nesmith, April 18, 1859; Pleasonton to Nesmith, April 23, 1859; National Archives, Bureau of Indian Affairs, Oregon Superintendency, Letters Received.

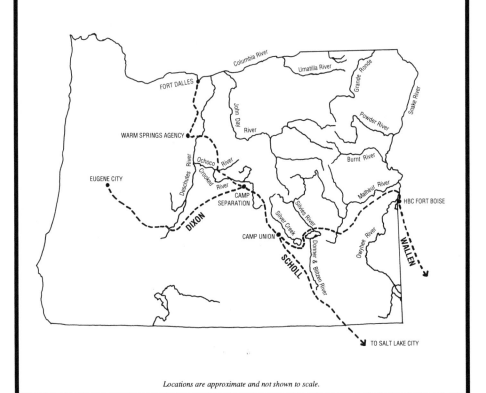

# CAPTAIN WALLEN'S 1859 ROAD SURVEY

*Locations are approximate and not shown to scale.*

# CHAPTER 93

# A SOLDIER AND A CIVILIAN

*. . . even among the Indians none knew more than a small
portion of the country we were to traverse and no white
man could be found who had any knowledge of the Blue
Mountains. . . .*

**Captain Henry D. Wallen**
June 2, 1859

Mounting hostility between two Indian confederations coupled with the
Oregon Volunteers' unauthorized attack on a peaceful Shoshoni encampment had
resulted in Capt. Henry Wallen's transfer to the Fort Dalles command. Wallen, a
combat infantry officer, was to command a battalion of army engineers on a road
survey through the most hostile country in the far west. He and his staff officers,
followed by loaded wagons, would blaze a trail from Fort Dalles, Oregon to Camp
Floyd, Utah in 28 days. The actual field time—interrupted by exploration, rescue
of wagon trains and Indian attacks—would vary in length from Lt. John
Bonnycastle's 12-day run from the head of Crooked River to Capt. Wallen's
73-day marathon to Great Salt Lake Valley. His entire command would cover
1,900 miles in four months and 16 days.

From this exercise, Wallen concluded that The Dalles could supply Salt Lake
City with ". . . all articles imported better and cheaper than they can be derived
from any other part of the Union. The entire land travel can be accomplished in
one month." Perhaps it could, but in retrospect it appears that Capt. Wallen was
more interested in getting into the war zone along the Oregon Trail than he was in
pioneering a military road across interior Oregon. What follows are the fortunes
and misfortunes of the men involved.

In briefings by Gen. Harney and Col. Wright, Capt. Wallen was told that
miners were pouring up the newly established Yreka Trail bound for the goldfields
in northeastern Oregon and western Idaho. At the same time, thousands of
emigrants—avoiding the dangerous western segment of the Oregon Trail—were
flooding the Applegate Trail to gain entry to the upper Willamette Valley. The two
trails intersected in south-central Oregon in the vicinity of Silver Lake. This
crossing was the scene of Has No Horse's vicious attacks. From Fort Dalles,
skirting the eastern base of the Cascades, it was six days' hard ride (330 miles) to

get into battle position. From Fort Crittenden, located 40 miles south of the Mormon citadel of Salt Lake City and headquarters for 20 percent of the entire United States Army in 1859, it was five days' hard ride (270 miles) to the trail intersection. A faster route had to be found.

The area north of the trail crossings had gained the name of Yreka Valley and was believed to be the main staging point and hideout of Wolf Dog's troops. This intelligence later proved to be false but not before the military squandered thousands of dollars and months of time in troop movements. Yreka Valley was located in a large basin bounded by Yreka Butte, Hampton Butte, Glass Butte, Wagontire Mountain and Horse Mountain. In the homestead period of 1910-16, the west end of Yreka Valley was renamed Imperial Valley; the north end, Misery Flat; the east end, Canary Flat, and the south end, Chicago Valley. The one thing the army did discover was that Yreka Valley was excellent horse pasture. So good that by the 1890s, settlers were trailing horse herds into Benjamin Lake—seven miles southeast of Yreka Butte—for winter range.[1] This practice would continue until the 1930s.

Harney's proposed route from Fort Dalles to Fort Crittenden—renamed Camp Floyd by order of Gen. Clarke in his effort to calm the War Department after the enormous expenditures on Fort Dalles—would take Wallen through 600 miles of the most hostile country west of the Rocky Mountains and the heart of Wolf Dog's territory. Earlier patrols, hounded by Snake dog soldiers, had made this ride in 12 days. Harney believed with a marked route it could easily be covered by supply wagons in 15 days. Based on this intelligence, Wallen was given 60 days to explore and establish a wagon road from The Dalles City to Salt Lake City and return. It would take twice that long to accomplish his mission.

The only man—soldier or civilian—at Fort Dalles who had any knowledge of the country Wallen was about to enter was Louis Scholl, the fort architect, who had been with Col. Edward Steptoe on his campaign against the Utes . . . and he had never been across the southern Blues. Scholl would be hired as chief guide and placed in charge of road design. Wallen, a perfectionist, studied his target in detail, asking and accepting advice of such men as Col. Steptoe who had attempted to establish a trail over the same route in 1853; A.P. Dennison, Indian Agent for eastern Oregon; and especially any man acquainted with the country. Here, he ran into trouble. As he put it, "The greatest difficulty under which I labored before starting out was in obtaining guides. . . ." The confederated tribesmen were ignorant of the land east of the Deschutes River and, in the absence of Hudson's Bay employees who weren't stepping forward with any information, Wallen couldn't find one white man, other than Scholl, who had been in the country he was about to explore. It was then, based on Dennison's honest belief that Wolf Dog wished

---

1    Benjamin Lake was named for Gen. Benjamin Alvord, at that time paymaster for the Oregon Volunteers.

to be on friendly terms with the Americans that Wallen—with misgivings—added Wolf Dog and Paulina to the army payroll as guides.

At the first light of dawn, Saturday June 4, 1859—eight days after his arrival at Fort Dalles—Wallen headed into the unknown. He may have been traveling blind but he was prepared to defend himself. Wallen thundered into Fort Warm Springs with the greatest fighting force yet to wander east of the Cascades. Backing Wallen on this venture were nine field officers, 184 U.S. Dragoons, 126 mounted infantry, army scouts and nearly 100 civilian employees.[2] They were trailing 155 extra saddle mounts, 344 pack mules, 60 head of beef cattle, supplies enough for 319 men for four months and 131 oxen to pull 30 wagons, two of which mounted 12 pound mountain howitzers.[3] The Dragoons were armed with Sharps carbines, sabres and navy colt revolvers; the infantry with model 1855 rifle-muskets and new model .52 caliber Springfields with elevated sights effective up to 800 yards . . . "all excellent weapons" according to Wallen. However, he believed the mounted men were carrying more arms than required "being an unnecessary weight to horse and rider." Wolf Dog would agree.

Beyond any doubt, Wallen was equipped for any emergency that should arise. Besides field artillery and food-stuffs, the wagons were transporting inflatable India-rubber pontoons, each 20 feet long, 20 inches in diameter and covered with a canvas deck for bridge construction. They also carried India-rubber inflatable boats 10 feet long for instant river crossings.

This preparedness didn't escape the watchful eyes of Wolf Dog and Paulina. It would become obvious that a head-on collision with a military power backed by unlimited resources such as this would not only be senseless but futile. From these observations, Wolf Dog would develop the hit-and-run tactics which helped to equalize the army's superior strength by reducing the effectiveness to a common level with that of the dog soldier. Second in command to Has No Horse, Paulina would learn much from this firsthand look at U.S. Army operations . . . knowledge which would benefit him in the years to come. It was said by those who knew him that Paulina—The War Spirit—loved to fight and killed more than one member

---

2   Besides Wallen, the officers were: Asst. Surgeon, Capt. John Randolph, medical staff officer; Lt. Joseph Dixon, U.S. Corps of Engineers; Lt. John Bonnycastle, 4th Infantry; Lt. Jacob Sweitzer, 1st U.S. Dragoons; Lt. Marcus Reno, 1st Dragoons; Lt. Henry Robert, Corps of Engineers; Lt. David Houston, command of sappers and miners (soldiers especially trained in constructing trenches, tunnels and underground fortifications); Capt. Charles Graham, quartermaster in charge of supplies.

3   Information on Wallen's expedition in letters received: John B. Floyd, Secretary of War to Hon. William Pennington, Speaker of the House of Representatives; Gen. Harney to Gen. Scott; Gen. Harney to Capt. Wallen; Gen. Harney to Col. Cooper; Capt. Wallen to Capt. Pleasonton; Capt. Wallen to Lt. Bonnycastle; Lt. Bonnycastle to Lt. Johnston; Lt. Bonnycastle to Capt. Pleasonton; Louis Scholl to Capt. Pleasonton; Capt. Thorn to Lt. Dixon; Lt. Houston to Capt. Wallen. (U.S. House Executive Document No. 65 and U.S. Senate Executive Document No. 34, Vol. IX, p. 51, 36th Congress, 1st session).

of his own tribe to enforce law and order. Some resented him for his determination to rise, his egotism, his scheming, but still they trusted him. They knew he was more than just smart and tough; he was contemplative, perceptive and honest. With these qualities, Paulina would absorb West Point skills not only from Capt. Wallen's command but from other military units they would encounter in the field.

Harney would now demonstrate why he was called "the scourge of the plains." With the cooperation of Brig. Gen. Albert Johnston, Commander of the Military District of Utah, Harney would insure that no serious harm befell his pet project. By spring 1859—counting Wallen's task force—there were four heavily armed military commands operating east of the Cascade Mountains in the area known to the fur trade as "The Valley of Troubles." These tactical units would intermingle and aid each other throughout the summer on a battlefront covering eastern Oregon, southern Idaho, northern Utah and northern Nevada, the undisputed hunting grounds of the Snake war tribes.

Their opponents were well aware of this increased military activity. Wolf Dog, although under army surveillance, was still the acknowledged head chief of the western Shoshoni nation and until instructed otherwise his followers would remain militant. Has No Horse, military commander of the Paviotso Confederacy was becoming increasingly dangerous. To date, his war chiefs, besides wreaking havoc on the Warm Springs Reservation, had forced the abandonment of the only supply outposts on the western half of the Oregon Trail. Fort Hall and Fort Boise were now in shambles. Because of this continued hostility, Major J.P. Reynolds' 3rd U.S. Artillery out of Fort Yamhill, Oregon, was rolling across the Cascades on orders to clean up the Oregon Trail; Capt. John Stark out of Camp Floyd, Utah, with the 2nd U.S. Dragoons was riding north to reinforce Reynolds' artillery; and Major Isaac Lynde, also stationed at Camp Floyd was assigned protection of the Applegate and Yreka Trails.

Although Capt. Wallen would write in his official road report that "I made the trip [from The Dalles City to Salt Lake City] with loaded wagons in 28 days," his journal would reveal that it took 73 days to make the trip.

At Warm Springs, Wallen added a detachment of Walla Walla scouts under the command of George Rundell to his already sizable force. The mixing of reservation scouts with Snake guides was inviting trouble but Wolf Dog and Paulina appeared to let bygones be bygones. On June 11, the engineers constructed a pontoon bridge across the Deschutes at the mouth of the Warm Springs River. Climbing the ridge west of Tenmile Creek (where the present South Junction Road is now located) Wallen began his march on the Ochoco. Eight days later, the expedition moved into the lower Ochoco Valley without incident. There was a reason for this lack of interference and quite likely Wolf Dog was aware of it.

Sometime between the March raid on Warm Springs and Wallen's entry into the Ochoco, Gourd Rattler's alliance with the Crows had gone sour. The forerunner of this split occurred in late October 1858 when Gourd Rattler found the Crows wintering on Shoshoni hunting grounds. His nerves already frayed from trying to deal with the U.S. government, Gourd Rattler lashed out killing 10 of the Crow trespassers. By March 1859, this union had deteriorated into open hostility.[4] Man Lost, chief of the Robber Snakes, aroused by war fever, burned Fort Thompson, the supply depot of the Pacific Wagon Company on Green River, causing the Americans to go into a state of panic. Meantime, the Crows—in open defiance of the Shoshoni—set up a large encampment in Big Wind River Valley near present Kinnear, Wyoming. Gourd Rattler, now in a militant mood, sent a message to the Crow camp demanding they get out of the country. The couriers—a dog soldier and his wife—were held hostage and the warrior killed but his wife escaped to report the atrocity.

Gourd Rattler was smart enough not to take on the Crow nation without assistance. When the call for reinforcements went out, Has No Horse put the Warm Springs raids on hold and along with Stiff Finger (Taghee), war chief of the Banattees, galloped off to join the fray. While the war chiefs of the two nations were sparring, (the Snakes were waiting for help to arrive), Big Robber, head chief of the Crows, was getting on Gourd Rattler's nerves by calling him a "squaw and an old woman" too cowardly to fight.[5]

The western allies arrived at about the same time that Capt. Wallen received orders to report to Fort Dalles for his new assignment. By now, the Crows had fortified themselves on Black Mountain near the head of Crow Creek. The battle got off to a roaring start when Gourd Rattler raised his hand to signal the attack and an arrow pierced it. At the end of three days of furious fighting neither side had made a gain. On the fourth day, in a grandstand play, Gourd Rattler challenged Big Robber to a duel . . . winner take all!

It is claimed that at the victory dance which followed, Big Robber's heart—which Gourd Rattler later ate to gain courage—adorned the end of his war lance. Under whatever circumstances this battle was won, it was decisive. The Crows were no longer a major problem. Besides settling Shoshoni hunting rights to the Wind River Valley, Gourd Rattler acquired a battle trophy . . . a girl, Crow Maiden, who later became one of his wives. Gourd Rattler, overjoyed to have put distance between him and the Oregon Trail, was unaware that the white man was already making plans to follow him with still another trail bringing further hardship to the eastern Shoshoni.

On June 18, 1859—as Has No Horse was approaching the eastern boundary of the Ochoco on his return from the Crow campaign—Wallen set up camp "on Achera (Ochoco) Creek a branch of Crooked River." It being Sunday, he took time

---

4    Lander's Report for the Year 1859, Senate Executive Document No. 36, pp. 49 and 69, 36th Congress, 2nd Session.

5    Irene Kinnear Meade, "Some Early Day School Events in the Wind River Valley," an unpublished account of the Black Mountain battle.

out to rest the livestock. Somewhere on this push from "Oswego (Trout) Creek," across the head of "Lohum (Willow) Creek" and down "Cottonwood (McKay) Creek," Wallen picked up two more guides . . . Yellow Jacket, chief of the Juniper Snakes and his war counselor, Kele, the Pigeon Hawk. No doubt, Wolf Dog vouched for their integrity.

Yellow Jacket—a likable but crafty gentleman often described as a happy-go-lucky wanderer—was Wolf Dog's master of espionage. He began his undercover career as a teenager when he sneaked Steve Meek back into the 1845 emigrant train and then arranged his escape along with Sol Tetherow's safe passage to the Deschutes River. He next shows up at the trial of the five condemned Cayuse warriors in Oregon City and later infiltrated Gen. Joel Palmer's 1855 peace conference at The Dalles touching pen to the treaty paper as a Dog River Wasco. Yellow Jacket would spend his life working as a double-agent, moving from army camp to Snake hideout with ease. A trusted dog soldier, he played a dangerous game.

Yellow Jacket—Potoptuah—would be known to Wallen as "Whitka." This was in keeping with Shoshoni custom of never revealing their true name to a stranger. A friend could introduce a person by name but the individual himself would never give his own name and it's unlikely either Wolf Dog or Paulina would disclose the true identity of their top agent. As a point of interest, Yellow Jacket—because of his venomous sting—was named for the insect not for an article of clothing.

Capt. Wallen now had the top aristocrats of the Shoshoni nation in his employ. Men who knew every crevice between Fort Dalles and Salt Lake City like Wallen knew the cracks in his worn infantry boots. If the Ghost People wished to establish a military route across the Ochoco, these men would know exactly where it was located and to some extent influence the course to their best advantage.

While camped at the confluence of the Ochoco and Crooked Rivers, the reservation scouts were having great sport slaughtering antelope. They killed so many that Wallen would name a swampy area in the vicinity of the camp—possibly where Prineville's Hidden Springs subdivision is now located—Antelope Springs. Even though no Shoshoni were encountered, Wallen moved with extreme caution as his troops worked their way up Crooked River to the forks. On this march, he would note ". . . had this part of Oregon been explored, it most certainly would have been settled long since in preference to other portions of the country more remote and less desirable as it possesses every requisite to make glad the heart of the farmer . . . for the past three days we have gone over the best stock-raising country in Oregon. I doubt if it can be surpassed in any part of the Union."

At the forks of Crooked River, the expedition discovered a small encampment of "Digger Snakes (Paiutes) who were not dangerous." From them, Louis Scholl—the head road locator—learned that a major Indian trail passed through a large landlocked prairie to the north and entered the John Day Valley. This information aroused Lt. Bonnycastle's curiosity and before another month had passed, engineers would be exploring that route for a possible link to either Fort Dalles or Fort Walla Walla.

A few hours after this meeting with the Paiutes and eight days after Wallen's arrival at the present site of Prineville, he worked his way some two miles south up a tributary to Crooked River and established a supply depot which he called Camp Division. Here, he split the command. More correctly, he fragmented it. Wallen knew from couriers passing through almost daily packing dispatches to and from Fort Dalles to the various commands in the field that there were dozens of army patrols in southeast Oregon. Because of this, he dispersed road locators in all directions, making it extremely difficult to trace the expedition's activities in any given area. Perhaps he did this to confuse the Snake guides as he really didn't trust them. Anyway, Lt. Bonnycastle would take command of Camp Division and oversee road construction from the south fork of Crooked River to the Columbia. Yellow Jacket, who for some reason Wallen did trust, would be assigned to Bonnycastle's command.

Lt. Dixon with a detachment of engineers was to check a route from Camp Division to the Oregon-California border for a tie-in with the Applegate and Red Bluff Trails. From there, he was to locate a route over the Cascades into the upper Willamette Valley. Rundell's Walla Walla scouts would serve as guides.

Louis Scholl, having the best knowledge of the desert to the south, was to locate a direct route from Camp Division to the Great Salt Lake Valley. Pigeon Hawk would accompany him to identify landmarks. Wallen himself, with Wolf Dog and Paulina as guides, would survey a trail from Camp Division to the junction of the Oregon and California trails.

On June 30, Lt. Sidney Johnston—son of Brig. Gen. Albert Johnston—on patrol out of Fort Dalles, arrived at Camp Division with a 15-man detachment of 1st U.S. Dragoons. He was attached to Bonnycastle's command.

The morning after Lt. Johnston's arrival, Capt. Wallen backed by Lt. Sweitzer commanding 85 1st U.S. Dragoons, Lt. Reno in charge of 27 4th U.S. Infantry riflemen, and Lt. Houston with 11 high explosive experts, headed deeper into the unknown. Marching up the south fork of Crooked River, his scouts discovered what appeared to be fortifications on the southeast slope of a sage-covered abutment, which, before another year passed, would be named Steen's Ridge. Since there was no record of the military having been in this area, the rock breastworks were dismissed as a natural formation. Had Scholl been present, he could have told Wallen they were man-made. The second day out, while crossing "Whirlwind Valley (Misery Flat)," Wallen was joined by Lt. Francis Mallory of the 4th Infantry Regiment out of Fort Reading, California in pursuit of Snake raiders. Attached to Wallen's command, Mallory relieved Reno—a cavalry officer—of the infantry detachment.

On July 5, 1859—three days after Mallory's arrival—Wallen found a definite fortified structure on a brooding basalt rim overlooking a warm desert stream called Silver Creek.

This discovery was disturbing to all the officers in the command. Unknown to them, they were finding evidence of Spanish colonization which had occurred 150 years in the past. Adding to their concern, Wolf Dog and Paulina—under cover of a moonless night—terminated their army career and disappeared, taking with them several cavalry mounts and two Sharps carbines.

Now, more than ever, Wallen believed this newly discovered fortress was a field fortification of Wolf Dog's rumored stronghold in Yreka Valley. Lt. Mallory, having chased Pipe and Burning Wagon up the Yreka Trail, was certain of it. Moving even more cautiously than before, the road locators continued east ". . . crossing into a sweeping valley where all the streams empty into a large landlocked lake of salt water, 9 miles wide and 20 miles long." Wallen named this body of water "Lake Harney." With no explanation, he named nearby Silver Lake "Whatumpa Lake." This may have been a corruption of the Shoshoni word *Kuaumpus*—Bear River—their name for Silver Creek. His scouts also reported an Indian encampment on the south shore of Harney Lake.

Mallory's infantry encircled the area as Sweitzer's dragoons charged the camp ready for a full-scale shootout with the suspected Snake deserters. To their relief, the suspected hostiles were "Digger Indians." It's to Wallen's credit that he checked first for he found the Paiutes to be "extremely shy of the white man and could not be induced to visit my camps." The term "camps" suggests that Wallen had sufficient manpower to cover any situation that might arise. What he didn't have was information on where Wolf Dog and Paulina were hiding or what they were intending to do. By the time Wallen reached Lake Harney, Wolf Dog had united with Has No Horse on his return from the Black Mountain battle and they were laying the groundwork for a renewed assault some 160 miles northwest of Wallen's line of march.

Puzzled over the peacefulness of the Shoshoni he had encountered, Wallen then discovered a wagon train camped on the north shore of Lake Harney. These poor lost souls had spent the winter at Lake Harney in such wretched condition that the Snakes ignored them. Now in a starving condition, completely bewildered as to what direction to travel and scared witless of an Indian attack, they had given up all hope of rescue. Wallen gave them supplies, a map and detailed instructions on how to reach Camp Division . . . which should have been no problem as all they had to do was follow his well-marked wagon tracks back to the Crooked River supply depot. As for an Indian attack, Wallen—in his own mind—felt there was little danger. In his push from the Deschutes River to Lake Harney, his scouts had found only two Shoshoni encampments and neither one presented any problem to white men.

Wallen's construction battalion had barely reached the eastern edge of Harney Basin when three things happened causing him to change his assessment of Shoshoni behavior. First, a messenger arrived with news of the Lane County miners ambushed on the headwaters of the Malheur River where they suffered an $8,000 property loss along with two men seriously wounded. Lt. Reno—a Yakima War veteran—with a cavalry detachment, was dispatched to scour the middle Blues in an effort to locate the hostiles and recover the stolen property. He was to continue his search northward to the mining camps along the Oregon Trail and then rejoin the main expedition somewhere along the Snake River.[6]

As Reno was leaving. Louis Scholl caught up with the command having been driven out of the desert by Snake raiders. More specifically, he retreated on the advice of Pigeon Hawk who made contact with Big Man. Always on the alert, Scholl had made an interesting discovery. On their dash across the Alvord Desert, Pigeon Hawk would show his German friend a reminder of eastern Oregon's volcanic past. A place held sacred by the Shoshoni, Pigeon Hawk called it *Chak-pahu,* the talking spring . . . it was a geyser surrounded by bubbling mud pots which would remain undetected by white men for another 132 years.[7]

Finally, as Wallen continued eastward, a detachment of dog soldiers—in answer to Has No Horse's request for reinforcements—forded the Snake River and moved into the Ochoco. On July 12, the two military units met on the Malheur River. This being Wallen's first contact with warriors of the Snake nation, he was due for a surprise. Somewhat disillusioned, Wallen would note ". . . they were athletic men, well armed and formidable. Doubtless these Indians are in the habit of visiting the valley of the Great Salt Lake and derive their supply of arms and ammunition from that source." He was right. They were also in the habit of picking them up from any other available source including unwary army patrols.

A few weeks later on Bear River, Wallen gained more insight on the militant Shoshoni. Here, he met Red Sand . . . "a chief who spoke broken English." Wallen believed Red Sand—a Ute war chief riding with the Paviotso Confederacy—had learned English from the Mormons as "he has never had intercourse with white people living west of the Blue Mountains." Wallen was now convinced that "these bands of Snakes are numerous and formidable, roving about in bands of 60 or 70

---

6     Reno's name does not appear again in Wallen's report indicating that he may have continued on to Fort Walla Walla. In 1876, Major Marcus Reno, along with Capt. Frederick Benteen would escape being killed on the Little Big Horn River where Gen. George Custer and 262 troopers of the 7th U.S. Cavalry made their last stand.

7     This geyser which spouts 200 degree water 6 to 8 feet in the air was discovered by Bureau of Land Management employees in March 1991. Located in the remote high desert country east of Steen's Mountain, its existence had been unknown. According to Mark Armstrong, spokesman for BLM, "the geyser runs every minute or so. It was once a churning spring or turbulent bubbling hot spring. Nearby is a series of small mud pots of the sort found in Yellowstone National Park."

and not having been impressed with the powers of the white man, are constantly annoying small parties. . . ." The problem wasn't a matter of the Snakes not being impressed by the Americans for they definitely were. The dilemma stemmed from the fact that they were too smart to tangle with superior man and fire power when the objective could be gained by other methods.

When Wallen left the dog soldiers on the Malheur, he proceeded to Fort Boise and found out just how annoying they could be. "In consequence of the Indian difficulties," Wallen would report, "the fort was abandoned and there was nothing now remaining but the adobe walls of the main building." This could spell disaster for the 1859 emigration. Putting road location on second priority, Wallen sent Lt. Mallory on a reconnaissance of Fort Hall. More bad news. Fort Hall was vacant and in a state of disrepair.

Between the mouth of the Malheur and Owyhee Rivers, Wallen made a curious discovery. Operating out of a run-down shack, Jacob Meyers and John Quitman were doing a thriving business in odds and ends picked up along the Oregon Trail . . . or so they claimed. Apparently, they had some sort of an arrangement with the Snakes who allowed them to carry on their trade without interference. Whatever the terms of agreement, Wallen was suspicious of this commercial enterprise in the heart of hostile territory. Before another month slid by, his doubts would be confirmed.

From this point on the Oregon Trail to its junction with the California Trail, road survey was getting dangerous. Couriers reported that Snake raiders were hitting the wagon trains without let up. With Wallen serving as a buffer between him and the Snake River, Scholl returned to the interior to check the Owyhee country for possible road location. He planned to make a fast march to the eastern base of Steens Mountain where he had been cut off two weeks before and continue his survey toward the Applegate Trail and Salt Lake City. This time, besides engineers, he was accompanied by a cavalry detachment under the command of Capt. Graham.

Scholl—Wallen's civilian counterpart—had an incentive for moving fast. The day after he left the main expedition on the Owyhee, his scouts reported that "horsemen had crossed and recrossed" their previous day's march. This was enough warning for Scholl to order a daylight start the next morning. As dawn tinted the sky, only two pack mules had been loaded when . . . "suddenly and with a yell, several Indians on horseback charged toward camp, swinging their spears and rifles." This excitement caused the dragoons' horses to stampede. At this point, Scholl found an unexpected ally who apparently had taken a liking to the German architect. "The Snake Indian [Pigeon Hawk] who accompanied me from Fort Dalles did me good service; after a few words of conversation between him and our enemies, they ventured nearer and came into our camp. One Indian [probably Pipe] had a fine silver mounted rifle in his possession which belonged to one of a party of 26 men who left The Dalles in late October 1858; only one of them survives and he reported to us in Salt Lake. . . ."

Scholl was favorably impressed with the dog soldiers. He would write with admiration that "these Indians are large and well made." No greenhorn when it came to Indian protocol, Scholl took them by surprise when he offered them presents of blankets and tobacco. In exchange, the warriors gave him a general description of the country and directions which he followed, thereby bypassing one of the bleakest areas in southeastern Oregon on his push to Steens Mountain.

Eight days after his encounter with the dog soldiers, Scholl reached Wildhorse Creek south of Steens Mountain on July 31, 1859. Here, as he put it, "Quite an exciting scene took place." The survey party had blundered onto a single Snake lodge hidden in a grove of aspen. As the soldiers debated over what action to take, a lone Indian woman charged them on a pony and ". . . without bridle or saddle, rode in full gallop toward the nearest mountain." The dragoons were so engrossed in this breakneck ride that they failed to see her husband who slipped in and stole a cavalry mount. Scholl would glumly report that "the Indian took advantage of our admiration about the horsemanship displayed by his woman and lassoed the best horse in the small band and followed her footsteps leaving a well-selected stock of winter supplies behind." He noted that among other things there were "buffalo robes, elk and deer and antelope skins; kouse, kamas and every variety of wild berries constituted their larder." This couple were not some of the under-privileged members of the Shoshoni clan. Fortunately for the soldiers, they didn't disturb anything.

The following day as the survey party moved south toward the Trout Creek Mountains—and a union with the Applegate Trail—they were overtaken by a Snake war party "yelling and howling like beasts." Within minutes they had the soldiers surrounded bringing the column to a halt. Capt. Graham and his dragoons with sabres drawn took up positions around the head of the stalled column while packers formed a barrier with the pack animals around the rear. Sharps carbines were readied for action as Pipe and his warriors circled the surveyors. In the tense moments that followed, Scholl and Pigeon Hawk rode out under a flag of truce to consult with Pipe. Pigeon Hawk explained what the soldiers were doing and that they were not out to cause trouble. Aware that the surveyors hadn't stolen or destroyed the Snake couple's belongings, Pipe called off the attack. Then, he and Scholl "smoked a pipe." As an offering of good will, Scholl presented Pipe with a "pair of new red blankets, tobacco and other minor articles . . . most likely knives, hatchets and mirrors." With this, Pipe showed Scholl the most direct route to Great Salt Lake and advised him to take it hinting of big trouble brewing in the Ochoco.[8]

---

8    Letter from L. Scholl, Fort Dalles, December 3, 1859 to Capt. Alfred Pleasonton, 2nd Dragoons, Hdqs. Military Department of Oregon, Fort Vancouver, Washington Territory.

Scholl took Pipe's warning seriously and arrived in Salt Lake City several days ahead of Wallen's main party.

On July 28, six days after Scholl disappeared into the Owyhee country, Lt. Mallory rejoined Wallen west of Raft River and reported that Snake war parties were attacking wagon trains on both sides of the Snake River. These acts of aggression extended from Fort Boise for several hundred miles to the east. That same day, Major Reynolds' 3rd Artillery and Capt. Stark's 2nd Dragoons intercepted Wallen's line of march. Stark would report that the dog soldiers were committing depredations as far south as the road leading from Salt Lake City to Sacramento. All of the emigrants the three army commands had encountered were in bad shape. Expecting to replenish supplies at Fort Bridger (burned by the Mormons), Fort Hall or Fort Boise, they were in a starving condition. Adding to their misery, white traders operating between the abandoned outposts were profiteering from the travelers' misfortunes.

Reynolds' artillery rolled out to escort wagon companies to Fort Walla Walla while Stark's dragoons began clean-up of the illicit business operations along the Oregon Trail. The word was already out that Jake Meyers was collecting a two dollar toll on wagons at the Snake River crossing for camping privileges and charging 50 cents a bucket for water out of his well. He had seen to it that all water nearby was polluted which Wallen could vouch for. Meyers was also doing quite well trading in used wagons. Capt. Stark paid him a visit, cleaned up the water and posted free camping signs. A short time later, Meyers was put permanently out of business when he got into an argument with his partner, John Quitman, who shot him.

On August 9, Wallen reached the California Trail and headed for Camp Floyd arriving on August 16 where he reported to Gen. Johnston. Four days later, after drawing supplies, he started back for the Columbia by way of the Oregon Trail and Fort Walla Walla. Enroute, he found Major Lynde camped on Bear River and borrowed Lt. Livingston and a troop of dragoons to guard his ox train back to Fort Boise. For all practical purposes, Wallen had completed his end of the road survey.[9]

Scholl, who had split from Wallen on July 22 at the mouth of the Owyhee River, was already in Salt Lake City when Wallen arrived. Not only had his surveyors made the best time but they had covered the shortest distance of all the engineering parties. Lt. Dixon would note that "the entire distance by land from Fort Dalles to Great Salt Lake Valley, following Scholl's route, is 630 miles." This distance would include Lt. Bonnycastle's survey on the northern section of the road from Camp Division to Fort Dalles. Capt. Wallen on his plunge from Fort

---

9    Information on Capt. Wallen's travel route from Fort Dalles to Salt Lake City, Utah, found in "Report on Wallen's Road Expedition," *Olympia Herald*, September 16, 1859, Olympia, Washington Territory.

Dalles via the Bear River ferry covered 902 miles; and on his return via Fort Walla Walla, the distance was 737 miles.

According to Lt. Dixon, this was a very accurate survey conducted under trying circumstances. "The distances were measured by an odometer which was carefully compared with the measurements by the chain from time to time.[10] Also a complete compass line from Fort Dalles to the ferry on Bear River was run by Mr. Streeter . . . taking numerous bearings each day on all mountain peaks and prominent land marks along the route."[11]

As it turned out, Harney's desire to have a marked trail between Fort Dalles and Camp Floyd was fulfilled by a civilian employee—not the Army Corps of Engineers. Meanwhile back at Camp Division on Crooked River, Lt. Bonnycastle was having his share of interruptions.

---

10    There are 66 feet to a chain and 80 chains (5,280 feet) to a mile.

11    Lt. Dixon to Capt. Pleasonton, *Office of Military Roads*, Department of Oregon, Fort Vancouver, Washington Territory, January 1860.

# CHAPTER 94

# FOR GOD'S SAKE SEND HELP!

*There are times when you have to betray your friends—but you don't have to do it with all this garbage about peace and democracy. . . .*

**James Burnham**
Doctor of Philosophy

By the time Wallen's courier of July 7 bearing news of the starving emigrants camped at Lake Harney arrived at Camp Division, Lt. Dixon had already made a probe to the south and determined that the Applegate Trail insofar as a military route was concerned, passed "entirely too far to the south to ever be a good thoroughfare to the state of Oregon." He also found out from Major Lynde that it was under heavy bombardment from Big Man and Burning Wagon's troops. It was also rumored that Burning Wagon had been killed in a wagon train raid.

Based on information he had obtained from the Paiutes about an Indian trail leading from the forks of Crooked River into the John Day Valley, Bonnycastle sent Lt. Johnston with 15 dragoons, Yellow Jacket and Samuel Johnston, wagon master, with 10 days rations to explore this route on July 1—the day Capt. Wallen left Camp Division. It was Bonnycastle's intention to link the trail with Scholl's survey. Meantime, Bonnycastle swept into Paulina Valley and went east without sighting an Indian but he did locate what would become the northern section of the Yreka Trail. Doubling back through Rabbit Valley, he united with Lt. Dixon and together they began exploration of Big Summit Prairie where they found evidence of a recent large Shoshoni encampment. Around the outer perimeter of the deserted camp were improved rifle pits and breastworks of logs. This was the first recorded evidence of an actual field fortification constructed by Indians—discovered some 22 years before Joseph of the Nez Perce was given credit for that military feat. Bonnycastle and his staff officers examined these fortifications with great care. They were more impressed over this discovery than the supply route they were searching for. From a military standpoint this was extremely valuable information for it gave the army forewarning of what type of people were defending the Ochoco. But this bit of intelligence was ignored in the belief that an Indian could not possess such knowledge of military tactics—much less apply it.

45

Here, they also observed mirror flashes from the top of a high flat-topped mountain and tracks of hundreds of horses which joined in Big Summit Prairie and proceeded north over a high divide between Lookout Mountain and the cone-shaped spire of Round Mountain. This would be the track of a large war party enroute to the upper Ochoco River Valley, the birthplace of Has No Horse. With this new information, Bonnycastle returned to Camp Division and Lt. Dixon proceeded westward looking for a military link to the mid-Willamette Valley.

Lt. Johnston, who entered Big Summit Prairie on July 6, just ahead of the Snake war party, returned to Camp Division on July 16 and reported that from Big Summit Prairie it was impossible to take wagons through the Mitchell country to the John Day River. He would also note that Yellow Jacket ". . . the Luake [Lohim] Indian proved of great service as the guide [George Rundell] was perfectly ignorant of the country. The information he [Yellow Jacket] gave me of the country before I passed over it proved to be correct." Lt. Johnston gave his course as being across ". . . Camas [Big Summit] Prairie on the left or north branch of Crooked River to Whoptaplas [Bridge] Creek, a stream emptying into the John Day; from thence to the Chopomgaz [Cherry Creek] another stream flowing into the John Day; and from thence to Scholl's Butte [Wagner Mt.] within two miles of the John Day River. From that Butte to the Deschutes bridge [the pontoon bridge erected on June 11] the country has been explored [by Louis Scholl] and found perfectly practicable for wagons." He also found the Indian trail from the John Day River to Trout Creek and it was in good condition for wagon travel.

With the arrival of Wallen's message from Lake Harney notifying Bonnycastle he was responsible for the safety of the starving emigrants of 1858, the Lieutenant was faced with a bad situation. He was charged, not only with a road survey to conduct, but the protection of American civilians from Snake attack. When they didn't arrive at Camp Division, he went looking and found they had lost Wallen's obvious trail and were again wandering in the central Oregon desert southeast of the head of Crooked River. There was only one thing to do and that was to escort them to The Dalles City before they died of exposure or fell victim to Has No Horse.

Pushed by necessity, Lt. Bonnycastle would discover the best and shortest route from Camp Division to Fort Dalles . . . the northern segment of Scholl's shortcut to Salt Lake City. It would lay down Crooked River to Eagle Creek; up Eagle Creek into the lower Ochoco Valley; thence up McKay and Lofton Creeks to Trout Creek with only two bad hills to cross—the Crooked River-Ochoco Divide and the ridge between Lofton and Trout Creeks. Following this route, it took Bonnycastle just 12 days to escort 17 broken-down emigrant wagons from Harney Basin to The Dalles. In his official report of the rescue, Bonnycastle would note ". . . had the route been known beforehand as to watering places, grass, etc., I should have brought the train in easily to The Dalles in 10 days which would have given me an average of 17 miles, or a little more, to the day. . . ."[1] In so doing, he had vindicated Steve Meek. This feat came as a shock to the 1845 travelers who 14 years before wandered for a month and a half to make the same journey.

Two days after Lt. Johnston reported back to Camp Division that it was impossible to take wagons through the Mitchell country; and the same day Capt. Wallen found Fort Boise in shambles, Indian Agent Dennison—in view of mounting Snake hostilities—requested that a detachment of U.S. Regulars be stationed at the Warm Springs Agency. This was on July 14, 1859. Before the month ended, Has No Horse had assembled nearly 300 dog soldiers—the largest single force yet to strike the Americans south of the Columbia—and began his march on the reservation.[2] Heavily armed with treacherous short bows, favorite war clubs, sacred shields, buffalo lances and the latest in modern rifles—.58 calibre army Springfields and .52 calibre Sharps, both deadly up to 800 yards—they were extremely dangerous.[3]

In keeping with Shoshoni custom, Has No Horse packed a ceremonial lance attached by an elk-skin sash to his neck. Under certain circumstances, he would take his place at the front line of his warriors and thrust the lance into the ground and there fight or await death; he could not retreat unless one of his own men should pull up the lance to which he was honor-bound.

As the Shoshoni moved leisurely down the Ochoco Valley, Lt. Dixon—unaware of what was happening—was paralleling their line of march a few miles to the southeast. Working his way toward Crooked River through a series of linking prairies, Dixon—a topographic engineer—gazed with awe on the panorama unfolding before him. The mountains—unlike the Cascades—were carpeted with pine grass, bunch grass, mountain brome and wild pea-vines while the prairies were a solid bed of red clover interspersed with fields of Camas whose roots when dried were pounded into meal by the Shoshoni, forming one of their main food supplies, *quamock,* their word for bread.

Upon these mountain meadows were grazing herds of antelope, mule deer and elk, so numerous that they had to be driven out of the way to allow the soldiers to pass. Prairie chicken, ducks, geese and several species of grouse scampered and flew over the prairies like hordes of mosquitoes. Black bear and silver-tipped grizzly bear roamed the timbered hillsides while big horn sheep fed at the 6,000 foot elevation on Lookout Mountain. This was a far cry from what the army had become accustomed to finding on their sporadic raids into eastern Oregon. Dixon

---

1   *U.S. Messages and Documents 1859-60,* p. 113.

2   In a letter written by Dr. Thomas Fitch, dated August 10, 1859, and addressed to Capt. Henry Black, United States Army, Fort Dalles, Oregon, Fitch claims he personally counted "about 250 Snake Indians." Shane, *Early Explorations Through Warm Springs Reservation,* p.21.

3   Berkeley, Lewis, *Arms and Ammunition 1776-1865 of the U.S. Service,* Smithsonian Institute Press.

was so enraptured over this wild life that his report turned to flora and fauna instead of topography. That would soon change.

Dixon wasn't the only one making exciting discoveries in the summer of '59. Back east, Edwin Drake was up to no good on the banks of a small creek near Titusville, Pennsylvania. He was drilling a hole. At 69 feet, the hole filled with oil—which signaled monumental changes in the development of warfare, not to mention world industry. Yet few could see much merit in Drake's accomplishment not the least of which was John B. Floyd, Secretary of War. The first newspaper mention came 17 days later, setting off a land rush much like that of gold in the John Day Valley three years later.

Meantime, on August 2, 1859 near the present site of Prineville, the Snake raiders claimed the first American casualties of the Warm Springs offensive. A party of miners headed for the Colville goldfields would never arrive. Now, fresh scalps adorned the rifles of Has No Horse, Wolf Dog and Paulina. Undoubtedly, the army was aware of this attack and most likely Lt. Dixon rescued the survivors. When Wallen's report of Dixon's probe into central Oregon appeared in *The Olympia Herald* dated September 16, 1859, he mentions five civilians killed by a Snake war party.[4]

It appears that Lt. Dixon sent a fast-riding messenger to warn the Warm Springs Agency because Dr. Fitch—post commander—would report that he was alerted to the approaching danger. Fitch immediately dispatched Simtustus and his rifle squad—reinforced by several hundred reservation Indians—to run them off. This would not be easy. The Snakes, believing they had been betrayed by their own kind when the Wascos and Walla Wallas volunteered to lead army personnel on punitive and exploratory raids into the Ochoco, were in an exceptionally mean frame of mind. Badly outnumbered, the dog soldiers slashed through the enemy lines on sheer nerve alone and pushed the Agency defenders to the very gates of the Warm Springs stockade. At this lonely outpost, the Shoshoni attracted the attention of the Oregonians.

Twelve hundred Agency Indians, hounded to the brink of doom, felt the galling sting of Shoshoni justice. The Confederated tribesmen fell like wheat before a sickle as the systematic search for Snake captives began. During this chase some of the braves commenced stripping the reservation of all livestock, rounding up 150 head of horses and 40 beef cattle in the first sweep. Tall Man and his warriors now running wild, murdered 13 Wasco women in payment of their own dead and mutilated daughters and wives. Included in this carnage was Simtustus' stepmother and sister.

The war chiefs stolidly setting their mounts against a backdrop of flaming long huts, watched their budding army with grim satisfaction as the sun god dipped

---

4    The bodies were identified as those of S.F. Shepard, his brother W.F. Shepard, W.C. Riggs, C. Rains, and E.C. Hall. *The Olympia Herald*, Washington Territory, September 16, 1859.

in silent salute behind a fuchsia-tinted Mount Jefferson. It was later reported that War Spirit, his eyes narrowed against the smoke and flames, glimpsed the ashen face of Dr. Fitch peering out of a window of his barricaded quarters. Kneeing his horse into explosive action, he charged the fortified cabin and in high good spirits flourished a white man's gory scalp in Fitch's face.

Dennison's fear of a Shoshoni uprising—precipitated by Fitch's unwarranted attack on Tall Man's camp—was fulfilled. On August 7, a winded Walla Walla messenger burst into his office bearing communications from Fitch. "Directed to any white man . . . for God's sake send some help as soon as possible. We are surrounded with Snakes . . . they have killed a good many Agency Indians and got all our stock . . . don't delay a single minute!" As this ominous message was being delivered to Agent Dennison, Louis Scholl galloped into Camp Floyd having surveyed and marked a military road from The Dalles to Salt Lake City in 64 days, thus proving to Gen. Harney and the United States that it could be done.

Dennison would also find out that 10 white families were now crowded into the stockade on Fifteenmile Creek while Indian refugees from Warm Springs—in a state of terror—were trying to force their way into the fortress for protection. Eastern Oregon from The Dalles to Warm Springs was in a state of shock. Gen. Harney now had his reputation to uphold.

As darkness engulfed the Cascades, the festivities began. While the dog soldiers entertained Fitch and his nervous companions with a scalp dance, Black Eagle—Paulina's brother—started the government horses moving toward the shadowy outline of Gray Butte. In this pandemonium, Fitch saw a chance to escape. He and four civilian employees slipped along the murky edge of the blockhouse wall and crawled toward the pack trail to The Dalles. Some distance from the howling mob, they spied one of the Agency Indians who supplied them with horses discarded from the main herd. Putting miles between themselves and the disaster-ridden Agency, they galloped straight in on a lone horseman . . . their fatal mistake of the evening. In a rapid exchange of gunfire, two more whites were killed. Fitch and the others broke free and made good their escape.

Three days after the arrival of the Walla Walla messenger, Dr. Fitch whipped his lathered horse into The Dalles City. At the Wells Fargo office he posted a letter to Capt. Black at Fort Dalles relating his "terrible experience." Among other things, he requested an immediate transfer from the Warm Springs Agency. "Finding myself in peril in following my vocation as resident physician at the reservation, I feel it incumbent to remain at The Dalles till the troubles are over as they [the Snakes] have threatened my life frequently. Hoping that this matter may meet with prompt attention."[5]

---

5  For more detail on the Snake raids on Warm Springs, see, *The War of Rebellion*, Vol. XIII, No. 59, Pt. 2, Series 1, Vol. 50, Pt. 2, pp.335-45; *The Illustrated History of Central Oregon*, p. 938.

Where were the Oregon Rangers assigned to defend the Warm Springs Agency when the Snake attack occurred? Shortly after Capt. Fitch and his Warm Springs militia returned from their misguided plunge into the Ochoco, Capt. Wilber—expecting trouble—decided to set up a buffer zone between the reservation and the Snake raiders. It was also his intent to guard Wallen's newly constructed pontoon bridge across the Deschutes River. Accordingly, the Oregon Rangers established an outpost on the east side of the Deschutes some 14 miles east of the Agency headquarters and nearly 10 miles downriver from the pontoon bridge.[6] This rock fortress constructed at the mouth of a large natural depression called The Pot was easily defendable but as a checkpoint it proved to be worthless. Stationed at this remote location, the Rangers were unaware of the present attack on the Agency buildings. Because of the fort's limited access—one way only—even if they had been conscious of what was taking place, three or four dog soldiers could have stalled any assistance for an indefinite period of time.

Following Fitch's arrival at The Dalles, it took Dennison a week to recruit a dozen men willing to go to the aid of reservation personnel. On August 22, with the Umatilla warrior Cut Mouth John acting as scout, they slipped into the deserted post and Dennison was much relieved to find that none of the permanent Agency buildings had been destroyed although all government arms, ammunition and other property had been stolen. Immediately, he sent Cut Mouth John out to gather his scattered flock and the work of restoration began. Holding top priority was the removal of the Agency headquarters to a more defendable location.

This begun, Dennison dispatched scouting parties to the east side of the Deschutes in hope of locating some of the 700 horses reported missing. Although a number of work oxen belonging to the Department of Interior were recovered not one horse or mule could be found. Dennison estimated the government loss at $9,000 and that of the Confederated Tribes at $7,000.

For some reason, during five months of Snake raids, Gen. Harney—the celebrated Indian fighter—was turning the other cheek. Maybe he was more interested in locating military roads and escorting more settlers into a crowded Willamette Valley; or perhaps he could see no reason to become involved in a conflict which pitted Indian against Indian. Then again, maybe he secretly believed as Gen. Wool and Gen. Clarke did before him that the Oregonians were instigating a disturbance to force the army regulars into a showdown with the Snakes in an effort to free eastern Oregon for settlement. Whatever the reason other disquieting actions were unfolding in both military camps.

James Nesmith—who thought the campaign to place the Confederated Tribes on the Warm Springs Reserve was "a damn farce"—resigned as Oregon

---

6    Evidence of rock fortifications located on the east bank of the Deschutes River between Swamp Creek and Cove Creek were discovered by an archeological survey conducted by the Bureau of Land Management in the late 1970s.

Superintendent of Indian Affairs to run for the U.S. Senate. He was replaced by the Rev. Edward Rachford Geary, a Presbyterian missionary and co-founder of Albany College.[7] A kindly man, Geary was ill-prepared to cope with an aggressive Indian nation and an equally belligerent white population. He would get his first briefing on the current situation from Courtney Walker who worked extensively with the Snake war tribes as Indian agent stationed at Fort Hall before they overran the outpost.

In a letter to Geary dated September 9, 1859, Walker asked some poignant questions ". . . in 1858 the Warm Springs Indians made ingress into the Snake country and committed most flagrant outrages. Were they reproached for this act? Or were they not encouraged to renew these damnable outrages by our people in 1859 . . . ?" He would further state that ". . . I was myself in the Snake nation a number of years and have known them, when it was completely in their power to slay the offenders, to suffer and endure wrongs without retaliation." Walker would give Supt. Geary much food for thought.

But the most troublesome news came hand-in-hand with Has No Horse's devastating raid on the Warm Springs Agency. Wolf Dog and Paulina—after leading Capt. Wallen's command into the war zone south of the Blues—had "decamped taking with them several horses and two good rifles."[8] This unpublicized communiqué would shatter Dennison's optimism that Wolf Dog intended to follow a course of non-resistance.

During this shake-up in the Oregonian's ranks, the Shoshoni also had other things besides Warm Springs to occupy their minds. In early summer One Moccasin, the Paiute holy man whose dream of peaceful bliss with his "white brothers" never faded, died—throwing the reins of command to his son-in-law Bad Face, who rode stirrup to stirrup with Has No Horse. This would bring the mounted Paiutes (erroneously called Bannocks by the Americans) into Wolf Dog's camp.

In a tragic offset, old Nevava—the northern Ute warlord—who was sympathetic to Wolf Dog's cause, was overthrown by a tough young Uncompahgre warrior, Ouray. Of mixed Ute-Apache blood, Ouray—The Arrow—would follow in Gourd Rattler's footsteps. The Arrow preferred talking to fighting. It was said that he liked to talk so much that he learned both English and Spanish and would sit for hours conversing with any traveler who would listen. Within four years, he would help the U.S. government gather many of the Utes onto the reservation and when Red Sand attempted to carry on the war in 1879—a year after Has No Horse's

---

7    "Memorial Life and Services of Edward R. Geary, D.D.," *Oregon Historical Quarterly*, LV, p. 148.

8    This escape would not become public knowledge until nine years later when John Webster Perit Huntington—appointed Superintendent of Oregon Indian Affairs by President Lincoln in 1863—revealed it in a letter to W.S. Taylor, Umatilla Indian Agency, December, 22, 1868. (National Archives, Bureau of Indian Affairs, Oregon Superintendency, Letters Sent.)

final defeat—Arrow refused to join him. He remained on his comfortable Colorado farm with his wife, Chipeta, and died "like a white man" a year later in 1880.[9]

Granted, both Oregonians and Shoshoni were facing difficult times, but Has No Horse in one daring raid had inflicted a $16,000 loss in government and Indian property while claiming an unrecorded number of human lives.[10] It was now obvious that Wolf Dog had officially declared war upon the United States.

9    Schmitt, *Fighting Indians of the West*, pp. 284-91.
10   *Bureau of Indian Affairs Report 1859*, p. 389.

CHAPTER 95

# CRY OF VENGEANCE

*Some people learn quickly, and others learn slowly; and preachers, school-teachers and military people most slowly of all.*

**Capt. John Bourke**
3rd U.S. Cavalry


In 1859, 30,000 people and 100,000 cattle took the Oregon Trail; one third of this multitude came to Oregon. Catering to the elite of the migration—and there were a few—the finer restaurants in The Dalles City were featuring a new treat on their menus ... "Saratoga Chips." It took six years for this delicacy to reach the Pacific Coast. In 1853, George Crum—an Adirondack Indian—was head chef at Moon Lake Lodge in Saratoga Springs, New York. As the story goes, one evening a particularly fussy guest kept returning his french fries to the kitchen complaining that they were too thick. In a fury, Crum grabbed a vicious-looking butcher knife and a Maine potato, sliced it into pieces as thin as newsprint and plunged the slices into boiling fat. Then, knife in hand, he personally served the golden, curling flakes to the stubborn diner who proclaimed them delicious. He wasn't dumb and the next time you enjoy potato chips, give thanks to Chef George Crum who invented them.

Other Oregon travelers weren't faring so well. Owing to the protection offered by Gen. Harney's numerous army detachments in eastern Oregon that section of the trail between Fort Dalles and the ruins of Fort Boise escaped serious attack. Those who took the southern route into Klamath Basin ran the Shoshoni gauntlet. One train was so completely cut off that their fate might never have been known but for information furnished by a Klamath Indian who related the affair to Lt. Henry Abbot. The men were all killed at the moment of attack and the children were removed with the plunder. The women, left to fend for themselves, apparently died of starvation for they were never seen again.

Another wagon train—against Capt. Wallen's advice—turned off the main route, intending to take the Crooked River Trail. It was driven back to the Malheur River with the loss of one man and four wagons.[1] Major Reynolds of the 3rd U.S.

---

1    *Oregon Argus*, September 24, 1859; *The Portland Oregonian*, October 15, 1859.

53

Artillery out of Fort Yamhill, with 100 riflemen and eight field pieces escorted the advance of the '59 emigration to Fort Dalles while Capt. Wallen with his engineers remained at Fort Boise to guard the rear wagons. From there, Lt. Mallory with 60 1st U.S. Dragoons, made a four-day ride back along the Oregon Trail to "... succor some belated and famishing people."[2] In answer to the pleas of distress, Col. Wright sent 250 sacks of flour, 50 barrels of pork and other necessities by army wagons out of Fort Walla Walla to later trains which were also destitute.

During Capt. Wallen's return from Salt Lake City to Fort Boise, an interesting episode took place near Camp Division. At the time the dog soldiers were staging their August raid on Warm Springs, Wolf Dog's spiritual advisor, White Cloud, disappeared with his family while on a hunting trip. In the ensuing search, five Snake warriors were found dead and it was believed that Walla Walla scouts had ambushed them and taken White Cloud and his family captive. This was a very bad omen.

Five days after White Cloud's disappearance, a strange looking group approached Wallen's camp at the mouth of the Boise River. A heavily armed Snake warrior "rather slight in build with most determined grey eyes and long braided hair" was followed by an equally armed woman with an infant strapped to her back. Although showing traces of former good looks, the woman "bore fearful evidence of the past suffering she had endured." There was a dent in her skull from an old bullet wound and a badly twisted arm gave silent proof that sometime in the past her arm had been broken and improperly set. Behind her, rode three more children . . . a boy, also packing a rifle, and two young girls.

As White Cloud, the Snake medicine chief, slowly rode into Wallen's camp it was noticed that his left arm was broken and bleeding from a recent bullet would. Later, he would report that he intercepted "a party of United States Surveyors nearly 150 in number" and one of them set his broken arm.[3]

Since Capt. Wallen's military road expedition was the only survey party operating between the Cascade Range and the Rocky Mountains in August 1859, it becomes obvious that White Cloud met Wallen's engineers. And the man who set his broken arm must have been Capt. John Randolph, Wallen's medical staff officer. However, in keeping with his reluctance to mention contacts with the Snakes, Wallen's official report makes no note of this chance encounter but 18 months later, it would make headlines when a reporter for the *Cleveland Weekly Plain Dealer* broke the story on January 30, 1861.[4]

---

2 A letter appearing in *The Oregon Herald*, Washington Territory, September 16, 1859.

3 James Kimball, *Eleven Years a Captive Among the Snake Indians*, p.11.

4 Short narrative of James Kimball, "Eleven years a captive among the Snake Indians," *The Cleveland Ohio Weekly Plain Dealer*, Wednesday, January 30, 1861. Twenty-eight copies reprinted for Friends of Charles F. Heartman, Metuchem, New Jersey, 1930.

In 1829, White Cloud was born James P. Kimball in Onondago County, New York. At the age of 19, he and his wife, Jane, joined a wagon company in Syracuse, New York and were taken captive by the Bear Killer Snakes in 1848.[5] After being with the Snakes for two years, joining them in the hunt and on the war trail, Kimball—now known as White Cloud—became a student of Red Wolf's (later Wolf Dog's) spiritual advisor, Cut Hair. Cut Hair was an old man and after studying with him four years, Kimball succeeded him as tribal medicine man and held that honorable position until his flight for freedom. During this period, the Snakes ranged throughout Oregon, Washington Territory, upper California and beyond.

To give an idea of the extent of their travels, Jane Kimball claimed she had met Olive Oatman who was taken captive by the Apaches in 1851 and sold into slavery to the Mojaves where she was finally rescued in 1856.[6] In these wide ranging forays, Jim Kimball met Kit Carson—possibly in New Mexico—who gave him the idea how to escape and it was on Carson's suggestion that Kimball began going on hunts with his family, thereby accustoming the Shoshoni to his absence. He, himself, had had many opportunities to escape, but none with his family.

During their 11 years as captives, Kimball had thought of escape but the opportunity for flight with his family was never offered. But over the years as he and Jane appeared perfectly content, the Snake's vigilance relaxed and Kimball was permitted many liberties. Then in August 1859—with the raids on Warm Springs occupying Wolf Dog's mind—Kimball saw his chance. At this time the Bear Killers were camped "about four days' ride from the mouth of the Columbia" which meant the Snake camp was very close to present-day Prineville, Oregon.[7]

At this camp, Kimball decided to make his escape with his wife and four children. He, his wife Jane and Warrior, their 10-year-old son, were armed with rifles. In addition, Kimball packed a revolver and a single-shot pistol which was used by his father, Major Newell Kimball in the War of 1812. On the fourth day of their flight they were met by five Snake warriors on the Malheur River. Not taking any chances of being detected, Kimball ambushed them, killing all five but in the process one of the Snake's bullets broke Kimball's left arm.

To throw off suspicion in case the bodies were found by other Shoshoni patrols, Kimball scalped the Indians in what he called "Walla Walla style" a method not well known to the whitemen. He would explain that "the Snakes cut off the scalp in a circular pattern while the Walla Wallas removed it in a triangular form." He was gambling that if the bodies were discovered, the Snakes would think it was the Walla Wallas and on the failure of he and his family's return would think they were prisoners of the Walla Wallas. It worked. Wolf Dog, now convinced that

---

5     See *Thunder Over the Ochoco, Vol. II*, Part 3, Chapter 62, "Death Rides Our Back Trail."

6     *The American Heritage Book of Indians*, p. 384.

7     James Kimball, *Eleven Years a Captive Among the Snake Indians*, p.9. When on the move, the horse Indians would cover from 60 to 80 miles a day.

the Walla Walla scouts had captured White Cloud, was more vicious than ever on his attacks on the Warm Springs Reservation.

The next afternoon after the Snake ambush, Kimball ran into Wallen's survey party where "one of them set his broken arm." From here, Kimball continued east with Lt. Mallory's U.S. Dragoons to Fort Laramie. Now on foot, faced with crossing the plains in the dead of winter and traveling to the north to evade any contact with the Shoshoni clan—namely the Comanches—it would take another year to reach the eastern settlements on the upper Mississippi River. During this journey two of Kimball's daughters died of exposure. Then on arrival at the settlements, his son Warrior, supplied with rot-gut whiskey, dropped dead in a Mississippi barroom.

Thus ends the saga of White Cloud, Wolf Dog's New York medicine man known to his family as James P. Kimball. Eighteen months had now gone by since his escape from Wolf Dog's camp.

Shortly after White Cloud's disappearance—back on the Warm Springs front—Agent Dennison received welcome word from Portland, on August 25, 1859, that Capt. Andrew Smith was bringing a company of 1st U.S. Dragoons out of Fort Lane to guard the Warm Springs Agency. He was also notified that a force from Fort Yamhill under the command of Lt. Phil Sheridan was being sent into the Ochoco in an effort to recover the stolen government property. Smith's orders were ". . . to insure no further depredation befall the reservation Indians." Sheridan's instructions directed him to ". . . sweep the country from the mouth of Crooked River to the headwaters of the Umatilla." Dennison, acting on advice from Cut Mouth John—the Umatilla army scout—suggested to Harney that Sheridan should search south of the Blues if he wished to have any luck in retrieving the government horses.

Heeding this suggestion, Sheridan attempted to penetrate the lower Ochoco Valley but was repulsed by hard-hitting dog soldiers led by the Snake war chiefs, Lean Man (Torepe) and Horse Trap (Hadsapoke). The dragoons—now wise to Shoshoni warfare—made no effort to engage them in a fight as it was certain that Has No Horse and Wolf Dog were farther in, ready to strike at a moment's notice.

The absence of Lt. Bonnycastle's command suggests that he had retreated to Fort Dalles at the onset of the August hostilities. For whatever reason, Sheridan would find the Camp Division supply depot abandoned. Slipping across the divide into Crooked River, he found where the horse herd had divided. Sheridan's scouts after following the tracks several hours brought back startling news. This was no ordinary raid but a well organized plan. Part of the stolen stock had been taken into Paulina Valley, some towards Bear Valley and the remainder went down the south fork of Crooked River—within sight of Camp Division—into Yreka Valley which tended to confirm Dennison's suspicions.

In his report to Supt. Geary of August 30, 1859, Dennison wrote: "I am satisfied from observation and what I can learn here that the stock stolen has been driven into Yreka Valley or that vicinity. . . ." In this same letter he also thanked Geary for his "express of the 17th instant" which contained a copy of Special Order No. 86 stating Harney's intent to station U.S. troops at Warm Springs.

Instead of following the horse tracks into Yreka Valley, Sheridan stayed within his orders and swung north toward the Umatilla Agency where he picked up Agent George Abbot and provided an escort to The Dalles. As Sheridan moved into the John Day country, Wolf Dog's troops entered the Warm Springs Reservation from the south. For the next two months it was touch-and-go with Paulina giving his undivided attention to the reservation while Has No Horse and Big Man kept the army busy in engagements along the Oregon and Applegate Trails.

Although Smith's dragoons amounted to little more than a goodwill token on Harney's part, whenever they sounded boots and saddles and came pounding to the rescue of the Agency Indians, the Shoshoni would vanish like mist in the sage. This soon gave the soldiers and their Indian allies a feeling of security that eventually brought about the complete demoralization of Warm Springs.

Night after night, Paulina's guerrillas, carefully avoiding the U.S. Dragoons, ripped through the Wasco-Walla Walla's weakening lines of defense. Under this constant hammering, the Agency Indians were driven into a near state of panic and had it not been for the timely appearance of the dragoons, Paulina would have twice succeeded in confiscating another large herd of Indian ponies. In early fall when these peoples' future existence was as uncertain as a flickering candle in the evening breeze, and when Dennison was offering every possible inducement to hold them on the reservation—Harney blundered.

Perhaps, because the dog soldiers were bothering no one but reservation Indians on the western front, he believed the U.S. troops could serve a more useful purpose on the southern and eastern battlefronts. Anyway, on October 8, 1859, Capt. Black alerted Dennison of Harney's intention to withdraw all army regulars stationed at the Warm Springs Agency with the deadline being set as November 5. Dennison rushed a message to Supt. Geary asking him to use all available influence on Harney to reconsider and if necessary, apply pressure on Gov. Whiteaker to prevent this recall from taking place. When Wolf Dog's spies made him aware of this proposal, he issued his own proclamation. If the Long Knives were withdrawn he would drive the Confederated tribesmen into The Dalles and if necessary, pursue them to Portland as punishment for joining forces with the Ghost People. Taking this warning at face value, all civilian employees at the Agency gave notice that if the soldiers left, so would they. Dennison classified these men as being "some of the best and bravest men in the country."[8]

On these grounds, Dennison pleaded with Geary to exert all his power to see that at least a small force remained at Warm Springs during the winter, if for no

---

8    Bancroft, *History of Oregon*, Vol. 2, Chap. XIX, "The Warm Springs Raids."

other reason, to give the reservation Indians confidence in the U.S. government. As for spring, Dennison would write ". . . it will require, in my opinion, a full company of dragoons to protect the reservation and secure the Agency Indian's rights. Please give this matter your earliest attention. . . ." Gen. Harney was not easily intimidated. "The Dragoons will be removed from Warm Springs on November 5, 1859—as stated!" And they were.

By mid-winter of '59-60, Wolf Dog fulfilled his threat. The moment the cavalry left, the Snakes struck the reservation with unleashed fury. Heading a three-pronged assault, Has No Horse, Big Man and Paulina put the Confederated tribes, Agency personnel and every white settler on the Deschutes Plateau into a complete rout; a dash for safety that didn't lose momentum until it spent itself on the rocky bench between The Dalles City and Fort Dalles. From here, to the consternation of their white benefactors, the reservation Indians couldn't be budged for the rest of the winter.

Come spring, Dennison was again faced with the weary task of gathering his reluctant wards and forcing their return to Warm Springs. During this regrouping of his scattered flock, Dennison thought "to hell with it" and quit the Indian service. George Abbot, agent from Umatilla, was quickly reassigned as special agent to the Warm Springs Reservation with William Logan—a physician—serving as his assistant. Finally, Harney relented in his stand of non-cooperation and sent Lt. John Gregg with 20 Mounted Rifles to aid Abbot in his far-flung roundup of Warm Springs residents. Harney then ordered Gregg to proceed to the reservation and remain there for the summer making one wonder what offense the lieutenant committed to warrant such punishment. Once the Agency Indians were again firmly ensconced within the reservation boundaries, action on the Warm Springs battlefield was relatively subdued for the remainder of the summer.

# CHAPTER 96

# MAKE PEACE!

*For more than two decades after 1849, the Superintendent of Indian Affairs in the territory and state of Oregon had only partial information about the Indians under his jurisdiction. . . .*

**Stephen Daw Beckham**
*Indian Distribution in Oregon*

By 1860, the United States was harboring 32 million restless souls looking for an opportunity to better their lot in life. To satisfy this craving, Harney made plans to firm up Wallen's route through central Oregon in an effort to open more lands for settlement. Already, 500,000 emigrants were living west of the Rocky Mountains and the Pony Express was established in April to carry the mail between St. Joseph, Missouri and the Pacific coast . . . a dangerous ride that would be made in 10 days.

The army was contracting for 43,000 bushels of oats while hay was being shipped in from San Francisco at $77 a ton to feed the cavalry mounts at Fort Dalles. Bids for up to 700 pounds of beef a month were being advertised at 9-3/4 cents a pound to feed the troops stationed at the fort. The widely known technique of getting rich on military contracts was pioneered in eastern Oregon by far west "sutlers," as the suppliers to army posts were known. A 300 percent markup was typical and it's a matter of record that one sutler supplying the eastern Oregon outposts parlayed $4,000 into $193,000 during a nine year period. Something had to be done to curb this profiteering.

Based on Wallen's report of central Oregon, it became imperative that the Ochoco be opened to crop and livestock production. Ironically, Capt. Smith and Lts. Bonnycastle, Crook and Sorrel—instead of chasing Shoshoni during the winter of '59-60—were in the meat business. They were having ammunition sent in from San Francisco at 66 cents a pound and becoming professional game hunters. While Crook and Sorrel did the hunting, Smith put up the money and Bonnycastle provided an outlet by selling the meat in Yreka, California where most likely it ended up in an army mess hall.

In early spring, Ed Geary—a minister by profession and superintendent of Indian Affairs by political appointment—attempted to alleviate strained relations between the Snakes and the Americans. He had been given Congressional permission to outfit a 40-mule pack train with tools, construction materials and agricultural implements along with a herd of Indian ponies to be delivered to the Flathead Agency in Montana. Geary knew where the real trouble lay and he authorized Agent Major John Owen to use some of the goods to negotiate a cease-fire with the Snakes. On this expectation, Owen set up a meeting with Wolf Dog in the northern Blues.

The Snakes weren't about to become farmers and the shipment diverted to this council might just as well have been left in Portland. Among other items delivered to Wolf Dog's camp were cotton shawls, threadbare blankets, rice, hard bread, pots, pans and coffee salvaged from a grounded steamer. In his report to Geary, Owen wrote in disgust: "Hard bread is the last thing Indians require. They might better get good breeding stock to improve their herds!"[1] A few more encounters like this and Major Owen would resign as Indian Agent.

At this council, it would become obvious to Owen that the ranking war chiefs were missing. While Geary and Harney—each in his own way—were trying to open the Ochoco, some Nevada miners with a yen for Paiute women got the ball rolling. In the final days of the Bear Moon—the Ghost People called it April—the party was about to begin. Since 1849, thousands upon thousands of emigrants had trudged past the mouths of two small Nevada ravines that sluiced down the side of a stark mountain three days' ride south of the Ochoco. Some travelers halted to prospect. They found gold. Early in 1859, on the western edge of Paiute country, a small group in Gold Canyon and another a short distance away across a ridge in Sixmile Canyon, almost simultaneously, made strikes at either end of what became known as the Comstock Lode.

With a handy work-force, the Comstock Lode was soon producing gold and silver bullion worth millions of dollars. The long-suffering Paiutes had their fill. Word was sent into the war camps of the Ochoco that two of their young women had been kidnapped and taken to the roaring, miserable collection of tents and shanties called Virginia City where they had been raped, beaten and then given back to the desert to die.

A foot-weary runner packed the message from Bad Face—known to the Americans as Young Winnemucca—to Wolf Dog of this latest outrage on Paiute kinsmen. On April 30, 1860, over 200 Snake warriors led by Has No Horse and Paulina rode into Bad Face's encampment on the north shore of Pyramid Lake, 197 miles south of the Ochoco. It was rumored that there were 3,000 Paiutes gathered at this sight.

Word of the dog soldiers' arrival was slow in reaching the white settlements because the first thing Has No Horse did was to isolate the Nevada community from the rest of the world by cutting off the Sacramento Overland Stage and the Pony Express out of Salt Lake City. In the process, seven Overland Stage stations

---

1    Owen to Geary in *Superintendent of Indian Affairs Report*, 1859-61.

were burned and 16 employees killed. For the first and only time, the Pony Express was brought to a halt, and William Russell—owner of the Overland and Pony Express—would report that Paiute depredations cost the company $75,000 in livestock and equipment. This attack would cause "Pony Bob" Haslam to ride 190 miles in 18 hours to spread the alarm. It was—as the Paiute chief Numaga put it—"the month blood flowed across the pony's path."[2]

Twelve days later on May 12—as Major Owen was attempting to negotiate a peace treaty with Wolf Dog—Virginia City reeled in a state of shock. It was inconceivable to the Americans that Paiutes could or would retaliate over the mistreatment of a "couple of squaws." A conglomeration of miners, merchants and gamblers were mustered into service under the command of an ex-army officer, Major William Ormsby and moved down the Truckee River to chastise this illiterate group of misguided natives. Enroute, they were joined by a company of California Volunteers led by Col. Jack Hays, an ex-Texas Ranger. This rag-tail militia now numbered 105 and ahead . . . lay Pyramid Lake.

Instead of the expected timid Paiutes, the volunteers were met by Snake dog soldiers. Early reports of the ensuing battle claimed 50 men dead (it was actually 46) including Major Ormsby.[3] For the next five days stragglers crept back to Virginia City, which was now under siege. They reported that the remainder of the volunteers were either wounded, hiding in the sage or dead! This was now the tenth day that the Pony Express had been unable to operate while the cry for U.S. Regulars resounded from Oregon to Utah. Meanwhile, the slaughter complete, Has No Horse's shock troops melted back into the Blue Mountains.

When Gov. Roop's message reached Fort Vancouver, Gen. Harney refused help on the grounds that "Nevada is a maverick territory which seceded from Utah and California and therefore is not under the jurisdiction of the Military Department of the Pacific." The plain truth was that Oregon was afraid to send troops and leave the Willamette Valley open to Indian raids which the military firmly believed would happen. However, Harney relented and on May 24—the same day Major Steen was dispatched out of Fort Dalles into eastern Oregon—544 California Regulars composed of the 6th U.S. Infantry Regiment, two companies of 1st U.S. Dragoons and a detachment of 3rd U.S. Artillery, all under the command of Capt. E.F. Storey, marched into northern Nevada.[4] This task force caught up with Bad Face on June 2nd near the Oregon state line. Without Snake support, it was a costly engagement for the Paiutes. Three hundred men, women and children died that day in Coleman Canyon but the California Regulars returned to Fort Reading minus a leader. Capt. Storey was killed in the first onslaught.

---

2    Nevin, *The Expressmen*, pp. 103 and 109.

3    Roe, "Slaughter at Pyramid Lake," *Real West*, Vol. 5, No. 24, July 1962.

4    Russell, *The Book of the American West*, p. 262.

Prior to this outbreak, Bad Face's daughter—16-year-old Sarah and her older sister Mary—had been taken to San Jose and placed in a Catholic school by their grandfather, One Moccasin. When word of the Paiute uprising hit the press, these neophytes were turned out onto the streets to fend for themselves. As a consequence of this, Sarah became very frightened with her father's association with Has No Horse and dedicated her life to breaking up that friendship.[5]

The same day the 6th Infantry marched toward Virginia City, Major Enoch Steen and Capt. Andrew Jackson Smith pounded out of Fort Dalles at the head of a column of cavalry and mounted infantry riflemen to further explore Wallen's route across interior Oregon. Accompanying them were Lt. Dixon and Wallen's chief guide, Louis Scholl. George Rundell, civilian army scout, again headed up a detachment of Warm Springs Indians.

Following Lt. Bonnycastle's back trail, they set up camp in the lower Ochoco Valley and began exploration of the area. Sixteen miles northeast of the mouth of the Ochoco River—on Mill Creek—they discovered the ancient Shoshoni altar to their sun god. An awesome rock column 358 feet high, it resembled an Indian pestle set on end—being smaller at the base than it was at the top. "That night we camped there," the soldiers later reported to their friends, "and the Major used it for his pillow." Thus, it became known as "Stein's Pillar," the German spelling of Steen's name. Over the intervening years, this spectacular rock monument was believed to be unsurmountable. White men by the score attempted to duplicate the Shoshoni maid's climbing of Stein's Pillar to no avail, as attested by complicated wooden ladders and rotting ropes attached to its outward sloping sides. Ninety years would pass from its time of discovery before five mountain climbers from the Swiss Alps conquered the monolith on July 18, 1950.[6]

Because the Snakes were involved in a personal vendetta, Steen's command moved from the Ochoco Valley across Comb's Flat into Crooked River without seeing an Indian. Pushing steadily upstream for about 25 miles, Steen set up a supply depot at Wallen's Camp Division, renaming it Camp Separation. At this point—like Wallen before him—Steen divided the command.

Captain Smith was to continue east a distance of 350 miles and establish a road from Crooked River to the forks of the Oregon and California trails. It was expected to take 18 days. Lt. Dixon—starting where he had left off in August 1859—would head west and open a trail into the upper Willamette Valley a

---

5    See Sara Winnemucca Hopkins, *Life Among the Paiutes: Their Wrongs and Claims*, privately printed in 1883.

6    Lenord Rice, Glenn Richardson, Don Boars, Rod Shay and Lloyd Richardson began the climb on July 11, 1950. Three men reached the summit on July 18 and the other two on the 19th. This climb has never been accomplished again. They found what appeared to be ancient bones on the dome of the pillar—bones too large to have been carried there by birds. Perhaps the Shoshoni legend is true. The *Central Oregonian*, Prineville, Oregon, July 20, 1950.

distance of 150 miles. He was to accomplish this in eight days. Major Steen would continue exploration of the Crooked River country.

Hacking a wagon trail over the east end of the Maury Mountains into Camp Creek—a road that was still visible in the 1970s—Steen turned west toward Bear Creek while Dixon continued southward toward the eastern face of the Paulina Mountains. Staying north of the Devil's Garden, Dixon entered the Cascades through a low gap between Sugar Pine Ridge and Big Hole Butte. He was searching for John Diamond's pass between Maiden Peak and Diamond Peak in the area of the Virgin Lakes—today named Odell, Crescent and Waldo lakes. From there, he followed the middle fork of the Willamette River to Eugene City establishing a supply link to Camp Separation.

Steen arrived back at Camp Separation on the night of June 14 and was not overjoyed when the following morning he was visited by a party of four white men and five Warm Springs scouts escorting Supt. Geary and Warm Springs Indian Agent George Abbott on a search for Wolf Dog. They were planning to negotiate a treaty or at least obtain a cessation of hostilities. Without the prestige of numbers, presents or display of any kind, Geary was pushing into the heart of the hostile Ochoco under the shadow of the military which, far from being extended for his protection, completely ignored his presence.[7] In the reports of military and Indian departments there is found a mutual concealment of this meeting, no mention being made by Steen of the presence of the head of the Indian Department of Oregon and Washington at Camp Separation in his communications to his superiors. Nor did Geary in his report confess that he had been disdainfully treated by the army as well as by the few Snakes to whom he had an opportunity of offering the friendship of the U.S. government. Through his interpreter, they replied that powder and ball were the only gifts that they desired and would accept from white men.[8] *The Dalles Mountaineer* would release this information on July 10 and it would reach Washington Territory through the *Olympia Pioneer and Democrat* on July 20, 1860.

During Geary's stay at Steen's camp, two refugees from a party of prospectors which had been attacked by the Snakes came in and reported the wounding of one man, the loss of 70 horses and the scattering of their company which fled into Harney Valley after being attacked a second time. This incident along with the general haplessness of his errand caused Geary to return to The Dalles while an express was sent forward to warn Smith, who was then two days into his march to the Oregon Trail. Steen spent two more days looking for Indians without finding any so he decided to move his command to Lake Harney.

Another interesting thing happened while Geary was at Camp Separation. Pigeon Hawk drifted in looking for his German friend, Louis Scholl who was

---

7    Bancroft, *History of Oregon*, Vol. II, p. 466.
8    *Bureau of Indian Affairs Report 1860*, pp. 174-75.

serving as guide for Smith's command. Recommended by Geary who was grasping at any straw to cement good public relations and aware of the faithful service he had given Scholl in 1859, Steen hired Pigeon Hawk as a guide. He would ultimately find out that it was one thing for Pigeon Hawk to work for a man who posed no immediate threat to the Shoshoni in his search for a trail to Salt Lake City and quite another to serve an army commander who was obviously out to cause trouble.

For the next 10 days, Pigeon Hawk led Steen on a game of hide-and-seek claiming to know where the Snakes were hiding but never quite catching up with them. Sixteen days out of Camp Separation, Capt. Smith was having better luck. On June 29, while moving down Butte Creek—some 20 miles west of the Owyhee River—he rode into the stragglers of the big Nevada war party. Smith—a veteran of the Rogue War—overjoyed at the chance for some action, sounded the charge and with 40 dragoons spread out behind him, hit some of the best light cavalry this country has ever produced. Led by the Buffalo Killer war chief, Broken Knife—brother-in-law to Has No Horse—60 dog soldiers put Smith into a complete route. He didn't have enough men to guard the supply train let alone fight. Taking cover under a rocky ledge, his troops fought like cornered wolves but were pinned down for nearly 10 hours. This near brush with death convinced Smith he would need reinforcements before continuing on. Come the protective cover of night, he gave up exploration and began a strategic withdrawal towards Camp Separation, sending an express to Steen and one to Fort Dalles.

On the evening of July 3—six weeks after Steen's expedition had left Fort Dalles—George Rundell whipped a dying horse into the army post with news of the Snake attack. He would report that Capt. Smith "had been no more than able to protect the government property in his charge" and was now in retreat toward Crooked River.[9] This news reached California fast as both the *San Francisco Alta* on July 13 and the *Sacramento Union* on July 20 printed the account with glaring headlines.

Twenty-four hours ahead of Rundell's arrival at Fort Dalles, Smith's other messenger caught up with Steen some 25 miles east of the upper Deschutes River. He swung back and made contact with Smith near the headwaters of Crooked River on July 4 at the southern point of a rocky hogback now called Steen's Ridge. Meantime, Lt. Dixon continued west and mapped the trail which, within five years, would serve as the military road between Albany and Fort Harney. Steen and Smith, now ready for combat, advanced to Silver Creek and dug in at Smith's old camp naming it Camp Union. It would later become Fort Currey. From this fortification, they made an unsuccessful stab toward the east again hoping to reach the Oregon Trail. When this failed, Steen waited at Camp Union for reinforcements. He was now witnessing firsthand the frustrations of carrying on a military campaign against the Shoshoni.

---

9    Report of Capt. Andrew Smith, *U.S. Senate Document 1*, p. 119, 36th Congress, 2nd Session.

In the midst of these setbacks, Gen. Harney was recalled to Washington, D.C. to explain Oregon's mounting war debt. Before leaving, Harney placed Col. George Wright in command pending the arrival of his replacement, Brig. Gen. E.V. "Bull" Sumner. Sumner, a tough old Unionist who had been in the army since 1819, would carry out the Secretarial Order of 1858 and move department headquarters to San Francisco.

Wright—a firm believer in swift retribution—on hearing of the attack on Steen's expedition, ordered Major George Andrews to roll to their assistance with three companies of wagon-mounted artillery. To protect Steen's eastern flank, Major William N. Grier with a squadron of dragoons out of Fort Walla Walla was sent to re-man Fort Boise.[10] The artillery reached Camp Union on August 4 and Steen marched toward a range of mountains south of Harney Lake where Smith believed the Snakes were hiding. Traveling with him were 100 dragoons and 65 artillerymen. The remainder of the command was divided between Major Andrews and Capt. Smith. Andrews was to march toward the forks of the Owyhee River while Smith was to cover the Malheur. With Major Grier now on the march to Fort Boise, Steen hoped to catch the Snakes in a trap, driving them into one or the other of these divisions.

Three days out of Camp Union, Steen's Warm Springs scouts while moving up the Little Blitzen River discovered a Shoshoni camp on the west slope of a massive desert upthrust which now bears the name of Steens Mountain. Steen launched an attack but on the morning of August 8, the Snakes fled to the very top of the mountain into the region of perpetual snow. When the dragoons arrived at the 9,700-foot summit, the descent on the north side—down which the Indians plunged—looked impassable but with more zeal than caution, Steen followed their path down a 6,000-foot drop through the narrow and dangerous Kiger Gorge with the loss of but one mule . . . and the trail of the enemy.

It can only be guessed that the dog soldiers paused for spiritual guidance at the sacred "Speaking Spring" before they split to reunite in the bleak Diamond Craters; and it can also be fairly certain that Steen's guide, Pigeon Hawk, knew exactly where they were going. Army scouts spent three days searching Steen's "Snow Mountain" for tracks during which time they brought in three Paiute men, five women and some children as prisoners of war.[11]

Thwarted in this effort to chastise the Snakes, Steen dispatched messengers to Smith and Andrews to regroup at Camp Union which they did on August 16. During their short stay at Camp Union, the Paiute prisoners of war suffered every indignity imaginable at the hands of the Warm Springs scouts without interference from the soldiers.

---

10 · *House Executive Document, No. 29*, pp. 84-5, 36th Congress, 2d Session.

11 Bancroft, *History of Oregon*, Vol. II, pp. 467-68.

Observing this, Pigeon Hawk—with no show of emotion—told Major Steen he could lead him to the dog soldiers' hideout. Steen explained, quite emphatically, that if Pigeon Hawk led him astray, he would be killed. No problem. The following morning with the whole command at his back, Steen began a 100-mile forced march on the supposed trail of the enemy. A grueling advance through a parched wilderness where there was no sign of water. Continuing on, into one of the most desolate regions Steen had ever encountered, he realized Pigeon Hawk had led them into a trap.

Lt. John Noble would later vividly recall what transpired: "When the Major asked why he did so when he'd been told he'd be shot, the Snake guide replied that he thought by leading the soldiers into this desert that they would all perish before they could reach water and by this means save his people and get revenge. He also told Major Steen he would never take the soldiers to where his people were but was leading them away from the Snakes and that most of the soldiers must now die of thirst. He was turned over to the Warm Springs scouts. When they told him to turn his face to the sun, he laughed. He was willing to die to save his people. They cut off his head." It was a messy operation performed with a war hatchet.

Lt. Noble would also note that the artillerymen "suffered most damnable. Their craving for water was so great that the means of relief is too horrible to write."[12]

On Steen's survival march back to Camp Union, the dog soldiers—in a remarkable display of psychological warfare—paralleled the column just out of range of artillery fire. By now, field artillery was found to be of no advantage in a clash with the Snakes. Great on amassed forces, it was hardly worth the effort to lob 12-pound cannonballs in the hope of hitting a single man. During this nervous trek back to Silver Creek, the Vanorman train left Fort Hall on August 24, expecting to pick up an escort from either Capt. Smith at the forks of the Oregon Trail or Major Grier at the Hudson's Bay Company post on the Boise River. They would be disappointed. Smith was now in retreat to Camp Union and Major Grier, unable to make contact with Steen, had returned to Fort Walla Walla.

Three days after the Vanorman party left Fort Hall, Steen's command arrived at Camp Union. For a month and a half, Steen had combed southeastern Oregon in an effort to clean up Shoshoni resistance with little success. On September 1, 1860, he decided to abandon road work—his primary objective—and return to Fort Dalles. To insure safe passage, Steen divided the command into three columns spaced 20 miles apart and began his march to the Columbia.

On the way out, Lt. Gregg with 20 dragoons out of Fort Warm Springs intercepted Steen and reported that the Snakes were hiding out in small groups

---

12    The thoughts of Lt. John Noble four years later when he passed through the same area—the Alvord Desert—in 1864. Lt. John F. Noble, 1864 Drake Expedition, 1st Oregon Cavalry, Third Notebook, diary entry, Thursday, June 23, 1864.

around the Warm Springs Agency watching and waiting for an opportune time to strike.[13] Major Steen refused to take the bait and continued on to Fort Dalles where the field troops were reassigned to their various posts for the winter.[14]

During Steen's retreat to the Columbia, messages were dispatched to Washington, D.C. In the understatement of the year, Supt. Geary would report to the commissioner of Indian Affairs that ". . . generally speaking the Indians of the Northwest are now peaceful. Menacing Shoshonis or Snakes are the exception. Hostile Snakes are causing trouble in eastern Oregon and in June, compelled Major Enoch Steen—who is conducting a survey in contemplation of opening an emigrant wagon road into the Willamette Valley by way of the Middle Fork of the Willamette River—to deviate temporarily from his routine tasks."[15]

Col. Wright in a report to Gen. Winfield Scott October 10, 1860, would see the situation in a somewhat different light: "Long scouts are made without ever seeing at one time more than a single Indian family. The difficulty we encounter in advancing is that we have no fixed objective point. We pursue an invisible foe without a home or anything tangible to strike at. The hardships these Indians undergo in war differ little from their privations in peace . . . they unite and disperse without inconvenience. Victories can easily be gained over such an enemy but they will rarely prove decisive . . . hence, their final conquest must be a work of time and patience."[16] Unfortunately, Wright's solution of "time and patience" did not anticipate the greatly increased travel and numbers of miners who would shortly cross or invade Shoshoni country.

Just after Steen's expedition returned to Fort Dalles and the combined force was dispersed to winter posts, news arrived of the massacre of most of the Vanorman party near Salmon Falls on the Snake River.[17] A short time later, the way Bancroft put it in his *History of Oregon* . . . "as usual, the Snakes ran off all the livestock from the Warm Springs Reservation."[18]

---

13   *The Olympia Pioneer and Democrat*, Washington Territory, September 14, 1860.

14   *U.S. Senate Document 1*, Vol. II, p. 131, 36th Congress, 2d Session.

15   Geary to Commissioner of Indian Affairs, October 1, 1860, *U.S. Senate Document 1*, Serial 1078, pt. 1, p. 395, 36th Congress, 2d Session.

16   *U.S. Senate Document 1*, "Affairs in the Military Department of Oregon," Serial 1079, pt. II, pp. 141-42, Washington, D.C., 1861.

17   *House Executive Document No. 29, pp. 84-85, 36th Congress, 2d Session.*

18   Bancroft, *History of Oregon*, Vol II, p. 468.

# CHAPTER 97

# SKELETON CAMP

*The body of Chase was exhumed and prepared for eating but before it had been tasted, succor arrived.*

**Joseph Myers**
Emigration of 1860

Once Has No Horse had the U.S. Regulars in full retreat, Paulina descended on the Warm Springs Agency. In one night of plunder, he turned the reservation into shambles and drove off all the remaining livestock. Caught in the cross fire, Jarvis Briggs, a packer, and his sons were ambushed and killed on the Barlow Trail.[1] The public backlash was quick in coming. Before the Shoshoni disappeared into the Ochoco, Wasco County citizens panicked and a sheriff's posse rounded up some vagrant Wascos and hung them at The Dalles City. This action failed to promote good will with the reservation Indians.

Wright immediately ordered Lt. Gregg and his 20 cavalrymen—who had returned to Fort Dalles with Major Steen—back to the reservation where they were ordered to dig in for a winter offensive. Furthermore, the Agency Indians were to be armed and given military training on the expectation that the Shoshoni revolt could be sidetracked before it gained momentum. For once, the military was backed by the residents of western Oregon who at last realized the dangerous situation they were facing. Prior to this last raid, it was deemed inadvisable to arm the Agency Indians on the belief that they could not be trusted not to join forces with the Snakes. It was now obvious that relations between the Confederated Tribes and the Shoshoni nation would never permit such an alliance. Also, it was thought that with the proper training, the Agency Indians could easily overcome the Shoshoni thus preventing the shedding of much white blood.[2] Trying desperately to fire them with false courage, the state of Oregon was placing its welfare in the hands of intimidated reservation Indians.

---

1    *The Puget Sound Herald*, October 26, 1860; late as always when it came to reporting Indian disturbances in eastern Oregon, *The Oregon Statesman* wouldn't report this incident until a year later on August 26, 1861.

2    *Bureau of Indian Affairs Report 1860*, p. 176.

On September 26, only days after Steen's return from the hostile interior, Wright reported to Gen. Sumner that the routes of emigration were "rendered perfectly safe" by the summer troop operations; and that nothing more needed to be done, or could be done with regard to the Shoshoni before spring when Supt. Geary would obtain a treaty which would serve every purpose.[3] He didn't elaborate on just how Geary was to accomplish this mission. Wright also urged the construction of a military post on the Boise River which had already been directed by the Secretary of War. However, Congress was slow in appropriating funds for this project because of rising tension between the northern free states and southern slave states.

A month before Wright's state-of-the-military address to "Bull" Sumner, the Vanorman Company—organized by Mark Vanorman and consisting of eight wagons, 54 passengers and a number of livestock—left Fort Hall on August 24 escorted by Col. Sam Howe and 22 U.S. Dragoons.[4] Because of the earlier Virginia City, Nevada, trouble Howe believed the Shoshoni were active along the California and Applegate trails. He was also aware that Steen, Andrews and Grier were in eastern Oregon. He didn't know that Steen's command was under attack and that Grier, on orders from Col. Wright, was retreating to Fort Walla Walla. Six days west of Fort Hall, because of no resistance, Howe decided that further escort was unnecessary; still he left two dragoons—Sgt. William Antly and Trooper Charles Kesner—to guide the train to the Boise River and contact with either with Major Grier or Capt. Smith. Also, there were four soldiers whose terms of enlistment had expired and who were to be discharged at Fort Dalles, traveling with the Vanorman party. All of the soldiers were riding U.S. Cavalry mounts and well-armed.

For two weeks after Col. Howe left, the Vanorman train proceeded down the Oregon Trail without incident. The night of September 12, they camped on Alkali Creek one day's travel from the Owyhee River crossing. The next morning at 9:30 a.m., a line of horsemen appeared on the barren slope of Blackjack Butte some two miles west of the Oregon Trail. Antly estimated the force to number upwards to 100 warriors and the train was corralled for action. A few moments later, Has No Horse with five dog soldiers rode in for a conference and demanded payment for safe passage across Snake hunting grounds. He met with Vanorman who offered food and clothing for payment. This amounted to little more than an insult to Has No Horse but he allowed the train to proceed. Obviously, he could see no advantage in an attack when the train was in a well-fortified position. When the train reached a ridge-top (some three miles south of present Adrian, Oregon) exposing it to attack, the Snakes opened fire with rifles. Unable to circle on the steep slopes, the train halted and returned the fire. For the rest of the day they were pinned down and Vanorman was wounded. Trooper Kesner and four other men were killed. All

---

3     *U.S. Senate Document No. 1*, Vol. II, 1860-61, p. 136, 36th Congress, 2d Session.

4     The Vanorman train is also referred to as the Otter (Utter) train. See *House Executive Document No. 29,* pp. 84-5, 36th Congress, 2d Session; and *The Book of the American West,* p. 212.

ni ght the Indians fired at random and fought all the next day killing Sgt. Antly, Jim Trimble and three more of the defenders. Toward sunset, Charles Utter, who assumed command of the train, decided to leave four wagons at the scene of battle and make a run for it with the other four wagons believing this would divert the Indians' attention long enough for them to escape. The remaining four soldiers were to ride in advance to keep the way open. Under heavy fire, the four broke free of the train but three more emigrants were killed. It was later learned that Sgt. Murdock and Trooper Chambourg were killed but Cpl. Chaffey and Trooper Snyder escaped.[5] The Reith brothers—both single men—went with the soldiers.

Has No Horse paid no heed to the abandoned wagons other than to have them torched, but followed the moving wagons and continued the attack. In panic, the emigrants abandoned the wagons in an attempt to hide. In this dash for safety, Abe Markerman, John Myers and Susan Utter were shot. John Utter, seeing his daughter killed, ran toward the raiders making signs of peace. He took a bullet through the head. There were now 19 dead. As darkness settled, Has No Horse—having looted and burned the wagons—rounded up the livestock and headed into the Ochoco. His mission was accomplished.

Seeing the Indians leave, the 37 survivors fled under the cover of darkness and made it to the Snake River. By walking at night and hiding under the riverbank during the day they reached the mouth of the Owyhee where they set up camp. During this flight, Sam Chase's wife took the only loaf of bread they had and disappeared never to be seen again. Two dogs which followed them were killed for food and a cow abandoned by an earlier party furnished scanty subsistence. On the Owyhee, the emigrants obtained a few salmon from the Digger Snakes in exchange for clothing and ammunition. Sam Chase died from eating the salmon.

From the Owyhee camp, George Munson and Christopher Trimble—a boy of 11—started downriver to look for help. At the mouth of Burnt River, they found the Reith brothers, Cpl. Chaffey, who was wounded and Trooper Snyder. These men were lost. Munson stayed with Chaffey, while the Reiths and Snyder continued the search for help and young Trimble returned to the Owyhee camp. On the way back, he was picked up by a Snake hunting party and made friends with them. These hunters began supplying the Vanorman Company with food. One day as Trimble was about to accompany the warriors back to their camp, Joe Myers told him to mark the trail so ". . . if the soldiers come to our relief, we shall send them in for you." It was an unfortunate statement as the Shoshoni believed the Americans were going to turn them over to the soldiers. On the way back to their camp, they killed Trimble and left his body to the wolves. Then they returned and raided the emigrant camp, carrying away all guns, ammunition and blankets. Fearing they would return with more deadly results, Vanorman—now recuperated

---

5 Joseph Myer's account of the attack in *The Olympia Standard*, Washington Territory, Nov. 30, 1860.

from his bullet wound—tried to persuade the survivors to move forward but most refused to budge on the grounds that they were too weak to travel. On September 29, Vanorman with his family, Sam Gleason, Charles Utter and Henry Utter started up the Oregon Trail hoping to meet a relief party.[6]

Three days after Vanorman left the Owyhee camp, the Reith brothers and Trooper Snyder reached the Umatilla Agency on October 2. Immediately Byron Davis, an Agency employee, headed for Fort Walla Walla with the news that a massacre had taken place three weeks previous and some 50 persons had been killed or scattered over the country to perish by starvation. At the time, Col. Wright believed the report brought in by the three known survivors might be exaggerated.[7] He would soon learn otherwise.

Early snowstorms were already threatening to block the Blue Mountain passes when Capt. Fredrick Dent—brother-in-law to Ulysses S. Grant—was ordered out with 100 cavalrymen and 40 horse-loads of provisions. About this time, Eagle From The Light—a Nez Perce who had been riding with Has No Horse—and four Snake warriors rode into the Umatilla Agency. The Snakes told Agent Cain that they knew of four white children who were alive. They later proved to be Mark Vanorman's children. Arrangements were made with the dog soldiers to bring the captives in and accordingly, they left their wives at the Agency and returned to the Snake River country for that purpose.[8] The Snakes had to give up the hunt because of heavy snow in the Blues but they did learn that the children were seen 159 miles southwest of the Flathead Agency and were sent for by Major Owen but never found.

Back on the Owyhee River things were getting grim. Without supplies from the Shoshoni, Elizabeth and Susan Chase died of starvation soon followed by Daniel and Albert Chase. At length, the remaining members were "compelled to eat the bodies of the dead." This determination, according to Joe Myers, "was unanimous and was arrived at after consultation and prayer!"

Pushing hard down the Oregon Trail, Capt. Dent found Munson and Chaffey on the Powder River. At the mouth of Burnt River he found the bodies of Vanorman, his wife and daughter, the two Utters and Sam Gleason. Jane and Alexis Vanorman had been scalped and the four Vanorman children were missing. Undoubtedly, they were the children sighted on the Little Salmon River.

On October 28, forty-five days after the attack on the Snake River, Capt. Dent arrived at the Owyhee just as the emigrants were preparing to eat the body of Sam Chase. When the soldiers rode into this camp of misery many wept and thought it

---

6     Bancroft, *History of Oregon*, Vol. II, pp. 473-74.

7     Col. Wright's report, *U.S. Senate Document No. 1*, Vol. II, 1860-61, p. 141, 36th Congress 2d Session.

8     Letter from Fort Walla Walla, Washington Territory, published in the *Oregon Argus*, December 22, 1860.

cruel that Dent—wise in the effects of starvation—would not permit them to distribute food without limit among the half-naked living skeletons stretched upon the ground or that he should resist the cries of the wailing, emaciated children.[9] Ten people were all that remained alive at the Owyhee camp. These, with the two rescued by Dent and the three who first reached the Umatilla Agency, were all that survived of a company of 54 travelers and the six soldiers assigned to the wagon train. Forty-five people had died in a span of six weeks, 21 of whom had starved to death.

By the time Dent arrived back at Fort Walla Walla with the survivors on November 1, the Blues were buried in snow. Had he been a few days later, he could not have crossed the mountains. News of this tragedy hit every major newspaper on the Pacific coast. Headlines in the *Washington Standard*, *Olympia Pioneer and Democrat*, *Oregon Statesman*, *Portland Advertiser*, *Oregon Argus*, *San Francisco Bulletin*, and *Sacramento Union* screamed the fatal event to the outside world, making it known that the Shoshoni were a force to be reckoned with.

The Oregon legislature was in session when the first reports reached Salem. Gov. John Whiteaker dispatched a letter to President Buchanan and a memorial to Congress requesting that military posts be established on the Grande Ronde, Burnt, Boise and Malheur rivers.[10] The forts on the Grande Ronde and Burnt rivers were to be manned by one company each of cavalry; Boise would be a four-company post; and the Malheur would be a two company post. He also requested that a treaty be made with the Shoshoni of interior Oregon whatever the cost and a military road be constructed through central Oregon to connect the post on the Boise River with Eugene City.

The committee that drafted the memorial evidently was under the impression that Major Steen had completed a reconnaissance of the middle route which was not the case, his time being spent as Steen expressed it "in pursuing an invisible foe."[11]

The Shoshoni were also suffering setbacks. On December 18, 1860, Wolf Dog's eastern ally, Peta Nocona—Comanche war chief—was attacked on the Pease River by 40 Texas Rangers and 21 U.S. Cavalrymen under the command of Capt. Sul Ross. Most of the warriors were hunting buffalo when Ross suddenly struck killing many and taking captives, among them Peta Nocona's wife, Cynthia Ann Parker[12] and their daughter Prairie Flower. Peta Nocona died soon after from

---

9    *Oregon Senate Journal 1860*, p. 63; *Hayes Scrapbooks*, Vol. V, p. 191; *Bureau of Indian Affairs Report 1861*, p. 155; *U.S. House Executive Document*, No. 46, Vol. VIII, 36th Congress, 2d Session; *Congressional Globe* 1860-61, Pt. II, p. 1324-25.

10   Special message of Gov. Whiteaker to the President of the United States, *Oregon Statesman*, October 15, 1860.

11   Steen's report, *Congressional Globe 1860-61*, pt. II, p. 1457.

12   For the story of Cynthia Ann Parker, see *Thunder Over the Ochoco*, Vol. I, p. 38, footnote 30.

an infected bullet wound and his son Pecos of disease . . . a bad omen. His other son, Quanah Parker, was now chief of the Nocona Comanches and proved to be a bitter antagonist to the advancing Americans.[13]

The Vanorman attack would also produce more speculation as to the identity of the war tribe leaders . . . something the Americans didn't really know. There is evidence that Has No Horse had acquired a new name. F.W. Lander, who was having his share of trouble along the Pacific Wagon Road, would report the massacre of a group of emigrants by "Snake Indians under the direction of Chief Jageoh—The Man Who Carries The Arrow."[14] Note the similarity in the pronunciations of Chochoco (show-show-ho), The Man Who Has No Horse, with Jageoh (jo-show-oh), The Man Who Carries the Arrow and beyond doubt, Has No Horse was carrying the arrow against the white men.

Lander would also speculate in his report of February 11, 1860, that Pashego (Sweet Root), "considered a wonderful prophet by the Snakes" now hiding out in the northern Blues was leading the Robber Snakes (Bannocks). C.H. Miller—Lander's partner in the Pacific Wagon Road Company—would further state that he considered Sweet Root to be "one of the most dangerous and desperate men now living west of the Rocky Mountains."[15] It was certain that the Department of Interior didn't know who was leading the Shoshoni rebellion.

In January 1861, Supt. Geary and Agent Abbott received most gratifying news. Both were being transferred. Replacements were William Rector—survivor of the 1845 emigrant train—Superintendent of Oregon Indian Affairs, to be stationed in Portland; and William Logan—reservation physician—Agent for Warm Springs. By May, Bill Rector in an artful move sponsored by Gov. Whiteaker, would unload most of his Indian problems onto the shoulders of Charlie Hale, unsuspecting head of the newly created Indian Superintendency of Washington Territory. During the formation of this latest bureaucracy, and through no fault of the dog soldiers, the Shoshoni war would be shoved onto the back burner.

---

13   Capps, *The Great Chiefs*, pp. 105-07; Douglas, *The Gentlemen in White*, p. 63.

14   F.W. Lander, Pacific Wagon Report, *Senate Executive Document No. 42*, 36th Congress, 1st Session, Series 1033, pp. 29-30.

15   C.H. Miller Report, *Senate Executive Document No. 36*, 36th Congress, 2d Session, Series 984, pp. 70-71.

# CHAPTER 98

# WAR OF REBELLION

*In your hands, my dissatisfied fellow countrymen, and not mine, is the momentous issue of civil war.*

**Abraham Lincoln**
Inaugural Address 1861

On April 12, 1861—with South Carolina cannons hurling destruction at Fort Sumpter—the nation was plunged into civil war. Senator Jefferson Davis took the helm as President of the Confederate States of America while the man who had refused the governorship of Oregon—only 19 days in office—was piloting the United States of America through troubled waters.

By telegraph and pony express, the paralyzing news spanned the continent and four days after the opening guns were fired, a weary horseman packed the communiqué down the rain-drenched streets of Portland, Oregon. In its wake came President Lincoln's call for 75,000 volunteers to put down the rebellion . . . a plea ignored by Oregon's governor, John Whiteaker.

In answer to the governor's reluctance to send assistance, Gen. "Bull" Sumner—in an effort to preserve the Union—began reduction of Oregon's military force by sending the U.S. Regulars to the eastern battlefront. As Oregon wallowed in self-pity, Col. Wright was forced to apologize for the army's abandonment at a time when the Shoshoni War was imminent.[1] Oregon was a seething hotbed of political unrest and a vast majority of her citizens had but four things uppermost in their minds . . . the complete destruction of the Shoshoni nation; increased emigration from the east to bolster their ranks; gold to finance a new republic; and cessation from the Union![2]

Rumor was that a secret revolutionary organization based in California was working in Oregon. Gen. Sumner believed plots for a Pacific Republic were more serious than people were inclined to think and as early as February—when the Confederate States of America were formed—sent additional troops into

---

1     Bancroft, *History of Oregon*, Vol. II. p. 488.

2     Joseph Ellison, "Design for a Pacific Republic, 1843-62," *Oregon Historical Quarterly*, Vol. XXI, No. 4, December 1930, pp. 319-42.

California from Oregon and stationed them in strategic places, especially in the southern counties around Los Angeles.[3] When war broke Sumner was hastily sent to relieve Gen. Johnson, commander of the Military District of California, and arrived unexpectedly on April 24, just 12 days after the Confederate guns shelled Fort Sumpter.[4] Col. Wright was promoted to brigadier general and placed in charge of the Oregon District. One of his first moves was to confiscate property of all suspected rebels in his command. He then placed Oregon under martial law and made the sale or transfer of private land by such persons illegal.[5]

Many of the newspapers including the *Albany Democrat, Portland Advertiser, Corvallis Union,* and the *Eugene Democrat Register,* were openly against the Union.[6] Prominent Oregonians were or had been slave holders. In striking contrast, Oregon's U.S. Senators—Edward Baker and James Nesmith—backed the war effort without question. Nesmith—very anti-slavery—was the only democrat in the Senate to vote for the Abolition Amendment. Baker, noted for his oratorical eloquence and intimate friendship with Lincoln, accepted a colonelcy in the Union army.[7]

While Senator Nesmith fought it out in the U.S. Senate, Senator Baker headed for Oregon and appeared on the floor of the state senate, resplendent in full uniform, where he made a ringing appeal for the Union. Successful in raising a regiment—the only Oregon unit to see action in the Civil War—Baker left for the eastern front.

Known as a man imbued with a streak of romance, Col. Baker rushed off to battle in a gay mood and light-heartedly told a fellow officer ". . . press where ye see my white plume shine amidst the ranks of war." By October 22, 1861, Baker was on Ball's Bluff overlooking the Shenandoah River in Virginia in charge of an advance against the Confederates. He waved to Col. Milton Cogswell, commander of the 42nd New York Volunteers—better known as the Tammany Regiment—and sang a couple of lines from Scott's *Lady of the Lake*: "One blast upon your bugle horn, Is worth a thousand men. . . ." A few moments later, Col. Baker—a partner in the law firm of Logan, Stuart and Lincoln and a veteran of the Black Hawk and Mexican Wars—was blasted from the saddle with a rebel bullet in his heart . . . the first northern officer to die in the Civil War.[8]

When word of Baker's death reached Oregon, Gov. Whiteaker immediately appointed Benjamin Stark to the vacant post. And so, the man who introduced Abe Lincoln to the crowd at the inauguration ceremonies in March was replaced by a

3    *San Francisco Alta,* February 17, 1861.
4    *Records of the Rebellion,* Series I. Vol. L, Part 2, pp.471-72.
5    *The Oregon Statesman,* March 3, 1862; *Oregon Argus,* March 8, 1862.
6    Bancroft, *History of Oregon,* Vol. II. p. 492.
7    Corning, *Dictionary of Oregon History,* pp. 17 and 174.
8    Cotton, *Mr. Lincoln's Army,* pp. 77-80.

strong pro-slavery advocate in October. Although this arrogant action on the part of Whiteaker provoked such a storm of protest from Oregon's Union supporters that it reached President Lincoln, Stark—whose only bid for fame was that he helped found the city of Portland—was seated.

Meantime, recruitment was at a standstill for the Oregonians were more concerned with promoting their first state fair than with problems of a war of rebellion. The sole purpose of this gala affair which was to be held near Oregon City was to lure more settlers to Oregon through the promotion of agriculture. On this count the fair was a booming success because of the 26,000 who joined the westward emigration of 1862, 10,000 came to Oregon. Unfortunately for these folks, instead of homesteading in the fertile Willamette Valley, they chose to settle east of the Cascades.[9]

Another fact which seemed to have escaped the Oregonians was the impact of civil war on regular army troops in the Pacific northwest. The young officers in the Pacific command hopefully wished that the war would last long enough for them to advance in rank. This wish was soon to be fulfilled for these men were entering into the most bloody conflict humanity had ever witnessed. Ironically, the revenue cutter *Jo Lane*, anchored at Astoria, was ordered to transport the Union troops from Portland to New York harbor.[10]

By August most of the regulars were on their way to the Atlantic front. Lt. Phil Sheridan, putting his knowledge of Shoshoni warfare to good use, was recognized as an outstanding horse soldier and promoted to Lt. Gen. in charge of all cavalry of the Army of the Potomac. Lt. Henry Abbot was placed in command of the 1st Connecticut Heavy Artillery and was wounded at the battle of Bull Run, July 21, 1861. Lt. George Crook entered the war with the rank of Lt. Col. in command of the 36th Ohio Volunteers whom he drilled to such a condition of efficiency, the other regiments nick-named them the 36th regulars.

Wounded in the battle of Lewisburgh, West Virginia, Crook then took command of the Army of West Virginia. Slashing deep into enemy territory, he was soon employing Shoshoni tactics of hit and run . . . ripping the enemy open and then letting him bleed to death. Crook was now riding against his old saddle-mate of the Yakima War, Capt. George Pickett, now a general in the Confederate Army.

Another Oregon warrior would become a force to be reckoned with. Sam Grant who Capt. Ord once told to "reform or resign" and who Capt. McClellan had labeled "useless" was trying to reinstate his commission in the Army of the United States. With misgivings, it was finally given. Then came the surprise. Grant may have been a part-time drunkard unlucky in his business ventures; lacking in

---

9    *The Olympia Standard*, October 11 and 25, 1862.

10   *The Oregon Argus*, June 29, 1861.

interests of a cultural nature; limited in his education—but he possessed that particular type of military genius that it takes to win wars.

For eight months after the disastrous battle at Bull Run neither side had made a gain. Then Grant was assigned a command and charged into the fray. His first act was to secure the unconditional surrender of Fort Donelson on the Cumberland River. He then struck Tennessee, gaining complete possession of most of the state, and by 1863 had began his terrible siege on Vicksburg. With its capture, Grant opened the Mississippi River to northern travel, cutting the Confederacy in half. Grant, the uncouth and unwanted, was now pitted against the southern aristocrat, Robert Edward Lee.

These were only a few of the West Coast soldiers thought to be incapable of protecting Oregon's interests from Indian depredations. Now they were gone and to make matters worse, Oregon successfully created another roadblock to a peaceful solution to Shoshoni hostilities.

Fort Hall—abandoned since 1859—was the only agency to deal directly with the Snakes. In a neat political move to rid Oregon of any responsibility for the area east of the Cascades (a tendency extended to the present day) a Washington Superintendency was cut off from that of the state of Oregon. Conveniently, it would include what is now Idaho and by virtue of the native inhabitants would encompass eastern Oregon even though it was by default. The new Superintendent, C.H. Hale, now sat in an office at Olympia, Washington, many miles farther away from Fort Hall than Supt. William Rector in Oregon.[11] With the increase in distance there developed even more ignorance of the tribes operating out of the Ochoco.

With the war tribes based in eastern Oregon, they could stage a raid on the Deschutes one week and 10 days later be in Idaho, Utah, Nevada or California ripping wagon trains apart while Washington Superintendent Hale faced a no-win situation. The map furnished to him by the Oregon Superintendency was a large expanse of nothing with the word "unexplored" printed across the middle and little more in the way of information except that it was inhabited by "Shoshonies or Snake Indians."[12] Oregon Agent J.M. Kirkpatrick in a letter to Supt. Hale would describe the mountain Snakes as a "mysterious people, living in rude lodges made of willow brush [the Big Lodges]" and the desert Snakes as "living amongst the sagebrush, hiding in the canyons, skulking behind the rocks." He also believed "both tribes" were operating out of Washington Territory as "the sphere of their marauding operations commences south of Fort Hall, and extends into the Blue Mountains."[13] In short, Agent Kirkpatrick knew little or nothing about his

---

11    Simeon Francis to Commissioner of Indian Affairs, Portland, Oregon, May 18, 1861, U.S. National Archives, *Letters Received by the Office of Indian Affairs*, 1824-81, Washington Superintendency, 1861-62, Micro Copy No. 234, Roll 907.

12    "Map of Washington Territory," *Annual Report of Superintendent of Indian Affairs, 1862.*

13    Report of Agent J.M. Kirkpatrick, Powder River, Oregon, July 22, 1862, in *The Commissioner*

assigned wards while doing his best to saddle Washington with the responsibility of treating with them.

The sad truth is that at the start of the Civil War and continuing thereafter, any supervision that the eastern Oregon Shoshoni received came not from their legally constituted government officials on the Pacific coast but from contact with a southern neighbor, the Indian superintendency based at Salt Lake City, Utah. Cognizant of this, Wolf Dog and Has No Horse were not about to suspend their Oregon campaign just because the Americans were squabbling amongst themselves.

of Indian Affairs Report 1862, p. 267; Report of Supt. C.H. Hale, Olympia, Washington Territory, October 19, 1862, *Commissioner of Indian Affairs Report 1862*, p. 399.

# CHAPTER 99

# THE LONG KNIVES

*The thoughts of others were light and fleeting,*
*Of lover's greeting and luck or fame,*
*But ours were of trouble and ours were steady,*
*And we were ready when trouble came.*

**A.E. Housman**
*A Cavalry Charge*

Thus were the thoughts of tense Shoshoni dog soldiers and equally nervous Oregon Volunteers at the start of the Civil War. Only James Buchanan could breathe easy during this chaotic period having bequeathed all responsibility to Abraham Lincoln less than a month before confederate artillery hurled destruction upon Fort Sumpter. Col. George Wright, Commander of the Military District of Oregon, did not enjoy such an enviable position. Within a matter of weeks his command was stripped of manpower; army posts were abandoned and any chance of quelling an Indian attack was remote. For a man charged with protecting civilian life and property from a hostile thrust, it was—like Washington Indian Supt. Hale's directive—a hopeless task. By mid-year, there were only 700 enlisted men and 19 commissioned officers in the entire Oregon country.[1] Much later, this fact gained national attention when Eva Emery Dye summarized the critical plight in a terse statement: "The United States owes much to its pioneer Indian fighters. They held Oregon country in escrow for years." It could be added, that's all they did.

In early June, Major Owen reported to Supts. Rector and Hale that at least two more tribes had joined the Paviotso Confederacy and this intelligence was correct. Bear Hunter pulled his Dog Ribs into the fold shortly followed by Yellow Jacket's Lohim Snakes. With the addition of the Juniper People and the Dog Ribs, Wolf Dog's forces now stood at 16 tribes making him superior in fighting strength to Wright's combined units of cavalry, infantry and artillery.

Without questioning Owen's report, Wright ordered a detachment into the field more as a show of bravado than an attempt at defense. On June 27, Lt. Alan

---

1    *Congressional Globe 1860-61*, Pt. II 1213, 1324-5, p. 362; U.S. Senate Document 1, Vol. II, No. 32, 37th Congress, 2d Session.

Piper of the 3rd Artillery stationed at Fort Umpqua took to the field with 65 men under orders to keep the emigrant road through southeastern Oregon open to traffic. This is how bad things were. As back-up, Lindsay Applegate—who with his brother, Jesse, had pioneered the southern route into Oregon—was dispatched with 40 Oregon Rangers to man Fort Klamath which was abandoned in 1857.

Fort Walla Walla, the sole protection for the western Oregon Trail had only four commissioned officers—Capt. W.T. McGruder, commanding, Capt. Thomas McParlin, post surgeon, Lt. Marcus Reno, and Lt. George Wheeler—with 100 cavalrymen to cover all the country between the John Day River and Green River in Wyoming Territory. Fort Dalles had two commissioned officers—Capt. Rowell, commanding, and Capt. West—with one company of infantry.[2] To bolster this force, Lt. Gregg and the 25 cavalry troopers at Warm Springs were recalled to Fort Dalles in May causing Agent Logan to beg Rector for their return. He also requested that the Superintendent make treaty with the Shoshoni . . . a plea that was turned over to Hale and ignored by both Superintendents. Then, on the possibility that the Modocs and Klamaths might join forces with the Snakes, Lindsay Applegate was appointed special Indian agent to forestall any trouble in southeastern Oregon.[3]

Once his meager forces were entrenched, Wright placed a requisition with the state of Oregon for a company of volunteer cavalry to serve for 90 days which would carry him through the major Shoshoni attack period. This company would receive the same benefits as the regular army with the exception that the volunteers would furnish their own mounts. The Oregon legislature, led by Ben Harding and Luther Elkins, was in favor of such action but former Warm Springs Indian Agent A.P. Dennison, the enrolling officer and Gov. Whiteaker—both accused of being southern sympathizers—so hindered the success of this undertaking that it was finally discontinued.

In desperation, Wright called for a meeting with the political leaders of Oregon. The outcome of this conference being that the legislators decided it was in the public's best interests to keep their weakened condition top secret. Immediately, the necessary precautions were enacted to suppress any information that a Shoshoni uprising was in progress; a ban that was to remain in effect throughout the Snake campaign. This censorship would serve a two-fold purpose. For the army, it would buy precious time to enlist and train a volunteer force under the guise of going to the Atlantic front; for the state officials, it would stave off possible uprisings in the Willamette settlements for it was no secret that a majority of Oregonians were openly pro-slavery. Somewhat puzzled over this renewed zeal for recruitment, the *Oregon Argus* on June 15, wondered how "the bureaucrats,

---

2    *Oregon Statesman*, August 11 and December 2, 1861; *San Francisco Alto*, November 4, 1861.

3    Bancroft, *History of Oregon*, Vol., II, p. 494.

with a swiftness uncommon to them, talked the taxpayers out of a 50,000 dollar appropriation for the forming of volunteers."

In a further effort to sidetrack any curiosity about the situation in eastern Oregon, Capt. Wallen's Road Report of 1859—which made no mention of Indian hostilities—was made public. This release was a tactical blunder on Wright's part as the report hinted of possible gold-bearing streams in the southern Blue Mountains. This rekindled interest in the Blue Bucket and Four Dutchmen gold strikes of 1845 and 1849. Stimulated by Wallen's report and the Union treasury's known need for gold (by 1865, the government was spending 3.5 million dollars a day to finance the war effort) several search parties were organized on the West Coast and unaware of the dangerous situation east of the Cascades, they plowed into the interior in quest of riches.

Meanwhile having failed in the attempt to enlist men through state authorities, the War Department sent Col. Thomas Cornelius to Oregon on orders to raise 10 cavalry companies. Arriving with him in November was Provost Marshall J.M. Keeler who was authorized to start a draft if the Oregonians refused to volunteer.[4] By now, the term of enlistment was three years. Previous to the battle of Bull Run in July, enlistment had been set at 90 days—that was how certain the North was that the rebels would be a pushover.

Notices were posted throughout the Willamette Valley and at The Dalles City which read:

### To Arms!

*Eighty-eight able bodied Union men are
wanted to enlist and form a Company of Volunteer
Cavalry; to be mustered into service of the
United States for three years, unless sooner
discharged.*

*When sixty men shall have enrolled their
names, one company will be called together
at Dalles City, Oregon for the purpose of
organizing and electing their officers; to whit:*

*One Captain, one first Lieutenant, one second
Lieutenant, four Sergeants, four Corporals, one
Farrier and Blacksmith, and two Buglers . . .
The pay of volunteers will be: for Privates, $31
per month; Sergeants, $36; and Corporals, $33. Each
volunteer must furnish his own horse. In addition to
the above pay, each soldier on being honorably discharged*

---

4    Bancroft, *History of Oregon*, Vol. II, p. 494.

*will receive a bounty of One Hundred Dollars and a*
*Land Warrant. The commissioned officers will receive*
*the same pay as in the regular army.*

The furnishing of their own horse was no small item. At the time, good cavalry mounts cost from $125 to $250 while their allowance, set by Congressional Act of 1861, amounted to 40 cents a day. Out of each volunteer's pay, the government withheld two dollars a month until the end of the enlistment and deducted 12-1/2 cents a month for soldier benefits and retirement fund. Still, cavalrymen did better than foot soldiers (who received only $13 a month). Artillerymen fared even worse. Oregon's volunteer artillery served without pay and each man of the battery contributed 50 cents a week for supplies and equipment. Although wages on farms and in the mines were very high, Col. Cornelius convinced men to enlist on the promise of going to the eastern battlefields. Because of the Shoshoni, few did. Oregon sent only 350 troops to the Civil War while California—besides sending soldiers into eastern Oregon—supplied 6,500 men. Lt. James Waymire, first Oregon cavalry officer to make contact with the dog soldiers in eastern Oregon, had this to say: "It was thought as soon as we should become disciplined, if the war continued and in the event it didn't reach the west coast, we would be taken east. For my own part, I would have gone to the Army of Missouri but for this understanding."

As soon as men were recruited, they were marched to Fort Vancouver and issued uniforms. The first item of issue was the jaunty Kossuth hat worn by all cavalrymen. Attached to the front of these hats was the crossed sabre insignia of the horse soldier with the number of their regiment in silver worn above the sabres and the company letter also in silver worn below. The troopers called their hat the "Jeff Davis" not in mockery but because it was Davis who had adopted the hat for army wear when he was secretary of war.

Since all new weapons were going to the eastern front, their poorest item of issue was their rifles, which consisted of .54 calibre single shot muzzle-loaders, totally inaccurate and valuable only as a crutch or a handy implement for pounding tent pegs. By the time they reached the Ochoco, Wolf Dog's warriors were armed with Henry model 1862, .44 calibre rifles which held 15 bullets in an under-barrel magazine and could fire 30 shots a minute with sufficient force to kill at 1,000 yards. An advertisement tacked on the stage office at The Dalles boasted that ". . . a resolute man armed with one of these rifles, particularly if on horseback, cannot be captured." As the Oregon cavalry would find out, this was no exaggeration. The Shoshoni had acquired a few of these highly dangerous weapons by confiscating a few arms shipments destined for the West Coast, specifically California. Before the end of the Shoshoni War, the dog soldiers would be packing

Winchester rifles loaded with a 200 grain .44 calibre bullet. The "forty-four forty" was equally as deadly as the Henry.

To offset their museum piece rifle, the cavalrymen were issued either a army model .44 calibre Colt or a navy model .36 calibre Colt both of which were single action, six shot percussion pistols with an 8-inch barrel and boasting an effective range of 300 yards.[5] However, accuracy was limited to about 50 yards. Backing up these hard-hitting weapons were the dreaded "long knives," the cavalry sabre with its razor-sharp blade ranging from 30 to 32 inches in length. These weapons the dog soldiers coveted and respected and should a man be so unlucky as to lose one, the government presented him with a statement of charges equal to a couple of months pay.

Their horses also drew a piece of government property namely the McClellan saddle. When Black Ice and Kamiakin cut off McClellan's railroad survey north of the Columbia, he was shipped to Europe as military attaché for the U.S. Government. In Hungary, he came up with his idea for a new type of cavalry saddle which was accomplished by mating a U.S. Army saddle with the Hungarian horse pad. This piece of equipment he pawned off on the army and consequently the cavalry was stuck with it for 90 years.

Lastly, the new recruits were given a company guidon of which no troop was complete without. This small banner was forked, half red, half white. On the red field in white lettering was the letters U.S. while on the white background was the letter of the company in red. They never got a chance to pack this into the Ochoco for by 1863, it was changed from the solid red and white to the stars and stripes so as not to confuse them with a Confederate outfit.

After drawing their initial supplies, the volunteers proceeded to Fort Dalles where they received intensive training. For the next two years, other than short raids into the Deschutes country, the Oregon cavalry did nothing but go through rigorous maneuvers preparing for the grand push into central Oregon.

During this, the Snakes—curious as to why the army had ceased harassment—were making the most of a welcome rest. Shoshoni hunting parties were probing deep into Wyoming territory laying in a supply of buffalo meat with only a token force left to patrol the two major emigrant trails. The mounted Paiutes in a contest over Carson River hunting grounds which had been going on for a year, ousted the Washoes and forbid them to ever again own horses. And so, while the Shoshoni were busy with domestic chores, a number of Americans were entertaining thoughts of breaching their vast storehouse.

---

5    Oregon Historical Society, Ordnance Returns to the War Departments, Washington D.C., Letters and Correspondence, Capt. John McCall, First Oregon Cavalry.

# CHAPTER 100

# TEARS FROM HEAVEN

*Those big white faces are telling us . . . "Then we found the
gold and took this last piece of land because we were stronger
and there were more of us than you . . ."*

**John Lame Deer**
Sioux Medicine Man

Between 1859 and 1861, vast deposits of gold had been discovered in
southwestern Oregon, Idaho and northern Nevada. Now a massive effort was being
undertaken to locate gold in eastern Oregon. In mid-July 1861, Jim Adams, Bill
Cranston, Allan Rodgers and Jim Clinton, aware that Capt. Keenly and Capt. Pierce
with two companies of Oregon Rangers were operating in Shoshoni territory, threw
caution to the wind and slipped into the Ochoco. Dr. Thomas Fitch—agency
surgeon recently stationed at Warm Springs—was serving as guide. On the divide
between Crooked River and Silver Creek they struck pay dirt one foot below the
surface and were run off by the Shoshoni.

But Indians weren't the only problem. In three letters to *The Portland
Oregonian*, it was brought out that claim jumping was in progress.[1] According to
Jim Adams, his party met a group by the name of Mattoon and Company with 30
heavily-laden pack animals who had been led into Crooked River by Pete Delore,
an ex-Hudson's Bay Company trapper and first settler in the Suplee country.
Mattoon jumped Adams' claim. Mattoon would later testify that Adams never got
to the gold claim on Silver Creek. Whatever the circumstances were, new trouble
was brewing in the Ochoco.

Out of all the parties that slipped into interior Oregon in the summer of 1861,
four had a dramatic impact on the settlement of the Ochoco. These separate groups
were organized and led by: Henry Griffin, who came out of the unknown past to
streak across eastern Oregon setting it aflame; David Littlefield, an ex-sailor in

---

1     One letter was written at Mountain House, September 5, 1861, signed by J.L. Adams and
Allen Rodgers; another written in Tygh Valley, September 10, 1861 and signed by E.D. Thom,
B.L. Mathews, Wm. Gamble, and E. Gilbert; and a confirmation letter also from Mountain
House signed by Fred Sievers. *The Portland Oregonian*, September 21, 1861.

search of the elusive Blue Bucket Mine; Edward Pierce, who "learned the ropes" in the California strike of '49; and Joseph Bailey, a popular politician from Salem.

Griffin outfitted at The Dalles and headed directly for Crooked River. With him was James Wilson Marshall . . . the man who discovered gold nuggets in the tail race at Sutter's sawmill on the American River in 1848.

At about the same time Griffin's party slipped up the Deschutes, Littlefield left Portland armed with firsthand information on the location of the Blue Bucket gold and slashed through the center of the state. Somewhere in the back country, while dodging Snake patrols, Littlefield and Griffin made contact and decided to join forces. Since there appeared to be more Indian activity to the south than there was to the north, they drifted toward the headwaters of the John Day River and lady luck rode with them.

Griffin discovered gold on a creek in Baker Valley which later became known as Griffin Gulch. Marshall hit it rich on the Powder River. Apparently Marshall was good at discovery but poor at development. On May 23, 1864, *The Portland Oregonian* passed along this bit of information: "J.W. Marshall, discoverer of the 1848 California strike is still living in Coloma, a poor but respectable citizen."

Dave Littlefield found the mother lode on the banks of Elk Creek soon to be known as the Auburn Strike. Griffin and Littlefield quickly pledged to keep their discoveries a secret. They were so excited by their good fortune that they were completely oblivious as to what was going on around them.[2] Ed Pierce with a party of 20 men who had come in from the north and—in a period of eight weeks—prospected a vast section of country west of Hells Canyon was at this moment moving through Griffin's and Littlefield's territory.

On the other side of the Cascade range, Joe Bailey decided to strike it big by another method as evidenced in the *Oregon Statesman* August 19, 1861. In its usual caustic manner the *Statesman* noted that ". . . Joseph Bailey, a member elected to the Oregon legislature, is leaving today to trail herd 800 cattle to the Nevada mines and (insofar as the *Statesman* was concerned) he is asking for trouble." This was a valid opinion.

Despite Lt. Piper's artillery and Capt. Applegate's Rangers which had been prowling the high desert finding no Indians, Little Rattlesnake ambushed the cow column south of the Blues on August 26, just seven days after it left the upper Willamette Valley. Bailey, a large and athletic man, fought desperately, killing several of Little Rattlesnake's braves before the war chief killed him. Two of Bailey's cowhands (Samuel Evans and John Simms) were also added to the American death list. The remainder of the herders escaped to Fort Klamath but the Shoshoni now had a couple of model '60, .56 calibre Spensers to add to their arsenal plus 800 prime beef.

---

2     Other known members of this strike were Henry Martin, William Stafford, George Scriber, and John Adams.

Unaware that Little Rattlesnake was staging an attack under their nose, the 3rd Artillery clanked back into the timber where a train of 32 wagons stumbled onto their camp and informed Lt. Piper that all was not well on the Applegate Trail. This was in early September. Not only had the Shoshoni stolen all their livestock but they had another train under siege east of Klamath Lake. These raiders were led by the adopted Comanche war chief, Big Man. Piper lit out with his cumbersome artillery wagons and was successful in bringing this train through with minor casualties to Fort Klamath.[3]

In the course of two weeks, the Shoshoni had acquired thousands of dollars in horses, cattle, arms and ammunition. The historian Bancroft would reflect that "the Shoshoni with their nomadic habits and knowledge of the country were at this point no despicable foe as the officers and troops of the U.S. army were yet to be compelled to acknowledge." However, despite their gains, all hell was about to erupt in the tribal holdings of the White Knife Snakes.

As Bailey rode to his death, Ed Pierce galloped into Fort Walla Walla and shouted to the world at large, "Eastern Oregon is underlain with gold!" According to this messenger of glad tidings, there was ample room for thousands of miners to pan from 3 to 15 dollars a day in every stream from the Grande Ronde to Crooked River. Two of his party had cleaned up 2-1/2 pounds of gold dust in six hours on the Powder River; another of the group had taken $6,000 in nuggets off the Burnt River in four days; one pan of earth from the banks of the John Day contained $150 in gold dust; and the Grande Ronde was embedded with placer gold.

This was earth-jarring news and it didn't take long to span the continent. *The Portland Oregonian* broke the news on August 27, 1861 despite efforts by military and civil authorities to keep it subdued. In general, the Oregon media was difficult to control. They had, in the period between 1851-1861, developed a free-swinging brand of personal journalism which came to be called the "Oregon Style," described by the eastern press as "a seething caldron of editorial invective which left their readers gasping." The editors pulled no punches in degrading one another or anyone else who evoked their ire. For example, Asahel Bush, editor of *The Oregon Statesman*, penned this missile against Thomas Jefferson Dryer's *Portland Oregonian*: "There is not a brothel in the land that would not have felt itself disgraced by the presence of *The Oregonian* of week before last. It was a complete issue of gross profanity, obscenity, falsehood and meanness. And yet it was but little below the standard of that characterless sheet." This trend was initiated by Bill T'Vault in his *Oregon Spectator* which went defunct in 1855 due mainly to the Colville gold rush in Washington Territory.

Small wonder that neither the army nor the politicians wished to get on the bad side of these newspapermen. However, they were somewhat successful for the news died down for almost two months. Apparently Gen. Sumner hadn't

---

3    Bancroft, *History of Oregon*, Vol. II, pp. 477, 489.

intimidated the editors on his end for the story broke the *San Francisco Bulletin* October 24, 1861; soon followed by the *Sacramento Union*, November 4 and finally the *Olympia Herald*, November 7, setting off a stampede which nearly cleared the West Coast of males and did much to hamper Oregon's bid for fame during the Civil War. Within a year fortune hunters were arriving from such diverse places as Portugal and China; Germany and Argentina; England and Mexico.

When the word went nationwide it was already November and winter was in the air but this had no effect on anyone. The Dalles City, having weathered a four-year depression, was once more a wide-open boomtown. Immediately, the Oregon Steam Navigation Company—composed of the major Columbia River boat owners—was formed for the purpose of carrying the added freight three times a week from Portland to The Dalles; and from The Dalles to Umatilla Landing for the country beyond. Heading their group was Captain John Ainsworth who incorporated in a deft move to monopolize all transportation into the inland empire—a monopoly which lasted for two decades. An all-out effort was made to complete a portage railroad around the Cascade Rapids in the Columbia. This project, located on the south side of the river, was started in 1859 with mules used to pull crude cars on wooden rails between boat landings. Gold assured its completion in the fall of 1861, but as a transport route it was never satisfactory.[4]

As Ainsworth had foreseen, river travel during the gold rush would be a money-making venture and by the end of 1861, his line was running the field and definitely out for profit. He also placed little value on paper money. It cost $40 in gold per ton on the Oregon Steam Navigation Line to move freight from Portland to The Dalles; to Umatilla Landing, $130 a ton in currency or $65 a ton in gold. Passage from Portland to The Dalles cost $75 currency or $7.50 gold with portage and meals extra. In May 1862, the *Tenino* on one trip from The Dalles to Lewiston, Idaho (Washington Territory) collected 18,000 dollars for freight, fares, meals and berths. Constructed in 1860 at an improvised boatyard on the Deschutes River, the 135-foot *Tenino* was the second sternwheeler to operate the Columbia above Celilo Falls.[5] As the rush for eastern Oregon gold continued, the Oregon Steam Navigation Company built other boats to handle the upper river traffic. These included the *Yakima*, the *Webfoot*, the *Nez Perce Chief*, the *Spray* and the *Okanogan*.

One of Capt. Ainsworth's moves to corner all river trade was to put a steamship at the farthest point of inland navigation on the Snake. Built at Fort

---

4    The Oregon Steam Navigation Co. then built the six-mile Bradford railway, which they located on the Columbia north shore. This improved railroad was opened to traffic on April 20, 1863. (McCoy, *Melodic Whistles in the Columbia River Gorge,* p. 43.)

5    The first to ply the middle Columbia was the *Colonel Wright,* a 110 foot sternwheeler, built and launched by Captain R.R. Thompson at the mouth of the Deschutes River in 1858. (All information on Columbia River boats contained in a letter from Keith McCoy dated White Salmon, Washington, December 7, 1995. Mr. McCoy has done extensive research on Columbia River shipping and is the author of *Melodic Whistles in the Columbia River Gorge.*)

Boise, the freighter was christened the *Shoshone*. The *Shoshone*—one of the greats in inter-river navigation—never paid for its initial cost but it made river history that has never been equaled.

"Built out back of beyond on the very edge of nowhere," as Stewart Holbrook so aptly put it, the little steamer lived up to its fighting name. No sooner was it constructed when the Idaho gold rush came to a half-hearted standstill, so there it sat, 600 miles from the main artery of traffic with 300 of those miles never before traversed by steamboat. In fact, it was thought impossible for a ship of its size to navigate Hells Canyon, a belief that was very close to being true.

But Capt. Ainsworth was not a man to let any of his ships lie idle and his orders were to "bring her down to the Columbia . . . or burn her where she stands!" One attempt was made and ended in failure with the report that Copper Ledge Falls on the Snake "could not be run by man or devil." Undaunted by this report, Capt. Sebastian Miller and engineer Don Buchanon convinced Ainsworth they could bring the vessel through come hell or high water. They experienced a bit of both in the days that followed. In mid-winter 1864—some two years after the eastern Oregon gold strike—Miller and Buchanon started for the *Shoshone* in a buckboard following the Canyon City trail into the Blue Mountains. High up on the rugged slopes, the road gave way to marching snowdrifts. Not about to admit defeat, the rivermen ripped the boards off their wagon and made a sled. This worked fine until they struck Burnt River where the snow suffered a setback on the warm southern foothills. Discarding the sled, they rode the horses for 50 miles. Then the horses gave up and Miller and his first mate arrived at the Snake on foot finding the *Shoshone* in her mountain prison in mid-April.

Drafting the two watchmen and one of the Delore boys who was trapping the tributaries of the Snake, Miller formed a crew. Although the boat was badly cracked from weathering, the craft was able to keep afloat and on the crest of the spring runoff, Miller headed for the open river . . . and the boiling waters of Copper Ledge Falls. He didn't even get off to a good start. Misjudging the power of the eddy at the falls, Miller plowed into it full steam ahead and the sternwheeler *Shoshone* swapped ends, straining her already aching seams to the breaking point before Miller could get her straightened out for the run through whitewater. In two quick dips and one split second, the steamer plunged over the falls, knocking a sizable chunk off the paddle wheel and grinding an eight-foot section off the bow; but the *Shoshone* had conquered Copper Ledge and was rarin' to go which is more than can be said for the crew.

After two days of repair, the *Shoshone* was ready for another round when the Sheep Killer Snakes spied the odd-looking craft anchored below Copper Ledge Falls and began peppering it with rifle fire. Casting off in a frenzy, the boatmen rode through hell where the canyon walls rose 7,000 feet above the river and the small craft shipped water until it ran out the hold onto the main deck, but it rode the rapids to Lewiston and safety where it had already been given up as lost.

For a brief time the *Shoshone* worked the upper Columbia and lower Snake as a cattle boat. Then, with Captain Ainsworth himself at the helm, the Shoshone plunged into the treacherous horseshoe shaped falls at Celilo; successfully rode the Dalles rapids; shot the Columbia Cascades (no mean feat in itself) and was put into service on the Willamette after being ignobly hauled on skids around Oregon City Falls. Sentenced to the quiet life of the settlements, like its namesake, the *Shoshone* could not long endure. Here, the rugged bark of the inter-mountain river lanes which had run waters never before navigated, struck a rock in the quiet Willamette near Salem and sank. In her eight year career—two spent in idleness—the tough freighter *Shoshone* had seen more rough life than any boat on the river . . . perhaps, any river.

While Capt. Ainsworth was capturing the river trade, a town sprung up around Fort Walla Walla, where miners could purchase horses, saddles, clothing, harness, provisions and cattle at inflated prices. Wood sold for $30 a cord and flour at $24 a barrel. Preparations were being made in every community from Seattle to San Diego for a grand exodus to the eastern Oregon goldfields.

Finally, the Shoshoni became aware that something vastly different was happening. Until now, their main worry had been the homesteaders and the Ochoco had been their strongest ally. Deep mountain valleys, ryolite bluffs, timbered ridges and basalt rims were not for the plow. Neither did the arid plateaus surrounding the Blues offer any encouragement to farming. As yet, the Shoshoni were unaware of the great trail herds and a different breed of men who were moving steadily towards the open rangelands of central and eastern Oregon. But now, the fickle Ochoco was courting the Americans with a Midas touch and thousands of prospectors were clamoring for her golden embrace. So enamored with the passion of yellow fever that even the war-axe could not instill enough terror in their hearts to keep them away.

When the tribes drifted back to the Ochoco after the summer's hunt, there were white men everywhere. For the first time since the Blackfoot invasion of the late 1700s, they were frightened . . . very frightened. Their combined tribal population—men, women, children, old, infirm—would, perhaps, total 10,000 at the most and they had never envisioned that many people, let alone seen them in one place.[6] But during the winter of 1861-62, an estimated 10,000 white men descended on the Ochoco like a plague of snow-spiders. In the first few weeks, the Snakes stood up under the pressure but their faith was severely tested.

Emigrants wintering at the eastern base of the Blues, lured by the promise of gold, broke camp to head for the John Day country. They were met by an

---

6    Lewis and Clark in 1805 estimated the Shoshoni population between the Cascades and the Rocky Mountains at "16,800 souls." (See Clark's *Map of Western America*, copied by Samuel Lewis from original drawings by Wm. Clark.) This was probably accurate, perhaps even on the high side. By 1850, disease and warfare had reduced this number to about 14,000. Gourd Rattler's schism in the mid-1850s took another 4,000 Shoshoni into the Wyoming country.

incredulous Has No Horse. Never had emigrants tried something this foolish and he quickly dispatched them to the Eldorado in the sky.[7]

But more whites were coming from all directions—Nevada Territory, California, Dakota Territory, Utah, Washington Territory but mostly from the hated Oregon settlement at the Celilo. More than the needles on the mountain pine. The land was gripped by *Pokunt* . . . the mystery or unseen force.

Baffled and terrified, the Inland People called upon their spiritual leaders to do something . . . anything to stop the advance of the Ghost People. Those who answered the call were White Man, the Paiute holy man; Turkey Buzzard, the Snake healer; Sweet Root, the feared Snake prophet; Death Rattle; Pipe; Buzzard Man; and Half Moon, Has No Horse's sister who had been touched by God.

They petitioned the spirit world and in the waning days of the Elk Moon (late November) a terrible cold befell the Ochoco and snow blanketed the mountains with increasing fury—so violent that even tribal elders could not recall a similar incident. All was over. The Sky Father had rejected their plea. And then, the winter winds turned to spring-like warmth caressing the earth mother. Riders were dispatched once more to the far-flung winter camps of the Shoshoni nation and this time Wolf Dog's request for fighting men would not go unheeded. The Paviotso Confederacy would grow like a mushroom in the warm damp soil to full strength. The year 1862 would hold no fear for the Saydocarah. Let the whiteman come. The Sky Father had given a sign that his people would not become *Nokonis*—reservation Indians.

Up on the Columbia a new development was gaining momentum. In the final week of November nature helped deplete the white population permanently. Cold gripped the interior with an icy grasp and no one knows how many perished in the terrible blizzards that raked the Columbia plateau from the mouth of the Deschutes to the head of the John Day. Snow drifted and swirled, piling ever deeper and the first gold seekers wondered why they had left home. Few, if any, reached the diggings of their dreams.

Abruptly on December 1, there came a sudden reversal . . . temperatures soared from the sub-zero to the high 50s and warm rains caressed the frozen land.[8] The Chinook wind—brother to the Shoshoni—arrived bringing with it the worst floods ever encountered by white men in the Pacific Northwest. Rains and more rains spawned floods from southern California to British Columbia; killing and destroying. What once were deserts were now waist deep lakes. Raging torrents born on the headwaters of the John Day, Spokane, Ochoco, Walla Walla, Umatilla

---

7    Those known to be killed were members of the James, Boll, Jagger, Moody, Gay, Miles, Jefferies, Wilson and Bolton families. Bancroft, *History of Oregon*, Vol. II, p 484.

8    This atmospheric phenomena repeated itself 103 years later. In 1964, the Pacific Northwest flooded from Washington to California causing millions of dollars in damage. At a weather station in Prineville, Oregon the temperature fluctuated from 34 degrees below zero on December 7 to 59 degrees above zero on December 14, a difference of 93 degrees in one week.

and Crooked rivers boiled into the swollen Columbia and smacked into the Willamette Valley.

Other gushers roaring off the slopes of the melting Cascades destroyed the town of Orleans on December 3, swept away Linn City and historic Champoeg. There was water four feet deep and one-fourth mile wide in the streets of Salem. The Deschutes—claimed to be the only river on the North American continent to never overflow its banks—rose six feet above flood stage and tore out the only man-made bridge to span its treacherous waters.[9]

So much water covered the Willamette Valley that some thought the Pacific Ocean had crashed through the Coast Range and many tasted the water to determine if it was salty. Captain Hunnington, skipper of the *S.S. Cortez*, reported in Portland that all the way from San Francisco, the coastal streams ripped paths to the ocean spewing debris 20 miles off-shore.

No stagecoaches ran for days because all bridges were out and the roads quagmires. Food supplies ran short. There was little flour because all grist mills were on rivers and destroyed. By spring, hay was selling for 40 cents a pound.[10] Even by present standards, $800 a ton is mighty expensive livestock feed. Want and misery rode the sodden land. By May 19, 1862, the *Oregon Statesman* would report that 71.60 inches of rain had fallen between October 1861 and March 1862, most of which fell in the opening week of December. Fort Hall, the white man's supply depot for the western section of the Oregon Trail, was swept off the banks of the Snake in the winter floods.

Again it turned bitter cold. January 13, 1862 saw the Columbia, a swift and free-flowing river, blocked with ice. No steamer could reach Portland from the sea and inland navigation was impossible. There was no communication by land or river with eastern Oregon. Ben Snipes, whose cattle empire stretched from central Oregon north to the Canadian border and from the Cascades to the Rockies, estimated that 90% of the cattle carrying the S brand died . . . and his herds numbered into the tens of thousands. Besides Snipes' tremendous loss, it was believed that the storm destroyed as many as 25,000 cattle bound for the goldfields. Hundreds of travelers lay down by the side of the trail and slept the sleep that is dreamless. The plateau of north-central Oregon was strewn with frozen bodies which washed down with the spring floods.

Temporarily, the Shoshoni holy men's prayers were answered. Because of this omen from the spirit world, the Paviotso Confederacy would fight like starving wolves to protect the final stronghold of the Shoshoni nation . . . the once invulnerable Ochoco.

---

9     The bridge, constructed by the Todd and Jackson Freight Company in the summer of 1860, spanned the Deschutes at Sherar Falls. It was rebuilt in 1862.

10    McNeal, *Wasco County*, p. 136.

# CHAPTER 101

# WHISKEY FLAT

*Gold! We leapt from our benches.*
*Gold! We sprang from our stools.*
*Gold! We wheeled in the furrow,*
  *fired with the faith of fools.*
*Gray beards and striplings and women,*
  *good men and bad men and bold,*
*Leaving our homes and our loved ones,*
  *crying exultantly, "Gold!"*

**Robert Service**
The Trail of 'Ninety-Eight

In 1862 while the rest of humanity held their breath awaiting the outcome of the battle of Fair Oaks—pitting the celebrated McClellan's 105,000 yankees against the unknown Lee's 90,000 rebel troops—the maddening cry of "gold!" reverberated across eastern Oregon luring 10,000 argonauts to Whiskey Flat where stringers of the fabulous metal had first been discovered in the fall of 1861. Army recruitment came to a standstill and farmers in a feeble effort to combat mining companies were offering laborers $65 a month plus room and board, but this presented no competition to the $300 wages received in the mines.

During the winter of 1861-62, while the rest of Oregon suffered frigid snowstorms and drenching downpours, a group of miners and emigrants wintered in a valley ringed by granite peaks and protected from both weather and Shoshoni. In this charming locality a thriving town sprung up on the Powder River and in June 1862 an election was held. By July, a dusty rider carrying a buckskin pouch stuffed with 100 ballots and a petition for county status—signed by O.H. Kirkpatrick—made it known to the secretary of state that this was the "vote of Baker City, Oregon."[1] On September 22, 1862, the state legislature authorized a huge chunk of land to be named for Col. Ed Baker, Oregon's martyred senator. Baker City, county seat of Baker County would control what is now Baker, Union,

---

1    *The Portland Oregonian* belatedly made this news public on May 28, 1863. *The Olympia Standard* beat the Oregonian to the punch by six months when it announced the news first on October 11, 1862 and again on October 25.

Wallowa and Malheur counties. Mighty Wasco County was being cut down to manageable size.

Spring floods were still washing grisly human remains into the Columbia when William Aldred with 60 men left California bound for Florence, Idaho where it was rumored that nuggets covered the ground like fallen pine cones. At Fort Klamath, he hired Charlie McKay for a guide and slipped up the Yreka Trail into the Ochoco. On June 8, 1862, this group crossed Blue Canyon Creek and camped one mile east of the crossing at Hog Point. Aldred, certain that they were passing through virgin territory, went back to Canyon Creek, took off his long underwear and shoveled some gravel into them. Later, back at Hog Point, he panned five dollars in gold dust from his sample. Aldred thought they should do some more prospecting but McKay was persistent. "No by gawd! If we stop at every little stream that might have a speck of gold in it, we'll never get to Florence." The others agreed with McKay so they continued on, stopping four miles east of Hog Point at what became the rich "prairie diggings strike" and again found gold.

A week later at the Powder River gold camps, they learned that the Florence strike was just a pocket and was already cleaned out. After some argument, Aldred persuaded 17 of his original party to go back to Blue Canyon Creek. When they arrived back at their old camp they stared in disbelief. The shanty town of Marysville had sprung up at Hog Point and hundreds of men were frantically panning gold along a three mile stretch of Canyon Creek.

One day after Aldred's party left Hog Point, two Frenchmen struck the mother lode on Whiskey Flat where Aldred had first crossed Canyon Creek on June 8. Texas Ike Guker sluiced $50,000 from a 10' x 20' hole in a single day. In July more fabulous strikes were made on Dixie Creek, Granite Creek, the middle and north forks of the John Day River. Every quarter section of land along the streams was claimed and had a cabin erected upon it with preparations for permanent settlement.

Prospectors fanned out through the Blue Mountains covering the streams of the Ochoco. Within four years virtually every part of the country had been explored. Suppliers, freighters, dance-hall girls and ranchers turned to other pursuits to satisfy the mushrooming population. Way stations erected along essential travel routes were soon followed by sawmills. Stage and freight lines extended into the mountains and military roads were developed so soldiers could attempt—somewhat futilely—to protect the settlers from the aroused Shoshoni.

This road building was accomplished in part by forced labor. The legislature of 1862 saw to that. According to the spirit of Oregon's constitution all Negroes and Mulattoes were to be removed from the state. To insure their effectual exclusion, the legislature enacted a law whereby each and every Negro, Chinaman, Hawaiian and Mulatto residing within the limits of the state should pay an annual poll tax of five dollars or failing to do so should be arrested and put to work upon the public highway at 50 cents a day until the tax and the expenses of the arrest and collection were discharged.[2] This act would provide for some very cheap road construction.

Back in the eastern Oregon goldfields it was believed a perpendicular dike or vein of rich gold bearing rock ran from the head of the Ochoco River east through Canyon City to Florence, Idaho, a distance of 250 miles. As water poured over this dike, erosion followed, scattering the gold in every gulch below.

By the end of 1862, the miners had placered 20 million dollars in dust and nuggets and the surface had barely been scratched. One million dollars had been taken from Blue Canyon Creek alone and it would yield another seven million by 1870.[3] So feverish was this strike that the government began construction of a United States Mint at The Dalles City at an estimated cost of $110,000. It took six years to complete . . . and never minted a coin! At the height of production, the John Day, Burnt and Powder river goldfields turned out an average of one million dollars in dust a month with every settlement west of the Cascades vying for a share in the take.

On the banks of Canyon Creek, one-half mile south of Whiskey Flat, a hodge-podge of log cabins, muslin tents and board shacks mushroomed into the boomtown of Canyon City. There were stores and there were saloons and the ratio of saloons to stores was said to have been heavily in favor of the saloons. Boasting a population of 5,000, Canyon City was the largest center of population in the Pacific Northwest.[4] Two miles north on the John Day River Chinatown—called "Tiger Town" and known today as John Day—claimed another 600 inhabitants most of whom were Chinese laborers. Mining companies—such as the Humbolt Mining Association—were formed with shares selling at $1,500 each and the companies were further investing in large tracts of land to start cattle ranches. There was no sidestepping the issue—the Americans were crowding the Shoshoni.

---

2   Oregon General Laws, 1845-1864; Oregon Code, 1862 pp. 76-7.

3   *Ebey's Journal* M5, Vol. VIII, pp. 237-8; *Oregon Historic Landmarks*, Eastern Oregon Society D.A.R., 1959, pp. 18-19.

4   Portland wouldn't catch up with Canyon City until 1865 when its population reached 6,000.

# CHAPTER 102

# DESTINATION CANYON CITY

*America might well be the only nation passing from a primitive
society into decadence without ever having known civilization.*

**Sir Herbert Beerbahm Tree**
British Visitor

One of the first to capitalize on the gold discovery was William Gates who
organized and led the first pack train to the Oro Fino mines in 1861. He claimed
the John Day strike of '62 rivaled the California rush of '49 and surpassed the
Nevada strike of '59. Within seven years, Gates would become foreman for the
first big cattle outfit to enter the Ochoco.

Overland freighting—after overcoming many obstacles—would also
become big business. Although a stage line operated by Miller & Blackmore had
been opened from The Dalles City to Walla Walla in 1861, Hugh
McNary—member of the 1845 emigrant party who discovered the Blue Bucket
Mine—started the first wagons rolling into Canyon City and Boise in 1862.
Thomas Brent started the first Pony Express to Canyon City charging fifty cents
a letter; a dollar apiece for newspapers; and 3% of all the gold he could stuff in his
saddlebags.[1] Within a month, Brent was bought out by Wells Fargo but he
continued working for the company, not for the money but for the thrill of the
chase.

The Overland Pony Express had been out of business less than a year—closed
by the trans-continental telegraph service on October 24, 1861—when Wells Fargo
saw a chance to revive it. Countering Overland's boast with one of their own, Wells
Fargo now claimed the longest pony express run in the West . . . not measured in
miles but in hours of anxiety spent on the 225 mile dash between The Dalles City
and Canyon City with the average riding time running anywhere between 30 hours
and the gates of eternity.[2] Between the years 1862-64, the Pony Express averaged
one rider killed per week over this devilish run. Contributing to this high casualty

---

1   In 1923, Roy Gray of Prineville in an effort to duplicate the early day pony express runs made
    the 176 mile ride from Bend to The Dalles in 11 hours and 20 minutes for an average of over
    17 miles an hour.

2   McNeal, *Wasco County*, p. 141.

rate was the cargo itself. The riders often carried thousands of dollars in gold dust in their saddlebags and Wolf Dog's highwaymen were not always to blame for this increased death rate.

In 1862 most of the riders were armed with a five-shot .31 calibre 1848 Dragoon Colt, a gun much favored by gamblers of the period but it proved very ineffective at any distance greater than the length of a poker table. It was soon bolstered up to a .44 calibre six-shot equipped with shoulder stock so it could be fired either as a handgun or a rifle.

Even though express riders were held expendable, Wells Fargo wasn't making any profit. In order to stay in business, the company had to haul bigger payloads. Specially built coaches were the answer but there was too much money involved in a Concord to fiddle it away on an Indian's whim. However, the biggest problem was poor roads and the need for a relay station somewhere near the midpoint between The Dalles and Canyon City. It just so happened that this point lay in the tribal holdings of the White Knife Snakes, home tribe of Has No Horse and ruled by his cousin, the tough warrior Pogonip—Mountain Fog.

Also a new competitor had entered the field of transportation. In 1859, the War Department imported a herd of camels from Asia to be placed on desert service. Harney had acquired some of them and had placed them at Fort Walla Walla to pack supplies over the Mullen Trail to Virginia City, Montana. In 1861, the army unloaded them on a private speculator for $1,200 each and the camel express was now operating out of Umatilla Landing to Canyon City and Boise.[3]

The heavy demand for freight brought on the road-builders. In an attempt to keep trade firmly in control of Willamette Valley merchants, western Oregon entered steam railroading like a runaway freight train, leading the entire Pacific Northwest into that field of transportation. On May 10, 1862, the *Oregon Pony*—brought by ship from San Francisco to Portland and floated up the Columbia by barge—started hauling freight around the rapids between Bonneville and Cascade Locks to make connection with steamships from the port of The Dalles.[4] The *Pony*, 14 feet long and under two tons in weight, hauled 200 tons of freight and passengers daily from one boat landing to another until 1863 when it moved upstream to Celilo Falls. The locomotive awed both whites and Indians. Stock Whitley, rotund war chief of the Walla Walla tribe, was a daily passenger for months.

One of the first to enter the race for a direct link to the eastern Oregon goldfields was Eugene City, shoved to the forefront by a couple of local boys harboring a get-rich quick scheme. Selling beef to the mining camps was a high-paid racket as all miners seemed to possess a yen for solid, fresh meat. With this in mind in the spring of 1862, the Scott brothers—Felix and Marion—loaded

---

3    McNeal, *Wasco County*, p. 141.

4    The *Pony* now stands in front of Union Station in Portland, Oregon.

nine freight wagons with merchandise hooked to 80 yoke of oxen; gathered a trail herd of 800 beef cattle and planned to hit every mining camp between the John Day and Salmon rivers. There was only one obstacle to this venture . . . no road over the Cascade Mountains. On the promise of a lucrative trade-route, the Scotts talked the Eugene merchants out of a thousand dollars to open a trail from the upper Willamette by way of the McKenzie River Pass.

Felix Scott, captain of the Independent Rifle Rangers (an organization enlisted for the purpose of escorting emigrants into the Willamette Valley) convinced the Lane County farmers to donate labor for this undertaking and by June, they were hacking a road up the McKenzie River. Since they also had to hire men, the Scotts figured out a way to use the $1,000 subscription as a revolving fund. Every Saturday night, Felix would pay the laborers in full. Then Marion would get a poker game started. Before the night was over, the money would end up in the hands of the Scotts and another payday would be accounted for.

The Scotts played by their own house rules and in the early 1860s, a man could draw some weird combinations such as the blaze (all face cards); the Dutch straight (any sequence of even cards); or the notorious lulu, a one time play of any combination of cards which by dealer's choice could beat four of a kind. To indicate the dealer, a buckhorn handled knife was passed around the blanket. This weapon was also instantly available when an irregularity occurred and it can be certain the Scotts needed it on occasion.

The road building took more time than anticipated and near the Cascade summit, the Rev. Henry Spaulding—trail herding 600 beef cattle to Canyon City—overtook the Scotts. He would beat them to the gold camps by six months. By the time the Scotts reached Trout Creek in central Oregon winter was setting in. Not wishing to get caught in a repeat of the storms of the previous winter, they began searching for a place to shelter their merchandise and livestock. A suitable spot was finally agreed upon in a cave under the overhanging cliffs of Hay Creek Canyon.

While Eugene merchants fretted over the absent business boom that was supposed to gild their counters with gold dust, the Scott boys lounged in their cave practicing card techniques for the benefit of the gents in the goldfields and garnered the glory of latter day journalists; for the Scott brothers went down in history as the earliest white settlers in Crook County. Holing up under a bluff with a barrel of trade whiskey hardly amounts to a first class settlement!

While the Scotts struggled over the Cascades, Bakeoven got its lusty start. In the early spring, Joseph Sherar (a native of Vermont and a packer out of Arcata, California) with his partner, Jonathan Lyon (nephew to Major General Caleb Lyon, who was appointed by Lincoln as territorial governor of Idaho and described as "a polished misfit in a country of mining camps"[5]) decided to get in on the Canyon

---

5    Winther, *The Great Northwest*, p. 241.

City strike. Moving up the Trinity River to Jacksonville, they crossed the Cascades over the Barlow Trail, breaking their way through 20-foot snowdrifts in mid-June 1862. Along the way, they had rounded up a number of fortune hunters and offered their services for a fee to guide them to Whiskey Flat. Among the aspirants was a German trader loaded with flour and golden dreams of establishing the first bakery east of the Cascades. As Sherar's contingent was dogging across the treeless expanse of the Columbia plateau, they were spotted by a Shoshoni patrol. At this point, they were just south of Buck Creek and some 50 miles southeast of The Dalles City.

Here, the Shoshoni relieved them of their property except for the flour. Broke and with no transportation for his supplies, the resourceful German stayed behind while Sherar returned to The Dalles to re-outfit. In a few days, the German got tired of just sitting and twiddling his thumbs while musing over the central Oregon landscape so he constructed a rough stone and clay dutch oven and started baking bread. After turning out a dozen or so loaves, he began to wonder what to do with them when another pack train hove into sight. The packers were overjoyed to find fresh light bread in the middle of nowhere and took the whole batch off his hands. It didn't take the baker long to see the possibilities of setting up a business here on the trail. And so, in a roundabout manner, the Shoshoni were responsible for the first bakery in central Oregon.[6]

On his return trip to The Dalles, Sherar saw the possibilities in road construction. The bridge built by Todd and Jackson over the Deschutes River was being rebuilt in the spring of 1862. In 1871, Joseph Sherar bought the bridge for $1,040. He then expended $75,000 on improving roads on each side of it, 66 miles of which he kept in repair for the heavy freight wagons. It was a paying proposition. He also maintained a stage station and post office at the bridge where a little settlement—valued at $40,000—clung to the rocky banks of the Deschutes. Sherar then purchased the White River Flour Mill which manufactured 40 barrels of flour per day. He also constructed a sawmill cutting 2,800 board foot daily. By now, the California packer owned over 100,000 dollars in property including a 1,500 acre ranch 14 miles east of the bridge on which he pastured 6,500 head of sheep. Canyon City gold had made Joe Sherar an influential man.

With road construction in progress, all Wells Fargo had to do was build stage stations. Wells Fargo wasn't trying to hoodwink anyone. The company realized that stage stations in Shoshoni territory were inviting trouble and they would soon become a favorite target for Shoshoni snipers always in search of arms and horses. Besides the dangerous aspect, life would be dreary and the rewards of labor small. It would take tough men to fulfill qualifications for the company assignments—men willing to face some of the deadliest Indians in the United States at that time. The men who passed the test for the first stage station to be

6    *Illustrated History of Central Oregon*, p. 173; Bancroft, *History of Oregon*, Vol. II, p. 787.

constructed and manned between The Dalles and Canyon City were Christian Meyer born in Germany in 1812, a California immigrant of 1849; and Frank Hewot a hard-bitten French-Canadian trapper. These men soon became known throughout eastern Oregon as "Dutch" and "Alkali Frank."

The spot chosen for the mid-way station was on a grim, sun-washed bench called Alkali Flat some five miles west of the present town of Mitchell. From this vantage point it was nearly impossible for the Indians to carry out a sneak attack and while Has No Horse devoted his time to the destruction of Warm Springs, Meyer and Hewot began construction of one of the most famous road houses in the West. The main building and barn were made of stout juniper log frames, bolstered with adobe walls and topped with sod roofs to inhibit burning. Next to the station lay the peeled-log horse corrals and around the whole complex stood a four-foot-high rock wall serving as a battlement.

In connection with the stage station, Meyer operated a frontier dining room and gained the reputation of furnishing the best meals between the Cascades and the Rockies. Most stations of the day served either "hawg and hominy grits" or "beef and beans" and that was it. At Alkali Flat you were fed like royalty for Meyer, a farmer at heart, developed a producing garden, grainfield and orchard which supplied the table most generously. Also for the convenience of the traveler caked with dust or mud from the Canyon City trail, Meyer and Hewot kept a barrel of water outside the door along with tin basin and a dish of lye soap that would peel the hide off a bull elk. Beside this was a roller towel which bore evidence of grime from miner, Indian scout, trooper, freighter and gentlemen of fortune alike. They even furnished a comb for the dandy, minus more teeth than Hank Wheeler after he took a .44 slug through his lower jaw, but nonetheless, it served its intended purpose. Evidently, the station masters suspicioned some eastern souvenir hunters might take a fancy to it so they firmly anchored the comb to the bench with a three-foot rawhide string which supposedly no man of gentle upbringing would think to sever.

Inside the station was a huge fireplace which served the double purpose of heating and lighting, the only other means of illumination being a couple of sputtering tallow candles. Against one wall they had constructed four bunks, crisscrossed with horsehair ropes for springs and covered with a mattress stuffed full of dried grass. All in all, the Alkali Flat Stage Station was quite homey.

Hewot and Meyer withstood everything Wolf Dog had to throw at them, holding their station against terrific odds—sometimes aided by the cavalry but most often going it alone.[7] With Hewot and Meyer paving the way, the northern Ochoco soon blossomed with stage stations along the trail to Whiskey Flat. The

---

7    Meyer died February 3, 1903 at his home in Mitchell, Oregon. Hewot operated from his Eight Mile home east of The Dalles as a peddler and became well known to almost every old-timer in eastern Oregon.

same year they constructed Alkali Flat Station, Cottonwood was established near the head of gloomy Picture Gorge and Bakeoven at the German's bakery south of Buck Hollow.

After stations were constructed, the coaches wheeled a hundred miles or more a day in well-spaced changes while the Pony Express covered the route in 24 hour relays. At The Dalles City base, both freight and express service started from the Umatilla House built by Nixon Bros. in 1857. In its heyday, the Umatilla House boasted the largest barroom on the Pacific Coast. Within walking distance of the Umatilla House, the weary traveler could rest at the Wasco Hotel or relax at Vic Trevitt's Mt. Hood Saloon advertised as "a gentlemen's club" which frowned upon drunks, gambling and gunfights. This posed no problems for the sporting element. Next door to the Mt. Hood Gentlemen's Club, George Clayton operated the biggest gambling house in Oregon specializing in poker, faro and three-card Monte with liquor selling anywhere from 25 cents to 50 cents a drink.[8]

It's worth noting that Trevitt—a veteran of the Mexican War who rode with the Oregon Mounted Volunteers in both the Cayuse and Yakima Indian wars—was the only white man to be buried on Memaloose Island, where the lower Columbia Gorge Indians had placed their dead for centuries.[9]

Hauling nothing but guards and gold, Wells Fargo's fast Concord stages left Umatilla House daily bound for Canyon City. When the competing Wheeler Stage Line entered the fray, Wheeler's coaches left Umatilla House every Monday and Wednesday morning. During the summer these stages made only three stops between The Dalles and Canyon City. During the winter, due to poor road conditions they made nine.[10]

Until 1863, the Wells Fargo Pony Express riders were the only ones daring enough to risk the Canyon City run. Then Slavin & Co. Stageline and the H.H. Wheeler Co. entered the field and war began. Although Slavin was the first to operate coaches from The Dalles to Canyon City, Bannock City and Salt Lake City, Wheeler became Wells Fargo's main competitor. It is reported that the Pony Express in a race with the stagecoaches once traveled the 225 miles from Canyon City to The Dalles in 18 hours flat stopping only for the necessary changes of horses and riders who had been stationed along the way.

The minute Wells Fargo completed its stations, Wheeler and Slavin took to the field. Henry Wheeler—after whom Wheeler County is named—had been watching construction at Alkali Flat with interest. While Wells Fargo toiled to

---

8    McNeal, *Wasco County*, pp. 12, 15, 142.

9    McCoy, Keith, *Melodic Whistles in the Columbia River Gorge,* pp. 53, 55. For more on this interesting aspect of eastern Oregon history, see *Thunder Over the Ochoco, Vol. IV,* Chp. 184.

10   Summer stops west to east were Bakeoven, Alkali Flat and Cottonwood; winter stops (also west to east) were Pratt's Twelve-Mile House, Nansene, Sherar's Bridge, Bakeoven, Antelope, Burnt Ranch, Alkali Flat, Murderer's (now called Mountain) Creek, and Cottonwood (Dayville). McNeal, *Wasco County*, p. 143.

bring in rest stations, Wheeler quietly ordered a 2,400 pound stagecoach from Abbott, Downing & Co. of Concord, New Hampshire, paying the neat sum of a dollar a pound for the coach delivered at The Dalles. It was well worth the money for the Concord was sturdily built, guaranteed to never fail until completely worn out and that was no idle boast. Barring Indian attack it would do just that. A low-riding, ground-hugging mud-wagon, the Concord was preferred over the Lever Coach in the winter when rains made bad roads even worse. Hitched to a six-horse team (some drivers used four-or eight-horse teams depending upon the load and terrain), the coach was a sight to behold as it rumbled down Canyon City's main thoroughfare.[11]

Bells jangled on the shiny black harness as Wheeler manned the drivers seat, expertly guiding the horses through the jumble of freight wagons and packstrings; his only aids being a ten-foot bullwhip which never touched a horse and the jerk lines. These were leather reins running from each team to the driver's hands so that he was manipulating six separate ribbons. Each rein was split on the forward end and the right rein split ends linked to the right side of each horse's jaw; the left rein split ends hooked to the left side so a single pull directed both animals.

But no one was looking at the teamster, they could be seen every day. The Concord was something else for it was the very latest in modern transportation. Bright red, trimmed in gold, the coach glistened like a Blue Canyon nugget and it was huge, able to carry 12 or 15 passengers without crowding and as Wheeler later discovered, he could pack in as many as 23—which didn't make an enjoyable trip for the passengers but certainly helped the payload. Inside were three seats, two facing forward, the third facing back. In this particular coach, the middle seat could be lowered to form a bed so if there weren't too many passengers they could catch a nap between stations at least as far as Antelope. From there, the road pitched over the corner of Axhandle Ridge; bounced across Hell's Half Acre; dove into John Day Gulch; worried up Bridge Creek Grade; quieted down on Alkali Flat; banged over Monroe Roughs; twisted above Rock Creek Gorge; ducked between Waterspout and Rattlesnake gulches; crunched into Cottonwood; and finally thundered up the John Day Valley into Canyon City with everyone aboard wide-eyed and shaken.

If necessary, three seats could be mounted on the roof which was covered with a heavy canvas, painted and waterproof, but Wheeler never deemed it necessary to stick anyone up there. One good reason: they presented such a wonderful target when traveling through the Shoshoni shooting gallery. The dog soldiers usually hit the coaches in the vicinity of Potato Hills—south of Currant Creek and west of Muddy Creek—and would continue the attack into Cottonwood

---

11    Especially eye catching were the coaches brightly painted with flowers and landscape scenes which achieved popularity in the flush mining days of the 1860s and 70s.

Station. To driver and passenger alike, the Shoshoni were *hyus cultus* . . . bad medicine!

The coach doors, one on each side, were entered with the aid of hanging steel step-plates. On both sides there were windows beside the front and rear seats protected by canvas curtains. The curtains, rolled up on a stout slat, were held in place by a leather strap and when let down were firmly fastened with eyes and turnbuttons. Next to each window was a tug strap to cling to, as the seats were quite close together and those in the front seat riding backward often had to "dovetail" their legs, as the process was called, with the legs of those in the center seat riding forward. As might be expected, dovetailing was a cozy arrangement looked upon in high disfavor by the ladies making the trip.

Conspicuously posted—fore and aft—inside the coach were the stage-line's thoughts on proper travel etiquette noting that "adherence to the following rules will insure a pleasant trip for all." Among these pleasantries were:

1. Abstinence from liquor is requested, but if you must drink, share the bottle. To do otherwise makes you appear selfish and un-neighborly.

2. If ladies are present, gentlemen are urged to forego smoking cigars and pipes as the odor of same is repugnant to the Gentle Sex. Chewing tobacco is permitted, but spit WITH the wind, not against it.

3. Gentlemen must refrain from the use of rough language in the presence of ladies and children.

4. Buffalo robes are provided for your comfort during cold weather. Hogging robes will not be tolerated and the offender will be made to ride with the driver.

5. Don't snore loudly while sleeping or use your fellow passenger's shoulder for a pillow; he (or she) may not understand and friction may result.

6. Firearms may be kept on your person for use in emergencies. Do not fire them for pleasure or shoot at wild animals, as the sound riles the horses.

7. In the event of runaway horses, remain calm. Leaping from the coach in panic will leave you injured and at the mercy of the elements, hostile Indians and hungry coyotes.

8. Forbidden topics of discussion are stagecoach robberies and Indian uprisings. [This rule was strictly enforced.]

9. Gents guilty of unchivalrous behavior toward lady passengers will be put off the stage. It's a long walk back. A word to the wise is sufficient.[12]

---

12   This is an authentic set of rules posted in many stages in the old west. These rules may sound very humorous to us today but they were taken very seriously by the passengers of that day.

Outside the stage in gilt letters six inches high was the destination—Canyon City—painted above the right door panel; above the left was printed The Dalles City, noting the point of origin. On the panel under the driver's seat was the inscription. H.H. Wheeler Co. No. 1, showing that this was the first stage Wheeler owned. Square-sided oil-burning coach lamps set in brackets right and left just back and below the driver's seat. They provided some light at night though it must have been precious little. Many of the old stage companies did not travel at night. . . . The Dalles-Canyon City line did.

The driver's seat was set high on the front so he perched a good six feet from the ground. Under the driver's box was a leather shrouded boot for baggage and directly beneath his shelf-like seat was a smaller compartment in which he carried the valuable strong box—the iron money chest chained and padlocked. In the rear of the coach was a hinged, chain-supported platform, also leather or canvas hooded, which provided space for heavier luggage. Rails around the top provided space for still more luggage.

The driver of the coach, or whip as he was called, drove from the right hand side of the box where a powerful foot brake was provided. On his left rode an armed guard, sometimes hired by the stage line, sometimes provided by the express companies as a traveling agent in direct charge of valuable express shipments. These representatives typically packed a pair of .44 calibre Colt Specials and sawed off 10-gauge shotguns loaded with double-aught buckshot—a truly lethal combination. The most popular weapon for the stage driver was a needle gun—so-called because the firing pin passed through the charge for detonating.[13]

Making his first run on May 1, 1864, Wheeler charged $40 gold per passenger from The Dalles to Canyon City. Because of the high risks involved, the current rate of exchange didn't hold at the two-to-one rate. It was either $40 gold or $120 currency. He also received $12,000 a year for hauling mail. Wheeler made more runs than any stage driver on the Canyon City run, losing 89 horses and at least four coaches. Although severely wounded many times in Shoshoni raids, Wheeler lived to tell the tale.[14]

By 1871, the Northwestern Stage Co. had 22 coaches in transit between The Dalles, Canyon City, Pendleton, Walla Walla, Boise and up the Snake River into Kelton, Utah. The glamorous coaches beyond doubt were the ultimate in western transportation but the mundane freight wagons—hauling all worldly

---

13     Beside Wheeler some of the better known stage drivers on the hazardous run from The Dalles to Canyon City were: Hank Monk, Justin Chenowith, Big Bill Lockwood, Tom Vaughn, Hill Beasky, Jim Perkins (traveling horseshoer for Ben Holladay, one of the greatest stagecoach operators in the west), Jim Clark, Ad Edgar, and John Ward. *Illustrated History of Central Oregon*, p. 588; McNeal, *Wasco County*, p. 141.

14     Henry Wheeler married Dorcas Monroe and died in Mitchell, Oregon, March 26, 1915.

supplies—were the lifeblood of the frontier settlements; and along with other provisions, it was not uncommon for a few young ladies to arrive with the freighter now plying the inland sea of grass. Any delay in the scheduled arrival of groceries was accepted with a splendid stoicism, the philosophic admission that "oh well, such things will happen you know." But if anything happened to delay the arrival of the liquor supply it was looked upon as a major disaster, no doubt engineered by the enemies of liberty and "by gawd, somebody'll bleed for this!"

Beside the discovery of gold, another blow fell heavily upon the shoulders of the embattled Shoshoni. This was the passage of the Homestead Act of 1862. Under it, a settler—which included prospectors—could claim 160 acres in Oregon by cultivating the land and improving it in some fashion, usually by building a cabin (lean-to) which could mean a couple of boards thrown across a rail fence corner and setting up housekeeping. Thus, hundreds of thousands of acres in eastern Oregon were opened for settlement under easy conditions.

On the political front—as greenbacks devaluated to forty cents on the dollar—James K. Kelly was elected to the Oregon Senate and J.W. Perit Huntington, member of the state legislature, was appointed Superintendent of Indian Affairs in April 1862. Addison C. Gibbs, pro-Union republican, became Oregon's second governor and Ben Harding became U.S. senator while his brother Ed chased Indians across central Oregon in command of Company B 1st Oregon Cavalry. During this period, the Confederate army was riding roughshod over Lincoln's rag-tail forces but even so, support for the Union was growing in Oregon although many residents were apathetic and many hoped the Confederacy would win.

Then, on September 1, 1862 at the battle of Chantilly, Gen. Phil Kearny—who made the first U.S. military probe into the Ochoco—was killed along with Washington Territory's favorite son, Gen. Isaac Stevens. As for the Shoshoni, they were still reeling from the shock of a population explosion.

# CHAPTER 103

# THE OUTCASTS OF WHISKEY FLAT

*Kick away, old fellow; I'll be in Hell with you in a minute.*
*Every man for his principles—hurrah for Jeff Davis! Let 'er rip!*

**Boone Helm's last words to Jack Gallagher**
January 14, 1864

In 1862 justice around Canyon City was dubious at best. Thousands of dollars a day were being taken out of the ground and eastern Oregon swarmed with miners, gamblers, saloon keepers, dance-hall girls and desperadoes. It often seemed the criminals were better organized than the law-abiding citizens. It was said that Canyon City was a town "where some men died in the streets and others went home to read David Copperfield." And you had to be very careful what you said to the local residents. An Englishman visiting a friend on a John Day ranch inquired of the foreman, "Is your master at home?" The foreman looked him straight in the eye and replied, "The son of a bitch hasn't been born yet!"

It was also claimed that the citizens of Canyon City had little use for the finer arts but "they did dress fashionably on occasion." And one of the more stylish articles, always in good taste among the sporting element of Canyon, was the .31 calibre Allen & Thurber pepperbox. A sinister little gadget that felt perfectly at home in a vest pocket or tucked in one's waistband, this rapid-firing pocket pistol gained extreme popularity during the gold rush days of '49 and it was only a matter of time that it should find its way to Whiskey Flat. A percussion muzzle-loader consisting of six smooth-bore barrels three and a fourth inches long with an overall length of seven and three-eights inches, weighing one pound five ounces, it was without doubt a treacherous opponent. Although the effective range was only around 20 feet, for men of violence, it was just what the doctor ordered . . . better yet, the undertaker; for once blasted with a pepperbox at the sporting distance of one card table, it was mincemeat for the gentleman on the receiving end. As Mark Twain once observed, "The Allen was a cheerful weapon. If she didn't get what she went after she would fetch something else!"

In its heyday, Canyon City would harbor some of the more colorful personalities of the old west; a fact Oregon was uniquely successful in hiding.

Known only by names they chose to reveal, such as French Rita, Rattlesnake Jack, Two-Bit Sally, Arizona Sam, Velvet-Ass Rose, or Cherokee Bob, each in their own way contributed to eastern Oregon history.

Cultured Oregonians liked to believe that the state's eastern boundary stopped at the Cascade crest. They were very successful in convincing the outside world that this impression was true. In the American mind, Oregon is associated with the missionary movement, lots of rainfall, God-fearing farmers and genteel merchants. Therefore, it became easy to overlook that two-thirds of Oregon was taken up with desert mountains of scanty rainfall steeped in the rough and tumble romance of gold strikes, boomtowns, Indian raids, road agents, vigilantes and range wars. Although eastern Oregon shared as much violence as Montana, California, Wyoming, Nevada and Idaho, it has been seriously ignored in this respect.

In the spring of 1862, Henry Plummer—ex-lawman and baker by trade—drifted into Canyon City. With him was Dick Mayfield and Ned Ray who walked with a slight limp due to a bullet lodged in his foot received in his recent escape from San Quentin. Another traveling companion was a beautiful young lady who had abandoned her husband and children in Portland to help Plummer share the joys of Canyon City. He soon became known to the citizens of Canyon City as a gentleman with the "manner of a banker, the looks of a theater actor, the speech of a scholar, the carriage of an English lord and the fast draw of Wes Hardin." It was claimed that Plummer could fire six shots in four seconds with a .44 Colt and place each bullet where he wanted it. It wasn't long before Plummer had organized a gang of road agents to operate between Canyon City and Lewiston, Idaho to rob gold miners.

Another gentleman with similar ideas was Barry Wey. When he rode into Canyon City in the spring of '62, he already had several notches in his gun. Asked what he did for a living, he quietly replied, "I am a shootist," and with those words eloquently summed up a career dedicated to blasting his fellow men into eternity. A friendly gent who owned a packstring, Wey offered to see that gold shipments made it through to The Dalles without mishap. With his reputation as a gunman, it was believed he was the man for the job. The first shipment went through without a hitch and the miners were confident they had picked the right man. Then one morning Wey with Jack Gallagher as guard, left Canyon City with a gold shipment valued between sixty and eighty thousand dollars. When Wey arrived at The Dalles—minus his packstring—he calmly stated that Gallagher had bought him out on the trail and was coming with the gold shipment. No questions asked. A few days later a Canyon City bound party noticed "a peculiar juniper tree" and found a man's body under it believed to be the missing Gallagher.[1] The gold shipment never arrived at The Dalles and the rumor was that Wey had murdered Gallagher near the Antelope stage station and made off with the gold. He

---

1    Oliver, *Gold and Cattle Country*, pp. 47-8.

undoubtedly stole the gold but the charge of murder was false. A year later Gallagher turned up very much alive as deputy sheriff under elected sheriff Henry Plummer in Bannock, Montana.[2] A few months later, he was hanged along with Boone Helm, Haze Lyons and Frank Parish at Virginia City, Montana.

Meanwhile more gold shipments were being knocked off and it was obvious that Barry Wey had turned road agent. Within a few months, he had gained the reputation as being the "most feared outlaw in the west." Tom Brent, Pony Express rider, rode into a camp on Cherry Creek and to his dismay found it occupied by Barry Wey, his "wife" and Jack Gallagher. Unknown to Brent, they had just murdered a prospector on the headwaters of the Ochoco River. For some reason, they didn't harm Brent and he notified authorities in Canyon City of his chance meeting. A few days later—in the vicinity of Alkali Flat—Brent rode head-on into "the Greaser," a notorious outlaw named Romaine. He traveled the 112 miles to The Dalles in 10 hours flat.[3]

During Brent's narrow escapes, a young man still in his teens rode into Canyon City and within days had made his mark as a gambler and fast draw. Henry Vaughan was one of a special breed in the old west . . . a gunfighter. He and men like him lived (and usually died) with six-gun in hand. Some were outlaws and some were lawmen; frequently it was hard to tell the difference. But they all had one thing in common—they were bad news. Those who knew him ranked Vaughan along with Bill Langley, who had killed 32 men by the time he was 27 years old.

When Brent notified everyone in Wasco County that Barry Wey had gone bad, it was logical to try and convince Vaughan to accept the job as deputy sheriff for the eastern part of the county. Why he accepted is anyone's guess as the job only paid two dollars a day to keep the peace in the roughest town west of the Rocky Mountains. Apparently that was of small consequence, for Vaughan picked up Wey's tracks and backtracked him to a rocky canyon north of Stephenson Mountain known as The Devil's Holding Pen. It appeared Wey had hid out here for several days and some believed he buried at least part of the stolen gold at this spot. Vaughan continued on the track and eventually caught up with Wey at the Oro Fino mines in Idaho Territory where he arrested him (apparently Wey did not care to match draw with Hank) and returned him in chains to Canyon City to await transportation to The Dalles to be tried for the murder of Gallagher. Unfortunately, the Canyon City jail already housed a very dangerous man.

Just prior to Vaughan's pursuit of Barry Wey, Boone Helm—a Missouri knife artist—and David English—a notorious California outlaw—showed up in Canyon City. It was said that "if ever a desperado was all guilt and without a single redeeming feature in his character," Boone Helm was that man. Some of the Helm family, including a Methodist minister, had arrived in Oregon with the ill-fated

2    Dimsdale, *Vigilantes of Montana*, pp. 221-223; McNeal, *Wasco County*, p. 138.

3    McNeal, *Wasco County*, p. 136.

1845 emigrant train and it was commonly believed in the gold camps that "a relative furnished money to clear him [Boone] from the meshes of the law." Not overly intelligent, Helm—a medium sized, hard-featured man in his late thirties—had the reputation of a barroom brawler who had fatally stabbed or shot nearly a dozen men. In the winter of 1861-62, he killed a German prospector called Dutch Fred in a drunken spree at the Florence strike. It was on this charge that he was lodged in Canyon City's jail.[4]

Vaughan didn't have funds to hire another deputy (no one wanted the job) neither did he intend to stand guard over Wey night and day, so he chained him to a log for safe-keeping. That night he escaped. It was believed that "Little Dear Legs"—a Shoshoni girl named Running Deer and consort of Boone Helm—had smuggled him a file.[5] Again Vaughan recaptured him at Boise City and returned the outlaw to Canyon City. Having been put to considerable trouble chasing Wey, Vaughan refused to further inconvenience himself by taking prisoners to The Dalles to be tried . . . a journey of 200 miles through hostile country and the Shoshoni held no respect for even such a high official as deputy sheriff of Wasco County. Everyone was in favor of lynching Wey, everyone that is except Wey himself and Ike Hare.

Hare, a budding politician, made such an impassioned speech for justice that he finally quelled the mob spirit. In bombastic tones, he ended his oration with, "We will give him a fair and impartial trial. We know him to be guilty and we'll hang him anyway."[6] Couldn't argue with that and since this speech seemed to make everything legal, Vaughan proceeded to serve as judge, jury and executioner.

Undoubtedly, the county judge was more than happy when the Canyon City deputy took the law into his own hands, for the Oregon State Penitentiary was becoming overcrowded. It is interesting to note that by 1863, Wasco County was furnishing 35% of the inmates to that institution.[7]

Before hanging, Wey asked for his boots to be removed. The request was granted. In return, the deputy made his own request. Since where Barry was going, he would have no use for it why not tell Hank where the gold was hidden? Wey's answer was brief and to the point, "Where none of you sons-of-bitches will ever find it!"[8] His death was summarized in a couple of lines:

---

4    Dimsdale, *Vigilantes of Montana*, pp. 221-223; McNeal, *Wasco County*, p. 138.

5    Running Deer was a sister to Broken Knife and she later married the notorious Snake war chief Big Man.

6    Oliver, *Gold and Cattle Country*, pp. 47-8.

7    Bancroft, *History of Oregon* Vol.II, p. 645.

8    *The Dalles Times-Mountaineer*, 1898, "The Execution of Barry Wey at Canyon City, 1863."

*They took him down to Canyon town*
*and into jail they flung him,*
*Then they took him out again one day*
*and very neatly hung him.*

Barry Wey's boots were placed on top of his grave where they remained for years until weather and rodents destroyed them. The stolen gold was never found.

With the sad demise of Barry Wey, Henry Plummer left Canyon City and moved to Bannock, Montana Territory. There he was elected sheriff in 1863 and hanged January 10, 1864. His last words were, "Give a man time to pray."

However, with the passage of Plummer and Wey, other interesting characters were drifting into Canyon City to pay homage to the celebrated hurdy-gurdy girls. Mostly from Germany, these young ladies charged 50 cents to a dollar or whatever the traffic would bear to dance with the lonely miners. And that's all they did. Among the new arrivals to share in their companionship were Barney Prine, a high-roller at the poker tables spending as high as $1,000 a day; and John Wheeler, a gun artist and another big spender.

About the time Wey escaped from his log anchor another hard-pressed peace officer devised a cute little chunk of steel and brass weighing 16 pounds to transport criminals that would cause western Oregon to cringe with shame. This brass-steel combination which locked around a man's ankle became the infamous "Oregon Boot." Like all great inventions, the boot cannot be said to be the product of one mind. Necessity caused it to be constructed as a leg weight. Other improvements followed when a Salem man, William Leninger, improved the shackle and got a patent on it. Its main use was for the transportation of dangerous prisoners and—in aggravated cases—for punishment. By the 1880s it had replaced the whipping post at the Oregon State Penitentiary. Then around 1905, Gov. Chamberlain abolished use of the boot in prison.

The boot was simple in design: a 16-pound brass weight cut in half with sections coming together with enough room in the center for a man's ankle and locked with a screw device. When locked around the ankle, this brass weight rested on a lighter steel oval band attached to side pieces that reached below the foot and clamped under the heel, making it extremely difficult to walk and next to impossible to run. Some of the more dangerous Indian chiefs were outfitted with this torturous contraption when en route to the various federal prisons in the 1860s and '70s.

Harry Tracey, who wore one in the Oregon state prison, announced he would never wear one again—and he didn't. After he and his brother-in-law David Merrill escaped, Tracey, facing certain capture, committed suicide. Both Neil Hart and James Rathie—hanged for the murder of Pendleton sheriff Til Taylor—wore one.

Ray Gardener, another charged with murder, claimed, "It would be easier to escape from McNeil Island than from the boot."

One prisoner beat the boot by using a silk handkerchief. He pounded it into the screw hole and gradually loosened the screw. Another tried to burn it off with an acetylene torch. It served the purpose of cooking his foot so bad it had to be amputated.

While the citizens of Canyon City were engrossed in hanging Barry Wey, Boone Helm broke jail. Again Little Dear Legs was the means to escape but this was not known until Helm revealed it in his last confession. "When I was in Oregon I got into jail and dug my way out with tools that my squaw gave me."[9] She fled with him to Caribou, Montana. Again Vaughan took the trail and brought Helm back to Canyon City but witnesses were away when he was brought up for trial and civil authorities—among them saloon-keeper Bill Burton—were suspected of having substantial reason for letting him go.

Big Bill Burton had been on the Pacific Coast for a number of years where he was known as a gambler and sporting man—which meant he ran a house. He was absolutely fearless but was addicted to petty theft, which eventually led him into becoming involved with outlaws like Wey, Plummer and John Said. In the summer of 1862, he got into a fracas at a dance held on Copy-Eye Creek near Walla Walla and shot a miner named Dan Cogwell. Burton was arrested but made his escape on a fast horse and rode into Canyon City. Here, he opened the Elkhorn Hotel—Plummer was a steady patron—sporting such luxuries as Judy Hole Card, a faro dealer and Lousy Liz Cannary, sister to Calamity Jane. And there was Two-Bit Sally Ives who undoubtedly hoped to match the fame of Julia Bulette—the reigning courtesan of the Comstock Lode—who could receive as much as a thousand dollars for one night of pleasure.[10]

According to Bud Thompson, a Canyon City packer, Burton's "lady waitresses," as he called them, were "poor, faded, blear-eyed creatures in gaudy finery upon whose features was stamped the everlasting brand of God's outlawry." Maybe so, but Thompson wasn't so dumb as to voice that opinion to Big Bill. It was said that Burton, to insure order, kept a ten-shooter under the bar. Made in France by Le Mats for the Confederate army, the huge cylinder held nine .44 slugs while below the pistol barrel was a .60 calibre shotgun barrel which could be fired by flipping down the adjustable nose on the hammer. This weapon was enough to intimidate the most violent drunks.

Burton's days in Canyon City were also numbered. Lawless acts which went unpunished in eastern Oregon mining communities were coming to an end. Over Dixie Pass at Auburn—at that time the second largest city in Oregon—two men were poisoned. Their partner, a Frenchman, was held to be the guilty party. A

---

9    Dimsdale, *Vigilantes of Montana*, p. 139.

10   Reiter, *The Women*, p. 18.

A typical stagecoach of the 1860s.

*Courtesy of Crook County Historical Society, Bowman Museum.*

Freight wagon on the Dalles-Canyon City Military Road.

*Courtesy of Crook County Historical Society, Bowman Museum.*

Col. Benjamin Bonneville

Elijah White

**Col. Benjamin Bonneville** was in command of troop movements in eastern Oregon in 1861.

**Elijah White**—physician, politician and Oregon Indian agent.

**Kit Carson**—mountain man, Indian scout, and military man, was with Fremont's expedition when it explored central Oregon.

Kit Carson

Gourd Rattler (Washakie)

*DAP; courtesy of Mercaldo Archives.*

Wovoka

*DAP; courtesy of Mercaldo Archives.*

Black Kettle

*DAP; drawing by Herschel Lee,*
*courtesy of Library, State Historical Society of Colorado.*

**Gourd Rattler** was the head chief of the eastern Shoshoni nation. After Red Wolf died, Gourd Rattler and Wolf Dog competed for control over the Shoshoni nation; the result—Gourd Rattler and his peaceful followers splintered off and settled on the Wind River Reservation in Wyoming, while Wolf Dog, along with Has No Horse, led the rest of the Shoshoni in their continued fight against the white man's invasion of their territory.

A Northern Paiute Indian, **Wovoka** was a spiritual leader and originator of the Ghost Dance, which ended in the massacre at Wounded Knee.

**Black Kettle**, Cheyenne chief, was murdered by Custer's 7th Cavalry on the Washita River.

Tecumseh

*DAP; courtesy of Bureau of American Ethnology, Smithsonian Institution.*

Looking Glass

*DAP; photo by William Henry Jackson, courtesy of Bureau of American Ethnology, Smithsonian Institution.*

In 1811, Shawnee chiefs **Tecumseh** and his brother The Prophet fought together to protect their lands from white advances led by Gen. William Henry Harrison. After Harrison became president in 1841, the curse The Prophet placed on him would come true (see pages 261-262).

**Looking Glass**, Nez Perce chief, was an enemy of the Shoshoni, and plotted treachery during the treaty negotiations of 1855.

**Ouray** was head chief of the northern Utes; Has No Horse had a price on his head for being a traitor.

Ouray

*DAP; courtesy of Mercaldo Archives.*

Captain Jack

Chief Joseph

Quanah Parker

**Captain Jack**, Modoc chief, supplied the Shoshoni with arms and ammunition.

Nez Perce **Chief Joseph** remained neutral during the Shoshoni war.

**Quanah Parker**, Comanche war chief whose mother was a captive white woman (Cynthia Ann, see third picture section), was believed to have sent aid to the Ochoco Shoshoni.

Pres. James Buchanan (1857-61)

*DAP; engraving by John C. Buttre.*

Pres. Abraham Lincoln (1861-65)

*DAP; photo by Alexander Gardner,
courtesy of New-York Historical Society.*

At the dawn of the Civil War, **President Buchanan** breathed a sigh of relief as he turned the government over to Lincoln.

Six days after Lee surrendered to Grant, **President Lincoln**, who had brought the Civil War to an end, was assassinated by a brooding southern sympathizer (see following photo spread).

**Secretary William Seward's** acquisition of Alaska was arguably the most valuable achievement of the Johnson administration. Scoffed at as "Seward's Folly" and "Seward's Icebox," the vast northern territory proved worth far more than its purchase price of $7.2 million.

Sec. of State William Henry Seward

*DAP; photo by Mathew Brady,
courtesy of U.S. Dept. of State.*

Pres. Andrew Johnson (1865-69)

*DAP; engraving by Alexander H. Ritchie.*

Pres. Ulysses S. Grant (1869-77)

*DAP; photo by Alexander Gardner, courtesy of Peter A. Juley & Son.*

Julia Grant

*DAP; courtesy of Library of Congress.*

Facing impeachment from a radical Republican Congress, **President Johnson** appointed **General Grant** as secretary of war in 1867. Two years later Grant, who had served military time on the Oregon Indian frontier, became the 18th president of the United States. Suffering from fatal cancer, Grant wrote his memoirs to provide support for his wife, **Julia**, and his family.

John Wilkes Booth

Mary E. Surratt

*DAP; courtesy of New-York Historical Society.*

Six southern sympathizers conspired in the assassination of President Abraham Lincoln in 1865, including **John Wilkes Booth**, **Mary E. Surratt** and **Samuel Arnold**. John Booth, a well-known Shakespearean actor, carried out the plot by shooting President Lincoln as he watched Booth perform at Ford's Theater in a production of *Our American Cousin*.

Samuel Arnold

*DAP; photo by Alexander Gardner, courtesy of New-York Historical Society.*

Gen. George Crook (North)

*DAP; courtesy of Library of Congress, Brady-Handy Collection.*

Gen. Henry Halleck (North)

*DAP; Engraving by Alexander H. Ritchie.*

Gen. George McClellan
(North)

*DAP; courtesy of New-York Historical Society.*

All three of these outstanding officers saw action during the Shoshoni conflict.

**General Crook** finally brought the Shoshoni war to an end in 1868, and Crook County was named after him.

**General Halleck**, who served on the West Coast, was an expert in military fortifications and was Army chief of staff until 1865.

In 1864, **General McClellan**, running on the Democratic ticket, challenged Lincoln for the presidency. He picked up 21 electoral votes to Lincoln's 212.

Gen. George Armstrong Custer
(North)

Lt. Marcus Reno
(North)

Generals **Custer** and **Sherman**, stationed east of the Rockies, were instrumental in preventing other hostile tribes from joining forces with the Shoshoni.

**Lt. Reno** was with Drake's command when they established Fort Maury in the upper Crooked River valley.

Gen. Wm. Tecumseh Sherman (North)

*DAP; courtesy of New-York Historical Society.*

Gen. Robert E. Lee
(South)

Gen. Stonewall Jackson
(South)

Gen. George Edward Pickett (South)

**Robert E. Lee** was in command of the Texas Cavalry (fighting Comanches) when the Civil War broke out. President Lincoln offered him field command of the Union forces but he declined and joined the Confederacy. Thomas Jackson, commonly known as **Stonewall Jackson**, earned his nickname at the first battle of Bull Run. In 1863 he was accidentally shot and fatally wounded by his own men. Captain **George Pickett** was the man sent in to rescue Captain McClellan's survey party when it was cut off by the Indians east of the Cascade mountains. As a Confederate general, Pickett would gain immortality at the battle of Gettysburg, Pennsylvania, when with 4,500 troops at his back, he charged the Union lines and lost three-fourths of his men in the attack.

James Butler Hickok
(Wild Bill Hickok)

*DAP; courtesy of Mercaldo Archives.*

William F. Cody
(Buffalo Bill)

*DAP; courtesy of New-York Historical Society.*

These photographs are representative of the adventurers who roamed the West during the Indian wars. **James Butler Hickok**, a stage coach driver, was said to have tangled with a grizzly bear, killing it with a bowie knife. He served as an army scout, supply train wagon master and performer in Buffalo Bill's Wild West Show. **William F. Cody** was a pony express rider, army scout, and showman. His Buffalo Bill shows toured the United States and Europe. By the early 1890s, Cody was a millionaire. **Jenny Lind**, also known as the "Swedish Nightingale," was typical of the entertainers who visited the western gold camps. Following her tour of the United States, Jenny returned to Europe and settled in London.

Jenny Lind

*DAP; courtesy of New-York Historical Society.*

Mark Twain

Bret Harte

Joaquin Miller

Considered three of the best writers of their time, Mark Twain, Bret Harte, and Joaquin Miller explored new frontiers in their writings of the West.

**Mark Twain** had President Grant's memoirs published in book form. He then turned over a half million dollars in profit to the destitute Grant family.

**Bret Harte**, first editor of the *Overland Monthly*, wrote *The Outcasts of Poker Flat* and *Plain Language from Truthful James* while touring the western gold camps. His most famous story, *The Luck of Roaring Camp* (a tear-jerker) was published in 1868.

**Joaquin Miller** was a Shoshoni war veteran, journalist, poet, and the toast of Europe.

Henry Wells

*DAP; courtesy of Wells Fargo Bank, History Room.*

William Fargo

*DAP; engraving by E.G. Williams & Bro.*

**Henry Wells** and **William Fargo** established the Wells Fargo Stageline in 1852 to transport gold from the mining camps of northern California and eastern Oregon.

**John Sutter** owned the land where gold was first discovered in California, which began the gold rush of '49.

John Sutter

*DAP; painting by Samuel A. Osgood, courtesy of New-York Historical Society.*

Henry Comstock

Gen. Grenville Dodge

*DAP; engraving by Alexander H. Ritchie.*

Hubert Howe Bancroft

**Henry Comstock** was described as an unscrupulous fast-talking character who conned two penniless Irish miners out of their silver claim, the famous Comstock Lode in Nevada.

**Gen. Grenville Dodge**, commander of the Department of the Missouri, in 1865 sent four columns (the Powder River Expedition) up the Missouri to prevent any hostilities from hampering Col. Drake's command in eastern Oregon. Dodge would describe these soldiers as "mutinous, dissatisfied and inefficient."

**Hubert Howe Bancroft**, premier historian of the Pacific Northwest between 1875-1912, chronicled the tales of fur traders, emigrants and Indians. He maintained a library of 60,000 volumes and 500 manuscripts, dealing mainly with the history of the American West.

Joseph Smith

*DAP; courtesy of Church of Jesus Christ of Latter-Day Saints.*

Brigham Young

*DAP; courtesy of Church of Jesus Christ of Latter-Day Saints.*

Three of the most prominent men in the Mormon church, **Joseph Smith** founded the Latter Day Saints in 1830. Smith was murdered in an Illinois jail in 1844. His prodigy, **Brigham Young**, moved the Mormons to Utah to avoid the continuing persecution.

Brigham's right-hand man, **John Lee**, was thought to have been the man who carried out Brigham's instructions which led to the massacre at Mountain Meadows in 1857. Lee, known as "Brigham's Avenging Angel" was aided in this attack by the Big Lodge war chief Three Coyotes and some 50 Shoshoni dog soldiers.

John Doyle Lee

citizen's committee named a jury and counsel for each side (this didn't happen with Barry Wey) and a trial followed. The suspect was found guilty and hanged . . . and the vigilantes of eastern Oregon were born! It was understood that the well-equipped vigilante should carry: "A pair of revolvers, a rifle or shotgun, blankets and some *rope*."

His services no longer required, Hank Vaughan headed for the gaming tables at The Dalles. Immediately, some of the leading citizens of Canyon City left town for easier pickings in the Virginia City gold camps but there miners would soon take their cue from Canyon City, Auburn and Baker City and in the fall of 1863 formed the equally dreaded Vigilance Committee of Montana.

One of the first to leave eastern Oregon was Henry Plummer soon followed by Bill Burton, Steve Marshland and Aleck Carter. Marshland, a college graduate, was known to be a thief in Canyon City but no murderer. As a cover, he went to work on the Big Hole Ranch northwest of Bannock and was gathered up by the Montana vigilantes and hanged January 16, 1864. Marshland's last words were, "Have mercy on me for my youth."

The big surprise to the citizens of Canyon City was Aleck Carter. Carter went to work for Joe Sherar as a packer in 1862. He was a "good and honest man" and large sums of gold were frequently entrusted to his care to be transported to The Dalles "which he accounted for to the entire satisfaction of his employers." He never lost a shipment. On leaving Canyon City, he turned outlaw and became leader of a Montana gang. Carter was hanged at Hell Gate, January 25, 1864. As the noose was being placed around his neck, Carter shrugged and said, "Well boys, let's have a smoke." When the news of the hanging reached eastern Oregon those who knew him were shocked. "He left [Canyon City] with an unstained reputation. It is sad to think that such a man should have ended his life as a felon, righteously doomed to death on the gallows."

But not all with questionable character had left. Canyon City was due for its second hanging in a matter of days and the victim didn't even have the temptation of a gold shipment for a prize. William Kane got mad at his employer for paying him off in paper money. The miners sympathized with Kane but they couldn't quite accept this as an excuse for killing the man. Kane, with ankles and arms chained, was placed in a buckboard and hauled to the gallows—conveniently located at the cemetery. On the way, Kane played a game of solitaire. With most of the townsfolk following to view the gala occasion, some children eager to get there on time, passed the buckboard. Kane looked up and called . . . "Boys! Boys, there's no hurry. They can't do a thing 'til I get there."[11]

Observers said he won his game of solitaire. That evening while everyone celebrated Kane's confirmation of law and order, John Said (alias Rattlesnake Jack) Arizona Sam Rush and five colleagues instigated one of the more brazen

---

11   Oliver, *Gold and Cattle Country*, p. 49.

robberies of the period and had it been successful, they would have been set for life.

It was Saturday and dusk was falling as the miners working the sluice-boxes sacked up their week's take of dust and nuggets. Suddenly seven masked riders appeared with shotguns leveled and took two 25-pound sacks of gold each which amounted to over $50,000. Mounted on fast horses, they soon eluded pursuit. Going down The Dalles-Canyon City trail, the gang stopped long enough to rob the Wells Fargo safe at Cottonwood Stage Station of another $10,000 in gold coin and then disappeared into the Ochoco Mountains. The vigilantes were able to track them to a spring some 20 miles southwest of The Dalles-Canyon City trail—now called Bandit Springs on the headwaters of Marks Creek—and here the track was hopelessly lost. The desperadoes were never seen again.

Four days after the robbery an unidentified man crawled into Alkali Flat Stage Station, his arm shattered by a bullet and an arrow driven through his leg. He was already in the advanced stages of gangrene and delirious. Before dying, he motioned that he had come from the south over some of the roughest terrain in central Oregon. He told of "tossing some gold into a deep mountain spring flowing from the base of a large pine to hide it from the Indians."[12] Neither Meyer or Hewot could make out where the man came from other than the Ochoco Mountains and they nor anyone else ever connected him with the sluice-box robbery.

Some 50 years would pass before a government surveyor would wander into the little glade now called Burglars Flat near the summit of the Blues northeast of Prineville, Oregon. He discovered the skeletons of seven horses tied to a log where they had died of starvation. The log had been scalloped out in front of each skeleton where the horses, in their effort to survive, had gnawed on the wood. As late as 1944, remnants of the saddles and bridles along with most of the skeletons and the partly eaten log could still be found—giving mute testimony to the tragedy of the horses left to struggle against hunger and thirst before death ended their sufferings.[13]

The big robberies quieted down until 1872 when the big strike on the Ochoco River was made. Ad Edgar left the boomtown of Scissorsville with a large gold shipment. North of Grizzly Mt., Frank Thompkins, William Bromlette and

---

12    This story as remembered by descendants of Christian "Dutch" Meyer, station master at Alkali Flat in 1863.

13    See "Burglars Flat," Old Timers Edition, *Central Oregon Shopper*, August 4, 1949. At the time of first discovery, the glade was named Seven Horse Prairie. When the author first saw the area in 1944, it was obvious as to what had transpired. Now all signs have been obliterated by vandals. In the vicinity of the horse skeletons were scores of excavations made by those who searched for the gold cache. Perhaps this search was more successful than anyone realizes. Julius Cornez, who settled on Marks Creek some seven miles southwest of Bandit Springs, was born in California in 1850 and roaming the streets of Canyon City at the age of 13.

F. Huston robbed the stage. They were caught in Antelope Canyon and taken to the Oregon State Penitentiary in chains.

Some other engaging gentlemen to wander the streets of Canyon City in the 1860s were William (Bud) Thompson, a gun-toting news-hound and his sidekick Cinncinatus (Joaquin) Miller, an avowed southern sympathizer. They were on the law-abiding side of the fence—but not too far. Between the two of them, they began printing the *Canyon City Journal*. Miller then became a Canyon City lawyer. When Thompson first arrived in Canyon City, he would note that the "restless, surging, throbbing throng of humanity drawn thither by the glittering dust that lay hidden beneath the ground" also attracted those "human vultures that feed and fatten upon the frailties of their fellowmen." It was his guess that there were six saloons to every legitimate business house. These dens of iniquity were only too frequently the scene of awful tragedies and the sawdust floors "drank up the blood of many a poor unfortunate crazed with an overdose of double-distilled damnation" who fell victim to the revolver or knife. He would recall one unhappy event relating to Canyon City's floating population that couldn't be blamed on rot-gut booze.

In 1863, a young musician named Brown arrived in Canyon City with his beautiful wife and infant daughter. Seemingly, Brown was a man of good morals who never drank nor had an enemy in the world. Seven nights a week, he played the violin at the various saloons for $10 a night. One morning he left the Eldorado Saloon at 2:00 a.m. and was never seen again. Whether he was murdered and the body concealed or whether he left the country remained an unsolved mystery. The latter theory had few or no believers as he was tenderly attached to his wife and child.

Soon after Brown's disappearance, a young physician—described as handsome, accomplished and talented—rode into Canyon City and set up practice. It wasn't long before he was spending much time with the attractive widow and when sufficient time had passed and no word was received of the missing husband, a divorce was granted and the young doctor married the widow Brown.

As the years rolled by and the mines played out, the doctor and his wife moved to the Willamette Valley where he took an active interest in political and public matters. In 1874, he received the nomination of his party for state senator and was the odds-on favorite to win the election. About that time, the Oregon press exposed to the world the indiscretions of Oregon's U.S. Senator, John H. Mitchell. To offset the charges of financial dishonesty and bigamy, Mitchell's backers tossed out dark hints and innuendoes about the disappearance of Brown and the quick marriage of his widow to the young physician; the outcome being that Dr. Hendricks withdrew from public life forever. It was claimed that but for his connection with the Brown tragedy at Canyon City he would have achieved a name equal of his distinguished brother, Senator Thomas A. Hendricks . . . vice president of the United States during Grover Cleveland's administration of 1885-89.[14]

---

14    Thompson, *Reminiscences of a Pioneer*: pp. 59-61.

In 1871, Bud Thompson—now the 23-year-old editor of the *Roseburg Plaindealer*—was caned and shot by Henry and Thomas Gale who published the competitive *Roseburg Ensign*. They picked the wrong man. Quick-draw Thompson shot and killed Henry Gale but the other brother escaped. By 1882, Bud Thompson had organized and was leading the Crook County vigilantes based in Prineville, Oregon. Joaquin Miller, his erstwhile partner, gave up the practice of law and gained international fame as a writer and poet.

During this hectic period, the lawful and the lawless were trying their damnedest to ignore the native sons of the Ochoco. It wasn't going to be that easy.

# CHAPTER 104

# BARD OF THE OCHOCO

*The red men rose at night,*
*They came, a firm, unflinching wall of flame;*
*They swept as sweeps some fateful sea*
*O'er land of sand and level shore*
*That howls in far, fierce agony.*
*The red men swept that deep dark shore*
*As threshers sweep a threshing floor.*
*I kneel to all the gods I know. . . .*
*Great Spirit what is this I dread?*
*Why, there is blood! The wave is red!*

**Joaquin Miller**
Captain of the Canyon City Volunteers

Born in Liberty, Indiana, March 10, 1839, Cinncinatus Hiner Miller came west with the ill-fated Clarke Train of 1851. A restless youth, he was working in the California goldfields as a cook at age sixteen. This being a little too tame for his adventurous spirit, he headed north and joined the Oregon Volunteers during the Rogue Indian War. Near Klamath Lake, he was seriously wounded when he took an arrow in the head and a bullet in his body. Left to die, a Shasta girl nursed him back to health. They were married by a passing missionary in 1857 and to this union a daughter—Cali Shasta Miller—was born. At the time, Joaquin and his Indian wife were living with the Modocs. Shortly after Cali Shasta was born, Miller abandoned his wife and daughter and enrolled in the Columbia University in Eugene where he studied law.

Admitted to the bar, he was again hit with wanderlust. Arriving at Fort Walla Walla in the winter of 1862, he took a job riding pony express between Walla Walla and the goldfields of eastern Oregon and Idaho Territory. Dodging Wolf Dog's raiders and Plummer's road agents temporarily satisfied his yen for high adventure, and he returned to Columbia University where he became a classmate and friend of John Douthit. Douthit, another restless soul, would become one of the first settlers on the upper Ochoco River where, in 1876, he hacked out a ranch on Douthit Creek two years before the last violent outbreak of the Shoshoni War.

During his sojourn at Columbia University, Miller became editor of the *Eugene Democrat Register*, a political organ openly against the Union. *The Register*, sometimes called *The Herald*, changed names periodically to avoid suspension by the federal government for its pro-Confederate editorials.[1] It isn't known that Miller was especially sympathetic with the South, but he was against authority of all kinds so he believed the South had a right to secede if it wanted to. He also took on other controversial issues. About this period, Joaquin Murietta, a Mexican bandit was making a name that was used to scare little children into good behavior. Miller wrote an article defending the outlaw—a sort of poetic apology for murder, rape and plunder. It sold only because the populace was shocked that anyone would dare to stand up for such a person. By the time the *Sacramento Union* got through bombasting Cinncinatus Hiner Miller, he was known throughout the west as "Joaquin" Miller. Miller rather enjoyed the new name. As for Murietta, his head was pickled in spirits and placed on exhibition at San Francisco.

Meanwhile, Brig. Gen. Ben Alvord who had just taken command of the Military District of Oregon, was not about to humor this young radical. In July 1862, he ordered Captain William Rinehart, commander of the Union troops in Lane County, to shut down Miller's anti-government press and to be "damn quick about it!" Rinehart complied with vigor. As the troops were moving in for the kill, Miller accepted a dinner invitation at the home of Judge George Dyer where he was introduced to the judge's gifted daughter Theresa. Three days later, they were married.

The Miller's spent their honeymoon three jumps ahead of the Union cavalry, heading for the Confederate stronghold at Canyon City where Miller planned to practice law. Rinehart—at whom Miller was still miffed—followed him to Canyon City but for no more sinister purpose than to take over as city postmaster and distiller of rot-gut whiskey.

It is interesting to note that before his hasty marriage to Theresa Dyer, Miller's literary works, which included both short stories and poems, had gained little recognition. On the other hand, Theresa was fast becoming well known as a talented author.[2] Soon after sharing ink pots, Theresa's sonnets went unnoticed while Joaquin's rhymes soared to the very heavens. Two of his best known poems were "Columbus" and "The Passing of Tennyson." In a way, Miller described his own brilliant rise to fame in the immortal "Columbus": "He gained a world; he

---

1   Karolevitz, *Newspapering in the Old West*, p. 135.

2   Writing under the pen name of Minnie Myrtle Dyer, Theresa contributed to early Oregon periodicals before her marriage to Joaquin. Some of her best known poems were: "Sacrifice Impetro," "To a Poet," "Plea for the Inconstant Moon," "Chansons," "Have Mercy; My Boys," and "The Last Portrait." At age 37, destitute and in poor health, Theresa traveled to New York City in 1882 in search of Joaquin and help. He sent her to a physician only to learn she was dying. Theresa Dyer Miller was buried in Evergreen Cemetery, New York City, a forgotten woman. Peterson, *Joaquin Miller, Literary Frontiersman*, pp. 51-84.

gave that world its grandest lesson: On! Sail on!" and Joaquin did just that, winning international acclaim as The Poet of the Sierra.[3]

Again, he returned to Columbia University where he exhibited his first love for odd dress causing John Douthit to observe: "Joaquin wore rather queer garb for those days. He would show up in class wearing knee boots and a velvet overcoat trimmed with fur." Such strange attire didn't hamper his mind for Miller was valedictorian of the class of 1863 and the address given was critically acclaimed to be one of his best works.

Following graduation, Miller and his brother Jim—accompanied by Theresa and their infant daughter Maud—trail herded 800 head of cattle through the hostile Ochoco to the beef-hungry miners at Canyon City. That summer, Joaquin took credit for planting the first orchard in eastern Oregon. Back in Canyon City, he was once again in his element and his head was bursting with wild, poetic ideas of sun, waves, love, mountain streams, stars, men and nature. These thoughts were all pretty chaotic. He could be seen all up and down Blue Canyon Creek, sometimes drunk, sometimes sober, but always with a notebook in his hand. The miners didn't know quite what to make of Miller but European nobility would think he was pretty hot stuff, a child of nature full of sunlight and mountain air. The miners suspected he was full of Rinehart's mountain dew.

At Canyon City, Miller wrote an account of the Idaho gold mines putting the Shoshoni name *Eldahow* (Sun Marching Down the Mountains) into print.[4] The word first appeared in this form when used by Joaquin in the *Washington Statesman*, March 18, 1862.

In 1866, Miller was elected judge of the newly created Grant County. When he aspired to be judge of the Supreme Court this august body told him he better "stick to poetry." Whether this advice was taken seriously is hard to say but for whatever reason, Miller wrote a tantalizing little article which would appear in the long-deceased *Pacific Monthly* (edited by his sister-in-law, Lischen Maud Miller) entitled "The Most Beautiful Girls in the World."

"Where are the most beautiful women to be found?" asked Miller, "And why are the women of this or that favored spot so passing fair?" He then gave two reasons:

Look about earth for tall women and you'll find tall women are of the woods where they partake somewhat of the stately glory of the aspiring trees. The second thing to consider in contemplation of womanly beauty, if it is not really the first in most cases, is the matter of complexion. The difference in races is largely only a difference in texture and delicate seashell tints. And where does the beautiful woman get her seashell and rosebud beauty? She gets it from rain,

---

3   All poems taken from Miller's *Poetical Works*, New York, 1923.
4   McNeal, *Wasco County*, p. 136.

the beauteous moisture in the air. The entirely beautiful girl must be of the woods, the water and the grasses.

He then declared California girls were the "daughters of God" but Oregon girls "Ah!, Oregon girls are the most wondrously beautiful of all. Oregon is the garden of beautiful girls. . . ." Mighty flowery prose for a pony express rider.

At this point Miller became so excited over his literary genius that he deserted Theresa—by now they had three children—and headed for George Himes' printing office in Portland with manuscript in hand. According to Himes, it was "The craziest manuscript ever offered to any publisher." Himes was unimpressed but "here and there" there was a gem of expression so he offered to work with Miller to make sense out of it. At intervals, Miller would shout "full many a flower is born to blush unseen and waste its sweetness on the desert air." Then he would slap his chest and yell, "That's me!"

In spite of these outbursts, Himes finally got Miller's first book of poems, *Specimens*, published in 1868. When *Specimens* came out, *The Oregonian*—digging deep for its most blistering editorial adjective—condemned it as drivel. But as one writer commented, "It is doubtful if Joaquin read *The Oregonian*. Why waste time reading what other lesser men wrote when eagles were screaming in his brain?"

Fired with enthusiasm, Miller armed himself with more notes and charged back east in search of more worldly critics. About the time he arrived in New York City, the philanthropist Peter Cooper died which inspired Miller to write a memorial poem. With same in hand, he contacted a publisher. A bewildered employee yelled, "Boss! There's a feller here to see you; says his name is Walkin' Miller." The outcome being that the publisher bought Joaquin's poem for $25. Its haunting last line . . . "and all he could hold in his cold dead hand was the things he had given away" gave Miller the recognition he craved.

Soon thereafter, Joseph Lawrence—a San Francisco businessman—bought the *Golden Era*, a weekly magazine, and proceeded to turn it into San Francisco's *Literary Journal*, catering to western writers—among them Mark Twain from Nevada; Brete Harte from California; and Joaquin Miller from Oregon.[5] In 1869, Lawrence promoted Twain's *The Innocents Abroad*, Harte's *The Outcasts of Poker Flat* and Miller's *Joaquin et al.* pushing them to the forefront as gifted writers.

Following the publishing of *Joaquin et al.*, Miller sailed for Europe in 1870. With long hair flowing, dressed in high-topped boots and bearskin robe; singing of wild freedom, wild winds and wild love, Miller took England by storm. Hailed as Oregon's gift to mankind he became the literary lion of London . . . the Byron of the Ochoco. A London book firm published *Songs of Sierra,* making Miller an overnight sensation.

---

5    Stone, *Men to Match My Mountains*, p. 246.

The Franco-Prussian war was in full swing when Miller—famous beyond his wildest dreams—hit the European mainland. In true Miller style, he managed to get arrested by both the French and the Germans as a spy. In Paris he became the guest of Victor Hugo who had recently written *L'Homme quie rit* and lived for several weeks at the home of Verdi, the great composer who was working on *Aida* at the time. On August 25, 1870, he attended the wedding of Richard Wagner to Cosima von Bulow, daughter of Franz Liszt.

By 1871, Joaquin was back in eastern Oregon living in an Indian lodge where he wrote *Unwritten History: Life Among the Modocs*. Published in 1872 while Miller covered the Modoc War as a newspaper reporter, it not only made him rich but did much to arouse sympathy for the Indians. He also penned *Shadows of Shasta: The Modoc War*. He then went to China as a news correspondent to cover the Boxer uprising and then spent a season in the Klondike during the Alaska gold rush.

While Joaquin was flitting around the world making an international name for himself, Jim Miller—his older brother—was carving out the vast Keystone Ranch in central Oregon with headquarters on the Ochoco River. Located 12 miles east of Prineville, it became one of the major cattle ranches in eastern Oregon. His sister-in-law, Maud Miller—riding on Joaquin's coattails—was making big bucks publishing poems and magazines devoted to women's interests.[6] His daughter Maud—known locally as Juanita—was also writing poems carrying much of her father's style. She was also every bit as flamboyant. Juanita would come to Canyon City during the big '62 celebrations to preside over ceremonies and on one of these visits gathered some notoriety of her own by marrying—in a mystic ceremony—the man in the moon![7]

Miller wrote most of his poems and stories from three log cabins: his original home in Canyon City which was made into a museum in 1922; a log cabin he constructed in 1885 on Meridian Hill near Washington, D.C. which was bought by the California Historical Society and kept in his memory; and a log cabin near Mt. Shasta called The Heights. The Bard of the Ochoco died February 17, 1913 and with his passing, there passed an era.

Now back to Wolf Dog, Has No Horse and Paulina, the true unblemished free-roaming mountain spirits of the Ochoco.

---

6    Gaston, *Portland, It's History and Builders*, pp. 509-10. For other information on Joaquin Miller see Power, *History of Oregon Literature*, pp. 229-46; *Oregon Historical Quarterly XLVII*, pp. 165-80.

7    Oliver, *Gold and Cattle Country*, p. 43.

# CHAPTER 105

# MURDERER'S CREEK

*they hav war with the indians all the time there has bin war everry since the fall of fifty four all through oregon. . . . I hav left my claim several times on the account of the danger of being massecred by the read devils ther is danger all the tim . . . but the whites ar getting to strong for them wher I live but they are fighting on the frounteers all the tim*[1]

**Josiah March**
Letter to his father

Although the 1st Oregon Cavalry—mustered into service in 1861—was called upon to guard roads, escort emigration trains, pursue hostile Shoshoni, avenge murders, protect gold miners and patrol the Ochoco, its first years of existence consisted of nothing but maneuvers. It would take two long years of rugged training before the volunteers would be trusted to tangle with Wolf Dog's waiting dog soldiers. During this period, the volunteers did pursue and arrest horse thieves and whiskey peddlers; men who could seldom be apprehended without the assistance of the cavalry. Because of this the cavalry's horses were kept worn down by long marches to recover both private and government property and leaving them ill-prepared for Indian attack.

With Captain—soon to be promoted to Major—Rinehart actively engaged in the illicit liquor trade, it is hard to believe the army was entirely innocent of the part whiskey would play in softening up the red military. The Shoshoni themselves did not understand this fact. With slow poison eating away his stomach and numbing his brain, the dog soldier was in no condition to withstand a well organized cavalry charge. The army was fully aware, if officially blind, to the swift sword it wielded in the lethal trade liquor of the eastern Oregon frontier.

When the white man drank the same brew he sloughed off onto the Indian, he didn't function so well either. Rinehart's recipe for Ochoco bourbon speaks for itself: one quart of raw alcohol, one pound of rank chewing tobacco, one handful of red peppers, one bottle of Jamaica ginger, one quart of black molasses, mixed

---

1    Copy of original letter in possession of Wasco County filed in The Dalles City Museum.

to any degree of strength with river water but—dependent upon the whim of the distiller—usually consisted of two gallons of mix to seven gallons of water. This rot-gut whiskey—known by such names as tangle-leg, white-lightning, forty-rod, Canyon City dew or tarantula-juice—was white civilization's most potent ammunition against the Indians and they were going to need it.

The gold discovery of 1861 forced the Shoshoni into an unexpected situation. Prior to this, the Americans had only been passing through the Ochoco. Now they were crawling over the country like ants looking for food. At first the prospectors presented some very interesting targets and the approaches to the goldfields were left open to the extent that the Shoshoni allowed enough traffic to satisfy their wants. Picking off travelers and pony express riders as they saw fit, the Shoshoni acquired gold, arms and other incidentals which made life zestful for all involved.

Beginning in the summer of 1862, Has No Horse set up a constant patrol of all trails leading into eastern Oregon. Broken Knife and Little Rattlesnake were raiding the Yreka Trail; Paulina, Yellow Jacket and Horse Trap were making life miserable along The Dalles-Canyon City Trail; Pipe and Big Man were prowling around the eastern Oregon gold camps while Has No Horse joined forces with the Dog Rib war chief, Bear Hunter, and was striking far to the east along the Oregon Trail. This was to bring on internal conflict in a hurry.

Gourd Rattler, attempting to uphold his pledge to the Americans to remain neutral, sent word to Has No Horse to knock off hostilities in his territory. Has No Horse refused to honor this request and to keep from getting embroiled in a family squabble, Gourd Rattler fled to the Mormon settlements near Fort Bridger for protection. This only served to arouse the ire of Has No Horse and he sent Bear Hunter into the Mormon settlements to insure Gourd Rattler stayed in hiding.

On the western battlefront, Paulina was having a field day interrupting supplies from The Dalles bound for Canyon City and beyond. His favorite point of ambush was on Currant Creek about halfway between Antelope and Alkali Flat Stage Station. Here the trail squeezed into a narrow, brush-choked gully with Currant Creek gushing along one side and a low rock ledge hemming it in on the other. In early summer 1862, Antone Nelson—a Canyon City packer—with three men and a 40-mule pack train was returning from The Dalles heavily laden with tools, canned goods, ammunition, black powder and other vitally needed supplies for the gold camps on Whiskey Flat. This was the first pack train into the new found Eldorado and they held little concern for Indian attack. At the head of the narrow Currant Creek descent, Nelson halted the packstring. He and his partner were busy adjusting packs when the rider of the bell mare yelled, "Indians!" The men, armed only with revolvers, dove into the jungle of wild currant bushes and willows along the creek and the startled pack animals stampeded down the narrow trail. Paulina, more interested in supplies than killing four white men, took off in pursuit. Nelson and his drivers escaped but all merchandise was lost. The incident would cast a new light on the supply line to Canyon City and Auburn.

Traces of gold had also been discovered on Beaver Creek—a tributary of the south fork of Crooked River—where many tribesmen reported prospectors firing upon them and raiding their camps for women captives. Big Man cleared Beaver Creek from Dutchman Flat to Miner Flat of all opposition then swung east across the south fork of the John Day and headed north toward Whiskey Flat. On the bank of a turbulent mountain stream he found what he was searching for. When he and his warriors rode off that evening another eastern Oregon landmark had received a name . . . Murderer's Creek!

Jim Davis lived long enough to get his wounded partner, Sam Porter, to the diggings on Blue Canyon Creek. There he died from a slight arrow wound in the arm. The war head had been dipped in poison. Porter, who remained a cripple for life, told of that 10 minutes when a golden creek ran red with blood.

We had finished supper and was returning to work the sluice boxes when this godawful big Indian rode around a bend in the creek. Instead of runnin' he drove his horse straight for us and before anyone could lift a rifle, shot Richardson. By that time the rest of the howlin' mob was following on his heels and young Vehrs had an arrow rip clear through him. It was every man for himself and the last I seen any of 'em as me and Davis headed up stream, they was trying to make it up a rock ledge back of camp. One man, I think it was Hoffman, fell screaming off the ledge with an arrow in his neck. About this time we ran square into five more Indians coming down the canyon. We dropped two of them but Davis was hit in the arm with an arrow and that's where I picked up the arrow in the side. [Porter was also packing three chunks of lead in his body when picked up on Canyon Creek.] Guess they figured we was done for because they went on down the creek to join in the fun. Me and Davis crawled into the bushes along the creek and could hear the rest of the boys shooting for about five minutes, then a lot of yelling and hollering. By now I was near paralyzed and crawled under a log to die when I could hear them coming back for me and Davis. Must have passed out for it was dark when I next remember anything and Davis was packin' me. . . . Oh gawd, the pain! I wished then thy'd of finished me. . . .[2]

Seriously wounded, Richardson and Vehrs struggled down the creek to the south fork of the John Day River. Here Vehrs gave out, crawled off into the willows and died. Richardson finally made it to the China Ranch on the John Day River where he died the next day "in great agony." Whiskey Flat was now alerted that Snake dog soldiers were in the area.

---

2    Files of the *Blue Mountain Eagle*, John Day, Oregon.

Simultaneous with this attack, Has No Horse and Man Lost were closing in on a wagon train. They drew blood on August 10, 1862, 12 miles west of American Forks on the Snake River. At this spot the Oregon Trail passed along the south bank of the river winding between two high palisades of solid basalt . . . Hell's Gate! It was near sundown when 11 wagons carrying 25 Iowa families dipped into the bottleneck on their final weary miles to eastern Oregon. For five days, Has No Horse's scouts had dogged their tracks waiting for them to reach this spot. In a swooping charge that caught the train in a wicked cross-fire, Snake rifles spit destruction at the rate of one death per minute. Nine people were killed and all of the survivors wounded.[3] The price for settling the Ochoco would not be cheap for either side.

These were the same Indians who two years before, in 1860, Oregon Superintendent of Indian Affairs Edward Geary had described to the commissioner of Indian affairs as:

> . . . being generally armed with bows, they cannot be formidable, yet they are the terror of the surrounding tribes, and alike a mystery to the red man and the white. As to the declivities of the Blue Mountains, it is barren desert. Our government could well afford to permit them to possess it without molestation, would they but cease their incursions into more favored regions and suffer the traveler to pass unmolested.

> To this, however, they will not consent, till overtaken and taught by sincere chastisement the white man's power, then made the recipients of our bounty, they may be brought to appreciate and enjoy the benefits of peace and honest labor.[4]

By no stretch of the imagination were the Snake war tribes going to accept or "appreciate and enjoy the benefits of peace and honest labor."

During the August raid on the Iowa train, the gates of hell swung open near Fort Laramie. Enraged over broken treaty promises, the Santee Sioux went on the warpath and a real bloodbath followed. Besides killing 93 volunteer soldiers, they slaughtered 644 white men, women and children.

Not only were the Indians consolidating forces but so were the Oregonians. As a direct result of Big Man's raid on the Canyon City miners, Umatilla County was created from Wasco on September 27, 1862, and a county seat was established

---

3    Sixty years later in 1922, a monument was erected at Hell's Gate renaming it Massacre Rocks.
4    Edward R. Geary, *Report*, October 1, 1860, I.O.R.; *Report of Commissioner of Indian Affairs*, 1860, pp. 176-77.

at Swift's Station.[5] By 1863, Swift's Station—now Umatilla City—boasted a log jail to accommodate all the renegade Snakes that sheriff Alfred Marshall was expected to arrest. Marshall had the good sense not to try to enforce this silly ordinance—which was just as well for all concerned.

---

5    The county seat was moved to Middleton in 1868 and the county court renamed the new county seat "Pendleton" after Major George Pendleton a democratic hopeful running for vice president of the United States that year. Raley, "Reminiscences of Oregon Pioneers," *The Oregon Journal*, September 24, 1962.

# CHAPTER 106

# NITS MAKE LICE

*Five years later, the bleached skeletons of scores of noble red
men still ornament the grounds. It is regrettable that Pocatello
[Man Lost] and his gang had not also been annihilated.*

**The Utah Desert News**
May 20, 1868

By mid-November 1862, Bear Hunter had inspired such terror in the
Mormon settlement of Franklin on the Idaho territorial line that these people
appealed to the military for help. Not only was Gen. Wright having trouble trying
to keep Oregon under control but the fiery Col. Patrick Connor—commander of
the Military District of Utah—was becoming a thorn in his side. Therefore, he
decided to honor the request for military aid in the hope of solving two problems
with one solution: send Connor in to pacify the Saints and also to chastise the
Shoshoni.

Earlier in the year, Connor had been ordered to establish a garrison in the
Nevada desert midway between Salt Lake City and Carson City to protect the
Overland Stage route from Shoshoni attack. At a time when all military outposts
were bleak, Fort Ruby—manned by 700 troopers of the Third California Infantry
Regiment—was downright grim. Connor and his men were so upset with this
assignment that Connor wrote to Gen. Halleck, army chief of staff in Washington,
D.C., complaining that "the men enlisted to fight traitors and as far as the Indians
are concerned it is entirely unnecessary to keep troops at Fort Ruby." Connor's
comment about the Shoshoni was wishful thinking. He also assured Gen. Halleck
that the soldiers were willing to give up back pay just to get out of the
garrison—which says much for living conditions at Fort Ruby. The way Connor
put it, the regiment "will authorize the paymaster to withhold $30,000 of pay now
due if the government will order it east and it pledges Gen. Halleck never to
disgrace the flag, himself or California."[1] The Salt Lake *Desert News* being less
sympathetic to Connor's request believed the only reason the troops wanted to

---

1    Hart, *Old Forts of the Northwest*, p. 94.

abandon Fort Ruby was that "they have little interest in freezing to death around sagebrush fires."[2]

In November, Wright ordered Connor to Salt Lake City only to cause more trouble. Connor didn't like Mormons and in his estimation Camp Floyd, 40 miles south of Salt Lake City, was too far away to keep a watchful eye on Brigham Young's recreants (his orders were to observe Shoshoni activity in the area). Anyway, Connor established Fort Douglas on the outskirts of town where he planned to become so well entrenched he could say to the Saints of Utah "enough of treason!" The feeling was mutual. The Mormons went to the courts to have Fort Douglas removed as a public nuisance.

Connor would continue to get bad press. On November 19, the *Desert News* commenting on the Third California Infantry Regiment's march across the Nevada desert announced to the world "from the nature of orders given by the Colonel commanding, it is but reasonable to suppose that all natives found had been killed whether innocent or guilty" of any crime against white settlers. Connor in a fit of rage financed the first daily newspaper in Utah, *The Daily Union Vedette*. Published at Fort Douglas, it was both a post publication and an outspoken critic of the Mormons. Most of the funds for this tabloid came from Connor's pocket.[3]

While Connor and the Mormons were heckling each other more reports were coming in from the Idaho-Utah border that the Shoshoni, showing no fear of military intervention, were raiding at will. Bear Hunter and his braves had settled in for the winter at Battle Creek Hot Springs, only 10 miles from the town of Franklin. In early January 1863, a party of miners from Grasshopper Creek, Montana, en route to Canyon City, Oregon, blundered into this camp and Bear Hunter quickly took pursuit in an effort to keep his hideout a secret. One miner was killed and several wounded but they made good their escape and the word was out.

The chief justice of the Utah Supreme Court issued a warrant for the arrest of Bear Hunter, Old Snag and Little Foot and asked the military to support the U.S. marshall in serving the warrant.[4] Casting aside all caution, Bear Hunter and a dozen warriors rode into Franklin and demanded supplies. They received 24 bushels of wheat, but the Shoshoni needed more—and rather than run the risk of being killed, the merchants gave without an argument. This was January 25, 1863, the same day Connor began his three-day forced march from Salt Lake City to Bear River, 110 miles to the north.[5]

---

2 *The Desert News*, October 15, 1862.

3 Hart, *Old Forts of the Northwest*, p. 23.

4 *The Desert News*, January 28, 1863.

5 Bear River, known to the Shoshoni as *Bia Ogoi,* was a popular camping spot. They often gathered along its banks in January for the Warm Dance, an annual winter ritual to drive away the cold. The Shoshoni imitated animals and birds in dances to frighten away bad spirits, to bring rain, or to insure good hunting. Some of the more popular dances were the Love Dance, Sun Dance, Warm Dance, Rain Dance, War Dance and by the 1880s, the Ghost Dance.

The night of January 27, Tin Dup—a tribal elder—awoke from a nightmarish dream: the white man's pony soldiers were slaughtering his people. Convinced that this was a warning from the Great Spirit, he told anyone who would listen to get out of camp. Few believed his gloomy prediction.[6]

Meantime, Connor and his frostbitten troopers were closing the gap. Orrin Porter Rockwell, Connor's Mormon scout and personal body guard to Brigham Young—who would watch the coming bloodshed from the safety of the river bluffs—assured the colonel that upwards to 600 Snake warriors were camped on Bear River and battle-ready. This was sweet music to Connor's ears. As a career soldier looking for recognition—and body counts were important—his assignment to protect Mormon settlers from Shoshoni attack was galling. If Rockwell was telling the truth, now was the chance to make a name for himself. Attacking an Indian village was a poor substitute for battlefield glory but it was all the ambitious Connor had to impress Gen. Wright and impress him he would.

In a swirling blizzard, Col. Connor with 200 Third California Infantrymen and 75 Second California Cavalry, arrived in Franklin the night of January 28 and was told the location of Bear Hunter's winter camp. Fearing the Indians might leave before he could get there, depriving him of a fight, Connor ordered a forced night march. There was no need to hurry—Bear Hunter was waiting.

Shortly before dawn, January 29, Connor's scouts located their objective at the base of a 200 foot bluff towering above Bear Hunter's still-sleeping encampment. With the temperature holding at 23 degrees below zero, Connor planned the attack. It was to be a deadly three-pronged assault with no avenue of escape. One group was to strike the Shoshoni from the upstream side, one to hit from the downstream side, while Connor would lead the fatal frontal attack. It was then that Connor issued the command . . . "kill everything—nits make lice!"[7]

The Shoshoni were entrenched across the ice-choked Bear River on Battle Creek and had they been awake would have been prepared to fight. As it was, the attack was ruthless. Bear Hunter fell in the first onslaught and in the next 20 minutes, 14 infantrymen were killed and twice that many wounded. In the next four hours, it was nothing but a slaughter. Many Shoshoni—some of them women with infants strapped to their backs—tried to escape by plunging into the icy river. Most drowned, others were shot as they swam. Few escaped.

Back in camp, soldiers took babies by the heels and dashed them to death. Women, helpless from their wounds, were raped even as they were dying. Bear Hunter endured a savage beating. His wife, Beshwaachee, who watched from her concealment in nearby willows recalled that Bear Hunter did not cry out even when soldiers rammed a heated bayonet through his head from ear to ear. Old Snag's

6    As remembered by Mae Parry, Shoshoni historian and direct descendent of Sagwitch (Old Snag).

7    Hull, William, *Autobiography*, p. 2, Daughters of the Utah Pioneers.

12-year-old grandson—Yeager Timbimboo—escaped slaughter by playing dead.[8] For some reason, Old Snag was not killed, but held as a prisoner of war by the California Volunteers.

Connor's losses were 23 dead, 53 wounded and 79 disabled with frozen limbs. Death counts of Bear Hunter's force varied from 224 in Connor's official report to 255 reported by James Doty, superintendent of Indian Affairs, to 368 recorded by James Hill and other Utah citizens who visited the battleground the next day. Of this, at least 90 bodies were identified as women or children. The Shoshoni claimed that two-thirds of those killed were women and children. The army had taken 160 women and children captive; destroyed 70 tipis; captured 175 horses and collected over 1,000 bushels of grain. Many other articles gathered obviously came from emigrant trains.

Estimates of how many Indians died at Bear River vary because, for obvious reasons, no official count was made. Tradition has it that Connor counted bodies from horseback and recorded 220-270 dead. Settlers who went later found many more bodies in ravines or under deep snow and put the number as high as 500. Connor would describe the Battle of Bear River as a glorious struggle won by classic military tactics and superior firepower. Ignored were persistent Shoshoni claims to the contrary. Survivors recounted Connor's "battle" as a day of savagery in which soldiers smashed infants' skulls, raped dying women and dispatched the wounded with bullets, clubs and axes. News of this atrocity was pushed out of most newspapers by dispatches from the Civil War listing American casualties suffered at Fredericksburg, Virginia, and Stone's River, Tennessee.

Edwin C. Bearss, chief historian for the National Park Service, Washington, D.C., says after extensive research that "a good case can be made that there were more Indian casualties in the Bear River attack than any other by U.S. forces west of the Mississippi. Bear River was much more grim than the highly publicized massacres at Sand Creek in Colorado Territory where 133 Cheyennes were killed by troopers November 28, 1864, or at Wounded Knee, South Dakota, where soldiers slaughtered 153 Sioux on December 28, 1890."[9] On April 3, 1990, Bearss would recommend that the Bear River battlesite be granted national historic landmark status.

Of the estimated 60 survivors, a handful of dog soldiers under the command of Little Foot made their way to Wolf Dog's winter camp in the Ochoco. He told of the terrible massacre on Bear River, a loss keenly felt by Has No Horse and Paulina. One of the survivors, Buffalo Horn, still a child, would return to Man

---

8   This is the testimony of Mae Timbimboo Parry who has spent much of her 70 years gathering the tribe's oral history. Mae Parry is the granddaughter of Yeager Timbimboo who was Old Snag's (Sagwitch Timbimboo) grandson. "We have never recovered from the massacre," Parry said. "We've never quite recovered."

9   The Kalispell, Montana, *Whatcom Reveille*, March 21, 1990, p. 4.

Lost's camp to nurse his wounds and plot later destruction on the whites. This setback would only serve to make the dog soldiers more dangerous.

According to *The Oregonian*, this was not a slaughter but a brilliant military victory that would end the Shoshoni raids. Others were not so certain. One journalist had this to say about the Bear River Battle:

> John Reed's hunting party from Fort Astoria in 1814 was attacked and all murdered by the Snakes. In August 1826, William Sublette with 250 trappers almost annihilated the band on Green River. In the summer of 1836, Jim Bridger with a force of trappers gave them another severe chastisement. But among these incorrigible banditti the lesson of a thorough beating does not last long, so forgetting one disaster, unapprehensive of the next, and recruited to fighting, they are soon ready for fresh depredations.[10]

He spoke the truth.

Ecstatic that he had crushed Wolf Dog's uprising for all time, Col. Connor—soon to be brigadier general—marched back to Salt Lake City proudly waving the scalp of Bear Hunter, which was hung in the officer's quarters at Fort Douglas.[11] Instead of crushing the Shoshoni, his action set the Pacific Northwest aflame.

---

10    W.J. Ghent, *Road to Oregon.*

11    Brigham Young, *Manuscript History*, February 3, 1863.

# CHAPTER 107

# AN EMPIRE IN DISTRESS

*Last night when the land was being cleansed by the moon,*
*I saw a vision. White men, like maggots on a dead carcass,*
*were crawling over the Ochoco.*

**Left Hand**
Snake Prophet

Connor's destruction of the Dog Rib Snakes only made Has No Horse more determined to clear the Ochoco of trespassers. However, no matter how well intended, nothing could have stopped the white tidal wave that was to engulf Wolf Dog's domain. Canyon City reigned supreme while Auburn—queen of the Powder River strike—was now the second largest city in the state, putting The Dalles in third place. Wasco County's assessed valuation, in spite of heavy property damage caused by blizzards and floods of 1862, skyrocketed to 1.5 million dollars.[1] The increase in population east of the Cascades was unequaled in the history of northwest settlement and continuing discoveries of gold would bring in more people. Snake hunting grounds now contained upwards to 45,000 white inhabitants and was estimated to reach 50,000 by the end of the year.[2] With all available manpower going to the mines, farmers were having trouble harvesting crops. In an effort to get laborers, employers started contacting the Chinese tong societies on the West Coast.[3]

The first Chinese to arrive on the Pacific coast—two men and one woman—arrived from Hong Kong on the brig *Eagle* in 1848. In a span of 10 years, they sent money to relatives and friends, and by 1860, thousands of Chinese nationals were living in Seattle, Portland and San Francisco. Willamette Valley farmers enticed them to come "to thriving Oregon" for 80 cents a day. The Chinese soon discovered that the mine owners would triple this pay and they too, flooded to the goldfields.

---

1    *Oregon Argus*, September 28, 1863.

2    J.M. Edwards to the Secretary of Interior, October 22, 1863, *House Executive Document 1, Serial 1182*, p. 14, 38th Congress, 1st Session.

3    Those contacted were the Sam Yap, Kong Chow, You On, Hip Kat, Ning Yeung and Hop Wo tong societies.

To many Chinese people, eastern Oregon was *Gum San*—the land of golden mountains—but it would prove to be as full of hardship and oppression as it was of industry and opportunity. The goal of those who immigrated to the gold camps was to labor and save for a number of years, then return to their homeland where their modest savings could provide a measure of financial security and a better life for themselves and their families. Few Chinese attained this goal but no one tried as hard as they did.

The Chinese worked their way across the Sierras and the deserts of Nevada in the construction camps of the nation's first transcontinental railroad; they labored in the goldfields from California to Montana; they hired on as chuck wagon cooks on high desert ranches and cannery workers on the Pacific Coast and performed a variety of domestic jobs within the settlements and cities. In short, they were active and essential participants in the development and settlement of the West and Tiger Town on the outskirts of Canyon City became one of their main bases of operation. Unfortunately for them, the Shoshoni held a particular fondness for Chinese scalps.

The demand for supplies in eastern Oregon was astronomical. In the first budding days of spring, William Flett left The Dalles with thousands of dollars in merchandise bound for Canyon City and points beyond. Among other things in Flett's saddlebags was a handy little item which had just arrived on the scene in 1863. It was called a Derringer pistol with an effective range of around 15 to 20 feet. A few miles east of Bakeoven near the head of Ochoco Canyon, Has No Horse stole the entire pack train including Flett's $10 Derringer which, by the way, was a real fancy price to pay for a weapon of that size. Re-outfitting at The Dalles, and backed by armed guards, Flett attempted the trip again in April. The packstring made it as far as Bridge Creek where everything was lost to Snake raiders.[4] Fortunate to be alive, Flett retired to the Willamette Valley and took up saddle making.

In May 1863, a party of miners led by Michael Jordan left Placerville in the Boise Basin to search for gold in the Crooked River country where rumor had it that nuggets were being used by emigrants as weights on fishing lines. Crossing the Owyhee Mountains, Jordan—on May 18—discovered gold on what is now named Jordan Creek. He would pay for this indiscretion with his life, but the discovery sparked the Owyhee gold stampede. Within days, 2,500 prospectors jammed into Jordan Valley, and Ruby City, clinging precariously to the narrow canyon walls of Jordan Creek under the brooding summit of New York Pass, was born. Plagued by violent winds—according to some, the spirits of the Indians—it soon gave ground to Silver City. Located a half mile upstream, nestled between the protective shoulders of War Eagle and Florida mountains, Silver City would

---

4    The first attack on Flett's pack train occurred in March 1863. *Illustrated History of Central Oregon*, p. 588.

boast the first telegraph line east of the Cascade summit. Raw ore in the Jordan strike was running as high as $87,000 a carload and Silver City rated second only to the Comstock Lode in Nevada.

Boomtowns were sprouting like mushrooms from the headwaters of the Ochoco to the Malheur. Eldorado City, Amelia, Whitney, Greenhorn, Auburn, Bourne, Malheur City, Granite, Arthur, Sumpter, Copperfield, Scissorsville, Cornicopia . . . are today but a memory of lust, laughter and gold. Sumpter Valley produced nine million dollars in gold in 1863 and that was just the beginning. Within seven years, the Cornicopia mine was employing 350 men and between 1870 and 1938 it alone produced ten million dollars in gold. The Mayflower on the headwaters of the Ochoco would produce another seven million dollars.

With Has No Horse wreaking havoc on supply trains along the Canyon City trail, Paulina renewed attacks on the Warm Springs reservation. Earlier, Agent Bill Logan had sent a sarcastic message to Superintendent Rector in Portland stating: "I will call the attention of you to the fact that the U.S. troops stationed at the Warm Springs reservation have been removed leaving the reservation without protection. I would suggest that you request General Wright to have a company of cavalry stationed at that place as it will be impossible to keep the Indians on the reservation without protection against the incursions of the Snake Indians."

He got no reaction and the reservation was now under a siege which would last for eight months. Logan didn't waste any more time in contacting Rector. Instead, he sent his request direct to Brig. Gen. Ben Alvord, commander of the Military District of Oregon. Alvord, having higher odds at stake, chose to ignore him. Not only were the dog soldiers stopping commerce to the gold camps but other Snake raiders were striking as far west as the Umpqua Valley. Capt. Remick Cowles, Co. H Second Battalion First Oregon Cavalry, was having his hands full keeping them out of the upper Willamette Valley settlements. Learning of this, Gen. Wright pulled all stops and began his delayed plans of setting up a network of forts throughout eastern Oregon and Idaho. Idaho, still part of Dakota Territory in early 1863, was given territorial status and placed under Wright's command. In June, four cavalry units were ordered into eastern Oregon to engage the Shoshoni in combat and this meant the construction of military forts.

Capt. James Kelly, Co. J Second Battalion, was ordered to re-man Fort Klamath in an effort to stop the Snake raids into southwestern Oregon.[5] Fort Klamath had experienced an on-again, off-again existence since it was first established in 1856. Abandoned in 1857, the post was re-activated in 1859 and again abandoned in 1861. Located in big timber in Wood River Valley north of upper Klamath Lake, it consisted of a log stockade of which 12 log cabins with

---

5    Klamath took its name from the French *clairmetis* meaning *light mist of clouds*. The Shoshoni
     called it *ivkak* meaning *within* which referred to the lake being close to or between the
     mountains.

rifle ports formed the major part of the stockade walls. The outpost could not only guard the southern passes over the Cascades, which the Snakes were using to gain access to the Umpqua Valley, but it also provided protection for the Applegate, Red Bluff and Yreka trails under constant attack from Pipe and Burning Wagon.

At the same time Capt. Kelly marched out of Camp Baker, Lt. Col. Reuben Maury—backed by Capt. Tom Harris and Sgt. Silas Pepoon of Company A Northern Battalion First Oregon Cavalry—left Fort Dalles with a 150-mule pack train to negotiate a treaty with the Snakes. Capt. George Currey with a 20-man detachment of Co. E Northern Battalion, headed toward the Hampton Butte country—guided by Charlie McKay—to patrol the Yreka Trail.

McKay had been serving time in the Fort Dalles stockade and fined $200 plus costs for being drunk and disorderly. Since he couldn't pay, Major Drew—post commander—palmed him off onto Capt. Currey as an Indian scout. Acting in the same manner, Gen. Henry Wager Halleck, army chief of staff, was doing his best to hamper U.S. Grant as he would do three years later with Crook when he arrived in Oregon to take command of troop movements against the Snakes.[6]

To round out Gen. Wright's four-pronged assault on the Ochoco, Capt. Richard Caldwell, Co. B Northern Battalion and Major Pickney Lugenbeel, Co. I, galloped out of Fort Walla Walla to establish linking forts between Canyon City and Silver City. Attached to Lugenbeel's command were 40 Umatilla scouts under the leadership of Cut-Mouth John, the Umatilla warrior who led the Wasco County posse to the Ward massacre in 1854. By June 10, Lugenbeel had established Fort Logan near the Prairie Hill diggings some 12 miles east of Canyon City. Leaving Lt. John Noble in command, Lugenbeel headed toward the Snake River to start construction on Fort Boise. He had barely gotten out of sight of Fort Logan when Has No Horse and Fox—son-in-law to Left Hand—plunged into their pool of horses and with 75 cavalry mounts splitting the breeze, lit out for the Ochoco Valley with Lt. Noble in hot pursuit. At the south fork of the John Day River, Fox proceeded on with the horses while Has No Horse set up an ambush. Riding with the Snakes was Lone Otter, a Umatilla mercenary and brother to John, the cavalry scout.

After exchanging shots for about 15 minutes, the Snakes—stalling for time to give Fox a lead—signaled they wished to parley. Noble sent John to negotiate and Has No Horse countered with Lone Otter. As Umatilla John would later reveal, "I knew for many months that my brother was riding with Has No Horse but never expected to meet him at opposite ends of a rifle."

Lone Otter spoke first, telling his brother that the cavalry was outnumbered and except for Lt. Noble, they didn't wish to kill the scouts. He then told John to go back to the fort. John refused and tried to talk Lone Otter into joining the Umatilla scouts on the promise that the soldiers wouldn't harm him. As John later

---

6    Colton, "This Hallowed Land," *American Heritage*, Vol VII, No. 6, pp. 33-34.

told Gen. Howard, Lone Otter stood impassive during this speech then in a sad voice said, "No, I will shoot you if you come another step closer."[7]

This ended the discussion and Noble sounded the charge. John led the first wave. Lone Otter stood up, laid his revolver on his arm, aimed and fired. The bullet smashed into John's face, plowing a deep furrow from the corner of his mouth over and beyond his right eye, ripping away lip, teeth and bone. John lived—but for the remainder of his life his expression was a constant leer. Because of his brother's shaking aim, he would go down in frontier history as "Cut Mouth" John.

When John fell, the Umatilla's decided Has No Horse had won the day and no amount of coaxing from Lt. Noble would get them to rally. Without their aid, further attempts by the cavalry to unseat the Snakes was futile so he gave up and returned to Canyon City. Has No Horse carried three of his dog soldiers to the burial ground on Mt. Pisgah that day, one of whom was Lone Otter.

Cut Mouth John fought throughout the Shoshoni war, ending his army career as scout in the Salmon River Mountains in 1879 . . . the final phase of the Shoshoni rebellion. His reward for nearly 30 years of faithful government service was to be made a five-dollar-a-month policeman on the Umatilla reservation. He remained a steadfast friend of the white men at all times even to the end when, sick and neglected, he died a beggar's death.

During Gen. Howard's tour of duty, Cut Mouth visited him in Portland in 1876 as a witness against whiskey peddlers on the Umatilla reservation. For this public appearance, he was wearing "a lieutenants' cast-off coat with shoulder straps, a red sash around his waist, a pair of dirty white gloves full of holes and a slouched hat." He was very much ashamed of his poor shoes and general signs of poverty. He said he had brought this to the attention of the Indian agent but "no luck." Howard goes on to comment, "Poor fellow, in his shabby finery he presented a truly ludicrous spectacle, yet I had a feeling of great compassion for him when I looked at the sad disfigurement of his visage and remembered that it was a wound received from a hostile brother on account of his fidelity to the white men who have never been very faithkeeping to him or his people."[8]

While Lt. Noble was being harassed by the Shoshoni, Major Lugenbeel arrived at the Snake River without mishap and on July 1 selected a site 40 miles up the Boise River from the old Hudson's Bay Company post to establish another fort.[9] Work began on July 4 with Major J.S. Rinearson in charge of construction. Lugenbeel then took off to make contact with Lt. Col. Maury whom he found camped at the mouth of the Boise River. Maury had made contact not only with various Shoshoni tribes but (now General) Patrick Connor as well. It would soon surface that during Maury's treaty plunge into the Snake River country, Bad Face

7    Howard, *Famous Indian Chiefs I Have Known*, pp. 350-51.

8    Howard, *Hostile Indians*, pp. 265-66.

9    Bancroft, *History of Oregon*, Vol. II, p. 495.

had slipped into the *Eldahow* on a two-fold mission. First, to dilute the effect of any government peace proposals and more important, to squelch all rumors that Connor's Bear River campaign had intimidated the Paviotso Confederacy.

By late spring of 1863, Bad Face and his warriors were in Montana Territory and camped about a mile north of Bannack. The townspeople called a meeting to organize a group for the purpose of attacking and murdering the whole band. This recommendation was met with such high approval that a celebration was in order. The chosen leaders of the Bannack vigilantes and their enthusiastic recruits got so drunk there wasn't enough sober men to stage a decent attack. Alarmed at this turn of events—and on second thought, somewhat ashamed—the town fathers reversed their decision and the enterprise was abandoned. In the meantime, a half-breed warned Bad Face of the situation and the wily dog soldier lost no time in preparing a reception for the white war party. He sent the women and children to the rear and posted his warriors . . . "to the number of three or four hundred on the right side of a canyon in such a position that he could have slaughtered the whole command at his ease. This he fully intended to do if attacked and also to have sacked the town and killed every white in it."[10] As an impartial bystander would later observe: "This would have been achieved but for the drunkenness of the leaders and no attack by the townsmen."

Once again, the sons of liberty escaped the scalpel of Snake practitioners only by the whim of luck. A few days after this playful interlude, a party of miners—accusing the Shoshoni of stealing their horses—rode into Bad Face's camp and started shooting into the tipis. Within minutes, the dog soldiers killed all nine and took their possessions. At this time, Old Snag—survivor of the Bear River massacre—was camped with Bad Face. After witnessing the horrible consequences of Connor's raid, this latest exchange of gunfire made Old Snag extremely nervous. In fact, he became so worried that he decided to ride into Bannack and make peace with the whites.

As Old Snag rode into town, Haze Lyons shot one of Old Snag's followers—whether "for luck, on general principles or for his pony" was uncertain. A number of citizens, thinking it was an Indian attack, ran out and joined in the shooting. When his horse's leg was shattered by a bullet, Old Snag jumped from his mount in an effort to escape but was shot in the hip. Badly hurt, he limped into the willows lining the creek, looking for a miner named Carroll who was living with a Shoshoni girl. By the time Old Snag arrived at Carroll's cabin he had been joined by his son and daughter. Carroll told him that there was no way he could protect him and that Old Snag better run for his life. Tiovan Duah, his son, ran but Old Snag, using his rifle for a crutch, stood his ground. He had his war axe in hand and was talking to his daughter, Catherine, when Buck Stinson stepped out of the cabin and without saying a word shot him in the side with a revolver at the distance

---

10    Dimsdale, *Vigilantes of Montana*, p. 43.

of four feet. Old Snag raised his hand and yelled, "Oh, don't!" The answer was a bullet in the neck accompanied by the remark, "I'll teach you to kill whites!" and then Stinson shot the old warrior again in the head.[11]

At this, Old Snag's band scattered in flight. One who was wounded plunged into the creek trying to escape but was killed as he crawled up the opposite bank. Old Snag's body was mutilated and his scalp taken to a Salt Lake City banking house where it was placed on public display.

As Old Snag was being blasted into eternity, Lt. Col. Maury charged into Fort Bridger and on July 2, 1863 convinced Gourd Rattler that it would be wise to touch pen to a treaty of relinquishment. Twenty-eight days later at Box Elder Creek, Utah Territory, Maury—with the help of Gen. Connor who rounded up the stragglers, Utah Superintendent of Indian Affairs James Doty, and Agent Luther Mann—for the promise of $2,000 worth of provisions negotiated three separate treaties with 10 Shoshoni tribes.[12] These treaties were lumped into one document touted as "The Treaty of Peace and Friendship" and signed by Man Lost (Pocatello), Stiff Finger (Tag-hee) and The Climber (Tendoy).

According to the treaty officials, Sagwitch (Old Snag) who was supposed to have signed the document had been shot by a white "friend" while under arrest by the "California Volunteers" and was unable to leave his tipi but "agreed to all the provisions" of the treaty. No doubt this claim was made to add dignity to "The Treaty of Peace and Friendship" for Old Snag was beyond the signing of any document and it is certain all participants were aware of that fact.

The combined treaty provided for freedom of the building of certain travel routes into the new gold strikes in eastern Oregon; the guarantee of safety to stage passengers; the erection of military posts and relief stations; and the construction of telegraph lines and railroads across Shoshoni soil. The tribes involved were to receive annuities and compensation for loss of game but no definite move was then made toward reservation restrictions.

By signing the 1863 treaty, Man Lost—claiming Utah Territory and Idaho Territory—transferred Shoshoni title to the Americans. A month later at Ruby Valley, Fish Man (Numaga), a minor Paiute head man signed away Nevada Territory. Fish Man's signing of the Ruby Valley treaty would spark a 129-year

---

11    Dimsdale, *Vigilantes of Montana*, pp. 44-45.

12    The Box Elder treaties were signed by the following Shoshoni chiefs on July 30, 1863: Pocatello (Man Lost), Toom-ont-so, Sanpitch, Tasowiz or Te'yue-wit (Good Man), Yah'no-way, We'era-hoop (War Hoop), Pahra-gooshd or Paru'gin (Swamp), Tak'ke-too-nah or To'ho-um (Cougar Tail), and Omrchee or Oderie (Walking Rock). Utah Superintendent Doty would negotiate another treaty at Soda Springs on October 14, 1863 signed by Tasok-wain-berakt (The Great Rogue), Tah'gee or Targee (Stiff Finger), and Mat-i-gerd or Muinyan (Big Porcupine). James Duane Doty to Commissioner of Indian Affairs, Great Salt Lake City, November 10, 1863, U.S. National Archives, *Letters Received by the Office of Indian Affairs, 1863-1865*, Utah Superintendency, Roll 901.

battle between the western Shoshoni and the federal government.[13] Before winter could set in, the 275 pound Great Rogue (Le Grand Coquin)—a sometimes disciple of Gourd Rattler and chief of the Robber Snakes—clinched the deal by relinquishing claim to all Shoshoni lands from the Rocky Mountains as far south as the Humboldt River in Nevada. He was soon relieved of command.

Upon receipt of these sell-outs, Wolf Dog declared war upon the treaty signers. He was now fighting the Americans, the Confederated Tribes of Oregon, the Mormons and the eastern Shoshoni.

During the hostilities, Wolf Dog was especially annoyed with Man Lost who, because of his mixed blood, was now considered a traitor. Around 1830, a Blackfoot warrior named Big Top led a raid on a Shoshoni hunting camp and captured a Snake girl whom he held hostage. He had a son by her before her brother came and negotiated her release and rescued the girl. However, the girl was again seven months pregnant. According to Beverly Hungry Wolf, a direct descendent of Big Top, Big Top let her go but kept the son—and the son he kept was to become her great-grandfather, Little Bear, a Blood Warrior. The child the Snake woman had after her rescue from the Blackfeet became Man Lost, a well-known Shoshoni chief after whom the city of Pocatello, Idaho is named.[14]

---

13   As late as December 1992, a group of western Shoshoni were continuing their dispute with President-Elect Clinton over the terms of the 1863 treaty of Ruby Valley. In 1979, Congress in an attempt to settle this agreement, appropriated 26 million dollars to purchase title to 24 million acres of tribal lands. By 1992, this sum with interest had grown to 75 million dollars and continues to grow. During a meeting at Battle Mountain, Nevada, on December 11, 1992, tribal chiefs Frank Temoke and Frank Brady were adamant in their refusal of a government pay-off. Temoke was certain that the Shoshoni would forever end their claim to tribal lands if they accepted the funds. "I did not sign any agreement for money." In Temoke's words, "The actions of the federal government are unconstitutional, immoral, genocide and against international law." Brady also urged his people to refuse settlement. "The people need land, not money." But chiefs Temoke and Brady—like Has No Horse and Wolf Dog before them—were facing a sell-out from their own people for many of the Shoshoni wanted the money. "Some say we've lost the land already and that may be so," Brady said. "But we still have a fighting chance if we don't take the government payment." (*The Bulletin*, Bend, Oregon, Associated Press release, December 14, 1992.)

14   Beverly Hungry Wolf, *The Way of My Grandmothers*, pp. 71-72.

# CHAPTER 108

# BE DISCREET

*Ever since men grouped themselves in tribes, peace treaties have walked hand in hand with war.*

**Lawrence W. Beilenson**
*The Treaty Trap*

As Lt. Col. Maury collected treaties, Wolf Dog gathered supplies. In July, Broken Knife with 20 men, women and children, rode down Blue Canyon Creek and camped on the outskirts of Canyon City where he visited with his sister, Running Deer. Running Deer had parted company with Boone Helm and was now married to Big Man. Well known in Canyon City, she could come and go without interference and often spent weeks in town gathering vital information for the Shoshoni war effort. Now, her brother had boldly ridden into Canyon City leading a pack train loaded with lead ore which he wanted to trade for grain, blankets, knives and beef. The merchants were quick to make a deal. Obviously, they didn't want any trouble but above all, they needed lead for bullets. The mystery was where did the Shoshoni get it. Because of the weight involved, it undoubtedly came from nearby, but prospectors to this day have never been able to locate lead deposits in eastern Oregon.

When he got what he came after, Broken Knife left peacefully but within days, Snake raids on isolated camps, livestock herds and supply routes increased in intensity. The general public, not realizing the danger that existed or ignoring it, were adding to the explosive situation. Many discouraged in the goldfields were attempting to locate homesteads in the Ochoco. It was never known how many died but one of the fortunate ones was George Millican. Having tried his luck in California, Washington and eastern Oregon with little success, he decided to try a different pursuit. In the summer of 1863, Millican entered Shoshoni country with the intent of settling. Some 20 miles south of Crooked River in the shadow of Pine Mountain, he found what he was looking for and attempted to lay the groundwork for the first cattle ranch in what is now Deschutes County.[1] Only the arrival of Capt. Currey's cavalry detachment kept him from becoming another statistic.

---

1    Cary, *History of Oregon*, Vol. III, p. 714.

To gain a perspective of the political climate existing in Oregon in 1863, it is necessary to retreat to the hub of power—the Willamette Valley—which by no stretch of the imagination represented the majority of the population. Addison C. Gibbs—elected in 1862—took office as Oregon's governor on September 10, 1862. Painfully aware of the dangerous Indian situation east of the Cascades, he soon gained the reputation of being Oregon's "war governor" when he called for a state militia. This appeal didn't set well with many of his former constituents. Gibbs had been a democrat when he served in the territorial legislature but split with his party on the slavery issue and became a republican though he still held strong ties to the south. Surprisingly, it was only through his efforts that Oregon remained on the side of the north . . . officially at least but hardly in practice. As for eastern Oregon, it didn't exist.

Four months after taking office and only 18 days before Col. Connor's bloodbath on Bear River, Gov. Gibbs issued a proclamation on January 10, 1863, calling for more volunteers to form six additional cavalry companies for Indian service in eastern Oregon. Ashland democrats responded by calling a protest meeting. The North and the South may have been locked in a death struggle but in "remote Oregon," why in heaven's name was there a need for more soldiers? These agitators seemed to forget that the only thing separating them from the war zone was the Cascade range and Snake dog soldiers were already breaching that barrier.

By the end of September 1863, all of eastern Oregon was an armed camp. Superintendent of Indian Affairs J.W. Perit Huntington was jarred into reality when an Indian runner delivered a message to his Salem office. Dated October 10, 1863, it read: "On the night of the 8th, a party of Snake Indians made a raid on the herd of this reservation and drove off about 120 horses belonging to the Indians of this reservation and eight or so horses belonging to the Dep't; also they did shoot a Dep't mule with an arrow; the mule will probably die, or be unfit for service."

This was but a preamble to Agent Logan's real concern. "Something has to be done about this. A party of 20 of our Indians have gone in pursuit of these Snake Indians. . . ." They were never seen again. Working through the governor's office, Huntington dispatched a detachment of Oregon Cavalry and one of Washington Infantry to Warm Springs. Under the command of Capt. Tom S. Harris, these reinforcements arrived in the latter part of October on orders to remain there until relieved. Within three days, Paulina again raided the Agency and despite the troopers made off with 200 horses and a couple of Wasco scalps. The cavalry, their nerves keyed for revenge, gave chase.

Lt. James Halloran, in command of the punitive force, made the mistake of all inexperienced Indian fighters. Gaining yardage on the retreating Paulina with every mile, he saw the dust cloud he was pursuing disappear along the base of a towering basalt upthrust on Crooked River. Galloping into the dim-lit gorge, Halloran and his men were literally blasted out of the saddle by Wolf Dog's reinforcements who were guarding Paulina's back trail. Five Warm Springs scouts were killed and eight of the soldiers wounded. Dazed but not out, Halloran and his men burrowed into the rocks and for an hour sporadic rifle fire kept them pinned down. Then all was deathly still. Finally, Pvt. Voke Smith volunteered to scale the 3,200 foot ridge on the northeast side of Crooked River from which vantage point he could scan the surrounding country for Indian signs. Halloran granted permission and Smith began the tremendous ascent. Near the summit, he stepped on a rock, lost his footing and plunged to his death.[2] This was enough misfortune for Lt. Halloran and he gave up the chase.

At the close of 1863, all that stood between the citizens of Oregon and the thrust of a Snake war lance were six lonely outposts on the extreme rim of the inland plateau. These fragile little garrisons patrolled an outer perimeter of defense some 870 miles in length and caught within their scope of operations lay 64,000 square miles of relatively unknown Indian territory. The nucleus of this vast wilderness was the inner Ochoco or more specifically, the Crooked River basin . . . a river known to the Shoshoni as *Paga Tubic*, the Weeping Water whose winding course glided across Shoshoni land like a glistening snake. If the Oyerungun was Wolf Dog's domain, the inner Ochoco was Has No Horse's private hunting ground.

The Indian-fighting army, undermanned, ridiculed by the general public, vilified by the press and hamstrung by politics could stall no longer. It had to react. Gen. Alvord quietly dispatched messengers from Fort Vancouver to the widely separated frontier outposts instructing the commanding officers to obtain all available information pertaining to Wolf Dog's activities. Fort Dalles, 60 miles northwest of the Ochoco, was to be the point of rendezvous. On October 26, Charlie McKay—now special agent for Lt. Col. Buchanon—left the fort on orders to ferret out every Shoshoni encampment between the mouth of the Deschutes and the mouth of the Ochoco River.

This would be no easy task. Three years earlier, Oregon Superintendent of Indian Affairs Ed Geary had told the commissioner of Indian Affairs that the Snakes were an unknown force. "Their country has no indication they are numerous; few trails and seldom an old camp are found."[3] At Fort Walla Walla, 143 miles upriver from Fort Dalles, Major Lugenbeel dispatched Donald McKay—half-breed son of Tom McKay and one-time war chief of the Cayuse nation—toward the ragged north slope of the central Oregon Blues. His mission

---

2    Halloran named this unique formation on the north bank of Crooked River some 15 miles west of Prineville, Oregon, Smith Rock in memory of Pvt. Smith of Linn County. In the diary of Capt. John Smith—ex-sheriff of Linn County and state representative at the time of Voke's tragic fall—he states that stringers of gold were found on the rock in the early 1870s. Capt. Smith (no known relation to Pvt. Smith) was Indian Agent at Warm Springs from 1866 to 1884.

3    Edward R. Geary, "Report," October 10, 1860, in *Report of Commissioner of Indian Affairs 1860*, pp. 176-77.

was to search every ravine between the Umatilla River and the mouth of the John Day for hostile movements. At the same time Lugenbeel sent Major John Owen—Shoshoni trader and former Indian agent—into the vast area between the headwaters of Powder River in eastern Oregon and the Salmon River in Idaho Territory to determine if the Sheep Killer and Robber Snakes planned on joining forces with Wolf Dog.

At Fort Logan, 114 miles south of Fort Walla Walla, Lt. Noble instructed Cut-Mouth John—leader of the Umatilla army scouts—to observe all Shoshoni activity along The Dalles-Canyon City trail.

Fort Boise, 130 miles southeast of Fort Logan, was the starting point for Archie McIntosh—half-breed Iroquois, ex-Hudson's Bay employee and scout for Major Rinearson. His orders were to scout every inch of ground between the Malheur and Harney basin.

Two hundred sixty-five miles west of Fort Boise stood the desolate stockade of Fort Klamath. Capt. James Kelly sent Sgt. William Moulder toward the southern slopes of the central Oregon Blues. His objective was to search each dip and knoll between Winter Ridge and the south fork of Crooked River.

Perched on the western edge of the Ochoco sat the battle-scarred Warm Springs Agency—159 miles north of Fort Klamath and 60 miles south of Fort Dalles. From here, Capt. Harris dispatched Capoles—Warm Springs war chief and army scout—to cover Crooked River from mouth to source.

By mid-November—traveling light and fast—the special agents reported to Fort Dalles and were taken by river packet to Fort Vancouver to meet with Gen. Alvord and his staff. The information gathered was startling.

Less than 40 miles from The Dalles City, Don McKay and Cut-Mouth John had run into Snake war parties riding insolently along The Dalles-Canyon City trail. Moulder, Capoles and McIntosh would report numerous Snake and Paiute camps ranging in size from 10-member family groups to 300-man encampments between the Owyhee Mountains and the John Day Valley. Heavy concentrations of Snakes were going into winter camps next to the eastern Oregon goldfields. The Harney Basin was swarming with mounted Paiutes. Owen would report that he had attended "one of the blackest war councils ever held on the Pacific coast."

Charlie McKay had met with Has No Horse when he visited a Shoshoni village in the upper Ochoco Valley. It was the largest concentration of Indians Charlie had ever seen. The camp stretched from the mouth of what is now called Mill Creek 12 miles upriver to the mouth of Canyon Creek and he estimated the number of Indians present at 4,000. Laughing Hawk, Man Lost's war chief, was also in the camp and confirmed Owen's report that the Robber and Sheep Killer Snakes were joining forces with Has No Horse even though (or perhaps because of) Man Lost had touched pen to Lt. Col. Maury's peace treaty less than four months ago followed by the Great Rogue's signing in October.

McKay also found out that Black Buffalo, the Big Nose war chief, had made a 750 mile ride to the North Platte where he had recruited 150 Comanche warriors to give support.[4] It was now evident that what the military had suspected since 1855 was about to happen. Wolf Dog was preparing for an all-out offensive which Gen. Wright and Gen. Alvord believed would be the most devastating Indian war the United States had yet encountered.

Not wishing to alarm the public, Alvord and his staff met secretly with Gov. Gibbs and the civil authorities of the state in January 1864 presenting the facts as they saw them. Both groups agreed that this information should not be made available to the public. Somehow, an alert reporter for the Portland *Oregonian* got wind of this high level meeting and within the week tossed an article on the editor's desk which was intended to make headlines across the nation. Instead, this newsbreak of the year was discreetly pigeonholed until May 28, 1864 . . . coinciding with the Oregon Cavalry's move into eastern Oregon.

On that day, these fateful words appeared on page 2, column 4 of *The Weekly Oregonian*: "It is believed by the army officials that the greatest Indian fight the United States has yet witnessed might take place in the valleys of the Ochoco and Crooked River basins, east and south of Camp Separation in interior Oregon."[5]

Oregon's center of population west of the Cascade barrier refused to believe the information given by the army scouts. One McKay was branded a drunkard and a liar, the other a half-breed troublemaker; McIntosh was classified as a traitor because of his association with the Hudson's Bay Company; Owen was held suspect because of his Shoshoni wife; while Capoles and Cut-Mouth John were beyond redemption. Only Sgt. Bill Moulder escaped criticism unscathed. Those poor souls east of the Cascades, facing the business end of a Shoshoni war lance, knew that Wolf Dog wasn't bluffing.

---

4    As remembered by Dave Chocktote, son of Black Buffalo, in an October 1938 interview.

5    Camp Separation on upper Crooked River was established by Capt. Wallen in 1859 as Camp Division. In 1860, Major Steen used it as a supply depot renaming it Camp Separation. It was abandoned that same year not to be re-manned until the late spring of 1864. At that time it became Fort Maury.

It is worth noting that as federal and state officials were meeting in January to formulate invasion strategy, Tiger Town became John Day City on January 20, 1864.

Between January and May, the military prepared for action. To sweeten the prospects of going into battle—hopefully making the troops more willing to face uncertain death—a promotion list was posted in Salem and Fort Dalles.[6] The outposts of Klamath and Boise were bolstered with the addition of two cavalry companies each; and Major Rinehart—made regimental adjutant—transferred from Fort Lyon to Boise to complete fort construction. Col. Justin Steinberger, commander of the First Washington Territorial Infantry was ordered to station his regiment at Fort Walla Walla. Capt. Rowell and Capt. West of the 4th California Infantry Regiment marched into Fort Dalles.

Following Lt. Halloran's defeat at Smith Rock, Warm Springs Agency had been abandoned in November 1863 and Capt. Harris transferred to Fort Boise. In January 1864, Co. A 1st Oregon Cavalry was ordered to re-man the Agency and with this order came the first repercussions. When Capt. Harris found out he was to return to Warm Springs to act as a buffer against a Shoshoni winter offensive, he balked. In his opinion, to send only one cavalry company was the same as committing suicide. Col. Maury believed one company was sufficient. Harris was not convinced and in mid-January resigned his commission.

Capt. Edward Harding, Co. B, was quickly summoned to replace Harris and on February 2, Harding, Lt. Stephen Watson and Donald McKay with Companies A and B left Fort Dalles for Warm Springs in a blinding snowstorm. Meantime, Gov. Gibbs voiced his doubts as to the integrity of the army "half-breed" scouts and suggested that more reliable sources of information be sent into eastern Oregon. Gen. Alvord, still catering to the political pressure groups of western Oregon, ordered Col. Maury to dispatch still another force into the Ochoco to gather more information on the chance the original scouts had been wrong in their predictions of a Shoshoni war. Maury reluctantly complied and this time he chose with deliberation for he wanted no more unfavorable remarks about the ineptness of military intelligence.

In mid-February, Sgt. James Waymire—battle-wise veteran of the Yakima War and personal secretary to Gov. Gibbs—was commissioned a lieutenant in the Oregon Cavalry and told to report to Fort Dalles. Here, he received orders to ride roughshod across central Oregon and establish a military post within the boundaries of Has No Horse's ancestral domain. Under his command were 26 riflemen of the 1st U.S. Cavalry led by Sgt. Robert Casteel; 54 Indian war veterans

---

6    Those deemed worthy of advancement in grade were: Lt. Col. Maury to Colonel; Major Drew to Lt. Col.; Captains Rinehart and Traux to Major; 1st Lts. Caldwell and Small to Captain; 2nd Lts. Hopkins, Hobart, McCall, Steele, Hand and Underwood to 1st Lts.; and Sgts. Waymire, Pepoon, Bowen and James Currey to 2nd Lts. Bancroft, *History of Oregon*, Vol. II, p. 496.

of Co. D 1st Oregon Cavalry; 15 Warm Springs scouts under Chiefs Kamilch and Soukup; Cut-Mouth John, army scout from Fort Logan; George Jacquith, civilian scout with six Hudson's Bay Company trappers; and Sgt. Henry Catley a regular army hospital steward. Waymire was given two weeks to whip this outfit into shape.

As Waymire drilled his reluctant gladiators, Gen. George Crook (commander of the Military Department of West Virginia and soon to be eastern Oregon's favorite son) was having his share of bad luck. It all began in September 1863 at the Battle of Lookout Mountain when Crook's volunteers hit the famous "Jeff Davis" Division and cut it to pieces. Flush with this victory, he began slashing deep into enemy territory employing Shoshoni tactics of hit and run. Returning from one of these forays deep into the hostile South, a growing career was nipped in the bud.

It was common knowledge that Cumberland, Maryland had for two years been headquarters of the Military Department of West Virginia and that Gen. Crook and his staff officers stayed in the Revere Hotel. With this in mind, a band of rebels set out to capture some Yankee officers. They would receive some unexpected help in this daring venture.

Late one evening as Crook's raiders rode past the Dailey plantation on the outskirts of Cumberland, the general met a southern belle who caused his breath to catch. Crook, the indifferent who had weathered Oregon socials without so much as a glance at Pacific beauty—white or red—was smitten. With no end of Southern gallants seeking her hand, the girl of Crook's dreams was not impressed with him.

Over the ensuing weeks, Mary Dailey alone knew why the young Yankee cavalry officer always managed to ride by her father's plantation on his spasmodic plunges into Confederate lines. A devoted adherent to the rebel cause, Mary saw her chance to help and lost no time going into action. It was common during the Civil War for Southern and Northern officers to mingle at parties under a gentleman's agreement to cease hostilities for the evening. Therefore, there was no suspicion when one day Crook stopped for his usual chat and Mary casually mentioned a party she was giving. A select group of "nawthen officials" were being invited. "Would you, sir, accept the honor of being my guest?" Jeb Stuart and his cavalry couldn't have held Crook back that night.[7]

On the evening of February 19, 1864, a party of 70 men left their rendezvous near Moorefield, Virginia and crossed the Potomac about four miles upriver from Cumberland, Maryland. These men were members of a guerrilla band known as McNeill's Rangers, led by Major John McNeill and his son Jesse. Among their

---

7    The Dailey plantation, called Oaklands, was only a half-day's ride from Washington D.C. After the Civil War it became a favorite mountain resort consisting of several large hotels and a number of furnished cottages all owned by John Dailey, Esq., Mary Dailey's father. (Gilliss, *So Far From Home*, p. 162.)

numbers was Lt. James Dailey of Cumberland whose sister Mary was at this moment entertaining Northern officers.

While Crook and his lady danced the See-Saw Waltz, Confederate soldiers surrounded the house. In the midst of gaieties—about 2:00 a.m. February 20—the Rangers struck, swift and silent as the magnolia scented night. Within moments, the United States officers—Gen. Crook, Gen. Kelly and their aide, Capt. Thayer Melvin—were prisoners of war. They were pursued immediately but the Rangers knew the country much too well and eluded all efforts to capture them. The captives—considered to be one of the greatest prizes of the Civil War—were sent to Richmond, Virginia.

Mary Dailey smiled as the prisoners were marched from the ballroom. Then she made the mistake of looking into the bleak eyes of her dance partner and suddenly she felt like screaming. In that instant, Mary realized she loved the man whom she had betrayed and who was now being sent to rot in the infamous Libby Prison. From that moment on she began doing penance. Never a day passed when she wasn't fighting to have Crook released and knowing this, his time in prison was more easily endured.[8]

On March 1, 1864, while Crook pondered over his indiscretions in a prison cell, 24-year-old Lt. James Waymire led the first tactical expedition into the heart of central Oregon . . . and down through the bloody pages of frontier history. When asked by his fellow officers why he got picked for this unwelcome assignment, Waymire, who expected to be shipped east to the Civil War battlefront, wryly commented: "I guess half a loaf is better than no bread at all."[9] Ensconced in the vermin infested Libby Prison, Gen. Crook may have disputed that claim.

On March 10—as Waymire steadily plodded toward a clash with the Shoshoni—a contrite southern girl struck pay-dirt and arrangements were made to parole Crook from the Confederate penitentiary. According to the custom of the day, he was sent home to await word of an official exchange of prisoners. Secretary of War Stanton—considerably peeved at the whole affair and irked by some remarks made by Crook after his release—did not want to make an exchange. Another Oregon warrior, Sam Grant—brother-in-law to Captain Fred Dent who rescued the Vanorman survivors in 1860—was breaking the Confederacy in half and he didn't see things in quite the same light as Sec. Stanton did. Grant wanted his old partner back in action. Wielding considerable political clout, he arranged

---

8   Carrie Strahorn would recall that Mary Dailey "deliberately planned the ball at her father's house at which Crook was captured. They were married at the close of the war and lived happy ever after but she never enjoyed having that affair referred to." (Carrie Adell Strahorn, *Fifteen Thousand Miles by Stage*, Vol. I. 1877-1880, pp. 181-82.) The Strahorns were intimate friends of General and Mrs. Crook.

9   *Daily Oregonian*, April 22, 1864, letter from south fork of John Day River dated April 17, 1864, signed "Hyus Cultus."

for Crook's exchange and sent him back to command the Military Department of West Virginia.

During Crook's confinement, command had been given to Gen. Winfred Hancock by order of President Lincoln, and liking his new assignment, Hancock was in no mood to give it up. Crook went ahead and resumed command without any formality. Hancock deemed this a gross breach of discipline and without further inquiry ordered Crook's arrest and confinement. Crook, however, was simply acting on Grant's orders and assumed the proper instructions had been given. Sam had forgotten and in the meantime decided to use Crook to command the cavalry of the Potomac replacing Sheridan and issued another order for Crook to report to Sheridan for his new assignment. This put Crook in danger of arrest by Hancock's order. It became necessary for the President to intervene, suggesting Hancock forget the whole affair.

Hancock then wrote Crook saying he took pleasure in believing that Crook had acted without malice, purely in ignorance and without knowledge of the actual situation. By the end of March, the tangle finally unsnarled with no one being arrested and by the end of the same month, Lt. Waymire had confirmed that the Shoshoni, in reality, were uniting into a force to be reckoned with.

# CHAPTER 109

# NO SIGNAL SUCCESS

*Up to the blackened ceiling the sunken eyes were cast—*
*I knew on those lips, all bloodless, my name had been the last;*
*She called for her absent husband—O God! Had I known—*
*Had called in vain and in anguish, had died in that den alone.*

**George R. Sims**
*Christmas Day in the Workhouse*

A young Indian woman watched in silence as horsemen rode up the narrow river canyon and came to a halt on the small brushy flat at the mouth of Deer Creek. A guidon hanging limply in the snow-filled air identified them as soldiers—tired, cold, sick men who for the past 16 days had pushed ever deeper into Shoshoni territory. Men who welcomed the signal to dismount and exercise their numbed limbs.

The woman frowned. Her husband would not be happy to receive this news for he was war chief of the Buffalo Killer Snakes and as such would feel honor-bound to make contact with these American dog soldiers. Half Moon made a decision. What Broken Knife didn't know he could not be concerned about and with that, she quickly dismissed the passage of the cavalrymen from her mind.

Lt. Waymire, a tall, raw-boned man, stepped wearily from his horse and gazed at the rutted wagon tracks etched across the flat. He knew he was on the south fork of the John Day River, therefore this must be the Yreka Trail and his point of destination. It was mid-day, March 17. One of the trappers in his command had come down with measles and others were showing symptoms of sickness. He had to select a campsite and soon. When he reached the top of a small knoll, he sank down beside a snow-covered rock, studying every inch of ground in minute detail. Suddenly, he was alert. Across the river to the west something moved like a phantom along the base of the timbered ridge. He assumed it to be a deer and settled back against the rock. His attention was drawn to a bench a quarter of a mile above the ice-choked river. . . a defendable spot that would command a view of the river canyon and the Yreka Trail.

Twelve days before Waymire's frostbitten attack force arrived at the Yreka Trail, Oregon was linked with the rest of the war-torn United States by telegraph line. The Oregon Telegraph Company, formed in Portland in 1855 as a local means of communication, now gave way to the Pacific Telegraph Company. On March 8, 1864, Governor Gibbs wired a congratulatory message to President Lincoln in which he emphasized: "We want no Pacific Republic; no compromise with rebels in arms; and no slavery." Nine days after this message was sent, President Lincoln would have his name temporarily engraved on the central Oregon frontier.

The following morning after Waymire's troops arrived at the mouth of Deer Creek, the sound of axes echoed across the John Day canyon as the cavalrymen began construction of log huts and a stockade. This god-forsaken outpost guarding the Yreka Trail would become Fort Lincoln. By March 20, the fort was nearly completed when a group of miners stopped and reported that California packers had just lost 100 head of pack mules to the Shoshoni on the outskirts of Canyon City, 33 miles to the east. Leaving Corporal Perry McCord in command of Fort Lincoln, Waymire with 20 riflemen, 20 days' rations and George Jacquith as scout headed for Canyon City. When he arrived at Canyon City, he found out the Indians had a four-day head start but 65 well-armed miners led by Joaquin Miller were on their track so he sent an express that he would join them and headed south on the Indian trail to Harney Valley.[1]

Meantime, Cpl. McCord sent out scouts from Fort Lincoln to scour the surrounding country for signs of hostile Indians. Within the week, two Warm Springs scouts—Kamilch and Soukup—located Broken Knife's winter camp on Wind Creek south of Wolf Mountain. McCord's order to all scouts was to report back to Fort Lincoln where he would decide what action, if any, to take—but the Warm Springs scouts had other ideas.

On the day of discovery, Broken Knife and his braves had ridden out on a hunting trip and the camp was deserted except for women and children. Most of these were out foraging for food. The women had drifted some distance from camp when discovered by the scouts. Gathering reinforcements, Soukup and Kamilch fired on this group and later reported they had killed them all. Not quite. One, Half Moon, lived long enough to crawl back to her lodge and sleeping child. Clutching her sobbing daughter to her bleeding breast, she died. There, her stiffened body was found by Broken Knife.[2]

Upon discovery of Half Moon's body, Broken Knife with his daughter clasped in his arms, rode at breakneck speed for Spring Valley on the head of Crooked River and the main encampment of Has No Horse. A costly mistake had been made, for the murder of Half Moon closed all doors to peaceful negotiations. Prior to this butchery, Broken Knife had been semi-friendly and on occasion had

---

1    Waymire's Report to Gen. Alvord, pp. 68-77; *Report of the Adj. Gen. of the State of Oregon 1864-66*, Salem 1866; *War of the Rebellion, Vol. XIII*, pp. 309-15; Letter from south fork of John Day's River, dated April 17, 1864, signed Hyus Cultus, *Daily Oregonian*, April 22, 1864.

2    As remembered by Mattie Shenkah, Half Moon's daughter. She was approximately seven years old at the time.

served as an army guide. With the slaughter of Half Moon—sister to Has No Horse, and sister-in-law to Pony Blanket and Big Man (three of the ranking war chiefs of the western Shoshoni alliance)—vengeance was now riding the American's back-trail.

Waymire, unaware of the army scouts' vicious attack on women and children, tracked the Snake raiders from Canyon City across the head of Deer Creek onto the Yreka Trail a few miles south of Fort Lincoln and from there back across Snow Mountain to the Silvies River. Here, he found where the miners had camped and a note that they were headed toward Harney basin. On the evening of March 27, he caught up with the Canyon City miners at the Malheur silver ledge, dining on "a roasted horse head which they found to be very delicious." Shortly before Waymire's arrival, they had slipped up on "a lone Snake tipi, wounded one Indian, captured two horses and confiscated their evening's meal."

Six of Waymire's cavalrymen were sick with measles so it was decided to set up a base camp at the silver ledge and scout the area from there. The next day, army scouts spotted signal fires in Harney basin and the chase was on. Unfortunately for the white warriors, Broken Knife had made contact with Has No Horse and Big Man, both of whom had led the raid on the California packers.

At 3:00 a.m., the morning of March 29, the combined forces of Waymire and Miller now totaling 87 men, took off in a blinding snowstorm.[3] Lt. Waymire with 15 cavalrymen and 30 civilians started around one side of Harney Valley and Joaquin Miller with Wendolen Nus—first white settler in Klamath County—acting as scout took the remainder of the force around the opposite side. At daybreak, Waymire spotted a smoke and Sgt. Casteel with four men was sent to scout it out. By now, another one of the soldiers in Miller's company had come down with measles so Miller used this as an excuse to return to the base camp. In the vicinity of Dry Lake, Cpl. Meyers, who was attached to Sgt. Casteel's scouting party, bumped into Miller's volunteers. Meyers had spotted the smoke in the distance so Miller sent George Jacquith (who owned a ranch on the upper John Day River) to investigate it.

At 10:00 a.m. a single rifle shot rang out and somebody yelled, "There's Indians everywhere!" and mass confusion took over. Meyers' smoke turned out to be steam and Jacquith was never seen again. Then Miller's militia charged a rock formation thinking it was Indians. Hearing the shooting and seeing dim figures in the gloom which he took to be Snake dog soldiers two miles away . . . Waymire charged a flock of wild geese! Soon both parties were scattered over six or seven

---

3    Some reports state there were only 54 miners with Waymire's force but the official record numbers 65 civilians which is most likely correct. Also, there are conflicting dates on the day of the battle. Some say the fight occurred on March 29, 1864, others give the date of April 9, 1864. Based on later dates of troop movements it is probable that March 29 is the correct date.

miles in small groups of from three to five men. Their horses soon wore out on the frozen ground and they were ripe for an attack.

During this tragic comedy of errors, Has No Horse was joined by Pony Blanket and Natchez, son of Bad Face. Again, the frantic cry of "Indians" bounced across the Harney Valley floor, only this time it was for real. The cavalry which had trained nearly three years for this glorious climax hit the Shoshoni at a full gallop and gained firsthand knowledge of an Indian charge. It was the bitter sensation of overwhelming defeat.

The Oregon Cavalry had ridden into an estimated 200 dog soldiers who, according to Lt. Waymire were "well armed and brave. They also had plenty of ammunition." In the Americans' split-up condition it was every man for himself. Waymire, with only 11 troopers—the civilians had already taken off on their own—fought a circuitous, retreating battle toward the base camp. It took him 11 hours to reach there at 9:00 p.m. without the loss of a man. Along the way, he picked up a wounded civilian. As near as Waymire could tell, the only losses he had inflicted on the Shoshoni was the shooting of many of their horses.

By 10:00 p.m., none of the civilians that had left with Waymire that morning had returned to the base camp and there was no word from Sgt. Casteel. The next morning, Lt. Waymire searched for Casteel and the missing civilians. At mid-morning, he traced a smoke which turned out to be steam from the hot springs north of Warm Springs Butte. A day's search found nothing. Miller with his militia and the wounded civilian from Waymire's command returned to Canyon City. Waymire stayed one more day. It was now March 31. Sgt. Robert Casteel, Scout George N. Jacquith, Pvt. Cyrus R. Ingraham, Pvt. John Humbert and the 29 missing miners were never seen again. That night, Waymire made a 22-mile forced march in a raging blizzard and on April 2, arrived back at Fort Lincoln to find it in a state of siege.

Broken Knife had made repeated raids on the fort stealing horses and attempting to burn it. One of the guards had a bullet pass through his great coat but escaped injury. Two Canyon City civilians—Wilson and Overton—were killed. The night Lt. Waymire arrived seven more horses and one pack mule were taken.

With only six hours of rest, Waymire and his saddle-sore troops again took to the mountains pursuing an invisible foe. Battered by wind, snow and rain, mired in mud, crippling horses on the frozen slopes of the Ochoco, Waymire finally gave up the fruitless chase. On April 15, 1864, the lieutenant and his jaded troopers rode into Canyon City. Since first leaving Fort Lincoln on March 20, they had been in the saddle for 26 days. During this push into the Shoshoni stronghold it had stormed almost continuously, hammering the weary horse soldiers with 14 days of blinding snow and three days of freezing rain.

Before another 10 days had passed, Fort Lincoln came under such heavy bombardment that Waymire, in defeat and unaware that reinforcements were on the way, abandoned the outpost to the Shoshoni. The next day a black column of smoke drifted ominously down the John Day Canyon as Has No Horse put it to the torch. And so, Fort Abraham Lincoln—the first military outpost within the boundaries of Old Crook County—was relegated to the forgotten past.[4]

At the very moment when Lt. Waymire sacrificed Fort Lincoln to the enemy, Captain John Drake with the largest military force yet to enter central Oregon, was marching toward Crooked River. Well aware of all troop movements, Paulina and his warriors, serving as a decoy for Has No Horse's activities, burned a ranch house on the John Day River about a mile below the mouth of Bridge Creek. Irate white settlers and prospectors—joined by a party of Wascos whose chief had been recently killed by the Shoshoni—pursued the raiders and caught up with them near the head of McKay Creek. Paulina successfully repulsed them and made good his escape.[5]

Some 24 hours later, on April 28, Lt. Waymire joined Capt. Drake's command on Trout Creek. In his official report to Capt. Drake, Waymire spared all details on his aborted plunge into the Ochoco with this blunt statement: "We fought killing some but achieving no signal success. . . ."[6] Because of the broken-down condition of Waymire's horses and men, Drake sent him to Warm Springs.

---

4    As late as 1979, remains of old Fort Lincoln located in T16S, R27EWM, SEC 7 SESW, could still be found. There were stumps of ax-fallen trees most likely used for the stockade walls; the rotted outline of what was believed to have been log structures inside the stockade; and what appeared to be two unmarked graves on a grassy bench overlooking the south fork of the John Day River a short distance east of the fort.

5    Report of the Commissioner of Indian Affairs 1867, *Congressional Documents, Serial 1326*, pp. 51-53

6    *Drake's Report of the Waymire Expedition to the Adj. Gen. of Oregon 1864; Waymire's Report to the Adj. Gen. (Cyrus A. Reed) of Oregon, 1864-66*, Salem 1866, pp. 68-72.

# CHAPTER 110

# PASSAGE TO CROOKED RIVER

*I and the Indian scouts struck up a very steep, long, rocky gulch in places almost perpendicular. We were compelled to pull each [other] up and then haul up our horses . . . I never traveled over a worse country.*

**Lt. John Noble**
May 14, 1864

It would now surface that Lt. Waymire and his troops were the sacrificial lambs of the Ochoco offensive. Waymire's preliminary probe into eastern Oregon was nothing more than a cover to keep the Shoshoni off-guard while the main offensive was being put into motion. Both the Northern and Southern Battalions of the First Oregon Cavalry and the Northern Battalion of the First Oregon Infantry would be placed in the field to deliver a knockout blow. Also being considered were plans to enlist two more battalions of infantry to be shoved into the front if the need should arise. However, there were strong differences of opinion in the high command as to how this invasion would be accomplished with volunteer officers opposing regular army officers on both strategy and tactics.

A few days before the Expeditionary Forces were to engage the Shoshoni in combat, a select group of volunteer officers came up with a provocative solicitation. Major Rinehart, Captains Drake, Spencer and Small along with Lt. Watson signed a joint request to the secretary of war asking that a board of officers be convened in Oregon to examine them for commissions in the United States Colored Troops[1] (what they were after was a reservation Indian regiment). Against their better judgment, Col. Maury and Gov. Gibbs—perhaps with ulterior motives in mind—recommended them for such service and Gen. Alvord forwarded the application to Washington, D.C. with the endorsement: "These are all valuable and efficient officers. Most of them are going into the field in a few days against the Snake Indians which will keep them out all summer. I recommend a Board of Officers to be ordered to convene here for their examination as requested on the 1st November next." Gen. Alvord who held the same reservation as Maury and

---

1    The William V. Spencer *Collection*, Oregon Historical Society files.

Gibbs was no dummy. By the time November 1864 rolled around most of said officers' terms of enlistment had expired and one was dead.

But there was another force to be reckoned with. Captain George Currey, co-commander of the Snake Expeditionary Force, who was engaged to Jessica Clarissa Gaines—granddaughter of ex-gov. Gaines—held the political advantage.[2] A Rogue River Indian war veteran, he was also a very popular man in western Oregon. These citizens were strongly in favor of having Indians fight Indians. Such action, they believed, offered the advantages of practicality, economy and the substitution of Indian blood for white blood. Currey, acting as their voice, was pushing hard to muster 100 reservation Indians into the fight against the Shoshoni.[3] The regulars who had seen the reservation Indians in action knew it was poor military strategy. Their acts of brutality would only serve to make the Shoshoni more determined to fight to the death when the army hoped to gain a cease-fire out of the campaign. As one officer put it, "The military use of Indians against other Indians engendered warm debate."

To even further complicate the chain of command, the Oregon Volunteers—ignoring U.S. military authority—were taking their orders from Gen. Cyrus A. Reed, commander of the Oregon Militia based in Salem. Gen. Reed's most outspoken critic was Col. Maury, a U.S. Regular. While not a graduate of West Point, Col. Maury had served in the Mexican War where he received his field commission and he held the beliefs of the professional military about using Indians against Indians in combat.

When it became obvious that Capt. Currey meant business, Col. Maury wrote to Gen. Alvord, February 17, 1864: "I do not approve of the idea of having a company of Indians. Their manner of warfare is repugnant to our civilization and they would be a constant source of anxiety and perhaps trouble to the commander of the expedition."[4] Alvord agreed, but caught in a political cross-fire with Gov. Gibbs and Samuel May, secretary of state, he allowed Currey to recruit 100 friendly Indians as light mounted irregular cavalry.

That issue settled, a course of action designed to "find, disperse or destroy the Snake Indians" was put into motion. Lt. Col. Drew, field commander of the Oregon Regiment, would throw all available troops into eastern Oregon in a huge

---

2  There were two unrelated men named George Currey (or Curry) who were prominent in Oregon history. Territorial governor George Law Curry who spelled his name without an "e" and after whom Curry County was named; and George Byron Currey, the Indian fighter. Captain Currey held a law degree from Wabash College and would resign his commission in 1865 to practice law, first in Eugene, then in Canyon City. He later became editor of the La Grande *Observer* and author of *The Tribute to the Ox Whip.* (Carey, History of Oregon, Vol. II, pp. 628, 641-41.) Jessie's sister, Amanda Susannah Gaines, was engaged at this time to Major William V. Rinehart. Jessie and Amanda were the daughters of Albert P. and Sarah Barlow Gaines.

3  *War of the Rebellion*, Series I, Vol. L, Pt. 1, p. 317.

4  *War of the Rebellion*, Series, I, Vol. L, p. 758.

pincers movement. Captain John Drake, commander of the Northern Cavalry Battalion with half of the infantry would march into the country south of Crooked River still believed to be Wolf Dog's main stronghold and set up a line of defense. Captain Currey with the Southern Cavalry Battalion and remainder of the infantry would move onto the Oregon Trail and close in from the east. The plan was simple. Whatever direction the Shoshoni moved, they would be cut off from retreat and left with two alternatives: either sue for peace or be exterminated by summer's end.

The new recruits mustered for the Snake Campaign began arriving at Fort Dalles on April 6 where they were to receive their first pay. This sparked another conflict. Promised $31 a month, the soldiers were very unhappy when they were paid $25 and then in greenbacks valued at 50 cents on the dollar. Even so, this was considerably more than the regular army troops were receiving.

The cost of maintaining the regular army in eastern Oregon based on 1865 military records was as follows:

### *Pay Scale:*

| Rank | Pay Per Month |
|------|---------------|
| Colonel | $75 |
| Lt. Colonel | $65 |
| Major | $55 |
| Captain | $45 |
| 1st Lieutenant | $30 |
| 2nd Lieutenant | $25 |
| Sgt. | $13 |
| Cpl. | $10 |
| Pvt. (artillery) | $8 |
| Pvt. (cavalry) | $6 |
| Pvt. (infantry) | $5 |

A company was made up of 50 enlisted men plus officers although 75 men was desirable. Ten companies constituted a regiment and a battalion was normally part of a regiment consisting of a headquarters and two or more companies. Officers and non-commissioned officers assigned to a company were: 1 captain, 2 lieutenants, 10 sergeants and 6 corporals. A regiment had 1 colonel, 1 lt. colonel, 2 majors, 1 adjutant (usually a captain), and 1 quartermaster of the lieutenant rank.

Supplies for one cavalry regiment cost $600,000 a year; supplies for one infantry regiment came to $300,000 per year. When in the field, this cost jumped to 1.5 million dollars a year. During the period 1864-1869, there was a minimum of eight regiments in eastern Oregon at all times (4,000 men) and the cost of supplies, salaries, etc. was in excess of two million dollars per year. This was the cost to the United States government to subdue the Shoshoni rebellion. When offered greenbacks, many volunteers refused to accept their pay and when Gen. Alvord got word of this, he ordered disbandment of these companies. Col. Steinberger, fort commander, refused to let them off so easy. He coolly informed the malcontents if they didn't accept their pay, he would "consider it as mutiny and sedition and treat it accordingly."[5] They got the message but shortly thereafter, Col. Steinberger—under intense political pressure—was relieved of duty by the secretary of war and recalled to Washington, D.C.

Anyway, this hassle placed the dissenters three days behind the main expedition so Steinberger dispatched two companies to Canyon City under the command of Capt. Charles Crandell. Staff officers for this disgruntled group were Lt. Cyrus Walker, son of the Rev. Elkanah Walker and Lt. John W. (Watermelon) Redington, ex-editor of *The Oregon Statesman*. They were to reinforce Major Lugenbeel at Fort Logan.[6] Another 50 troopers of B Company, First Oregon Cavalry, led by Capt. Richard Caldwell, were sent to Warm Springs where the rest of B Company was stationed under the command of Capt. Edward Harding—brother to Benjamin Harding, who at that time, was Oregon's outspoken mouthpiece in the U.S. Senate.

Hamstrung from the start, Capt. Harding—a tough campaigner of the Yakima War—arrived at Warm Springs on February 10, a month and a half behind schedule. That is how long it took to whip his cantankerous troops into some semblance of order and as yet they were untried in battle. Adding to his discomfort, his woefully inexperienced executive officer, 2nd Lt. Stephen Watson could think of nothing else but leading "a glamorous cavalry charge into the midst of the howling red throng." There was only one problem. Watson didn't like horses. Harding was also blessed with a detachment of H Company and bloodthirsty Donald McKay who would serve as official army scout. The arrival of Caldwell's squad would come as no great source of joy.

On April 20, the commands of Drake and Currey were ordered into the front. In both outfits were a hodge-podge of volunteer and regular army officers who didn't see eye-to-eye on anything. Currey with Louis Scholl, the German architect, as guide left from Fort Walla Walla to effect the eastern barrier. Drake with "Cayuse George" Rundell as guide marched south from Fort Dalles choosing the Crooked River route because "Cayuse George" thought by going that way . . . they could avoid contact with the Snakes![7]

---

5   *The Daily Oregonian*, April 22, 1864, letter from Fort Dalles dated April 20, 1864 signed "Co. G."

6   Fort Logan was established June 16, 1863 by Major Lugenbeel on Strawberry Creek six miles south of Prairie City, Oregon. An old box stove from the fort was still in use at the Prairie City Grange Hall in 1963—one hundred years later.

7   George Rundell, an Ohio farm boy, helped guide Wallen in 1859 and Steen in 1860. At the time he was 26 years old. (*War of Rebellion*, Vol. L, Part I, p. 336.) When Rundell served as

The two commands presented an awesome sight to the haggard Shoshoni. Drake's column alone consisted of pack trains, freight wagons, artillery wagons, field ambulances and was trail-herding hundreds of beef cattle and extra horses. He was transporting enough equipment and supplies to last 200 army personnel, 125 Indian scouts and 100 civilian employees for six months of field duty. To help keep track of this motley crew, Drake had eight cavalry officers under his command, some of whom were misfits.

Born December 21, 1830, John M. Drake was educated at the Pennsylvania Stroudsburg Academy and was more literate than most of the personnel in his command. At the age of 18, he had been in on the '49 gold strike and worked three years in the California mines. Mustered into the service at Camp Baker, Oregon as a 1st lieutenant on December 19, 1861, Capt. Drake was 33 years old at the time of the Snake Expedition. Before resigning his commission, Drake would advance in grade to the rank of Lt. Colonel.[8]

The first cavalry detachment—under the guidance of Captain Henry Small—to join Drake's command at Fort Dalles arrived on the steamer *Julia* which was well supplied with liquor. In fact, on the trip from Fort Vancouver, one trooper in high good spirits jumped his mount over the deck rail and both horse and rider became sacrifices to the river god.

On the brighter side, Captain John Darragh—sometimes Wasco County school teacher and sometimes lawman—took charge as pack master of the endless military supply train and more or less did a good job. He would later serve as chief of scouts in Gen. Crook's command.

And then, there was Major C.C. Dumreicher, one of the more colorful gentlemen to be attached to the Crooked River arm of the Snake offensive. At the time he came under Drake's command, Chief Surgeon Dumreicher seemed to have turned professionally from the patching of battle wounds and various other ills common to soldiers on campaign duty to the research field, in which he was carrying on an experiment in the effects of alcohol on the human body with himself as the subject.

The Major and the Captain held a mutual distrust of each other but fortunately for the troopers, Dumreicher had Dr. William H. Robertson, a contract surgeon and 1st Sgt. Henry Catley, the hospital steward who had been with Lt. Waymire, to take care of his more mundane chores.

On the first day out many visitors arrived in camp, among them Col. Maury with the disquieting news of Waymire's failure. Maury expressed the opinion that "Waymire had pursued the Indians too far," an allegation which rightfully deserves

---

scout for Gen. Crook in 1867, Crook thought him "utterly worthless and demoralized." (Crook, *Autobiography*, p. 144.)

8    *Oregon Adjutant General's Report, 1865-66*, p. 215.

to rank as the understatement of the whole campaign. If that was Waymire's first mistake, his second was in catching up with them.

Because of Waymire's recent defeat, both Drake and Currey would move with extreme caution. Their mere presence in the field was enough to stir up much civilian activity. In mid-April, Ralph Bruney and Dr. William Dain, who was hoping to do better than mining chunks of lead from prospectors' bodies, organized a party of adventurers and left The Dalles City heading for Crooked River in search of the Blue Bucket gold. They planned to travel with Drake's command but because of heavy wagons and pack animals the military column moved too slow so the miners pushed on without the protection of an army escort.[9]

On May 1, Henry Wheeler—taking advantage of Drake's military force—launched his big Concord stagecoaches on the first passenger and mail run to Canyon City. Wolf Dog was more impressed with these potential bearers of gifts than he was with Oregon's show of military strength.

Meanwhile Drake, with all his problems of logistics, was making good time. In the first week, he covered 70 miles. Lt. Jesse Robinson in charge of the cattle herd was having difficulties in keeping up and Drake was having no small amount of problems with his new recruits. The old Roman military axiom that "a good soldier should fear his officers more than the enemy" certainly didn't apply to the members of the First Oregon Cavalry, especially not to Major Dumreicher, who in spite of his rank was subordinate to Captain Drake.

The second day out, Drake would note that "the Doctor was pretty tight." Two days later he got drunk and couldn't find his way back to camp.[10] Happily, at least for Drake, Pvt. Love came down with measles, then followed by a civilian packer and Dumreicher soon had has hands filled with medical problems. However the cooks got into his liquor supply and got "very drunk." No supper that night.

Capt. Drake was also bogged down in paperwork not the least of which involved Sgt. Barton, who had to make a sworn affidavit as to why Pvt. Russell had neglected to report that he lost his cavalry horse 15 days before the command left Fort Dalles. To make things more uncomfortable it was snowing. At least the expedition was saving on supplies by living off the land. The Indian scouts were killing game—ducks, deer, geese, antelope, sage hens—while the officers were having a great time fishing. At Cross Hollows, Drake had 600 lbs. of supplies stored for later use.

An express had been sent to Lt. Waymire to meet the command at Trout Creek and on the evening of April 28, Drake set up a permanent camp to await his arrival

---

9    *The Daily Oregonian*, July 27, 1864—letter from Camp #35, Harney Valley dated July 2, 1864, signed John M. Drake, Capt. 1st Oregon Cavalry, Commanding to A.A.A. Gen. Hdq. District of Oregon, Fort Vancouver, W.T.

10    Private journal (unpublished), Captain John M. Drake, *Expedition from Fort Dalles, Oregon into the Indian Country*, journal entries for Thursday, April 21, 1864 and Saturday, April 23, 1864.

and also the arrival of Lt. Watson with dispatches from Warm Springs. That evening, Don McKay, leader of the Warm Springs scouts; Stock Whitley, Walla Walla war chief; and Simtustus, a Walla Walla war chief who wore a wolf head for a hat, rode into camp with 15 Walla Walla scouts followed by Lt. Watson, Indian Agent Bill Logan and Dr. William McKay, agency physician and half-brother to Don McKay. Logan would add to Capt. Drake's woes when he happily presented him with "Kit," an Indian boy servant.[11]

The following morning, Watson, Logan and Waymire—because of the broken down condition of his horses and men—returned to Warm Springs. Major Dumreicher went with Dr. McKay to attend not only to Waymire's sick crew but Capt. Caldwell's troops who had also contracted measles. Before leaving, Drake ordered Watson to rejoin the column as soon as he could.[12] Eager as he was to slay redskins, Watson was—according to Lt. John Noble—an ex-sailor and didn't particularly enjoy horseback riding and he was "much disgusted at the news of his accompanying us to Crooked River."[13]

Shortly after Lt. Watson left, the command got excited when they spotted a large smoke. Believing they may be under Indian attack, Lt. Noble was ordered out with a cavalry detachment to check it out. Drake's irregulars were holding true to form. The smoke was caused by the packers who had gone fishing. A campfire had escaped and was now burning up their supplies.

In a few days, Lt. Watson and Major Dumreicher caught up with the command on Hay Creek. The doctor was in a "delightful mood." At Warm Springs, Logan had made him a gift of "Henry" an Indian servant boy and a bottle of booze. Henry would learn firsthand how to become a medic. It should be noted that the Indian boys so generously given as personal attendants were Shoshoni children who were fortunate enough to survive torture by the Warm Springs scouts.

On Hay Creek, Lt. Noble made an interesting notation in his diary. He reveals in his entry for May 3 that he "wrote to Che-what-ne in chinook." Che-what-ne was the Snake war chief Black Buffalo. Noble, a career army soldier, had been in Oregon since 1849 and had fought in every Indian war since that time. There is no doubt he was well acquainted with Black Buffalo but what was the message? Was

---

11     Drake's journal entry April 28, 1864. "Marched 12 miles over rough country and camped on Trout Creek. Visited by Mr. Logan who brought me an Indian boy for a servant."

12     Watson was described by his good friend Lt. John Noble as 5' 10" tall, grey eyes and brown hair. Born in New Brunswick, Watson immigrated to California during the gold rush. Naturalization papers were issued at Yreka in 1852 at the age of 23. In 1858, he was elected to the Oregon Territorial Legislature. In 1861, Watson enlisted in the First Oregon Volunteer Cavalry and served under Capt. Drake for 17 months as 1st Sgt. in B. Company. He was commissioned a 2nd Lt. April 9, 1863.

13     Quotations, unless otherwise noted, are from Lt. John F. Noble's first dairy dated April 20 to May 27, 1864, The Drake Expedition, 1st Oregon Cavalry into eastern Oregon.

he inviting him in for a peace parley; perhaps notifying him not to fight; or just passing the time of day? No one will ever know.

Moving up Hay Creek in a snowstorm, Drake's poor luck was still holding. Kit, his Indian boy servant ate some poison parsnips and Dumreicher had a difficult time keeping him alive. As Noble put it, ". . . had six convulsions—singing good time!" Maybe the good doctor was experimenting with Indian medicine chants.

Whatever the case, on the evening of May 8, the column camped at Lt. Bonnycastle's old depot at Cedar Springs on Willow Creek which the Indian scouts called "Stinking Springs." Shortly before dark, a 110-mule packstring—40 days out of Stockton, California—camped with them. It was made up of French and Spanish miners who were bound for Canyon City. One of the owners, a Spanish lady, was traveling with the train. She told Drake that 19 days out of Yreka, they lost the trail and came in on the head of Crooked River and had traveled down river to this point. They experienced no trouble and saw no Indians from Fort Klamath to Hay Creek. This was encouraging news.

In the high divide between Willow and McKay creeks, Lt. Noble celebrated his 36th birthday on May 9, 1864. His only complaint was "not one drop to celebrate the day with." Apparently, the cooks had drunk all the liquor. But Noble guessed he was "all the better for it." On this day 15 years before, Noble had rode out of Fort Leavenworth, Kansas, for Oregon Territory with the U.S. Mounted Rifle Regiment.

The next day, as the advance column descended into Mill Creek Valley, Cayuse George galloped up with an express from Fort Dalles and gleefully dropped a high explosive on Drake's weary shoulders in the form of Special Order No. 70. Dated May 6, 1864, it flatly stated: "The command of Captain Drake will proceed to the northeastern end of Harney Lake and effect a junction with the force of Captain Currey, 1st Oregon Cavalry, who will command the whole force. Captain Currey will decide when the two commands shall again separate." Signed, General Alvord, Fort Vancouver, Washington Territory.

When the commands left Fort Dalles it was the announced intention of Gen. Alvord that each expedition was free to act on its own as circumstances might dictate. Now, as Drake would comment, "At the eleventh hour an order is received that will destroy the effective strength of both."[14]

To add insult to injury, Richard Barker of Salem arrived with Cayuse George on the pretext that he was delivering some books from Agent Logan. It soon became apparent he was to stay with Drake's command and make a firsthand report to the governor's office as to how the Snake offensive was being conducted.

A personal letter from a friend was no more heartwarming. Smallpox was raging up the Columbia River from Portland to Umatilla Landing with seven deaths being reported at The Dalles. Drake would sadly note that "two young ladies,

---

14    Drake Collection, Oregon Historical Society, Portland, Oregon.

friends of mine, the Misses Gaines, are at Lt. Apperson's both having been sick with measles and are sick now again, some think with smallpox." This information would also cause distress to Capt. Currey who had asked for Jessica Gaines' hand in marriage; and her sister, Amanda had the same arrangement with Major Rinehart, Canyon City's head brewmaster.

A few hours after the express had arrived, Drake's column reached Ochoco River where they had difficulty crossing. It was the belief of the cavalrymen that the Ochoco—a tangle of willows lined with wild rose bushes—should be called "Briar Creek." That evening, the column bivouacked near Steen's old campsite in the vicinity of the present Keystone Ranch.

The trail up Veazie Creek and down Horse Heaven Creek to Crooked River was extremely difficult. The cavalry officers were not favorably impressed with Steen's military road. The trail up Crooked River was no better. Badly washed out from the 1862 flood, the military expedition was forced to make four treacherous river crossings in six miles. Pack mules mired down and had to be dragged out while the heavy freight and artillery wagons were brought to a stop. The column finally ground to a halt on Shotgun Creek. During this torturous leg of the journey, Lt. Watson was making scouts up all the side streams but any Indian sign found was at least two months old. That evening on Shotgun Creek, the cavalry mounts stampeded in a lightning storm. The dozing guard was unaware that anything had happened until Capt. Drake came out to get his horse and found the herd gone. Lt. William Hand, officer of the day, suffered for this lack of attention. The troopers lost 52 cavalry mounts—including Drake's prize gelding—and one pack mule.

Capt. Henry Small and Lt. Noble with a detachment of G Company took off in pursuit of the spooked horses. They tracked them over terrain so steep that they had to dismount and pull each other up. In places it seemed impossible that the runaway horses could have made the ascent but they did. On Lost Creek they found one shod horse which had been killed by Indians near a large petrified tree. Undoubtedly the horse was crippled. The troopers also found traces of gold in a nearby stream.

The round-up crew finally caught up with 41 head of horses on the upper Ochoco River below the mouth of Marks Creek. The rocky knob—located between Salmon Creek and Owl Hollow—where they recaptured the horses was named "Stampede Butte." By now, the troopers own mounts were so broken down that Lt. Noble decided to take an easier route back with the horse herd while Small headed across the mountains to unite with the main command. At Keystone Flat, Noble found a supply train out of Eugene City. This train had left Eugene City on March 17 and spent the next 58 days lost. Noble provided an escort to the army's Trout Creek depot.

Here Sgt. Barton, in charge of the escort detail, learned that as the army moved toward Crooked River, prospectors had began construction on The Dalles-Canyon City Military Road. It was a hasty operation for the road was declared open in May while the toll road out of Sherar's Bridge was improved only to the extent that it was usable. The numerous freight wagons, pack trains and tramping feet of miners moving to and from the John Day Valley gradually hammered it into a fairly good surface. A federal land grant to the organizers of The Dalles-Canyon City Military Road became law February 27, 1867 awarding them alternate sections of land along a route six miles wide from The Dalles to Boise City. The company acquired 49,932 acres in Wheeler County alone, but the road was never completed between Canyon City and Boise. Canyon City was made a U.S. post office in the spring of 1864 with Major Rinehart appointed postmaster.

While Small and Noble chased horses, the main column reached the North Fork of Crooked River—called by the Warm Springs scouts "*wah pass*" meaning the separation of waters—on May 14. Drake camped here for two days and his scouts discovered much evidence of recent Shoshoni activity. Interspersed with the Indian pony tracks they found shod horse tracks. The scouts determined the shod horse tracks were made by Bruney's prospecting party. Bruney had made it to the head of the South Fork three days before Drake reached the North Fork and he would later report that his party had been under constant Shoshoni surveillance.

Capt. Small had seen more than enough evidence of Shoshoni activity on his way back across the mountains to convince him that the command was in dangerous territory; and on the morning of the 17th as the main column pushed toward Steen's Camp Separation and their intended destination, Small again went on scout and found . . . nothing! That evening, 28 days out of Fort Dalles, Drake arrived at Camp Separation. In celebration, the exuberant troopers fired off all the pistols in the command—which must have alerted every Shoshoni in central Oregon of their arrival.

Since Capt. Small had found no indication of hostile activity south of Crooked River, Drake dispatched Don McKay and a dozen Warm Springs scouts to again comb the area to the north. Lt. Noble had just relieved Lt. Watson as officer of the day when around 7:00 p.m. a rider thundered into camp with a message from McKay reporting he had located a hostile camp. The scouts had counted a dozen lodges and had also found a large band of horses grazing nearby.[15] It was the general practice of the army to estimate from three to five warriors per lodge so that could mean there were close to 50 dog soldiers in the Shoshoni encampment.

At this point, the volunteers went berserk in their frenzy to be chosen for combat duty. As they waited impatiently for the assignment roster, Drake and his staff officers planned the attack. Two cavalry detachments and a squad of Warm Springs scouts would make a forced night march from Camp Separation and be in position to strike the hostile camp at the first hint of dawn. The remainder of the command was to split at daybreak. Half of the troops would remain at Camp Separation to begin construction of a fortification to be named Fort Maury and the

---

15    *The Daily Oregonian*, May 26, 1864, Capt. Drake's Report from Camp Maury.

other half were to march 12 miles to the east and set up an outpost to guard the Yreka Trail.[16] Tentatively referred to as Camp Union (in reference to the junction of Steen's military road with the Yreka Trail), this bastion was to include a stockade large enough to hold any captives from the Crooked River raid and other anticipated engagements of the coming summer. Camp Union would soon give way to Fort Dahlgren.

At 10:00 p.m. on the night of May 17, 1864, Lt. John McCall—commander of the attack force—and Lt. Stephen Watson thundered out of Camp Separation to unite with Don McKay in the vicinity of the Shoshoni camp. Following in their wake were 39 regulars of Companies B and D, 1st Oregon Cavalry and 10 Warm Springs scouts. Dick Barker, the Salem watchdog, John Campbell, a reporter for the Portland *Oregonian* and Cayuse George Rundell with 11 more Indian scouts decided to tag along and join in the fun.

---

16    Construction of Fort Maury began on May 18, 1864. It was located some three miles south of Crooked River on the west bank of Rimrock Creek at its confluence with Maury Creek. Standing guard at the mouth of Rimrock Canyon under the north slope of Arrowwood Point, the fort was concealed by a heavy growth of pine in which could be found many clear, cold mountain springs. The main fortification consisted of stone walls four feet high surrounded by rifle pits. Inside the enclosure were log officer's quarters, troop barracks, field hospital, guard-house, and mess hall. Also enclosed by rock fortifications was a huge log corral for the cavalry mounts. Serving as a backdrop to the fort was the southernmost tip of the Blue Ochoco's now named the Maury Mountains in commemoration of the fort. The main mountain peaks are Arrowwood Point named for the Arrowwood shrubs (syringa) growing on the summit; Tower Point on which the cavalry maintained an outpost; Drake Butte named for Capt. John Drake; and West Maury Mountain named for Col. Reuben Maury.

# CHAPTER 111

# TAPS IN RABBIT VALLEY

*I little thought when I relieved him as Officer of the Day on the 17th instant that I would have to have his grave dug and command his funeral escort—but such is life.*

**Lt. John Noble**
Fort Maury, May 19, 1864


Drake's command did not arrive in central Oregon unannounced. Shoshoni scouts picked up their trail on Trout Creek and from that day forward every move was under surveillance. Paulina returning from Klamath Marsh with a herd of stolen horses had been warned that soldiers were moving up Crooked River and it was his tracks army scouts discovered on May 17, less that two miles west of Camp Separation. He was bound for the springs at the head of Rabbit Valley where Wolf Dog and Has No Horse would make a stand. Since the first intelligence of troop movements reached them, they had selected and prepared this spot for their intended fight. They had chosen well.

Twelve Snake lodges sat in a semi-circle on a small flat a few yards east of the northernmost spring. A brush corral in a grove of juniper would hold all the horses. Directly back of the lodges was a solid rock ledge some 200 yards long. In front of this bluff Has No Horse had constructed a barricade of rocks and logs making it nearly impregnable. East of the rim, the juniper-choked base of Trapper Butte presented an impenetrable barrier for horses. On the north, a pine-covered butte formed a natural fortress in case of retreat and from there it was a short ride into Paulina Creek and easy escape into Big Summit Prairie. Bordering the area on three sides for a distance of one to two miles was a lava field covered with three-foot high sagebrush and rocks ranging in size from cobblestones to boulders two feet in diameter. It could be crossed by horses only at a walk and then with extreme difficulty. Immediately south of the rim fortress, the springs formed a swamp over a mile in length and a quarter of a mile wide. On the east, the saw-toothed rims of Sabre Ridge, running north to south and dividing Rabbit Valley from Paulina Valley, formed a high barrier some six miles long—so narrow at the summit that in places it was less than 10 feet wide. To approach the Shoshoni camp, the cavalry would have to move directly north up what is now named Watson

Creek into the Shoshoni guns. All the dog soldiers had to do was wait and time was on their side.

At noon, May 17, Paulina with his horse raiders arrived at the fortress adding 15 warriors to the 35 already in camp. At dusk, Broken Knife rode in with 20 more. Has No Horse had now doubled his fighting force. The strategy was quickly planned for he was well aware that Warm Springs scouts had located the camp earlier in the day as had been anticipated. Wolf Dog and Paulina with most of the dog soldiers would man the fort. Has No Horse and Broken Knife with three men would position themselves on the pine-covered butte north of the rock ledge to cover the escape route in the event Wolf Dog and Paulina should be forced to retreat. Black Eagle—Paulina's brother—and Pipe would patrol the outer perimeter of the camp and keep the war chiefs briefed on troop movements.[1]

Near midnight, May 17, McCall and Watson were joined by the uninvited guests—Barker, Campbell and Rundell with their 11 Wasco trophy hunters—bringing their total force to 65 men. With the addition of McKay and his Indian scouts this number would increase to 77. The two opposing combatants were now evenly matched. By now, the Shoshoni war dance was audible for two miles. McCall advanced up Sabre Ridge to within 600 yards of the hostile camp and waited for dawn to break. From this vantage point, he could make out the bluff to the rear of the Snake lodges and based his attack on the belief that this rim would serve as a barrier, blocking the Shoshoni's retreat to the north.

About 2:00 a.m. all became quiet in the Shoshoni camp and it was assumed they had bedded down for the night. McCall, who had been with Crook's 4th Infantry in the Yakima Campaign, laid out the plan of attack. McKay, in command of the Warm Springs scouts, would cross the valley and strike from the west. McCall with D Company, followed by the *Oregonian* reporter, would advance from the east. Watson with Company B would charge from the south in a frontal assault, the idea being to force the Shoshoni into McKay or McCall and certain annihilation. Barker—Gen. Reed's informant—decided to go with Watson.

By 4:00 a.m., the military units were in position. As dawn broke, the bugle sounded "attack!" and Lt. Watson, his sabre flashing in the morning sun, charged . . . into the swamp! Horses floundered in the mire throwing riders as Watson, shouting, "Pour it to 'em boys!" wallowed into Wolf Dog's waiting guns. McKay found the western approach filled with boulders "almost impossible to travel over without harm at any speed other than a slow walk." Advancing on foot, he had gotten close enough to see the Snake fortifications and yelled to Watson not to attack. The bulk of the men in B Company—bogged down in the

---

1     Noble, in his diary entry for Thursday, May 19, 1864 at Camp No. 18 (Fort Maury), names the Indian chiefs as Yak-we-wah (which could be either Wolf Dog or Black Eagle), Pe-li-ni (Paulina), Ot-se-hoe (Has No Horse) and Chong-yo (Pipe) of the Snakes.

marsh—heard this warning and retreated leaving Watson with only nine men. Apparently Watson thought McKay said, "Advance! There are the Indians!"[2]

Lt. McCall—cut off by a juniper thicket, and having swerved further south than intended—rode into the swamp and Watson's line of fire forcing him to retreat. He then tried to get north of the rim but was stopped by thick brush and rocks. Realizing the soldiers were in bad trouble, McCall dispatched messengers to Capt. Drake for reinforcements. This was about 4:30 a.m, May 18. The first messenger would reach Drake—en route to establish Camp Union—at 6:00 a.m. Immediately, Drake sent Capt. Small with 40 men to the battle site. They would arrive at 8:30 a.m.

Meantime McKay's scouts, entrenched among the rocks, fired volley after volley into the Snake lodges. Instead of being panic-stricken, the Snakes fell back to their fortifications . . . "rallied and fought like devils." By then, Watson had reached the lodges. Sgt. Balch's horse was shot out from under him a few yards from the bluff. At the same moment, a rifle bullet shattered Watson's left leg above the knee and plowed into his horse. As the horse fell, Watson took a bullet in the head, killing him instantly. Pvts. Harkinson and Kennedy riding on Watson's flank were also killed. Richard Barker was galloping in on Watson's right when his horse was wounded and fell on him, breaking his leg. While trying to crawl out from under his mount, a bullet smashed into his thigh fracturing the bone. Cayuse George and some troopers from D Company rushed in and dragged Barker behind some rocks. During this rescue mission Cpl. Dougherty took an arrow through the shoulder. Pvt. Freeman, seeing Sgt. Balch, down attempted to reach him and had an arrow driven through his chest. Pvt. Weeks had his wrist slashed open by an arrow when he reached out to support Freeman from falling off his horse. Pvt. Level was down with an arrow in his side and Pvt. Henline was laying in front of the Shoshoni barricade with a bullet wound in the shoulder.[3]

Seeing Watson go down, Stock—the Walla Walla war chief—made a dash from his position in an attempt to drag him to safety yelling to the scouts, "Our lieutenant is down! Rush 'em!" Before he could reach Watson's body, a rifle slug tore through his right arm and rendered it useless. Cimmas, a Walla Walla brave, seeing that his chief was wounded, jumped up to assist him and was shot in the head. Drawing his knife with his left hand, Stock charged the rock fortification

---

2    Noble's first diary, dated Wednesday, May 18, 1864.

3    Even a slight arrow wound was serious, for the Snakes were using arrows tipped with barbed agate, nearly as hard as diamond and poisoned by plunging them into a liver bitten repeatedly by rattlesnakes. Shot from a Shoshoni short bow, they were as effective as gunshot. In fact, most arrow wounds were worse than gunshot. The Shoshoni arrows were so constructed that the head and one or more sections of the shaft were joined together with moist sinew. When the arrow came into contact with the warm blood of the body, it came apart so when the shaft was removed the head and the first joints of wood were left in the body. To make sure this happened, the head of the arrow was barbed so it would hold fast.

shouting at Paulina to come out and fight. Paulina stepped out from behind a rock, blasting away with an army model Colt .44. The first bullet hit Stock in the left shoulder turning him around; the next struck him in the back of the neck coming out his mouth; he took another bullet through the leg; one in the body and one in the right shoulder. Stock now had six bullets in him but was trying to drag himself back to safety. Simtustus and Cayuse George made a run to drag him off the battlefield. They were successful but Simtustus was shot in the leg. When Stock regained consciousness, he got mad at Cayuse George for not picking up his rifle and pistol and insisted Rundell give him a horse in payment for them.

Suddenly, Has No Horse, Broken Knife and three dog soldiers, all mounted on war horses thundered around the northern end of the barricaded ledge and charged McKay's position. Gray Fish, one of the Walla Walla scouts, whirled around to shoot and took an arrow in the throat. This so unnerved the Warm Springs scouts that they took off in retreat and didn't stop until they arrived back at Fort Maury in mid-morning. On questioning by Lt. Noble, they claimed they didn't meet Capt. Drake or Capt. Small in their flight from the battlefield. Perhaps not and as Noble observed, "They appeared somewhat dissatisfied and much broken down."

Crippled by the desertion of his Indian scouts, McCall—seeing the futility of the fight—sounded retreat and secured a staging area for the wounded near the lower springs one and a half miles south of the battle site. In retreat, McCall found one scout who had been disemboweled hanging from a juniper tree. Following this grisly discovery, he sent Pvts. Barney and Wilcox with more dispatches to the main command. When Drake received the depressing news of battle casualties, he immediately sent an express to Warm Springs ordering Lt. Waymire into the field—leaving the reservation unprotected. By the time Drake received his first report from the front at 6:00 a.m., McCall had gotten the wounded off the battlefield.

When the Indian scouts—who were expected to keep the Snakes pinned down—were routed by Has No Horse, Paulina canvassed the battlefield for supplies. The dead were robbed, stripped, shot full of arrows, mutilated and then thrown over a cliff. Paulina and his warriors were in the act of collecting their booty when Small's reinforcements arrived at 8:30 a.m. Only three hours had passed from the time McCall's first expressmen had left seeking help until Small reached the battle site . . . a round trip of some 40 miles over rough terrain. At the sight of Small's additional troops, the Shoshoni retreated but in going, four of their wounded comrades were taken captive.

The first thing Capt. Small did was to recover the bodies of the fallen soldiers. While this was in progress, McKay with the few remaining scouts captured 65 horses. Watson's horse, valued at $300, was so badly wounded it had to be killed. During the round-up, Small's troopers set fire to the lodges and burned all Shoshoni property which consisted of a "large number of saddles, clothing, skins, ropes, blankets and large quantities of Couse and Cammas roots." With the loss of the horses, it was believed that the Shoshoni were severely crippled.

Only two dog soldiers were known to have been killed but from the blood on the rocks many were thought to be wounded. One warrior was buried underneath a dead horse to avoid discovery. The Shoshoni had also butchered one horse for meat. In 15 minutes of actual battle, the army suffered its worst single loss since the slaughter of Warner's troops 15 years before on the Oregon-California border.[4] It was a battle which began at the break of dawn and ended at the crack of doom.

Among the hostile captives was a light-haired, blue-eyed warrior about 18 or 20 years old. Great surprise was expressed at seeing a suspected American with the Snakes and the soldiers were eager to "make short work of the white renegade." However, it soon became evident that not only was he as much a dog soldier as any of the braves but he honestly believed he was an Indian. Because his age coincided with the passage of the lost 1845 emigrant train and the fact he had no recollection of white parents, it was obvious he had been taken captive as an infant. Surprisingly, he could speak fairly good English and said his name was Warm Spring. He soon became known to the troopers as "Johnny Warm Spring." Not trusted, he along with the other three captives was turned over to the Warm Springs scouts for safe-keeping on the return to Fort Maury. For the interim, the hostages were taken a few hundred yards from the staging area, securely bound, severely beaten, and tied to a juniper tree.

While this was going on, Major Dumreicher, Dr. Robertson and Sgt. Catley dressed the wounded soldiers first and then went to work on Barker who had to be placed under chloroform. Chief Stock was in the poorest condition of all. One bullet which entered just under his ear and came out his mouth, carried away most of his teeth. Another fractured his collarbone and he also had a .44 slug embedded in the fleshy part of his back and flesh wounds in both arms. Stock showed himself a brave man and like an old grizzly bear—though shot to pieces—walked to where he could receive assistance.

Barker had to be packed the entire 18 miles back to Fort Maury on the men's shoulders as he was unable to ride in a hospital wagon. He would have much to complain about in his report to Salem. Stock was packed nine miles until they met the ambulance and then a litter was swung in it for him to ride more comfortably. On reaching Fort Maury, he made a request to Lt. Noble that in the event he should die, "Bury me alongside Lt. Watson," whom he thought was a very brave man.

---

4     The casualty list was sad: Lt. Stephen Watson, Pvt. James Harkinson, Pvt. Bennett Kennedy, army scout Gray Fish, Walla Walla brave Cimmas, and an unidentified army scout . . . dead! Other casualties, some of whom would later die included: war chief Stock Whitley, civilian Richard Barker, Cpl. Ralph Daugherty, Pvt. George Freeman, Pvt. Jasper Weeks, Pvt. John Level, Pvt. William Henline, civilian John Campbell, and war chief Simtustus . . . wounded! Total casualties were six dead and nine wounded. Eleven of these men were from B Company, 1st Oregon Cavalry.

About all the Oregon Cavalry succeeded in doing on their raid into Wolf Dog's territory was to confiscate 65 Shoshoni ponies. When they arrived back at Fort Maury, Drake took all the horses except for 25 broken-down ones which he gave to the Warm Springs scouts who had captured the horses in the first place. Happy to receive any handout from their benefactors, the scouts headed for their camp a quarter mile west of the fort with the gift horses and four Snake captives in tow.

That night, the troopers got little sleep as the scouts indulged in a war dance. The following morning, Simtustus sadly reported to Capt. Drake that during the festivities all the prisoners, except for Johnny Warm Spring, had escaped. Later, Johnny would reveal just how they "escaped." It was shortly past midnight, May 19, when his comrades-in-arms were securely tied to a juniper with green rawhide and a mass of sagebrush collected and placed around them. The three Snake warriors were then roasted alive. The probabilities are that the cavalrymen were too busy with their own troubles to pay any attention to what was going on in the camp of their allies.[5]

The soldiers who fought in the Rabbit Valley offensive and witnessed the treatment of casualties firsthand were very despondent. In their minds, the hospital department—like the whole command—was "illy prepared" for battle conditions. Lt. Noble would remark, "God help the one who is taken sick or wounded on this march. . . . Someone must suffer for the manner we have been started into the field." So they did—but it was the troopers who felt the pain.

Before the day was over another sad duty had to be performed. The dead were "prepared and dressed neatly as possible and rolled in their U.S. blankets" for burial in a grove of three pine trees south of the fort. It was noted in the eulogy that Pvt. Harkinson was a spinner from Scotland and Pvt. Kennedy an Illinois farmer. "This battle will not soon be forgotten by any of this command for today in solemn procession, we carried to their last resting place three of our comrades and fired over their new graves. The tribute due to the bodies of those who die in the service of their country. . . ."[6]

Prior to the funeral, many of the Indian fighters commented that though public opinion did not so agree, it was just as deserving a praise to die on the

---

5   During his forced stay on the Warm Springs Reservation, the Americans began calling Johnny Warm Spring "Warm Springs Johnny" instead of his Shoshoni name, Warm Spring. He served as an army scout during the second phase of the Shoshoni rebellion—the Bannock War—where his knowledge of Snake customs and language was of great value. But beyond that, he was described by Col. William Thompson as "an arrant coward and could not be depended on when danger threatened." More likely, Johnny had no stomach to kill what he considered to be his own kinsmen. He married a Shoshoni woman taken captive to the Warm Springs Reservation and moved to the Willamette Valley where he lived and died an Indian. (Thompson, *Reminiscences of a Pioneer*, pp. 151-52.)

6   Nobel's first diary, Thursday, May 19, 1864.

battlefields of eastern Oregon in the discharge of one's duty as it would have been to fall at Shilo or Gettysburg. After the funeral Sgt. James Balch—a college graduate, school teacher and photographer—described by those who knew him as "a great lover of music and a melancholy man" penned his fallen saddle-mates epitaph:[7]

> *Where they fell let the mountains remember*
> *Where they bled let the turf be more green*
> *Where they lie in the last sleep of mortals*
> *Let the proofs of their prowess be seen.*

And then, the dead of Rabbit Valley were laid to rest in unmarked graves on the north face of the Maury Mountains.

Within three days, John Campbell—school teacher by vocation, news-hound by avocation—was stirring up trouble. In his report to the Portland *Oregonian*, he would charge that Lt. Watson was shot through the head "by some strange mistake." This statement was in reference to Lt. McCall's failure to reach Watson and an opinion held by much of the command that McCall was a coward. According to Campbell, "McCall was never under fire."[8] Apparently Campbell received this information in confidence for on May 20, Lt. Noble notes in his diary that he gave a letter to John G. Campbell and "asked him to send it to Logan and Humason and not to publish any statement from my letter."

The Humason referred to in Noble's diary was Orlando Humason who as a member of the Oregon legislature introduced the bill creating Wasco County. He also acted as emergency editor for the *Oregon Statesman*. At this time he owned freight lines making the dangerous run to the eastern Oregon mines.[9]

Campbell's implied claim of McCall's dereliction of duty would firmly imbed in the Oregonians' minds that regular army officers were inferior to volunteer officers. This line of thinking would serve to further hamper the Shoshoni war effort.

---

7    Sgt. Balch's son, Frederic Homer Balch, was the author of the most famous Oregon book ever written, *The Bridge of the Gods.*

8    These statements were confirmed in a letter from J.G. Campbell, Schoolmaster Warms Springs Indian Reserve to Wm. Logan, Indian Agent Warm Springs Agency, dated May 23, 1864.

9    Corning, *Dictionary of Oregon History*, p. 120.

CHAPTER 112

# NIGHT PATROL

*One lamb white cloud appeared to browse*
*In the azure above the aspen boughs,*
*When suddenly on the western rim*
*Thunderheads loomed, majestic, grim,*
*As lightening forked through the stormy wrack*
*And black was piled on deeper black.*

**Ethel Jacobean**
*Mountain Storm*

On May 23, 1864, Don McKay with the wounded arrived at Warm Springs Agency where war correspondent Campbell alerted the world that all was not well on the eastern Oregon front. During the Rabbit Valley encounter—now called the Battle of Watson Springs—Capt. Currey, meeting little resistance, forged into eastern Oregon and on May 25, established Fort Henderson on Gibbs Creek near the Owyhee River placing it under the command of his brother Lt. James Currey. Capt. Drake was not having it so easy.

Beginning on May 19 and continuing for the next eight days, Fort Maury was under siege. Protected by armed guards, many soldiers were busy cutting and hauling logs for a stockade and corrals while others were cutting down the high sagebrush encircling the camp. At the start of the project, one trooper enthusiastically described the fort area in this manner: "On the whole it was rather a romantic and pretty spot and very capable of being made safe as far as Indians are concerned." This observation would soon change. Construction crews would quickly find out that although Fort Maury was "a beautiful military depot with wood, grass, timber and fine water in abundance," it was next to impossible to defend. Paulina's warriors had them pinned down and were stealing cavalry mounts nightly, sometimes riding within 60 feet of the fort. During one of these skirmishes, Otter Bear—a Big Lodge chief—was severely wounded and later died . . . a loss keenly felt by the Snakes.

Although Drake, Small and Porter were leading patrols in all directions, it was impossible to get anyone to carry a message through to Capt. Currey's command for reinforcements and the most reluctant were the Warm Springs scouts. The cavalry officers were dismayed to find that their 25-man patrols were not

181

sufficient to make an attack upon any of the Snakes' fortified camps. Then on May 28, orders arrived from headquarters at Fort Dalles to stage a full-scale offensive against the waiting guerrilla forces.[1] This unpleasant mandate was delivered by Lt. James Waymire with a 22-man escort.

Waymire also brought news that "terrible fighting has taken place in the East." In a four-day battle on the Rapiden River between Grant and Lee, some 4,000 Rebels were killed or wounded while the Yankees' casualty list hit 15,000. In spite of the heavy Northern losses, it was Drake's opinion that "Grant seems to meet with a steady success thus far." Branded a merciless killer by the South, Grant—the general who usually wore a private's uniform with his stars tacked any-which-way on his stooped shoulders—so hated the sight of blood that he could not eat meat unless it had been cooked to a blackened crisp.

The weather had been unseasonably hot when on the morning of May 28, Lt. McCall with a detachment of 25 men left for the South Fork of the John Day River on a five day scout; and Lt. Noble with 25 troopers, a hospital steward, two civilian packers, six Warm Springs scouts and Cayuse George Rundell as guide, rode out of Fort Maury on orders to intercept Wolf Dog's warriors.[2] In six days of night riding—hiding in dense pine thickets during the day—Noble covered some 90 torturous miles.

Noble's scouts found fresh Shoshoni tracks a few miles west of the fort and the soldiers immediately took cover at the mouth of Sheep Rock Creek when an excited guard reported a signal fire on the south side of Crooked River. This succeeded in scaring the inexperienced troopers to such an extent that Noble would later report "the men were much frightened, constantly making alarms and reporting supposed noises."[3] This reaction to danger so unnerved the scouts that they refused to leave the command to check the signal smoke and the most obstinate was the Walla Walla war chief, Pipsher Simtustus.

Although most of his family had been killed by Snake raiders, it was obvious Simtustus held the whites responsible for Snake hostilities and was doing his utmost to hamper the success of the patrol. This coupled with his allegiance to Queapama, the only Wasco chief who refused to sign the treaty of '55 and currently held in irons at the reservation, would explain his reluctance to help Noble locate Wolf Dog's camps. According to Noble, Simtustus was "perfectly worthless and only a stone around my neck—a most arrogant humbug!" By now, the volunteers were referring to Simtustus as "General Washington."

---

1     Order No. 24, Headquarters Fort Dalles to Expedition to the Indian Country, Camp Maury, Oregon.

2     Drake's journal entry for Sunday, May 29, 1864.

3     Unless otherwise noted, all quotes taken from Lt. Noble's diary entries from May 28 through June 7, 1864.

Plagued by a violent lightning storm, Noble's patrol was doomed from the start. Not only did the storm cause miserable night travel—spooking horses and men alike—but the sudden drop in temperature accompanied by drenching rain sparked a flu epidemic and caused Noble to lose a day and two nights sneaking up on a Shoshoni camp which turned out to be a large lightning struck juniper burning on the crest of Sheep Mountain.

Undermanned on scouts, the detachment made little progress. Travel over treacherous terrain in inky darkness was slow and Noble, near the point of fatigue, complained that during the day he could not get any rest "as the men have to be constantly watched to see that they care for their horses properly and to prevent any surprise" by Wolf Dog's patrols. He would also note that most of his troopers couldn't be kept awake even when they lost only an hour's sleep nor could they be trusted on guard duty to alert the main body of danger. In his opinion, it was doubtful that their reports were of any use whatsoever. Even the civilian packers could not control their mules, which would stampede and cause enough ruckus to alert every hostile within miles of the soldiers' approach.

However, the patrol did make some interesting discoveries. They located a large winter campground on the west fork of Camp Creek which had been recently occupied by a Snake war party. On the headwaters of Bear Creek and also on their descent of Pine Creek, ex-miners in the detachment found strong indications of gold. On Shotgun Creek they discovered fresh tracks of deer that "were near run down" being pursued by an Indian who "was running bare-footed" . . . an almost certain sign that Big Man (the soldiers would call him Big Foot) had joined forces with Has No Horse and Paulina. Big Man, because of his size and speed, seldom rode a horse and was known to have outrun mounted patrols on many occasions.

By the fifth day, the cavalrymen had "no meat and but two scanty meals of bread" forcing Noble's return to Fort Maury. The only significant discovery on the return trip was that Big Man with a large war party had passed eight miles west of the fort. When reaching Crooked River, the war party split into small groups and the scouts could no longer track them.

Lt. Noble was happy to learn that Don McKay had arrived at Fort Maury with an additional 67 Warm Springs scouts described as "a well-mounted, good looking set of fellows who can be of much service to us if they do not take some Indian notions in their heads. They are strange beings at best. . . ."

On receiving Noble's report, Drake ordered Lts. Waymire, McCall, Hand and McKay into the field that night. The second night out—some 25 miles northwest of the fort—the scouts discovered a Shoshoni camp on the top of a high rocky mountain. They also reported that it would be almost impossible to get at the camp, the approach being so steep and rocky. Nonetheless, McCall gave the order to attack; eliminating a camp of women and children. The survivors were taken captive. Drake would dryly remark that "the Chitike Cavalry returned this morning with three squaws and eight children taken prisoner during their late raid."[4] McCall admitted that had there been even a few warriors present, the cavalry would have suffered heavy losses.

The officers were quite favorably impressed with the Shoshoni children. Lt. Noble who had campaigned from the Mississippi to the Pacific, would write: "I never saw a better looking lot of children—really all good features and intelligent looking." One of the captives, Old Woman, had her granddaughter with her. She said that the girl's parents had been killed 18 days before in the fight at Watson Spring. According to Old Woman, the Snakes' only losses were two men and two women. Under questioning, another captive—Sorrowful Woman—daughter of Wolf Dog and the wife of Lean Man, a Walpapi warrior, admitted that this was the third time she had been taken prisoner by white men since her capture at Tall Man's camp in 1859 where she became the "private property" of Pipsher Simtustus. She informed Simtustus that he now had taken his own child prisoner. On hearing this Simtustus became quite indignant accusing Sorrowful Woman of being "a damn liar."

They also learned from the captives that the men from their camp were with Paulina and Big Man while other dog soldiers had joined Has No Horse who was riding to intercept Currey's command on the Owyhee River. Wolf Dog was dug-in in the vicinity of Harney Lake to affect a blockade between Drake and Currey. The Oregonians were soon to learn what Shoshoni warfare was all about.

Arriving with the prisoners of war, an express rider delivered ballots for the election of national, state and county officials to be held Monday, June 6 at "Camp Union." At this time, headquarters was still referring to Fort Maury as Camp Union. Actually, Camp Union—where construction had come to a halt due to the Rabbit Valley battle—was the packer's camp located a few miles east of Fort Maury on Beaver Creek meadows.

Out of 110 men eligible to vote in the national election only six votes went to the Democrats. It was stated that only three men in the command were "not sound on the Union question" and one of these was a personal friend of Gov. Gibbs, a suspected southern sympathizer. Most of the soldiers refused to vote for state or county officials, thus expressing their disgust for Oregon and its politicians. It was their contention that Oregon had never recognized the existence of her soldiers and had done less for the country in a time of danger than any state in the Union. In short, Oregon manifested no public or patriotic spirit which according to Capt. Drake was a true assessment. Harboring such bitter resentment, the Indian-fighting army would not be overzealous in their pursuit of Shoshoni dissenters.

During this political bickering, Stock Whitley—the Walla Walla chief who had ridden with Yellow Serpent against Red Wolf's brigades—was suffering greatly from the wounds received May 18 and it was feared he was going to die.

---

4    *Shitaikt* was the Walla Walla name for the Shoshoni sentenced to the Warm Springs reservation, and Drake misspelled it as *Chitike*. Hodge, *Handbook of North American Indians North of Mexico*, Vol. 2, p. 606.

Black Ice, tough leader of the Yakima campaign and brother to Kamiakin, was watching over him. "He [Stock] seems to appreciate it which is indeed a rare quality in an Indian," so observed Lt. Noble who ranked Stock on a par with Yellow Serpent.[5] Stock wanted to get back to his wife at Warm Springs whom he believed could do him much good as, "She is strong medicine." But Major Dumreicher wouldn't allow it believing the ride would be fatal. Growing weaker from loss of blood, consumed by gangrene, his neck wound bleeding freely, Stock Whitley—who had once been arrested by Gen. Wright and imprisoned in the Fort Vancouver guardhouse—died at 9:00 p.m. on June 6, 1864, in the service of the United States Army.

His brother who supported his head as he was dying remarked that he preferred to see Stock go this way instead of in a drunken brawl, as the old man was very fond of his "toddy" and frequently "got on a spree." Just before Stock drew his final breath, several Snake warriors were seen near the fort and during the Walla Walla's ruckus of mourning, the captive Shoshoni girl untied her grandmother Old Woman and they escaped.

Immediately upon receiving the news of Stock's death, the Indians at Warm Springs mustered a war party of some 70 warriors; took what provisions and ammunition that Agent Logan was authorized to furnish them; and proceeded to join Drake's command. Drake, fearing that he would have to feed so large a party, refused to accept this new company of red reserves. It was his opinion that if the Warm Springs Indians did encounter the Snakes "the first little skirmish will flatten them out; they will wilt like a leaf and stampede for the Warm Springs like a herd of deer." Drake referred to the Warm Springs war party as the "Chitike Cavalry."

On June 7, 1864, in compliance with Special Order No. 24, Capt. Drake's full command took to the field.

---

5    Noble, who fought in the Yakima War and was well acquainted with all the war chiefs, would note: "One of his men, Son-ney-way (Black Ice) is very attentive to him almost devoted. . . ." Noble's diary entry for Thursday, June 3, 1864.

# CHAPTER 113

# NEWS FROM THE FRONT

*You no doubt think our prospecting party have all been killed off by the Snakes but I am happy to inform you that such is not the case.*

**R.W. Bruney**
Rattlesnake Creek, July 2, 1864

The Shoshoni were now involved in total war. Snake war chiefs, fighting more or less independent of each other but under the influence of Has No Horse, were striking from the California line to the Idaho border. Pack horses loaded with rifles and ammunition slipped into the Ochoco supplied by the Paiutes, Utes and Comanches. Nothing in the dog soldiers' path of destruction was being spared. Isolated ranches, thriving settlements, dusty trail herds, weary emigrant trains, heavily guarded stagecoaches, avenging military detachments; all were feeling the sting of Shoshoni resentment.

The army was reacting in kind. By June, Gen. Alvord—after three years of dalliance—increased the Oregon cavalry to full regimental strength and requisitioned Gov. Gibbs to supply 40 mounted riflemen to patrol The Dalles-Canyon City road. This rifle company under the command of Nathan Olney would prove to be worthless. Alvord also had Drake and Currey converging on Harney Valley; Lt. Col. Drew marching on south central Oregon; and ordered Capt. Richard Caldwell out of Warm Springs for manning Fort Lapwai and guarding the Mullen Road into the Idaho and Montana goldfields.

Still under the misconception that the Shoshoni were operating out of southeast Oregon, army scouts—among them Archie McIntosh attached to Olney's command—were scouring the Owyhee country and leaving the Ochoco untouched.

Military depots bearing such names as Three Forks, Maury, Logan, Henderson, Rattlesnake, Alvord and Wright were sprouting like mushrooms on the eastern Oregon frontier. Soon to follow would be Dahlgren, Gibbs, Rock Creek, Watson, Ochoco, Steele, Harney and Warner. Mule trains loaded with ammunition were waiting at the mouth of Owyhee Canyon to make contact with Drake and

Currey. Other supply trains loaded with food and medical supplies were rolling out of Fort Dalles, Fort Walla Walla and Fort Boise bound for eastern Oregon.[1]

Adding to the confusion, vast trail herds out of Utah, California and Nevada were converging on the military outposts and mining settlements trampling everything in their wake. Under intense criticism from eastern Oregon ranchers, Gov. Gibbs was applying pressure on the legislature to enact a law making the owners who drove cattle in from other states liable for trespass and damages caused by their livestock whether lands trespassed upon were fenced or not.

The governor's wife was also doing her share to aid the war effort and make Oregon a more desirable place to reside. While the Governor rode roughshod over the state legislature, Margaret Gibbs organized a Ladies Sanitary Aid Society to clean up the Willamette Valley. By mid-July, the Society had collected $676.78 for this worthwhile cause.[2] Presumably a clean environment would discourage Shoshoni trespassers.

Meantime, the Shoshoni—side-stepping the army—were wreaking havoc. Emigrant trains were ambushed. Prospecting parties were annihilated. Local defenders were cut to ribbons. Eager reporters, in an effort to keep abreast of the news, were publishing letters from unnamed soldiers, distressed citizens and irate miners.[3] These literary missiles, under the guise of public information, were causing as much or perhaps more damage to army morale than the dog soldiers themselves. Capt. John Drake, a sensitive man, vented his frustration in a private journal. Wounded by constant media harassment he would write:

> By looking over the Oregon papers and private letters published I find that I am becoming an object against whom all the spleen and abuse of the country is being hurled. The people of The Dalles seem to be the most abusive, and their conduct amounts to a systematic defamation of character. I have been informed that the common topics of conversation in the parlors, whiskey shops and other places of resort in Portland is the "strategy" as they are pleased to term it of the expedition. Gen. Alvord in his efforts to retain or acquire a popularity with the people has belittled himself enough to publish in the [The Dalles] "Mountaineer" a whole column of correspondence in which he endeavors to show how much he has done to secure the safety of the Canyon City road, but says not one word of the orders received May 10 which sent me

---

1    *Portland Daily Oregonian*, July 29, 1864, letter from Camp Maury dated July 20, 1864, signed "Hyus Cultus;" *Portland Daily Oregonian*, July 28, 1864, letter from Currey's expedition, Camp #49, Silvies River, dated July 8, 1864, signed "Sojer Boy."

2    *Portland Daily Oregonian*, July 19, 1864.

3    *Portland Daily Oregonian*, July 14, 1864, letter from Rattlesnake Creek, Harney Lake Valley Oregon, dated July 2, 1864, signed R.H. Bruney; *Portland Daily Oregonian*, July 14, 1864, letter from Canyon City dated July 10, 1864, signed R.H. Bruney; *Portland Daily Oregonian*, July 20, 1864, second letter from Canyon City, dated July 10, 1864, signed R.H. Bruney. Others would be signed Sojer Boy, Hyus Cultus and Company G.

a flanking towards Lake Harney. The fact of the matter is I am being systematically slaughtered.[4]

The article to which Drake refers is worth examining in its entirety.[5] From a "sense of duty" the editor, Wm. H. Newell, feels compelled to remark:

". . . there is something wrong in the management of the troops now in the Indian Country. Capts. Drake and Currey—as we understand—have some 300 men under their command, sent out for the especial purpose of protecting miners and others against Indian depredations. In view of this fact it is somewhat strange that the officers named keep clear of the scene of all the Indian outrages. Capt. Drake is supposed to be somewhere on the Crooked River—a part of the country that has rarely been visited by white men, and where he can be of no possible benefit. This, too, at a time when life and property on the Canyon City road is constantly exposed to destruction. One half the troops under his command, stationed on the road, would have been amply sufficient to protect the trade and travel, and shutting the Indians off from the opportunity to plunder, the savages would have been forced from sheer necessity to come to terms. At the time the two commands now out took the field, it was understood that the purpose was to protect the trade and travel, but instead of this the country where their services are required is literally given up to the Indians, whilst the soldiers are allowed to amuse themselves in a wild goose excursion up Crooked River. Take the record of Indian outrages on the coast for the last year, and the whole catalog will not show a destruction of life and property equal to that on the Canyon City road."

Drake and Currey knew why they were headed for a union in the remote southeastern corner of Oregon. It wasn't by choice but on the whim of their commanding officer, Brig. Gen. Alvord. They were also well aware that the "Indian outrages on the coast" were part of the Snake offensive, a bit of intelligence that the good citizens of the Willamette Valley seemed to be quite ignorant of. However, there was one warrior east of the Cascades who didn't have to tip-toe in the presence of Ben Alvord and he was about to explode.

Dr. William H. Watkins who was with Capt. Caldwell's troops attached to Drake's command, decided to hit the newspaper editors from a position that had clout. On July 26, he wrote to his brother-in-law, the Honorable Addison C. Gibbs, governor of the state of Oregon. Watkins was so mad, he neglected to dignify his message with punctuation.

---

4    Drake's Private Journal, Wednesday, July 20, 1864.

5    *The Dalles Mountaineer*, July 1, 1864, p.1, "More Indian Depredations on the Canyon City Road."

... if it comes handy will you not see Pittock [Henry Lewis Pittock, publisher of the *Portland Oregonian*] and tell him it is unjust to publish adverse reports as to operations of troops out here—letters from some private who to get even because he has been in the guardhouse rushed to the papers. Currey has followed these Indians around 1,200 miles trying to bring them to bay and a fight but yet has been unable. Drake and command have been on the move all the time—Waymire's raid was bold and as full of danger as Sheridan's around Richmond how he managed to get back with his scalp is more than I can imagine now that I know all about it five men have been killed and one officer as many more wounded—and chasing these Indians over an empire in extent and then have adverse stories published in the papers by those who know nothing about it is not agreeable.[6]

Governor Gibbs now faced opposition on the home front.

In the battle of the media, some of the more informative reports were coming from Ralph Bruney. Thirteen days before sending his first scoop, Bruney had been shot through the thigh and was writing in a prone position. He had organized a 15-man party to search for the Blue Bucket mine and left The Dalles in April with Drake's command.[7] Bruney originally planned to travel with the military for protection but becausse of heavy freight wagons, pack animals and cattle, the army moved so slowly that the miners pushed on without them. By the first week in May, they had prospected the Crooked River basin finding traces of gold but were constantly in sight of Shoshoni signal fires. At one point, they had to "change course for fear of utter annihilation." On May 8, at the Yreka Trail crossing of Crooked River, the miners met an emigrant train from Shasta Valley bound for Canyon City.

J.W. Williamson, leader of the wagons, told Bruney they had been under Indian surveillance since leaving California. For a week both parties camped on Crooked River afraid to venture out. Large and small war parties trailing stolen horses were seen entering the mountains north of Crooked River. From this camp, five of Bruney's prospectors with four days provisions headed west to look for the 1845 emigrant trail. They were turned back by Snake patrols. On May 15—three days before the cavalry's fatal encounter with the Shoshoni in Rabbit Valley—the two groups decided to make their escape in a heavy rainstorm. Bruney, still eager to find gold, moved west again searching for the 1845 emigrant trail. Williamson's train turned east for Fort Boise.

---

6   Gibbs Collection, Oregon Historical Society, Portland, Oregon.

7   Bruney's party consisted of: Dr. William Dain (co-organizer), John Jackson, George Beals, Rufus Perkins, John Sherwood, A.K. Gird, Edwin Stone, C.W. Chadwick, J.H. Deadmond, Simm Lundry, William Conroy, G.H. Caine, Alexander Swan, Daniel Gross, and David Dewitt who joined the main party 60 miles out from The Dalles.

That afternoon, the miners hit a fresh Indian trail and spotted a large smoke about one mile distant. Well-armed and of sufficient strength, the miners attacked the camp, but the Shoshoni seeing them approach disappeared into the hills without firing a shot. The next morning, the miners were joined by three packers from Canyon City who reported much Indian activity along the south fork of the John Day River.[8] The two groups joined forces and headed for the California line and safety.

At the trading post on the Red Bluff-Humboldt Trail, they learned that two Paiutes with a pack train of ammunition had passed there recently heading north into central Oregon. While at the trading post, a detachment of Lt. Davis' 2nd California Cavalry out of Fort Crook arrived, tracking a war party under the leadership of Little Rattlesnake which had destroyed an emigrant train in eastern Oregon. When Bruney decided to join them, the miners mutinied and led by Dr. William Dain, they returned to The Dalles via the Willamette Valley. Only Alex Swan stayed with Bruney.

Moving into Warner Valley, their luck ran out. Unknown to the cavalry, they were riding into a Shoshoni ambush. Crossing a small creek, the soldiers stopped in midstream to water their horses. Little Rattlesnake's warriors fired at a distance of 10 feet. Swan was hit twice. One bullet passed through his right hip and another slashed through his right arm above the elbow gouging a three-inch wound in his ribs. One of the troopers was shot through the body, the bullet then shattering his right hand as he was in the process of cocking and pulling his rifle from the saddle sling. Bruney took a bullet in the right thigh which embedded in his saddle.

In a state of shock, the cavalry detachment galloped eight miles to a rocky bluff and took a stand on top. Having done his damage, Little Rattlesnake disappeared into the mountains. Lt. Davis then led the 2nd California Cavalry on a course to intercept Drake's command which he believed to be somewhere in Harney Valley. With the wounded, it took Davis 10 days to cross the high desert. Ten days without water except for what could be found in rock depressions after a rainstorm. On July 1—68 days after they had left Drake's command on the Deschutes River—Bruney and Swan rejoined it at Camp Rattlesnake in Harney Valley.

Other reports filtering into the press from the far reaches of eastern Oregon were equally grim: ranch houses burned to the ground, stagecoaches robbed, livestock stolen or slaughtered, miners murdered. And Has No Horse had just begun his campaign.

---

8    These packers were E.A. Heath, William Farmer and V. Selly of Yreka, California.

# MILITARY DEPT. OF THE PACIFIC 1858

**HEADQUARTER LOCATIONS**

| | |
|---|---|
| 1854-1858 | Fort Vancouver |
| 1858-1868 | San Francisco |
| 1868-1880 | Fort Vancouver |

MILITARY

DISTRICT OF

OREGON

FORT VANCOUVER

FORT SIMCOE

FORT WALLA WALLA

FORT LAPWAI

FORT DALLES

FORT WATSON

FORT STEELE

FORT LOGAN

FORT MAURY

FORT CURRY

FORT HARNEY

FORT BOISE

FORT ALVORD

FORT WARNER HDQS.

FORT KLAMATH

FORT C.F. SMITH

FORT LYON

FORT HALL

FORT BIDWELL

FORT McDERMIT

FORT CROOK

MILITARY DISTRICT OF CALIFORNIA

By order of the secretary of war, the Department of the Pacific was subdivided into the Military Districts of Oregon and California on September 13, 1858 with department headquarters in San Francisco. The Military Department of the Pacific was again placed under one command with headquarters at Fort Vancouver, Washington Territory, June 1868, and renamed the Military Department of the Columbia.

*Locations are approximate and not shown to scale.*

# CHAPTER 114

# HIGH WATER MOON
## (TWENTY-THREE DAYS IN JUNE)

*I wish to correct an erroneous impression that seems to have gone abroad that the great Indian fight is to take place in the vicinity of the lake about 100 miles southeast of this camp. Now the facts are simply this: that all the Indians who have created so much disturbance in the John Day country are to be found in the vicinity of this camp!*

**Captain Henry Small**
Fort Maury, June 21, 1864

On June 7, Capt. Drake with five staff officers, 50 enlisted men, five Warm Springs scouts and an assortment of civilian guides, packers and teamsters marched into the desert south of Crooked River to intercept Currey's command. Capt. Small—with one staff officer, one medical officer and 58 enlisted men including the sick and wounded—was left in charge of the depot and supply train at Fort Maury. Drake did leave one army scout, Jim Luckey whose brother Warren—a Eugene blacksmith—was traveling with Drake's command as a farrier.[1] By now the in-fighting had started.

At the start of Oregon recruitment, Gov. Gibbs had proclaimed that whoever enlisted the most volunteers would be made captain of that company. Noble, Small and Hand had all undertaken to raise companies for the First Oregon Cavalry but it became apparent that none could completely fill their quota. Since Noble had raised the most men, Small and Hand agreed to act as first and second lieutenants. Shortly thereafter, Small changed his mind and in the interim Noble became involved in difficulties with Gen. Alvord and was court-martialed. Gen. Wright intervened in Noble's behalf and he was acquitted of charges but reduced in rank from captain to 2nd lieutenant and Small was made captain of Company G, Noble's

---

1    Another brother, John Luckey, would serve as a Wasco County Deputy Sheriff based in Prineville, Oregon during the vigilante reign of terror. (Information on the Luckey brothers is contained in a letter to the author from Eugene E. Luckey dated June 10, 1988, Burns, Oregon.)

former command.[2] This reprimand fueled the personal grudges already present in Drake's command.

In light of this, Small refused to have Lt. Noble as his staff officer at Fort Maury. However, he used a different approach when presenting his request to Capt. Drake. Small had been grand chaplain of the Marion County Sons of Temperance before the war. Although he still thought Noble a "wholesouled fellow," he was not about to have Noble with "his dissipated habits" second in command at Fort Maury.[3] Drake was not going to have an easy campaign.

As Drake's column moved out of Fort Maury, Capt. Currey—operating out of the newly constructed Fort Henderson in southeast Oregon—was making raids on the Owyhee country. Drake was expecting to meet Capt. Alfred Pleasonton—who was riding south from Fort Walla Walla—somewhere between the head of Crooked River and Silver Creek but Pleasonton had already joined forces with Currey. At this time, it was boasted in the newspapers that Drake and Currey would now make up for the mistakes and shortcomings that characterized the opening of the Shoshoni campaign.[4] Nothing could have been farther from the truth. Before the summer was over, the expedition would be an absolute failure. Much of the time, the commands were searching for each other and the blame could be placed on Gen. Alvord. Alvord's imprecise orders that they meet somewhere in Harney Valley at no specified date was at best risky and could have proved fatal. Also his stubborn insistence that the Shoshoni were operating in that area when his officers knew differently was giving Wolf Dog's troops free rein in the Ochoco. Drake would privately complain, "If I was not hampered with instructions and orders . . . I could do something with these Indians that are infesting the country. But under the present arrangement I can do nothing. Gen. Alvord has undertaken to say for himself that the Indians are in such a place and there the military must go."[5]

Drake, apprehensive that Currey would beat him to Harney Valley, was overlooking obvious signs of Shoshoni activity. On the head of Crooked River the expedition met Giles Wells trail herding 1,000 cattle from Jackson County to Fort Boise. He told Drake that they had met with little Indian trouble except for losing

2    *War of Rebellion*, Vol. L, Part II, p. 510, Gov. Gibbs statement of July 2, 1863; Alvord to Gibbs, September 12, 26; December 30, 31, 1863; January 20, February 6, 1864 in "Oregon War Crimes: Senate Executive Document" No. 70, 50th Cong., 2nd Session, Serial 2680; 51st Cong., 1st Session, pp. 190-91.

3    *Oregon Statesman*, Oct. 14, 1861; Oct. 13, 1862; H.C. Small to Gibbs, March 12, 1863 (Gibbs Collection).

4    *Portland Daily Oregonian*, July 25, 1864 reprinted from *The Dalles Mountaineer*. June 23, 1864.

5    All quotes in this chapter unless otherwise noted are from Capt. John M. Drake's Private Journal, Expedition From Fort Dalles, Oregon into the Indian Country from June 7 to July 3, 1864; and Lt. John F. Noble's Second Diary, Drake Expedition, 1st Oregon Cavalry dated June 7 through July 3, 1864.

horses until they came into the Crooked River drainage. Drake chose to ignore this intelligence placing the blame on Klamath Indians. For some reason, Drake seemed surprised that Wells had encountered Snake resistance on Crooked River, but he was convinced that the Shoshoni had "united themselves under able leadership for the purpose of plunder."

Belatedly, the Snakes' military cunning under the leadership of Has No Horse and Paulina was being recognized by both army and Indian office personnel. It comes as no surprise that Superintendent of Indian Affairs Huntington considered Paulina the Snakes' "most celebrated war chief and their most efficient leader" while Agent Meacham thought Paulina was "probably the most daring and successful leader the Snake Indians ever had."[6] It appears that Has No Horse was purposely keeping a low profile to insure that Paulina became the prime target for retaliation. Considering the American inclination to identify and destroy the ranking war chief, this was a smart military move.

It was during the push to join Currey in Harney Valley that Drake's staff officers came to the conclusion that he was a poor commander. It was their belief that Drake—a squadron captain—was incapable of handling a command and that he was showing marked favoritism to some men and outright hostility toward others.

One flare-up occurred as they were leaving Fort Maury when Drake refused to let Dumreicher take all of his personal gear into the field. Livid with rage, the doctor informed Drake that he was nothing more than a captain in the Oregon Cavalry while he was a major on the general staff. "You intend to put me on a level with these lieutenants?" Drake did. As one officer put it, "He does not seem to think officers of his command have any sense or are entitled to any respect or consideration." He would further comment that Drake's greatest fault was a "lack of experience—no regularity in anything and entirely too vacillating. Time proves a man and I am sorry—in this case—all is for the worst."

The feeling was mutual. Only two days out of Fort Dalles, Drake had this to say: "The officers of this command need a good deal of instruction for campaign life, particularly Hand and Noble." He also questioned Waymire's and McCall's ability to make a decision under fire. "What can I do with such officers, they know nothing at all about their duties and Hand I don't think wants to learn anything. Noble is willing enough but is too flighty entirely to rely upon in any contingency."

However, Drake would later change his mind about Lt. Noble. When the troops were down with measles and everyone was in a state of gloom upon receiving word of a smallpox epidemic in western Oregon, he wrote: "If it were not for Noble I do not know what we would do; buffoon though he is, our time would frequently hang heavy but for his rollicking fun. I think better of him the

---

6    *Report, Commissioner of Indian Affairs 1867*, Cong. Doc. Series 1326, p. 73; *War of Rebellion Series I*, Vol. 50, Pt.1, p. 341.

more I see him and think he will make a good officer for this kind of service, which is a good deal more than I am willing to say of some others that I have with the expedition."

Later in the campaign when they were stalled in the desert waiting for Capt. Currey, Drake would remark, "Nothing whatever to relieve the monotony of camp life except Noble's unremitting gas. I do think I would dry up entirely but for him. He always has something fresh and original—true, it is not of the most chaste and refined quality, but better than none, a good deal. The most versatile man I ever saw. I cannot help liking the fellow, though he is of no account as an officer. . . ." Drake was not so forgiving with Lt. Hand. "Of all the worthless fellows that ever I saw, he excels."

And so, this was the happy group of officers who were marching into the Ochoco to conquer Wolf Dog's guerrilla warriors.

As Drake moved toward Harney Valley, the advance guard was encountering much evidence of recent Shoshoni activity and the scouts were reporting war camps in the southern Blues. Two days out of Fort Maury, Drake and Hand attacked one of these camps and much to their regret captured a young woman with a baby strapped to her back. They would later discover that she was Funny Bug (Leli Otu) wife of the Snake warrior Black Eagle and sister-in-law to Paulina. Lt. Hand thought Funny Bug was a "perfect devil" while Drake described her as "the most vindictive piece of humanity I ever saw." But he also gave her credit for showing "a good deal of spirit and grit." She fought like a cornered wolf when the Warm Springs scouts attempted to take her child. They got much joy out of manhandling her and even Drake admitted that it "seemed cruel to take the little thing away from her forcibly" but it "had to be done."

Back in camp, Funny Bug was referred to by the officers as Hand's "Maid of the Juniper" and coveted by the enlisted men as "Madam Hum-tits." Undaunted, Funny Bug ridiculed them all. In a voice dripping with venom, she shouted, "If it takes a company of soldiers to take a woman captive how many companies will it take to capture a warrior?"

Under questioning, Funny Bug told the officers that Paulina—with all of his fighting men—was riding on Canyon City to "commit robberies, murder, anything else he can do." She also told them that Paulina had recently killed a Snake warrior, suspected of being an army spy, to prevent him from giving information to the soldiers and furthermore all Shoshoni including women and children "would fight the whites till they died." She also admitted that Paulina had his extra horses hidden near Snow Mountain [in what is now the southeast corner of the Ochoco National Forest] where the women were guarding them. Glaring at Capt. Drake, she told him if he wanted women so badly there were plenty there. "Go take them and leave me alone!" On this outburst, Drake turned Funny Bug over to the Warm Springs scouts for safe-keeping. When he later found out what they did to her, he vowed never again to take an Indian woman prisoner.

The monotony of waiting for Currey's command to arrive in Harney Valley weighed heavily on the soldiers' nerves. To stave off boredom, they gathered around campfires telling stories and singing battle hymns. Here, as everywhere, sentiment was divided. Isolated groups wearing the dust-covered blue of the 1st Oregon Cavalry sang the southern airs of "Take Me Home," "Nut Brown Maiden," "When Johnny Comes Marching Home" and they matched the vigor of their companions' "Battle Hymn of the Republic" with the stirring "Dixie." Many bellowed a "Free America" into the booming melody of "The Dying Volunteer" which had been taken from an article in *The New Orleans Times* and set to music in 1861.

Like their counterparts on the Atlantic front, the eastern Oregon troopers were deeply sentimental and sang a great deal to pass the listless days of march. Not patriotic songs but slow, sad tunes that expressed loneliness and homesickness of boys who had been uprooted and sent out to face death. Some sang "The Bonnie Blue Flag" which toasted the southern states which joined the cause to follow the "Bonnie blue flag that bears a single star." Others sang "The Girl I Left Behind Me," an old Irish tune made famous by the U.S. Cavalry. Another great favorite was "The Belle of the Mohawk Valley," a haunting ballad which like "The Girl I Left Behind Me" became the last memory of hundreds of volunteers to the loving hearts they left . . . some forever. This ballad reached its peak of popularity in the 1890s when Alice Nielson, star of the light and grand opera used it as her encore in her first public appearance on the West Coast.[7]

While Drake twiddled his thumbs on the western front, Capt. George Currey, operating out of Fort Henderson on the eastern front, was staging raids in the Owyhee country. On the same day that Drake was fighting the battle of Funny Bug, Currey surprised and killed six Shoshoni on Jordan Creek, three of whom were women. The next morning a miner reported 60 mounted and well-armed warriors on the Jordan Creek Trail 20 miles above the spot where Currey had killed the Indians. This was Has No Horse, returning from raids on the Idaho mining settlements, moving west to link up with Paulina near Canyon City. Lt. Silas Pepoon, guarding the supply wagons out of Fort Boise, was traveling on a collision course with Has No Horse's raiders. Inasmuch as their food supply was at stake, Currey moved with all units as he put it "to save our bacon." He found no sign of Shoshoni or the supply train in a 50-mile march. Four days later Capt. Currey arrived back at Fort Henderson only to find the supply wagons hadn't arrived.

He immediately dispatched his brother, Lt. Currey (post commander), with a 20-man escort to try and locate Lt. Pepoon. When another two days passed and

---

7    The hit tunes of 1864: "Rosa Lee"; "Dear Evelena"; "Listen to the Mocking Bird"; "The Lone Fish Ball"; "Those Evening Bells"; "Tramp, Tramp, Tramp the Boys are Marching"; "Sally in Our Alley"; and "Buffalo Gals." (*Heart Songs—Melodies of Days Gone By*, contributed by 25,000 people.) Drake's Journal entry of May 5, 1864, tells of the officers gathered around a campfire in front of Capt. Porter's tent telling stories and the soldiers singing battle hymns.

still no wagons had arrived, Major Rinehart took to the field out of Fort Boise to scout the country along the Owyhee north of the big bend. Rinehart found nothing to report except that there were no Shoshoni in the area nor had there been. Finally, on June 15—the same day Capt. Drake arrived on Rattlesnake Creek at what would become the site of Fort Harney—the supply train rolled into Fort Henderson. It had been stalled by Snake snipers. The next evening, Rinehart and his troopers galloped into the fort, making it the first time Currey's command had been together since leaving Fort Walla Walla in April.

Farriers and blacksmiths began repairing horses and wagons in preparation for the big push on Harney Valley. Umahowlitz, Umatilla war chief in charge of Currey's Indian scouts, did a scalp dance for the entertainment of the troops. His warriors had taken three women's scalps in a raid on the lower Owyhee River.[8] Laying over two days at Fort Henderson, Currey then marched across the Alvord Desert to the eastern base of the Steens Mountains. Traveling with him were 20 miners.

Drake's column—pushing through a June snowstorm—was meeting many wagon trains and trail herds of cattle, all reporting Shoshoni attacks. Freezing and short on supplies, Drake dug in on Silver Creek and established Camp Currey. The men, without tents, short on blankets, ropes frozen, dug holes in the ground for protection from the elements. At this point, Lt. Noble heartily wished that "Old Ben [Alvord] might enjoy the pleasure of his pet campaign." From here, Cayuse George was dispatched to Fort Dalles with reports of their progress and the fervent wish of Capt. Drake that Gen. Alvord would abandon this fruitless search of the southeastern Oregon desert.[9]

The express had barely left Camp Currey that night when the cavalry's horse herd was stampeded, and during the commotion Funny Bug (who was bound hand and foot) escaped with her baby. Kah Kup who claimed her as his private playmate was "much disgusted at losing the squaw." For some strange reason, he blamed the baby for turning her loose. It was more likely that Funny Bug was released by a Snake warrior or perhaps it was even Capt. Drake. He would later admit that had she not escaped, he intended to affect her release the next morning. Whatever had happened, Lt. Noble (in high good spirits) believed that Kah Kup would "cut his throat in a fit of jealousy when he found his betrothed gone."

Down in the Klamath region, Lt. Col. Charles Drew was having no better success at locating Shoshoni than Drake or Currey but that didn't stop him from alarming the populace to eminent danger. Drew, possessing a near fanatical hatred for Indians and an outspoken critic of the regular army, was regimental

---

8    Portland *Daily Oregonian*, July 28, 1864, letter from Currey's Expedition, Camp #49, Silvies River, dated July 8, 1864, signed "Sojer Boy."

9    *The Dalles Mountaineer*, June 23, 1864.

commander of the Oregon Cavalry.[10] Stationed at Camp Baker, Jackson County, he had received orders from Gen. Wright—commander of the Military Department of the Pacific—in March to man Fort Klamath. The strip of country lying along the Oregon-California-Nevada line between Klamath Lake and the Owyhee Mountains was now treated as a separate invasion unit, being in fact a part of the Military District of California.

It was the end of May before Drew's expedition could open a road through the snow-clogged Cascades arriving at Fort Klamath, May 28—the same day Noble took off on his night patrol and 10 days after Drake's defeat in Rabbit Valley. These reinforcements were confined to Fort Klamath for a month or as Drew would put it: "The Indians being turbulent in the vicinity of the fort, it became necessary to remain at that post until the 28th of June."[11] The reason for this date of departure becomes painfully obvious.

On June 23, a group of prospectors from Shasta Valley bound for Canyon City blundered into a Snake war party near Silver Lake, 85 miles north of Fort Klamath. Known as the Richardson Train—consisting of 15 men and their families in seven wagons—they had been pinned down for four days when Lt. Davis with a detachment of 2nd California Cavalry out of Fort Crook arrived in time to prevent a massacre. Already several men had been killed, three wounded, and seven others driven off along with 3,500 pounds of flour stored in one of the stolen wagons. A messenger was sent to Fort Klamath for an ambulance to bring in the wounded while Lt. Davis pursued the war party toward Harney Valley and a union with Drake's command. Drew would later report that the miners, still determined to get to Canyon City, traveled under his protection to Fort Henderson on the Owyhee.

When the messenger arrived at Fort Klamath with news of this latest Snake attack, the lid blew off the kettle. Rounding up a force of miners, ranchers, and frontier riff-raff, the Klamath Volunteers marched off to lay siege to some Indians—any Indians, whether associated with the Shoshoni or not. The Yanas, a peaceful people, had gathered south of the Oregon state line in northern California for their annual summer seed-gathering. The whole tribe (about 3,000) were spotted by the volunteers and in several days of heavy fighting, the Oregon Militia killed all but 50 of the Yanas. Yet another Indian tribe was headed for extinction.[12]

During the Yana fracas, Drake marched into Harney Valley. On the Silvies River he was joined by Jacob Evans who was trail herding 500 head of cattle and escorting a wagon train to Bannack, Idaho. Crossing the high desert, Evans had

---

10    For more on Lt. Col. Drew's hatred of the Indians and his contempt for regular army personnel see Drew, "An Account of the Origin and Early Prosecution of the Indian War in Oregon," *Senate Misc. Doc., No. 59, 36th Congress, 1st Session.*

11    Drew, "Official Report of the Owyhee Reconnaissance," published by the *Jacksonville Sentinel,* (Jacksonville, Oregon) in 1865 as a 32 page pamphlet. The original publication appeared in the newspaper from January 28 to March 11, 1865.

12    Stoutenburgh, *The American Indian,* p. 454.

lost most of his herd to Snake raiders. He also reported that he met a detachment of 2nd California Cavalry on the head of Crooked River looking for a wagon train that was under Shoshoni attack. Drake—obeying Special Order No. 24 like it was engraved in stone—offered no assistance but instead began a thorough exploration of Harney Basin.

It now became obvious that Capt. John Drake was out to prove a point: "I am convinced that there are no Indians in the vicinity. From appearances, I am deposed to think this valley is not a haunt of their's. Maybe 20-30 families winter here but they do not live here during the summer. I have found the country over and around Harney Valley, not more than 1/10 of which is fit for any useful purpose whatsoever, uninhabited." The woman prisoner at Fort Maury had—along with Gen. Alvord—given him false information when they both insisted that Wolf Dog was operating out of Harney Valley and Drake would make certain that this misinformation became public knowledge.[13]

Finding neither Shoshoni nor Capt. Currey in Harney Valley, Drake headed into the Steen's Mountains. He was now being hampered by the lack of reliable scouts. "I wish," Drake would lament, "I had about two officers who could do something in the way of scouting. I have not got an officer that is worth a curse for such service." Lt. Noble had drawn the same conclusion about the enlisted men.

On the Malheur River, the Warm Springs scouts were certain they were riding into an ambush so Drake ordered all the pistols in the command fired off, presumably to frighten the Shoshoni although none were seen. As one officer glumly noted, "It was rather a strange move as not a shot was left in the command should there have been an Indian attack." Quite likely Drake suspected his jittery scouts were imagining things and hoped to instill some confidence so the expedition could continue on. Moving again into the desert toward the big bend in the Owyhee River, they stumbled onto a desert spring and found a fresh human skull believed to be that of a white man.

Some 50 miles to the south, Currey—guided by the old mountain man, Joseph Gale, who had been in the region 25 years before—arrived at the eastern base of the Steens and found Waymire's old camp established in March while pursuing Broken Knife. Located in a valley some 50 miles long and from two to five miles wide running north and south along the base of the Steens, Currey decided Waymire's camp was ideal for a permanent army base. Currey was now some 150 miles southwest of Fort Boise. At the northern end of the valley, Has No Horse had attacked Capt. Smith's 1st U.S. Dragoons in 1860 driving them back to Harney Lake. This was also the land of mirages and Currey blamed this phenomenon for Waymire's chasing geese earlier in the campaign.

On June 21 as Currey was hastily digging rifle pits on the eastern face of the Steens and dignifying the star-shaped breastworks as Fort Alvord; and while Drake

---

13    Portland *Daily Oregonian*, July 27, 1864, letter from Capt. Drake, Camp #35, July 2, 1864.

marched across the northern end of the valley to Skull Spring; Capt. Small had Watson's body exhumed and placed in a metallic coffin sent to Fort Maury by citizens of The Dalles.[14] The intent was to ship the body by wagon to The Dalles but Shoshoni activity around the isolated outpost put a stop to that venture. Knowing wagons couldn't get through to The Dalles, Small had Watson's body escorted by heavy guard over the military road through Little Summit Prairie to Camp Rock Creek—Capt. Caldwell's depot on The Dalles-Canyon City road—where the body was buried.[15]

It was becoming apparent to both commands that the greatest Indian threat lay in the southern Blue Mountains along The Dalles-Canyon City and Yreka trails. Drake had the added worry of getting supply wagons into Fort Maury. Should the wagons come under attack, the garrison would be placed in a critical position as they were entirely without rations. Scout Jim Luckey had gotten a message through to Drake alerting him to the dangerous situation that Small was now in. In his communiqué to Capt. Drake, Capt. Small reported that he was sending out scouts daily and they never failed to report Shoshoni activity in the locality of the fort. In a 24-hour period covering June 21-22, the Warm Springs scouts saw numerous war parties, some as high as 40 in number, crossing Crooked River not 10 miles from the fort. These hostiles were riding in the general direction of Big Summit Prairie. Leaving barely enough men to guard the depot—most of whom were the sick and the wounded—Small had taken to the field.[16]

Ironically, on June 22 as Small was leaving Fort Maury, Congress made a $20,000 appropriation to cover the cost of a treaty with the Shoshoni of southeastern Oregon.

Back in Alvord Valley, Drake found a note from Currey on June 26 stating that he had passed through four days earlier . . . on June 22, 1864. Disgusted with having missed him, Drake's scouts found where Currey had headed north toward Harney Lake. The two commands had missed each other by six miles. Following Currey's trail, Drake found where he had camped and a vast amount of newspapers. The news from the East was most interesting. "Old Abe was renominated for President with Andy Johnson for Vice President." According to Drake, the ticket "suits me exactly. It will be elected by a large majority not withstanding John C. Fremont's nomination by the crew who called themselves radicals: sore-heads would be a better name."

Scouts were dispatched to intercept Currey, and Drake again marched toward Harney Lake. On July 1, the two commands finally met on Silvies River—72 days

---

14    Portland *Daily Oregonian*, July 4, 1864, letter from Camp Maury dated June 21, 1864, signed Co. G 1st Oregon Cavalry.

15    Small's order to move Lt. Watson's body to Camp Rock Creek, dated Camp Maury June 21, 1864 appears in the Portland *Daily Oregonian*, July 9, 1864.

16    The Portland *Weekly Oregonian*, Vol. XIV, No. 34, July 9, 1864, p. 1, col. 3.

from the time they had separated at Fort Dalles. In this interval, Currey had covered over 700 miles and Drake nearly 600 miles searching for each other without having accomplished anything. On the Silvies River, they were joined by Capt. Alfred Pleasonton commanding a detachment of the Second Battalion Oregon Cavalry who, on Currey's orders, had been scouting the Trout Creek Mountains.

Capt. Barry, 2nd Washington Infantry, had been left in charge of Fort Alvord with 96 pack mules, all the disabled cavalry horses and enough supplies to last for a month so Currey decided to stay with Drake and stage an invasion of the southern Blues. The two commands would travel together but not consolidate their forces.[17] Before starting, the captains planned to lay over at Camp Rattlesnake (site of Fort Harney) to celebrate the 4th of July but since there was no liquor in either camp they decided to move out immediately, as scouts were reporting much Indian activity to the west.

And so, on July 2, 1864, the pride of the Oregon Cavalry marched on the southern Blues—Wolf Dog's stronghold of defense.

---

17    The Portland *Daily Oregonian*, July 28, 1864, letter from Currey's Expedition; Bancroft, *History of Oregon*, Vol. 2, p. 497; Portland *Daily Oregonian*, July 27, 1864, letter from Drake dated July 2, 1864 to AAA Gen. Fort Vancouver, Washington Territory.

# CHAPTER 115

# BLOOD MOON
## (THE AMERICANS CALLED IT JULY)

> *General Alvord told him [Capt. Caldwell] a plain, palpable
> falsehood to the effect that I was empowered to act according
> to my own judgment in all things. The damnedest lie the old
> hoary-headed scoundrel ever told in his life.*
>
> **Captain John M. Drake**
> Camp Gibbs, July 30, 1964

Gen. Alvord was stubbornly sticking to his original plan for Drake and Currey to remain in Harney Valley although it was common knowledge that Wolf Dog's forces were raising havoc along The Dalles-Canyon City road and especially around Canyon City. On June 27—three days before Drake and Currey joined forces 30 miles north of Harney Lake—Alvord reported to department headquarters in San Francisco that he was "averse to calling Drake and Currey in and breaking up their plan on account of these attacks in the rear."[1] In short he was going to keep them away from any action. By July 12, however, complaints from irate businessmen about the safety of The Dalles-Canyon City supply route reached a point which forced Alvord to approve Currey's plan to invade what he called the northern Ochoco.[2] Alvord was unaware that Currey, without prior approval, began his campaign to "scour out the Blue Mountains west of Canyon City" on July 3.[3]

One reason Currey was in a rush to get into action was to counteract Lt. Olney's "90 day wonders." The three-month volunteers who had been mustered into service in March to backup Capt. Caldwell on the Canyon City front were just entering the field and Currey wanted to head off their operation before they all got

---

1   Alvord to R.C. Drumn, June 27, 1864, *War of Rebellion, Vol. L*, pt. II, pp. 879-80 and 906. It should be remembered that it was not *their* (Drake's or Currey's) plan to remain in Harney Valley but Alvord's direct order to do so.

2   By 1864, the Shoshoni Ochoco which stretched from the Deschutes River in central Oregon to the Snake River had, in the minds of the Americans, been reduced in size to that area of eastern Oregon lying west of Canyon City.

3   All direct quotes in this chapter, unless otherwise noted, are taken from Capt. Drake's private journal and Lt. Noble's third notebook diary entries dated from July 1, 1864 to July 31, 1864.

killed. Actually, Olney's volunteers had enlisted for four months or until the cavalry should be able to relieve them of duty, whichever came first. In an effort to encourage enlistment, the citizens of The Dalles whose businesses were hurt offered to make up a bounty to pay anyone who joined. Even so, only 40 men signed on and this company never left The Dalles until July 19.[4]

When Drake and Currey decided to disobey orders and invade Wolf Dog's inner line of defense, Drake sent an express to Fort Maury—which arrived at one o'clock the morning of July 1—advising Capt. Small of their plan. Drake's column would march northward toward Canyon City on a course that would bring them to Fort Maury in three weeks.[5] The whole expedition under the command of Capt. Currey—numbering over 500 cavalrymen plus Indian scouts and civilian employees—began their push on the Ochoco in a heavy rain shower with many of the troops suffering from malaria, including Lt. Hand and his son, Pvt. Charles Hand. Lt. Hand would become so sick that they would transport him through the Ochoco by horse litter. There was much suffering from cold weather as the temperature plunged forming ice on the camp gear. By July 5, the temperature inside the officers' tents stood at 20 degrees and outside at 16 degrees. The enlisted men had no tents. It would be mid-July before Drake noted that "for the first time during the summer's campaign we had dusty roads today." Prior to that the soldiers had slogged through mud, rain and snow.

In this bleak weather, Currey ordered Lt. Waymire with 30 troops to make a reconnaissance to the northern Blues. With the old frontiersman Joe Gale as guide, Waymire pushed through Bear Valley—so named because they killed a 300-pound cinnamon bear while crossing the valley—on a course which took him into the Strawberry Range where he discovered a well-used Indian trail which Gale said was the main hunting route from the Umatilla and Walla Walla rivers into the Ochoco range. On July 7, Waymire moved to the summit and discovered Strawberry Lake, but no hostiles.[6] From Strawberry Lake, he proceeded north as far as Dixie Pass before returning to the John Day Basin.

Some 180 miles southwest of Waymire's line of March, Lt. Col. Drew was staging an all-out assault in the region which Gen. Alvord believed was harboring every hostile Indian in the western United States. Making slow progress, Drew was reporting little contact with the enemy as he wandered back and forth between Warner Valley and the Black Rock Desert. During this march, he found Warner (Hart) Mountain to be unequaled for military defense and as such was held by the Snakes. The summit was located on a general elevation with an area covering more

---

4    Bancroft, *History of Oregon*, Vol. II, pp. 496-97.

5    *Daily Oregonian*, July 12, 1864, letter from Camp Maury dated July 6, 1864 signed "a volunteer."

6    *Daily Oregonian*, August 4, 1864, letter from Lt. Waymire, commanding The Dalles Expedition, Camp #38, dated July 8, 1864.

than 100 square miles. Dotted with "miniature mountains, grassy valleys, lakes and streams of pure water, groves of aspen, willows and mountain mahogany and gardens of service berries made it a complete haven of refuge where its possessors could repel any foe."[7] Unknowingly, Drew had found Has No Horse's southern base of operations.

While admiring the flora on Warner Mountain, Drew's column narrowly missed attack by Paulina. Drew, a resourceful man, had cleverly chained a couple of mountain howitzers fore and aft in a covered wagon to form his own field artillery unit which traveled a short distance away from the main expedition. He was certain this lethal machine disguised as a lonely emigrant wagon would tempt any red-blooded Shoshoni into an attack on a seemingly harmless victim. Wrong! Paulina—at a treaty council held at Fort Klamath—would accurately describe Drew's line of march, the method of encamping, the order of picketing and the placement of guards with all the details of an advance through enemy territory showing that nothing escaped his observation and what was worth copying he could easily duplicate.

On the push from Fort Klamath to the Pueblo Mountains, Drew's reports contain few incidents of a military character in relation to the Shoshoni. In fact, according to the historian Bancroft, ". . . these appear to have been purposely left out."[8] Although he avoided any and all skirmishes with the Indians, Drew deemed it prudent to come up with this profound observation which has been a curse to the Shoshoni ever since: "It is virtuous to seize and ravish the women of the other tribes with whom they are at war—often among themselves—and to retain or sell them and their children as slaves." This may have been an apt description of Drew's Klamath scouts but held little application to the Shoshoni dog soldiers. Lt. Col. Drew, the Indian hater, liked to spit verbal venom but had no stomach for open warfare with the "brutes."

While the regimental commander took his troops on a scenic tour of the Oregon and Nevada deserts; and while Lt. Waymire scouted the backbone of the northern Blues; Lt. James Currey, with 20 cavalrymen, rode into Canyon City and found it in a state of siege. Shortly before their arrival, Has No Horse had attacked a corral within sight of town, killed two men and stole 40 horses. A group of townspeople took pursuit with disastrous results. Eight of the party were killed and six wounded.[9] Another raiding party under the leadership of the Big Lodge dog soldier Woman Helper—son-in-law of Has No Horse—had made a descent on Bridge Creek west of Alkali Flat and ran off all of the stage-station livestock. At the same time, Yellow Jacket and Elk Calf had virtually stopped all traffic on The Dalles-Canyon City road. It was the belief of the Canyon City citizens that all the

---

7    Drew, *Official Report of the Owyhee Reconnaissance 1864.*

8    Bancroft, *History of Oregon*, Vol. II. p. 503, footnote 27.

9    Noble's diary entry for Thursday, July 7, 1864, Camp #38, Bear Valley.

Snake war-tribes were concealed in the Ochoco mountains west of town. Their observations were more correct than the desk soldiers would like to believe.

Charged with keeping The Dalles-Canyon City road open for safe travel, Capt. Caldwell—whose C Troop was beat into the ground—was tempted to lead a cavalry raid on Drake and Currey. Unaware of Gen. Alvord's instructions, he believed they were purposely staying away from a fight with the Snakes and the residents of Canyon City were on the side of Capt. Caldwell.

Offsetting this depressing situation, Lt. Currey would bring news from the Atlantic front which to the majority of Canyon City's populace was most elating. At the battle of Cold Harbor, 10 miles northeast of Richmond, Gen. Grant—suffering 7,000 casualties—had been outflanked by Lee and was forced to retreat to Chancellorville. On the eastern Oregon frontier, the heavy betting was that Lee would be in Pennsylvania within 10 days.

To keep western Oregonians abreast of the times, expressmen were dispatched to the Willamette Valley with news from the Snake front. Caldwell's 26-year-old scout, John Luckey—brother to Jim and Warren—headed for Eugene where on July 21, 1864, he married Samantha (Ella S.) Miller, sister to Joaquin. Tired of Indian fighting, he took a job as county clerk for Lane County and would remain at Eugene City until 1866 when he joined Gen. Crook's column serving once again as an army scout.[10]

The Snakes, aware of what was going on, began a new diversion. Paulina and Wolf Dog headed west to make life at the stage stations a little more zestful. Howard Maupin—a native of Kentucky—and his 22-year-old wife, Nancy McCullum, had come to Antelope Station in 1863. Almost immediately, Paulina stole 22 head of company horses—but more pranks were in store. In late July 1864, within sight of Antelope Stage Station, Paulina and Wolf Dog attacked the Tower & Company freight train, killing two guards and taking 350 head of cattle which Paulina drove to Warner Mountain. Entrenched on Warner Mountain, Paulina's troops feasted on beef and kept watch on Drew's expedition for most of August.[11] Wolf Dog continued to harass traffic on The Dalles-Canyon City trail.

Has No Horse and Big Man with 100 warriors rode east where they were joined by Laughing Hawk with another 100 warriors. Laughing Hawk, operating out of the Raft River country, had been stalling traffic on the Salt Lake-Boise City road. Shortly after midnight July 9, Has No Horse raided the Jordan ranch, killing one man and capturing 40 horses. At daylight, Mike Jordan—discoverer of the richest gold strike in the Owyhee country—with 13 volunteers took to the trail. The next day, reinforced by eight miners from Ruby City, Jordan caught up with

---

10    Luckey family records No. 12133, Lane County Oregon.

11    Drew, Official Report: 14, 24.

Has No Horse in a rocky canyon. In five minutes of furious gunfire, Jordan was shot through the heart and two others critically wounded. The fight was over.[12]

When word of this attack reached Fort Boise, Col. Maury dispatched Lt. Charles Hobart with 20 men to pursue and chastise Has No Horse. Fortunately for Lt. Hobart, he never caught up with the Shoshoni warriors who true to form, had broken up into groups of two or three men and were again headed for the Ochoco. Hobart was expecting to make contact with Currey's force but it would be September before he would receive any help from Capt. Currey.

On receiving intelligence of this latest Snake raid which reached Fort Gibbs on July 31, Capt. Drake would sarcastically comment: "Gen. Alvord could not have botched matters worse if he aimed at it direct." Drake's only comforting thought was that out of this most recent farce "Currey may come in for his share of blame on account of this Jordan Creek matter." As for Lt. Col. Drew, who should have been in the area, no one but Paulina knew for certain where he was.

Lt. Jim Currey's report from Canyon City that the army was now definitely in hostile territory jarred the command into a nervous state of readiness. Aside from a few officers and a handful of enlisted men, the troops were untried in combat. The order was hastily given to muster for target practice. Each man was issued 40 rounds of rifle or carbine ammunition and 20 rounds of pistol ammunition and the fun began. Lt. Noble would caustically remark that "from 24 revolvers of Co. G, 84 balls (out of a possible 480) struck a two-foot-square target at 40 yards." Not exactly sharpshooting. However, Noble was quite elated when on the third time the pistols were fired, only two barrels misfired. Heading back towards Crooked River a mutiny broke out among the civilian packers when Capt. Porter ordered one of them to walk when he refused to accept his share of the cooking duties. Porter didn't fool around. He ordered Lt. Noble to arrest all of the packers and put them on foot under armed guards. He then marched them 17 miles over some of the roughest country in central Oregon from Canyon Creek to the South Fork of the John Day River. After that, the packers were quite willing to do their share of KP duty in the hope they could once more become mounted on horseback.

Moving into Beaver Creek, Drake and Currey discovered the Yreka Trail was cut off to Canyon City. The outline of the road was very dim and, with the exception of a herd of cattle, there appeared to have been no travel on it this year. Currey dug in at what would become Fort Dahlgren and patrols were dispatched in all directions. Capt. Porter, Lt. Hand and Sgt. Kelly with nine cavalrymen, three packers, 40 pack mules loaded with supplies including the command tent and poles, all the empty ammunition boxes, the beef cattle and 10 days' rations rode west to reinforce Capt. Small's starving troopers at Fort Maury. Drake—remaining with Currey—split his command, sending Lts. Noble, McCall, Bowen and Mackey with 120 troopers, 10 civilian packers and 40 Indian scouts south toward Snow

12    *The Dalles Mountaineer*, July 13, 1864, correspondent from Ruby City, Idaho.

Mountain. With the uniting of the two commands, there were now Wasco, Walla Walla, Umatilla and Nez Perce scouts aiding the army in its fight against the Shoshoni while Klamaths were riding with Drew's column.

Lt. Noble, in command of the southern probe, would make first contact with the hostiles. On the head of Crooked River in the vicinity of Ibex Butte Noble's scouts reported signal fires to the north. He sent them to check it out and moved the rest of the detachment to the Yreka Trail crossing of Grindstone Creek. From there, he advanced up Grindstone Creek and camped on Twelvemile Table. Because of the size of his command, Noble set up two camps. Here, on high ground, he awaited a report from the scouts. It was July 11, 1864.

At midnight a shot rang out and one of the Nez Perce scouts riding fast, galloped into Noble's camp soon followed by several more. They reported that near sunset on the main branch of Crooked River along the Yreka Trail, they found Shoshoni tracks and decided to return to camp and notify Noble as to what they had discovered. Almost at the same moment, they were attacked by 25 Snake warriors, many of whom were mounted on large, sure-footed mules. Their leader, identified by the Umatilla scouts from the brass key and tin plate he wore in his hair was Lame Dog—one of the more dangerous Snake war chiefs.[13] A half-breed Nez Perce-Snake and brother-in-law to Black Eagle, he had given much trouble to the Cayuse and Wascos during the 1850s. According to the Umatillas, he was an exceptionally desperate man. The Warm Springs scouts who had dealt Funny Bug misery little more than a month before would become increasingly nervous. Lame Dog was Funny Bug's big brother!

Lame Dog, operating out of Wolf Dog's camp—which Noble had missed by less than two miles on his push to Twelvemile Table—had been paralleling Capt. Porter's line of march, waiting for him to get sufficiently far from the main command to attack when the scouts came blundering in. Believing them to be reinforcements for Porter's detachment, Lame Dog attacked the scouts. Noble was certain that the arrival of the army scouts "was all that saved Capt. Porter and party" from being annihilated. In the running fight back to Noble's camp, one of the Nez Perce scouts was shot in the thigh and left behind. Another had his horse shot out from under him and took off into the brush along Grindstone Creek. Lame Dog paid little attention to them, continuing the pursuit almost into the soldiers' camp.

Now back to the single shot that shattered the silence as the winded army scouts burst into camp. In a volunteer's typical disregard for military procedure, Lt. Bowen had slipped out of camp for some night hunting. He claimed he didn't realize that there might be hostile Indians close by. Had Lt. Bowen not fired his rifle, Lame Dog would not have seen the enemy camp until it was too late for him and his warriors to escape being shot down. Warned that there were many soldiers

---

13     Noble's third notebook diary entry for Tuesday, July 12, 1864. The Umatilla scouts would call Lame Dog by his Shoshoni name, She-apchis.

in the area, he retreated into the nearby mountains. Noble would comment that "this is truly unfortunate" as he believed the cavalry could have dealt the Shoshoni "a telling blow."

At daybreak July 13, couriers were dispatched to alert the main command of this new development. Currey immediately dispatched a cavalry unit toward Hampton Butte. Their commanding officer would claim that they had "forced Paulina into the desert." Six days later an expressman from Fort Alvord barely escaped death in the Steens Mountains—again blaming the attack on Paulina.[14] Since Paulina was holed-up on Warner Mountain keeping an eye on Drew's column, it seems more likely that Bad Face—whose main hideout was the Steens Mountains—had entered the fray.

Meantime Noble—leaving Lt. McCall in command of both camps—took out after Lame Dog and also to search for the missing scouts. Fortunately for the scout whose horse had been shot, the troopers were close enough on Lame Dog's trail that he was found in good shape. The other was not so lucky. Twelve miles from camp, they found his body dangling head down from the limb of a juniper. It appeared from the many knife wounds in his body that there must have been a hand-to-hand fight. Besides a broken arm, he had been shot in the leg, the heart and the head. Although his body was mangled almost beyond recognition, he had not been scalped which indicated that the Nez Perce army scout had fought bravely.[15]

Continuing on, Noble found Lame Dog's camp on Little Mowich Mountain. The Shoshoni had burned everything which they could not take with them including their lodges and other vital equipment.[16] Here, the tracks split and Noble with the main force headed north while Lt. Mackey with eight Umatilla scouts veered south. Mackey caught up with a small encampment at Doe Springs east of what is now known as Mackey Butte. It would be his final engagement. Mackey and six of his scouts were killed.

Pushing hard on Lame Dog's trail, Noble stumbled upon Wolf Dog's main encampment in what is now named The-Hole-In-The-Ground just west of Izee. He would describe it: "The place was a perfect hole. . . . Had the command have gotten there not one could have escaped." Following this discovery and with night fast approaching, Noble with 40 Warm Springs scouts reported to Capt. Currey, now dug in on Beaver Creek.

Noble's own commander, Capt. Drake, had split his force into fast riding patrols—one of which was Lt. Noble's—and it was these patrols which thus far had made contact with the Snakes. Capt. Currey on the other hand had kept his

---

14    *War of Rebellion*, Vol. L, Pt. I, pp. 333, 339.

15    Noble's diary entry for Wednesday, July 13, 1864, Camp #41, Twelvemile Creek.

16    *Daily Oregonian*, July 29, 1864, letter from Camp Maury dated July 20, 1864, signed: Hyus Cultus.

command intact and they had been sitting on Beaver Creek for a week doing nothing but constructing a log stockade which soon would become Fort Dahlgren. Upon receipt of Noble's intelligence, the two commanders were at odds on how to attack Wolf Dog's camp. There was no need for concern. Aware that his camp had been discovered, Wolf Dog lost little time in evacuating The-Hole-In-The-Ground. Although impregnable, The Hole could also prove to be a death trap for the Shoshoni. Enemy forces couldn't attack without facing terrible losses but they could easily seal off all avenues of escape and in time starve the Shoshoni into surrender. Wolf Dog was too shrewd of a strategist to let that happen—especially when Has No Horse and Paulina, with two-thirds of the fighting force, were carrying on a campaign far to the south.

When scouts reported that the Snakes were on the move, the two army commanders were again at loggerheads. Drake believed Currey moved too slowly to be effective and he was right. It was Currey's plan to take the whole command numbering over 400 men, complete with mess wagons, supply wagons, ambulances and pack train to pursue Wolf Dog at the rate of . . . two miles an hour! Drake wanted to take 30 men with 10 days' rations and run them down. Without giving any reason, Currey denied permission. And so, with the whole command in tow, Currey began pursuit on the morning of July 15, two and a half days after Noble's discovery of The-Hole-In-The-Ground.

The fleeing Snakes led the cavalry over an almost impassable country to the south fork of the John Day River. Crossing Hardscrabble Ridge, Wind Creek Canyon and Elbow Gulch, they circled Wolf Mountain and crossed the river at the mouth of Black Canyon, described by one of the troopers as "the bottom of an awful chasm over 3,000 feet in depth." Into this canyon the Indians had descended with their horse herd and all their earthly belongings and into it followed the Long Knives with the trail getting ever fresher. The alert Wolf Dog—a skilled antagonist—had gone up Aldrich Gulch on the opposite side of the river by an easy ascent. While the front halted for the remainder of the column to complete the descent of Black Canyon, the Snakes suddenly appeared on the bluff almost directly overhead and began firing. Many of the cavalrymen panicked and the officers had much difficulty in forming them into skirmish lines. During the initial confusion, Major Rinehart became the first casualty when he was thrown from his horse and had to be transported by horse litter to Fort Maury where he spent nearly three weeks in recovery.

Currey then sent Capt. Pleasonton with 30 men from Co. A back to secure the rear of the column which was still struggling down Black Canyon and under attack. Drake with 30 men from Co. D was ordered forward "to seize" the bluff opposite of the Indians and hold it "at all hazards." Under Drake's covering fire, Currey—with 50 more troopers—began moving by a circuitous route to reinforce him at the top of the bluff. Firing at a distance of 1,000 yards, neither side suffered any casualties but Wolf Dog, having lost his advantage yet having won his objective of gaining time for the women, children and horse herd to escape, was again on the run.[17]

The Black Canyon clash lasted nearly an hour with no one other than Major Rinehart getting hurt. One horse was slightly wounded and the soldiers thought they had hit one Indian. This was due to the great range and angle of trajectory. The Snakes, being above were out of range of the cavalry rifles, but because they were firing straight down, the Indians overshot their targets.

Sending Drake back to Fort Dahlgren, Currey continued the chase still encumbered by wagons and pack animals. It was a futile effort. Wolf Dog led him on a tortuous route which again circled Wolf Mountain as he crossed and recrossed the south fork of the John Day River. Capt. Currey who was now thoroughly disgusted with this game of hide and seek sent an express to Col. Maury at Fort Boise: "This day's chase should prove the impossibility of doing any good by pursuing these marauders when they once know that you are upon their trail for they prefer running to fighting. They can only be punished by catching them unawares and that can only be done by rarest chance." The field officers of the First Oregon Cavalry were beginning to realize that Shoshoni military tactics didn't coincide with the army's accepted rules of warfare.

While Currey stalked shadows, Drake explored the colorful hills above Beaver Creek in Paulina Valley and discovered acres of prehistoric relics. John Drake, a well-educated man, suspected he had found something of importance so he collected a few fossil specimens and sent them to Dr. Thomas Condon, pastor of the Congregational Church in The Dalles. Condon, an amateur geologist, immediately sought and received permission from Gen. Alvord to accompany Drake on Indian patrol. Chasing Shoshoni through the John Day country, Drake showed Dr. Condon more fossilized mammal bones which, incidentally, the good reverend lost no time in shipping off to Europe. He then took credit for discovery of the John Day fossil beds, depriving Drake of even this little recognition.[18] Dr. Condon went on to become Oregon's foremost geologist and paleontologist while Drake, as usual, received nothing but criticism.

Currey arrived back in Beaver Valley in a grouchy mood and put a stop to Drake's fossil expedition. Having climbed in and out of Black Canyon for the third time, he was firmly convinced that the cavalry pursued the Snakes with about the same success as the dog pursues the timber wolf. In desperation, Currey again split the invasion force with Drake and his command returning to Fort Maury. Capt. Caldwell with 50 regulars and Olney's four-month volunteers would return to the

---

17    Bancroft, *History of Oregon*, Vol. II, pp. 497-98.

18    Located in the John Day Valley, the John Day fossil beds—now a historical monument—are the second largest paleontological repository in the world. Fossils from all of the geologic ages have been found there, and the geologic structure of the earth from its remote beginnings have been revealed.

John Day Valley and establish an outpost at the mouth of the South Fork on orders to keep The Dalles-Canyon City road open to traffic. Currey himself with the remainder of the troops would work the headwaters of the John Day, Malheur and Crooked rivers. . . an ambitious undertaking.

Forty-two days from the time he had left Fort Maury, and over 600 miles of hard riding, Capt. Drake arrived back on July 18 to find all the grass eaten out around the outpost. Because of this and the difficulty of defending it from Snake attack, he decided to change location. He chose an open meadow on Drake Creek north of the timber line where he had a clear view of Crooked River Basin. Within two days this outpost, located six miles west of Fort Maury, was under construction. Named Fort Gibbs, in honor of the governor, it too would be of short duration.

Two days after Drake arrived back at Fort Maury, he again received marching orders. A courier arrived with instructions to make a drive to the west. In May, Gen. Alvord had issued orders to make a raid on "Sheep Rock." At the time, Drake thought that Alvord's mind was no longer vigorous. Lt. Noble had been given this task and although there are presently two landmarks in the vicinity of Fort Maury named Sheep Rock, Noble never knew where he was supposed to go. In his diary, Noble would note that "no one knows where Sheep Rock is or what it looks like." Now, Currey's orders were to go to "Sheep Rock and engage the Snakes." Since none of his officers or scouts were acquainted with such a spot, Drake decided to take the mission to avoid further criticism but he readily admitted "Sheep Rock was a rather mythological locality and could not be identified by me if seen." After a nine day scout that proved to be another goose-chase, Drake ruefully wrote, "I do not know whether I ever reached there or not."

This patrol which took Drake to the eastern base of the Cascades was over some of the most desolate country in central Oregon: a search for Snake war-parties which covered the Maury Mountains to Little Bear Creek and then west to Big Bear Creek. The cavalry then probed Bear Creek to Crooked River following the river westward to the mouth of Rocky Canyon where they climbed up onto the northern end of the "Great American Desert" southeast of Powell Buttes. Suffering from heat and thirst, the column arrived at the Deschutes River in the middle of the night and were unable to descend the jagged bluffs to obtain water. The next morning, they rode upriver three miles to the present site of Bend, crossed the river and proceeded some 20 miles downstream following Fremont's old track to the McKenzie Trail, crossing the river at what is now Lower Bridge.

On this sortie the cavalrymen discovered that large cattle herds were being moved north from California to the Canyon City road. This indicated two things. One, that Lt. Col. Drew apparently had the area around Klamath Lake secure for travel; and two, that Wolf Dog was not operating this far west. To make certain, Drake pushed north to the mouth of Squaw Creek before retracing his tracks to the McKenzie Trail where he again crossed the Deschutes at Steamboat Rock. He purposely stayed clear of the lower Crooked River Valley because Lt. Waymire was searching that area. By now, the cavalry horses were nearly done in. "Gaunt flanks and wild staring, protruding eyeballs greeted us on every side."

Moving back onto the desert, Drake again rode southeast toward Powell Buttes, passing the present site of Redmond. Searching for water, the scouts discovered Tracy Spring on the east slope of Powell Buttes and here, they also discovered where a small party of Snakes had been hunting in the pine timber near the summit of the buttes. From this vantage point, the Snakes had been able to watch Drake's column for their entire march from Bear Creek to the Deschutes River and return. Since their presence was known, Drake knew it was wasted effort to continue the search. He dispatched Lt. Noble with five troopers to alert Lt. Waymire while he and the main patrol returned to Bear Creek in a spectacular lightning storm. This electric storm was so violent that from Crooked River rim, the Maury Mountains were seen as "the mountains afire." Riding through smoke and flame, Drake arrived at Fort Gibbs on July 30, 1864.[19]

Drake would describe his push to the Deschutes River as "the hardest scout I have ever had on the plains." Noble, who thought it the worst country he had traversed in 14 years of Indian fighting was more blunt. "I was satisfied that we had no business being here." During Drake's absence, Capt. Small—on another gamble—rode into the headwaters of the unexplored Ochoco River and made a startling discovery. Here in the lush valleys and high mountain meadows of the upper Ochoco—no more than 30 miles north of Fort Gibbs—he found hundreds of winter campsites. . . the actual homes of the Snake war tribes.[20]

Before Drake could digest this latest intelligence, Capt. Currey rode into Fort Gibbs the afternoon of July 30 with more discouraging news. On his march to the east, he had found evidence of much hostile activity. On Buck Creek near the head of Crooked River one of his patrols found a wrecked wagon, all the livestock missing and it was believed that the passengers had been killed. Another patrol reported 250 head of cattle stolen by the Indians near Hampton Butte. On July 28, Currey returned to Caldwell's outpost on the John Day River where he met Lt. Olney and "his company of mongrels." The day previous, Capt. Caldwell had found four dead prospectors staked out on Mountain Creek some five miles southeast of the present town of Mitchell. Fearing more depredations on The Dalles-Canyon City road, Currey turned west and charged into the Cherry Creek hills meeting no resistance. In fact, he never saw an Indian on the entire ride.

Now back at Fort Gibbs, Currey and Drake—on the evening of July 30—were wondering what to do next when an express from Fort Dalles arrived at 10:00 p.m. The express rider had made a round trip from the now abandoned Fort Maury to Fort Dalles and back to Fort Gibbs in eight days. . . "the quickest trip ever made"

---

19    *War of Rebellion*, Vol. L, Pt. 1, pp. 332-33.
20    *The Weekly Oregonian*, Saturday, July 30, 1864, letter from Camp Maury, dated July 30, 1864 signed: Hyus Cultus.

between the two army posts. He was packing the news of Has No Horse's raid in Jordan Valley and orders for Capt. Currey to march on the Owyhee country.

Waymire, who returned to Fort Gibbs the following day, had found more evidence of hostile acts. About the time he was intercepted by Lt. Noble, a sobering discovery was made. In a narrow draw some 10 miles west of the Ochoco River, they found evidence of a terrible massacre. Although the cavalry officers believed this tragedy to have happened 15 to 20 years in the past, it confirmed that the Shoshoni had a history of hostile acts against the whites. What they had found was the remains of the 1845 attack on a segment of the "Lost Emigrant Train." Because of the gruesome appearance of the area, Waymire would refer to it as Skull Hollow. Ironically, both officers had strong ties to the fragmented wagon train of 1845.[21]

It was now midday, July 29, 1864. That afternoon, while making a search of the lower Ochoco Valley, Waymire came upon a recent scene of total destruction. In a small sage-covered basin south of the union of Ochoco and Crooked rivers, surrounded on three sides by the sheer bluffs of Rimrock Mesa and Viewpoint, lay the wreckage of three wagons and the twisted bodies of 10 men, women and children. Waymire buried the luckless emigrants in a unmarked grave at the attack site.[22]

When Lts. Noble and Waymire arrived back at Fort Gibbs on July 31, they found things in a mess. Capt. Porter was almost blinded testing quartz for gold when a bottle of concentrated ammonia blew up in his face. Lt. Hand was still delirious with fever and causing "some little fuss." In all of this misfortune, Lt. Noble—whose thoughts had been far removed from Indian clashes—would receive some welcome news. Earlier in the month, his wife in a difficult childbirth had presented him with a daughter, but she remained in critical condition. The July 30 express from Fort Dalles which bore ill-tidings for Capt. Currey would ease Lt. Noble's anxiety. "Was greatly relieved—rec'd a letter from Mrs. Noble—says she had nearly recovered. . . ."

And so, the interminable month of July ground to a faltering halt.

---

21  Lt. John Noble's uncle, Henry Noble, had attempted to kill the wagon guide, Stephen Meek, on the 1845 passage across central Oregon. Lt. James Waymire—nephew to John Waymire one of the wagon scouts—had missed being a passenger on the wagon train by a stroke of fate. His father, Stephen Waymire, died on the west bank of the Missouri River in Kansas Territory April 4, 1845. Because of this, Jim and his mother didn't join the migration but came to Oregon Territory in 1853.

22  In 1907, some of the skulls of these unfortunate people were unearthed by accident when trying to farm the basin. This area is now covered by the Crestview housing subdivision in southwest Prineville and lies within sight of the Meadow Lakes Golf Course.

# CHAPTER 116

# THE PURITAN REGIMENT

*The cavalry is not accomplishing anything besides incurring a vast amount of expense to the Government and disgusting all good soldiers who wish to do their duty. . . .*

**Letter from Camp Maury**
*Weekly Oregonian,* July 2, 1864

By mid-summer 1864, Wolf Dog was winning the war by default. Between April and August less than a dozen Snake warriors had been killed or captured. The Americans had not fared so well. All livestock between the Deschutes River and the Idaho frontier had been confiscated by the Snakes and an unknown number of white men had died in guerrilla raids. Newspapers would proclaim that nothing but a continuous wall of troops could prevent these occurrences. For some unexplained reason many civil authorities were recognizing Sweet Root (friend of Bad Face) as the leader of the Snake war tribes. What he had accomplished—no small feat in itself—was to convince many of Gourd Rattler's warriors to join the cause.[1] Although holding much sway as a man touched by God, Sweet Root had stopped pounding the war drum following Bear Hunter's defeat in 1863 when it was claimed that in places the bodies of dead Shoshoni were "piled eight feet deep." That was enough to cause Sweet Root to return to the shadows where he could advise Wolf Dog in comparative safety.

In three months of futility, Currey, Drake and Caldwell had pushed their cavalry squadrons to the limits of endurance and the enlisted men were bitterly complaining that they were forced to face unbearable hardships for no pay. In a way this was true. Privates received only a dollar and a half a day including horse rental and combat pay—the terms agreed to at the start of enlistment.[2] The commanding officers of the expedition were hardly to blame for their failure to carry out a successful campaign. Not only were they pitted against an exceptionally wily and dangerous adversary but they were being hamstrung by general staff

---

1    Trenholm and Carley, *The Shoshoni*, p. 189.

2    Bancroft, *History of Oregon*, Vol. II, p. 496; *Weekly Oregonian*, Vol. VII, No. 37, letter dated July 9, 1864 from the Snake River Indian Expedition, signed: Co. G, 1st Oregon Volunteer Cavalry.

officers who were politically motivated by the state of Oregon. With Democrats in control of the state legislature, a majority of Oregonians—including the governor—were sympathetic to the southern cause and doing their utmost to hamper any military effort which might be beneficial to the preservation of the Union. A few field officers and enlisted men were aiding in this disruption. Also, American political philosophy, from discussions of the Revolutionary era onward, has notably dealt with the rights of the citizen and not with the duties of the subject.

Oregon would also have a hand in the political affairs of Idaho. Heaping more criticism on the Oregon cavalry, the citizens of Idaho, speaking through Territorial Gov. W.B. Danick—a recent political appointee from Yamhill County, Oregon—accused Gov. Addison Gibbs, State Adjutant General Cyrus Reed and Oregon Indian Superintendent J.W. Perit Huntington of ignoring their Indian responsibilities in eastern Oregon. In desperation, the Idaho legislature passed a resolution for the extermination of all Indians in eastern Oregon and Idaho. Among other things it resolved that:

> ... three men be appointed to select 25 men to go Indian hunting, and all those who can fit themselves out shall receive a nominal sum for all scalps that they may bring in. . . that for every buck scalp be paid $100, and for every squaw $50 and $25 for everything in the shape of an Indian under 10 years of age.

To insure that everything would be legal the resolution further defined "that each scalp have the curl of the head, and each man shall make oath that the said scalp was taken by the company."[3] Brunettes beware!

This hunting of men, women and children—placed on a par with the extermination of noxious weeds—would not be taken lightly by the dog soldiers. Neither would it help the military in its attempt to bring the Snake rebels to the negotiating table.

Oddly enough, news reporters—who held a special loathing for regular army personnel—touted the virtues of the Oregon Volunteers, lavishly extolling their habits of temperance and morality. To their loving fans in the Willamette Valley the Oregon Volunteer Cavalry was known as "The Puritan Regiment." The media arrived at this conclusion because the enlistees were largely composed of the sons of well-to-do farmers, merchants, doctors and lawyers. According to the press, "No regiment in the regular army had stood the same tests so heroically."[4] Maybe, maybe not.

As late as 1961, local newspapers were advancing the theory that members of the 1st Oregon Cavalry made up of Oregon's finest families were beyond reproach. "A peculiar feature of the Oregon Cavalry regiment that distinguished

---

3    From the introduction to Col. Richard Irving Dodge's, *The Plains of the Great West.*

4    Bancroft, *History of Oregon*, Vol. II, p. 508.

it from other military organizations is the men who composed it pledged themselves at the beginning to temperance and pure living."[5]

Perhaps this was true but the record would tend to dispute these claims of valor. Reluctant to follow orders, it took more than two years to train these offspring of an elite society into some semblance of a fighting unit. On the battlefield many panicked under fire and by the close of the 1864 campaign, 51 of them would have deserted. The west side newspapers would quickly explain this away by claiming the deserters were "from the floating population of this country" meaning the fugitives were from eastern Oregon and that "only three" were from the "privileged class."

On the Crooked River and John Day fronts, a different story was unfolding. On August 2, 1864, Capt. Currey with half of the expeditionary force left Fort Gibbs for Jordan Creek to reinforce Col. Maury's troops in an attempt to trap Has No Horse. Has No Horse, following his raid on the Jordan Ranch, had defeated the scalp-hunting Idaho militia, mowed a swathe of destruction across northern Utah and Nevada and was now heading north into the Ochoco miles from Currey's line of march.

On Crooked River, Capt. Drake was in good spirits now that Currey had received his marching orders. Not that he objected to serving with Currey for they were good friends—but as long as Currey was around, Drake was placed in the unreasonable position of having command of an expedition without having any control over it. Operations were going to change and the first order on the agenda was some house cleaning.

Spring cleaning began the day after Currey left when Drake was investigating a charge made by Sgt. Fortney that Assistant Pack Master Bowers had stolen a box of tobacco from the supply train. During the investigation, Drake intercepted a letter addressed to the editor of *The Oregonian* signed "Company G" once again berating Drake's ability as a commanding officer. (Capt. Drake was a regular army officer.) Checking the daily field reports, he was able to identify the handwriting as being that of Sgt. Christopher Garrett, the company clerk. Drake's first inclination was that Garrett was the author of all the abusive information being leaked to the press but he decided to withhold punishment until conferring with his staff officers. During this meeting he gained some more disquieting information.

Capt. Henry Small had been observed recording everything the officers discussed among themselves—mainly gossip, scandal and rumors—noting dates, places and names. Apparently he was reporting this information to Salem and Vancouver. Small, a prominent Marion County businessman and friend of Gov. Gibbs was not a popular man with the other officers and Drake was not surprised

---

5    *Central Oregonian*, May 4, 1961, "Saga of Fort Watson."

that he would do such a thing. As far as Drake was concerned, Small certainly had "the faculty of being as mean a man as anyone I know."

Although he would never admit to it, it was obvious that Small was connected with the Co. G letter that appeared in *The Oregonian* on July 4, which implied that if Drake would have stayed on Crooked River instead of going to Harney Valley, the Snakes would have been defeated within a month.[6] At the time of publication Small reportedly expressed his concern about the contents of the letter and its harmful affect on Drake's command. His professed anxiety had aroused Drake's suspicions and now he was convinced that Small knew more about the letter than he pretended to at the time. Although he may not have written it with his own hand, Drake believed he dictated it and "induced some soft-headed fool to send it in," most likely Sgt. Garrett.[7]

Beside the proliferation of hate mail, other disturbances were occurring within the ranks. For some undisclosed reason, Sgt. Thomas Baker—one of the best soldiers in the command—was intensely disliked by the enlisted men. In mid-August, Sgt. Baker was placed in charge of a detail to escort the supply train to Fort Dalles. On the return trip, his men mutinied at Cedar Spring north of the present town of Madras. In the ensuing fight, Sgt. Baker was severely beaten. So bad in fact, that he had to receive medical treatment when he got back to Fort Gibbs, thus bringing the quarrel to the attention of the commanding officer. Drake arrested the whole detail, had them placed in chains and confined to the guardhouse. In a move to justify the beating of Baker and an obvious attempt to keep those responsible from being punished, one of Small's men—Pvt. John Adams—requested permission to speak to Capt. Drake. He told Drake that he was a wanted criminal, confessing that he and Sgt. Baker had committed robbery at The Dalles prior to the expedition's departure for Crooked River in April. Drake was certain that Adams, "an accomplished villain at the age of 19," was turning states evidence to wreak further vengeance on Sgt. Baker by ruining his reputation. He also believed someone applied pressure on Adams to surrender with this information. It appeared to be a conspiracy against Baker to punish him if he was in fact guilty or to persecute him if he was innocent. As Drake would observe, "soldiers are not apt to take such deep interest in incriminating their fellows without some strong impelling nature." He would never find out what was prompting this new cause of unrest but it certainly wasn't helping his stand against the Shoshoni.

Things were faring no better among the other officers. "Pills," as they called Major Dumriecher, the command's medical officer, was trying to cause trouble between the staff members and he nearly succeeded. Described as "a stiff, aristocratic old fool morbid in his sensibilities and contemptible," Dumriecher was

---

6 *Daily Oregonian*, July 4, 1864, p. 2, Col. 2. The letter dated Camp Maury, June 12, 1864, mentions Capt. Small prominently.

7 Drake, Private Journal entry for Saturday, August 27, 1864.

one of several officers in the command who would rather have seen the campaign a failure than otherwise. During the course of the summer, he noticed that Capt. David Porter—an efficient and respected officer—and Drake had become good friends. On the night of September 2, he proceeded to get Porter rip-roaring drunk from his ample liquor supply in the medical tent. As the evening wore on, they staggered down to visit with the grand chaplain of the Sons of Temperance, Capt. Small, where they were joined by Lt. Noble (who could smell alcohol a mile away). By 3:00 a.m. the party was getting boisterous to the point it awakened the whole garrison, including Capt. Drake. Drake—assuming Noble was the cause—charged into Small's quarters and put a stop to the gaiety in short order, berating Noble's condition as unbecoming to an officer and a gentleman.

That morning Porter, who had been sharing meals with Drake, appeared quite surly and was taking mess with Capt. Small. Drake never realized until then that Capt. Porter had also been doing some heavy drinking and it appeared that he was drunk enough to take Drake's reprimand directed at Lt. Noble "all on himself and got mad as the devil." Pills had successfully driven a wedge into their friendship. Two days later, Porter was still sulky but Noble was as jolly as ever. He invited Drake down to his quarters for a drink and "evidently does not feel hurt much over the little affair that transpired two nights ago." At least Drake had one officer he could trust in a pinch. Drunk or sober, Lt. Noble was regular army.

Six days before the Dumriecher episode, Capt. Caldwell rode in from the John Day front as disgusted with Oregon's nobility as Drake was. He told Drake he was having a great deal of trouble keeping any kind of discipline among what he called "the enterprising part" of his command.[8] Olney (recently promoted to captain) was giving so much trouble that Caldwell threatened to put him under arrest and throw his whole company of volunteers into the guardhouse. He even wrote Gen. Alvord recommending the disbanding of Olney's detachment as being "utterly worthless and unmanageable." This proposal caused Drake much concern as he was afraid he would get stuck with them.

On this happy note, Drake and Caldwell were trying to keep traffic open to Canyon City while Currey and Maury maintained a low profile on the southern front.

---

8    Ibid.

CHAPTER 117

# SHADOWS IN THE PINE

*I believe I am capable of better things than wearing out my life running over the mountains and desert, hunting down Snake Indians as one would wild beasts.*

**Capt. John M. Drake**
Fort Gibbs, August 1864

Two days after he resumed control of his own command, Capt. Drake ordered all available men into the field, covering central Oregon from the base of the Cascades to Harney Valley. Drake with 42 men and 15 days' rations headed southeast for the head of Silver Creek where it was rumored that Broken Knife and Lame Dog were hiding out. In 12 days of hard riding which took him within 25 miles of Harney Lake, Drake could never catch up with them.

Lts. Noble and Waymire who were working the western sector from Fort Gibbs to the Deschutes River had no better luck. Now that the Snakes were aware that the cavalry was making war on women and children, they couldn't even locate where the families were being hidden—and for good reason. The war chiefs were moving the young, the old and the infirm with them. On the Deschutes River foray, scout Billy Chinook swore that he killed Death Rattle, the medicine man whose mystical powers were believed to make Paulina invulnerable to bullets.[1] However, this claim was open to dispute.

Capt. Small with a detachment of 32 men and 15 days' rations was ordered to open the Yreka Trail from Beaver Creek to Canyon City. From there, he was to make contact with Caldwell and offer whatever assistance needed. Lt. McCall and Lt. Hand were to scout the desert south to Drew's sector and ride west to Warner Valley. Capt. Porter was placed in charge of the supply trains while Major Rinehart—now attached to Drake's command to recover from his injury suffered at the Black Canyon skirmish—remained at Fort Gibbs.[2]

Drake, besides chasing after Broken Knife was also scouting for a suitable site for a permanent military fortification. Fort Gibbs, some 25 miles due west of

---

1    *Daily Oregonian*, November 28, 1864.
2    *Washington Historical Quarterly*, No. 22, p. 94.

the Yreka Trail, was too far away for adequate protection and by the end of July, the 400 head of cavalry mounts had trampled and eaten all the grass around the fort for an area covering five square miles. By mid-August, Drake found what he was looking for on a strategically located promontory overlooking the north fork of Beaver Creek. Ironically, it was the June staging area where Currey had begun construction of a stockade. This jutland less than a quarter of a mile from the Yreka Trail and some 200 feet higher in elevation commanded an unobstructed view of the trail for a distance of nearly 14 miles. Logs for additional construction were readily available. Beaver Creek and its tributaries would supply ample water and from the site, they could observe some 40 square miles of grazing land.

On his return to Fort Gibbs, Drake met Capt. Small in Paulina Valley who by his own admission had been everywhere except the places he was supposed to have been. He had ridden directly into Canyon City for some joyous times in the saloons and dance-halls. Then he joined with Capt. Olney for a social gathering and ignored orders to make contact with Capt. Caldwell. Drake routed him out again.

Small had barely gotten out of sight when another annoying situation had to be dealt with. It seems that Lt. McCall had more pressing things to search for than some obstinate Shoshoni. Two of his Willamette Valley elite got lost while out hunting and couldn't find their detachment. They wandered into Drake on Beaver Creek. Drake figured McCall was having some uneasy moments on their absence but he believed that any officer in Indian country who would let two privates separate from the rest of the command for the mere purpose of hunting game deserved to be court-martialed. . . an idea he would pursue with some other disgruntled officers in his command.

Drake had cut his scout short by three days expecting an important express from general headquarters. The expressman—Cayuse George Rundell—hadn't arrived by the time Drake got back to Fort Gibbs, causing much concern over his safety, although there was always the possibility that the express had been detained by Gen. Alvord trying to come up with some new strategy to please the armchair commanders in Salem. In Drake's judgment, Ben Alvord (who celebrated his 51st birthday on August 18, 1864) was senile—he called it "superannuated"—and should be retired. The only message of importance was an express from Capt. Small reporting the defeat of a large citizen force (the Idaho Militia) by Has No Horse on Jordan Creek.

When several more days passed and Rundell still hadn't reached camp, Drake was certain the general would not detain him that long and feared he had been ambushed by the Indians before he ever reached Fort Dalles. Finally, the express arrived 10 days late but it contained both bad and good news. On the plus side, Alvord gave his approval for Drake to carry out field operations as he saw fit and on August 22, Drake began preparations to abandon Fort Gibbs and move to Beaver Creek. However, Alvord's approval wasn't put in official form, which led

Drake to believe Alvord was leaving an opening to escape criticism from the press in case something went wrong.

The most important information to arrive at the Crooked River outpost was that Gen. Irvin McDowell—graduate of West Point and veteran of the Mexican War—had reported to Fort Vancouver on August 12 to reorganize the Oregon Cavalry. Unfortunately, Gen. McDowell arrived under a cloud of suspicion. Commander of the III Corps of Gen. Pope's Army of Virginia, McDowell had been relieved of command after the second battle of Bull Run when Confederate Gen. Longstreet—in a surprise attack—broke through McDowell's flank and routed Pope's army. The outcome: the Union suffered 14,500 casualties and Washington, D.C. was threatened with capture. McDowell was now assigned to the Pacific Department to succeed Gen. Wright as commander so that Wright could replace Alvord as commander of the Military District of Oregon. Gen. Alvord would become paymaster-general of the army, placing him out of harm's way.

The express also brought the unwelcome news that by act of Congress, effective May 30, 1864, all cavalrymen who furnished their own horses were to be dismounted and then remounted on government horses. This was going to cause serious problems especially if the troopers horse rental was stopped retroactive to June 1.[3] Previously the cavalrymen supplied their own mounts, usually horses that they had trained and were used to, and the army gave them extra pay for doing so. Much preferring their own choice of horses as well as additional money, the soldiers threatened mutiny, but Drake finally got them cooled down. When the word reached Currey, Drew and Caldwell, they too would face grave resistance.

Ten days before Drake moved his depot to Beaver Creek, Currey arrived at Fort Alvord with 106 men out of 134 down with dysentery, including Capt. Thomas Cochrane, the company surgeon.[4] With his command crippled, he was unable to reinforce Maury which presented no problem as all of Maury's field officers were pulling duty in the newly constructed Overland Hotel in Boise City. Anyway, Currey's scouts assured him that the Shoshoni had gone south into Nevada for the summer. Currey took this opportunity to write a letter to Gen. Alvord recommending that troops be stationed in southeast Oregon during the coming winter.[5] He was certain he could make both men and animals comfortable during a desert blizzard. In fact, even though half of his command was due to muster out in December, Currey believed they would be just as satisfied to receive their discharge at Fort Alvord as they would at Fort Vancouver. Maybe. According to the Captain, many of his troopers were desirous of locating land claims in the Alvord Desert. He neglected to mention that there was a selfish motive in this

---

3    Oregon Adjutant General's Report, 1865-6, p. 47.

4    Bancroft, *History of Oregon*, Vol. II, p. 502.

5    This letter from Currey dated August 20, 1864 from Fort Alvord appeared in *The Daily Oregonian*, October 28, 1864.

recommendation, for Currey had staked out a 40 acre claim for himself in June and now wanted some neighbors for protection.

Among the reasons he did list for making such a request were:

1.   The winter is the most effective time to operate against the Indians.

2.   A small force stationed in Alvord Valley would have the effect of fostering a permanent settlement.

3.   Thirty-five miles south of Fort Alvord, miners have opened the Pueblo Silver Mines. With a little protection from the cavalry a rich mining district will develop in the haunt of the Indians. Such a settlement would be of military advantage.

4.   There is no evidence of severe winter weather in the valley and wild grass is so abundant that a responsible citizen now employed as pack-master of my train, offers to cut hay within a short distance of any point selected in this valley at $25 legal tender per ton. [At this time, hay from Jordan Valley, if it could be delivered, cost $300 a ton.] With plenty of hay and a small amount of grain for extra storms, horses and mules could be kept serviceable all winter.

5.   And finally, by returning from the country in the fall, the labor of the summer will be lost no matter how successful the latter part of the campaign may be.

These were all valid points but the fact remains that Capt. Currey was more interested in homesteading than he was in chasing elusive red men in a winter white-out. Perhaps his superiors were aware of this, for his request was denied.

Lt. Col. Drew, plodding along the southern sector, didn't arrive at Fort Alvord until August 31. At that time, he established an outpost two miles east of the fort. Leaving the bulk of his command with Currey, Drew with 19 men proceeded to escort emigrant trains from California to Fort Boise. About all he had accomplished during the summer campaign was to open a line of communication from Fort Klamath to Fort Boise which was deemed well worth the labor and cost of the expedition as it shortened the Applegate Trail into the upper Willamette Valley by nearly 300 miles.[6]

While Currey's plague-ridden troops recuperated and Drew took on the duties of a wagon guide, Drake began the move to Beaver Creek amid the usual bickering within his command. Just before departure, Small and Rinehart—barely able to sit his horse—returned from a scout of the southern Blues that had taken them as far north as Bridge Creek and the Painted Hills, Small reported he thought he had picked up Paulina's fresh trail but when the trackers checked it out, the

---

6    Hay, *Scrapbooks*, Vol. III, p. 121-2.

tracks were over a month old. So, no action was taken. This made Small mad and he refused to leave Fort Gibbs. Apparently he had made some deal with Olney because Olney showed up at Fort Gibbs looking for pack mules and supplies to make a raid on Harney Lake. Drake denied this request.

The moment the main command arrived at the new fort site—which Drake would name Fort Dahlgren in honor of Col. Ulric Dahlgren killed in a cavalry raid near Richmond, Virginia—Dumreicker, higher than a kite, started complaining about the location and raising hell about the water supply. At this time, the water was not the best as the creek was choked with beaver dams—in fact, the soldiers would name the nearest tributary to the north fork of Beaver Creek, Beaverdam Creek. Capt. Pleasonton, in charge of building the fort, soon corrected that problem by dynamiting all the obstructions. Nonetheless, Dumreicker was treading on shaky ground from this latest drunken outburst as Drake seriously thought of placing him under arrest for insubordination.

This was not the first time Dumreicker had questioned Drake's authority. On July 22, the day Drake set out on his scout to the Deschutes, he had countermanded Drake's orders to Hospital Steward Henry Catley. After the flare-up at Fort Dahlgren, Dumreicker, on September 4, wrote district headquarters without Drake's knowledge, charging that Drake interfered with the medical department and stated that he was "preparing new charges of even more serious character." When Drake got wind of this, he brought court-martial proceedings against his senior medical officer.[7]

With Co. A busy constructing fortifications, Drake took to the mountains to survey a military route from Fort Dahlgren to The Dalles-Canyon City road. Capt. Porter would accompany him, serving as quartermaster, and Sgt. James Miller acting as wagonmaster. Heading northwest out of Fort Dahlgren, Drake intercepted the centuries-old Shoshoni trail from the John Day River to the head of Crooked River on Hewed Log Creek and followed it to its intersection with the Canyon City road at the Mountain House Stage Station 145 miles east of The Dalles.[8] The distance across the Ochoco Blues was only 22 miles and would shorten the distance from Paulina Valley to The Dalles City by some 30 miles and make a better travel route than Wallen's road up Crooked River. This trail, when improved, would open a route of communications between the John Day country and the vast area south of the Blue Mountains enabling the citizens of the John Day valley to penetrate the Crooked River basin in a single day's travel at any time of the year for the purpose of pursing any small band of Indians running off livestock.

---

7    Military District of Oregon, General Orders No. 24, November 11, 1864, is an account of Major Dumreicker's court-martial.

8    Mountain House, constructed as a Wells Fargo stage stop, was located on Badger Creek near the summit of Mitchell Mountain some eight miles east of the present town of Mitchell, Oregon.

Eager to get started, Capt. Porter (with a 19-man work crew) was detached to road construction on orders to open the new route as quickly as possible. Foreseeing a good opportunity to alleviate some of his problems, Drake also assigned Capt. Small the task of manning an outpost on the trail to insure the road remained open to travel once completed. This lonely garrison surrounded by four-foot-high rock walls and rifle pits sat 12 miles northwest of Fort Dahlgren, which would serve as a reinforcement and supply depot for Small's new command. Drake would note in his journal that this military buffer was located "three miles east of the May battlefield" where Lt. Watson was killed. This would place it on upper Paulina Creek in the vicinity of the old Roba ranch. This tiny outpost would be referred to only as the camp "in Kamas Valley."

In keeping with his stubborn nature, Capt. Small would direct activities at the "Kamas Valley" outpost from Caldwell's depot at Camp Watson. Drake would dejectedly observe: "I never have been able to get that man to do what I wanted him to do or go where I wanted him to go. I am unable to determine whether from instinctive obstinacy or systematic design, but certain it is that he is adept at evading the wishes of his commanding officer."[9] Drake was in a rush to get the road open because almost daily private citizens were crowding into Fort Dahlgren looking for lost horses in the army's captured herds and causing even more disruption to the military's main objective. To speed things up, Lt. Noble was sent to Camp Watson to take charge of road supplies. Suspecting that there "probably was some old rye" at Caldwell's camp, Capt. Porter volunteered to accompany Noble as an escort.

On the evening of September 22, Porter returned from Camp Watson at 9:00 p.m., a little under "the influence of onions" as he called it. He would report that he and Noble had taken a shortcut and were attacked by Indians in a narrow canyon on Rock Creek. Porter had previously directed the expressman to take the same route and he was pinned down in those woods overnight. As the old saying goes, "when the cat's away the mice will play."

Major Rinehart—Canyon City brewmaster par excellence—so saddle-sore he could barely walk, was the happiest man in camp when Cayuse George, the express rider, escaped with his scalp intact. In Rundell's mail pouch were several letters from Rineart's girl, one of which contained her picture. It was rumored that Bill and Amanda would be married in October.

The entire month of August and most of September had been spent in internal bickering: decisions on where to build outposts, chasing stolen livestock, guiding emigrant trains, and not one military engagement with Wolf Dog's troops who were now striking as far west as the Umpqua Valley. Many soldiers, knowing their

---

9    Unless otherwise noted all direct quotations for this chapter have been taken from Drake's private journal entries dated from August 1, 1864 to September 22, 1864.

term of enlistment would be up in December, were not eager to face the Snakes on any terms—but things were about to liven up.

Col. Maury—in two letters from Fort Boise dated September 5 and 17—notified Gov. Gibbs that there was "a larger immigration than has ever been received in one season in Oregon." They were mainly Southerners and Maury suggested it might be wise to pass a law prohibiting those who had borne arms against the Union from voting. This became a hot issue. On October 21, 1864, the loyalist *Oregon Statesman* in an article entitled "Can Immigrants Vote" complained that Copperhead Journals were acting on the presumption that a large proportion of recent emigrants were Northern sympathizers to the Confederate cause and they were trying to convince readers that such emigrants were legal voters. The *Oregon Statesman* was of the opinion that Copperheads should be barred from casting ballots in the coming election. Even so, these newcomers had to be protected from Indian attack.

In the aftermath of Maury's intelligence, orders arrived on the eastern Oregon front in late September to stage an all-out effort to locate and destroy the ranking war chiefs before they disappeared into their winter hideouts.[10] This would prove to be easier said than done.

---

10    *War of Rebellion*, Vol. L, Pt. 1, p. 340.

# CHAPTER 118

# MOON OF FALLING LEAVES[1]

*You say that your warriors can fight,*
*that they are great braves.*
*Now let me see them fight*
*that I may know your words are true.*

**Yellow Hand**
Snake Medicine Chief

Capt. Alfred Pleasonton, whose Co. A had been detached to finish construction of Fort Dahlgren, was due for an unpleasant surprise. While the rest of the command chased shadows in the Ochoco and surveyed new routes of travel into the Crooked River basin, Shoshoni snipers were wreaking vengeance on the timber detail. In the final days of September, Pleasonton, with a detachment from Co. A and Small's Co. G, took the scent and surprised Broken Knife's hostiles at Soda Springs a mile north of Suplee. In a running battle, Broken Knife lured Pleasonton into a trap on the scorched slopes of Iron Mountain—the soldiers named it Pleasonton Butte.

Here, Broken Knife was joined by Has No Horse and 50 veterans of the Jordan Creek battle. It was a complete rout. By some stroke of luck no soldiers were killed but many were wounded—including Cpl. Jacob Deen of Co. G—before they broke free and retreated to Fort Dahlgren.[2] For reasons unknown, this disgrace was not leaked to the press. . . or if it was, it got suppressed. Such clumsy action would not reflect well upon the good name of the so-called Puritan Regiment. Capt. Small, whose Co. G suffered the most casualties, was not about to advertise this fact, especially when he was looking for a command of his own. Neither would it surface in Drake's report, for he was saddled with enough criticism without adding this inept show-of-arms to his discredit.

---

1   See *Thunder Over The Ochoco, Vol. II—Distant Thunder*—Appendix B, page 351 for an explanation of Shoshoni moons and calendar months.

2   Testimony of Joseph H. Deen who settled two and a half miles north of Suplee on the south fork of Beaver Creek in 1893. His father, Jacob Deen, fought in the Shoshoni wars and told of this defeat suffered by the First Oregon Cavalry. Joseph Deen married Bertha Rush in 1899. Bertha didn't see a cook stove until she was 16 years old.

Three weeks before Pleasonton's defeat at Iron Mountain—some 104 miles north of Currey's position—Currey, acting on the advice of his scouts, galloped toward the Oregon-Nevada line on September 2, 1864 searching for Has No Horse. Near the Pueblo mines, he found some prospectors working a small quartz mill fired by sagebrush. They told him a small band of Indians had passed through the day before and volunteered to join forces with the soldiers, as most of Currey's troops were still recovering from dysentery. In a hard ride which took them some 40 miles south into northern Nevada, they surprised a Paiute camp and took them prisoners without firing a shot. Among the captives were five Snake dog soldiers. Currey had accomplished more than he realized at the time.

Whenever possible, miners slaughtered Paiute livestock and any Paiutes attempting to live peaceably were needlessly slain.[3] One of the objectives of these unprovoked attacks was to capture young women, who were then sold to the houses of prostitution in Canyon City, Oregon, Virginia City, Nevada and Silver City, Idaho. In late July, some miners had captured two Paiute girls north of Pyramid Lake to be sold into bondage. After a long search, they were found imprisoned in a mining camp root cellar by their fathers. In retaliation, Bad Face killed the miners, raided the white settlements along the Truckee River, stole a supply of provisions, and burned what he couldn't take and headed north to the Oregon line.

Shortly after the Jordan Creek raid, Has No Horse received word that Bad Face, pursued by the Nevada Cavalry, was hiding out in the Black Rock Desert. He dispatched five of his top warriors to offer assistance. Three Coyotes—leader of the Snake warriors in the 1857 Mountain Meadow massacre—Yellow Jacket, veteran of the Yakima War and three White Knife dog soldiers had stopped for provisions at a Paiute camp when they were captured by Currey. Currey had given the order to hang them when the Pueblo miners intervened. With Nevada only a month away from statehood (it was granted October 31, 1864) its citizens didn't want to get involved in Oregon's Indian war. They also believed if they showed mercy toward the captives, the Snakes would not attack them. Against his better judgment, Currey, after issuing a stern warning to the miners to get out of the country while they had the chance, released the five dog soldiers. He then headed into the Black Rock Desert.[4] A day later, Three Coyotes and Yellow Jacket ambushed the fleeing miners and killed them.

On his probe along the border, Currey found out that the drought which was baking California was also affecting northern Nevada and southeastern Oregon. The heat and alkali dust of the Black Rock Desert forced Currey and his sickly troopers to a standstill. At Mud Lake they gave up the chase and returned to Fort Alvord, arriving on September 16 where orders awaited to abandon the outpost and return to Fort Walla Walla for emigrant train duty.

---

3    *Political History of Oregon from 1864 to 1867.*

4    Capt. Currey's report appearing in *The Report of the Adjutant General of Oregon 1866*, p. 46.

After a sluggish beginning, the final days of September were becoming quite active. Under orders of the secretary of war, a revengeful Col. Justin Steinberger arrived in Portland to take command of his old regiment, the First Washington Territorial Infantry, most of whom he had recruited in California. Part of his regiment was now stationed at Camp Watson under the command of Capt. Caldwell where they were charged with keeping The Dalles-Canyon City road open to traffic.

Col. Steinberger had commanded the Military District of Oregon from May to July 1862 when Brig. Gen. Alvord relieved him of duty. Steinberger then moved to Fort Walla Walla, headquarters of his regiment. During the period of early recruitment, he had made enemies among the Copperheads of Oregon and in a smear campaign they made it appear that he was one of their staunchest supporters. Because of these unfounded rumors, he was called east and dismissed from service in January 1864. However, Col. Steinberger had influential friends—among them, Gen. Grant, Gen. Sheridan and Senator James Nesmith—and he was restored to full military rank and active duty by July.[5] Now in the sunset of September, Steinberger was again riding the war trail.

About the time Steinberger's ship docked in Portland and six days after Currey received orders to retreat to Fort Walla Walla, Lt. Col. Drew rode in from Fort Boise on orders to return immediately to Fort Klamath where a meeting had been arranged to hold a peace council with the Indians of eastern Oregon. Apparently this order didn't meet the Colonel's approval. He failed to show up and by November had sent in his resignation from the First Oregon Cavalry for reasons unstated, but possibly because of his close relations with the Confederate cause. He was also at odds with "men of some importance" in southeastern Oregon—namely Lindsey Applegate and Amos Rogers—over his location of Fort Klamath, some 15 miles north of Agency Lake where they wanted it constructed. In return, they accused him of awarding army contracts to pro-southern sympathizers instead of "sound local businessmen," which he probably did. Neither did it help when Major Gen. Halleck aired his opinion that the cost of construction of Fort Klamath was "entirely disproportionate to its importance." Whatever the case, on November 21, 1864 by Special Order No. 252, Drew was relieved from duty and authorized to make out his report of the Owyhee reconnaissance at Jacksonville, Oregon.[6]

---

5    Heitman, *Historical Register; Steinberger and Nesmith Collections*, Oregon Historical Society.

6    Drew's actual resignation did not become effective until January 31, 1865 having been accepted by Special Order No. 22. At this point, Lt. Col. Charles S. Drew fades from history leaving a blank as to where he went or what he did after leaving the First Oregon Cavalry. (*Introduction to Drew, An Account of the Origin and Early Prosecution of the Indian War in Oregon, Washington, D.C., 1860*, in Senate Miscellaneous Document No. 59.

Although Drew had missed all engagements with the Snakes, his expedition was termed a great military success presumably because he had discovered one of the hostile hideouts on Warner Mountain making it a necessity to establish an army post south of Warner Valley. The site chosen was Surprise Valley—scene of the Warner massacre—where California, Nevada and Oregon intersect. Fort Bidwell (as it would be named) was only a few months old when cavalry troops joined the local militia to fight some peaceful Shoshoni camped in Guano Valley just north of the state line in what is now Lake County, Oregon. They attacked at daybreak, killing 81 men, 15 women and their children claiming it "was impossible to distinguish one sex from the other."[7]

In one of these raids on women and children, Small's celebrity squadron took a young Shoshoni boy captive and sent him to Warm Springs. He would be given the name William Henry Harrison in mockery of the ninth president of the United States who according to popular belief died as the result of an Indian curse. These unwarranted attacks on non-combatants convinced Wolf Dog that the Long Knives—nearing their term of enlistment—had no heart for a legitimate fight with the dog soldiers, so he turned up the heat. Lt. Col. Steen, in command of all supply trains into the combat area, was being constantly harassed and by late September it was a gamble whether his supply wagons would make it through unscathed when they left Fort Dalles. The situation got so bad, that Steen—deciding he had done enough for his country—retired from the service on September 23, 1864 and in the minds of the enemy another victory had been won.

It was because of the supply train raids that Capt. Drake was concentrating all efforts to open a road from Fort Dahlgren to Mountain House to shorten the link between upper Crooked River and Fort Dalles. During road improvement, it would come to light that Small was engaged in more political intrigue along with Olney. The two command captains Drake and Caldwell—out for vengeance—would set a trap and Camp Watson would become the bait.

Originally established as Camp Rattlesnake, a supply depot on lower Rock Creek, it was renamed Camp Watson with the arrival of Watson's body in late June. In early July, Caldwell was authorized to move the camp and re-establish it "at the most expedient point on the Canyon City road."[8] He moved the camp to the head of Rock Creek some 13 miles east of Mountain House Stage Station near the present site of Antone and named it Camp Rock Creek. It was not much better located than Camp Rattlesnake.

Well known to both Drake and Caldwell, Capt. Small was after his own command at any price, which would explain the adverse publicity they were receiving in the press and the lack of support from Gen. Alvord. Small had influential friends in positions of power and was not above using them to his

7    Hart, *Old Forts of the Northwest*, p. 128.

8    *War of Rebellion*, Vol. L., Pt. II, pp. 877, 879-80, 894-95.

advantage. For example, when Drake asked the editor of the *Oregonian* for the letters signed Co. G so he could compare handwriting, he was told that the *Oregonian* had either "lost or destroyed the original manuscripts."[9] Working through Gen. Reed, Small was about to get his own command, but it wouldn't be quite what he expected.

On September 28, Capt. Porter having completed the military link between Fort Dahlgren and Mountain House, rode into Drake's camp with orders from headquarters. Captains Drake and Caldwell were to report to Fort Dalles and Captain Small with G Co. was to report to Camp Rock Creek and there, take command of the post, the Washington Infantry and Capt. Olney's "Forty Thieves." Furthermore, he was to upgrade the depot to permanent fort status and . . . dig in for a winter campaign! Although Drake and Caldwell were snickering up their sleeves, they did feel a little sorry for Small and wished him well. Drake was certain that Small, who was out on patrol when the order arrived, would be "the most downhearted man in camp when he arrives. And what will Hand say? It will nearly kill him!" Lt. Hand being Small's executive officer, he was also caught up in this order and Lt. Noble was ecstatic. He liked the arrangement simply because it would be such a "terrible punishment to Small and Hand." However, Noble's mirth was short-lived. Three days after Small got his orders, Noble was ordered to report to Camp Rock Creek and assume the duties of quartermaster and take charge of the commissary at that post . . . under the command of Capt. Small!

To complicate matters, Capt. Caldwell had also been told to start upgrading the post. On September 24, Lt. Hopkins—Alvord's acting adjutant general—had written Small that although Caldwell had recommended that Rock Creek was the ideal location, Small was "to select the site he thought best." Apparently Hopkins had second thoughts on the matter for he continues: "If by any accident this letter gets to you too late, after you have made a commencement at Rock Creek, you will make no changes. In whatever place you establish yourself you will call it Fort Watson."[10]

Small did not approve of the Rock Creek site and neither did Drake. By some strange coincidence they both agreed that an open meadow on a tributary of Mountain Creek four miles west of Camp Rock Creek was a more suitable location. From this position, an outpost would not only command a view of The Dalles-Canyon City road but it would also be within striking distance of the Shoshoni trail connecting the John Day and Crooked River valleys. Setting nine miles east of Mountain House, this garrison on what would become Fort Creek could also provide protection for the beleaguered stage station.[11] However, since Caldwell had already started work on Camp Rock Creek it put Small in the

---

9   Drake's Private Journal, Friday, September 16, 1864.

10   *War of Rebellion*, Vol. L., Pt. II, pp. 988-89.

11   Oregon Adjutant General's Report 1865-6, p. 52.

awkward position of disobeying orders on his first command if he moved locations. But, until he arrived at Caldwell's depot, he was still under Drake's jurisdiction so Drake—in a forgiving mood—approved the new location on September 25 without comment from Caldwell who had greater things on his mind. He had just received word (compliments of Capt. Olney) that his pay had been stopped because he wasn't holding muster properly. Drake fully expected the same to happen to him.

On this happy note, Drake and Caldwell turned over their commands to Capt. Small and headed for Fort Dalles. Watching them leave, Henry had the nagging feeling that perhaps he had swallowed more than he was prepared to digest.

# CHAPTER 119

# FORTRESS OF THE FORGOTTEN DEAD

*On a high shoulder of the Ochocos, Lt. Watson and his comrades sleep today in graves sunken and uncared for. No flag flies from the weathered staff. Their only memorial is the shaft of towering Spanish Peak. Their eternal requiem is the west winds of the pines.*

**Lettie Powell Putman**
June 15, 1925

Four miles west of the old Rock Creek campsite where The Dalles-Canyon City road crossed a swift flowing mountain stream, Capt. Henry Small staked out a tract of ground encompassing more than three acres of level ground. This would become Fort Watson, the military hub of central Oregon. Strategically located on a divide where the waters flowed both to the John Day and Crooked rivers, it sat 154 miles southeast of Fort Dalles, 45 miles west of Canyon City and a scant 40 miles northeast of the Ochoco Valley—winter hideout of the Snake war tribes . . . and by October, winter was already approaching.

On October 1, 1864—as peace feelers were being sent out to the war chiefs—with two troops of Oregon Cavalry and two companies of Washington Infantry serving on work detail, Small began construction on a grand scale. Although no mention is made of him, one can see the hand of Louis Scholl in the design and layout of the fort. Scholl was acting as courier for Currey, the same as Rundell was for Drake and it is certain his route to Fort Dalles would take him through Drake's various camps.

Laid out in a huge rectangle 500 feet long by 300 feet wide spanning Fort Creek, the walls consisted of a log stockade 15 feet high encircled with catwalks and equipped with gun ports. By completion, the north wall—running east and west—would have two rows of 12 cabins each to be occupied as barracks for the enlisted men and officers' quarters. The south wall would contain three divisions of corrals, stables and hay storage sheds. Along the west wall was a map house, hospital, guardhouse, orderly room, commissary and quartermaster store. The east wall consisted of a laundry, blacksmith shop, suttler's store, livery stable, bakery and stage station complete with dining room and bar. Running through the middle of Fort Watson was The Dalles-Canyon City road. Due to a lack of proper tools, the severity of mountain storms and constant patrols after Wolf Dog's raiders who were doing their utmost to discourage this venture, Fort Watson was not completed until mid-January 1865.

Once again, Lt. Watson's body was moved to what would become its final resting place. On a gentle, pine covered slope west of the fort, Small established a military cemetery. He also had memorial markers placed for all the soldiers killed in the Shoshoni campaign through September 1864 now lying in unmarked graves throughout eastern Oregon. The headboards hewed from pitch pine and inscribed with a hot iron would be the only recognition these men would receive.[1]

Small little realized that the military cemetery would also become a civilian burial ground. During the winter of 1864-65, Wolf Dog's troops in a fit of frenzy killed over 100 travelers between The Dalles City and Canyon City. They too, their sunken graves still discernible in the 1960s, were laid to rest in the Fort Watson memorial park.

Today, few people are aware of the existence of Fort Watson, the frontier army post that once was a flourishing settlement. More than a century of the ravages of time and man have wiped it from memory. All that remains are a few weathered boards, fallen headstones and some rotting, fire-charred logs—mute evidence of a more recent attack. The stockade walls and the crumbling cabins were burned by the Forest Service in the early 1900s. In their defense, forest personnel rationalized that Fort Watson—once considered for recognition as a National Historic Site—constituted "a fire hazard."[2]

Following this unfortunate incident, Lettie Powell Putman did much to stir interest among the residents of Crook, Wheeler and Grant counties to at least maintain the graves. She wrote many impassioned articles—now on file at the Oregon State Library in Salem—appealing to the Pioneer Association of Oregon and the American Legion to help preserve the cemetery. In an emotional speech in Prineville in the 1920s, she pleaded:

These men who lie in neglected, all but forgotten graves are our soldier dead! They fought for this country and for civilization! They assisted those men and women who blazed the trail through the wilderness and started homes that make it possible for a rising generation to live and to have!

1 Lt. Watson's headboard was still very legible in 1904. Testimony of D.E. Trent, May 4, 1961. Trent lived near Fort Watson in 1904.

2 *Central Oregonian*, May 4, 1961, p. 6A; for more information on Fort Watson see *The Bulletin*, May 1 and May 4, 1961; the *Oregon Journal*, May 1, 1961; *Sunday Oregonian*, April 16, 1961.

On June 15, 1925, Lettie Putman and Elizabeth Davenport got a group together for the purpose of fencing and cleaning the cemetery.[3] It was they who discovered that many graves lay outside the known cemetery on a rocky knoll overlooking the fort parade ground. It was from this same vantage point in 1865 that Has No Horse took his deadly toll of the soldiers as they exercised on the drill field. They also established in fact what had been in doubt for years, that this was the final resting place of 2nd Lt. Stephen Watson killed in Rabbit Valley May 19, 1864. Many would not accept this, believing his body had been taken to Fort Dalles and later transferred to Fort Vancouver. Finally, in March 1957, the Oregon Historical Society would admit there were no records to be found to support this belief. However, they attempted to qualify their research by claiming "it is not the Government's policy to sell ground which holds the remains of any of our fighting forces." The site of Fort Watson lays on private lands a scant half mile north of the Ochoco National Forest boundary.

Ultimately, on June 26, 1932, at a dedication service sponsored by the American Legion posts of Prineville, Mitchell, John Day, Canyon City, Prairie City and Fossil, markers were placed on seven American soldiers' graves. Nothing more was ever done and the dust of the Ochoco is now mingling with the dust of the forgotten dead.

---

3    Elizabeth Davenport Houston and her husband, Lem Houston, were very close friends of the author. They spent many hours describing the old Fort Watson military site.

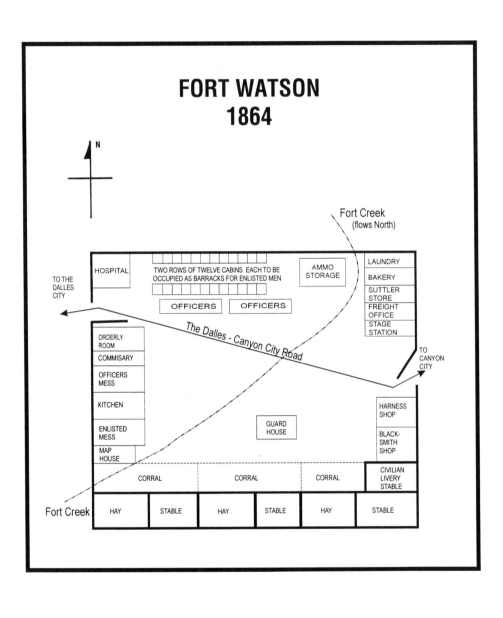

# FORT WATSON
# 1864

CHAPTER 120

# BETRAYAL AT COUNCIL GROVE

*We want your hunting-grounds to dig gold from, to raise grain on and you must move on. Here is a home for you. You must not leave this home we have assigned you. When the march of our empire demands this reservation of yours, we will assign you another, but so long as we choose, this is your home, your playground, your prison.*

**Samuel Bowles**
Editor, *Springfield Republican*[1]

Two weeks after Capt. Small began construction of Fort Watson, a new county was carved out of Wasco and Umatilla in an effort to bring civil obedience to the lawless mining settlements strung out from Crooked River to the headwaters of the John Day. On October 14, 1864, Grant County was formally declared with Canyon City as county seat. Not wishing to tarnish its new respectability, Canyon City quickly divorced itself from Lower Town—better known as Tiger Town—which was mostly composed of Chinese laborers, prostitutes and the less desirable elements of the community. These citizens, not to be outdone, proudly proclaimed that Lower Town was to be renamed John Day City on January 20, 1865.

The only thing that disturbed the population of Grant County—a seething hotbed of southern supporters—was the name of their new community. After all, a name like Grant didn't fit well with such local landmarks as Dixie Butte, Jackson Gulch, Pickett Canyon, Stewart Crossing, Bull Run Rock, Rebel Hill and Jeff Davis Creek, to name just a few. In fact, in 1864 Prairie City was called Dixie City. Even Lookout Mountain on the outskirts of Chattanooga where, in the fall of 1863, Grant's forces suffered 16,000 casualties in two days of bitter fighting was commemorated by a central Oregon landmark. Even though it was hailed as the "battle above the clouds," the Tennessee Lookout Mountain was nearly 5,000 feet lower in elevation than the Ochoco Lookout Mountain.

---

1    Sam Bowles also believed that it was the Indians' "destiny to die." In 1865, the role of hunter and hunted was reversed. Snooping around the Colorado Rockies looking for a headline story for the *Springfield Massachusetts Republican*, editor Bowles was scared out of his wits by a Ute war party. In fact, he came very close to losing his life.

Fearing that the Oregon rebels would stage an outbreak during the presidential election, Gen. Alvord placed the eastern Oregon field commands on alert. If anything could infuse some energy into the volunteer cavalry it was the prospect of putting down a confederate rebellion. Couriers, carrying messages of this new threat, were dispatched to the far-flung outposts of interior Oregon.

At this point in time, Capt. Drake—traveling at a leisurely pace—was taking all of G Company's horses to Fort Vancouver for the winter leaving Small with a dismounted cavalry and the Washington Infantry. All officers agreed that if Wolf Dog should make an attack on the Canyon City road during the winter "a bunch of men on foot would be worse than useless." They would only serve as a temptation to the dog soldiers. In the minds of his sarcastic field officers, Gen. Alvord's strategy for fighting the Shoshoni or quelling a rebel uprising was "becoming remarkable."

The same day Grant became a county, Capt. Currey—en route to Fort Walla Walla—was intercepted on the Oregon Trail and told to disperse his troops, while he was to report to Fort Dalles and link up with Drake's B Co. and Caldwell's C Co., already marching in that direction. Within two days, Currey arrived at Fort Walla Walla where Capt. Pleasonton's A Co. went into garrison; Capt. William Matthews' F Co. was dispatched to Fort Lapwai; and Currey's E Co. headed for Fort Dalles. Two weeks later, Capt. Small received orders to turn over the construction of Fort Watson to Capt. Olney's volunteers and report to Canyon City with G Co. to cover the November election.

Lt. Col. Drew, whose L Co. was marching west toward Fort Klamath, turned over the southern front to the California Cavalry.[2] His orders were to suppress an anticipated Snake outbreak at the Council Grove Treaty Conference. The state of Oregon and the federal Indian Bureau had came up with a novel idea. To paraphrase John O'Sullivan—editor of the *New York Post*—the Interior Department sought to soothe matters by releasing a document which was the nearest thing to divine revelation that the modern world could boast . . . a peace treaty, signed with an X. They hoped this would bring an end to all present and future Indian hostilities in eastern Oregon.

---

2    In July 1861, Congress passed legislation directing federal officials to reimburse states for expenses they incurred in providing troops for the Civil War. Three months later Secretary of State William Seward wrote California Governor John Downey, urging the state to raise war funds while assuring Downey that California would have no trouble getting compensated. Unfortunately for California most of their volunteers were marched into eastern Oregon to fight the Shoshoni. Since they never engaged Confederate troops directly and because the Shoshoni rebellion didn't count in the war effort, California, like Oregon, never received any federal bounty for enlistments. At the time (1861) California sold 668,000 dollars in war bonds and then refinanced that amount with a 2.3 million dollar bond sale in 1873. By 1995, some 134 years later, the debt had reached nearly 82 million dollars with interest and there is no indication that the debt will be paid anytime soon. "California Chases Feds Over Civil War Debt," *The Bulletin*, Bend, Oregon, November 28, 1995.

Therefore, after a preliminary conference held in August—which none of the Snake chiefs attended—Oregon Indian Superintendent, J.W. Perit Huntington sent out messages to the concerned parties calling for a meeting of all eastern Oregon tribes not already confined to a reservation.[3] The "concerned parties" singled out for invitation were Lalake, chief of the Klamaths, Old Schonchin, chief of the Modocs, Motcunka Sket, half-blood Shoshoni leader of a mixed band of Snakes and Klamaths, and Paulina, war chief of the Walpapi Snakes. Why Paulina was chosen over Wolf Dog, ranking chief of the Snake war tribes or Has No Horse, war chief of the Paviotso Confederacy will never be known. At any rate, even though Drew had not yet arrived, the peace council convened at Council Grove on the Sprague River, some 12 miles southeast of Fort Klamath on October 9, 1864. California Superintendent of Indian Affairs A.E. Wylie was unable to attend, so those aiding Huntington in this diplomatic endeavor were Deputy Agent Bill Logan of Warm Springs who took Wylie's place; Lindsay Applegate, Klamath basin politician and William McKay, Warm Springs physician who would act as interpreter. In the absence of Lt. Col. Drew who would not arrive until the sixth and final day of negotiations, Capt. William Kelly with a detachment of D Co. out of Fort Klamath and Lt. James Halloran with a squadron of Washington Infantry from Warm Springs were to provide military protection.

Over 1,000 Indians were crowded onto the council grounds with another 500 camped nearby. Those on the council grounds were identified as 710 Klamaths; 339 Modocs; and 22 Yahuskin Snakes. In truth, there was only one Snake present at the treaty of 1864 and he was a half-breed. The designation of "Yahooskin" is of no known Shoshoni tribe and the 11 men, five women and six children so recognized denied most emphatically that they were Snakes. Most likely, they were a destitute Washoe family who got caught up in the excitement of the white man's offer of presents and decided to join the party. The Yahuskin classification for Shoshoni which would cloud the record for 91 years appeared for the first time in Huntington's treaty documents. In fact, the name Yahuskin appears only in Indian Affairs reports not in army records, with the exception that Capt. Kelly did use the name in his official report to army headquarters on the 1864 treaty proceedings.[4]

According to Dave Chocktote, Yahuskin was the Shoshoni name for the Klamath Indians.[5] It meant "the water bellies" because they lived by the lake and

---

3   *Report of Commissioner of Indian Affairs 1864; Congressional Documents Series 1220*, pp. 228-29, 256-57; *Report of Commissioner of Indian Affairs 1865*, Series 1248, pp. 269-72; *War of Rebellion* Vol L, pp. 991-92.

4   For a full account of the fallacy of the Yahooskin being a representation of the Snake tribes see Voegelin, *Northern Paiutes of Central Oregon*, pp. 96-115.

5   Dave Chocktote—interviewed by the author—was the son of the Snake war chief Black Buffalo, whose Shoshoni name appears in the various records as Chockto-te, Tchaktot, Chock-toot, Chaw-wat-nanee, Che-whatney, Che-what-ne, Choc-chack-chuck and Tchatchaktchokok.

many had protruding stomachs. The Shoshoni specifically applied this name to the war-like Klamath under the leadership of the mixed blood Shoshoni, Motcunka Sket, who became known as Moses Brown after attending the 1864 treaty council. Following Shoshoni tradition, Moses Brown had settled with his mother's people, thus becoming the chief of a hybrid band of Snakes and Klamaths. In an effort to translate Yahuskin into Klamath, the interpreters came up with "people from far away" which may explain why Huntington did not connect the name with Motcunka Sket's Klamath followers but applied it to the wandering Washoes, believing they were Snakes.[6] (Yahooskin was incorrectly spelled by the treaty officials; Yahuskin is the correct spelling.)

Drew, in his official report for July 1864, would classify Motcunka Sket's (he spelled it *Moshun-kask-kit*) tribe as Snake Klamath. Noticing the Shoshoni within the band, he was quick to note that: "They are physically superior to any of the Indians about the borders of Klamath Lake and possess more man-hood." At that time they were friendly but in Drew's opinion in the event of a general Indian uprising "they would doubtless prove more dangerous and troublesome than any of the other Indians" in the Klamath region.[7]

A few days before Drew's arrival at the treaty grounds, Paulina had ridden into Motcunka Sket's camp and tried to persuade him to join the Paviotso Confederacy. Although the Klamath war chief Chiloquin claimed he was eager to enter the fray, Motcunka Sket was reluctant. Like Gourd Rattler, he reasoned that there might be more advantage to remaining neutral in the event Wolf Dog's revolt should fail. On this note, the meeting ended with Motcunka Sket knowing he had made an enemy of Paulina for life, and thus none of his Snake followers would attend the treaty conference at Council Grove. Captain Jack of the Modocs also failed to appear.

At least during the preliminary peace feelers, Gourd Rattler was not offering any advice on the joys of treaty benefits. He was involved in a free-for-all with the Crows over hunting rights in the Wind River country but he did take time out to confiscate 19 head of horses from the Sheep Killers and turn them over to the army at Fort Bridger.[8] Unknown to him, many of Gourd Rattler's warriors were now secretly defecting to ride with Has No Horse. Or perhaps he did know and was merely keeping up appearances with his American allies. After all, the return of 19 broken-down miners' ponies was little more than a gesture of goodwill.

And so with the usual amount of confusion, the treaty of 1864 got underway. It would contain the standard provisions of cession of all lands claimed by the Indians present for a berth on Upper and Middle Klamath Lakes; said Indians to

---

6      Gatschet, *Klamath Indians*, Pt. 2 pp. 71 and 99; Spier, *Klamath Ethnography*, p. 23.

7      Drew, *Official Report*, pp. 2-6.

8      James Doty to Commissioner of Indian Affairs, June 13, 1864 and Luther Mann to Acting Commissioner of Indian Affairs, June 20, 1864, Record Group 75, Office of Indian Affairs, Washington, D.C., Indian Office Records.

This picture of Has No Horse was taken in 1869 when he and Iron Crow traveled south into Nevada. Union Pacific took this picture, and although they knew his correct name, they had no idea that Has No Horse was head chief of the Paviotso Confederacy, and leader of the Shoshoni in their war against the United States Army.

*Courtesy of the American Heritage Center, University of Wyoming.*

This is an example of a typical willow tray used by the Big Lodge Shoshoni to gather seeds and grasses.

Oliver Applegate and Joaquin Miller were veterans of the Shoshoni war. Applegate, Indian agent, army scout and politician, was a captain in the Mountain Rangers, a local militia formed to fight the Shoshoni, and for a time he was editor of the *Ashland Tidings*. He occasionally wrote poems and this perhaps brought on his meeting with Miller, Oregon's famous author and longtime newspaper editor.

About 800 people lived in Portland when this picture of Front Street was taken in 1852. Ten years later, when the gold stampede got under way, the population was around 2900, yet during the opening 3-year period of the gold rush it is estimated that 82,000 people passed through Portland en route to the gold fields in eastern Oregon and Idaho.

*Caption and photo courtesy of The Ore Bin, Vol. 40, Number 4, State of Oregon Department of Geology & Mineral Industries.*

The portage at the Cascades in 1861 (now known as Cascade Locks) was 6 miles long. When steamers from Portland unloaded their up-river freight at the Cascades for transport over the portage during the gold rush, the mule-drawn flat cars were so slow that freight sometimes piled up for days before it could be loaded onto steamers above the rapids for transfer to The Dalles.

*Caption and photo courtesy of The Ore Bin, Vol. 40, Number 4, State of Oregon Department of Geology & Mineral Industries.*

The Cascades of the Columbia in 1898.

*Courtesy of Keith McCoy,* Melodic Whistles in the Columbia River Gorge.

Umatilla House pool room and bar.

*Courtesy of Keith McCoy,* Melodic Whistles in the Columbia River Gorge.

The dining room of the Umatilla House.

*Courtesy of Keith McCoy,* Melodic Whistles in the Columbia River Gorge.

# NEW UMATILLA HOUSE,

### THE DALLES, OREGON,

HANDLEY & SINNOTT, · · · Proprietors.

The largest and finest hotel in Oregon. Ticket and Baggage office of the O. R. & N. Co. and office of the W. U. Tel. Co. are in the hotel. Fire proof safe for the safety of all valuables. Trains depart from this house for Walla Walla and the East, and for Portland and San Francisco.

An advertisement portraying the outside of the Umatilla House hotel.

*Courtesy of Keith McCoy,* Melodic Whistles in the Columbia River Gorge.

This small engine, on display at Cascade Locks, was named "The Pony." It was built in San Francisco, then shipped to the Cascades in 1862 to help speed up the traffic over the portage. The rails were made of wood covered with strap iron. This was Oregon's first railroad.

*Caption and photo courtesy of The Ore Bin, Vol. 40, Number 4, State of Oregon Department of Geology & Mineral Industries.*

The Dalles was the jumping-off place and last outfitting headquarters for the gold-seekers heading east, and the *Harvest Queen* pictured here was one of several boats plying the river between the Cascade portage and The Dalles. The famous Umatilla House is in the background. More money reportedly passed over its bar during this period than over any other bar in the Pacific Northwest.

*Caption and photo courtesy of The Ore Bin, Vol. 40, Number 4, State of Oregon Department of Geology & Mineral Industries.*

Interior of a red light cabin typical to gold rush towns such as Canyon City and Tiger Town, in the mid to late 1800's. Perhaps it was the living quarters of those Canyon City doves known only as French Rita, Two-bit Sally and Velvet-ass Rose.

Warren H. Luckey

*Courtesy of Gene Luckey.*

Jim Blakely supplied beef to eastern Oregon military posts during the Shoshoni war.

*Courtesy of Crook County Historical Society, Bowman Museum.*

James, John and Joseph Luckey

The Luckey boys served as army scouts during the Shoshoni war. Several members of their family along with General Wright were lost at sea when the *Brother Jonathan* crashed into Dragon Reef and sank off the coast of northern California.

*Courtesy of Gene Luckey.*

The Oregon Boot, or Gardner Shackle as it was known in those early days, was a restraining apparatus invented in 1865 by Portland prison warden J.C. Gardner. Patented in 1866, the shackle was made in the prison blacksmith shop. Above the boot is unassembled, and below it is in place on a prisoner's foot.

*Courtesy of Jon and Donna Skovlin,* Hank Vaughan, *and the Oregon Sheriffs' Association.*

The difficulties of the portage above The Dalles and past Celilo Falls were lessened by the construction in 1863 of the 15-mile-narrow-gauge "portage" railroad. Built on the Oregon side of the Columbia River at a reported cost of $50,000 per mile and in service until the 1880s, this railroad constituted an important link for river boats plying the Columbia between Cascade Locks and The Dalles and those plying the up-river run from Celilo to Umatilla Landing and Lewiston.

*Caption and photo courtesy of The Ore Bin, Vol. 40, Number 4, State of Oregon Department of Geology & Mineral Industries.*

The river steamer *Tenino* on the upper Columbia. With stops at Umatilla Landing, Wallula, and Lewiston, this vessel is credited with having taken in $18,000 on one up-river trip in 1863.

*Caption and photo courtesy of The Ore Bin, Vol. 40, Number 4, State of Oregon Department of Geology & Mineral Industries.*

A sketch of the first house built in Auburn, Baker County, in the fall of 1861, built by D. Littlefield, H. Griffin, Wm. Stafford, and G.W. Schriver. Sketch is by Isaac Hiatt, 1893 from memory.

*Courtesy of Baker City Library, McCord Collection.*

Express Stage Station

*Courtesy of Baker City Library, McCord Collection; Jon and Donna Skovlin,* Hank Vaughan.

Blacksmith shop in Auburn, Oregon in 1863. The Blacksmith is said to be the grandfather of Lilith Allen.

It was under the cover of a smoke screen such as this from a forest fire in the Ochoco Mountains that Has No Horse attacked the Ochoco Blockhouse on Mill Creek in July of 1868 (see Chapter 147).

Unknown mine in Cornucopia District.

*Courtesy of the Baker City Library, McCord Collection.*

Panama Placer in the Cornucopia District.

*Courtesy of the Baker City Library, McCord Collection.*

Baker City as it appeared around 1867. The large, unpainted building in the foreground served as court house and the repository of the county records removed from Auburn. With Auburn on the decline, Baker went on to become the Queen City in the eastern Oregon gold belt and the center for all heavy mining equipment.

*Caption and photo courtesy of The Ore Bin, Vol. 40, Number 4, State of Oregon Department of Geology & Mineral Industries.*

Bourne, once known as Cracker City, is situated 6 miles north of Sumpter on Cracker Creek and is surrounded by some of the best mining property in the state. Founded in 1890, Bourne soon had a population of 1500, with 2 hotels, 4 saloons, 7 general stores, 2 newspapers, and 3 restaurants.

*Caption and photo courtesy of The Ore Bin, Vol. 40, Number 4, State of Oregon Department of Geology & Mineral Industries.*

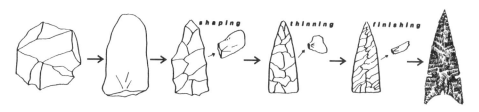

Diagram of the making of a Shoshoni arrowhead.

*Courtesy of Carrol B. Howe,* Frontier Stories of the Klamath Country.

This is a replica of an eastern Oregon military fort, constructed in 1960 for a movie set where Sunriver, Oregon is now located.

*Courtesy of Gale Ontko.*

In this area on the lower Deschutes River Captain Hiram Wilber, in command of two companies of Oregon Rangers, constructed a fort on the east side of the river to guard the Warm Springs Agency and Captain Wallen's newly constructed pontoon bridge, which was built across the Deschutes in 1859 (see Chapter 93).

*Courtesy of Gale Ontko.*

receive $16,000 in supplies and another $80,000 to be paid over the next 15 years (presumably they would be self-supporting by 1879); all white people except government officials and employees were forbidden to reside on the reservation; and finally, when ratified, the government would pay an additional $35,000 for farming equipment, education expenses and general welfare of the Indians signing the treaty. At the same time, the United States reserved the right to place other Indians on the Klamath Reservation.[9] Lindsay Applegate was appointed Indian Agent. However, for almost a year after the signing of the October Treaty, the Klamath Reservation existed only on paper and had no agent.

The Klamaths and Modocs, under constant raids from the Snakes, could see a strong ally in the United States Army. Twenty-one Klamaths and four Modocs—including Lalake, Old Schonchin, Allen David, Chiloquin and Motcunka Sket (Moses Brown)—willingly gave up all rights to tribal holdings from the headwaters of the Deschutes River in south-central Oregon to the ridge between the Pit and McLeod rivers in northern California for some protection. But the tragic outcome of the 1864 treaty was the signing by two so-called chiefs—Kiletoak and Skyteocket—of the "Yahooskin Band of Snake Indians." By touching pen to the treaty they sold title to all Shoshoni lands south of the 44th parallel from the eastern base of the Cascades to Harney Valley and extending from the southern Blues in central Oregon to the Oregon-California-Nevada state line. And thus, without representation or reimbursement, the United States government acquired nearly 22 million acres of Shoshoni tribal lands . . . 33,700 square miles of land which Kiletoak and Skyteocket readily admitted they had never seen. (For a partial reproduction of the 1864 Treaty, see the appendices.)

The Klamath chief, Waualaix (By The River), soon to be known as Dave Hill, took it upon himself to verify the mark of Kiletoak and Skyteocket as being authentic Shoshoni acceptance. Has No Horse was a long time in catching up with Dave Hill for this treachery but he would never live to celebrate his 50th birthday. In the early spring of 1892, Dave was found near Linkville (Klamath Falls) . . . with a Shoshoni scalp knife embedded in his chest.[10]

Captain Jack, to show his contempt for his fellow tribesmen, began selling rifles and ammunition to the Snakes. When he found out about it, Allen David, one

---

9     *Treaty Between the United States of America and the Klamath and Modoc Tribes and Yahooskin Band of Snake Indians, concluded October 14, 1864, United States Statutes at Large*, Vol. 16, p. 383. Twenty-seven "chiefs and headmen" signed the treaty. Identified as a Klamath chief, Moses Brown (Mo-ghen-kas-kit), whose father was a Shoshoni, was the seventh person to touch pen to the treaty; the twenty-fourth signer was Kiletoak and Skyteocket was the twenty-sixth. These two were the so-called Yahuskin Snakes who transferred title of 22 million acres of Shoshoni tribal land to the U.S. government. This sell-out was witnessed by R.P. Earhart, treaty secretary, Capt. William Kelly, 1st Cavalry, Oregon Volunteers, 2nd Lt. James Halloran, 1st Infantry, Washington Territory Volunteers, William C. McKay, M.D., and Robert (his mark) Biddle.

10    The *Ashland Tidings*, April 14, 1892.

of the Modoc signers, squealed to the authorities and Captain Jack had him marked for execution.[11]

By the Klamath Treaty of 1864, the Indian signers relinquished their right to leave the reservation for the purpose of hunting, fishing, gathering berries and grazing of horses except on permit issued by the agent. They did not understand that there would be any difficulty in obtaining these permits. There was. It has been stated that the treaty was fraudulently negotiated with the Indians because they were deliberately allowed to misunderstand the terms. Even the old Indian-hater, Lt. Col. Drew was happy that he had no hand in the treaty process for he was certain the government would fail to meet its promises. Other critics who were more outspoken soon found themselves in the same unwanted category as those whom they tried to defend. Perhaps that is why Drew disappeared from public sight.

A journalist, looking back on a century of questionable dealings with the native population, would criticize not only the actions of the aggressors but also those of the defectors who so willingly surrendered to the advance of American domination. This writer would tartly comment:

> The Indians, fighting to retain what they had owned for ages, were unmitigated rascals, but the whites, fighting to possess what did not belong to them, were splendid soldiers of God. The Indians, often driven to actual starvation, and striking back desperately, were yelping and unvarnished assassins; but the whites, eager to lay the camas meadows under agriculture, were approved by all the centuries of plunder in which right has been on the stronger side. And not only that: those Indians who, deserting their own traditional people, came to the aid of the whites are today commemorated in monuments; but the few whites who went over to the Indians were held in unspeakable infamy.[12]

On the deficit side of the Indian ledger, a prime example occurred in May 1863 when Nevada Agent John Burche—on the promise of a Spanish sombrero, a red silk sash and a pair of heavy red blankets—talked Bad Face into using his influence to prevent the mounted Paiutes from joining forces with Has No Horse.[13] Bad Face himself, a staunch friend of Has No Horse, rode heel to heel with him in battle. . . not once but hundreds of times. Yet history would portray Bad Face—even when he was caught red-handed in hostile acts—as a man of peace while Has No Horse was reviled as a savage renegade equaled in barbarity only by "the brutal devastator" Paulina.

In the near future, these two incorrigibles would inflict much pain on the happy treaty signers of Council Grove.

---

11    Letter, Lindsay Applegate to Stephen B. Thoburn, Fort Klamath, September 19, 1869. Applegate Collection, Oregon Historical Society.

12    Idaho's Writer's Project, *Idaho*, p. 11, New York, Oxford University Press, 1950.

13    Report of the Commissioner of Indian Affairs 1864, pp. 288-92.

# CHAPTER 121

# I COME IN PEACE

*I saw the white man. He said he was my friend. He abused
our women and children and told us to go from the land. Still
he gave his hand in friendship. . . . I feel the irons in my heart.*

**Paulina, The War Spirit**
Fort Klamath, November 1864

No doubt Huntington was disappointed that the Snake war chiefs rejected his offer of reconciliation but the fortunes of diplomacy were about to shift in his favor. Aware that the army was in a state of confusion with enlistments expiring in December and paying little attention to duty, the Shoshoni took this opportunity to prepare for winter. Raids came to a standstill as the tribes fanned out in all directions to gather winter provisions. With Drake, Caldwell and Currey marching toward Fort Dalles and Drew preoccupied at Fort Klamath, Wolf Dog, Has No Horse and Paulina moved into their winter headquarters in the Ochoco.

At the Walpapi camp in Beaver Valley, Falling Star, Paulina's wife, Cactus Fruit, his sister and Tiny Ant, wife of the dog soldier Sun Hunter, decided it would be an excellent time to slip into the Cascades to gather a supply of venison, elk and huckleberries. To insure protection, Burning Wagon (Paulina's brother-in-law), Death Rattle (Paulina's medicine man), Lean Man (whose wife was taken hostage by Lt. McCall in May and was now slave to Simtustus), Magpie Man (a Tukaricka brave), and Horse Trap (Paulina's ranking lieutenant) would accompany the women on this food-gathering mission. Horse Trap was described as a natural born killer. Restless as a stalking puma, he was the self-elected bodyguard and personal hatchet man for Paulina—the only man for whom Horse Trap ever held any affection. Before three summers could cross the land, Horse Trap would die in an attempt to save Paulina's life.

As this small party got underway, Huntington was putting the final touches on the treaty of 1864. After distributing presents and depositing 16,000 pounds of flour at Fort Klamath, the treaty members under escort of Lt. Halloran's Washington Infantry and a cavalry detachment under the command of Lt. Charles Underwood, headed back to Fort Dalles on the Klamath trade trail along the eastern base of the Cascade Range. This route was now called Huntington's Road. On the headwaters of the Deschutes, the advance guards surprised and captured Lean Man and Magpie Man who were fishing on what Huntington called "Mill-ke-ke Creek at the crossing of the Deschutes River." After their capture, Underwood sent out McKay's scouts to search for the main camp which was found 15 miles to the east on a side stream emptying into the Deschutes. The scouts reported that there were only three men, three women and two children in camp. The soldiers quickly encircled the little encampment and took everyone prisoner.

When Huntington found out from the Warm Springs scouts that one of the women was Paulina's wife he was elated. He immediately issued orders to have them all taken to Fort Dalles where he would use Falling Star as a bargaining chip to make direct contact with Paulina. On hearing this, the warriors made a desperate attempt to seize weapons and horses from the guards. In the explosive action Burning Wagon, Magpie Man and Death Rattle were killed. Lean Man and Horse Trap, although badly wounded, mounted horses and made good their escape. In an effort to confuse pursuit, they immediately split up with Lean Man serving as bait. After several hours of tracking, the soldiers finally caught up with Lean Man who had died from loss of blood. Unable to locate Horse Trap and believing that he also had died, they gave up the chase. This would turn out to be a mistake. Through him, Paulina learned of the loss of four warriors and the capture of his wife and sister. Huntington would later claim that he sent the Klamath chief Lalake to Paulina with a peace message.

On arrival at The Dalles City, Logan—worried about Snake retaliation on the reservation—refused to imprison Paulina's wife at Warm Springs. Apparently unaware that Cactus Fruit was Paulina's sister and that they had made a double coup, he accepted her and the two children, one of whom was Paulina's son. The military, not happy with holding women as prisoners, advised Huntington to get Falling Star out of eastern Oregon as they too feared retaliation on The Dalles. At the end of October, Falling Star was taken to Fort Vancouver and placed under the custody of Gen. Alvord to be held hostage until peace was obtained.[1]

En route back to the Warm Springs Agency, Cactus Fruit and the two children escaped.

Paulina immediately sent a messenger to Fort Klamath protesting the killing and capturing of his people.[2] Surprisingly, Lalake and several other Klamath chiefs

---

[1]    There are several versions of this affair varying in details. Paulina's own account, delivered through a messenger to Capt. Kelly at Fort Klamath is found in a letter in the National Archives, Bureau of Indian Affairs Oregon Superintendency, Letters Received, Wm. Kelly to J.W. Perit Huntington, Fort Klamath, Oregon, November 1, 1864. Huntington's account is found in Report to the Commissioner of Indian Affairs 1865, Congressional Documents Series 1248: 269-70. Other references are: National Archives, War Department Command Department of the Pacific, K-30, K-77, 1864; Wm. Kelly to E.P. Waite, Ft. Klamath, Oregon, November 10, 1864; National Archives, War Department Commands, Department of the Pacific, A-176, 1864, Benjamin Alvord to R.C. Dunn, Ft. Vancouver, Washington Territory, November 25, 1864; *War of the Rebellion*, Vol. L, Pt. 2: 1144; Bancroft, *History of Oregon*, Vol. II: 507.

[2]    Paulina's messenger, the Togwingani war chief, Yellow Badger, is referred to by Capt. Kelly

expressed deep concern over "the outrage done to Paulina." A good guess for this unexpected reaction is that they, like Agent Bill Logan, were deathly afraid of Snake revenge.

Fearing for his wife's safety, Paulina then dispatched riders to Wolf Dog's and Has No Horse's camps telling them to cease hostilities until he could negotiate Falling Star's release. Has No Horse was willing to comply but Wolf Dog and Black Eagle—their faces slashed with white and red stripes over the capture of their sister and death of their brother-in-law—vowed they would burn the Warm Springs Agency to the ground. Amassing a small army, they headed for the white settlements. On the Agency Plains, they found Cactus Fruit and the children thus averting the Agency's destruction, but they then turned to The Dalles-Canyon City thoroughfare. During the winter of 1864 and 1865, these vengeful warriors filled the Fort Watson cemetery with fresh graves.

One of the fortunate few to get through was Marion More. The *Daily Oregonian* would announce on November 28, 1864 that "Marion More arrived in Portland last night on the stage from Owyhee with 600 pounds of bullion in seven bricks from the Oro Fino and Morning Star Ledges." That shipment alone was worth over $86,000. The next day, 130 Cheyenne were gunned-down at Sand Creek in western Colorado.

Meanwhile, as his brothers rode west to exact vengeance, Paulina, in the cold grey dawn of a November snowstorm, headed for Fort Klamath—160 miles southwest of his Crooked River camp. From Horse Trap's report it was his belief, perhaps even hope, that Falling Star was imprisoned there. Traveling day and night, he arrived at the fort in three days, where the military would get their first unhampered look at the man feared throughout four western states as "the Brutal Devastator." If they were expecting—as portrayed by artists and news reporters—a classically bronzed, splendidly proportioned warrior decked out in an eagle feather war bonnet, hip-length fringed buckskin leggings and beaded moccasins, mounted bare-back on a small, high-strung, multi-colored Indian pony, carrying a feathered battle-lance and laminated sheep-horn bow; they were due for a surprise.

In appearance, Paulina was rather ordinary. He approached the stockade gate mounted on a rangy, durable bay gelding that looked as though it had seen too much riding with too little grass. Like the horse, his saddle was practical but had known little care. It, along with the faint trace of a brand on the horse's hip, indicated that both had been quietly lifted from some settler's pasture, corral or barn on a moonless night.

---

as Sky-ti-at-tilk. Notice the similarity in spelling with Skyteocket, the Washoe headman who signed the 1864 treaty just 17 days before Yellow Badger's arrival at Fort Klamath. National Archives, Bureau of Indian Affairs Oregon Superintendency, Letters Received, Wm. Kelly to J.W. Perit Huntington, Fort Klamath Oregon, November 1, 1864; *War of the Rebellion*, Vol. L, pt. 2: 1068.

Wound about his head was a bandanna that once had been red but neither color nor pattern could now be clearly distinguished because of long accumulations of dirt and sweat undisturbed by washing. From under this headband, two braids of black hair hung over his shoulders and down the front of a ragged cotton shirt, which hung outside denim trousers, both unmistakably the products of the white man's loom. Over the tattered shirt, he wore a heavy dark blue army coat with the insignias of a U.S. cavalry major. Speculation ran high as to the identity of the unfortunate person who provided this garment large enough to fit Paulina's broad shoulders but it was believed that he was an officer of the California cavalry. His moccasins, worn to the point of no covering at all, were without decoration. Nestled in the crook of his arm was a Sharps .52 calibre carbine and tucked into a well-oiled holster on his right thigh was a .44 calibre army model Colt. What Paulina lacked in fine clothing, he made up for in modern weapons.

Nearly six feet tall, Paulina gave the impression as he rode in that his legs were too short for his body. When he dismounted this illusion became obvious. With his thick chest, extremely broad shoulders and lumpy body running to paunch, the big warrior's appearance contradicted his height. Although he approached Capt. Kelly with a friendly eye, Paulina left the impression that he possessed a fierce animal nature. Kelly observed that when Paulina first arrived "he looked very sullen, his brows were knit heavily but before he left he got cheerful with the hope of getting his woman back."[3] When invited to the officer's mess, he consumed twice as much as any man at the table. It was also obvious that when he fasted he could go many days without food.

The fact that Paulina had a reputation of some magnitude is evidenced in how quickly a photographer, which was quite rare on the eastern Oregon frontier, was brought into Fort Klamath. This photo was more revealing than the usual frontier portrait.[4] It shows a determined man, squat, solid and dark with high cheekbones and unrelenting eyes. It also reveals how a brave man faces death. Paulina—an unlettered product of rimrock and sage—had never heard of a camera let alone seen one. He believed it was some kind of gun and waited impassively for death as the army photographer tripped the shutter. Thus how Paulina placed himself in position to have his photo taken is an insight to his character; and his presence before the camera—a man searching for his wife—shows him to also be a man of sentiment, which is alien to his reputation as a cold-blooded killer.

With the social amenities taken care of, Capt. Kelly and war chief Paulina got down to business. It quickly became a stand-off. Paulina refused to sign a treaty until his wife was safely returned to him. Kelly was equally certain that once

3    National Archives, Bureau of Indian Affairs Oregon Superintendency, Letters Received, Wm. Kelly to J.W. Perit Huntington, Ft. Klamath, Oregon, November 10, 1864.

4    See article by Early Deane, "Chief Paulina the Red Raider," *Northwest Home Garden*, February 13, 1966.

Falling Star was reunited with her husband, he would not sign. Paulina readily admitted he had been fighting the soldiers during the summer and was in the fight in which Lt. Watson was killed and that he had returned to the Indian fort (in Rabbit Valley) afterwards. But now, he assured Kelly, he was tired of war. All he wished was his wife's safe return and a place for him and his people to live in peace "between Fort Klamath and The Dalles, east of the trail [Huntington's Road] where it crosses the Deschutes and near the big mountain [Lookout] east of the trail." He also told George Nurse, a fort civilian employee, that he had "500 warriors under his command both great and little," meaning men and boys.[5] In this discussion, treachery was working on both sides.

A message was dispatched to Salem notifying Huntington of Paulina's offer. It also urged the release of Falling Star . . . not to Paulina but to Fort Klamath where they would both be held in captivity until Huntington could arrive the following summer to witness the signing of an official treaty. Simultaneously with Paulina's arrest at Fort Klamath, the mysterious hostile visitations in the Rogue and Umpqua valleys—200 miles from the Snakes' main line of defense in the Ochoco mountains, and which had been a source of puzzlement—immediately stopped. This caused Kelly to believe that Paulina was sincere. On Capt. Kelly's conviction, Supt. Huntington promised to arrange Falling Star's release from the Fort Vancouver prison and return her under armed guard to Fort Klamath which he did . . . nearly a year later in August 1865!

Meantime, Gen. Alvord was overjoyed to hear that Paulina had "sued for peace." In a letter to Huntington, Alvord gives an interesting bit of information about Paulina and how the army and Office of Indian Affairs decided who would be chiefs. Alvord writes, "Mr. Logan, agent at the Warm Springs Reservation, said that the Indian women said that Po-li-ni's brother was the principal chief, he being only war chief. No doubt it will be our policy to treat Po-li-ni as the head chief if he is friendly and peaceable, to increase if possible his power and to make use of him in controlling all the Snake Indians."[6] And that is how chiefs were made by the white men!

Major Rinehart, in a somewhat cloudy state of mind, would pen in his memoirs: "Paulina, the terror of the whole frontier, surrendered before Christmas at Fort Klamath after being reduced to the verge of starvation. Paulina's Indians never took the warpath again but gave up their life of vagabondage and settled on the Malheur Reservation where as Indian Agent I cared for them for six years. . . ."[7]

---

5    National Archives, Bureau of Indian Affairs Oregon Superintendency, Letters Received, Wm. Kelly to E.P. Waite, Fort Klamath, Oregon, November 10, 1864; George Nurse to Mr. Huntington, Fort Klamath, Oregon, November 10, 1864; *War of the Rebellion*, Series I, Vol. L., Pt. 1: 337-38.

6    *War of the Rebellion*, Series I, Vol. L, Pt. 2: 1072.

7    W.V. Rinehart, Manuscript, Oregon Historical Society, Portland, Oregon.

Rinehart must have been sampling some of his own whiskey when he wrote this. Paulina was shot to death four years before the Malheur Reservation was formed in 1871 and Rinehart served as Indian agent during the years 1878-1883—after the third and final phase of the Shoshonean wars.

During the winter of 1864-65, Paulina remained at liberty but was warned to keep the peace and not go near the Warm Springs Reservation.[8] Out of deference to his wife, Paulina would honor this request. But unfortunately for the military and any stray civilians, Wolf Dog and Has No Horse were not bound to such a foolish agreement.

---

8   *War of the Rebellion*, Series I, Vol. L, Pt. 2: 1114-1115.

CHAPTER 122

# WARFARE GRINDS TO A HALT

*The people of the Willamette Valley have persistently heaped*
*odium and reproach upon their own troops . . . sneering at*
*the sight of an officer of the cavalry on the streets. . . .*

**John M. Drake**
Captain, First Oregon Cavalry

With enlistment of the original six companies of cavalry due to expire in December 1864, the military was in a state of confusion. Troops were ordered from the field with more than half the veterans being mustered out of the service and the remainder awaiting reorganization. Flooded with southern sympathizers who could be expected to join any effort to defeat or harass the Union, Oregon, which was now under the strong influence of the Copperhead party (a name applied to northern Democrats who advocated peace with the Confederacy) was a volcano ready to erupt.

Adding to Oregon's growing discomfort was the threat of possible attack by the British, who embraced the southern cause and were casting covetous eyes on the Oregon empire lost in 1846. Those who remembered the British alliance with Indian tribes in the Revolutionary War feared some like move by the South, and the specter of a general Indian uprising throughout the West hung over the area. The Union, busy with civil war, would not be able to send help.

Many incidents gave Oregon residents cause to worry. A cannon in Albany used to fire military salutes disappeared, which caused an uproar among the loyalists. It was later learned that southern sympathizers wheeled the howitzer down a hill, loaded it on a ferry and dumped it in the middle of the Willamette River.[1] A Confederate flag was hoisted over a Canyon City hotel where it flew for days before residents of the mining town got up enough nerve to haul it down. In a shocking political defeat, Gov. Addison Gibbs in a bid for the U.S. Senate, didn't even have his name offered for nomination. This came as a heavy blow to his brother-in-law Capt. Watkins, medical officer for Co. C, which was guarding the Canyon City road. Watkins, sensing the adverse effect on military operations, was

---

1    *The Oregon Journal*, "Centennial Countdown," Friday, April 3, 1959.

more anxious about the endorsement than Gibbs himself. Then in August with the presidential election fast approaching, Gen. George McClellan—darling of the Union army—won the Copperhead nomination for president at the Democratic convention in Chicago. It was widely believed that should McClellan succeed in getting into power with Congress at his back, the Civil War would be lost. The polls were showing a strong vote in his favor and it was by no means certain that he would be defeated—particularly if Grant failed at Richmond or Sherman met with disaster at Atlanta.

When officers of the Oregon Cavalry—many who had served under McClellan in Oregon—learned of his nomination, they were dumbfounded. Drake would voice their outrage when he angrily declared that McClellan was "a demagogue of the first water, an ambitious political intriguer incapable of a patriotic emotion who would not hesitate to put the people of the United States under his heel."[2]

Five days after the creation of Grant County, the newly elected sheriff, in no mood to play games with Johnny Rebs, dispatched a rider to Fort Dalles requesting the cavalry be present in Canyon City on election day. The southern influence was so strong in Canyon City that loyalists believed Jeff Davis' name would be penciled into all the ballots and Grant County would elect him President of the United States! In uncommonly swift action, three days after receiving Grant County's plea, an expressman galloped into Fort Watson on October 27 with the following message for the commanding officer:

> Captain Henry C. Small—If this reaches you in time before the election of Tuesday, the eighth of next month, you will proceed in command of two-thirds of your company to Canyon City to be there election day. The object of your repairing there is to aid the civil authority in the suppression of violence on that day. . . . You will not, however, use military force except in subordination to the civil authority, and, if any firing on a mob occurs, let it be from the express requisition of the civil authority. . . . You will not permit any interference by the military to influence, much less to control or restrain, anyone in the full and free exercise of his right to vote for whomsoever he pleases. If your men are entitled to vote, let them go without their arms to the polls, if you can spare them from the ranks.
>
> Headquarters, District of Oregon,
> Fort Vancouver, W.T., October 24, 1864
> Benj. Alvord, Brig-Gen.,
> U.S. Volunteers, Commanding

---

2  Drake's Journal entry, September 9, 1864.

Having sent all horses to Fort Vancouver for the winter, Small immediately started for Canyon City on foot with 40 cavalrymen and 10 Washington infantrymen. He barely made it on schedule. On the evening of November 7, his troops slogged up the muddy streets of John Day City into Canyon City singing "Hang Jeff Davis to a Sour Apple Tree." Small then proceeded to cover the town with hand-painted posters which read:

### *To The People of Canyon City and Surrounding Country*

The presence of the military in your midst is not for the purpose of influencing much less to control or restrain anyone in the full and free exercise of his right to vote for whomsoever he pleases.

H.C. Small
1st O.V.C. Comd'g

To make certain no outbreak would occur later, the soldiers remained in town for three days after the election and on November 12, wallowed back to Fort Watson in driving rain and freezing snow.

With the changing tides of fortune, speculation ran high as to who would command the Oregon cavalry following reorganization. Col. Reuben Maury was the odds on favorite but there was a chance that Capt. Currey with his political clout could take over. Most of the field officers had been told they would be relieved of duty at the expiration of their three-year entry into Oregon service in 1861. On their return to Fort Dalles, they received word from the War Department that contrary to Oregon District orders, they would not be mustered out of the service. Many, including Major Rinehart and Capt. Currey, both of whom planned to get married, and Lt. Waymire who had a political career in mind, were very disappointed.

Drake's command arrived at Fort Dalles October 11, Currey a few days later, and Drew marched into Fort Klamath on October 16, bringing to an end the invasion of Wolf Dog's domain which was intended to squelch the Shoshoni rebellion for all time. The military—in direct opposition to civilian thinking—knew the campaign was a failure. Soldiers warned the public that "the different tribes of Shoshoni Indians would confederate together under the leadership of some Pe-li-ne and the white settlements from the head of the Columbia to The Dalles would be swept out of existence."[3] Strangely, army intelligence had never uncovered the fact that Has No Horse was the leader of that suspected confederacy and had been since the late 1850s. It was also military belief that it would take a minimum of "3,000 men and 10 million dollars" to suppress

---

3    Drake's Private Journal: 97.

the Shoshoni revolt. For this heresy, the army was subject to public ridicule. Drake would dourly comment "they [the people of the Willamette Valley] don't think so, however, and never will until the Indian is at their door or in wait for their freight trains." He further expressed the feelings of officers and enlisted men: "Were it not for the helpless women and children, I would rejoice to see the Indians wipe out the Columbia River country just to let the people of Portland and The Dalles know what slippery ground they stand on." If it accomplished nothing else, the campaign of '64 brought officers and enlisted men together in a tight-knit brotherhood of mutual respect.

Arriving at Fort Dalles and with the dust of the trail still on their uniforms, the cavalry found a much needed ally in Brig. Gen. Irvin McDowell. McDowell would instill in the Oregonians some respect for his weary Indian-fighting troops. Gen. Alvord—quick to note the change in attitude with McDowell's arrival—issued a news release commending the eastern Oregon soldiers for arduous service under battle conditions and put the public on notice that the officers and enlisted men of the First Oregon Cavalry had prevented an Indian uprising while "developing a part of Oregon heretofore marked on our maps as unexplored."[4] He also for the first time expressed a genuine interest in what his cavalry officers thought of their troopers. In a report on the Indian scouts, Currey, who had suggested their use at the start of the campaign, was enthusiastic about their performance. Drake's only comment was "our Warm Springs scouts are good spies but their capabilities as scouts have been overrated."

Then in an unexpected move, Gen. Alvord brought charges against Major Dumreicker for countermanding Capt. Drake's orders. Dumreicker's court-martial convened at Fort Dalles on October 25. The court, led by Major A.R. Egbert, Surgeon, United States Volunteers, would find Major Dumreicker "generally not guilty."[5] Gen. Alvord disapproved of the acquittal stating his reasons at some length but Major Egbert decided it was "not convenient" to reconsider the case.

During the Dumreicker hearing, Major Rinehart—still stricken with Amanda Gaines—was assigned to court-martial duty. Since he had what he called "four days leisure," he slipped off to Oregon City and got married. A month later, Captain Currey took the plunge with Jessica Gaines. Their father, Albert Gaines, was a Virginian loyal to the South and he was not happy about this northern invasion of the family. A truce was finally proclaimed a year later when both daughters announced the arrival of his first grandsons—one born at Fort Klamath, the other at Fort Hoskins.[6]

The pony soldiers would now find out the fate of the First Oregon Cavalry. Gen. McDowell entered Oregon's morass of political back-stabbing at a full gallop.

---

4    *The Daily Oregonian*, November 1, 1864.

5    Military District of Oregon General Orders No. 24, November 11, 1864.

6    *Washington Historical Quarterly* No. 22: 94-95.

Gen. George Wright had been the first casualty. Although retaining command of the California District, he was relieved of command of the Military Department of the Pacific by McDowell in early July. Following a whirlwind tour of Fort Dalles, Fort Walla Walla and Fort Boise, he would make sweeping policy changes. Arriving back at Fort Vancouver in October, he went into conference with Gen. Alvord, Gen. Reed and Gov. Gibbs. In a heated session, McDowell gave state officials a choice. Either they voluntarily brought Oregon forces up to acceptable military strength or he would order a draft to restore the Oregon Volunteer Cavalry to full regimental strength; commandeer a second full regiment of cavalry under regular army status; and raise a regiment of infantry—ten companies of 82 privates each—all to be filled with a full compliment of regimental and staff officers. Acting on orders of the War Department, Gen. McDowell was going to bring Oregon into step with the Union or die trying.

When word of McDowell's proclamation reached the volunteer cavalry, they were ecstatic. The thought of 4,000 draftees chuckled one soldier, "will make the webfoot nation squirm." And squirm they did. Oregon was in a state of shock. It was obvious the west-siders were not anxious to be "out there hunting Pe-li-ne." Perhaps, as Capt. Drake hoped, this would "place a different estimate upon brass buttons by the time they have worn them two or three years."

After reading Lt. Col. Drew's report, Gen. McDowell ordered the Applegate Trail to be taken as a pattern for an Oregon Central Military road. Organization, construction and maintenance would be done by a corporation of Lane County citizens. He also started construction of a Willamette Valley and Cascade Mountain military road into the Crooked River Valley.

Drake, promoted to major and ordered to winter at Fort Vancouver was not overjoyed with this assignment, believing he could be put to better use backing up Small on the Canyon City road. Currey, also promoted to major, was shipped to Fort Hoskins to ride herd on Copperheads. Waymire, who was Gov. Gibbs' private secretary before enlisting in the First Oregon Cavalry, was detailed to special service at the state capital and then reassigned to the regular army as a second lieutenant in 1865.

The *Portland Oregonian* on November 30, 1864, boldly announced that "there will be 10 companies of volunteer infantry in the field by 1865." (Oregon would reach eight companies by April 1865.) The governor—in a state of distress—appealed to county officials to avoid the draft by "vigorously prosecuting the business of providing volunteers." The 1864 legislature—in hope of stalling off McDowell's draft—quickly passed a new bounty act to encourage enlistment. It gave every man who would enlist for three years as part of the state quota under the laws of Congress, $150 in addition to other bounties and pay already provided, which was to be raised by a tax on all private property in the state. At the same time, an act was passed setting aside a $100,000 fund out of which to pay five dollars a month additional compensation to volunteers already in service. This bounty would also provide a 160 acre land warrant to veterans.[7] Oregon, shaken to its foundations, was taking Gen. McDowell's warning quite seriously.

During this feverish activity, the regular army got another lowering of morale when Portland received news on the newly installed telegraph of a crushing defeat suffered by the enemy. The message read: "Great Battle with Indians! The savages dispersed! 500 Indians killed. Our loss nine killed, 38 wounded." In the cold gray dawn of November 29, 1864—one day after an $86,000 gold shipment had successfully run the Shoshoni gauntlet between Canyon City and The Dalles—Black Kettle's Cheyenne village on Sand Creek was attacked by a force of blood-hungry civilians under the command of Col. John M. Chivington, a former Methodist minister and Gen. Reed's counterpart for the Military District of Colorado. Chivington would note, "I am fully satisfied that to kill the red rebels is the only way to have peace and quiet."[8] And that he did. Men, women, and children.

At the time Black Kettle, White Antelope and Little Robe were camped on Sand Creek (according to army instructions), they believed themselves to be under the guardianship of the government. However, the citizens of Colorado wanted them removed. Gov. John Evans was absent from the territory when a political henchman under his authority planned the attack. Chivington led 100-day volunteers—hailed as the Colorado Militia—by night to Sand Creek and let fly with grapeshot and carbines at 600 sleeping Cheyenne, two-thirds of whom—by eyewitness report—were women and children. Shot down like jackrabbits, by noon hundreds lay dead as some of the volunteers began hacking off parts of women for souvenirs. They heaped mats on one woman so old she could not walk and burned her alive. One of the officers seeing her charred body yelled: "Boys, kick some sand over that old thing—it looks bad!" Chivington bragged that he had killed Black Kettle. He lied. Black Kettle escaped, only to die four years later under the guns of Custer's 7th Cavalry on the Washita.

A great victory had been won—impressing the Oregon citizens with the value of volunteers who knew much better how to dispose of reluctant trespassers than did the army. After all, the butchering of an entire tribe was infinitely more efficient than leaving a few survivors to produce seed for a new crop of human weeds.

---

7    Oregon Laws 1866: 98-110.
8    Capps, *The Indians*, p. 192.

# CHAPTER 123

# POTATOES AND ONIONS

*The Snakes though composed of many bands are not formidable.*
*I do not see any new source of danger is to arise from these*
*Indians.*

**Gen. George Wright**
October 10, 1860

For some reason, Oregonians believed Huntington's dubious Klamath treaty had ended Indian hostilities in eastern Oregon. In view of the continuing raids on Canyon City traffic, this assumption was beyond logic. Oregonians stubbornly refused to give little more than token aid to their beleaguered kin on the Shoshoni frontier. Even under threat of a military draft and the *Portland Oregonian's* editorial crusade to "join the army and kill Indians" enlistment lagged far behind schedule. At least Canyon City, isolated by a Shoshoni blockade, did its share.

Encouraged by recruiting officer, Capt. A.J. Borland, the first organized infantry company came from Grant County. Polk County, through the added incentive of an extra $1,200 bounty, was the next to be formed in December followed by Yamhill County. Although Josephine County offered a $2,500 bonus and Clackamas County a like amount, they were having few takers. Ironically, the two counties doing the most complaining about protection and with the most at stake—Jackson in the heart of the southern Oregon goldfields and Wasco, supply depot for the eastern Oregon strikes—were the last to come up with volunteers.[1]

Gov. Gibbs, knowing that Gen. McDowell's pledge to enforce mandatory draft was no idle threat, reminded the male population of their patriotic duty but response was less than enthusiastic. Then the axe fell. In January 1865, McDowell converted the First Oregon Volunteer Cavalry Regiment to regular army standing, placing it under the control of United States Army personnel. Rogue Valley to Owyhee Canyon was removed from Gen. Wright's command and attached to the Military District of Oregon. Gen. Alvord—under the influence of Oregon politicians—was transferred to the East Coast and Col. Reuben Maury placed in

---

1     A list of the infantry companies formed and their officers appears in the *Report of the Adjutant General of Oregon 1866, pp. 217-221.*

command of the Oregon district. Western Idaho and northern Nevada were made a subdivision of Oregon under Drake who was advanced from major in the volunteers to lieutenant colonel in the regular army. This realignment left the military affairs of Oregon entirely in the hands of her own citizens under the overall command of Brig. Gen. McDowell.[2]

Oregon lawmakers also received another incentive to open the eastern routes of travel. In January 1865 Congress appropriated $100,000 to build a United States mint at The Dalles. Work commenced immediately, providing employment to a large number of men and an excuse not to enlist in the army. The three-foot-thick walled building—50 feet wide by 60 feet long by 35 feet high—was made of granite from a quarry on Mill Creek (five miles from the site) and by July the first story was completed.

With all the shifts of military personnel taking place, Fort Watson was the only active post during the winter of 1864-65. Duty at this isolated outpost was anything but pleasant. Surrounded by six-foot snowdrifts, short on rations and without horses, Capt. Small could do little to stop Wolf Dog's raids on the supply lines into Canyon City and points east. To make garrison life a little more bearable, several women moved into the fort to work in the laundry, commissary, mess hall and hospital. Stage company records show that other women visited the army post from time to time to bolster troop morale. Among these were the wives of Capt. Walker, medical officer, and Lt. Noble, quartermaster, who spent most of the winter at the outpost.[3] On one trip, Noble's wife brought their two children. The youngest, born while Noble was on Crooked River, he had never seen.

By the first week of January, most of the command—suffering from influenza and scurvy—was bedridden without medication. George Rundell was dispatched to Fort Vancouver with an urgent request for help, only to be told that all available medical supplies were at The Dalles and would be forwarded immediately to the stricken camp. This rush shipment didn't arrive at Fort Watson until April 1.

On January 11, two days after Cayuse George had left for Fort Vancouver, a pony express rider reported that Cottonwood House—a stage station near the present town of Dayville—had been attacked by Has No Horse the previous evening. In a blinding winter storm, Small and Lt. Hand with 20 infantrymen mounted on snowshoes marched to the rescue. For three days, they followed Has No Horse's trail through the snow-clogged passes of the Ochoco Mountains, but never made contact. As soon as they returned to Fort Watson Has No Horse resumed his raids on the stage station, mining camps and nearby ranches, plundering at will. By the end of February, settlers were demanding protection which Small was powerless to give. By now, Henry Small was cursing the day he

---

2   Bancroft, *History of Oregon*, Vol. II, pp. 509-10; *The Portland Oregonian*, November 30, 1864, February 14, 1865.

3   Capt. Walker's *Report to the Adjutant General of Oregon 1865-66*, pp. 50-60.

had requested his own command—at last realizing what Drake and Caldwell had faced during the summer campaign.

Another commander was also facing tough odds. Once again Grant was pitted against his old classmate, the aristocratic Robert E. Lee, and in early spring with Henry Abbot directing the heavy artillery fire, he began his assault on Richmond.[4] Small was making a less spectacular assault on a farm wagon.

On March 1, in an effort to discourage Has No Horse's repeated attacks on the stage station, Small re-manned Caldwell's summer fortification at Cottonwood with 10 cavalrymen under the command of Lt. Hand. Three days later with nearly half the garrison down with scurvy, Small commandeered a civilian wagon and headed for Alkali Flat Stage Station to remedy the situation as best he could. On a government requisition, he purchased all the potatoes and onions that Meyer and Hewot could spare but before he could reach Fort Watson, Pvt. Matthew Fitzsimmons, his body covered with livid spots, died begging for a fresh potato through swollen and bleeding gums.

Adding to Small's misfortune, Sgt. Daniel Garber—leading a patrol into the northern Ochoco Mountains—ran into an ambush on Badger Creek. In an attempt to reach Mountain House, two of the soldiers were wounded and Sgt. Garber was killed. On the request of his family, Small had the body sent to Fort Dalles by pack mule and downriver by barge for military internment at Fort Vancouver, which started the rumor that Lt. Watson's body was removed from the fort cemetery.

In mid-March with the situation critical, Capt. Small—taking what healthy men he could spare—started on foot for Fort Vancouver to obtain supplies, regain the company horses and pick up additional men. Already, the Oregon cavalry—manned with regulars—was riding into eastern Oregon and the few available infantry companies without any training were coming with them. Lt. Col. Drake, with 240 battle-trained cavalry troopers and two detachments of veteran infantrymen, was marching on Fort Boise. From this post he was to liberate and maintain the 450-mile road system leading into Virginia City, Nevada, Silver City, Idaho and Canyon City, Oregon. The infantry detachments under joint command of Capt. Edward Palmer and Lt. Cyrus Walker were to establish a military post (Camp Lander) at the site of Fort Hall on the Oregon Trail to escort western emigrants and guard the roads to Salt Lake City, Utah, Virginia City, Montana and Boise City, Idaho.

Capt. Borland with Co. G of the 1st Oregon Infantry and Lt. John Cullen with a 20-man detachment of Co. E 1st Oregon Cavalry were ordered to Fort Watson to reinforce Capt. Small. Arriving with them was a detachment of Warm

---

4    Brig. Gen. Henry Larcom Abbot graduated from West Point in 1854 and on October 1, 1854 was assigned as assistant to 1st Lt. Williamson for Pacific Railroad surveys. For two years Abbot conducted a major part of the work, covering central Oregon from the Klamath Basin to Fort Dalles. *Pacific Railroad Reports*, 1857.

Springs Indian scouts. Major Rinehart with Co. A 1st Oregon Cavalry was dispatched to Fort Klamath to take command and reinforce Capt. Kelly's Co. G who had remained in garrison during the winter to issue subsistence to the new residents of the Klamath Reservation. Rinehart's orders were to open all routes of travel from Red Bluff, California to Jacksonville, Canyon City and the Pueblo mining district in Oregon. Though the combined forces of Drake, Rinehart and Small totaled nearly 800 men, they couldn't keep the roads into eastern Oregon and the Montana goldfields free from Shoshoni attack.

As Small's heavily laden pack-train ground its way toward Fort Watson, the Battle of Five Forks raged across the Virginia countryside as Sheridan and Pickett were going for each other's throat. They had fought side-by-side in the Yakima War. Another old Indian-fighting comrade, Brig. Gen. Crook in command of the Army of West Virginia, lost all but 50 of his men at the Battle of Appomattox before Lee accepted Grant's terms of surrender on April 9, 1865. Small's column was a day's march from Fort Watson when, at daybreak April 12, a ragged Confederate army laid down its arms at Appomattox Court House. After another month of die-hard resistance in remote sections of the Confederacy, the Civil War was over. It had killed some 360,000 Union soldiers and 258,000 Confederates. It had left 500,000 men from both sides with wounds and scars they would carry to the grave. It had sunk hundreds of ships, ripped up miles of railroad and destroyed a flourishing part of a nation's commerce . . . but it had restored the Union.

Unaware of what had happened, Small arrived at Fort Watson on April 13 with horses, beef cattle, food, medical supplies and two detachments of untrained infantry. The arriving foot soldiers were also packing something new in their knapsacks. Marketed by Blackwell, Ginnis and Durham, it was smoking tobacco packaged under such fancy names as Bull Durham, Sitting Bull, Pride of Durham, Duke of Durham, Ridgewood and Duke's Mixture.

As the new recruits shared pipe-fulls of this aromatic weed with their less fortunate comrades, Capt. Small received orders from Lt. Col. Drake to link up with patrols he had sent west from Fort Boise. The campaign of 1865 had begun.

Small was inspecting his warriors prior to taking the trail when President Lincoln in a special meeting warned his cabinet members that there was too much talk of continuing bloodshed. People in high office were demanding that all rights be taken away from the defeated southerners putting them on a level with the Shoshoni. "I do not sympathize in those feelings," said Lincoln who was once more in fact—as he had always been in spirit—President of the whole United States.

# CHAPTER 124

# INDIAN CURSE

*Some day Harrison, you will become leader of your nation.*
*You will not live to finish your duty. After you, every twenty*
*years, the man the people choose to lead them will also bear*
*this curse and die in office. . . .*

**Ten Skwa Tawa**
Shawnee prophet

Morning dawned cold and clear as Small made preparations to join Drake's detachment east of Canyon City. Leaving Olney and his volunteers in charge of the fort, Small with Co. G mounted on fresh horses, a squadron of Indian trackers and Borland's foot soldiers following in his wake, headed out in the hope of trapping Has No Horse's warriors between the two columns. An express was sent ahead to Camp Cottonwood instructing Lt. Hand to proceed up the main fork of the John Day River as an advance guard. Small would spend the night at Cottonwood and with the remainder of Hand's troops join him in the vicinity of Prairie City the following day. Plans would change—which probably was just as well since Hand, instead of going upriver as ordered, went downstream.

In a bad case of timing—for Small—just before sunset, Has No Horse and Broken Knife raided a ranch near Cottonwood House, wounding a herder and driving off 16 head of cattle. For the Christian faithful, it was the eve of Good Friday, April 14, 1865. Before this night would pass, Oregon, along with the rest of the nation would be thrown into the deepest despair.

For the past three days, the country from New York to San Francisco had reeled in unbridled celebration. News of Lee's surrender was flashed by telegraph to Portland on April 11. Victory bonfires blazed along S.W. Front, 2nd and 3rd avenues. Barrels of burning tar, pitch and turpentine sent up black columns of smoke as men carrying torches ran down the streets, while flaming lights in front of houses and business firms illuminated the whole city. Mayor David Logan named Henry Failing, a prominent businessman, to head a committee to direct the victory program. A 100-gun salute was fired, followed by ringing of bells. A military and two civilian bands filled the air with music and hundreds of soldiers, firemen and citizens moved through the streets in a torch-lit procession. Gov. Gibbs, Col. Maury and other officials made impassioned speeches.

In the nation's capital, President Lincoln seeking relaxation entered Ford's Theater. He had invited Gen. Grant to accompany him and his family but at the last moment Grant declined in order to catch a train to Philadelphia to see his children. All eyes were on the stage when a shot rang out through the auditorium. The President slumped forward, unconscious and dying. John Wilkes Booth—a crazed southern zealot and star of the theater production—leaped from the Presidential box to the stage waving a knife which he had intended to use on Grant after shooting Lincoln. He escaped through a side door.

In the shock which followed, some would recall the curse of a Shawnee medicine man made in 1811 upon William Henry Harrison—then governor of Indiana Territory. At the time, Ten Skwa Tawa (The Prophet) was one of the many messiahs springing up among a people beginning to smell the numbing odor of genocide. Speaking of The Prophet's brother, the famed Shawnee war chief Tecumseh, "He is," said Harrison, "one of those uncommon geniuses which spring up occasionally to produce revolution and overturn the established order of things. . . ."[1] The Prophet would also overturn the order of things and make his presence felt on the course of history.

At the battle of Tippecanoe, The Prophet was defeated by an army force under the command of Gen. Harrison. Angry over the terms of Harrison's treaty, Ten Skwa Tawa, a proud and haughty warrior, leaped to his feet and placed a curse on Harrison.[2] He predicted that Harrison would become the leader of his nation but he would not live long enough to carry out his duties. Furthermore, the man chosen by the people to lead the nation on 20-year intervals after Harrison had been elected would also bear the curse and suffer the same fate.

Twenty-nine years later, Harrison was elected president of the United States in 1840, inaugurated March 4, 1841, and died of pneumonia a month later. Twenty years later, Abraham Lincoln was elected president in 1860. Sworn into office for his second term in March 1865, he was assassinated in April. Was it coincidence or would history bear witness to the accuracy of an Indian curse? No one knew but it left many with an uncanny feeling. The future looked bleak.

Following Lincoln, "zero-year presidents" as they were soon to be called were: James Garfield, William McKinley, Warren Harding, Franklin Roosevelt, John Kennedy and Ronald Reagan.

Garfield, elected in 1880, was shot in a Washington railway station in July 1881 and, while the bullets themselves didn't appear life-threatening, he developed an infection and died in September. McKinley, elected in 1896 but re-elected in "zero-year" 1900, was shot while attending the Pan American Exposition in

---

1    Brandon, *The American Heritage Book of Indians*, p. 202.

2    Research on the legend of Ten Skwa Tawa's curse was published in the *Eugene Register Guard*, October 2, 1960. The newspaper would refer to Ten Skwa Tawa—The Prophet—as Olliwackica, another spelling of his name.

Buffalo, New York. Eight days after the shooting he was dead. Harding, elected in 1920, fell ill during a trip to the Pacific Northwest in 1923. He developed pneumonia and died in August. Roosevelt, elected in 1932 and re-elected in 1936, 1940, and 1944 could not escape the hex completely. Within three months of his fourth inauguration, he died April 12, 1945 of a cerebral hemorrhage. Kennedy, elected in 1960, was killed by an assassin's bullet in 1963 as his motorcade wound through the streets of Dallas, Texas. Reagan, elected in 1980, was struck in the chest on the 70th day of his administration by a bullet during an assassination attempt outside a Washington, D.C. hotel on March 30, 1981. But Reagan proceeded to make a recovery that astonished doctors, and gained him the name "the Teflon president."

After the passage of 140 years had Ten Skwa Tawa's curse finally been broken? Only time will tell. The year 2000 is only a stone's throw away.

# MILITARY DEPT. OF THE COLUMBIA

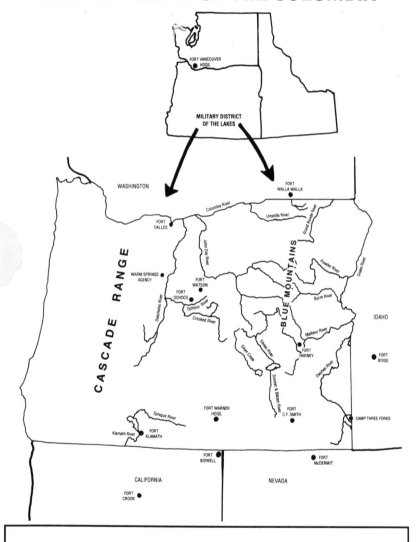

The Military Department of the Pacific was established in 1854. On September 13, 1858 the enormous Department of the Pacific was divided into two smaller districts, the Military Districts of Oregon and California. The Military District of Oregon was then further divided into the districts of the Columbia, the Owyhee, and the Lakes in 1867. But in June 1868, the Military Department of the Pacific was again put under one command and renamed the Military Department of the Columbia, which was headquartered at Fort Vancouver, and Major General Crook was commander.

*Locations are approximate and not shown to scale.*

# CHAPTER 125

# BATTLE RIDGE

*The steepness of the mountains allows a small number of Indians to cause great execution among any troops seeking to ascend. I feel thankful that we succeeded in driving off the enemy with so few casualties. . . .*

**Captain Henry Small**
April 16, 1865

Yes, the Civil War was over. The Union was preserved but all the nation had to show for it was 600,000 dead and one assassinated president. It was a blow to the Shoshoni also, for they had lost a potent ally. Shortly before his tragic death, President Lincoln had promised: "If I live, this accursed system of robbery and shame in our treatment of the Indians shall be reformed."[1] Such was not to be.

On the morning of April 15—with the nation's flags fluttering at half-mast—Capt. Small dispatched a messenger to Lt. Hand (whom he had difficulty in finding) informing him of Has No Horse's attack and to act on his own initiative until he received further orders. The trail of the stolen livestock led up the South Fork of the John Day. Moving cautiously and expecting an ambush at any moment in the rugged confines of the river canyon, Small covered some 16 miles before dusk without meeting the enemy.

Has No Horse, certain the cavalry would be on his back-trail, was moving fast. Having a 12-hour head-start on Small, who was further burdened with the infantry, Has No Horse was some 20 miles upstream on the Red Bluff-Yreka Trail by daylight. With the cattle near the point of exhaustion, he decided on a new tactic. Three warriors would continue up the trail on an easy route and deliver the beef to the hungry camps in Big Summit Prairie. Has No Horse and Broken Knife with 30 dog soldiers would act as decoys. Their scouts would report that they had ample time to rest and select the site for battle. It was now Holy Saturday.

At daybreak, Easter Sunday, Lt. Noble with eight soldiers and five Warm Springs scouts found where the Shoshoni crossed the south fork. Tracking them another six miles, he located where the cattle had separated from the war party.

---

1    Seton, *Gospel of the Redman*, p. 60.

The war party's tracks headed northwest toward Wolf Mountain and the newly formed Rock Creek Mining District. Believing that to be the next target of attack, Noble continued pursuit over some of the roughest ground in central Oregon. At 5:15 p.m., the cavalry rode into an ambush on the ridge between Wind Creek and the south prong of Black Canyon.[2] The spot chosen for entrapment was where Half Moon—Broken Knife's wife and Has No Horse's sister—had been murdered by Waymire's scouts in April 1864 . . . just one year in the past.

Small, who had set up a base camp at the junction of Elbow Gulch and the south fork, heard the distant shots. Taking the medical officer and nine cavalrymen, he rushed to Noble's assistance. About a mile and a half up Elbow Gulch, Small met a runner who told him the Snakes had attacked Noble some two miles further up the canyon on the head of Squaw Creek and several men had been wounded. Noble was now fighting a retreating battle towards Small's position. Sgt. George Dichtl and five troopers rode up a narrow trail clinging to the south side of Elbow Gulch to gain a position 800 feet higher in elevation to cover Small's advance. When some 250 feet from the planned advantage point, the Indians fired upon them from above. With three horses shot out from under them, the advance party dove under the bank of the trail for protection. A second volley seriously wounded Dichtl and Pvt. Sam Church. Charging to their rescue, Small's detachment made it only about 30 yards up the hill when they were stopped by a hailstorm of bullets. By now, some of the Shoshoni had crossed the canyon—flanking Sgt. Dichtl's advance and successfully cut off their retreat. Dismounting the troops, Small took to the north side of the gulch and with bullets whizzing all around, a rider was sent to the base camp for reinforcements.

Meantime, Lt. Noble had made it to the head of the gulch. Under his covering fire, Capt. Small finally gained the summit and drove the Indians from their fortifications, killing three. Small would later report that a 15 minute delay in reaching Noble's position would have been fatal to the whole operation.

With reinforcements on the way, Small nearly blundered into another trap. Broken Knife, seeing more soldiers arriving, retreated about six miles to where Has No Horse had dug in on what would become known as Battle Ridge south of Wolf Mountain. The cavalry heard his signal shot alerting Broken Knife of his position and thus averted riding into a deadly cross-fire.

Capt. Walker spent Easter night attending to the wounded. Hand litters were prepared and infantrymen detailed to pack the most seriously injured to the base camp on the South Fork. From there, they were packed 20 miles to Cottonwood Stage Station to be transported by wagon to the fort hospital. The 10 men dispatched with the wounded would make contact with Lt. Hand a few miles west of Cottonwood Station. They told him of the fight raging on Battle Ridge and

---

2    Small's report to District Headquarters from the Canyon City Road Expedition, Fort Watson, April 20, 1865.

suggested he return to the defense of Cottonwood which apparently he didn't do. However, Hand had some interesting news.

On his wrong-way plunge down the John Day River, Lt. Hand visited the Clarno Ranch. In 1858, Andrew Clarno—a Lane County farmer—and Bill Snodgrass had paid an Indian $10 to guide them into the lower John Day Valley to become the first white settlers in that region. In 1859, Clarno formed a partnership with Bill Trosper and brought 600 head of heifers and 1,000 horses into the John Day Valley. In preparation of moving his family from Eugene City to the John Day claim, Clarno hauled lumber in by ox-team from the Cascades but because of Indian hostilities, the family would remain in Eugene until 1864. By that time, Clarno had become good friends with the Shoshoni and acted as their unofficial agent in negotiations with the whites. During this period he maintained contact with the outside world through letters delivered by Joaquin Miller's pony express at 50 cents each.[3]

The first trouble Clarno had with the Snakes—which was a bad omen—had occurred within the past week. On April 8, one day before Lee surrendered to Grant, Wolf Dog stole his saddle horse and milk cows. There was good reason for confiscating the dairy herd. Clarno and John Staley—a Hudson's Bay Company trapper—had taken a contract to furnish the army outposts with cheese. One of Wolf Dog's raiders advised Clarno to "take your women and children away. The man without a horse is coming here to kill you." Believing Fort Watson was going to come under heavy attack, Clarno and his family went to Howard Maupin's fortified stage station in Antelope Valley.

When Small received Hand's communiqué, he was certain that the Shoshoni would stage an all-out attack on every white settlement in the John Day Valley. Leaving the main force on Battle Ridge under the command of Lt. Noble, Capt. Small—the only man who knew the snow-covered mountain passes between Wolf Mountain and Fort Watson—decided to try and reach the fort. It was now April 17, 1865. Dr. Walker would accompany him on this treacherous journey.

At sundown on the head of Rock Creek less than eight miles from the fort, they spotted an Indian sitting on his horse in the middle of the trail. From his size, it was certain that this warrior was Has No Horse. Since he appeared to be alone, they spurred their horses into a dead run in an attempt to ride by him but nearly collided with a dozen or more braves who were within 40 yards of the trail. Small and Walker reined in as the Indians hadn't as yet seen them and retreated some 50 yards when a war whoop split the air and the chase was on. After a three-mile run, the army officers escaped only because they were mounted on thoroughbred

---

3     Information on the Clarno family was obtained by Fred Lockley in an interview with Lucinda Clarno Evans (daughter of Andrew Clarno) in April 1929; The *Oregon Journal*, April 23, 1929; the *Fossil Journal*, June 6, 1941.

cavalry horses which, when it came to a race, were much more than a match for the wiry little Indian ponies weak from lack of winter feed.

They returned to Noble's camp on Battle Ridge where Broken Knife's sporadic rifle fire echoed throughout the night. An hour past midnight, the two officers with a three-man escort again started for Fort Watson. A little beyond where they had encountered Has No Horse the previous evening, they found three civilians who had been killed. Apparently Small and Walker had interrupted this affair as only two of the men had been scalped. This bloodshed prompted Small to detour to the mining camps on Rock Creek fearing that they too had been wiped out.

A year earlier on March 18, 1864, five Mexicans discovered a lode of silver-bearing quartz about one and a half miles southeast of Camp Rock Creek on The Dalles-Canyon City road. Calling themselves the Tonita Company, Stephen Ruiz, Francisco Yquera, Modesto Gutieraz, Ignacio Soto and Jose Rico also claimed 160 acres each for ranching in the vicinity of their mining claims.[4] They were soon joined by Antone Francisco who started the community of Antone some four miles east of Fort Watson. News of their silver strike traveled fast and by the summer of 1864, American miners swarmed over the area making rich gold and silver strikes in Spanish, Mule and Hope gulches.

Arriving at Spanish Gulch, Small found log barricades erected and the miners preparing for a state of siege. The only ones missing were three men named Potter, Nichal and Vihrs. Assuming these were the bodies found by Small, the high mountain pasture where the slaughter took place was named Potter Meadows because the only corpse with hair intact was identified as Potter.

Arriving at Fort Watson shortly after sunrise, Capt. Small sent out a team and wagon to recover the bodies and bring them in for burial. He then sent out patrols into the John Day and lower Crooked River valleys. They discovered that Has No Horse was being joined by dog soldiers coming from the North Fork of the John Day River. They also found the pass between Bear Skull and Wolf Mountain plugged with snow and therefore stalling any Shoshoni attack from that direction.

The detail sent out to locate Lt. Hand—who had never shown up at Cottonwood House—returned on April 22 having found no sign of him. Information picked up from the mining camps indicated that Hand had gone down the John Day toward Bridge Creek. The search party had traveled downriver through very mountainous country a distance of 65 miles and returned by way of Alkali Stage Station where they found Hewot and Meyer in good shape. This cavalry patrol traveled a distance of 170 miles in four days and saw fresh Indian sign all the way but no Indians.

---

4    *Grant County Mining Records 1864-65.* During this period the richest strikes were made by J.M. McCoy and A.S. Sutton for whom Sutton Mountain is named.

The Wheeler Stage was blockaded on Rock Creek and Small had to send a squad to escort the stage and passengers to the fort. Small would report to headquarters: "From what I now know respecting the number of Indians, I fear the forces under my command will prove insufficient to afford the necessary protection to travelers and settlers. . . ." His scouts reported that Wolf Dog's warriors were scattered along The Dalles-Canyon City road for 60 miles causing Small to further lament, "It has been thought heretofore, that they [the Snakes] did not exceed 35 or 40 in number, but I am now satisfied that there are twice that number at present around Fort Watson, alone." He was correct but even so, he had sorely underestimated the manpower Has No Horse had at his command.

A hundred miles to the east, Big Man and Pipe were dealing Lt. Col. Drake an equal amount of misery in this efforts to keep traffic flowing between Canyon City and Boise while to the south, Major Rinehart—guarding the Applegate and Red Bluff trails—was being harassed by Little Rattlesnake and Bad Face who had effectively stalled all commerce to the Jacksonville and Nevada mines. In deference to Capt. Kelly, Paulina (The War Spirit)—impatiently awaiting Falling Star's release from prison—was staying in the background.

Henry Small—Drake's outspoken critic—was now becoming schooled in the fine art of guerrilla warfare. "I most respectfully request," he would petition, "that the forces may be increased on this road, at least for the present. I could easily manage them with the number of troops I have if they would remain together; but they scatter in all directions, rendering it impossible to trail them with any degree of certainty. Both men and horses are much fatigued having been almost constantly on the march for the past eight days and nights."[5] It was only mid-April and the campaign of '65 had barely begun.

Col. Maury was trying his best to fulfill the demands of his field officers but Oregon still lacked two companies of filling its quota of infantry and all available cavalry—10 companies—were now engaged on the eastern Oregon battlefront. Something more had to be done and done quickly.

Early in April, Paulina—worried over his wife's continued captivity—sent word to Capt. Kelly through Moses Brown (Motcunka Sket) that he had been among several tribes of the Snakes and advised them, as well as his own people, to be friendly with the whites. He also wished to make arrangements with Huntington for peace as soon as the snow was off the ground . . . a cease-fire which he had no intention of honoring once Falling Star was out of harm's way. He also said he would come into Fort Klamath and wait there until his wife was returned to him. Moses Brown also informed Kelly that the Snakes were suffering from starvation.[6]

---

5    Small's report dated April 23, 1865, Report to the Adjutant General Oregon 1865-66.

6    National Archives, Bureau of Indian Affairs Oregon Superintendency, Letters Received, George Nuse to J.W. Perit Huntington, Fort Klamath, April 6, 1865.

Moses Brown often served as a go-between for Huntington, Lindsay Applegate, the military and the Snake hostiles but his loyalty to the whites was "somewhat questionable."[7] In fact, Moses was serving in the same capacity as Yellow Jacket . . . a double-agent playing a dangerous game. To make his cover even more uncertain, Moses knew that Paulina didn't trust him.

---

7    Ibid, W.V. Rinehart to J.W. Perit Huntington, Fort Klamath, July 2, 1866; Lindsay Applegate to Huntington, Klamath Indian Sub-agency, Oregon, October 25, 1866.

# CHAPTER 126

# THE AXE AND RIFLE SQUAD

*All that can be done now is to chastise the Snakes as well as
we may, to facilitate communications by opening roads, to
occupy points from which to control them and give protection
to the annual immigration. . . .*

**Gen. George Wright**
Commander, Military Dept. of the Columbia

By May 1865, the Snake war tribes were once more rulers of the Ochoco. To
the west, Wolf Dog and Black Eagle were striking from Antelope to Warm Springs;
to the north, Has No Horse and Broken Knife were ripping into The Dalles-Canyon
City traffic; to the east, Big Man and Pony Blanket had cut off communications
between Canyon City and Boise City; and to the south, Little Rattlesnake and Bad
Face were raiding the Red Bluff-Yreka Trail.

In the heart of the Ochoco red hell lay waiting in the form of seasoned shock
troops—men who had won their eagle feather in campaigns from the Umpqua
Valley in western Oregon to the Wyoming plains. The situation was so critical that
the secretary of war found it necessary to upgrade the Military District of Oregon
to full departmental standing separate from the Military Department of the Pacific.
Under this new realignment, Col. Maury resigned from active duty and Gen.
Wright was named commander of the Military Department of the Columbia with
headquarters at Fort Vancouver, Washington Territory.

Because Huntington, superintendent of Oregon Indian Affairs, seemed more
concerned with business in western Oregon, George C. Hough, U.S. attorney for
Idaho Territory, was placed in charge of Indian affairs for Idaho and eastern
Oregon.[1] His first act was to order William Logan, U.S. Indian agent at Warm
Springs to proceed immediately to San Francisco and petition Congress for
sufficient money to negotiate equitable treaties with the Snake war tribes.

Col. Maury, in one of his last official acts before turning over command to
Brig. Gen. Wright, authorized Major Rinehart to recruit special forces into the

---

1    Testimony of Hough's son, A.C. Hough, September 3, 1939. A.C. Hough was an attorney in
     Grants Pass, Oregon. George Hough served as first U.S. Attorney for Idaho Territory from
     1863 to 1868, the period covering the first phase of the Shoshonean wars.

United States Army with full military rank. He did this without confirmation or official sanction of the War Department and this unauthorized enlistment would come to a boiling head in October 1866.

In mid-May, while Rinehart was working on this project, Capt. Nathan Olney—who for 10 months had been making a sorry spectacle in his attempt to help Small guard the Canyon City road—was relieved of duty by Lt. Col. Drake. Drake then assigned Capt. Edward Palmer's Co. B 1st Oregon Cavalry to escort all supply trains from Fort Dalles to Fort Boise. To make certain that Palmer got through, he sent in Capt. Robert Williams with Co. H Oregon Infantry and Lt. Jim Currey with a squadron of cavalry to clear the Canyon City road for traffic.

At this time, The Dalles merchants were refusing to make shipments into the interior, and the mining communities of eastern Oregon were facing even more serious problems. They could ship gold and silver to The Dalles and risk forfeiting it all to Wolf Dog; or they could ship to Salt Lake City and watch Pony Blanket ride off with the proceeds; or they could hold it and pray that Has No Horse would not ransack the camps.

With Palmer, Williams and Currey backing up Small, Drake ordered Capt. Charles Hobart's mounted infantry into Jordan Valley to establish a military outpost (Fort Lyon) on Jordan Creek. En route, settlers in Harney Valley told Hobart that the Snakes were rustling cattle and they wanted him to investigate the matter. On the Malheur River, Hobart was attacked by Pony Blanket and Big Man. In a four hour fight, two infantrymen were wounded and most of the army pack-horses were run off. Hobart later caught up with the holding crew of the stolen merchandise (mostly old men, women and children) and killed or wounded many of them. Hobart had recovered the army horses, some of the settlers' stolen cattle and captured a part of the Indian horse herd.[2] He had also saddled the army with more misery. Among those killed were Bad Face's wife and his daughter Mary. No longer would The Man With a Bad Face honor a promise given to Nevada Indian Agent John Burche in 1863. From this day forward, he would exercise all of his powerful influence to bring the mounted Paiutes into the fray.

While Capt. Hobart stirred up more unrest, B.J. Pengra—president of the newly formed Oregon Central Military Road Company—began surveying a right-of-way from Eugene City, Oregon to Silver City, Idaho along the general route of the Applegate Trail. This survey party was under heavy military guard consisting of two companies of cavalry commanded by captains John McCall and Jim Kelly; two companies of infantry under the command of Capt. Arthur Borland and Capt. Franklin B. Sprague; and a detachment of Co. C Oregon Infantry under Lt. Patrick McGuire.[3] To secure even more supply routes into the military outposts, the Willamette Valley and Cascade Mountain Military Road Co. was gearing up

---

2    *Boise City Statesman*, July 13, 18, 1865.

3    Bancroft, *History of Oregon*, Vol. II, p. 810.

to drive a road from Albany over the Santiam Pass through the Crooked River Basin to Boise City, Idaho.

To guard these new routes of travel, Major Rinehart was busy enlisting new recruits at Fort Klamath. Soon to be feared throughout eastern Oregon—not by the Shoshoni but by the very people they were sworn to protect—was the dreaded U.S. Army Axe and Rifle Squad under the command of Captain Oliver Applegate, 20-year-old son of Lindsay Applegate, who was co-founder of the Applegate Trail and U.S. Indian agent for the Klamath Reservation. The Axe and Rifle Squad was hailed as the most unique company of men to operate on the border in the initial days of conflict. Of the 50 men who constituted the squad, 49 were Indians; including seven tribal chiefs, one head chief and one war chief.

For his staff officers Capt. Applegate chose Allen David (Wal-aik-ski-dat), a Klamath tribal chief to be commissioned a first lieutenant in the United States Army; Dave Hill, head chief of the Klamaths—better known to the Shoshoni as Chief By The River (Wa-ua-laix)—commissioned a second lieutenant; and Big Belly (Monish Mukusk Getko), a Klamath war chief that would serve as master sergeant of the squad. This elite outfit made up of Agency Klamaths and Modocs was recruited for the express purpose of escorting army supply trains, road survey parties and itinerant emigrant wagons safely through eastern Oregon. The recipients of their protection, especially the emigrants, were not quite so sure of their intended purpose. The psychological effect of seeing a mounted patrol of screeching Indians bearing down on them after close encounters with the Shoshoni was enough to offset any benefit they had to the trains. Worse yet, the Axe and Rifle Squad was mostly bluff.

When entering hostile country, the special forces usually found it advisable to go on a scout en masse and while the wagons wallowed blindly into the Crooked River country—perhaps to meet Has No Horse head-on—the stalwart bodyguards circled onto the high desert and picked up their charges miles beyond the danger zone . . . that is, if they survived. For the moment, the Axe and Rifle Squad was assigned to Pengra's survey party as the war reached the boiling point 200 miles to the north and east.

The first to travel the western leg of Pengra's Oregon Central Military Road was Capt. James Blakely of Brownsville, Oregon. Besides road agreements, many government contracts were being let to supply the army outposts in eastern Oregon, southern Idaho and northern California with beef. Cove and Carrick, cattle buyers out of Sacramento were supplying beef to Fort Watson, Fort Boise and Fort Lyon. Hoping to pick up some of this loose federal change, Capt. Blakely, young Jim his son and Billy Chinook rounded up 500 head of three-year-old steers and trailed them to California for army consumption. These daring buckaroos followed the military road to Fort Klamath where Major Rinehart provided an escort through the mountains to Pit River, Little Rattlesnake's area of operation. At Fort Bidwell, Capt. Blakely sold his herd to Cove and Carrick for $20,000 in gold—not a bad month's wages. Staying clear of the Shoshoni front, Blakely put the gold in flour sacks and returned to Brownsville by way of Yreka and Mount Shasta, traveling only at night.

Up on the northern line of scrimmage, Wolf Dog forced Howard Maupin—the celebrated Indian fighter—into moving the Antelope Stage Station to a more defensible location at the junction of Big and Little Trout creeks. With the aide of his five children—Perry, Elizabeth, Rachel, Garrett and Nancy—he accomplished this move in jig time. Maupin would be granted 13 more years to heckle the Shoshoni before gasping his final breath in 1878 during the second phase of the Shoshoni war.

# CHAPTER 127

# DRAGON REEF

*Tell them that if they had not overloaded us we would have gotten through all right and this would never have happened.*

**Captain Samuel DeWolf**
July 30, 1865

Six hundred miles southwest of the eastern Oregon front a badly overloaded steamer lay at anchor in San Francisco Bay. The *Brother Jonathan* was no stranger to the treacherous ocean currents battering the rocky coastline from California to Alaska. Built in Williamsburg, New York in 1850, the 220-foot long, 36-foot wide vessel had Oregon white oak in her hull, California redwood in her decks and towering above all were three huge masts of Douglas fir. After rounding the horn, the *Brother Jonathan*, had plied the Pacific sea lanes between San Francisco and ports of the northwest since 1852. A stern driven side-wheeler—originally owned by Cornelius Vanderbilt—the *Brother Jonathan* which could accommodate 750 passengers, was touted as the finest luxury liner in the Pacific fleet. It was so popular that the Cascade peak now known as Mt. Bachelor was named Brother Jonathan to distinguish it from the Three Sisters peaks, which were then called Faith, Hope and Charity.

In addition to passengers, her main cargo (which frequently ran into six figures) was shipments of raw gold . . . millions of dollars of the precious metal to finance a government involved in civil war. The files of the *Portland Oregonian* give some clue to the value of gold carried by the *Brother Jonathan*: September 24, 1863—$315,000; October 12, 1863—$203,835; October 28, 1864—$500,000; November 15, 1864—$339,000 just to name but a few entries in the ship's log. In fact there was so much gold that the *Brother Jonathan* couldn't handle all the shipments. For example, on December 4, 1863, the *S.S. Oregon* shipped out of Portland with $750,000 in the cargo hold. These figures will also serve to illustrate the magnitude of gold transported by pack mule, stagecoach and pony express out of eastern Oregon and western Idaho over the dangerous trails held hostage by the Snakes. So much gold was arriving from Canyon City, Sumpter, Silver City, Auburn and Malheur City that a new United States mint was under construction at The Dalles in the spring of 1865.

On this July day in 1865, the *Brother Jonathan* was loaded beyond her limits with sawmill equipment and heavy industrial machinery bound for the gold mines of eastern Oregon. Other items on the manifest would include two camels for use by the military in the deserts of southeastern Oregon and 100 barrels of imported whiskey for the finer saloons in The Dalles City, Canyon City and Boise City.[1] This overloading would cause much controversy between the ship's captain and the owners.

Furthermore, there was an estimated one million dollars in gold and silver on board. Maritime records listed only $375,000 in the ship's safe which didn't include the army payroll or the Congressional appropriation to purchase the Snakes' hunting grounds. Neither did it include the gold wrestled from the California diggings laying in passengers' carpetbags, money pouches and coat pockets waiting for its power to be released in The Dalles, Canyon City and Baker City . . . money to be gambled in business investments such as first class saloons, large cattle ranches or promising mining claims.

Apparently, the ship's owners convinced Captain DeWolf that she would sail with or without him, for at noon, July 28, 1865 and against DeWolf's better judgment, the *Brother Jonathan* steamed from San Francisco Bay into the path of a summer nor'wester on her scheduled run to Portland, Oregon. The passenger list was impressive. Gen. Wright and his staff were on board to take command of the Shoshoni war. In addition to his aides, the general was accompanied by his wife and his favorite cavalry horse. He was also packing the $200,000 army payroll for the troops in eastern Oregon.

An adjoining cabin was occupied by Indian Agent William Logan and his wife. Logan had been successful in his mission. He boarded the *Brother Jonathan* with $105,000 in gold coin locked in steel boxes to compensate those Shoshoni tribes who would make treaty with the United States and sell out their birthright—the Ochoco.[2]

Anson G. Henry, governor of Washington Territory, was returning to Fort Vancouver to insure that the followers of Kamiakin, Black Ice and Young Chief didn't join ranks with Wolf Dog, Has No Horse and Paulina.

And also joining this group was Gen. Henry Logan, veteran of the Cayuse War and newly appointed director of The Dalles Mint.

Among some of the lesser known passengers were members of the Luckey family, who had strong ties to eastern Oregon. Jeremiah (Jerry) Luckey, who came west in 1863 to join his nephews (John, Jim and Warren Luckey) in the Snake campaign, had sent word for his wife Catherine and their two children to join him at Fort Dalles. On July 27, Catherine, accompanied by her father-in-law Samuel

---

1    Drawson, *Treasures of Oregon*, "They Called Her *Brother Jonathan*," pp. 44-49.

2    Rieseberg, "Last Voyage of the *Brother Jonathan*," *Grit Magazine*, December 24, 1972.

Nelson Luckey, his wife and daughter, boarded the *Brother Jonathan*. They would never arrive in Oregon.[3]

Two days out of San Francisco, the laboring ship, bucking a stiff head-wind and rolling in choppy seas, passed Crescent City, California and fired her usual one gun salute. All was gaiety on board. Although it was dark as night at mid-day, the passengers were unaware of any hazard. In the brightly lit salon many were dancing to the music of a five-piece orchestra. In the bar, Gen. Wright, Gen. Henry Logan and Gov. Henry were offering toasts to success. Cheers and raucous laughter drowned out the sound of the groaning engines below deck, which were straining against the fury of the storm. On the bridge, a different mood prevailed.

Within sight of the Oregon coastline, Captain DeWolf ordered the ship to turn back and make for a snug harbor at Crescent City. In fog and smoke, the *Brother Jonathan* passed Seal Rock and within minutes ground to a halt on the undersea rocks—appropriately named Dragon Reef. It was 1:50 p.m., July 30, 1865. Shrieks and curses echoed through the ship as it shuddered in a twisting, rendering terror of destruction. So great was the impact that the main mast plunged through the deck clear to the yard arm. Pandemonium reigned and with only six lifeboats, the captain ordered everyone to look out for himself.

Their riches forgotten, men, women and children fought for space on the lifeboats. Gen. Wright's wife refused to leave him. The seat she gave up turned out to be in the only lifeboat to survive the tragedy. It took 45 minutes for the *Brother Jonathan* to break up and sink beneath the angry sea. The wreckage was strewn on a plateau under 270 feet of water nine miles off Crescent City. As Lt. Harry Rieseberg—chief, U.S. Bureau of Navigation—would later comment: "Ironically, the miners on the *Brother Jonathan* who worked so hard and dreamed so big, who pried gold from the earth where it had been imprisoned since the dawn of time, succeeded only in burying it even deeper beneath the sea."

Like a clarion call from the deep, Captain DeWolf's last words, "Tell them if they had not overloaded us. . . ." spoken in anguish to quartermaster Jacob Yates, pilot of the surviving lifeboat, must have struck a sensitive chord among shipping magnates everywhere.

Out of 232 people believed aboard, only 19 in one lifeboat survived. The sinking of the *Brother Jonathan* was the greatest maritime disaster in Pacific shipping up to that time and it would have major impact on the course of eastern Oregon's economy.

With the death of Gen. Wright and his staff, Drake, Small, Rinehart and Currey were moving without direction. Superintendent Hough's dream of buying off the Snake war tribes in an effort to stop further bloodshed was doomed forever. The loss of business investors, with their infusion of private capital, without doubt altered the pattern of settlement in eastern Oregon. Production in the mines would

---

3    Information from Eugene E. Luckey, Burns, Oregon, July 22, 1988.

be stalled for months for lack of machinery. The Dalles Mint would never coin any money due in part to the death of its director.

Once again, Oregon was floundering in its crusade to rid the world of the heathen Snakes all because of an Indian sea-god called . . . Dragon Reef!

# CHAPTER 128

# WALK A HEAP

*The war dance is on—they're loose again*
*all along the Oregon Drive,*
*And the orders are out for Uncle Sam's men*
*to bring 'em back dead or alive.*
*So it's through the Blues, boys—*
*dead injuns or bust!*
*But oh! for the dust, the dust, the dust*
*and that alkali thirst in the morning.*

**Owen Wister**
Western Poet

On August 8, 1865, with one million acres of virgin timber blazing out of control in the Silverton holocaust northeast of Salem, the state of Oregon was engulfed in lung-searing smoke. In this gloomy setting, Major Currey was rushed out of Fort Hoskins, promoted to Colonel and placed in command of the Military Department of the Columbia. His first order was to build more forts.

Work on The Dalles Mint came to a standstill. It was rumored that, without a director, some of the $100,000 appropriation designated for construction was being funneled into political channels to defray campaign expenses of "a certain corrupt" candidate who had run on the mint bill and was defeated by one vote. Whatever the circumstances, the mint never went into production, which caused some irate backers to reason that as long as the building was there, "the government had damn well better use it." There certainly wasn't any lack of raw material, for during 1865 in the glory hole at Silver City, 30 million dollars in gold was taken from just one shaft.

Using the loss of Agent Bill Logan and the Shoshoni treaty appropriation to his advantage, Oregon Indian Superintendent J.W. Perit Huntington (sidestepping Idaho Superintendent Hough's authority) frantically called for another round of peace negotiations with the Snakes to be held in August at a place called Yainax on the Klamath reservation. He was basing his success on the long shot that Paulina would keep his promise given nine months before at Fort Klamath, and reaffirmed by messenger in May.

Meanwhile, the troops in eastern Oregon had been taking a beating. The stage companies, disenchanted with army protection, were constructing more fortified stations to shorten the interval between stops. Among these were Howard Maupin's famed Antelope Station on Trout Creek and Jim Clark's equally famous Burnt Ranch on Bridge Creek. Between the two stations lay the dreaded Hell's Half Acre, favorite ambush spot for both road agents and Snake warriors. Captain Small was charged with protecting the Overland Stage Company employees and livestock at Antelope, Burnt Ranch, Alkali Flat, Mountain House and Cottonwood. He couldn't do it. Lt. Jim Currey had the unenviable job of escorting the mail and gold shipments between Canyon City and The Dalles. Sometimes he was successful, sometimes not. Fortunately, he made it to The Dalles with a shipment from the Poor Man Mine at Silver City. A 500 pound chunk of ore made up of solid ruby-silver crystals, this gem was so unique that specimens were sent to the Paris Exposition in 1866.

Capt. Williams with two companies of First Oregon Infantry was stationed at Fort Watson where, because of lack of experience, they were undergoing extensive combat training. Has No Horse on one of his periodic raids of the John Day country spotted this untrained reserve and as a gesture of disregard, slaughtered two settlers and left their bodies on The Dalles-Canyon City road. Driving off all their livestock, he then rode across the mountains to Fort Watson.

The foot soldiers, little expecting an Indian in the vicinity of the fort, marched onto the parade ground for dismounted drill. Secluded in the timber on Cemetery Hill, Has No Horse grimly watched these new antics of the Walk-a-Heaps as they marched in close-order drill and charged in mock battle tactics, unaware that they were about to witness the real thing.

The dog soldiers were armed with Colt carbines .36 to .58 calibre. These carbines with a revolving cylinder were not very popular among the whites because they had a nasty habit—when one cylinder was fired, they might all go off and many a red brother packed the scars to prove it. Scouts would discover that Has No Horse was armed with a Confederate model '63 Enfield calibre .577 sighted to 900 yards and he was fairly certain to hit at that distance.

Gen. Crook could attest to the Shoshoni's ability at long distance shooting. In the late 1850s, his mounted infantry learned from deadly experience that it was best to engage the Snake dog soldiers at close range. As Crook would recall, "We invariably charged right in their midst and confused them and had them miss more than once at no greater distance than 10 feet, where they could hit a man every time at 60 yards."[1] The regular army scouts Howard Maupin and Baptiste Delore would state that the only limitations to the Snakes' deadly accuracy was the effective range of their weapons.

---

1    Hart, *Pioneer Forts of the West*, p. 122.

Now—back to the parade ground. One minute the soldiers were perfecting maneuvers, the next in a hail of rifle bullets, they were in the midst of war. In their confusion to clear the drill field, two infantrymen were killed and eight wounded, two of whom would later die from wounds received. Sending a messenger to Capt. Small to alert him of this latest raid, Capt. Williams with a detachment of Co. H took pursuit immediately. The tracks headed toward the South Fork of the John Day River and though afoot, Williams doggedly pressed on. As soon as Small received the message, Lt. Joseph Bowen and 25 veteran cavalrymen were sent to join Capt. Williams. But before Bowen could arrive the inexperienced infantry, in their debut performance, surprisingly executed some of the best fighting the Snakes had yet encountered in their dealings with the army.

They were so contemptuous of soldiers on foot, they made no effort to hide their trail and traveled at leisure. To the complete surprise of Has No Horse and his warriors, the foot soldiers caught up with them some 35 miles southeast of Fort Watson between Sunflower Flat and Snow Mountain. Still unalarmed, the mounted Indians surrounded Williams' detachment and in a screaming cavalry charge aimed for the kill. In disbelief, they found men who could hide in the rocks as well as they and who were equally deadly at long-distance shooting. Not only did the infantry repel the attack with the loss of only one man and two wounded, they killed 15 Snake warriors including the war chiefs Yellow Badger, Snake Hawk (whose wife Prairie Flower had threatened to kill Kit Carson on his tour through central Oregon in the 1840s) and Elk Calf, who had ridden with Has No Horse during the Warner massacre.[2]

This was the first infantry engagement in the Shoshoni war and Capt. Williams deserves much credit for his fighting ability. Has No Horse had suffered a serious defeat. No longer did he hold the Walk-a-Heaps in contempt and because of this he would change battle tactics in future clashes with foot soldiers.

During this engagement Col. Currey moved into action outlining a bold plan for a winter campaign against the Snakes. This would require winter outposts and he selected nine sites for the purpose. One of these was 40 miles west of the confluence of the Ochoco and Crooked rivers. It would sit on the Santiam Trail, which was now under construction as the Willamette Valley and Cascade Mountain Military Road. Charles La Follette, commander of the company of Oregon Volunteer Infantry that was providing protection for the road builders, was ordered ahead to establish headquarters on Squaw Creek, which La Follette named Camp Polk. La Follette and his eager volunteers were confident they would come to grips with the Snakes and laid in enough supplies to last all winter.

Currey, once more reverting to the use of volunteers, was still certain that the Shoshoni could be herded against the western slope of the Steens Mountains, broken up into small bands, then waylaid by the volunteers operating out of these

---

2    Captain Williams' report in *Report of the Adj. Gen. Oregon 1865-66*, pp. 82-98.

new winter bases and destroyed. With this in mind, he ordered all troops now in the field to converge on Harney Lake.

Drake—not so confident as Currey—was following orders and started a push from the east. Camp Reed was established near Falcon Falls on the Snake River to guard the Oregon Trail. From this outpost, Lt. John W. Cullen with 20 cavalrymen would patrol the emigrant road west to the crest of the Blues. Capt. Edward Palmer established Camp Wallace on Big Camas Prairie and from this point, Lt. J.H. Walker with 22 men patrolled the Oregon Trail for 110 miles to the east. Fort Logan, sitting 15 miles east of Canyon City and abandoned in 1864, was re-manned with a cavalry company under the command of Major Pickney Lugenbeel. Fort Logan (named for Major General John Logan of Illinois who resigned his post in Congress in 1862 to join the Army of the Republic) would cover Slaughterhouse Gulch, which was a major death trap on the Boise-Canyon City trail. Some 75 miles east of Fort Logan, Drake established Camp Colfax at the Boise-Canyon City road crossing of Willow Creek (another favorite ambush spot) six miles east of Ironside Mountain. This outpost under the command of Sgt. William Hilleary, Co. F First Oregon Infantry would also cover the gold strike areas of Eldorado and Malheur City. Capt. Charles Hobart's mounted infantry were stationed at Fort Lyon on Jordan Creek to guard the approaches into Ruby City and Silver City, Idaho Territory.

Col. Charles McDermit was ordered to establish a military outpost on the Quinn River three miles south of the Nevada-Oregon line to guard traffic between Virginia City, Nevada and Boise City, Idaho. Known as Camp 33 and manned by a company of 2nd California Cavalry, it was the first outpost to come under attack. On the morning of August 7, 1865, Bad Face and Pony Blanket hit the camp and made off with a large number of cavalry horses and headed for the Santa Rosa Mountains. McDermit took pursuit and rode into an ambush on the East Fork of Quinn River at a place called Devil's Gate, less than a quarter of a mile from the Oregon state line. Among those killed was Col. McDermit, Drake's field commander for the Nevada District. On August 11, Drake renamed Camp 33 Fort McDermit in honor of his fellow comrade-in-arms.

The following morning, in an unexpected turn of events, Paulina—with a few Snake warriors in attendance—rode into Fort Klamath and without fanfare touched pen to a treaty of relinquishment on August 12, 1865. In so doing, he signed away title to all Shoshoni holdings in eastern Oregon not already ceded by the Yahuskin imposters. Another 20 million acres of Indian lands now belonged to the United States government. (See the appendices for the treaty reproduction.)

It appears that Huntington lost no time in going to Fort Klamath. In fact, he must have been halfway there when the tragic loss of the *Brother Jonathan* was made public. Huntington had been relieved of all responsibility concerning eastern Oregon Indian affairs by Idaho Superintendent George Hough in May yet in late July Huntington, in a report to the commissioner of Indian Affairs, states that he had arrived at the Warm Springs Agency with four Indian captives under armed guard. These hostages were identified as "Paulina's wife and son, his sister and another woman." He then quickly explains that Cactus Fruit (Paulina's sister) and his son young Paulina "being too sick to travel were left at Warm Springs." From here, Huntington proceeded to Fort Klamath with Paulina's wife and the other woman captive.[3]

This brings up an interesting question: Was Huntington unaware that while Falling Star was being escorted to Fort Vancouver under army guard, Paulina's sister and his son escaped from their captors on the return to the Warm Springs Agency in November 1864 nearly a year ago? Or, did he wish to conceal the fact in his report that through the ineptness of their guards, they eluded capture? There is convincing evidence that Huntington had no desire to advertise this blunder. Later at Fort Klamath, he would report that "through the two woman captives" he made contact with Paulina. Chances are the second woman mentioned was Sorrowful Woman, who was taken captive at Fort Maury in May 1864 and confined at the Warm Springs Agency.

Jim Luckey, army scout, who had met Falling Star in the Crooked River Valley in 1864 would describe her as "a very beautiful object around 30 years of age. She had a black silk handkerchief over her head, a brilliant dash of red ribbon around her throat and was wearing an old tawny buckskin dress and moccasins covered with rows of colorful Hudson's Bay Company beads."[4] Quite likely, she was dressed much the same way when she arrived at Fort Klamath in early August 1865. There is little doubt as to why Paulina was so eager for her safe return.

On August 12, Paulina with 10 warriors rode into Fort Klamath and signed the treaty. His entourage was a mixed group of Mountain, Bear Killer and Pony Stealer Snakes. The two men who could have added substance to the treaty—Wolf Dog and Has No Horse—didn't appear.[5] Little is known about this meeting as no minutes of the treaty council can be found. This is based on the supposition that records were kept.[6] With a single stroke of the pen, Paulina—without receiving payment of any kind, not even basic supplies—ceded to the United States a chunk of ground running from the head of the North Fork of the John Day River south to

---

3     *Report of Commissioner of Indian Affairs 1865*, Congressional Document Series 1248, pp. 650-651.

4     As remembered by Luckey's sister-in-law, Mrs. John (Sarah) Luckey in an interview in Prineville, Oregon, September 1956.

5     Signers of the 1865 treaty were: Paulina (Pahnine); Little Lizzard (Nuninooey); Cold Wind (Kinowney); Snake Hawk (Waakchau); Black Buffalo (Chokkosi); Lame Dog (Shezhe); Cow Lick (Nowhoopacowick); No Ribs (Kepoweetka); Tobacco Root (Cheonma); Biting Bear (Hauneshastook); and Buffalo Meat (Ahtootoowe). National Archives Record Group No. 98, U.S. Army Commands Military Department of the Columbia, 9-K-1868, Wm. Kelly to George Williams, Camp Harney, Oregon, June 25, 1868.

6     Vogelin, *The Northern Paiute of Central Oregon: A Chapter in Treaty Making*, p. 106.

Crooked River; east to Harney Valley on the headwaters of Malheur and Burnt rivers; and north to the headwaters of the Grande Ronde River. In short, the whole Ochoco. For this, the 1865 treaty would provide "beneficial objects for the Walpapi, such as would advance them in morals and knowledge of civilization."[7] Just what they needed!

Immediately after signing, Agent Applegate—on Huntington's orders—sent Paulina out to contact Big Man. It's unlikely Paulina even attempted to do so but regardless, it was unsuccessful. Huntington in his report to the commissioner of Indian Affairs would note that "Howlock (Big Man) declared himself for continuation of the war and attempted to persuade Panaina (Paulina) to leave the reservation and join him."[8] Paulina was then moved into the upper Klamath Lake region and the Klamaths moved to safer territory down by the agency. In a swift move unbefitting to Congress, this secretive treaty was ratified July 6, 1866—less than one year from the time of signing.[9]

By an ironic twist of fate Snake Hawk, riding night and day from Fort Klamath to alert Has No Horse of Paulina's foolishness, arrived at Sunflower Flat just in time to get shot to death by Capt. Williams' foot soldiers.

Gloating over his latest coup, Supt. Huntington was certain that the Shoshoni war was ended but already Wolf Dog and Has No Horse were gaining fresh allies. The death of Yellow Badger, highly respected war chief of the Buffalo Killers who had recently been killed in an engagement with Currey's troops, brought the Bannock Snakes into the fray. Black Beard, Man Lost's war chief; Ground Owl, war chief of the Dog Ribs; Little Foot, chief of the Root Gatherers; and Laughing Hawk of the Honey Eaters rode into the Ochoco pledging their support. The Bannock guardian spirit was the dragonfly, powerful in flight, eater of insects and a serpent of the air. This symbol, which all Bannock warriors painted on their war shields, let the enemy know of the strong medicine they received from this killer—and Williams' infantry was the enemy.

Col. Currey, to insure that Huntington's contract went unchallenged, continued his plan of winter fortifications designed to eliminate all Snake resistance. On the strength of these forts and the fact that Drake had things fairly well under control, The Dalles to Salt Lake City mail, express and passenger run of 800 miles was established in August 1865.[10] As the stagecoaches began rolling,

---

7    At some future day, the Snakes were to receive $2,000 for five years and $1,200 annually for the 10 years following. The government also promised to expend $5,000 for fences, cultivation of land, seed and farming implements and to hire teachers, mechanics, a physician and a farmer none of which it ever did. *Walpapi Snake Treaty 1865, Congressional Documents Serial 4624,* 57th Congress 1st Session, Vol. 2, pp. 671-72; *The Statutes at Large and Treaties of the United States 1851-1875,* Vol. 14, p. 683, Article 7.

8    *Report of the Commissioner of Indian Affairs 1866,* Congressional Doc. Series 1248, p. 89.

9    *The Congressional Globe 1865-6,* Part V, p. 402.

10   McNeal, *Wasco County,* p. 14.

Capt. Williams—because of his successful rout of Has No Horse's troops—was ordered from the Sunflower Flat battlefield to construct a string of forts into Harney Valley. His first priority was to establish a permanent outpost some 35 miles south of Fort Dahlgren at Drake's old depot at Currey Springs, the junction of the Willamette Valley and Cascade Mountain Military Road—now under construction—and the Red Bluff Trail.

On this march to Currey Springs, Williams ran into the Snake reinforcements on Deliment Creek and the battle was on. This time on the advice of Has No Horse, the men with the dragonfly war shields used a different mode of attack. Williams and his celebrated infantry dug in and prepared for the dog soldiers' mounted charge. It never happened.

Black Beard set fire to the grass and calmly awaited the result—which was not long in coming. The surrounding timber exploded into a fiery inferno and only because their guardian spirit was watching over them, the infantrymen were able to escape through the smoke and flame, but suffered many burn injuries. Believing they had roasted the foot soldiers, Black Beard and his war party continued north bent on more destruction.

An expressman was dispatched to Fort Watson requesting help after this attack and work hurriedly began on the construction of Fort Currey. When completed, Fort Currey would consist of forty 10 by 12 foot cabins surrounded by log breastworks reinforced with rock. Sitting alongside the Shoshoni trail from the Ochoco to Nevada, it was under constant attack. The little cemetery on the barren hillside north of the fort was soon sprinkled with graves, three of which were still visible in the 1970s.

Rushing to fill Williams' request, two companies of 4th California Infantry, a detachment of 1st Washington Infantry and a squadron of 1st Oregon Cavalry, all under the command of Capt. L.S. Scott (of the 4th California Infantry Division), arrived September 30 to hold the position. By November, Lt. Frank Perry (brevet major) moved in with Co. E, Second Battalion, 14th U.S. Infantry to take command of the post.

Before Capt. Scott arrived, Capt. Williams with a construction crew again moved out in mid-September under orders to build a similar post on the Silvies River, another important stopover on the Willamette Valley and Cascades Mountain Military Road. He began construction on September 18. Known as Camp Adobe, it was destined for a short life. Under repeated attack, the workers were having difficulty protecting their own lives. As a means of defense, the soldiers excavated a hole 75 feet square by three feet deep, heaping the dirt up around the outer perimeter another three feet high to form a sod blockhouse and hence, the name Camp Adobe. Williams finally had to give up and once again under orders, abandoned the project on October 3 and marched to Harney Valley where he began construction of a fort on the east end of Wright Point, a fringe of land jutting into Malheur Lake.[11]

Camp Wright consisted of sod cabins with juniper pole roofs covered with earth and surrounded by rifle pits. The main fortification was the lake itself which surrounded the fort on three sides. Williams also constructed and launched a log-framed flat boat, floored with lumber and put together entirely with wooden pegs to patrol Malheur Lake. You might say that this gunboat was eastern Oregon's first navy.

While Capt. Williams was struggling to build a line of defense, the troops at Camp Polk—three miles northwest of the present site of Sisters, Oregon—were anxiously awaiting Indians to come dashing into rifle range in their retreat from the battlefront. They never fired a shot. By the end of October, the Willamette Valley and Cascades Mountain Military Road crew had reached Camp Polk and with winter approaching decided to end construction for the year. Leaving all their equipment at the army camp under the care of William Smith, a company employee who would winter with the soldiers, the road crew returned to the Willamette Valley before snow clogged the passes. Capt. Newton White with a detachment of Co. B, 1st Oregon Infantry who had served as road escort, was attached to Capt. La Follette's command.

By now, the bitter winds of 12 winters had blown over the lonely platform in the high mountain pass that was Red Wolf's final camping ground. His successor's half-brother, the youth Red Wolf had known as The War Spirit was sitting docile on the Klamath Indian reservation waiting for a winter handout of food while his disgruntled followers—the Mountain (Walpapi) Snakes—were having second thoughts on the wisdom of their leader's latest maneuver to overwhelm the white brothers.

In October, while Has No Horse attempted to do something constructive by eliminating a few army posts, Paulina rode into Fort Klamath. He told Major Rinehart that "all the Indians of his tribe who stipulated to come in" were camped in Sprague River Valley (Moses Brown's private hunting grounds) and that he wished to talk to either Huntington or Applegate. As usual, when something of a serious nature was in progress, Supt. Huntington was unavailable and Agent Applegate had gone into winter quarters in Ashland. However, Applegate did return to Fort Klamath as a result of Paulina's request. Instead of listening to Paulina's problem, Applegate tried using him, Lalake and Moses Brown as intermediaries to persuade Big Man to report to Fort Klamath and make peace. This attempt failed.

Moses Brown, already on Big Man's blacklist, refused to go. Paulina and Lalake did go into hostile country and returned with Black Buffalo and Pony Blanket. Sensing victory, Applegate extolled the joys of reservation life and

---

11    *Oregon Adj Gen. Report 1865-6*, p. 82.

outlined the boundaries of the federal reserve stressing that their people must stay within those boundaries. It made little impression on either Pony Blanket or Black Buffalo. They had no intention of being corralled in the white man's pasture for they had come to Fort Klamath mainly to convince Paulina of the error in his present thinking. Perhaps it worked. Paulina remained on the reservation but by the end of December, the only Shoshoni on the reserve besides him were seven women and eleven children. The rest had returned to Has No Horse's war camp in the Ochoco although Paulina assured Applegate that the Walpapis had "promised to rejoin him in the spring."[12]

On November 1, 1865 orders came from the War Department for Currey to abandon the winter campaign and relieve all volunteers of duty. The regular army would take over. By the time word reached the field, the snow was too deep in the Blues and Cascades for the volunteers to return and as a consequence, they spent a tough, cold winter in their makeshift camps without pay.

In December the Fort Wright navy with a crew of 10 sailed on an exploration of Malheur Lake. Coming to shore some five miles from the fort, the sailors were surprised by a Snake war party who set fire to the patrol craft, ending its service in a burst of glory. Fighting a retreating battle toward camp, Capt. Williams, out on wood detail, heard the gunfire and rushed to the rescue. But by the time the two detachments could make contact, the Indians had cut them off from the fort. An ugly column of black smoke drifting ominously toward the snow-covered ridges of the Blue Mountains signaled the demise of Fort Wright which burned to the ground. With no other choice, the remnant of Capt. Williams famed infantry slogged through a blinding snowstorm toward Fort Currey some 40 miles to the west. They arrived in time to celebrate a very dreary Christmas. Fort Wright was never rebuilt.

Col. George Currey's dream of linking forts to break the back of the Snake war tribes hardly put a dent in their frequent raids, for the main bases of operations in the high sheltered valleys of the Ochoco secluded under Lookout Mountain and Mount Pisgah remained undiscovered and therefore, untouched.

---

12   *National Archives, Bureau of Indian Affairs Oregon Superintendency, Letters Received*: W.V. Rinehart to Huntington, Fort Klamath, Oregon, October 6, 1865; Lindsay Applegate to J.W. Perit Huntington, Ashland Mills, Oregon, October 31, 1865; Lindsay Applegate to J.W. Perit Huntington, Ashland Mills, Oregon, January 20, 1866.

# CHAPTER 129

# REQUIEM FOR THE VOLUNTEERS

*And though you be done to death, what then?*
*If you battled the best you could;*
*If you played your part in the world of men,*
*Why, the critic will call it good.*

**Edmund Vance Cooke**
*How Did You Die?*

Weeks before the War Department's order came down to stop the winter campaign, Currey's strategy was taking a beating. The field troops who were supposed to be herding Has No Horse's raiders into the waiting guns of the various forts were having no success. Commerce was stalled on The Dalles-Canyon City-Boise Trail, and traffic over the Oregon Central Military Road had come to a virtual stop between Fort Klamath and Fort Lyon on the Idaho border. Little Rattlesnake and the Big Lodge war chief Storm Cloud, working out of the Warner Mountains north of Fort Bidwell, were striking anything that moved on the west end of the military road, while Big Man and Four Crows (a walking memento of the 1845 emigrant train) were keeping things lively around Fort Alvord on the eastern end.

Capt. Franklin B. Sprague, escort for the Oregon Central construction crews, had spent a pleasant summer wandering around the southern Cascades. On one of his sightseeing jaunts, Sprague discovered—or so he thought—Crater Lake on August 15, 1865 naming it Lake Majesty. Actually John Hellman, a prospector, discovered it first on June 12, 1853 and christened it Deep Blue Lake. It has been known at times as Mysterious Lake and Lake Mystery but on August 4, 1869 it was named Crater Lake by a party of visitors from Jacksonville, Oregon.

East of the Cascades, progress for the road crew was not so gratifying. The only leisure time the infantry riflemen had was spent in fending off Shoshoni attacks. Inspired by unfriendly interruptions, construction of the Oregon Central Military Road was completed to Fort Alvord moving at double-time. There was only one problem. No traffic was forthcoming. Suspecting the reason, Sprague's infantry backed by a squadron of cavalry took to the back trail, first following Four Crows, then Big Man and finally, hot on the trail of Little Rattlesnake, he arrived back at Fort Klamath in October.

The weary foot soldiers had barely shaken the dust out of their uniforms when Major Rinehart ordered them back to Fort Alvord in a further attempt to intercept the hostiles. Picking up the tracks of a war party almost at the stockade's gate, Capt. Sprague followed them on a circuitous route to the Nevada line. On October 28, he met Capt. Robert Starr of the 2nd California Cavalry south of the Steens Mountains. Starr was post commander at Fort Bidwell, California located 17 miles south of the Oregon line and 10 miles west of the Nevada border.

During the 1865 campaign, Gen. McDowell—unimpressed with Oregon's war effort—was leaving all decisions strictly in the hands of Col. Currey and his volunteers. In mid-October, Gen. McDowell ordered Capt. Starr—who had been helping Lt. Col. Drake—to return to Fort Crook, California before snow blocked the mountain passes, which left only 25 regulars to man Fort Bidwell for the winter. In view of this order, Starr was not eager to assist the Oregon Volunteers. Sprague, certain that he would catch up with the Snakes at any moment finally talked Starr into sending Lt. John Backus with 10 cavalrymen to help him find the Indians. After a three-day march no Indians had been sighted so Backus left Sprague at Warner Creek and headed for Fort Bidwell to catch up with Starr.

An hour after Backus departed, Sprague walked into a trap two miles south of the Oregon Central Military Road. Little Rattlesnake and Storm Cloud with 125 warriors were entrenched in a rock slide on the west side of Warner Mountain. Trapped in a narrow corridor between Hart Lake and the steep hillside, Sprague dug in. During the battle, he observed that the Indians' front line was armed with rifles while the rear had only bows. Concentrating his attack on this weak back-line, Sprague made an end run and was able to escape with the wounded to Fort Bidwell some 40 miles to the south.

Leaving Sgt. Orson Stearns with the wounded at Fort Bidwell, Sprague made a forced march back to Fort Alvord. South of Catlow Valley, he bumped into Lt. John Dimick with more bad news. Four Crows had raided the fort corrals leaving half of the cavalry stationed there dismounted. The mounted half, led by Lt. Dimick, were now tracking Four Crows toward the southern Blues. Pvt. James Alderson, who was on horse guard, had been killed.[1] On this sour note, Sprague bypassed Fort Alvord and continued on to Fort Lyon on Jordan Creek where he and his discouraged infantrymen spent the winter.

While Capts. Sprague and Williams were taking a beating in the southeastern Oregon desert, the first Civil War veterans arrived from the east, marching overland into Fort Boise. Major Jesse Walker, commanding two companies of the 14th U.S. Infantry Regiment, relieved the volunteers of duty and those who could out-distance the winter storms marched to Fort Vancouver where they were mustered out of the service. At the same time Major Walker took command of Fort Boise, Capt. John McGregor and Lt. John Snell with Troop A First Oregon

---

1    The *Portland Oregonian*, December 4, 1865.

Cavalry, manned with regulars, relieved the volunteers at Fort Klamath. Col. Currey retired and Lt. Col. Drake took command of the Military Department of the Columbia.

As soon as he took command, Drake married Angeline Robb on November 20, 1865.[2] In less than a month, he too, was relieved of command by Major Gen. Fred Steele. Disgusted with military life and not wishing to be separated from Angeline (at least not so soon), he resigned his commission and along with William Kopus—regimental adjutant of the First Washington Territorial Volunteer Infantry—opened a grocery and bakery shop in Portland.

Col. Currey went back into law practice at Salem and then moved to Canyon City where he practiced law from 1872 to 1880. It was here, perhaps under the influence of Joaquin Miller, that he began writing *The Tribute to the Ox Whip*.

Captain James Waymire was reassigned to the regular army as a second lieutenant. When he resigned his commission at the end of the Shoshoni war, he studied law and was admitted to the Oregon bar, subsequently moving to San Francisco where he became a federal judge. In 1879, Waymire was suggested for a cabinet post in the McKinley administration.[3]

The regulars had barely arrived when Jim Clark, driver of one of the Wheeler stagecoaches, stopped to visit with some wagoneers camped near the mouth of the Owyhee River. Black Beard and Four Crows joined forces and hit them at dusk. Clark was one of the first to go down with a nasty bullet wound in the left shoulder. He was one of the lucky ones for he escaped. Apparently, the volunteers stranded in the winter outposts were doing little to protect life or property. Shortly after the Owyhee attack thirty-four horses were stolen near the Boise Ferry on the Snake River and in late December all the pack mules at Fort Alvord were driven off. Capt. Sprague, for lack of something better to do, later searched for and recovered the mules.

On The Dalles front, the Scott brothers took advantage of the newly constructed Willamette Valley and Cascade Mountain Military Road—a trail they had pioneered three years before—and with five riders trail herded 400 cattle from the Willamette Valley to Trout Creek.[4] They intended to supply the new military outposts with beef. On Trout Creek, Wolf Dog stampeded the cattle, stole seven horses and all the camp gear. Thus another dream of riches fell through.

Hoping to get in on the cattle trade, Abe Mitskie and Hank Gussil followed the Scotts with 200 head of heifers to start ranching operations in the heart of the battle zone. Learning the fate of the Scott's cattle drive, they quickly turned north

---

2    *The Oregon Statesman*, Salem, November 27, 1865, p. 2, col. 6.

3    Scott, *History of Oregon*, Vol. V, p. 273; Smith, Bethel, *Polk Co. Oregon*, p. 66; *Gibbs Collection*, Oregon Historical Society Scrapbook 5, p. 73.

4    The cattle herders who later settled in Crook County were: Charles Hardesty, John Evans, Thomas Evans, Lem Jones and Ike Miller.

and sold out to Ben Snipes, Wasco County cattle baron who was operating out of The Dalles.

Although the Snakes were still holding their own against all comers, the eastern members of the clan weren't faring so well. The Comanche war chief Medicine Walker had gone into winter camp on the Canadian River directly in the path of Lt. Col. Andrew W. Evans, who was marching downriver with six companies of cavalry and two companies of infantry at his back. On Christmas day 1865, he hit Medicine Walker's village and destroyed everything in sight. For this victory, Evans was promoted to brevet colonel.[5]

By the end of December there were still 872 volunteers abandoned in the snow-covered battlefields of eastern Oregon.[6] It was time to usher in a new year.

---

5   Monaghan, ed., *The Book of the American West*, p. 230.

6   Those still left in the field included 553 infantrymen and 319 cavalry troopers. Bancroft, *History of Oregon* Vol. II, p. 519.

# CHAPTER 130

# HAPPY NEW YEAR!

*Stranger in town: try the Stark Street entrance to the Bella Union Saloon. Drinks are 25 cents and the most attractive ladies will always be found.*

**Advertisement**
*Portland Oregonian,* December 30, 1865

As 1865 drew to a close, the growing city of Portland boasted a population of 4,000 strident souls. The rest of the United States struggling with reconstruction in the aftermath of civil war would hardly notice. More important things were happening. The world's first oil pipeline—six miles long—was completed in Pennsylvania. Word arrived on the newly completed Atlantic cable that a cholera epidemic was sweeping across Europe which claimed 60,000 lives in Paris alone. The citizens of Richmond, Virginia, fearing a Negro uprising, gave birth to the Ku Klux Klan in Pulaski, Tennessee. The Mississippi legislature was in Washington, D.C. to petition for the pardon of Jefferson Davis, who was now held in a federal prison. And on the literary scene Lewis Carroll's *Alice's Adventures in Wonderland* had hit the New York market.

But the eager young city of Portland could not be bothered with such mundane matters. The city fathers were planning a glorious party to celebrate the return of Oregon's volunteers from the rigors of eastern Oregon. The time set for this gala affair was New Year's night, Monday, January 1, 1866. And the big social event would take place at the Turn Verein Hall honoring the officers and men of the Oregon Volunteers—more fondly known as the State Militia.

The newly arrived U.S. Regulars—neither welcome nor invited to this prestigious affair—would take the rest of Portland by storm on their last big fling before going into Shoshoni country. Even though their eastern border was ablaze with war, Oregonians—fiercely proud of their volunteers—refused to accept the presence of regular army personnel. Both the public and the press, loathing the Shoshoni war and its effects on Pacific Northwest commerce, wanted no involvement nor help from United States soldiers—whom they considered to be the scum of the earth. By the end of the first Snake campaign in 1869, the army would fall so low in public esteem that Congress cut army strength by half to appease their constituents. Now these unwanted warriors were roaming the streets of Portland on New Year's night. It would be three years before the regulars again had cause to celebrate.

In contrast to the "Puritan Regiment," the regulars made no denials that they enjoyed a shot of liquor. In fact, the Indian-fighting army was the rowdiest of all time. A high percentage of the enlisted men were habitual drunks and few of its officers shunned the bottle. Payday brought on a mass spree lasting till the money was gone or the hangover refused to quit. Even a $13 a month private could satisfy his wants this New Year's night. Money was no object—not with the best whiskey going for two bits a shot and a steak dinner for one dollar. The gay blade could rent a horse and buggy for the evening for $1.00 and dazzle the local cuties the whole evening for less than $10 dollars. If he really wanted to cut corners, he could dip his face to the eyebrows in a schooner of Weinhard's beer from the Portland City Brewery for a solitary nickel.

Soldiers with finer tastes could dine at the freshly renovated new Columbia Hotel which advertised a fireproof safe to protect your valuables. The troopers from the East would discover that this was not a bad idea as "those Stark Street girls could be covetous." And for those who went for that sort of thing, the Empire Restaurant had dining rooms for ladies.

It is doubtful that the veterans from the Atlantic side of the country were interested but on New Year's night 1866, the Willamette Theater was offering *Toodles! Or, It's So Handy to Have Him in the House,* a pretty racy farce described by an anonymous reviewer as "screaming" and featuring A.R. Phelps as Toodles.

However, Portland's finest would be arriving by carriage at Turn Verein Hall to help the Fenian Guards—Co. F of the State Militia, Capt. Sprague's old command—tout the exploits of their brothers-in-arms with Gov. Addison C. Gibbs at the head of the receiving line. To show how exclusive this party was, it required a cover charge of $5 to admit "a gentleman and his ladies." In these progressive times, as an *Oregonian* reporter would put it, "a man-about-town took his female companionship in the plural or risked some rather painful criticism the next day down at the livery stable."[1]

Among those attending was Lt. Col. John Drake and Angeline Robb, his bride of six weeks; Col. George and Jessica Gaines Currey; Major William and Amanda Gaines Rinehart; and Capt. James Waymire, newly commissioned second lieutenant in the United States Army. Being a part of the in-group, Waymire was tolerated if not forgiven for this indiscretion.

By daylight January 2, the party was over for the U.S. Regulars as they shuddered and faced their new assignment with a little help from a bottle of Constitution Water guaranteed to cure "diabetes, general debility and physical prostration." Before the Snake campaign was over they would need all the

---

1    Early Deane, "New Year's was a Dizzying Affair in 1866," The *Sunday Oregonian*, December 26, 1965.

assistance they could get. Desertion rates would be higher than in any period since. In one garrison alone, 54 of 86 men went over the hill in the summer of 1866. The U.S. secretary of war cynically remarked that it might be the easiest way to get the far west populated.[2]

The pacifists who today encourage draft-dodging and desertion and harbor fugitives are nothing new in United States history. There were like-minded idealists in Oregon, Idaho and Nevada in 1866. When a trooper deserted, citizens paid him upwards to $200 for his horse, rifle, uniform and saddle instead of turning him in for the $20 reward.

The living conditions at Fort Watson, Fort Boise and Fort Harney were cramped and bare. The food issued to the regulars and methods of supply were unbelievably cheap. In fact, no soldiers since the American Revolution had been so poorly served. The issue consisted of salt pork, dried beans, green coffee, brown sugar, a small amount of white flour (often wormy and moldy) and the cheapest soap that could be bought. Some kind of fresh meat was sometimes issued twice a week. If the troopers wanted fresh fruit or vegetables, they had either to grow them or steal them . . . they did both. It's small wonder that they lived off the land and in so doing—perhaps by government design—they nearly exterminated all game animals in eastern Oregon by the 1880s a blow that the deer, elk and antelope never fully recovered from.

Rather than being uniformed as one, the Indian-fighting army was what is now called permissive. All soldiers did not dress alike. Some commanding officers like Custer dressed in buckskin shirts; others like Crook preferred light duck clothing and pith helmets. The uniform codes in each unit were pretty much set by the ranking officer. He was given the power and he used it. It's also interesting to note that the cavalry did not carry the Stars and Stripes until 1887. Prior to this time they carried the national Cavalry Standard, a yellow flag bordered in gold with the American eagle in the center.

Many of the troopers gave false names on enlisting. They did it either to cover up an unsavory past or because their families and friends regarded army service as socially degrading. These were the men who would march into the Ochoco in the spring of 1866 to wrest it from the grip of the Snake dog soldiers.

Fresh from the battlefields of the Civil War, the regulars—harboring no love for civilian apathy—were not in eastern Oregon to play games. Their commanding officers had reached the top through a tough school. Having learned to kill their white brethren without remorse, the officers and men with few exceptions would show no mercy in slaughtering Indians. They had fought a civil war to unify the country and were still committed to that purpose. However, on one count, they would fall short. Trained for trench-fighting and massive frontal assaults, they

---

2    Brig. Gen. S.L.A. Marshall, "Disorder not new to U.S. Army," *The Oregonian*, May 30, 1969.

knew little about Shoshoni warfare and like the Americans in Vietnam 100 years later, they would make many costly mistakes.

But for a start, Gen. Steele would make some sweeping changes. By June 1866, the whole volunteer force—except for Waymire's Co. B First Oregon Cavalry and Sprague's Co. I First Oregon Infantry—was relieved of duty. All camps were abandoned in Oregon except Fort Watson and Fort Alvord which was moved a few miles and renamed Fort C.F. Smith.[3] These remained open only because the merchants at The Dalles would not permit their closure. Fort Lyon and Fort Boise were allowed to remain active in Idaho but Fort Lapwai and Fort Walla Walla, both miles north of the battle zone and serving no useful purpose, were abandoned. In general, there was a complete change of priorities to make an opening for a new campaign under a new department commander.

The first reconstruction year of 1866 was a bitter one in Oregon politics and it would affect the military. In November 34-year-old George L. Woods, Republican, was elected third governor of the state and the Democrats, still smarting under the firm war leadership of Gov. Gibbs, demanded a recount. Woods stood off the challenge but had a hostile legislature on his hands.

Also, one of the most important industrial steps came in 1866 when the manufacture of paper from wood pulp was started in Oregon City. This gave Oregon the edge in paper production for newspapers and magazines. It likewise set the stage for the expansion of the timber industry.

And western Oregon was still dutifully ignoring the Shoshoni war. Portland papers would report that Oregon residents kept worried watch on major outbreaks in Idaho, Montana and Wyoming but there was only minor Indian trouble in "parts of eastern Oregon." So be it. Some residents, namely the settlers in eastern Oregon, were not quite so steadfast in their western allies' beliefs.

---

3    *The Dalles Mountaineer*, April 20, 1866.

# CHAPTER 131

# DUEL ON FLORIDA MOUNTAIN

*I would have the winds to envelop my body;*
*I would have the sun shine upon my body;*
*The whole world I would have to make music with me.*
*When thou wouldst slay me, O Shining One!*
*Let it be day*
*When I sing the last song!*

**Hartley Burr Alexander**
*Let It Be Day*

Seven days before Gen. Steele arrived in Portland to take command of the Military Department of the Columbia, the Snakes drew blood on the Oregon-Idaho border. After 14 months of self-imposed exile, Paulina had returned to the fold.

Under cover of a December blizzard, Paulina and Falling Star—facing starvation—left the Klamath reservation and once again pledged support to the Paviotso Confederacy. Following their arrival at Has No Horse's camp in mid-January, a large war party slipped out of the Ochoco Valley and moved south into the storm-lashed rims of the northern Great Basin. From this position the raiders worked in a huge circle, striking every settler's cabin and mining district from northern Nevada to the Snake River Plain in southern Idaho. In command of this well-armed group of Snake warriors were Paulina, Big Man, Four Crows and the feared medicine man Gray Head.

Back in the snow-clad inter-mountain valleys of the southern Blues, the very old and the very young were dying for lack of nourishment. For the past few years, bogged down in fighting the Americans, the tribes had been unable to make their annual hunts to buffalo country; what supplies they did cache were systematically destroyed by the invading soldiers and the local game was fast disappearing— wantonly slain by the white men's guns. Therefore the sole purpose of this winter foray was to capture horses and cattle in a desperate attempt to stave off starvation. Whenever a herd was separated from its owner, it was driven back to the inhabitants of the Ochoco. In this manner, the war party steadily decreased in size with each successive raid.

The second week in February found the raiders crossing the Owyhee Mountains on their return to the Ochoco. By this time their numbers had dwindled to a mere handful. Moving down Jordan Creek, sharp eyes raked each knoll and gully searching for anything which would fit into the tribal stew-pot, but in this remote section of the Oregon-Idaho border the pickings were mighty slim. Then on the late afternoon of February 13, Gray Head stumbled onto a small ranch house nestled under the rims of Trout Creek Canyon, on a tributary to Jordan Creek. A hurried scout soon revealed that this homestead was well worth the risk of attack.

Meanwhile in the broken land south of Trout Creek, Andrew Hall loaded a freshly killed deer onto a long-legged sorrel gelding, happy in the assurance that he would have enough meat to last until the first warm days of spring. Not another thought entered his mind as he faced his horse into the bitter north wind and rode towards his snug cabin on the ice-locked stream five miles away.

The raw winter evening was fading into semi-darkness when Hall saw a crimson glow against the northern sky. Cautiously he topped the crest of a low ridge and the nagging fear became verified. What once had been a house and barn were now twin fire brands in the glistening snow. Seething with rage, the young settler jerked his rifle from its well-oiled scabbard, laid whip to his horse and charged toward the flaming buildings.

Hall hit the creek at a lunging gallop but before he had reached mid-stream, the sixth sense of a frontiersman told him to take heed. Somewhere out in the crusted snow muffled hoofbeats were bearing down on him at a rapid pace. Self preservation took precedence over anger and with hardly a second to spare, Hall drove the rangy sorrel into a clump of frozen willows. Moments later, he cursed helplessly as his life earnings thundered by—50 of the finest horses in Idaho Territory were being pushed downstream toward the grim foothills of the distant southern Blues.

Following in their wake came a half-dozen Snake warriors. One of these braves swerved so close to Hall's hideout that he could plainly distinguish the Indian's horribly scarred face; a twisted mass of scar tissue puckered into an unmistakable brand. Etched in a series of vivid welts were the well-defined numbers 1845 running from the right side of the man's forehead to his lower left jawbone.

Andy Hall had spent four years in the western wilderness and was accustomed to gruesome sights but this man's tortured countenance was enough to turn his stomach. Instantly, the story came to mind of how members of the 1845 lost emigrant train had caught an "Injun brat" and burned the date of their passage through central Oregon on his face. Almost reluctantly, Hall remembered how he had thrilled to the story at The Dalles; laughed over it at Canyon City; joined in its discussion wherever men gathered to drink and boast but never in all its gory detail had he taken any stock in the farfetched tale.

Now, the skeptical rancher knew the truth but he had neither the time nor the sympathy to waste on an ignorant savage so he quickly dismissed the image from his mind. First and foremost, he must save his house and barn if possible and then, there was always the unpleasant consideration that his own hide was at stake.

Anxious as Hall was, he waited until the Indians disappeared around a bend in the canyon before abandoning the ice-box he had picked for shelter but the precious minutes lost in hiding would spell destruction for the blazing cabin. A few minutes after his arrival, the roof and one wall buckled to the ground in a dancing shower of orange sparks.

The primitive structure so ruthlessly destroyed had been the white man's only claim on the unfriendly land. Now that grasp was broken. Dazed and heartbroken, Hall wandered aimlessly over the trampled area around the smoldering ruins of his home, his mind plagued with indecision. Midway between house and barn his eyes came to focus on a track in the snow . . . an imprint which jarred him back into reality. Spaced evenly along a 50-foot path and sunken deeply into the hard packed snow were tracks of a man measuring over 17 inches in length!

Climaxing this ominous discovery, a lonely Shoshoni war whoop screeched through the dark corridors of night. Unexpected and terrible, this eerie cry forced Hall into immediate and decisive action. Though it could mean death, he must try and reach the nearest white settlement and somehow send word to Capt. Frank Sprague at Fort Lyon to be on the alert for he had learned something of extreme importance. The huge footprints now caked in ice were those of the 300-pound Big Foot (Big Man), Has No Horse's eastern commander and number two war chief of the allied Snake tribes. The way Hall saw it, the evidence could prove but one thing—Has No Horse, the relentless head chief of the Paviotso Confederacy, was carrying on a full-scale winter offensive.

Fear and frustration gave way to an all consuming rage as he returned to his horse. With an impatient tug, the angry rancher untied the deer carcass and let it drop to the ground. No more need for fresh venison he thought bitterly as he cast a final glance at his smoldering cabin. He then mounted and with the temperature hovering at 10 degrees below zero, Hall turned his horse eastward toward Ruby City, 1,500 feet higher in elevation than his ranch.

Although only 15 miles away, Ruby City perched on the north slope of Florida Mountain at the 6,000 foot level and buried in 10 foot snowdrifts from four to six months out of the year, would take many torturous hours to reach.[1] To the north, just inside the Oregon line, sat Fort Lyon some 12 miles north of the Chico Trail and 18 miles northwest of Silver City, Idaho. The fort—nearly bisected by the Oregon-Idaho boundary—was an equal distance from the ranch but so far as Hall was concerned it was as inaccessible as the moon. Through the frontier

---

1    Ruby City, Idaho, a suburb of Silver City, averaged two feet of snow on the level with winter temperature averaging 10 degrees to 13 degrees and having winter winds up to 50 miles per hour. *Silver City Final Environmental Statement*, USDI-BLM, Lenard, May 1978, pp. 2-1.

grapevine, he was aware that the Snakes had all but isolated that post from the rest of the world.

Like Paulina, Man Lost had seen the folly in signing a white man's peace agreement. In early January he and Spotted Elk—in a bold attempt to shield Has No Horse's weakened position—had thrown their warriors into a tight circle around the fort and making it all but impossible for an infantry troop to get out without facing the possibility of total annihilation. So, a lone civilian had about as much chance of sneaking into Fort Lyon as Has No Horse had of becoming governor of Oregon.

Hall rode out, holding to the windswept ridges where he could make better progress for he knew that no one, least of all a superstitious Indian, would follow him on a night such as this. Shortly after midnight February 14, he had covered nearly six miles. Ahead lay the snow-choked Jordan Canyon knifing its way through the Silver City Range and the hardest part of the trail. Figuring that he could make this last jaunt on his hands and knees, if necessary, Hall reined in the weary sorrel for a much needed rest.

The next two miles were covered at a slow pace. Then in the pale glow of a sinking moon, the young rancher spotted a ghostly rider on his back-trail. Hall urged his horse into a halfhearted trot and again glanced over his shoulder. Surely he was imagining things for there wasn't another white man this side of the Owyhee River and no Indian would be on the prowl this late at night. At least that was what Archie McIntosh had told him and he should know. McIntosh, born in Canada, had worked for three years in Snake country as a Hudson's Bay trapper and was now employed as an army scout.

Nevertheless, Hall looked back once more and this time there was no mistaking what he saw. Archie McIntosh had been wrong! Yanking his old .50 Sharps from its saddle scabbard, Hall breathed a silent prayer as he lashed the weary horse toward Ruby City and the promise of safety.

If ever a war chief was nervous, it was Big Man. As yet he had left no survivors to tell of his 600-mile raid but now, under the rims of Trout Creek Canyon, luck had run out. Above all, he wanted no report of this last escapade to reach the soldiers. As long as the army believed the Snakes were holed up for the winter so much the better for the battle-weary dog soldiers of the Paviotso Confederacy. Like his own men, they were sick, hungry and badly in need of rest.

A mile west of Andrew Hall's glowing cabin, Big Man ordered a halt and immediately went into consultation with his warriors. Four Crows, his scarred features drawn into a permanent leer, was the first to voice an opinion. Always searching for the peaceful solution to an issue, he stressed the point that they had captured the horses without a struggle and therefore, the most sensible thing to do was to stop worrying and make tracks for the Ochoco. Why risk losing everything when there was so little at stake. At the very worst, by the time the white man reached Fort Lyon—taking into consideration the unlikely prospect that he could slip through Man Lost's warriors—they would be safe in the snow-locked valleys of the Ochoco.

This made sense to Gray Head and the others but Big Man was not so easily convinced. He was all for turning back and checking the next morning although he knew in his own mind that it would be too late to stop the white man if he should decide to go to Fort Lyon. His next suggestion which involved sending a messenger to Man Lost was also thrashed out and discarded as being impractical.[2]

Finally, Gray Head came up with a solution. A crafty huntsman who knew every trick in frontier warfare, he was certain that the white man was close to the ranch when they put it to the torch. How close, he could not say but in all probability at this time of evening, he was close enough to see what was going on. It was also a safe bet that he had identified the war party. In that event, there could be no alternative. Someone had to get him even though it meant taking the scent after dark.

It was ancient Shoshonean belief that to pursue one's enemies after dark was the most hazardous thing a warrior could do. According to their religion, if a person should die in darkness his soul would be lost forever—wandering throughout eternity between the four winds, never to enter the spirit land. This age-old belief placed the war chiefs in an uncomfortable position. At last, Four Crows put into words what was running through all their minds. No white man was going to pack the tale to Fort Lyon that any Snakes were in the vicinity and it was worth risking a life to protect the rest of the tribesmen.

At this stage of the game it was unanimously agreed that it would be unwise to tempt the demons of darkness with Big Man's hulking spirit for he was a key leader in the Paviotso Confederacy; and the needless loss of Big Man would constitute a crushing blow to Has No Horse's well-laid plans for victory.

Four Crows, although he was one of the toughest warriors in the group when the odds were against him, was also turned down on the grounds that he was too soft-hearted to be sent on a delicate mission such as this.

This left only Gray Head, who being a medicine man, was by far the best qualified of the three to cope with the spirit world. With his comrades blessings echoing in his ears, old Gray Head mounted on one of Hall's thoroughbreds, set out to eliminate any possibility of their whereabouts being turned over to the enemy. He was also painfully aware that Idaho—with the exception of the governor—was as rabid as Oregon when it came to inciting civilians to slaughter Shoshoni.

The frigid night winds moaned up the bleak canyon as Gray Head circled to pick up the track of his intended victim. Within an hour, he found where Andy Hall had pulled off the trail to let the war party go by and with a mournful war cry, Gray Head disappeared into the foreboding realm of night.

---

2    Testimony of Dave Chocktote whose father, Black Buffalo, was with the raiders.

Seven hours later on the cracked lip of Jordan Canyon two shadowy riders raced in the dark. Two straining horses matched each other step for step in the ever-deepening snow and the gap between never varied as the throbbing minutes stretched into anguished hours. A dull gray streak in the eastern sky promised the approach of an early dawn; the out-rider increased the pace and the exhausted lead horse, pushed to the very limit of endurance, sensed that the end was near.

The horses, wallowing in chest-deep snow, could go no farther. Hall's gave out first and Gray Head closed the gap to within 20 feet before his mount went down in a cascade of snow.

As the first orange tint of a winter sun caressed the frozen Silver City range, a solitary shot splintered the icy stillness with the fury of bursting thunder. The Indian reeled, then straightened and his war axe arched through the air. A sobbing scream, borne on the wings of agony, climbed the red-streaked dawn . . . then came terrifying silence.

On the evening of January 31, Archie McIntosh—half-breed Chippewa, ex-Hudson's Bay man and army scout since 1855—slipped out of Fort Lyon under the cover of a blinding snowstorm and headed west toward the hostile Blues.[3] He soon discovered that Man Lost had lifted his cordon of braves that had been hovering on the outskirts of the post but with the ever present threat that Has No Horse might be on the prowl, McIntosh traveled mostly by night.

For two weeks, McIntosh roamed the snow-drifted plateau but other than a few Paiute winter camps he found nothing of importance until the early morning of February 12. At the Crooked Creek Crossing of the Chico-Boise City trail, he found where a large number of livestock had crossed headed toward Harney Valley not over 24 hours ahead of him, confirming his suspicion that the Snakes were plundering during the winter. In fact, had he not known otherwise, the scout would have bet that the Walpapi war chief Paulina had left the Klamath reservation and was again riding with Has No Horse. Not many weeks would pass before this nagging thought would be verified. For the present, McIntosh had doubts that Capt. Sprague, weary commander of the Oregon Infantry, would take advantage of this

---

3    Archie McIntosh was the son of John McIntosh and a Chippewa woman. Born at Fort Williams, Canada in 1834, he came west with his parents to Fort Vancouver where he worked for the Hudson's Bay Company from 1847 to 1850. In 1852 he was in the Snake country and by the mid-1850s, Archie's connection with the army was established as packer, interpreter, drover and scout. Although he drank to excess whenever the opportunity offered, Gen. Crook would note that "Archie proved himself a wonderful man in any country." He served in the Yakima War in 1855 and enlisted in Capt. Nathan Olney's detachment of Oregon Volunteer Cavalry in the summer of 1864. He proved so valuable to Crook as a guide in 1866-67 that Crook later employed him in Arizona against the Apaches. He died at the San Carlos Indian Reservation in 1902. A brother died with Custer on the Little Big Horn River, June 25, 1876. Juana Fraser Lyon, "Archie McIntosh, the Scottish Indian Scout," *Journal of Arizona History*, VII, (Autumn 1966), pp. 103-22; Crook, *Autobiography*, p. 147; "Gen. Crook's Indian Campaign," *Portland Daily Herald*, December 10, 1867; *Owyhee Avalanche*, August 3, 1867.

information for he was waiting for the spring melt-off so he could march back to Fort Vancouver. Technically, Sprague and his foot soldiers had been mustered out of the service over a month ago. Nevertheless, this was the kind of intelligence for which the army was paying him so he considered his scout a success and turned east toward Fort Lyon. On the return, he discovered tracks of a large horse herd south of Jordan Craters which was also headed toward Harney Valley.

Shortly after dawn on February 14, McIntosh went into hiding near the desolate summit of Florida Mountain, almost within ear-shot of Silver City (only a half mile up Jordan Canyon from Ruby City). No sooner had he gotten comfortable when a rifle shot shattered the morning calm. This unexpected noise transformed McIntosh into a stalking animal. Crouched in the frost-ribbed sage, he waited, every muscle geared to danger. Nothing stirred. Even the mountain seemed to hold its breath. Five minutes passed while an awesome quiet hovered over the land like the soundless wings of death.

From his high lookout with the temperature hanging at zero, McIntosh could not place the distance of the lone shot. Perhaps it was only a few hundred feet, and again, it could have been five miles—of one thing he was certain, it came from the north in the direction of Jordan Canyon. Like a gaunt timber wolf, the stocky half-breed glided across the sullen land because if anyone was in the vicinity—white or red—he intended to find out who it was.

Around 7:30 a.m. he spotted a sorrel horse standing head down in the feeble rays of the morning sun. Frozen sweat encased the animal's half-dead body telling the scout that this suffering brute had carried someone on a terrible ride. From the appearance of the saddle and bridle, it could have been a white man but in this remote territory it could have just as easily been ridden by a Snake brave. His dark eyes swept the terrain in an effort to solve the riddle as he back-tracked the horse over a tree-studded ridge and some 10 minutes later they caught and held on a fascinating scene. Simultaneously, his ears picked up the low agonized chant of a Shoshoni death-song.

Twenty yards ahead on a sun-washed bench, a Snake warrior clawed his way to a rocky outcrop and with an excruciating effort pulled himself erect. During those tortured movements, McIntosh recognized an old friend turned enemy by conflicting loyalties . . . Gray Head, spiritual leader of the Motsai Snake tribe. Slowly, the old medicine man raised his head and for an instant looked at McIntosh who automatically raised his rifle and just as quickly lowered it, for Gray Head's glazed eyes were seeing no one but the Mighty Chief above.

The frozen blood from waist to ankle gave mute testimony that a heavy calibre rifle slug had entered his body just below the pelvis, almost severing his right leg at the hip, and had come out his back above the left kidney. At this moment, the blood ties were very strong as Archie McIntosh watched his red brother travel the Sun Down Trail into eternity.

Sadly, he placed the old chieftain's body high on a rocky ledge where no animal could reach and where the winds of the western desert could whisper over his last remains. This done, he turned to the task of finding the other participant in this frontier duel.

He followed Gray Head's bloody trail for perhaps 300 feet when he was jarred into action by a sobbing groan. Draped in the gnarled arms of a frozen sagebrush, Andy Hall lay just as he had fallen . . . his head split open like a porcelain bowl. Although more dead than alive, Hall recognized the familiar face of the half-breed scout and tried to raise his arm but it wouldn't move.

Gently as he could, McIntosh moved Hall to a sheltered spot; kindled a fire; took a pot from his saddle pack and brewed some coffee, trying to make the dying man's last moments comfortable. They were a long time in coming. In a voice grown dim with suffering, Hall haltingly told what had taken place from the time he shot the deer to his last agonized hours on earth. Then, along about noon—with a long, shuddering spasm—the strong body, which for 30 odd summers had carried the man named Andrew Hall, gave up his spirit to the unknown horizons of forever.

His last request was that McIntosh tell Capt. Sprague everything that had happened so that soldiers would be sent to punish the Snakes in general and Big Man in particular. The scout promised but he knew that Sprague, a man whose command had been mustered out of the service in December, would do little to avenge the death of one homesteader.

Archie's Indian blood told him that there was nothing to gain in taking Hall's body to Fort Lyon. Neither could he leave him on Florida Mountain for it was impossible to dig a grave in the frozen ground and he suspected that the white man's soul would not rest as serenely on a rock outcrop as would the spirit of Gray Head. He knew that Hall hung out around Ruby City, maybe even had relatives there. At least that was where the man was headed—so the Indian scout with a stiffening body draped across his saddle headed up canyon to Ruby City some three miles away.[4] It was now 1:00 p.m.

---

4    *The Boise Idaho Statesman*, February 17, 1866 and March 4, 1866.

# CHAPTER 132

# THE ADA COUNTY VOLUNTEERS

*Encouraged by Oregon Senator James Nesmith, Idaho settlers are listening to barroom advice to murder, scalp and use Shoshoni Indians for revolver practice. . . .*

**Idaho Governor Caleb Lyon**
Letter to the secretary of the Interior,
February 17, 1866

February 14, 1866 arrived in the rowdy settlement of Ruby City with a promise of better things to come. For the past six days a moaning north wind had whipped through the high pass between Florida and War Eagle mountains holding the town in an icy grip. Although the temperature still hovered close to the zero mark, the wind had subsided and a golden sun beamed its feeble rays onto the snow-drifted trail which ran an erratic course through the center of town. From the tarnished Eldorado Dance Hall and Saloon on the west end of town to the immaculate Butterfield Stage Station on the north, the citizens of Ruby City hustled about their morning chores making hurried preparations for the St. Valentine's Day celebration in Silver City which was expected to be well under way by mid-afternoon.

Although Ruby City was the Owyhee County seat, there was not enough room to grow and what few development lots were available sold for exorbitant prices. In protest, Silver City was born one-half mile up the canyon and competition between the two towns was intense as they fought for supremacy. Silver City had two advantages over Ruby City. First, it was located near the larger mines and second, it was nestled between War Eagle Mountain and Florida Mountain, which protected it from the violent winds that plagued Ruby City. Slowly, the population shifted to Silver City and one-by-one the businesses followed and before another year had passed it would become the major town in southwest Idaho and county seat of Owyhee.[1] It was also the first Idaho city to have telegraph service and a daily newspaper, the *Owyhee Avalanche*, and it was one of the first towns to have full electrical service.[2]

---

1    Johnson, Lonnie, *An Historic Conservation Program*: Silver City, ID, 1975: p. 1.
2    McCroskey, William B., *An Architectural Survey of Silver City, Idaho*, 1977.

Boasting a population of 3,000, Silver City's business district included 10 general stores, four hotels, six saloons, one brewery, two furniture and cabinet makers, two meat markets, two stationary stores, two music stores, one stove and tin shop, two assay offices, one notary public, four lawyers, one doctor, a drug store, a stable, a photo shop, a Wells-Fargo Bank, one laundry, a shoe shop, a bakery and a jewelry store. There were also two schools and two churches.[3]

Now, on Valentine's Day, these warring cities on the Oregon-Idaho border were trying to outdo each other with a celebration. Despite bad weather, Ruby City and Silver City had been greeting early arrivals for the past three days and on this morning of the gala event both were crowded to the hilt with more people drifting in with each passing hour. However, the big excitement would explode in the lower town.

At exactly 9:05 a.m., the Boise stage, driven by William Younger, thundered into town disgorging a load of thrill-seeking miners. Thirty minutes after his arrival, Major Jesse Walker with 39 regulars of the 14th U.S. Infantry Regiment, having learned a large amount of property had been stolen in eastern Oregon, marched into town.[4] Recognizing a good opportunity when he saw it, Major Walker decided that here was a good place to bivouac for the next 24 hours.

Around 10:00 a.m. the Snake war chief Yellow Jacket and four braves drifted in from the south and proceeded to trade 25 horses—which they had stolen from the Mormons—for three gallons of rot-gut whiskey and $20 in gold coin. Following this brisk transaction, the Indians set up camp in front of the Silver Slipper where they declared war on John Barleycorn[5] with a stubborn vengeance. Before long, Yellow Jacket drifted into the Silver Slipper with the $20 clutched in his hand and was joyfully accepted at a nearby gaming table.

It was no secret in the community that the good-natured Shoshoni was a proven hostile although on occasion, he was also known to scout for the army. But as the townspeople had come to find out, Yellow Jacket (whom everybody knew as "Shoshoni Jack") for all of his no-account injun ways, was a likable cuss and—while still sober—one of the best poker players east of the Cascades. Because of this questionable virtue and the well-known fact that Idaho governor, Caleb Lyon, frowned on mistreatment of the Indians for any reason, Yellow Jacket was tolerated as an equal among the rough inhabitants of the Oregon-Idaho frontier. In fact, in quarrels with some of the leading citizens including James Reynolds, editor of the Boise, Idaho *Statesman*, Gov. Lyon roused so much controversy with his defense of the Shoshoni that his chance of earning any tenure in Idaho politics seemed little short of miraculous.[6]

---

3    Department of Interior, *Prospector, Cowhand, and Sodbuster*, 1967: p. 1.

4    Bancroft, *History of Oregon*, Vol. II: p. 518.

5    John Barleycorn is an old-fashioned name for whiskey.

6    Madsen, *The Northern Shoshoni*: p. 44.

By high noon, every rancher and miner in Owyhee and Ada counties had arrived in the twin cities and the stage was set for a rip-snorting free-for-all. Nevertheless, as the day progressed everything went fairly smooth considering that this diversified group had but a single purpose in mind . . . to see if they could drink the local saloons dry. As of yet it was a stand-off.

By mid-afternoon, the weather had developed into a full-scale blizzard but two-thirds of the population was so bleary-eyed they couldn't have told what was happening and the remaining third just plain didn't give a damn.

With a raw mountain wind ripping up main street, a hunched rider threaded his way through the motley collection of wagons, buggies and unattended saddle horses and came to rest at the Eldorado Saloon. A sudden hush fell over the crowd as Archie McIntosh entered with a frozen body draped over his shoulder; stood for a minute in the open door staring at the awkward mob; then deposited his grisly burden on a faro table; and without a word to anyone picked up a half-filled whiskey glass and drained it in one gulp.

John Lawrence, one of the celebrants who had been staring intently at the body blurted out, "My gawd! It's Andy Hall!" Word quickly spread to upper town and as the story unfolded, the crowd's mood turned ugly. At the Silver Slipper, a buckskin-clad figure unobtrusively slipped out the back door, his liquor befuddled brain still clear enough to pick up the full impact of McIntosh's report.

This was the final straw so far as the citizens of Ruby City were concerned. In a matter of minutes a revenge-fired mob staggered out into the street and headed for upper town to lynch Yellow Jacket and his braves. The Indians who had been holed up in front of Gary's Confectionery Store had suspiciously disappeared. Francis Gary, a blind man, could give no clue to their whereabouts. Soberer heads intervened and it was decided to wait until morning before going off half-cocked to slay the whole Shoshoni nation.

The following morning, the crowd was still in a dangerous mood and a notice was posted in the *Owyhee Avalanche* asking for volunteers to help slaughter Shoshoni. News of this reached Gov. Lyon's office almost immediately and he fired off a letter to the secretary of the Interior on February 17, attacking Senator James Nesmith of Oregon for his proposal to the people of eastern Oregon to "kill all Indians wherever they can be found." This unsolicited advice was making a deep impression on Idaho settlers who, according to Lyon, were using Shoshoni "for revolver practice." He included a clipping from the *Owyhee Avalanche* which was offering bounties of $100 for an Indian man's scalp; $50 for a woman's scalp; and $25 for the scalps of children under 10 years of age; which were the prices set by the Idaho legislature in 1864.[7] The *Idaho Statesman* printed a copy of the letter.

---

6     Madsen, *The Northern Shoshoni*: p. 44.

7     Caleb Lyon to James Harlan (Secretary of the Interior), Boise City, February 17, 1866, Idaho Superintendency, Roll 337; *Idaho Statesman*, May 12, 1866.

However, editor James Reynolds took it upon himself to change Lyon's salutation "with burning indignation" to "with cursing indignation" and concluded that Lyon "as much a villain as a fool" was already virtually removed from office.[8] It appears that Reynolds was a strong supporter of the Nesmith theory on Indian management.

One of Lyon's staunch backers was Boise attorney, Judge I.N. Smith who with his son, Captain John Smith—a commissioned officer in the Black Hawk War—had arrived in Ada County in 1865. Capt. Smith, who had served as sheriff of Linn County, Oregon from 1852 to 1864, was appointed Indian agent at Warm Springs on November 14, 1865.[9] Capt. Smith would also be unimpressed with the way Oregon was handling its Indian problems.

At the same time Gov. Lyon was addressing his complaint to Secretary Harlan, John Holgate, a Silver City miner and Charles C. Gasset, a Boise rancher, raised 25 volunteers and on February 18 rode into eastern Oregon bent on destruction. Among others in the Idaho militia were Jim Beard and Joe Miller (teamsters from Chico, California), Thomas B. Coson, Aron Winters and Charles Webster (all three Ada County ranchers), and Bill Younger and Bill Waltermire (driver and shotgun guard for the Overland Stage Company). All would receive much more than they had bargained for.

McIntosh, who hadn't drawn a sober breath since arriving with Hall's body four days before, was cordially invited to lead the volunteers into the Snake stronghold. He just as politely declined. John Lawrence, the first to identify Hall's body, offered to scout for the party and was quickly accepted. Having a mining claim at Canyon City and a homestead on the John Day River, he was well qualified for the job and he also had a personal stake in the affair.

Major Walker, anticipating mob reaction, had already left on a reconnaissance of eastern Oregon. On Crooked Creek—in what is now Malheur County—the soldiers were joined by the Ada County volunteers. Soon thereafter, the combined forces found Yellow Jacket's winter camp consisting of 12 lodges. It made little difference that Yellow Jacket had taken no part in the raid on Hall's ranch. The infantrymen, goaded by the volunteers, attacked. With the soldiers swooping down from the north and the volunteers plowing up from the south, the camp was soon in shambles. In the confusion, Yellow Jacket and two warriors escaped. Every lodge was destroyed, 30 horses captured and 18 Shoshoni killed, including six women and children. Walker lost one man killed and one wounded.[10]

8   *The Idaho Statesman*, March 1 and June 14, 1866; J.H. Walker to Commanding Gen., Department of Columbia, Fort Boise, March 1, 1866, Idaho Superintendency, Roll 337; Caleb Lyon to Commissioner of Indian Affairs, Boise City, March 13, 1866, ibid.

9   *Illustrated History of Central Oregon*: p. 244; Letter, Clayton E. Earl, Acting Superintendent, Warm Springs Agency to Andrew G. Ontko, June 3, 1966.

10  Bancroft, *History of Oregon*, Vol. II, p. 518.

Walker would later report that the Indians "fought with desperation asking no quarter." He was quoted in the *Idaho Statesman* as saying he wanted "no better sport" than to set out on another such expedition, which made him the hero of Idaho Territory.[11]

Flushed with success, Walker returned to Fort Boise but the volunteers dreaming of becoming rich with scalps, continued on destroying four- to six-member family groups of starving Paiutes without suffering a single casualty. Justice was being done.[12] But the letter writing war between Lyon and Reynolds continued without abatement. In the heat of passion, the governor wrote that "a greater scoundrel never lived" than Reynolds for inciting the "massacre of 16 friendly Indians at More's Creek of whom 14 were women and children." The editor had expressed his opinion that "we long to see this vile race exterminated. Every man who kills an Indian is a public benefactor." Reynolds later claimed he hadn't written the article but admitted he had advocated the extermination of all Indians in the area known to be inhabited by hostile bands . . . in other words, the Ochoco.

The United States Regulars were facing some exciting times.

---

11    Madsen, *The Northern Shoshoni*, p. 44.

12    *Indian Affairs Report 1866*, pp. 187-88; Austin Reece, *River Reveille*, March 13, 1866.

# CHAPTER 133

# THE OWYHEE FRONT

*. . . our brothers are killed, our women are killed for crimes*
*we did not do. Stop this and we are your friends. We will give*
*you the country where the white men now live but leave*
*us in peace where we are. . . .*

**Always Ready**
Snake chief, April 10, 1866

During the Idaho tempest between Gov. Lyon and editor Reynolds, Major General Fred Steele arrived in Portland on February 24, 1866. Beside the 870 Oregon Volunteers now wedded to the regular Army whether they liked it or not, he had the 14th U.S. Infantry Regiment (793 men); two companies (150 men) of the 1st U.S. Cavalry; and three companies (225 men) of 3rd U.S. Field Artillery to throw into battle against Has No Horse's dwindling forces.[1] At his beck and call was the full military might of Major General Henry Wager Halleck's Department of the Pacific.

To Has No Horse's advantage, Steele made the continuing mistake of listening to and believing Oregon's General Cyrus Reed that all of eastern Oregon's Indian problems originated in and were centered in the Owyhee country; a falsehood started in the 1850s and stubbornly held to in spite of evidence to the contrary. Ironically, Paulina's and Big Man's recent raid into northern Nevada and southwestern Idaho added substance to this myth.

By March 2, Steele elevated Fort Boise with its dependency camps of Lyon, Reed and C.F. Smith into a full United States Military District under the command of Major L.H. Marshall who arrived at Boise City on March 20. His first action was to requisition Steele for three more combat companies. Steele was quick to react. On the same day he heard from Marshall, Steele wrote to Halleck that the Shoshoni had commenced depredations with such signs of continued hostility in the southern portions of Oregon and Idaho that he recommended the establishment of two more posts. One at or near the burned-out Camp Wright in Harney Valley and another in Goose Lake Valley where the Yreka, Red Bluff and Chico trails

---

1    Bancroft, *History of Oregon*, Vol. II, p. 519.

diverged into southeast Oregon and frequented by hostile Snakes, Utes, Paiutes and Modocs.[2]

In a flurry to get southeast Oregon covered, Col. James B. Sinclair of the 14th Infantry Regiment took command of Fort Currey on Silver Creek. Arriving with him was Lt. Col. John J. Coppinger—Fort Dalles Commander—with an infantry company and Capt. Hinton with a battery of 3rd U.S. Field Artillery which had been guarding the mouth of the Columbia. This now put the strength at Fort Currey at 375 men with a full compliment of combat field officers. Fort C.F. Smith in Alvord Valley received a cavalry troop under command of Capt. David Perry who marched into Oregon from the south by way of the Chico Trail, placing its strength at 150 men. Fort Lyon received another cavalry troop under the command of Capt. James Hunt who entered Oregon by the Humboldt Trail. There was already one company of 14th U.S. Infantry under Capt. Patrick Collins and one of the 1st Oregon Infantry under Capt. Sprague, stationed at Fort Lyon bringing it up to 225-man strength.

Wolf Dog, Has No Horse and Paulina were smart enough to figure out that by staging a few sporadic raids along the Oregon Central Military Road, they could operate with impunity along the John Day front. Accordingly, 10- and 20-man war parties would slip into the Owyhee country, cause enough disturbance to keep the army interested and then melt back into the Ochoco where the real objective lay. In the process, the Snake tribes who were trying to remain neutral were targeted for destruction. Their choice became increasingly clear. Either join the war tribes or face extermination and those who were suffering the most were the unmounted Paiutes—the pitiful family groups of Earth Eaters who caused no harm to anyone in their endless struggle for survival.

Thundering across the Owyhee country soldiers and civilians alike, facing no resistance, were slaughtering men, women and children at will. In desperation, these terrified tribesmen would offer whatever help possible to the embattled dog soldiers from the Ochoco . . . mainly by providing information on army troop movements and hiding raiders in their camps after they dispersed from a battle engagement.

During these trying times, Gourd Rattler continued his love affair with the enemy. Aware of Has No Horse's bitter stand against all odds, the Crow, Cheyenne and Sioux tried to enlist Gourd Rattler's help in ridding the country of Americans. He refused. Infuriated by Gourd Rattler's loyalty to the invaders, the Sioux and Cheyenne attacked his camp on the Sweetwater, stealing 400 horses, destroying lodges and killing several braves, one of whom was Snow Bird (Nannaggai), Gourd Rattler's favorite son. Then, within sight of his father, the attackers mutilated Snow Bird's body.[3] Has No Horse would offer no assistance on Gourd Rattler's

---

2    Bancroft, *History of Oregon*, Vol. II, p. 520.

3    Trenholm and Carey, *The Shoshoni*, p. 214.

retaliatory strike against the Sioux. Even if he had wanted to—which he didn't—things were getting too active on the Owyhee front to spare the manpower.

In the final days of March, Major Marshall led an expedition in a sweeping circle from the Owyhee to the Bruneau River in southwestern Idaho, covering some 110 miles. By his own admission, he found only small groups of unarmed young and old of the Snake tribes.[4] He eliminated 150 of these non-combatants which set the stage for treaty negotiations with Always Ready who, with the exception of his war chief Biting Bear, had thus far remained neutral in the conflict.

On April 12, 1866—following a two day meeting—the document known as the Bruneau Treaty was signed by Always Ready and 41 of the Indians present, surrendering the land south of the Snake River between Goose Creek in Idaho and the Owyhee River in Oregon in return for a promise that the 14-mile-long Bruneau Valley be reserved for the Shoshoni. The seven articles of the treaty included a proposed payment of $80,000 for the cession. The Bruneau Treaty was never ratified. In fact, according to some, the terms of this treaty were so questionable that the land cession was later renegotiated.[5]

Two weeks prior to the treaty signing, the *Idaho Statesman* was carrying on its usual vendetta against Gov. Lyon, one of the peace commissioners. The editor, Jim Reynolds, was worried sick that Lyon would select a more favorable spot. In a scathing editorial, he advised the governor to "give up his insane idea" of planting a reservation in the midst of thick settlements along the Boise River.[6] Under his strong influence, the desolate stretch of ground selected by the peace commissioners held little inducement for whites to settle on so therefore it was suitable habitat for the Indians. However, there was one slight flaw in the negotiations. The "questionable" part of the treaty was the reservation of the Bruneau Valley—small as it was—for the exclusive use of the Shoshoni. That could not nor would it pass muster. Even Biting Bear was aware of what was taking place for he reminded the commissioner that the Snakes "know there are bad white men as well as bad red men."[7]

While Always Ready was being forced into Has No Horse's armed camp, Marshall ordered Capt. Collins to remove all Shoshoni and any white men who might be with them from the mouth of Reynolds Creek in Owyhee Canyon to the head of Burnt River in the northern Blues using a cavalry detachment and a squad

4       Bancroft, *History of Oregon*, Vol. II, p. 520.

5       Caleb Lyon to Secretary of Interior James Harlan, Boise City, April 12, 1866, Idaho Superintendency, Roll 337; Wells, "Caleb Lyon's Indian Policy," *Pacific Northwest Quarterly*, October 1970, pp. 193-200; *Caleb Lyon's Bruneau Treaty, April 12, 1866*, Idaho Historical Society, Reference Series No. 369.

6       *Idaho Statesman*, March 27, 1866.

7       Biting Bear would also question why "the Great Father at Washington" couldn't make his white children do better. Madsen, *The Northern Shoshoni*, p. 45.

of infantry. Collins' orders were to hang any he found without further ceremony. It was an exercise in futility.

Finding nothing in the Reynolds Creek area, Collins and his hangmen moved north into the Blues on May 3. On May 4, 60 loaded pack horses were stolen on Reynolds Creek less than eight miles from Ruby City. None were recovered and the loss was estimated at over $10,000.[8]

Following this slap in the face, Collins returned to Fort Boise. Now more than ever determined to punish the hostiles whatever the cost, Major Marshall with 84 men rode out of Fort Boise on May 11, and Col. Coppinger with the 3rd Artillery rolled out of Fort Currey to clean up the headwaters of the Owyhee. They joined forces on May 18. This military activity hadn't gone unnoticed. Broken Knife and Pony Blanket rode out of the Ochoco with a sizable force to join Big Man, Bad Face and Natchez, south of the Steens Mountains, who were riding toward the Idaho border at the request of Biting Bear and Little Foot. Dog soldiers and pony soldiers[9] would soon make contact.

On May 20, the American force found the Shoshoni at the three forks of the Owyhee, strongly entrenched between the south and middle forks. The river being impassable at this place, Marshall and Coppinger moved eight miles downstream, and had their men cross by raft near the mouth of Field Creek. As they were about to advance up a bluff, the soldiers were fired on by Indians concealed in the rocks. In four hours of furious fighting punctuated by artillery fire, seven Indians were killed but the remainder refused to give ground. In desperation, Marshall was forced to retreat across the river, losing his raft, a howitzer and one non-commissioned officer killed. Provisions and ammunition were thrown into the Owyhee to keep them out of the hands of the Indians. The army, used to slaughtering unarmed Paiutes, was in a state of confusion.

During the battle, Capt. Waymire, commander of the Oregon Cavalry, charged Major Marshall with inhumanity. Sgt. Kenneth Phillips, a cavalryman, was lassoed by the Shoshoni and drawn up a cliff to be tortured and mutilated. Lt. Silas Pepoon volunteered to go up to his rescue and was forbidden to do so. In the retreat, Marshall also left four men stranded on the opposite bank of the river when they were cut off by the swamping of the raft. The soldiers were in a complete rout with an estimated 500 Shoshoni hounding their back-trail.[10]

It was during this campaign that Fort C.F. Smith—named for Gen. Charles Ferguson Smith—was established on White Horse Creek near the Pueblo mines to guard the Oregon Central Military Road.[11] It would not be successful in its first mission.

---

8    *The Dalles Mountaineer*, May 18, 1866.
9    Another name for the U.S. Cavalry.
10   *U.S. Messages and Documents 1866-67*, p. 501, 39th Congress, 2nd Session.
11   Established in May 1866, Fort C.F. Smith was officially recognized by General Order 19,

Coppinger and Marshall had barely gotten their troops rallied when an express arrived informing them that on May 19, a day before the Owyhee defeat, a party of Chinese laborers bound for the Silver City mines were cut off by Paulina on the Oregon Central Military Road between Fort C.F. Smith and Fort Lyon, close to where Mike Jordan had been killed in 1864. A frightened Chinese boy had dashed into Fort C.F. Smith yelling, "Me good Chinaman! Me no fight!" When he finally calmed down, he told Capt. Starr, of the 2nd California Cavalry and post commander, that his party was under Indian attack. Meanwhile, excited travelers reported over 60 bodies lying along the road. Starr immediately dispatched an express to Marshall to take action. Lt. Pepoon hastened to the spot but found only dead bodies strewn along the road for six miles. Apparently the scalps of the Chinese were too inviting for Paulina and his warriors to pass up. Pepoon gathered the remains—150 in all—and buried them in a common grave.[12]

While searching for the Snake raiders along the Owyhee River, Marshall came upon a party from Auburn, California on their way to the Montana goldfields. In the party was Jean Baptiste Charbonneau—son of Sacajawea—who first entered the Oregon country on his mother's back in 1805 with the Lewis and Clark expedition. Charbonneau, the half-breed Snake who had received a formal education in St. Louis, who spent six years in Europe as the guest of Prince Paul of Wurteinberg, and who had served as scout and guide for Lt. Col. Phillip St. George Cooke's famed Mormon battalion during the conquest of Mexico, was dying of malaria. He was buried in an unmarked grave at Inskip Stage Station on Cow Creek.[13] Charbonneau's grave would remain unidentified until 1965 when Clyde H. Porter of New Mexico traced him to his final resting place.

The Chinese slaughter was followed by a raid on the horses and cattle near Booneville, west of Ruby City, in which the Shoshoni obtained more than 60 head of prime saddle stock. Six days after this raid, Jim Beard and Joe Miller—the Chico teamsters who had joined the Ada County Volunteers in February—were attacked, losing 421 head of beef cattle out of a herd of 460. The Shoshoni desperately needed these animals for food. Two weeks later, Charles Gasset—one of the organizers of the Ada County Volunteers—was murdered at his ranch near Ruby City and 100 head of livestock driven off. Eight days later, John Holgate—another organizer—had 20 horses stolen from his claim on War Eagle Mountain.[14] The Idaho militia was beginning to pay for the error of their ways.

---

Military Division of the Pacific, August 3, 1866.

12   Butler, *Life and Times*, Manuscript, pp. 11-12; Starr, *Idaho*, Manuscript, p. 2; *U.S. Secretary of the Interior Report 1867-68*, p. 97, 40th Congress, 2nd Session; *Owyhee Index*, May 26, 1866; *Owyhee News*, June 1866.

13   *Owyhee Avalanche*, Silver City, Idaho, May 1866; *Placer Herald*, Auburn, California, May 1866. The *Avalanche* notes that a J.B. Charbonneau, age 63 died of pneumonia. The *Herald* attributes his death to mountain fever.

14   Bancroft, *History of Oregon*, Vol. II, p. 521, footnote 8.

Blaming the army for not stopping these attacks, another volunteer company was formed by Capt. Isaac Jennings, a Civil War veteran. Among those eager to join were Aaron Winters, Tom Carson and Charles Webster who had made big money scalp-hunting in February. While this group was getting organized, the Snakes struck a ranch on the Snake River near Weiser, driving off all the livestock and capturing an army supply train encamped there. Has No Horse now had plenty of ammunition to carry out a summer defensive.

Despite this reversal of fortune, Jennings' dedicated mob marched into eastern Oregon and on July 2 found what appeared to be a peaceful Paiute camp on Boulder Creek. Fired with revenge, they swooped in for the kill but were soon surrounded by dog soldiers. Jennings and company dug in and the battle began in earnest. Carson fortified himself in the rocks for two days, killing fifteen Indians. He was keeping good count for that amounted to $1,500 in bounty money. It was never collected for he too was killed. As a messenger galloped to Fort Lyon for help, Winters and Webster were seriously wounded. By the time help arrived it was too late. Jennings was already in retreat but he claimed the volunteers had killed 35 Indians who, most likely, were women and children cut down as they first rushed the camp.[15]

Marshall, suspecting that Always Ready and Biting Bear had joined forces with Has No Horse, established a fort on the Bruneau River to stall off an expected invasion from eastern Oregon. The Boise *Idaho Statesman* raised enough fuss about "expending thousands of dollars erecting a permanent post where there were no hostiles" that Gen. Steele ordered Marshall to suspend operations.[16] However, Steele did allow him to keep one company of infantry in the area which effectively kept them from getting into trouble in eastern Oregon.

Once their favorite son, Marshall—now under heavy criticism and accused of shirking his duty—was finding out that the citizens of Idaho were no more grateful than those of Oregon when it came to an attempt to make peace with the Shoshoni.

---

15    *Secretary of Interior Report 1867-68*, 40th Congress, 2nd Session, Pt. 2, p. 97; *Idaho Statesman*, July 7 and 10, 1866; *Sacramento Union*, July 28, 1866.

16    *Idaho Statesman*, July 20, 1866.

# CHAPTER 134

# THE OCHOCO FRONT

*We kill ten . . . a hundred come in their place!*

**Has No Horse**
Snake war chief, July 5, 1866

The fighting in the Ochoco was continuing unabated. During the winter of 1865-66, the garrison at Fort Watson didn't venture outside the stockade walls for good reason. Has No Horse was striking anything that moved . . . every stage, pony express rider or pack train that dared to make the journey from The Dalles to Canyon City and Boise City was fair game.

Word of the Shoshoni winter raids lost no time in reaching Portland. With business at a standstill, something had to be done. Using this as a stimulus, two dozen young men gathered in a warehouse on a cold February night and in the hours which followed, Oregon's First Volunteer Artillery was born. Battery A, 965th Field Artillery, 41st Division was to be the oldest National Guard outfit in the entire west. It consisted of two "Napoleons"—smooth-bore brass cannons—a Gatling gun and several muskets. But what the boys lacked in arms, they made up for in spirit. Led by Capt. F.C. Paint, they waited patiently for the call to send grape-shot screaming into the ranks of the Snake army. Wiser heads could envision the Shoshoni firepower, bolstered by the capture of the Napoleons, pouring rocks and scrap-iron into soldiers and settlers—so that call never came.

By March, the Overland Express, Wells Fargo and Wheeler stage companies refused to travel The Dalles-Boise Road. Running the gauntlet was so uncertain that Joe Sherar sold his entire packstring to Robert Heppner for $6,000. On his second trip to Canyon City, Heppner lost his entire outfit to the Shoshoni with a total loss of nearly $20,000.[1] Gold shipments piled up in Canyon City, Auburn and Eldorado for lack of transportation. The Dalles merchants were frantic as California took over the market, shipping supplies in from the south. And Gen. Steele, on the advice of his western Oregon counselors, issued orders to abandon Fort Watson. This caused so much public outrage expressed in *The Dalles*

---

1    *Illustrated History of Central Oregon*, pp. 256-57.

*Mountaineer*, the *Blue Mountain Eagle* and the *Idaho Statesman* that he was forced to rescind the order.

In mid-March, he sent two companies of 1st U.S. Cavalry under the command of Major Edward Myers to reinforce Capt. Small's beleaguered troops. Col. Eugene M. Baker, also of the 1st U.S. Cavalry replaced Small as post commander. Although this put Fort Watson's strength at 300 men, there was no way they could guard the 400 mile stretch of road between The Dalles and Boise City. Baker's arrival seemed to make little difference. In a half dozen successful raids, Has No Horse looted six more coaches and put them permanently out of commission before the first of May. Meantime, the Weahwewa brothers—Wolf Dog, Black Eagle and Paulina—made certain he would have no interruptions by keeping Fort Watson under constant siege.

This brings up an interesting side note on Paulina. Apparently Indian Superintendent J.W. Perit Huntington was unaware that Paulina had abandoned Howasti—site of the first Klamath Agency—in December.[2] In all likelihood, Major Rinehart—watchdog of the southwestern front—staying warm and cozy inside Fort Klamath, knew nothing of what was going on out in the wilderness. Neither would Agent Applegate, spending the winter on the west side of the snow-blocked southern Cascades at his Ashland home, be aware of what his Shoshoni wards were up to. Therefore Huntington, making the social rounds in Salem, would never give the Snake war chief a second thought. It would be spring before he received the unwelcome news.

On April 22, 1866, Huntington would report to the commissioner of Indian Affairs that Paulina and Black Buffalo with their followers had left the Klamath reservation. He would further state that a messenger from Moses Brown alerted Rinehart a few days after the fact that the Snakes had left as the result of a summons to war from Big Man. (If Moses did send a message, it was more like three months after the fact.) Then, according to Huntington, two Indians were sent out to track them but the trail had disappeared into the Ochoco. Lalake assured Rinehart that Paulina "has broken the treaty. He has gone not to return."[3]

Huntington was hopeful that Paulina had merely gone to the Crooked River Valley for the summer. This, however, was a vain hope. While on the reservation, Paulina and his people never received any of the benefits specified under the 1865 treaty and he would never return to the white man's reserve.

Back on the Ochoco front, Col. Baker based a detachment of cavalry at Jim Clark's stage station . . . soon to be known as Burnt Ranch. Located one-half mile

---

2    Voegelin, *The Northern Paiute of Central Oregon: A Chapter in Treaty Making*, p. 107.

3    *Report of the Commissioner of Indian Affairs 1866*, Congressional Document Series 1284, p. 77, 89; National Archives, Bureau of Indian Affairs Oregon Superintendency, Letters Received, W.V. Rinehart to Huntington, Fort Klamath, Oregon, April 24, 1866 and May 3, 1866; Gatschet, *Klamath Indians*, pp. 28-31.

downstream from Byrd Point on the south bank of the John Day River and with Bridge Creek flanking it on the east, Clark's station was considered to be the most easily defended on the entire run from The Dalles to Boise City. However, only a few miles to the west lay Horse Heaven Mountain, Sandrock Gulch and the dreaded Hell's Half Acre, the favorite hold-up point for Indians and road agents alike.

In May, the pits of hell were opened. Riding into the cross fire were the Thompson boys, Frank and William (Bud). Bud Thompson—a good friend of Joaquin Miller whom he called "Heinie"[4]—was hiding out from the law and he planned on joining Miller in Canyon City. Thompson had worked for Miller as a "printer's devil" on the *Eugene Democrat Herald,* a weekly newspaper that Miller and Anthony Noltner had started in 1862. Here, he first met Major Rinehart who was thinking strongly of "providing Mr. Miller a residence at Fort Alcatraz with board and lodging at the expense of the U.S. government." Shortly thereafter in the final days of the Civil War, Henry Mulkey—also a friend of Thompson's—was arrested for a "political offense" by order of Rinehart. Thompson arranged an escape for Mulkey but as he put it "that the arrangement miscarried was due to Mr. Mulkey, and not to the prudence of Major Rinehart or the failure upon my part to carry out the program." Mulkey was recaptured and Thompson's arrest was ordered. After hiding out for nearly a year in the Willamette Valley, he drifted into The Dalles in the spring of 1866, joined a Canyon City pack outfit and headed into the war zone with Frank, who was a teamster for the Overland Express Company.[5]

East of the Deschutes River it was necessary to travel at night while during the day a careful guard was kept and no fires were allowed. At Bridge Creek, Thompson's group joined another pack outfit and decided to lay over a day or two and rest their animals. As they were setting up camp, Jonathan Patterson, one of the drivers on The Dalles-Boise line was attacked on Cherry Creek—gateway to the stage-trap. John Mead, one of the Canyon City packers, heard the shots and sent his son Archie back to Clark's Station to alert the soldiers.[6] As soon as the cavalry rode out, Tall Man hit the stage station and robbed the Overland safe of $300. Eight miles up Bridge Creek another war party jumped Frank Thompson. He saw them coming and managed to escape to the packers' main camp but the Snakes got his team and loaded supply wagon. At the same time, another war party raided John Witner's ranch on the John Day River, killing him and running off all his livestock. To the west, Wolf Dog charged onto the Warm Springs reservation, killing and looting.[7]

---

4    Joaquin Miller was born Cincinnatus Hiner Miller, hence the name "Heinie."

5    Thompson, *Reminiscences of a Pioneer,* pp. 46-48.

6    Archie Mead would later marry Olivia (Livie) Vanderpool, granddaughter of Dr. Larkin Vanderpool, Prineville's first physician and surgeon. *Illustrated History of Central Oregon,* p. 267; *The History of Crook County Oregon,* p. 245.

7    Bancroft, *History of Oregon,* Vol. II, p. 523 footnote 13.

By the time Col. Baker could get his forces into the field, the Shoshoni had scattered like a covey of quail, leaving nothing but charred buildings and dead bodies to show they had been in the area. In an effort to shorten attack time, Baker ordered Lt. A.B. Ingram to re-man Fort Lyon with 60 men of Troop A 1st U.S. Cavalry. Ingram had barely gotten into position when Has No Horse raided the sluice boxes south of Canyon City, making off with an unknown amount of raw gold. It was becoming obvious that gun-runners were supplying the Snakes with arms and ammunition in exchange for stolen gold.

Ingram with 24 troopers took pursuit and picked up Has No Horse's trail in Bear Valley. Riding with Ingram were two civilians: James Perry, a miner and one of the best trackers in eastern Oregon; and his partner, Joseph Green. Groups kept splintering off from the raiding party in an effort to confuse the tracks but Perry was able to follow the main group across the South Fork of the John Day into Gray's Prairie. Here, they found where Has No Horse had camped but again he slipped out ahead of the cavalry. Perry located his avenue of escape which led over the summit of Lookout Mountain. Reaching the north point on Lookout late in the afternoon, the tracks led down a long steep ridge toward the head of Ochoco Valley. Ingram, suspecting this route to be a likely spot for an ambush, sent Perry, Green and Pamah Tamna (a Tygh Indian chief and Warm Springs scout) ahead to search out the area.

Perched some 3,000 feet above the valley floor, Ingram could see a huge Indian encampment, the largest he had yet witnessed since coming west with the First United States Cavalry in the late autumn of 1865. From North Point, it looked as though the Shoshoni horse herds stretched for miles. It was not an encouraging sight. When the scouts hadn't returned by the following morning, the whole detachment nervously descended toward the waiting valley. They had traveled some three miles following a well-defined trail over a high timbered butte when they came upon a sobering scene. In the middle of the trail with both arms and legs chopped off, his body pinned to the ground with a Snake war lance lay Joe Green. On an eerie flat covered with twisted and bent three-foot diameter pine trees, none of which grew in the same direction, they found the mutilated body of Jim Perry.[8] On the far side of what is now called Crooked Tree Flat, pinned upright against the twisted trunk of a pine, sagged the headless body of Pamah Tamna, his body held in place by a cavalry sabre driven through his chest. The sabre was driven so deeply into the tree that it took two men to remove it. Lt. Ingram gave up the chase,

---

8   This incident is mentioned in a footnote in Bancroft's *History of Oregon*, Vol. II, p. 521. Members of Perry's family settled in Prineville in 1881. He was killed two miles south of the present Ochoco Ranger Station on the Lookout Trail under the north slope of Green Mountain named for Perry's partner, Joseph Green. In the 1950s the forest service changed the name of Green Mountain to Duncan Butte for a local settler in that area.

returning to Fort Watson with the bodies. He had been out nine days and lost three men without inflicting any damage on the Shoshoni.

While Ingram was chasing Has No Horse, orders came down from headquarters to recapture Paulina. Lt. Reuben F. Bernard—a former army blacksmith and veteran of the Civil War—was assigned the task. On the fourth of July, Bernard with 45 men of Troop I 1st U.S. Cavalry, left Fort Currey and headed west toward Crooked River. Searching the Crooked River Basin with no luck he rode east circling Harney and Malheur lakes still without success. Bernard was not even close. As he moved southeast, Paulina and 35 warriors moved southwest with revenge in their hearts.

In early April when word first reached Major Rinehart that Paulina had flown the coop, he quickly scoured the reservation to verify the report. In a letter to Huntington, he would admit that there were only two Snakes on the reservation . . . and they were, and had been, locked up in the fort guardhouse for the winter. Rinehart identified one of the prisoners as "Gil-te-was who is blind in one eye."[9] This was One Eye, a White Knife dog soldier who had tangled with a grizzly bear and came out second best in the battle.[10] When the 1865 treaty was ratified on July 10, 1866, One Eye and his cell mate were the only Shoshoni present for the momentous occasion.

Convinced that Paulina was back on the battlefront, Rinehart took to the field with the Axe and Rifle squad, raiding Paiute camps and taking a number of women and children captive.[11] Rinehart—anxious to redeem himself—was out to capture as many Shoshoni as possible and he assured Huntington that all the Klamath chiefs had promised aid in doing so except for the half-blood Moses who "would therefore be closely watched."[12] Agent Applegate was also losing faith in Moses, believing that his Shoshoni ancestry was coming to the fore.

During this flurry of excitement, Paulina was steadily closing in on his target—the Klamath Agency and specifically Old Schonchin of the Modocs who he believed had betrayed him into signing the 1865 treaty. At dawn July 10—the day of ratification—Paulina attacked Old Schonchin's camp on Sprague River. Many Modocs were killed but Old Schonchin, mighty spry for a 70-year-old, escaped and made a run for the Klamath Agency at Howasti. Paulina followed and attacked the agency. Again Old Schonchin escaped to safety at Fort Klamath. With

---

9   National Archives, Bureau of Indian Affairs Oregon Superintendency, Letters Received, Rinehart to Huntington, Fort Klamath, May 3, 1966.

10  National Archives, Bureau of Indian Affairs Oregon Superintendency, Letters Received, George Nurse to Huntington, Fort Klamath, April 6, 1865; Capt. Kelly to Huntington, April 8. 1865.

11  *Report of the Commissioner of Indian Affairs 1866*, Congressional Document Series 1284, p 89.

12  National Archives, Bureau of Indian Affairs Oregon Superintendency, Letters Received, Rinehart to Huntington, Fort Klamath, July 2, 1966.

all the reservation Klamath and Modocs huddled around the fort, Paulina gave up and headed back into the Ochoco. This raid on the Klamath Agency brought on the establishment of Fort Warner on the east shore of Warner Lake on July 15, 1866. As for the Axe and Rifle Squad, wild horses couldn't have dragged them away from the protection of Fort Klamath, much to Rinehart's disgust.

Meanwhile, Lt. Bernard continued his southeastern search for Paulina, heading into the Steens Mountains where he found the first Shoshoni sign on his long march. Taking the trail which led toward the head of the Malheur River, he captured two women who informed him they were with Wolf Dog's band. Bernard with 15 troopers, believing they were close to Wolf Dog's camp, searched for a day finding nothing.

On July 17, Sgt. Michael Conner of the 14th Infantry (out of Fort C.F. Smith) headed toward the Ochoco on a scout with 19 men. The next morning, he discovered Wolf Dog's camp at 8:00 a.m. on Rattlesnake Creek north of Malheur Lake. Conner estimated the number at 80 warriors and 220 women and children. In a surprise attack, the infantry killed 13 and wounded more. Among the wounded was the war chief Broken Knife, brother-in-law to Has No Horse.

Amidst the tangle of women and children, Wolf Dog rallied his troops. In the bitter fight which followed, Corporal William Lord was killed and the Indians were able to gather most of their property, losing only a few horses and mules before retreating toward the South Fork of the John Day. Sgt. Conner with his dead and wounded returned to the base camp, arriving the evening of July 18. During his absence, a volunteer company of 47 citizens from Auburn, also in pursuit of Wolf Dog, had joined Bernard's command.

With the addition of these men, Bernard renewed the chase and found the Indians encamped in a deep canyon surrounded by perpendicular walls about a mile from where Sgt. Conner had attacked them the day before. This camp had been further fortified with log and rock breastworks but with many of his warriors wounded or dying, Wolf Dog abandoned his position, leaving all provisions and camp equipment behind while escaping only with horses and arms. The loss of all property would badly disable Wolf Dog's campaign but by summer's end, the Utes and Modocs would be smuggling in Model '66 Winchester repeating rifles—the latest innovation in frontier warfare.

During this clash in which many prisoners were taken, the soldiers plainly heard the English language spoken. Bernard would report that there were white men in Wolf Dog's camp. He did not understand that after 50 years of contact with British and Americans, most Shoshoni were well-versed in the English language.

Leaving the Auburn militia to help guard the army pack train, Bernard, with 30 troopers and dragging a mountain howitzer, followed Wolf Dog for 60 miles over broken and timbered country. Some of the wounded warriors and those whose horses had been shot out from under them were scattered along the trail, but Bernard passed them by refusing to engage in battle in his effort to catch up with

Wolf Dog's main force. This march took him on a circle around Snow Mountain and that night he camped on the head of Silver Creek, some 20 miles north of Fort Currey. During the night, the dismounted Shoshoni passed his camp. Come daylight, Bernard took the bait but succeeded only in capturing two women and their children while losing a day's march on Wolf Dog's trail. The following day, he sent for the army pack train and told the Auburn volunteers to go home.

He then trailed Wolf Dog for another twelve hours but by now the tracks were so split up that Bernard gave up and returned to Fort Watson. When only seven miles southeast of the fort, at what would become known as Leggin's Spring, he was attacked by the Big Lodge war chief Storm Cloud in an attempt to liberate the prisoners of war—which Storm Cloud did. Riding with the shock troops and accompanied by his father, the Paiute war chief Natchez—eldest son of Bad Face—was a young boy on his first venture into manhood. Known to his fellow warriors as Leggins, he would gain the admiration of Bernard's cavalry when he rescued Storm Cloud, whose horse was shot from under him in the first clash.

Minus most of his prisoners, Lt. Bernard rode through the stockade gates at Fort Watson 26 days after he had left Fort Currey on July 4, 1866. In that period, he had covered 630 weary miles.[13] Unknown to him, his greatest accomplishment—or perhaps the credit should go to Sgt. Conner—was the killing of Broken Knife.

Broken Knife, who had been wounded by Conner's riflemen on Rattlesnake Creek, lived to reach Has No Horse's camp and died in his daughter's arms. Seven-year-old Mattie Shenkah was now an orphan. Her mother, Half Moon—Has No Horse's sister—had been killed two years before by Lt. Waymire's Warm Springs scouts. Since that time, she had been living with her uncle and aunt, Pony Blanket and Evening Star who was also a sister to Has No Horse.

Prior to the murder of Half Moon, Broken Knife had been on friendly terms with the army, serving as a guide through eastern Oregon, Idaho, Utah and Nevada. In 1864, he joined the Paviotso Confederacy. Now, shot through the intestines and suffering terrible pain, he left this last impression on his daughter who related it to Gen. Howard in 1876 when she was 17 years old.[14]

> I have a picture of him, very sad, very sad, in my heart. He was so strange—so different from all the rest. I know now that he was strange because he was leaving us . . . for always. My father had been hurt in battle! He was very pale and his eyes very bright, looking far away. I am sure he knew when he spoke to me that he could not live to see another sun. He was lying down on the ground and he took me and pressed me tenderly in his arms against his breast.

---

13    *U.S. Messages and Documents Abridged 1866-67*, p. 501; Alta, California *Daily News*, August 22, 1866.

14    Howard, *Famous Indian Chiefs I have Known*, pp. 240-41.

Chief Egan [Pony Blanket] my uncle was kneeling by my father's side and bending over us with tears in his eyes. At last my dear father spoke and said, "Egan, my brother, the Great Spirit calls me away—I must go. I cannot take my little child with me. The Great Spirit does not call for her to go now. I wish I could take her with me to meet her mother but I cannot. My brother, I leave her to you—be her father."

My uncle, Chief Egan, gave my father an answer but I do not quite remember what he said but he laid his hand very gently on my head while my father added a few words which like his others have always been in my mind: "My daughter, my little dove, you cannot know what this parting means; to me it is a bitter one, but you and I will meet again; your good uncle will be a father to you and you must be a good daughter to him." After a few minutes of silence he gave his last words: "Now I go in peace."

While Lt. Bernard's search for Paulina was in progress, the Axe and Rifle Squad was escorting Snake prisoners of war to the Fort Klamath guardhouse for safe-keeping. On July 8, they captured Lake Hunter—a Buffalo Killer dog soldier—slipping into the Sprague River Valley for a meeting with Moses Brown. Three others with him escaped. Major Rinehart, determined to populate the Klamath reservation with Shoshoni subjects one way or another, sent 10 soldiers and 10 Klamath Indians led by the war chief Blow to round up the escapees. Seeing a good opportunity to get out of the guardhouse, One Eye volunteered his services as a guide. This party succeeded in taking four Paiute men, two women and five children hostage. The men were imprisoned at Fort Klamath, the women and children left with Moses and One Eye vanished![15]

By the end of July, Agent Applegate reported to Huntington that Rinehart had captured 16 Snake warriors on the headwaters of Sprague River. Two had gotten away and one was killed attempting to escape. By now, there were 13 Shoshoni women and 30 children living on the reservation. Applegate would note that "these women and children belong to the prisoners at the fort." He would also attribute Rinehart's success in arresting non-combatants to "the war farther north which probably drove these people to take refuge in the Summer Lake country."[16]

With the Shoshoni war again heating up, orders came down from the secretary of war to recruit a troop of Warm Springs Indians into the regular army. Known as the First United States Warm Springs Scouts, their first official act—which they carried out with enthusiasm—was to execute 14 Snake prisoners of war. In retaliation, the Snakes hit The Dalles-Boise road with renewed vigor.

---

15    National Archives, Bureau of Indian Affairs Oregon Superintendency, Letters Received, Rinehart to Huntington, Ft. Klamath July 9, 1866; July 13, 1866.

16    Ibid, Lindsay Applegate to Huntington, Ashland Mills, Oregon, July 24, 1866.

Advertisements paid for by Wells Fargo, Lockwood, Wheeler and Overland stage companies were now appearing in local papers:

*Wanted —*
*Young skinny wiry fellows not over 18.*
*Must be expert riders willing to risk death daily.*
*Orphans preferred. Wages, $25 a week.*

Orphans they may be but not many were dumb enough to take the challenge.

The word was already out that Has No Horse had gone berserk. In the summer of 1866, Dawn Mist had left the big Shoshoni encampment on the upper Ochoco River to gather berries. Less than two miles from camp she wandered up Canyon Creek and was murdered by a party of prospectors in search of the Blue Bucket gold. They too would pay the supreme penalty.

# CHAPTER 135

# DEATH RIDES
# THE CANYON CITY TRAIL

*The warriors return singing.*
*My man has scalps at his side.*
*His proud strength strides to us,*
*Sits by my side, smiling;*
*Smiling sinks to earth*
*Which reddens with his secret wound. . . .*

**Lilian White Spencer**
*Shoes of Death*

Following in Bernard's wake, Major Marshall with 160 battle-hardened veterans, marched from the Goose Creek Mountains in southwestern Idaho to the southern Blues killing small family groups wherever he found them. Having killed 30 Indians by the time he reached the head of Crooked River, Marshall turned south toward Fort Warner, which had been established 20 miles east of Warner Lake by Capt. Patrick Collins' Co. D 14th U.S. Infantry on July 15, 1866.[1] At Ram Lake, north of Yreka Butte (in present Deschutes County) his scouts located Black Eagle's camp.

Striking at daylight the following morning, Marshall made up for the losses and failures he suffered during the spring offensive. The Shoshoni fought furiously but it was mass destruction. Only Black Eagle and a handful of warriors escaped. Besides capturing all of their horses and provisions, burning lodges, killing men, women and children, Marshall took 35 dog soldiers captive whom he promptly hanged using the limbs of Juniper trees as a gallows. He then proceeded toward the forks of the Owyhee, turned back toward Warner Mountain, and killed unarmed Paiutes along the way until he arrived at Fort Warner on the first of October.[2]

During this bloody rampage, three more companies of the 14th U.S. Infantry Regiment under the command of Lt. Col. R.F. O'Beirne marched into Fort Watson and began a systematic scourge of The Dalles-Boise City road. With the army

---

1    Bancroft, *History of Oregon*, Vol. II, pp. 522-23.
2    *Yreka Union*, October 20, 1866; Hay's, *Scrapbook V*, p. 228.

pressing in from all directions, the inhabitants of eastern Oregon complained that all the soldiers were accomplishing was to drive the Indians into the settlements—which was true. Slaughtering all game animals as they found them, fouling water supplies and trampling out seed and root gathering areas, the Shoshoni were forced to raid the white settlements to avoid starving. When state officials complained to Gen. Steele of this turn of events, he calmly replied, "This can not always be avoided."[3]

State officials also claimed that Gen. Halleck was favoring California, using his main strength to protect the Red Bluff, Yreka and Chico trails into the mining settlements so that California merchants would be able to monopolize the trade while Oregon businessmen, dependent upon the Canyon City Trail, were left to suffer or protect it as best they could—which wasn't true. Oregon still hadn't sorted out in its collective mind that the Ochoco was the Shoshoni's main base of operations, not the arid southeastern high desert.

Despite all of the internal bickering, the state of Oregon and the United States Army would receive an added bonus at the expense of the Paviotso Confederacy. In mid-August, Man Lost and Black Beard joined Gourd Rattler's peace movement and got out of the fighting.[4] Even so, Oregon was having little success in herding Shoshoni onto the Klamath reservation. However, Huntington proudly announced that there were many Yahuskins (a people of questionable origin) residing near the agency headquarters, implying that they were Snakes.

Lindsay Applegate in his first annual report dated August 6, 1866 admits there were no Snakes on the Klamath reservation, showing he did not consider the Yahuskins to be Shoshoni. Although he refers to them officially as "Yahooskin Snakes" it is evident he didn't believe this. He states: "There are at present *no Snakes proper* on the reservation unless we except some prisoners in the custody of the military at Fort Klamath. . . . I am led to believe that there is now a union of all the Snakes proper for a more determined war . . . the universal belief among the Klamath and Yahooskin is that the Snakes are all for war. According to Rinehart, the Klamath's, eager to vindicate their loyalty, are willing to become allies in an invasion of the Snake nation." According to Applegate, the Snakes were raiding the Klamath Agency daily.[5]

During the summer, Gen. Steele made a tour of inspection of the battlefront, covering some 1,200 miles on horseback. Leaving Fort Dalles with his aide, Capt. George Williams and a 10-man escort, he proceeded to Fort Watson where he took one company of cavalry commanded by Major Meyers and moved into Crooked

3     Bancroft, *History of Oregon*, Vol. II, p. 525.

4     *Desert News*, Salt Lake City, August 30, 1866.

5     *Report of the Commissioner of Indian Affairs 1866*, Congressional Document Series 1284, p. 89; National Archives, Bureau of Indian Affairs, *Oregon Superintendency Field Papers*, Letters Received, Box D, Applegate to Huntington, Fort Klamath, October 31, 1866.

River, Fort Currey and Malheur Lake. During this march, the Snakes made off with 52 army pack mules. They were pursued and retaken by Steele but not without the loss of supplies and ammunition. Steele then marched to Fort Lyon where he was joined by Gen. Halleck and his staff in mid-August. Halleck had traveled the well-protected Oregon Central Military Road and Chico Trail without incident. Together, the commanding generals made an inspection of Fort C.F. Smith and Fort Boise. Riding across the Blues with a heavy escort and when the Shoshoni were unusually quiet (being engaged in gathering food for the coming winter) they arrived back on the Columbia in mid-September unmolested. Perhaps their successful crossing of the Blue Mountains was due, in part, to the fact that Halleck was traveling with a new and deadly weapon.

Shocked at the horrors of the Civil War, Dr. Richard Gatling set out to invent a rapid fire weapon that would enable one soldier to do the work of a hundred and eliminate the need for large armies. Out of these honestly humanitarian motives, Gatling came up with the first practical machine gun in 1862, a weapon that could fire 250 .58 calibre bullets a minute. By 1867, Gatling had improved the gun to fire 1,200 rounds of .45 calibre bullets per minute. Ironically, the Gatling gun and its successors would cause the death of more people than any other single man-made device.

Two of these guns came west with Gen. Halleck to the Military Department of the Pacific in 1866 and eventually found their way by pack train up the Yreka Trail to Fort Watson for tests against enemy forces. On August 24, 1866, the Gatling gun was officially adopted by the U.S. Army for use against the Indians, specifically the Snakes. The army ordinance department ordered 100 of them and Dr. Gatling contracted with the Colt Firearms Company for production, which patented and manufactured all his guns from then on.[6] Originally, many of the Oregon field officers believed that the use of so devastating a weapon would cause them to lose face with the Shoshoni. Now, they didn't give a damn![7]

With reports of heavy Indian attacks along the Burnt and Powder rivers including the murder of Samuel Leonard, a Mormon Basin miner, Lt. Col. O'Beirne moved most of his troops into that area. No sooner had he moved out than Has No Horse raided all the stage stations west of Canyon City, running off hundreds of head of livestock. In the process, he hit Fort Watson, stealing 54 pack mules, 18 beef cattle, killing Pvt. Marion Wilcox and wounding Davis Gormon, a Canyon City miner.

---

6    Stern, Philip VanDoren, "Doctor Gatling and His Gun," *American Heritage Magazine*, VIII, No. 6, October 1957, pp. 51-105; Truby, J. David, "Hailstorm of Death," *VFW Magazine*, February 1972, pp. 16-18.

7    In the mid-1980s, Duane Mizer, a Prineville resident, found numerous .58 calibre Gatling gun shell casings in Big Summit Prairie indicating a terrific battle had taken place in that area in the late 1860s.

Riding to intercept the Fort Watson cavalry on its plunge into the Burnt River country was Donald McKay. McKay had been hired by Gen. Steele on August 6 at $125 a month to serve as an army scout under Lt. Col. O'Beirne's command.[8] Four days after signing on, McKay, accompanied by Major Walker and a detachment of mounted infantry blundered into Paulina with "a large band of warriors" on the head of Burnt River. Marshall, flush with confidence from his recent Paiute victories, gave the order to attack and was immediately driven back. When Marshall's horse was shot out from under him, he lost all desire for further combat and the fight was over.[9]

As O'Beirne's troops descended on Burnt River, a new threat arose and he would saddle McKay with this problem. Andrew Wiley, acting as chief guide for the Willamette Valley and Cascades Mountain Military Road, was having extreme difficulty preparing a strip suitable for travel up Crooked River Valley. The Snakes were giving the construction crews so much trouble that many segments of the road would exist only on paper, giving vent in future years for settlers to bring suit against the company, claiming that the road never existed. Wiley was now asking for military assistance.

Under McKay's guidance, a cavalry detachment was sent into the lower Crooked River Valley to establish an outpost at the mouth of McKay Creek, mainly to protect the overland route from Fort Dalles to the military camps in southeast Oregon.[10] Protection of the road crew was a low priority item. This short-lived post was named Camp Steele. Billy Chinook, who served as scout and guide for Lt. John Fremont when he passed through central Oregon in 1843, joined McKay at Camp Steele with a detachment of Warm Springs scouts. He also was to provide protection for the road construction crew.

In late August, McKay with 20 "Long Knives" and Billy Chinook with the Indian scouts discovered Black Buffalo's camp on Dry Creek some 13 miles northeast of the present site of Prineville. They attacked at daybreak and the whole band numbering 32 men, women and children were either killed or captured, including Black Buffalo. On the ride back to Camp Steele, herding the captives before them, Black Buffalo escaped. Although his arms were bound behind him and his legs tied beneath his pony, the wily chief outrode and outmaneuvered his pursuers and disappeared into the timbered slopes to the north.

During the Dry Creek battle, Swamp Man—a White Knife dog soldier—made a run for reinforcements and he was followed by Sebastia and

---

8    *Special Order No. 49*, Report of Persons and Articles Employed and Hired at Fort Boise, Idaho Territory, Capt. T.J. Eckerson, September 1866.

9    *Report of the Commissioner of Indian Affairs 1867*, Congressional Document Series 1326, p. 78.

10    McKay Creek was named for Donald McKay's father, Tom McKay, a Hudson's Bay Company employee who had traversed the creek before Donald was born.

Wasanska, two of the most valued Warm Springs scouts in the business. McKay later found Swamp Man's body with a bullet in his right breast. Some 50 feet away, lying side by side, were the Walla Walla braves . . . one with a gaping hole in the face, the other with a bullet hole over his heart. Both had been shot with a .44 calibre revolver still clutched in Swamp Man's hand. Each side had suffered losses this day.

As September crested the horizon, Major Rinehart found the Fort Klamath guardhouse overpopulated with Shoshoni prisoners and against Agent Applegate's better judgment moved them to Sprague River under the guard of Moses Brown. It was not a good idea. Applegate correctly believed that Moses couldn't be trusted and through him the prisoners were kept in "constant communication with the war parties."[11] Applegate tried to convince Rinehart to place them closer to the agency where he could keep a better watch over them. By the time Rinehart decided to react it was too late. On the night of October 4, the released dog soldiers seized horses and guns belonging to the Klamaths and then stole a wagon train of supplies sent out by Capt. Sprague to feed the reservation Indians for the coming winter.

The Axe and Rifle Squad—led by Sgt. Orson Stearns who was attached to Sprague's command—was dispatched to apprehend the miscreants but their heart wasn't up to the assignment. The trainload of supplies disappeared into the Ochoco. Fortifications were quickly thrown up around the Klamath Agency in anticipation of a full-scale Snake attack. Meantime Moses Brown—supposedly afraid of retaliation from Has No Horse and Paulina—moved his followers next to the agency headquarters and "became involved in a plot to do-in high chief Lalake." Suspecting a revolution, quick amends were made to keep Moses peaceful.[12]

At the start of the summer offensive, Gov. George Woods and the Oregon legislature were being urged to take some action on eastern Oregon's depressed economy. After three months of discussion, a joint resolution was passed on October 7 proclaiming that if the federal government did not within 30 days from that date send additional troops for the protection of eastern Oregon, the governor was authorized to call out a sufficient number of volunteers to afford the necessary aid to the citizens of that war-torn area. Soon after, Gen. Steele met with Gov. Woods and agreed to recruit a cavalry unit in the Willamette Valley to be known as the 8th U.S. Cavalry Regiment. Instead of being an improvement, insofar as placing additional troops in the field, it was a complete failure. No one would enlist.[13]

---

11    National Archives, Bureau of Indian Affairs Oregon Superintendency Field Papers, Letters Received, Box D, Applegate to Huntington, September 30, 1866.

12    Report of the Commissioner of Indian Affairs 1867, Congressional Document Series 1326, pp. 91-92; National Archives, Bureau of Indian Affairs Oregon Superintendency Field Papers, Letters Received, Box D, Applegate to Huntington, October 31, 1866; Applegate to Huntington, January 31, 1867.

13    Woods, George L., *Recollection*, Manuscript; *The Portland Oregonian*, July 14, 1866; *U.S.*

Maybe this reluctance was due to the fact that Has No Horse, Paulina, Wolf Dog and Big Man were striking in unison along The Dalles-Boise City road where they made life uncertain for all involved. Getting September off to a roaring start, Has No Horse hit Antelope Stage Station, which nearly resulted in the death of Howard Maupin's son, Garrett, by his father's own hand. After the Ochoco raiders had taken all of the horses—thoroughbreds recently imported from the Willamette Valley—Maupin in a boiling rage took pursuit. Before leaving, he warned his wife not to permit Garrett to follow.

Near the present site of Antelope, Howard Maupin was nearly blown out of the saddle when the Indians began shooting at his form outlined against the stars. Later that night he heard a horse approaching and the jingle of metal. Seeing a rider outlined against the sky, Maupin carefully took aim and was pressing the trigger when an awful thought struck him. Only a few days before, he had given Garrett a knife on a chain which made a jangling noise. Risking all, he called in a low voice and prepared to hit the ground the instant he voiced it. "Is that you, Garrett?" "Yeah, Pa," came a shaky voice from the darkness. Maupin gave up night fighting on the spot.[14]

As Has No Horse and Big Man struck the western and eastern ends of The Dalles-Boise City trail, Paulina and Wolf Dog worked the middle sections, insuring the complete breakup of the army's forces.

At daybreak, September 9, Henry Wheeler, driving a four-horse team and a Lever coach—accompanied only by Henry C. Paige, special agent for Wells Fargo Express Company—was making the run between Mountain House and Alkali Flat. Aboard the stage, in addition to U.S. mail, were $10,000 in greenbacks, a number of valuable diamond rings, $300 in gold coin and 1,200 ounces of gold dust in buckskin bags. Three miles east of the present site of Mitchell, Paulina launched his attack as the coach reached Keyes Creek. The first shot struck Wheeler in the face, the bullet going through his cheek carrying away several teeth and a part of the jawbone. Despite this injury, Wheeler jumped to the ground and while Paige kept up a rapid fire with a .38 Colt revolver, managed to unhitch the lead team.

Noticing this maneuver, Tall Man (brother to Broken Knife) riding low in the saddle, swooped in and cut down on Paige. As was often the case in those days, his pistol misfired and on such small matters battles are won or lost. With an anguished look on his face, Tall Man rode into the happy hunting ground with a hole in his head you could drive a freight wagon through . . . leaving his seven-year-old daughter an orphan. Her mother, Little Shadow, had been shot on the John Day River near Clark's Stage Station by the Warm Springs volunteers in 1859.

---

Messages and Documents 1877-67, pp. 503-4, 39th Congress, 2nd Session; Oregon Senate Journal 1866, pp. 51-55.

14    As told by the Maupin family in *The Illustrated History of Central Oregon*, 1905.

This girl would become known in Prineville as Annette Tallman. Now, Pony Blanket had two orphan girls (who were first cousins) to raise.

Paige and Wheeler mounted the lead team, neither of which had been ridden before, and Paige was quickly bucked off. Before the Shoshoni could take advantage of his misfortune, Wheeler returned and double mounted they escaped to Alkali House. In 1887, Oregon Secretary of State George McBride, presented to the State of Oregon a long tin box which is still in the state archives. It contained a .38 Colt, a bowie knife made from a butcher's knife, two pairs of bullet molds, two ramrods and a pistol belt. These were the possessions of Henry Paige on that fateful day in 1866.

After Meyer had dressed Wheeler's wound, he, Paige and Hewot returned to the scene of the attack.[15] All they found was the stagecoach with its top ripped completely off, the slashed mail bags with the contents scattered over 10 acres and the gold dust poured on the ground. They were able to recover most of the dust. Apparently Paulina had no use for it, as he had taken the horses, the diamonds, the greenbacks and the gold coins. As Paulina's guerrilla forces headed back into the Ochoco mountains, Has No Horse descended on Clark's Stage Station. He was going to make certain the stage companies had more to worry about than the loss of a few horses and mules.

James M. Clark filed a land claim on the John Day River about a mile below the mouth of Bridge Creek in 1865, making him the third man to settle in what became Crook County.[16] A few days before the attack on Wheeler, Clark's wife had left the stage station to visit her parents in the Willamette Valley. Less than 48 hours after Paulina swooped down on Wheeler's stagecoach some 25 miles southeast of Clark's station, Clark—a driver for the Wheeler stageline and his brother-in-law, 18-year-old George Masterson, forded the John Day River to cut driftwood on the north shore. Glancing across the river, Clark spotted a group of Indians riding down the high ridge between John Day Gulch and Coyote Canyon south of the stage station. For reasons which defy explanation, Clark and Masterson had left their rifles at the station but they thought there was a chance to reach it ahead of the Shoshoni. Unhitching the team and climbing on bareback, they crossed the river and headed for the house. However, when they realized that the Indians were going to get there first, they swerved up Bridge Creek with the enemy in close pursuit.

It took but a few miles of hard riding to use up Masterson's work-horse and he told Clark to keep going and save himself. Masterson then jumped from his

---

15    At this spot on State Highway 26, the citizens of Wheeler County erected a monument commemorating the attack. It is the only marker in the Ochoco country showing where the Shoshoni pulled off one of their spectacular raids.

16    Bridge Creek received its name from Shoeman and Wadley, California packers, who constructed a small bridge of juniper logs over the stream when en route to the Canyon City mines in 1862. Bancroft, *History of Oregon*, Vol. I, p. 787.

horse into Bridge Creek and, swimming downstream a short distance, found a deep hole overhung with thick willows where he hid. Has No Horse chased Clark a few miles farther, but knowing a detachment of army scouts were patrolling the road between Alkali House an Clark's station, he turned back to finish Masterson. Fortunately Masterson had the good sense to remain submerged in his concealed waterhole but when later rescued, he was described as being more dead than alive, "his long bath in the water rendering him practically helpless."[17] After hunting all around for him, Has No Horse gave up and returned to the stage station.

Eight miles up Bridge Creek, Clark caught up with a party of Canyon City packers under escort of Pvt. Skanewa, Co. B 1st Warm Springs Scouts.[18] Among others in this group were William (Bud) Thompson, Perry Maupin (Howard's son), John Atterbury (who settled in Prineville in 1880), Emil Stoube (who later settled in Mitchell), and John Bonham (a freighter). At Clark's request, these men joined forces with the Warm Springs Scouts and went in search of Masterson. Failing to find a body, the awful possibility began to dawn upon the rescue party that he may have been captured alive. Clark lost control. Had he found the teenager dead, it would have been nothing compared to the thought of his capture and slow agonizing death at the stake. A search now began for the tracks of the Snakes, especially those of Has No Horse who, according to Clark, was mounted on a powerful black gelding. While this was going on, some of the men found Masterson in a state of shock mumbling "Oh Lord! Oh Lord!"

About then, some two miles to the north, an ominous black column of smoke blotted out the sky. By the time the relief party arrived, the house, stables and corrals were engulfed in flames which burned them to the ground. It was certain that everything worthwhile had been stolen, even to the ripping open of beds in a search for anything of value. The contents of feather mattresses covered the yard like new fallen snow. The main barn storing 50 tons of hay and a thousand bushels of grain went up in smoke while the livestock and extra changes of horses, four of which—valued at $600—belonged to Wheeler, were driven into the southern Blues.[19] Clark's stage station was now . . . Burnt Ranch!

That evening back at the packers camp, Clark was positive that there were no more than 15 or 20 warriors in the raiding party and he begged the Canyon City freighters to help him recover his property or at least take revenge on the Indians. Since the Warm Springs Scouts had returned to Fort Watson, seven men—including Perry Maupin, John Atterbury, Bud Thompson and John Bonham—volunteered to ride with Clark on this mission. Starting at daybreak September 12, Clark and his seven-man army struck Has No Horse's trail and were in for a hard day's journey, and quite likely an ambush. Has No Horse, expecting

---

17    Thompson, *Reminiscences of a Pioneer*, p. 51.

18    Within nine months. Pvt. Skanewa would die of tuberculosis on May 23, 1867.

19    Secretary of Interior Report, 1867-8, Pt. 2, pp. 95-100.

to be followed, led them on a tortuous chase. His trail led south up John Day Gulch; crossed over into Cherry Creek; wound up Stevenson Mountain nearly to the summit; then headed west to the head of Opal Creek; and again turned south toward Bull Mountain—not an easy route to follow.

Near sunset, Clark located an Indian camp on Trout Creek about a mile up the west fork between Cougar Rock and Ingram Point. If they had met resistance along the way, Thompson, who recorded the journey didn't admit to it. However, being a self-centered young man, Thompson was the last person in the world to confess that the volunteers may have blundered into a trap. But within 12 hours it would surface that Clark and his Indian-fighters numbered only six men out of an original eight and it is recorded that John Bonham, a member of the party, was killed by the Snakes in September 1866.[20] Who the second missing man is is anyone's guess. Thompson would later note that "three others [Bonham was one of them] whose names I cannot now recall, volunteered for the undertaking making seven in all."[21] Jim Clark, their leader, would make the eighth man.

Satisfied that the Snakes would remain on the West Fork of Trout Creek until morning, "no doubt feasting on some of the stolen livestock," the Canyon City militia decided to await daylight before making an attack.

Now it is necessary to back up for a few days. With Paulina and Has No Horse dealing misery along The Dalles-Canyon City road, Wolf Dog and Big Man were intent on striking the Warm Springs Agency just so the confederated tribesmen wouldn't feel neglected. En route, the Snakes ran into the Scott brothers in Hay Creek Canyon, stampeded their trail herd and moved on. When still 15 miles from the agency headquarters, their scouts reported a Wasco hunting camp on the West Fork of Trout Creek poaching on Shoshoni soil. This was an infraction which could not be ignored.

Seven days before Has No Horse's destruction of Clark's stage station, the Wasco chief Poustaminie had received permission from Warm Springs Agent John Smith to cross the Deschutes for the purpose of hunting. Accompanying him were his brother Queapama, seven men and their wives and children. Upon learning that Wheeler's stage had been attacked by Paulina, Poustaminie became alarmed and started back to the reservation, camping a few miles east of the Scott's trail herd. On the morning of September 12, all the men except two were out rounding up their horses when Wolf Dog rode through their camp shooting. Queapama was wounded in the arm and a woman was hit in the foot. Wolf Dog ordered a cease-fire and asked to what tribe they belonged. Upon being told, he informed the Wascos that he was Wolf Dog and that Big Man was but a short distance behind him.

---

20    Ibid; National Archives, Bureau of Indian affairs, Oregon Superintendency Field Papers, Letters Received, Smith to Huntington, Warm Springs Agency, September 26, 1866.

21    Thompson, *Reminiscences of a Pioneer*, p. 51.

Hearing the shots, the rest of the Wascos returned on a gallop. Seeing that the ruckus was caused by Snake dog soldiers, Poustaminie told his men to lay down their arms. Tying a white flag to a pole, he started forward to meet Wolf Dog when Big Man rode out of a nearby ravine and dropped him in his tracks. Mortally wounded, Poustaminie told his brother, who had run up to him "now we must fight!" Queapama wasn't that foolish and Wolf Dog rode off with 77 of their horses.[22]

At 3:00 a.m. the morning of September 13, Jim Clark and his volunteers (following a circuitous route) dismounted in the darkness and approached to within 150 yards of the Indian camp on Trout Creek. At the first streak of dawn, they mounted and at a full gallop, yelling like demons, hit the sleeping camp with revolvers blasting. Scarcely had they began their charge when several Indians, already scared out of their wits by the dog soldiers, sprang up and rushed toward the attackers with hands up yelling at the top of their lungs: "Warm Springs! Warm Springs! Wascos, Wascos!" Recognizing them as not being Snakes, both Clark and Maupin called out, "For God's sakes boys don't shoot!"[23] The last thing the stage company employees wanted was another hostile Indian tribe to deal with.

Queapama told Clark of his encounter with the Snakes and he believed the Indians Clark was trailing were the same as those who attacked the Wasco camp. He was wrong. Has No Horse with his loot was already riding up the Ochoco Valley. During their discussion, the Scotts with five buckaroos rode into the Wasco camp looking for lost cattle. Clark talked them into joining his party and was trying to do the same with the reservation Indians. They were quite certain that Paulina was nearby and they wanted no part of him, as they honestly believed the Mountain War Chief was bulletproof. Several of the Wasco men swore they had shot Paulina in the middle of the forehead but the bullets bounced off without harming him. Finally Clark convinced the seven men who hadn't been wounded in the previous day's battle to go along as trackers (which they were very good at).

Picking up a supply of dried venison from the Wasco camp, Clark's disciplinary squad—now numbering 20 well-armed men—took to the trail. Wolf Dog had made no effort to hide his tracks. The trail led in a southerly direction up the West Fork of Trout Creek and within four miles, the trackers found where the Snakes had spent the night. Their fires were still burning, showing Wolf Dog's utter contempt for the reservation Indians. It was now obvious that he was unaware of the white men's presence in the area.

Again, the track turned west, passed through McKay Saddle and headed down Little McKay Creek toward Crooked River. About 3:00 p.m., the Warm Springs trackers announced that the Snakes had gone into camp about a mile ahead at the junction of Allen and McKay creeks. They had counted 16 warriors. With plenty

---

22     Shane, *Early Exploration Through Warm Springs Reservation*, p. 26.
23     Thompson, *Reminiscences of a Pioneer*, pp. 52-53.

of white artillery to back them, the Wascos were eager to attack. Jim Clark, not yet 30 years old, being the oldest man in a party of youngsters barely in their twenties, was looked to as their leader. With evening near at hand, Clark was not fully convinced that a head-on clash was the smart thing to do but finally gave the go-ahead. "We are getting into the Snakes' territory. They might move again tonight and we would be compelled to go further on." He then warned, "We might bite off more than we can chew," but his young warriors were ready to attack.

Sneaking up on Wolf Dog's relaxed camp, Clark divided his troops so they could strike from two directions. At the first rifle-shot, the Warm Springs trackers were to stampede the Snakes' horse herd. With that, the battle began. Bragging as usual, Thompson noted: "Though this was to be my first real Indian fight, I felt no fear and not so much excitement as when stalking my first buck." He would also imply that he had "done in" Big Man. "I remember taking deliberate aim at a big fellow. At the crack of the rifle he sprang into the air and fell and I then knew I had made one good siwash."[24] Whoever he had redeemed, it wasn't Big Man.

Taken by surprise, the Snakes in a running fight regrouped in the timber and even Thompson was aware that to have pursued them "would have been madness." Already, two of the Wascos were wounded when Clark called a halt to the affair, knowing if they tried to follow it would result in "some of us getting killed." His riflemen had killed four Shoshoni, including one who had his leg shattered by a rifle ball and couldn't get away from the Warm Springs allies who were having a great time scalping their foe alive. The youthful Indian-fighters found it to be a gory spectacle. As Thompson put it, "The operation of lifting a scalp was a simple one. A knife was run around the head just above the ears and the skin peeled off." He had no desire to see the operation repeated.

After destroying everything of value in Wolf Dog's camp, the three groups parted company. The Canyon City volunteers going back to Bridge Creek for a week's rest; the Scotts back to rounding up stray cattle; and the Wascos back to the reservation where they arrived on September 17, packing their wounded and the remains of Poustaminie.[25]

In this two day contest, the score would read: Home Team, four dead, no known wounded; Visitors, three dead, four wounded. No great victory for either side. One might wonder what the soldiers stationed at Camp Steele—within rifle sound of the McKay Creek skirmish were doing. Perhaps they were on Veazie Creek (near the present Keystone Ranch) guarding the Willamette Valley road construction crew. Maybe not.

---

24  *Siwash* is the Chinook jargon name for Indian. All the old-timers of eastern Oregon referred to Indians—any Indians—as siwashes.

25  Thompson, *Reminiscences of a Pioneer*, pp. 53-57; Smith to Huntington, Warm Springs Agency, September 26, 1866.

Agent John Smith in his report to Supt. Huntington dated September 26, 1866 would again plead for protection. "The Indians upon this Reserve are in great dread of an attack from the Snake Indians: And this fear is not diminished in the least as a day does not pass that this fear is not increased by the reports that Snake Indians have been seen somewhere upon the Reserve. I will respectfully request that this Agency be furnished with arms as there are not guns sufficient to arm the employees."

And so as September, rimmed in gunsmoke, drifted toward an end, a group of Willamette Valley homesteaders ignoring the obvious danger, slipped into the Ochoco Valley and erected the first settler's cabin in present Crook County at the junction of Mill Creek and the Ochoco River . . . an act they were to regret.

# CHAPTER 136

# MAD MOON

*Few of us will soon forget the wail of mingled grief, rage and*
*horror which came from the camp 400 or 500 yards below us*
*when the Indians returned to it and recognized their*
*slaughtered warriors, women and children.*

**Col. John Gibbon**
7th U.S. Infantry

In 1866, Congress passed a bill authorizing the army to attach Indian scouts to the regular forces engaged in fighting hostiles. The number of scouts to be enlisted was apportioned among those states and territories where hostilities existed, Oregon's share being 100. When word reached Salem, Gov. Woods decided that Oregon's allotment should be organized into two companies of 50 each to be sent into the battlefield as commandos independent of regular army personnel. He further requested that the Indian regulars be ordered to kill hostiles without regard as to sex, age or condition. In short, the campaign against the Snakes was to be a war of extermination.[1] Gen. Steele declined Woods' request on the ground that the army bill intended the employment of Indians as scouts only, and their numbers to be limited to no more than 10 or 15 to a command. And this was the way he would implement the bill.

Enraged, Woods appealed this decision to Gen. Halleck who also refused to honor such a demand, using little courtesy in declining. Then, on October 8, Halleck sent a telegram to Steele: "The Secretary of War agrees with me that the law does not authorize the appointment of special officers to command Indian scouts but you can select hired interpreters for that purpose. Limit the pay to that of second lieutenant of cavalry." Acting on Halleck's telegram, Steele offered commands simultaneously to William McKay, John Darragh and James Halloran. Halloran, a lieutenant in the 1st Washington Infantry, declined.[2]

---

1    National Archives, Record Group 393, Microfilm 2, Roll 10:211.
2    National Archives Record Group 393, Department of Columbia, Letters Received, Box 7:78 and Box 6:138, Halloran to Steele, October 13, 1866.

Not to be thwarted in his obsession to eliminate the Shoshoni, Woods telegraphed the secretary of war and requested authority to carry out his plan of fighting Indians with Indians—a pet project of Oregon since the 1850s. Secretary Stanton immediately ordered Halleck and Steele to conform with the wishes of the governor or be relieved of their commands. They complied but their hatred for Oregon's interference in military affairs would not go unnoticed.[3]

Lacking any basis in fact, Woods' justification for the butchery of Shoshoni women was rooted in the 1854 Ward massacre.[4] Even the most dedicated Indian-haters knew this atrocity was not committed by the Shoshoni. Nevertheless, Woods would contend that the Ward Massacre . . . "perpetrated by Snakes has demonstrated that Indian women are even more fiendish than the men; that they have initiated particularly revolting torture for white women and children; and that without extermination there can be no peace."[5] Unfortunately, public sentiment was on his side and, at least temporarily, military objection to the slaughter of women and children subsided.

Lt. William Borrowe, 2nd U.S. Artillery, with 30 1st U.S. Cavalrymen was ordered to set up headquarters at the Warm Springs Agency for the purpose of enlistment. Between October 29 and November 9, he inducted 74 Warm Springs Indians into the regular army and adamantly stated, "I will take no more! In making these enlistments I found it impossible to comply with the requirement of the recruiting service . . . the oath was administered to them . . . but I much doubt if the men knew what they were doing or the importance of the obligation taken. . . ."[6] These Indian recruits were marched to Fort Dalles and mustered into the regular army to serve under Lt. Col. George Crook who was scheduled to take command of Fort Warner, new headquarters for the Snake campaign.

Warm Springs Agent John Smith understood quite well why Lt. Borrowe was having trouble filling his quota. Most of the reservation Indians had the good sense to realize that operating on orders to kill Shoshoni women and children could only add to their woes and they didn't want any family members or friends volunteering to do so.

Within the past month, Has No Horse and Paulina—after demoralizing Wheeler and Clark—were hitting and hitting hard at the Yainax sub-agency on the eastern end of the Klamath reservation, known as the Paulina reserve since the abortive treaty of 1865. Capoles, chief of the Warm Springs scouts, was dispatched

---

3    *U.S. Secretary of Interior Report 1867-8, Vol. III, Pt. II, p. 101, 41st Congress, 2nd Session.*

4    George Lemuel Woods, a prominent Oregon lawyer, was Wasco County Judge in 1863. From that office he was elected state governor in 1866 at the age of 34. President Grant appointed him governor of Utah Territory in 1871. Corning, *Dictionary of Oregon History*, p. 273.

5    Bancroft, *History of Oregon*, Vol. II, p. 531.

6    Borrowe to Major S.A. Foster, Fort Vancouver, November 9, 1866. National Archives Records Group 393, Department of Columbia, Letters Received, Box 6:374.

south with a detachment of Walla Wallas to police the area and was immediately killed.[7] Agent Lindsay Applegate, fearing that the Klamaths would leave the reservation because of a loss of supplies, petitioned Supt. Huntington for help. Huntington was quick to accommodate mainly because these reported Snake attacks on the Klamath tribes had brought quick congressional action in ratification of the treaty of 1865.[8]

Besides one of the largest trail herds of cattle ever to cross the low desert, he sent a wagon train loaded with $30,000 worth of clothing, blankets, flour, potatoes, cooking utensils and farm equipment. This mammoth supply train made such an indelible track across central Oregon it became permanently known as The Huntington Road. To make certain the train arrived with only minor difficulty, Applegate sent his son, Capt. Oliver Applegate with the Axe and Rifle Squad to escort it across the western Ochoco. Joining them at the Crooked River crossing were 60 U.S. regulars made up of cavalrymen and artillerymen. The train would get through!

Hounded by Gen. Grant and the War Department, Halleck and Steele were throwing almost the full power of the United States Army into the Shoshoni front. Fort Walla Walla and Fort Lapwai were reopened and manned with one company each of 8th U.S. Cavalry under the command of Lt. Oscar Converse and Lt. J.H. Gallagher; Col. Baker's command at Fort Watson was bolstered with an additional company of 1st U.S. Cavalry and one of the 14th Infantry under the command of Lt. Amandus Kistler. Fort Logan received an infantry company and one of the 8th U.S. Cavalry under Lt. Charles Western; Capt. Sprague with a company of Oregon Infantry marched into Fort Klamath; Major Walker moved into Fort C.F. Smith with a company of 14th Infantry; Capt. James Hunt brought a company of 8th U.S. Cavalry into Fort Lyon; and Lt. Col. John Coppinger moved to Camp Three Forks on the Owyhee with another company of 14th Infantry.

Capt. Patrick Collins marched into Fort Warner with two infantry companies and one company of cavalry commanded by Major Edward Meyers. Soon to arrive was Lt. Col. George Crook with the celebrated 23rd U.S. Infantry Regiment to make Fort Warner headquarters for the Snake Campaign.[9] And last, but by no means the least, Lt. Col. Albert Vincent with five batteries of 2nd U.S. Field

---

7     Those with Capoles employed by the government as Indian policemen included: Lt. Jake Thomas; Captain George (Shar-huk); Top-lash; Joe Sidwalder; Frank Sidwalder; Tahone; Sisson Jim; Pinause; Schooley; William Skineackee; and Jim Winnishett, a Snake warrior.

8     *Congressional Globe 1865-6*, Pt. V, p. 402.

9     Major General Crook, like many Civil War officers, had been reduced in rank to Lt. Col. in the War Department's effort to save money. Although receiving the pay of a Lt. Col., he still retained the brevet or honorary rank of a three-star general thus, he was of equal rank with both Maj. Gen. Steele and Maj. Gen. Halleck.

Artillery was ordered to keep all military roads into eastern Oregon open for travel.[10]

Altogether—not counting the forces already engaged against the Shoshoni—generals Halleck and Steele had thrown in an additional 2,200 troops. By sheer numbers alone, they would overwhelm the Paviotso Confederacy.

With the increased travel on The Dalles-Canyon City Military Road, the two bachelors at Alkali House found the household chores growing and they decided there was a need for the touch of a woman's hand. Being practical, Meyer and Hewot agreed to play a game of seven-up to determine which one would be the matrimonial victim. Meyer lost and headed for San Francisco as the most likely spot to find a girl who would settle at dreary Alkali Flat.

Dressed in his army Kossuth hat—gift of Baker's 1st U.S. Cavalry—gambler's frock coat and black string bow tie, baggy broadcloth pantaloons stuffed into his best cowhide freighter's boots, Dutch Meyer cut quite a striking figure strolling down Market Street. He soon struck up an acquaintance with a lady named Meta . . . and in a few weeks rode triumphantly home on the Wheeler Stage with a blushing bride. Meyer's new status forced his old partner out into the cold so he established the new Eight Mile Station south of The Dalles where he soon went the way of all good bachelors—he got married. Hewot was so thrilled over his newly acquired helpmate that he vowed: "Boys, if I ever have any kids, they're all going to be girls!" True to his word, Hewot became the proud father of two beautiful girls who in later years did much to attract the cowboy trade to his Eight Mile Stage Station.[11]

In late September, while Meyer took in the sights of San Francisco, Has No Horse—on his return from a raid on the Klamath Agency—was attacked by 50 cavalrymen near Abert Lake. In three hours of furious fighting, he was finally routed: losing 14 warriors killed, seven taken prisoner and hanged, while horses, rifles and winter stores fell into the hands of the pony soldiers. It was a serious loss.

By October, 60 Snakes—16 men and 44 women and children—had been captured and brought to the Klamath reservation. Among the prisoners of war were Biting Bear, Black Eagle, Lame Dog, Black Buffalo and Pony Blanket. Pony Blanket and Biting Bear met with Agent Applegate on October 3 and promised that all 60 Snakes (the women and children had been left at Moses' camp) would move down to the agency headquarters where the army could watch over them. Applegate assured the two war chiefs that if they did as told and remained faithful they might yet receive the benefits of the 1865 treaty. True to form, the Snakes quickly did the unexpected. The night of Pony Blanket's talk with Applegate, the men escaped to Sprague River, picked up the women and children, stole five guns,

---

10    *Official Army Register 1866-67*; Woods, George L., "Recollections," *Overland Monthly 1869*, Vol. II, p. 162; Bancroft, *History of Oregon*, Vol. II, p. 528.

11    Interview with Wheeler County pioneers.

two of Moses' horses and left the reservation. Lt. Harrison Oatman was sent in pursuit.[12]

As the Klamath escape was being planned, Has No Horse mustered his forces from the Abert Lake defeat and mounted a full-scale attack on the John Day settlements. Moving out of his main encampment in the upper Ochoco Valley, Has No Horse blundered into a mining camp on Canyon Creek. The big surprise was that this camp was on the very threshold of his winter village. This above all incurred the war chief's ire and he rode for one purpose only . . . to kill!

The prospectors—having heard the Indians coming up Canyon Creek—didn't wait to fight but attempted an escape into the heavy timber under the north slope of Round Mountain. Before they reached cover, two men were wounded and John Kester died on a rocky outcrop near the head of Fisher Creek. From here, the Snake raiders swooped down from Mount Pisgah and plundered the mining settlement in Spanish Gulch, a scant eight miles from Fort Watson. Putting the residents to flight, Has No Horse confiscated their livestock including 11 choice saddle horses and made off with their winter food supply. Continuing on toward Canyon City, he struck at outlying mining camps and ranches, he burned cabins; killed Matthew Wilson and severely wounded David Graham who later died from wounds received; captured a pack train; and made it to within one mile of Canyon City before being turned back by superior forces. Sgt. Conner with 20 troopers from Col. Baker's command took pursuit but never caught up with Has No Horse.[13]

During the attack on Canyon City, Lt. Oatman with 17 Oregon Infantrymen and 20 members of the Axe and Rifle Squad, left Fort Klamath on the morning of October 5 in pursuit of Pony Blanket and the escaped prisoners of war. Four days out of Fort Klamath when crossing the mountains west of Fort Warner, Oatman was intercepted by Lt. John Small with 27 8th U.S. Cavalrymen out of Fort Bidwell, California. Oatman's new orders were to join Lt. Small in clearing the Oregon Central Military Road of any hostiles. The army couldn't have picked a better man for the job than Lt. Oatman.

In 1851, most of his family had been killed in an Indian attack on the Gila River. His cousins, seven-year-old Mary Ann and twelve-year-old Olive Oatman had been captured by the Apaches and sold into slavery to the Mojaves. Their brother Lorenzo Oatman, left for dead, escaped and five years later through negotiations with the Yumas rescued Olive. Capt. Will (William F.) Drannan—whose many exploits filled two volumes—was in on the rescue. Olive became known as one of the West's most famous Indian captive but she never fully

---

12    National Archives, Bureau of Indian Affairs Oregon Superintendency, Letters Received, Lindsay Applegate to Huntington, Ashland Mills, October 11, 1866.

13    *Secretary of the Interior Report 1867-8*, Pt. 2, pp. 95-100; *The Dalles Mountaineer*, December 14, 1866.

recovered from the ordeal.[14] Cousin Harrison Oatman would not be easy on any Shoshoni.

Guided by Blow, a Klamath chief, Oatman marched toward Warner Lake. On October 15, 1866, he found his quarry. In a sabre-slashing attack, he hit the camp of Ground Owl, war chief of the Dog Rib Snakes, killing 14 (it seems 14 was an unlucky number for the Shoshoni) and wounding 30 including Ground Owl—all of whom were executed. Although several of Oatman's troops were wounded, he didn't lose a man.[15]

The day before Oatman moved out of Fort Klamath, Lt. James Patton, with 10 cavalrymen out of Fort Lyon, caught up with Bad Face's band—numbering 75 men, women and children—on the Blitzen River. In a retreating battle, the cavalry killed six Shoshoni with a loss of one man killed and four horses wounded.[16]

As Oatman and Patton caused trouble in the southern high desert, Has No Horse turned back from his assault on Canyon City and circled deep into the mountains to hide his trail back to the upper Ochoco Valley. On October 29, while crossing the high lava scabs on the head of Deep Creek his out-riders located an infantry camp.

Two weeks earlier, Major Jesse Walker with a detachment of infantry out of Fort C.F. Smith, split from Lt. Patton on the Blitzen River and was following an Indian trail into the southern Blues. On the evening of October 29, he set up what became known as Surprise Camp a few miles south of Big Summit Prairie. It was his intent to take the Indians by surprise from this depot and deliver a knock-out blow. At daybreak on October 30, amid war whoops and gunfire, Has No Horse ripped through the army encampment. Although he lost four warriors, he routed the infantry and cleaned out the depot—taking tents, blankets, tools, cooking utensils, grain and the pack mules loaded with ammunition. Walker finally organized his troops and got out of the country.[17]

The three creeks which drop away from this area were named Looney, Stupid and Crazy. Perhaps that was the method used by the soldiers to express their disgust with the commanding officer for picking such a campsite.

With Walker in full retreat, an express rider cut Lt. Oatman's campaign short when he was ordered back to Fort Klamath, which was now under siege by Paulina. Capt. Sprague, who had been brought in to defend the reservation, didn't have enough men to protect agency headquarters and search for the enemy at the same time. Early in November, Has No Horse joined Paulina for the purpose of targeting

---

14    *American Heritage Book of Indians*, p. 384; Reiter, Joan Swallow, "The Women," *Time-Life Books*, pp. 62-64.

15    *Jacksonville Reporter*, November 3, 1866; *The Dalles Mountaineer*, December 7, 1866.

16    *The Boise Statesman*, October 27, 1866.

17    *The Boise Statesman*, November 8. 1866; *The Owyhee Avalanche*, November 17, 1866; *The Dalles Mountaineer*, December 14, 1866.

the Axe and Rifle Squad. During their invasion of the Sprague River Valley, they made off with Schonchin's horses and winter food supplies. Schonchin took pursuit but succeeded only in capturing two Shoshoni women. He reported back to the Agency telling Applegate that he had met with Has No Horse and learned that he was planning to join forces with Big Man at Goose Lake, and to capture Fort Klamath, which was now in a weakened condition. The Shoshoni did in fact come within a few miles of the fort before being turned back by U.S. regulars, losing 13 men in the process.[18]

Meanwhile, the army was gradually and almost unconsciously surrounding the secret haunts of the hostile Shoshoni. As the Secretary of War would cynically observe, the army's success in battle was in direct proportion to how close they could get to the enemy and whichever side attacked first was usually victorious.[19]

Within a week of Has No Horse's raid of Major Walker's Surprise Camp, the Boise front exploded. Biting Bear and Spotted Elk joined forces with Bad Face and attacked the supply wagons headed from Boise City to the Owyhee mines, killing one teamster and wounding another. Then in a night attack, they fired on the Owyhee ferry and raided a cavalry camp—accomplishing nothing other than killing a horse and driving off 14 head of cattle. Moving on up the Snake River, the combined war party attacked a party of 68 miners, killing ten. In a panic, the miners headed into Montana where they were again attacked by Red Cloud's Sioux Alliance.[20]

Having routed the miners, the Snakes turned back into eastern Oregon and four miles west of the Snake River crossing ambushed the Owyhee stage. In the first volley, Bill Waltermire (the driver) took a bullet wound in the ribs, Wilcox (a passenger) was killed and another passenger, George Harrington was wounded in the hip. With the armed passengers firing into the Indians, Waltermire made a frantic effort to escape and ran his team two miles before the wheel-horses were shot and the party was forced to run for their lives on foot, escaping when a cavalry detachment arrived. Returning to the scene of the attack, they found Wilcox scalped and mutilated, the mail bags cut open and the contents scattered.

Continuing west, the war party raided a ranch on Cow Creek and took possession of the barn. From there, they riddled the ranch house with rifle fire and arrows. The inhabitants escaped after dark and the Snakes rode off with all the livestock. Lt. Col. O'Beirne took to the trail and in a surprise attack on a Shoshoni

18    Bancroft, *History of Oregon*, Vol. II, p. 530.

19    Secretary of War Report, i:481-2, 40th Congress, 2nd Session.

20    Among those killed by the Snakes were: Bruce Smith, Edward Riley, David Conklin, William Strong and George Ackleson. Killed by the Sioux were Collin Rice and William Smith. *Portland Oregonian*, November 28, 1866.

camp killed 14 and captured 10 whom he promptly hanged. In the fight, O'Beirne lost one man and S.G. Thompson, a news reporter, was killed.[21]

Meantime, Col. Baker's cavalry and infantry, working in unison with Lt. Col. Vincent's field artillery, were taking a heavy toll on The Dalles front. Baker, sweeping the John Day and Crooked River valleys, was concentrating on ferreting out small winter encampments. He killed some 60 Shoshoni with a loss of eight men.[22] While central Oregon was being raked with rifle-fire, Vincent's artillery blasted a hole in The Dalles-Canyon City road and by December, six million dollars in gold had been shipped to The Dalles. However, The Dalles citizens received another scare. On November 30, 1866, the first recorded earthquake felt at The Dalles rattled the city from one end to the other.[23] It appears that the Shoshoni earth god was voicing his disapproval.

By December, other militant tribes were taking serious note of the Snake's defiant stand against the might of the United States Army. Following their example, the Montana Sioux—just four days before Christmas—annihilated Col. William Fetterman's command of 80 officers and men. Someone would suffer for this and it would be the non-combatants.

Before a new year could arrive, hundreds of Earth Eaters—the peaceful and destitute citizens of the Shoshoni nation—were rounded up and placed in captivity in the vicinity of Fort Boise. On December 6, Agent George Hough wrote the governor of Idaho describing their pitiful condition, shivering in the cold, wrapped in threadbare and coarse horse blankets without sufficient food. Hough summed up by saying: "Their condition is most deplorable, and from a residence of 30 years among various tribes of Indians, I am constrained to say—these Bruneau Shoshonis are the most poverty stricken Indians I ever saw and unless they are fed—must necessarily starve during the present rigorous winter."[24] This was at a time when most eastern Oregon and Idaho citizens were applauding the suggestion of the *Owyhee Avalanche* that smallpox-infected blankets be distributed among the natives.[25]

Facing overwhelming odds, low on provisions, the Paviotso Confederacy was in for a bad winter. Even so, the final days of 1866 found the Indian situation in eastern Oregon much the same as it had been for the past eight years...extremely dangerous! Although suffering heavy casualties, Has No Horse's dwindling troops

---

21  *U.S. Secretary of Interior Report*, Vol. III, pp. 99-100, 40th Congress, 2nd Session; *Owhyee Avalanche*, November 10 and November 17, 1866; *The Boise Statesman*, November 17, 1866; *The Idaho World*, November 24, 1866; *The Dalles Mountaineer*, December 7, 1866.

22  U.S. Secretary of War Report, Vol. I, pp. 481-2, 40th Congress, 2nd Session; *The Dalles Mountaineer*, December 14, 1866.

23  This earthquake lasted for three seconds. McNeal, *Wasco County*, p. 14.

24  Report of Commissioner of Indian Affairs, 1866, p. 187, George C. Hough to D.W. Ballard, Boise City, December 6, 1866.

25  *Owyhee Avalanche*, January 20, 1867.

were still ripping and slashing at the settlements like a pack of hungry wolves. They were also on the prowl for some Shoshoni defectors.

The Climber's band of so-called Lemhi Shoshoni—actually a splinter group of Robber Snakes who had embraced Mormonism—volunteered to lead U.S. troops to the war tribes' winter hideouts on the promise of receiving some food.[26] Led by Six Feathers, a Snake mercenary operating out of Gourd Rattler's camp, these defectors pledged their allegiance to army scout Archie McIntosh, and in so doing were marked for execution by the dog soldiers.

Meanwhile, the Military Department of the Pacific which had changed commanding generals five times since the birth of the Paviotso Confederacy and sub-divided eastern Oregon into several military districts, was becoming bogged ever deeper in the quagmire of Oregon politics.

As for the Shoshoni, they had reached the end of the trail. Soon their native culture—born of the ages—would be snuffed out like the dying embers of a flickering campfire.

---

26    A branch of the Bannock (Robber) Snakes under the leadership of Tendoy, The Climber, became devout followers of Brigham Young. On June 12, 1855, the Mormons established a mission among them on the Salmon River. The Saints would name this group Lemhi Shoshoni in honor of Limhi, a neophyte Mormon king. (Ruby and Brown, *A Guide to the Indian Tribes of the Pacific Northwest*, p. 200). Most authorities claim Sacajawea was a Lemhi Shoshoni. This premise is open for debate, as Sacajawea (if she had lived) would have been approximately 64 years old before the Lemhi designation came into existence.

# Part V
## DYING EMBERS

# DYING EMBERS

## THE TERMINATION OF SHOSHONI SUPREMACY IN EASTERN OREGON

*Babes lashed to back in corded pain*
*Until their swollen bare legs bled,*
*But on and on their mother's led.*
*The starving mother's breasts were dry,*
*There scarce was time to stop and drink,*
*The swollen legs grew black as ink*
*There was not even time to die. . . .*

The Paviotso Confederacy and the United States Army were now locked in a death struggle in which no quarter was asked and none was given. In the final round of this uneven match the Americans would score a technical knockout but the fight was not yet over. Men defending their homes were executed as war criminals while women and children were sacrificed on the bloody altar of reformation to appease the insatiable god of progress. It was during this period of enlightenment that the anguished cry *"Nimma ne-umpu"* ("We too are human") echoed through the melancholy corridors of the Ochoco; and the Crooked River plunged into tribal history as the sorrowful Weeping Water. Once again the Saydocarah, powerful rulers of an inland empire became Nokonis, the homeless people. Bear in mind that no matter where you live in central Oregon today, you stand on the remains of an ancient and mysterious world whose roots go deep into the soil.

*Yet who, of all men that pursued*
*This dying race, year after year*
*By burning plain or beetling wood,*
*Did ever see, did ever hear*
*One bleeding Indian baby cry?*

**Joaquin Miller**
Shoshoni War Veteran

# CHAPTER 137

# THE WARM SPRINGS COMMANDOS

*It was one of the last human hunts of civilization,
and the basest and most brutal of them all. . . .*

**Hubert H. Bancroft**
Oregon Historian

The eastern Oregon battlefront now under the field command of Col. L.H. Marshall was about to undergo a radical change and Lt. Col. George Crook—six year veteran of Oregon Indian wars—was the man chosen to reverse the fortunes of war. Crook had been released from Libby Prison on August 21, 1865. The next day he married Mary Dailey, the girl who had betrayed him into the hands of his Confederate captors. Now a year later on November 5, 1866, Crook sailed from New York to take command of the 23rd U.S. Infantry Regiment stationed at Fort Boise and presently strung out across eastern Oregon from the Snake River to the Cascade Mountains.

Following a whirlwind inspection of Fort Dalles, Fort Watson and Fort Logan, he arrived at Boise City on December 11, 1866. To celebrate Crook's arrival three employees of the Overland Stage Company hanged Ada County Sheriff Dave Opdyke and left his body dangling along The Dalles-Boise City stage road. Crook was not impressed nor was he overjoyed with the mess he had inherited. He would grimly observe:

> When I arrived at Boise, Indian affairs in that country could not have been worse. That whole country, including northern California and Nevada, eastern Oregon and Idaho up to Montana, you might say was in a state of siege. Hostile Indians were all over that country, dealing death and destruction everywhere they wished. People were afraid to go outside their own doors without protection. There was scarcely a day that reports of Indian depredations were not coming in.[1]

---

1    Schmitt, ed., *General George Crook His Autobiography*, pp. 142-43; McConnell, *Early History of Idaho*, p. 250, "The Hanging of Sheriff Opdyke."

Despite Lt. Col. Crook's outstanding record during the Civil War, he would not be greeted with enthusiasm by the citizens of eastern Oregon and Idaho, for he was regular army. The citizens blamed the army, especially Col. Marshall and his staff officers, for all their misfortunes; totally ignoring the fact that their own interference was hampering the army's effort to gain control over the explosive situation. But there may have been some justification for this bitter resentment. To date, about all that Marshall had accomplished—and the volunteers had done no better—was to kill or capture a few poverty stricken Paiutes while the Paviotso war machine was still running in high gear. Now, to make Crook's new assignment even more unpleasant, the Warm Springs Regulars recruited in November and yet to be tested on the battlefield were placed under his command.

Leaders of this murderous squad were Lieutenants (later Captains) William Cameron McKay and John Darragh—two of the most unlikely candidates that could have been chosen for this bloody war of extermination. One was a licensed physician and the other superintendent of public schools for Wasco County.

Billy McKay—half-brother to Donald McKay, U.S. army scout—was resident physician at the Warm Springs Agency. Oregonians believed that by heritage and experience, McKay was particularly well-suited for this assignment. He was the grandson of Alexander McKay, partner of John Jacob Astor, who was blown up on Astor's ship *Tonquin* in 1811. After Alexander McKay's death, Billy's grandmother, a Chippewa Indian, married Dr. John McLoughlin. Billy's father, the famous trapper and guide Thomas McKay, was twice married. His first wife, a Clatsop girl was Dr. McKay's mother. Tom's second wife, a Cayuse girl (actually a Paiute captive) was the mother of Donald McKay.

Billy McKay's life reflected the profound changes brought on by American emigration to the Pacific Northwest. At an early age through association with McLoughlin, Billy wanted to become a doctor. Dr. Marcus Whitman learned of this interest and made an arrangement with Tom McKay that he would pay for Billy's medical education in exchange for goods and supplies delivered at Fort Walla Walla.[2] With two brothers, John and Alexander, Billy accompanied Jason Lee east in 1838 and enrolled in Fairfield College, New York.[3] He completed his medical training at age 19, too young for a diploma but was granted a license to practice medicine.

Intensely interested in his profession, McKay found little job security in the rapidly changing Hudson's Bay Company in Oregon so he took on various jobs. For a time he was employed as a Hudson's Bay Company store clerk, doctor, trader, miner, soldier, coroner and eventually practiced medicine exclusively. In 1852, he

---

2    Fred Lockley interview with Leila McKay, Portland *Oregon Journal*, October 21, 1927, p. 12.

3    Diary of Rev. Jason Lee, III, *Oregon Historical Quarterly* XVII, December 1916, p. 426.

established a trading post near the present site of Pendleton but during the Yakima War, the hostiles burned him out with a property loss of $19,941.[4]

Billy's first wife, Catharine, died in 1848 from complications after childbirth. A few months later he lost his seven-month-old son, Thomas. The elder McKay would write to his son from California, February 18, 1849: "Nothing gave me such pain to her the deth of the poor little boy. It is a blessing to us still that he is a long side of his mother."[5] Billy McKay then married Margaret Campbell, daughter of Colin Campbell, chief factor of the North West Company in the Peace River country, Canada. Margaret—also half Indian and educated in Winnipeg—was a sister to the wife of James Sinclair, Hudson's Bay Company trader killed by the Yakimas in the 1856 raid at the Cascades of the Columbia River. Billy and Margaret's marriage on October 3, 1856 is the first recorded in Wasco County.[6]

In 1855, McKay served as interpreter and council secretary to Gen. Joel Palmer and Gov. Isaac Stevens in the treaties of 1855. President Lincoln appointed him resident physician at Warm Springs in 1861. In 1864, under an army contract, he served as medical officer to Lt. Halloran's 1st Washington Infantry engaged against the Snakes.

Short and stocky with eyes, hair and skin of the Indian, McKay was blessed with a healthy constitution, a lively sense of humor from both sides of his family and a fondness for Scotch whiskey. It was said that he was always well dressed in a silk hat and Prince Albert coat. Through gold-rimmed spectacles, his dark eyes beamed with kindness and when he spoke, it was with those gentlemanly manners learned long ago at Fort Vancouver.[7] Enlistment at age 42 in the Warm Springs U.S. Regulars would have a profound effect on his life.

McKay's partner in this sordid affair was equally distinguished. John Darragh—36-years-old, a native of New York and well versed in Oregon politics—had served in various civilian capacities at Fort Dalles and was employed as an army packer in Capt. Drake's 1864 campaign.

Darragh arrived in Oregon in 1851 and married Mary Jane Gates, daughter of Nathaniel Gates, a prominent Dalles City attorney who served in both houses of the state legislature. Mary Jane died in March 1866, seven months before John's enlistment in the Warm Springs Regulars, leaving him with two small sons. A versatile man, Darragh served a term as superintendent of schools in Wasco County. After the Shoshoni war, he returned to New York in 1884 to engage in construction work with his brother, building the first skyscraper in New York City.

4    McKay Papers, Umatilla County Library, Pendleton, Oregon.

5    *Oregon Spectator*, June 1, 1848; McKay Papers.

6    Marriage Records, Wasco County Courthouse, The Dalles, Oregon.

7    Roger H. Keane, "Dr. William Cameron McKay," *Pacific Northwest Collection*, University of Oregon Medical School Library, Portland, Oregon, May 1933, p. 37.

Among the buildings he erected were the Vanderbilt mansion, the World Trade building and the Waldorf-Astoria Hotel.[8]

Darragh was highly esteemed by those who knew him, but he encouraged very few to come near enough to know him. He too, would suffer from his war experience. After the Shoshoni campaign, Darragh was described as "a morose, backward, unsocial man never mingling in any social affairs whatever. . . ."[9]

Both McKay and Darragh in giving a personal report of their expedition into the Ochoco, where their red cavalry killed women and children, stressed that it was done in accordance with written and verbal instruction from headquarters. By no means did they blame Lt. Col. Crook when they named headquarters, for Crook, when he found out what the orders were, washed his hands of this shameful mission. These bloodthirsty instructions were coming direct from the state capital at Salem.[10] At the beginning, Lt. McKay felt prestige as an officer in the United States Cavalry but that would soon change. When a similar position was offered a few years later, he flatly refused.

On November 1, 1866, the newly commissioned lieutenants marched their Indian cavalry to Fort Dalles where, for the next three weeks, the Warm Springs Regulars underwent intensive combat training in preparation for a winter assault on the Ochoco. Here, they were armed with .50 calibre Maynard carbines with elevated rear sights:[11] a deadly weapon which made its first appearance in the final days of the Civil War. They were also issued complete cavalry uniforms from the Kossuth hat with crossed sabres down to socks and boots. McKay and Darragh insisted on this regimental attire to distinguish their warriors from those friendly Snakes led by Archie McIntosh, chief scout for Lt. Col. Crook.[12]

The "friendly Snakes" referred to were made up of The Climber's (Tendoy) destitute Lemhi band and eastern Shoshoni mercenaries under leadership of the turncoat warrior Six Feathers. When Gourd Rattler finally caught up with Six Feathers when he returned to the reservation after the war ended in 1868, he killed him. It was commonly believed by the Americans that Gourd Rattler dispatched Six Feathers to the spirit world because of wife abuse. That may be but it's more likely the ex-dog soldier—while he himself believed in playing it safe with superior forces—didn't look favorably upon any of his followers who practiced armed aggression against his own kin and Has No Horse was a blood relative. Anyway,

8   U.S. Census for 1860 and 1870, Wasco County Oregon; *The Dalles Mountaineer*, March 14, 1866; *Oregon Historical Quarterly*, Vol. LXXIX, No. 2. Summer 1978, p. 133.

9   Lord, Elizabeth, *Reminiscences of Eastern Oregon*, Portland, 1903, p. 137.

10  *U.S. Secretary of Interior Report 1867-8*, Vol. III, Pt. II, p. 101, 40th Congress, 2d Session.

11  *Owyhee Avalanche*, August 17, 1867; *Portland Oregonian*, August 24, 1867.

12  National Archives, Record Group 393, Box 6, Roll 72, Letters Received; Lt. Borrowe to Lt. Sanborn, Department of the Columbia, October 27, 1866.

as an Episcopal bishop would slyly note, it cost "only one buck" to get rid of wife-beating on the Wind River Reservation.[13]

Three days before Thanksgiving, accompanied by their families, Gen. Steele, his staff and some prominent Portland businessmen arrived at Fort Dalles for an inspection of the highly-promoted Indian regulars. Dressed in their ceremonial finest, the Warm Springs Cavalry went through their maneuvers during which Steele presented them with the company guidons. At this presentation, he told the Indian troops they were now on an equal footing with the white soldiers to fight the Snakes without mercy as they were hereditary enemies and because of that, they were entrusted the battle flags which they should never surrender.[14] Dutifully impressed, the uniformed warriors performed a war dance for the entertainment of the inspection party.

On Thanksgiving day, Gen. Steele and party with four army deserters (shackled in chains and under heavy guard) returned to Fort Vancouver. Three days later in a drenching rain, the Warm Springs Commandos left for Crooked River. During this march, McKay and Darragh had split company. Lt. Darragh arrived at Camp Steele under cover of a blinding snowstorm on January 4, 1867.[15] As for Lt. McKay, the winter campaign had begun. It would be the beginning of the end for Has No Horse's half-starved army.

When Crook assumed command of the Boise Military District in December, the Snakes were already hemmed in by a cordon of camps and forts with infantry, artillery and cavalry detachments continuously in the field harassing and reducing them in numbers. One of Crook's first acts was to hire competent army scouts. In his opinion, Marshall's chief of scouts, Cayuse George Rundell, was "utterly worthless and demoralized." Heading his list of scouts was Sgt. Timothy O'Toole, Crook's infantry observer during the Civil War and a man to be feared by the Snakes—for nothing escaped his piercing eyes. Added to this roster were Cut-Mouth John whose Umatilla warriors knew the northern Blues almost as well as the Shoshoni and were willing to offer their services to the United States for no other reason than to see the Shoshoni in the same plight they were in. Howard Maupin, veteran of the Mexican War, Wells Fargo station master, and fourth man to take up a claim in the Ochoco also signed on. Rounding out this battery of army scouts was Pete Delore, first man with white blood flowing in his veins to be born upon Shoshoni soil; Donald McKay, brother to William; and Archie McIntosh,

13    Ethelbert Talbot, *My People of the Plains*, pp. 28-9.

14    William McKay, *Journal 1866-67: Indian Scouts*, entries for November 26, 27, 28, 1966; *The Dalles Mountaineer*, November 30, 1866; *The Morning Oregonian*, December 3, 1866.

15    McKay's Journal, Friday, January 4, 1867. Camp Steele was established by Donald McKay in August 1866. It was located on McKay Creek named for Donald and William's father, Thomas McKay.

ex-Hudson's Bay employee who was placed in charge of the Snake mercenaries. These men would serve as Crook's eyes and ears.

One week after his arrival in Boise City, the Snakes drew blood at the mouth of the Boise River. Crook and Capt. David Perry with 45 1st U.S. Cavalrymen, 10 Umatilla scouts and two civilian guides took to the field on December 18 to investigate this latest raid. All Crook packed with him was one change of underclothes and a toothbrush. It would be over two years before he again entered Fort Boise.

Has No Horse's scouts quickly reported the unbelievable news that pony soldiers—who normally stayed safe and snug in their winter fortresses—were riding toward the front. War chiefs prepared to meet this thrust head-on. Big Man with 60 warriors, accompanied by wives and children, moved onto the lower Owyhee River and set up camp. On the afternoon of December 19, McIntosh and Sgt. O'Toole located their hideout. Leaving 10 men to guard the soldiers camp, Crook made a forced night march in near blizzard conditions. Just after daylight, four days before Christmas, Crook attacked.

Slashing through Big Man's camp, the Long Knives killed many Shoshoni as they reeled from their lodges with sleep-filled eyes. The battle continued for three hours . . . an eternity of heartbreak for the dog soldiers as they had never before fought against such grim opposition. Big Man watched in anguish as he suffered his first major defeat. Not only had his wife, Running Deer, been killed in the dawn attack but during the course of battle 28 braves fell under the wicked cross-fire of the cavalry. There was nothing he could do but retreat, leaving some women, children and 30 braves behind. In a final defiant gesture, Big Man charged a soldier who was directing operations as much as Crook himself. They met head-on and when the tangle of horses broke free, the huge Indian—his lance red to the hilt—rode a zig-zagging course toward his defeated warriors . . . a shout of triumph on his lips. Sgt. O'Toole, survivor of 28 major battles in the Civil War, would no longer scout for Gen. Crook. Though Sgt. O'Toole was the only army casualty that day, Crook considered his loss a crushing defeat and both sides vowed there would be a balancing of the account soon.[16]

A few days later Lame Dog, ignorant of Big Man's loss, was moving a small force down the Canyon City-Boise City road to join him. Fifteen miles north of the Owyhee ferry, he camped for the night. At daybreak, January 3, 1867, Crook attacked. Five Shoshoni were killed and the remainder captured. Crook suffered the loss of a civilian guide and three soldiers wounded. Unfortunate for Lame Dog, McIntosh recognized him as one of the signers of the 1865 Walpapi Treaty. On the strength of Lame Dog's implied promise in signing the Klamath treaty "to

---

16 House Executive Document No. 1, 40th Congress, 2d Session, pp. 71, 81; Secretary of War Annual Report 1868, p. 58; Crook, *Autobiography*, p. 144; Bancroft, *History of Oregon*, Vol. II, p. 533.

refrain from warlike practices in the future" Crook had him shot for violating his parole.[17]

Later that same day, while moving up the Malheur River, McIntosh—who had now taken over as Crook's chief of scouts—discovered a hostile camp under the leadership of Storm Cloud, the tough Big Lodge war chief. There was only one problem. Because of a thick tangle of willows and rosebushes flanked by rock walls, there was only one approach to the Indian camp, and that was up a narrow trail nearly a half mile in length which presented one continual ambush the whole distance. Crook would later admit that in all his experience in Indian campaigns, this was the only time he could have used field artillery to advantage. In an unsuccessful attempt to breech the barricade, one soldier was shot but a horseshoe in his shirt pocket saved his life.[18]

By the following morning, Storm Cloud—as good a politician as he was a strategist—forced Crook into the galling position of calling for a truce. Storm Cloud and a few of his warriors came into Crook's camp where it became evident that they were not going to make any peace that was favorable to the Lt. Colonel. Although he toyed with the thought of killing the Snakes while in conference, Crook discarded the idea and called it a stalemate, thankful that affairs terminated as they did.

However, during the discussion, soldiers sneaked into Storm Cloud's stronghold and made off with his horse herd. At this stage of the game, the loss of the horses was like severing an artery to the Snake war tribes. From the Malheur, Crook pushed upriver toward Harney Valley and a rendezvous with Lt. McKay's Warm Springs Cavalry but the weather was so bad—fog, sleet, snowdrifts—that he was forced to turn back to Fort Lyon.

Since entering the bleak highlands of the Crooked River country, McKay's troops-in 26 days of hard riding—had bisected the Ochoco and completed one of the most destructive forays of the Snake campaign to date. The chase began on December 13, 1866, when McKay spotted a smoke toward the head of Crooked River. Leaving Darragh in charge of the pack train with instructions to meet at Camp Steele—north of the confluence of Ochoco and Crooked Rivers—McKay headed southeast toward the Maury Mountains. By now it was entering the holiday season and it seems somehow appropriate to paraphrase a Christmas carol submitted by T.L. Rodgers to the *Oregon Journal*, January 8, 1972:

---

17    *U.S. Interior Report 1867-8*, Vol. III, p. 188, 40th Congress, 2d Session; The *Owyhee Avalanche*, January 5, 1867. It is probable that Lame Dog Creek which flows off the southern breaks of Big Summit Prairie and drains into the North Fork of Crooked River was named for this Shoshoni who took the name "Lame Dog" after being badly crippled in the battle of Rabbit Valley where Lt. Watson was killed.

18    Crook, *Autobiography*, pp. 145-6.

*Hark, the herald angels sing!*
*While our rifles do their thing.*
*Peace on earth and mercy mild,*
*Nice warm grape-shot on your child.*
*Joyful all ye nations rise,*
*See our bullets fall from the skies.*
*With angelic host proclaim,*
*Peace and love for those we maim.*

Near Alkali Butte, McKay picked up a trail some 10 days old but was unable to follow it. However, his scouts located a small Paiute encampment on Bear Creek and all occupants were slaughtered. Moving out onto the high desert, three more peaceful Paiute camps were destroyed. Swinging around Glass Butte—marked as an Indian ammunition factory on army maps—without sighting the hostiles, McKay decided to cut back to the Crooked River valley as his horses, for lack of proper nourishment, were giving out. En route, more Shoshoni families were killed.

On January 4, 1867, McKay united with Darragh and set up winter camp at Camp Steele. That night, their horse herd was stampeded by the Snakes and the following morning—17 days after Big Man's defeat—McKay and Darragh made their move. Pete and Augustin (Quanah) Delore, serving as civilian scouts for the Warm Springs Cavalry, took to the trail.[19] On the morning of January 6, the scouts found a lone footprint track in the snow on the divide between Ochoco and Crooked rivers. Following the tracks, the commandos found a Snake family and killed them, taking their horses and ammunition. Against state government orders, they took two children captive. As Oregon Indian Superintendent Huntington would later report, "the Warm Springs Indians were reluctant to destroy captives whose economic value as slaves was considerable."[20]

Splitting their forces, Darragh headed up Crooked River while McKay took the high country. At daybreak January 7, McKay found Paulina in winter camp on the edge of Big Summit Prairie but the wily chief wasn't caught napping. Paulina had moved out with 50 men, women and children to the snow-covered crags of Round Mountain and there, nearly 2,000 feet above the valley floor, took a stand at timberline. The courage of Paulina backed by the fury of a mountain storm was more than McKay's troops could take. In four hours of intense fighting neither side

---

19   Augustin Delore's nickname "Quanah" was a Shoshoni name. The notorious Comanche war chief who rose to power in the late 1860s was also named Quanah. The Texans on whom he preyed would later call him Quanah Parker after his white mother, Cynthia Ann Parker. Captain Robert Carter, a battle-scarred veteran of the Indian wars blamed Quanah for "some of the foulest deeds ever recorded in the annals of Indian warfare." Capps, *The Great Chiefs*, Time-Life Books, pp. 101-3. Quanah (or Quanna) Delore died October 26, 1891 and was buried at Suplee, Oregon in what was known as the French Cemetery.

20   National Archives Microfilm 2, Roll 10, *Huntington's Annual Report*, August 20, 1867.

gained an advantage. The cavalry killed three Snakes while having one trooper and several horses wounded.

Seeing he could make no gain, McKay dropped down to the upper Ochoco Valley and stumbled onto Has No Horse's encampment on the Ochoco River. If nothing else can be said, McKay had nerve. Unknown to him, Has No Horse, hearing the distant gunshots, had ridden up Canyon Creek with every warrior in camp to give aid to Paulina. McKay with 40 men—one of whom was badly wounded—charged through the village at full gallop and was on his way toward Claypool and Smith's cabins at the mouth of Mill Creek before the Shoshoni knew what hit them. In his wake, he left 12 dead and was packing four women and six children to be sold as slaves at Warm Springs.[21]

In the Ochoco Valley, the snow was only 14 inches deep but the cavalry horses gave out and McKay took refuge on a small side creek where six months later the ill-fated Camp Brown was located. Here, he hid out until late evening and—missing the settler's cabins in the dark—drug into Camp Steele at two o'clock in the morning.

Meanwhile, Paulina and Has No Horse struck out on McKay's back trail for they suspicioned that a larger force was bringing up the rear. In the late afternoon, they hit Darragh on Crooked River. Badly outnumbered, Darragh was soon put to flight. He holed up in the rocks and managed to stave off the dog solders until darkness fell. And so, the same night that McKay was making his run down the Ochoco toward Camp Steele, Darragh—packing six Snake scalps—was riding for the same goal down Crooked River. He was also minus five men and carrying three wounded.

The major accomplishment on this raid—aside from killing 10 warriors and 14 women and children—was, that after nine years of warfare, the Warm Springs death squad had finally located the war tribes' main base of operations. Darragh in his report to headquarters, dated January 10, would reveal "... east was Paulina's and Ochoco's winter campground, and to it they retire after their predatory excursions toward the Canyon City road. They bring their booty to this place and subsist for the winter upon their plunder. . . ."[22] Fortunately for the Shoshoni, this intelligence would be ignored.

McKay and Darragh were continuously on patrol, working a huge semi-circle north to south of Camp Steele for they fully expected a retaliatory attack. It was also their duty to keep a constant check on the settler's cabins sitting deep within the hostiles bounds of Shoshoni territory. Some 12 miles east of Camp Steele at

---

21  McKay's Journal entries from Dec. 13, 1866 to January 8, 1867; Bancroft, *History of Oregon*, Vol. II, p. 533; Gregg, *Pioneer Days*, p. 32; Report of Commissioner of Indian Affairs 1867, Congressional Document Series No. 1326, pp. 99-100.

22  Bureau of Indian Affairs, Oregon Superintendency, 1866-69, Letters Received, Lt. Darragh to Lt. Borrowe, Camp Steele, January 10, 1867.

the mouth of Mill Creek, six white men had taken homestead claims in the fall of 1866; and only by the grace of God and the watchful eyes of the U.S. military had they lasted this long.

On January 19, eleven days after the raid on Paulina's camp, several gunshots could be heard in the close vicinity of camp. Quanah Delore and 10 troopers were dispatched to find out what was going on. Delore struck the tracks of a lone Snake on foot less than a half mile from the army outpost. Tracking the warrior some four miles, the trackers gave up the chase. Crossing a high ridge, they spotted smoke from an Indian camp some eight miles northeast of Camp Steele and returned to the outpost to report. They had also seen a single smoke to the west which Delore believed was the camp of the hunter they had been following. At midnight, Lt. McKay dispatched 30 Warm Springs commandos to attack the main encampment at dawn.

Twelve hours earlier, Wahi—The Fox—had left a cold and desolate circle of lodges huddled at the base of a dark bluff at the mouth of Allen Creek. The only sound in camp was the crying of a hungry baby. Each year since the arrival of the hated white men, game had become increasingly scarce and the winter of '67 was no exception. With most of the young men following Has No Horse and Paulina across the bleak winter battlegrounds of interior Oregon, provisions were even more limited, for the old men and women didn't have the strength to track game. But soon, there would be rejoicing for Fox was returning with fresh venison. With dawn's first light, he shouldered the deer carcass and joyously headed toward the Shoshoni camp knowing the hearts of the people would be lifted for today there would be fresh meat on the cooking fire and happiness in every tipi. Then he heard gunfire.

Everyone was slumbering peacefully when McKay's raiders—leaving horses and great coats behind—slipped into camp. They crept in so close that the Snakes were cut off from a fortification they had thrown up on the edge of camp, and as dawn streaked the sky, they commenced firing. In a brutal 10 minutes of savagery, men, women and children fell under the deadly fire of Maynard carbines. It was Sunday morning, January 20 and in the white settlements, church bells were calling the faithful to prayer.

Later that day, Lt. McKay dispassionately notes:

Still snowing at 7 1/2 o'clock left camp to join our scouting party. Met them coming back with 9 scalps had demolished and annihilated the camp & not one escaped them traveled 3 miles further killed 1 man 1 woman & child & surprised another camp and demolished it. Killed 5 women and 1 child. Still snowing we concluded to return to camp on Crooked River arrived 3 1/2 o'clock.[23]

---

23    McKay's Journal, entry for Sunday, January 20, 1867, *Oregon Historical Quarterly*, Vol.

Shortly after the Warm Springs Cavalry left the first Shoshoni camp, Fox arrived. Hoping, yet knowing, he searched frantically through the devastated lodges, then saw the familiar figure crumpled in the blood-stained snow. No longer was Hoctu—Willow Girl—beautiful. Willow Girl, the daughter of Left Hand, the fanatic Lohim medicine man, and Fox's wife was dead . . . her face crushed beyond recognition from the jarring impact of a Wasco war club. Holding her body aloft, Fox uttered the terrible blood-oath of the Shoshoni brave: "Hear me, Mighty One above! I will have blood for blood though twice ten snows whiten the ground before I find the ones who have wronged me and made desolate my heart. Hear me, Mighty One!"

Lowering Willow Girl's body into his arms, her lifeblood freezing to his chest, Fox made the lonely journey to Left Hand's camp. For this act of brutality, the invaders were to witness savagery at its very worst. Within weeks, soldiers and civilians were being stalked for the sole purpose of slow death. They who set the rules would now pay the penalty, for the all-consuming rage of Left Hand, driven by grief, could inflame the Shoshoni to do anything he desired.

Following this day of carnage, McKay and Darragh began a sweep of the lower Ochoco and Crooked River valleys. Finding small encampments of 10 or 20, they systematically wiped them out. The army couldn't have picked a better year for a winter campaign. Instead of bitter cold and snow, the weather was mild and raining. In a three day period in January, McKay would report: "Sun shone through the day. Nothing new. The snow is disappearing round the hills the creek is rising." The next day, "One of my horses perished in a mudhole. . . ." And the following day, "Very muddy bad as Wallomette incessant Rain. . . ."[24]

The Warm Springs special unit was also killing all game from the largest animals to the smallest. This was an official order that was sweeping the West . . . wipe out the Indians and also their food supply. Over to the east, a hide-hunter named Bill Cody was gaining a reputation, but the all-time champion was Tom Nixon. By alternating a Sharps "Big Fifty" rifle and a Springfield needle gun, Nixon dropped 140 buffalo at one stand in 40 minutes. In one 30-day stretch of sustained slaughter, sharp shooting Nixon rolled up the incredible score of 2,173 kills. On the westside, the same destruction took place on deer, antelope and elk. By the end of the Shoshoni campaign, the rimrock bighorn sheep had become extinct in eastern Oregon.

While Darragh and McKay continued their rape of the Crooked River Basin, Crook began his death march from the east. By April, William McKay and John Darragh—for their part in this gory conquest—would be advanced in rank to captain in the United States Cavalry by order of Gen. Steele.

LXXIX, No. 2, p. 152; Darragh's Report to Lt. Borrowe, January 31, 1867, Oregon Superintendency, Indian Affairs Records, Letters Received 1866-69, pp. 97-108.
24    McKay's Journal, entries for January 27, 28, 29, 1867.

CHAPTER 138

# SNOW WARRIORS

*My God! Have I got to go out and be killed in such cold
weather?*

**Capt. James C. Hunt**
1st United States Cavalry

After his unsuccessful bout with Storm Cloud, Crook jammed northwest to
tie in with the Warm Springs Cavalry. Finding the going tougher than he had
anticipated, he turned back near the head of the Malheur River and retired to the
nearest available army post to wait for a break in the weather. Although Fort
Watson was less than 80 miles away, it was impossible to reach it over the snow
clogged passes of the southern Blues so he turned south and headed for Fort Lyon,
where he arrived in early January.

Crook was not impressed with conditions at Fort Lyon under the command
of Capt. James Hunt, 1st United States Cavalry. It seemed that the garrison did
nothing more than drink and play with the Paiute house maids. Crook would dryly
remark, "From appearances and information, the normal condition of the officers
there was drunkenness."[1] Sending Capt. David Perry back to Fort Boise with the
Shoshoni prisoners of war, Crook, taking Capt. Hunt with two cavalry companies
and four civilian scouts, again marched toward Harney Valley on January 14. It
was on this forced march that Capt. Hunt complained of being forced out into the
cold to die. Ten years later, Capt. John Hale of the 7th Cavalry would voice the
same opinion as he rode to his death on Snake Creek, October 3, 1877.

At the eastern base of the Steens, Crook's scouts located Cougar Tail's winter
camp. Operating on the theory that a surprise attack was apt to weaken an Indian's
courage even more than that of a white man, Crook—shooting through the
tipis—struck at daylight. Hunt's cavalry, unused to such tactics, went ballistic.
Crook claimed that during the battle he was in more danger from his own troops
than he was from the enemy. Instead of obeying instructions, "they got excited and
the bullets whistled by me. My horse got excited and ran through the village so the

---

1    All direct quotations in this chapter, unless otherwise noted, are taken from *General George
Crook, His Autobiography.*

whole troop followed!" In an effort to gain some order, Crook leaped off his horse and ran back toward the village with Indians running to meet him.

Cougar Tail, a formidable man, was literally shot to shreds before he finally went down. During this suicidal charge, he was chanting: "Sky Father, I am going out to die. For Myself I grieve not, but for those who are left behind. Let not fear enter into my heart. I am going out to die." Crook would report that "one fellow, a big powerful man, surrounded by soldiers, singing his own death song was snapping arrows into the enemy. He must have been shot through and through a half dozen times before he fell." A civilian packer from Silver City—shot through the heart—was Crook's only casualty. The soldiers killed all the warriors but two, who escaped. Gathering up the surviving women, Crook delivered them to Major Jesse Walker at Fort C.F. Smith.

Picking up two more companies of cavalry, he started his march of destruction toward Fort Warner on January 21. By now, Crook had 200 cavalrymen at his back. Eight days after Crook left Fort C.F. Smith, General Order No. 5 (dated January 29, 1867) exploded across the eastern Oregon frontier when it discontinued the Boise Military District. A new combat area—the Owyhee Military District—had been formed made up of Forts Boise, Lyon, Winthrop, C.F. Smith, McDermit, Winfield Scott and Warner under the command of Lt. Col. George Crook.

When Crook's column left Fort C.F. Smith, they headed into a blinding blizzard bucking snowdrifts 15 to 20 feet deep. Horses sank out of sight in drifts and as fast as animals could be pulled free, the wind filled their tracks with sifting snow so that the cavalry column left no trail in passing. "It was," revealed Crook, "almost like traveling in the dark." The weather was completely baffling. They attacked a Paiute village in a blizzard but by noon everything "was serene and lovely" and as Crook marveled, "I actually saw grasshoppers jumping about this 24th day of January."

Crook was now moving with several converging columns, each able to take care of itself under any and all circumstances. Each column was provided with an effective train of pack-mules and with a corps of civilian guides. With beards and hair frozen with sleet, the snow warriors made certain that several bands of Paiutes were "cleaned up on the way."[2] Caught in a blizzard in Catlow Valley, the entire command was compelled to walk in small circles in the snow for two days and nights, not daring to lie down or sleep lest they should freeze. When the storm broke, Archie McIntosh found a soldier who had become lost and perished in the snow.[3]

---

2    Captain John G. Bourke, "General Crook in the Indian Country," *Century Magazine*, Vol. XLI, No. 5 (March 1891), p. 2.

3    The *Owyhee Avalanche*, April 6, 1867.

McIntosh, a half-blood, was no cast-off as were many of the self-styled guides on the frontier. He had been brought up by the Hudson's Bay Company and knew his business. On a bleak February afternoon, McIntosh—who had been in south central Oregon only once before and was roaring drunk at the time—led Crook's haggard column into Fort Warner more dead than alive. En route the winds were so strong that they nearly blew the soldiers out of their saddles, while 200 miles to the north, McKay and Darragh were experiencing unseasonably warm weather. Crook, a man of great physical stamina admitted he was never so near exhaustion in his whole life. "I was so much fatigued at the incessant blowing of the wind. It seemed to blow one's vitality out of him."

To his dismay, Crook found the garrison deserted. The barracks, haystacks and corrals were completely buried with snow. Sgt. Willey—one of the more experienced men who had served in the Oregon Cavalry—was sent to Warner Peak to check the surrounding area. He became lost and froze to death in a blizzard.

It was now obvious that Fort Warner was not located in the best of spots. Being inaccessible during most of the winter months, it had to be relocated. Warner Lake was 70 miles long and 15 miles wide but opposite Crook's camp it narrowed down to about 400 yards. In sub-zero weather, the troopers finally made a trail across to the western shore. A few months later, Capt. Darragh widened this access road enough for wagons to cross, which made a great saving in distance from Fort Klamath to Fort C.F. Smith.

During this project, McIntosh had been dispatched to Fort Bidwell to bring back a wagon-load of supplies. When he didn't show up in a couple of days, Crook figured the Shoshoni had gotten him. He finally arrived back, crossing Warner Lake on the ice. Perched in the supply wagon were two Paiute women whom Archie swore he had captured in battle. He told a glorious tale of attack and counterattack but being staggering drunk, Crook decided the hostiles seen and slain were mostly in Archie's mind.

Leaving 40 men to man Fort Warner, Crook again took to the snow drifted desert, arriving back at Fort C.F. Smith on February 22. Still on the prowl, he made a scout to the Pueblo Mountains, killing two warriors and capturing their wives and children. The snow was so deep in the Pueblo's he had to abandon that push.[4] With army messengers reporting near spring-like conditions to the north, Crook again made a drive on the Ochoco which, thus far, he'd been unable to reach.

During his winter hell on the southern front, the northern battlefield was inundated with rain. Lt. McKay would note on February 1—when Crook's column was bucking 15-foot snowdrifts—that he sank his boat while trying to cross the swollen Deschutes River and it was "raining like mischief the whole day."[5] His troops, having pretty well killed every Shoshoni in the lower Crooked River and

---

4    *Secretary of War Annual Report 1868*, p. 59.
5    McKay's Journal entry for Friday, February 1, 1867.

lower Ochoco valleys, were now methodically slaughtering all the game. Many of the Warm Springs soldiers' wives had left the reservation and were now staying at Camp Steele where they could join in on the sport. This interlude would soon come to a halt.

Crook sent a message ahead for McKay to renew attacks out of Camp Steele while Lt. Darragh was ordered to join him on the headwaters of Crooked River. On March 14, McKay made a noncommittal notation in his journal that "the women all left to day for the Reservation." Darragh and the death squad rode southeast. Before they arrived at Crook's camp the following day, an age-old weapon of warfare was unleashed upon the unsuspecting regulars. Crook was now tangling with the dog soldiers and the element of surprise would take a different turn.

As Crook's column moved north through Harney Valley, the weather became warmer and drier. By the time they reached the big prairie on the head of Crooked River a brisk warm wind was blowing and the stirrup-high grass—although new green shoots were appearing on the bottom stalks—was tinder dry. In this basin covered with ample horse feed, Crook set up camp to await Darragh's arrival. On March 15, shortly before noon, spirals of smoke popped up on all sides. The Shoshoni had torched the prairie and for a period of time it was chaos. Cavalry mounts stampeded, pack-mules threw off their loads and the Long Knives charged in all directions to find . . . nothing. Crook was not pleased.

It now became a forced march into the timbered canyons of the Ochoco. In seven days of grueling chase, covering some 200 torturous miles of vanishing trails, the cavalry managed to kill 24 hostiles with the loss of three men. Then on the evening of March 23, as Crook made a night ride into Fort Watson, a glaring light streaked across the sky followed by a sonic boom. Back at Camp Steele, McKay would record in his journal that "a meaterur [meteor] fell about half a mile from camp made a report like a cannon."[6] That did it for the Warm Springs Cavalry. This heavenly warning was a bad sign and they high-tailed it to the safety of the reservation. Lt. McKay would put it quite diplomatically. Since they were accomplishing little in the way of body-count, he granted his troops a furlough to return to Warm Springs where incidentally, they stayed for the next six weeks.

Seven days after Crook rode into Fort Watson to pick up fresh cavalry mounts for his saddle-weary troops, the United States on March 30, 1867—for the sum of 7.2 million dollars—acquired another 375 million acres for exploitation. William Seward, secretary of state, through negotiations with Alexander II, Czar of Russia, added Russian America to the vast public domain. Many American politicians and journalists criticized this purchase, dubbing it "Seward's Folly." Seward named the newly acquired territory Alaska, a corruption of an Aleut word meaning "a great country." The Aleuts, Eskimos, Tlingits and Athabascans would now come under American rule. This acquisition was of significance to Oregon because it

---

6     McKay's Journal entry for Saturday, March 21, 1867.

meant increased water trade with the northern region and Portland was to become a secondary gateway to the new territory.

Meantime, Lt. Darragh on his return to Camp Steele would set the stage for some unwanted trouble.

Paulina in 1864, taken at Fort Klamath when he went there to try to get his wife, Falling Star, after the army kidnapped her.

*Courtesy of Gale Ontko.*

Terr. Gov. John Gaines

*Courtesy of the Oregon State Archives.*

Terr. Gov. George Law Curry

*Courtesy of the Oregon State Archives.*

**John Gaines**, a veteran of the Mexican War, was a man of personal integrity but he rubbed his constituents the wrong way. Because of this he could get little cooperation in making a success of his governorship. During his term of office the first of a series of Indian wars broke out in Oregon.

**George Curry**, a newspaper man, had little formal education but was a natural politician. Curry County was named after him. His wife, Chloe Donnelly Boone, was a great-granddaughter of Daniel Boone.

**"Honest John" Whiteaker** was Oregon's first governor after statehood. He was usually described as an unschooled, self-educated, fringe-whiskered, and hot-tempered farmer politician.

Gov. John Whiteaker

*Courtesy of the Oregon State Archives.*

Gov. Addison C. Gibbs

*Courtesy of the Oregon State Archives.*

Gov. George Woods

*Courtesy of the Oregon State Archives.*

**Addison Gibbs**, a lawyer, was an antislavery Democrat who acted vigorously to keep Oregon in the Union. Before his tour of duty was over, he became a Republican.

**George Woods**, only 34 when elected, served in stormy times. The Shoshoni war was in full swing. Commerce and communications in eastern Oregon were severely crippled. In desperation, Woods urged a war of extermination. The War Department refused to carry out his order. Woods later served a four-year term as governor of Utah Territory.

Sen. Joseph Lane (1859-1861)

*DAP; engraving by John C. Buttre.*

Sen. Edward Baker (1861)

*Courtesy of the United States Senate.*

**Jo Lane**, first territorial governor, delegate to Congress and U.S. senator, was the Democratic candidate for vice president in 1860. Because of his pro-slavery attitudes and strong southern sympathies he never again held public office. Lane County is named after him. **Edward Baker** was elected Oregon's first U.S. senator after less than a year's residence. Statesman, orator, soldier and brilliant criminal lawyer, he was Abraham Lincoln's law partner. Baker was the first northern officer to die in the Civil War. Baker County is named after him. **James Nesmith**, a veteran of the Oregon Indian wars, was appointed superintendent of Oregon Indian Affairs in 1857. He then served in the U.S. Senate from 1861-1867. A strong abolitionist, Nesmith was the only Democratic senator to vote for the abolition of slavery amendment.

Sen. James Nesmith (1861-1867)

*Courtesy of the United States Senate.*

Sen. Benjamin Stark (1861-1862)

*Courtesy of the United States Senate.*

Sen. Benjamin Harding (1862-1865)

*Courtesy of the United States Senate.*

Sen. Thomas A. Hendricks (1867)
of Illinois.

*Courtesy of the United States Senate.*

**Benjamin Stark**, a Portland merchant, was appointed by Gov. Whiteaker to serve the unexpired term of Senator Baker. He was a strong pro-slavery advocate and opposed the establishment of public grade schools. He made a fortune selling town lots in Portland and Stark Street is named after him. **Benjamin Harding**, a Republican, was one of the ruling spirits of the Union cause. He also served as U.S. district attorney. Both Ben and his brother Edward served as captains in the 1st Oregon Cavalry during the Shoshoni war. **Thomas Hendricks**, a distinguished senator and vice president of the United States during Grover Cleveland's administration (1885-89), was brother to Dr. Hendricks, the doctor whose political ambitions were ruined because of his connection with the Brown tragedy in Canyon City (see Chp. 103).

Klamath Agency Indian Agent
Lindsay Applegate.

His son, Capt. Oliver Applegate was the
commanding officer of the U.S. Axe and Rifle
Squad, made up entirely of Klamath and
Modoc Indians.

*Courtesy of Carrol Howe,*
Unconquered, Uncontrolled.

George C. Hough

Special Indian Agent Hough, stationed
in Boise City, Idaho, tried to help the
eastern Oregon Shoshoni who were
being ignored by the
Oregon officials. He
would note that unless
they were given some
food, they would most
likely starve during the
severe winter of 1866-67.
Hough served as first
U.S. attorney for Idaho
Territory from 1863 to
1868, the same period as
the Shoshoni war.

*Courtesy of*
*Idaho State Historical Society,*
*photo #1108-H.*

William (Bud) Thompson

A Canyon City packer who claimed he had "done in" Big Man.

*Courtesy of Crook County Historical Society,*
*Bowman Museum.*

Cynthia Ann Parker with
Prairie Flower

The niece of Isaac Parker (a Texas legislator), Cynthia Ann, who had been taken captive by the Comanches as a girl, became the bride of Peta Nocona, a Comanche war chief. She bore him three children: two sons and a daughter. While camped on the Pease River in 1860, her tribe was attacked by government Indian hunters. Cynthia's husband and teenage son escaped. Quanah, the oldest son, would become a noted Comanche warrior (see first photo section). Prairie Flower died from a fever while in the white settlements. Devastated with grief over the loss of her family, Cynthia Ann starved herself to death (see *Thunder Over the Ochoco*, Vol. 1, pg. 38).

*Courtesy of the*
*Barnard (George) Papers,*
*The Texas Collection,*
*Baylor University, Waco, Texas.*

Allen David

Klamath chief and lieutenant in the U.S. Axe and Rifle Squad.

*Courtesy of Carrol Howe,*
Unconquered, Uncontrolled, *1992.*

Below:

Donald McKay

U.S. Army scout and brother to Capt. William McKay of the 1st Warm Springs U.S. Regulars.

*Courtesy of California History Section,*
*California State Library, Sacramento.*

Old Schonchin

Head chief of the Modocs and silent partner in the Shoshoni war effort.

*Courtesy of Carrol Howe,*
*Unconquered, Uncontrolled.*

Below:

Col. Charles McDermitt
and family

Commander of the 2nd California Cavalry, McDermitt was killed by the Shoshoni.

*Courtesy of Nevada Historical Society, Reno.*

Maj. William Rinehart

*Courtesy of Southern Oregon Historical Society.*

Lt. John Small

*Courtesy of Lake County Museum, Lakeview, Oregon.*

These men, all officers in the 1st Oregon Cavalry, made the first dedicated military attack on Has No Horse's defense of the Ochoco and. . . failed.

**Maj. Rinehart** later became the supervisor of the Malheur Reservation; **Lt. Small** constructed Fort Watson; and **Capt. Currey** shared joint command with Capt. Drake in the first assault on the Shoshoni-controlled Ochoco.

Capt. George Currey

*Courtesy of Oregon Historical Society*
*negative number CN 020568.*

Capt. John Drake

*Courtesy of Steve Lent
and the Crook County Historical Society.*

Lt. James A. Waymire

*From* The History of the
Bench and Bar of California, *1901.*

Maj. Henry D. Wallen

*Courtesy of Massachusetts Commandery,
Military Order of the Loyal Legion and
the U.S. Army Military History Institute.*

**Capt. Drake** led the first military expedition into the Crooked River valley and established Fort Maury.

**Lt. Waymire** established the short-lived Fort Lincoln on the South Fork of the John Day River and made the first armed contact with Has No Horse's dog soldiers. He would report "no signal success." Waymire later became a highly respected California judge.

**Maj. Wallen,** a combat infantry officer in command of a battalion of Army engineers, opened the first military road across eastern Oregon from Fort Dalles to Camp Floyd, Utah. He would discover evidence of Spanish colonization in Harney Valley which had occurred 150 years before his passage.

Gen. George Wright

Gen. Benjamin Alvord

**Gen. Wright** was in command of the Military District of Oregon at the start of the Shoshoni war. In 1861 he was sent to California but in 1865 was transferred back to Oregon. En route he was lost at sea aboard the *Brother Jonathan*.

**Gen. Alvord** was prominent in early Indian wars, particularly in eastern Oregon, where he was commander of the Department of Oregon. From 1872 until his retirement in 1880 he was paymaster general of the Army, and the Alvord Desert in southeastern Oregon is named after him.

**Col. Maury**, a career Army officer who received his field commission during the Mexican War, was in charge of the Army supply trains going into eastern Oregon. The Maury mountains in central Oregon are named for him.

Col. Reuben Maury

Major Enoch Steen

*Courtesy of Steve Lent*
*and the Crook County Historical Society.*

Major Andrew J. Smith

*Courtesy of Massachusetts Commandery,*
*Military Order of the Loyal Legion and*
*the U.S. Army Military History Institute.*

Lt. John McCall

*Courtesy of Steve Lent*
*and the Crook County Historical Society.*

**Maj. Steen** and **Maj. Smith** were sent to further explore Wallen's route across interior Oregon and make it safe for travel. They were chased back to the Columbia by hostile Shoshoni. Stein's Pillar (correct spelling) in central Oregon and Steens Mountain in southeastern Oregon were named for Maj. Steen.

**Lt. McCall**, a veteran of the Yakima War, was accused of causing Lt. Watson's death in the Paulina area. It was a false accusation.

The suspected grave of Lt. Stephen Watson, killed in Rabbit Valley on May 18, 1864 (Fort Watson Cemetery).

*Courtesy of Gale Ontko.*

The site of Fort Lincoln on the South Fork of the John Day River, which was the first military stockade erected in central Oregon.

*Courtesy of Gale Ontko.*

The Brennen Palisades on Mill Creek, some 16 miles east of Prineville, Oregon. This is typical of the rock fortresses used by the Shoshoni to ambush the U.S. Cavalry.

*Courtesy of Gale Ontko.*

Markers in the old Fort Watson Cemetery for the soldiers killed at the Battle of Watson Spring in Rabbit Valley, May 18, 1864.

*Courtesy of Gale Ontko.*

Headstones of civilians at the Fort Watson Cemetery.

*Courtesy of Gale Ontko.*

Another Shoshoni fortress on the John Day River, a few miles northwest of Dayville, Oregon.

*Courtesy of Gale Ontko.*

Fort Klamath

Fort Klamath was set in a well-watered natural meadow. The buildings were made of lumber and were much different from the concept of a traditional fort.

*Photo and caption courtesy of Carrol B. Howe,* Unconquered Uncontrolled.

Fort Klamath

U.S. Cavalrymen lined up in front of the barracks at Fort Klamath.

*Photo and caption courtesy of Carrol B. Howe,* Unconquered Uncontrolled.

CHAPTER 139

# INTENT TO KILL

*She heard the dead man say—*
*Look for me by moonlight;*
*Watch for me by moonlight;*
*I'll come to thee by moonlight,*
*Though hell should bar the way!*

**Alfred Noyes**
The Highwayman

When Lt. John Darragh arrived back at Camp Steele, he found the post abandoned. In his journal, Lt. William McKay would note that he and his troops had left the outpost on March 29 and arrived at the Warm Springs Agency at noon. He would also mention that the Indian cavalry held a war dance "principally amongst the Wascos around the [Agency] flagstaff." Low on supplies, Darragh also decided to return to Warm Springs, leaving his command at Camp Steele under the guidance of his chief scout, Billy Chinook, now going by the name of William C. Parker.[1] Darragh arrived at the agency on March 30 and the following morning started for Fort Dalles with the army pack train. Within five days, all hell would break loose on Dry Creek, some eight miles up Crooked River from Camp Steele. By coincidence, McKay with the Delore brothers would arrive at Fort Dalles on April 14 but make no entries on troop movements until May 14, 1867.

While the fire-bugs, Has No Horse and Paulina, were keeping things lively in the inner Ochoco, Lake Hunter with a small following of men, women and children in search of food, slipped into the lower Crooked River Valley and set up camp at the mouth of Dry Creek.[2] They had come to this area to take advantage of the spring salmon run in Crooked River and to gather bitter roots—a nutritious herb—which grew only in a few isolated spots in the western Ochoco.[3] Within a

---

1    Billy Chinook's headstone on the Warm Springs Reservation bears the inscription "William Chinook Parker, December 9, 1890."

2    This campsite was located in the vicinity of the present Stearns Ranch [Quail Valley Ranch, 1994] some five miles south of Prineville, Oregon. In the 1950s Bill Jackson found a rusted army Colt revolver in the rimrocks adjacent to this old Indian encampment.

3    These bitter root beds, southeast of Stearns Butte, at the head of Juniper Canyon and less than

few days, their camp would come under army surveillance.

Lake Hunter, in an unforgivable lack of precaution while in enemy territory, would pay dearly for this mistake. Believing all the Warm Springs Cavalry had returned to the reservation, he neglected to post guards. He was wrong. After Lt. Darragh had left, the troopers had lolled around camp, sleeping and gorging themselves on venison. Finally, Sgt. Parker went on a scout and spotted Lake Hunter's unguarded camp. Bursting with excitement, he returned to Camp Steele and didn't even wait for a dawn attack.

Dusk was coming to the Ochoco as the muffled hoofbeats of dozens of horses jarred the unsuspecting Shoshoni camp into hushed expectancy. Each person, even the children, paused as though suspended in air. Then the guttural Wasco war cry rent the air. Men had barely time to reach their weapons before they were clubbed from their hands by screaming warriors in U.S. Cavalry uniforms. . . . forty-six heavily armed soldiers against 27 Shoshoni men, women and children. Wives saw bullet-riddled husbands fall to the ground; husbands saw wives split from breast to thigh with razor-sharp cavalry sabres; mothers screamed as babes were trampled beneath horses' hooves; and children cried pitifully as mothers were dragged to death.

In ten minutes, the slaughter was complete except for three Shoshoni women, one old man and two children. As proof of their valor, the Warm Springs raiders would take these captives to the reservation for entertainment at the victory dance. By now, Sgt. Parker—sobered by this blood-orgy—began making hasty preparations to vacate the grim scene. There was always the possibility that dog soldiers were in the area and had heard the gunfire. As his men gathered scalps, Sgt. Billy Chinook Parker decided to head straight for the reservation.

The woman Bright Eyes had been held captive before and escaped. Because of this, she knew she was destined for a slow death. Suddenly, Bright Eyes was filled with confidence as a bloody hulk that once had been a Snake warrior, moved ever so slightly. Lake Hunter, her husband was alive. No emotion crossed her face to betray this as Lake Hunter deftly signaled to her in sign language . . . "I will come for you." She saw no more for a husky Klickitat brave slapped her harshly into line with the other captives and the march to Warm Springs began.

Painfully, Lake Hunter rolled his bleeding body to a sitting position, retched, maintained his balance, then after several faltering attempts rose to his feet and wrapped his scalp-torn head with a piece of dirty blanket. Through broken teeth, a thin whistle echoed up Crooked River Gorge . . . followed by the appearance of a crow-bait pony, unsightly enough even for Warm Springs tastes. Lake Hunter knew that Black Eagle, his brother-in-law was camped less than 10 miles away.

a half mile south of the present Prineville reservoir highway were still being harvested by the Warm Springs Indians as late as the 1970s.

He must reach that camp before he died. He didn't quite make it but Black Eagle, who had heard the rifle shots, intercepted the mortally wounded man and after gasping out what happened, Lake Hunter died.[4]

Three hawk-faced men took the Shoshoni oath of vengeance and with faces painted black, rode west—because the woman captive who was to provide entertainment for the reservation Indians was their sister. It is certain that Has No Horse offered the best men he could spare but this was a personal affair. The brothers must settle the score in their own way. Victories over women, and children, whose tiny scalps decorated Wasco lodges the same as a Snake warrior's would be avenged. Let the Bowl Makers and Little Rivers sing of their pitiful conquests—the days of celebration would be to be short-lived.

Before Monday, April 8,—the day Lt. McKay left for Fort Dalles—had slipped into night, the reservation was in chaos. The Warm Springs Regulars, joined by friends and relatives, were reveling in their latest victory: dancing, drinking and abusing Shoshoni slaves taken in earlier raids. Agent John Smith and Department employees were sickened but there was little that could be done to curb the Wascos' savage passion. Risking his own life, Smith milled with the Indians, talking in an effort to quiet frayed nerves for in their condition, the Warm Springs Cavalry could wipe out the agency and kill every white man in the near vicinity. Even their commanding officers—had they been present—would have held no sway over this frenzied mob. Agent Smith couldn't risk sending a rider to Fort Dalles for that would show the Indians that the whites were afraid. All that remained was to pray and await the whims of the crazed throng. All civilian personnel knew the agency was in for a night of raw emotional hell. Smith's nieces, who were visiting from the Willamette Valley, would record this night of terror in the family Bible.[5]

That afternoon three Shoshoni warriors glided through the lower Crooked River Valley, pausing long enough to set fire to the now abandoned Camp Steele. As darkness fell, they struck the familiar trail across Agency Plain as drum beats mingled with peals of laughter guided them to the hostile camp, sitting in a huge semi-circle around the Warm Springs Agency headquarters building. All they had to do was enter the largest concentrated camp of confederated tribesmen east of the Cascades, locate the lodge of their head chief and . . . assassinate him!

A Shoshoni woman spread-eagled between two upright poles—her body some four feet above the ground—watched stoically as a fire curled at her feet and licked hungrily at her ankles. Braves, drunk on victory and rot-gut whiskey, circled

---

4    As remembered by Dave Chocktote, son of the White Knife war chief Black Buffalo and Tom Ochiho, grandson of Has No Horse.

5    As remembered by descendants of Captain John Smith who settled in Prineville, Oregon. Captain Smith was agent at Warm Springs from November 4, 1865 to June 30, 1869; and again agent from May 7, 1871 to January 18, 1884 when he died.

the squirming figure, reaching out with lances to nick her body, now streaked with trickles of blood. In the barricaded agency headquarters, Smith's nieces could not sleep, thinking of this poor girl—not much older than they—and waiting for the screams that never came. To pass the agonizing hours, they wrote in the Smith family Bible.

As the tempo increased, Bright Eyes heard the lonely trill of a night hawk and sudden relief flooded her pain-wracked face. Eyes that had mirrored agony filled with thanksgiving. To her, that haunting call meant many things . . . happy childhood days in the Ochoco; the love of an Indian boy for his little sister; the promise of vengeance by a big brother who never failed; and above all, relief from torture . . . a call that begged forgiveness for what must be done and her heart answered that plea. Lifting her head, she smiled toward the darkness and in that instant, the Great Spirit took Bright Eyes' hands and lifted her into the Land of her Fathers.

Black Eagle's aim was true and merciful. The Warm Springs celebrants never knew until the following morning why the unflinching Shoshoni woman died with a smile on her lips. Beneath her left breast, barely visible in the morning light, protruded the haft of a miniature war arrow . . . hafted with black eagle feathers.

Near midnight, Queapama headed for his tipi. A drunken brave staggered into the darkness and a shadow, quick as a lunging puma, struck. The man sank to the ground with a low moan, his neck snapped like a pine twig. Wolf Dog grinned and awaited the next victim. Black Eagle, his hunting knife red to the hilt, was concentrating on men in cavalry uniform. Inside the tipi, Queapama paused as his eyes became accustomed to the fire's dim glow. A look of horror crossed his face as his eyes focused on the twisted features of Paulina, his teeth bared in a wolfish snarl. Before Queapama's scream could leave his throat, the avenging Snake had struck.

The drunken revelers were suddenly jarred back into reality by the mournful yip of the Shoshoni hunting call . . . a yell born on the very edge of camp as Paulina and his brothers galloped into the chilly void of pre-dawn. Rushing to Queapama's tent for instructions, they found their chief sitting by his dying fire—grinning hideously with his throat slit from ear to ear. They knew that Skookum—the evil spirit Paulina—had ridden among them that night.

For the Shoshoni avengers, this was a double victory. Queapama's soul, liberated during darkness, would never walk in the happy hunting ground with true warriors.

# CHAPTER 140

# DEVIL OR SAINT?

*Duncan is in his grave;*
*After life's fitful fever he sleeps well;*
*Treason has done his worst; nor steel, nor poison,*
*Malice domestic, foreign levy, nothing*
*Can touch him further.*

**William Shakespeare**
*Macbeth*

From Warm Springs, Paulina headed east in a grueling 800-mile ride that spanned 17 days. Averaging more than 50 miles a day, his mission was to pick up supplies—livestock, arms, ammunition—anything to prolong survival. The army's new policy of extermination had also wiped out their arsenal and recent engagements had been arrows against Model 1865 Spencers, known throughout the west as the "Indian Model" and by 1867, the sport model—which shot either a 56-50 or 56-52 calibre slug—had entered the scene.

The Shoshoni were now resorting to a trick picked up from the Sioux . . . an innovation that made one of the greatest contributions to the progress of modern firearms. Immediately after the Civil War, they captured a few breech loading .50 calibre rifles which had just been issued to the soldiers. Ammo was not readily available on the frontier and the army promptly clapped a ban on anybody selling to the Indians. But the Snakes were plunking away at the army like they had tons to spare and in a way, they did.

The soldiers finally figured out that the Indians were picking up the empty shells fired by the soldiers which had solid-head, non-reloadable jackets and performing something unheard of. Punching a hole in the head of the shell, they crammed an ordinary muzzle loader percussion cap into it, then dropped a little rock into the shell to serve as a striking surface. Then they filled it with musket powder and added a lead bullet (they could melt out plenty of lead) to the shell; the Indians had beaten Sam Colt and Oliver Winchester to the outside primer and reloadable cartridge. For this reason, Paulina was looking especially for Crook's battle sites over the past three months.

What kind of a man was Paulina that men, women and children, alike, cowered at the mention of his name? Why was he known throughout the western states as the "executioner of the Ochoco" and reviled as the "Brutal Devastator"? Residents of eastern Oregon, Idaho, Nevada and northern California swore he was a natural born killer—a sadist who reveled in wanton bloodshed. In correspondence with Lt. McKay, Lt. Borrowe would voice his fervent wish that McKay would kill Paulina: "... as to forage use what I have sent you and get your horses up as fast as possible so that you can make another dash at your old friend Paulina before you come in. I am particularly anxious to have you kill this man. It would pay for the whole expedition."[1]

Few men are born with the instinct for ruthless slaughter and Paulina was no exception. Big Man perhaps, but not Paulina. The Shoshoni looked upon him as a hero and to them, he was one of the greatest sons the Shoshoni nation had ever produced sharing equal footing with Twisted Hand, Red Wolf, Gourd Rattler and Has No Horse. Known as Paulina—The War Spirit—he was a kind but firm leader. His followers trusted him as a faithful husband who placed his life in jeopardy so that his wife might be freed from the damp cells of Fort Vancouver; a compassionate comrade who wept unashamedly when he saw the twisted fly-blown bodies of children at the McKay Creek massacre; a brave warrior who avenged the honor of the Shoshoni nation.

In 12 days, Paulina had swept through Harney Basin, dipped into the Pueblos, sacked Jordan Valley, raided Mormon Basin and was on his return to the Ochoco. During this marathon plunge into enemy territory, he was sending stolen beef cattle and horses back to the Ochoco. En route, he had stampeded a trail herd on the Idaho border, killing one drover and seriously wounded another; burned numerous ranch houses and barns, killing five ranchers and seriously wounding several more; killed a civilian packer on the Owyhee River; attacked the Inskip Stage Station on the Boise-Owyhee Road and burned the barns and corrals; and with only seven warriors left, he waylaid the Boise-Owyhee stage, destroying the coach and contents and killing the driver and all passengers. Following the stage attack, Paulina headed west for the John Day Valley and home.[2]

In the summer of 1866, two men had taken claims in the John Day Valley. One was Andrew Clarno who located on Pine Creek and the other was William Trosper who took a claim on Cottonwood Creek, some 20 miles to the east. Clarno, when he found out Trosper had moved in, rode over and complained, "Bill, don't you think you're crowding me a little?"[3] Another gentlemen thought both of them were a detriment to the neighborhood and in the final days of April 1867, he decided to correct that problem.

---

1    Bureau of Indian Affairs, Oregon Superintendency 1866-69, Letters Received, Lt. Borrowe to Lt. McKay, Fort Vancouver, February 5, 1867.

2    U.S. Secretary of the Interior Report, 1867-8, III, pp. 101-3, 40th Congress, 2d Session.

3    McArthur, *Oregon Geographic Names*, p. 132.

Trosper was hit first, his house, barns and corrals burned and all livestock driven off. Moving on to Clarno—who had built everything out of rock, including corrals—the evictors picked up 25 cattle and a like number of horses. It was still good daylight so Paulina decided on one last strike before heading for Has No Horse's camp in the upper Ochoco Valley. Antelope House, three miles north of Slaughterhouse Gulch and nestled beneath the gray cliffs that separated Antelope Valley from Trout Creek Canyon, was the next objective.

There are as many versions as to what happened at this lonely outpost as there are days in Paulina's final ride. Perhaps the most authentic is based upon the testimony of Thomas L. Childers, Paulina's grandson.

Darkness had fallen and from Sand Mountain, Paulina could spot the yellow square which marked Maupin's station. Like sights on a moving target, his eyes flicked from the station to the bobbing, blinking light topping the divide between Currant and Little Trout creek. These were the driving lights of Hank Wheeler's famed Concord coach still some 10 miles from the stage stop. The Dalles-Canyon City stage was behind schedule. It would arrive at Antelope House shortly before midnight giving him a good two-hour head start on any attempted pursuit. Drawing his faded blue army officer's coat tight against the sudden chill, he motioned his men forward and disappeared into the night. It was April 25, 1867 . . . a date that would go down in Oregon history as the beginning of the end for the most feared and hated man who galloped roughshod across the Pacific Northwest.

Slipping up on the corrals, Snake warriors stealthily opened the gates and relieved Maupin of the responsibility of taking care of a lot of horses. These, along with his dairy herd, were aimed toward the Ochoco Valley only 40 miles away. Staying clear of the stage road, the raiders rode up Sheep Hollow and, north of Blizzard Ridge, entered a small basin edged with cliffs lying between Paulina Butte and Sheep Rock. Here, in the lee of a high rim, Paulina's men—tired and hungry—persuaded their leader to stop and rest and enjoy the spoils of war. The wary chief was not all for it but his men had worked hard and there was small chance of pursuit with Crook a hundred miles to the south and the cavalry holed up at Fort Watson 45 miles to the east. Posting one sentry on the back trail, the war party prepared a feast—the first good meal they had eaten in over two weeks.

As the Wheeler stage crossed the divide between Long Hollow and Trout Creek, Jim Clark, the driver, spotted the glow of a fire some four miles to the northwest and was momentarily curious. When he arrived at Antelope House, his curiosity was satisfied. With the memory of his Burnt Ranch station still fresh in his mind, he volunteered to go with Maupin in pursuit of the stolen livestock. As they saddled up the stagecoach's lead team, Clark's lone passenger, William Ragan—a California prospector—asked if he could trail along. "It's your funeral," shouted Maupin, "but come on, the more the merrier." So the three men started out.

Maupin, well acquainted with the isolated country south of the stage station, knew there were two trails the Indians could have taken. One led up Trout Creek into the Blues; the other (further to the west) would travel the high country between Slaughterhouse Gulch and Devil's Canyon, up Blizzard Ridge and into the lower Crooked River Valley. Moving up Trout Creek they soon discovered that the livestock had not been driven over this trail. It was now certain the Snakes had taken the western trail and high ground. This was soon confirmed when Maupin found a knife along the trail which Clark identified as one that had been stolen from Burnt Ranch some seven months before. Maupin stuck the knife in his belt and before the day was over it too would take its place in history.

At daybreak, Maupin's sharp eyes spotted an Indian sentinel high on a rocky butte overlooking a small basin. Forewarned, the trio dismounted and took cover. It was rough going and Ragan unable to keep up—or perhaps for other reasons—kept lagging farther and farther behind. Maupin now took the lead, cautiously crawling toward a rocky outcrop directly above the campsite. From this vantage point, looking into the rock-walled cove—now known as Paulina Basin—Maupin sighted his intended victims. They were dining on his milk cow. A bundle of nerves, Maupin opened fire with a Henry rifle.

This rifle, given to him by Lt. Col. Crook, was the first repeating rifle to be used in central Oregon by a white man. It was a deadly weapon. The Henry was the forerunner of the famous lever action Winchester . . . the fastest shooting rifle the world had ever seen prior to the advent of the semi-automatic in the first half of the 20th century. Capable of firing sixty .44 calibre bullets a minute, the Henry was claimed to have an eight-inch penetration at 100 yards; five inches at 400 yards; and sufficient force to kill at 1,000 yards. Advertisements would confidentially state that "for a house or sporting arm, the Henry has no equal. Furthermore, a resolute man armed with one of these rifles, particularly if on horseback, *cannot be captured.*" It was also claimed that a Henry, when loaded on a Monday would shoot until Sunday.

As the barbecue fire tossed weird shadows on the jagged cliff in the rosy glow of dawn, the dog solders—in rare good humor—joked over their victorious raids. Suddenly, the voice of a rifle shot, screaming vengeance, echoed in hatred along the high rims of the basin wall. Paulina, who had just walked up to the fire, grimaced in pain and fell to the ground, his right leg shattered at the hip. More bullets rained down and the startled warriors huddled in shocked disbelief, then broke and ran for cover. Horse Trap, riding in from the north where he had gone to check the surrounding country, saw his friend go down and the men scatter. His shouts boomed across the basin as he tried to rally the dog soldiers—but the sight of the indestructible Paulina down and bleeding was more than they could comprehend. Panic was riding roughshod through their ranks.

Screaming in rage, Horse Trap charged the unseen enemy, his rifle spewing lead and with the Shoshoni war cry torn from his raw throat, took a .44 calibre slug through the chest that would have felled a war-horse. Literally blasted from the saddle, Horse Trap painfully crawled into a rocky depression. All was suddenly quiet. Then he saw the hated *Soo Yawpis*—two of them broke over the ridge and methodically poured lead into his beloved chief. Still Paulina remained in a sitting position, moving his head from side to side like a wounded grizzly. In these last moments he had spotted his boyhood friend and lifted his hand in farewell. Vainly, Horse Trap tried to raise his rifle but somewhere the strength of his arms, once so powerful, had left him. Numbly he watched them descend on Paulina and cursed himself for a weakling. Try as he might, he couldn't move and realized that for all practical purposes, he was about as helpful as a papoose. With a prayer to the Mighty Chief Above, he closed his eyes on the grisly scene below.

At the first shot, the Indians had broken and ran, heading across the nearly level floor of the basin toward a trail leading out of the cove. Shortly after Maupin shot, Clark came up in time to witness a curious thing. While the whole band rushed for the outlet, a lone horseman charged from the far side and with a wild shriek galloped straight toward the two white men. As his horse disappeared among the boulders, Maupin fired once more but thought he had missed.

Then, Clark and Maupin noticed that one Indian, apparently wounded in the leg was trying to get up. As the two men watched, he shouted to his retreating braves as he pulled grass from the earth and placed it on his head and chest. Unknown to the whites, Paulina was making his last will and testament. Then as Paulina turned his head, Clark grabbed Maupin's arm. "My gawd! That's the same Indian that chased me all over Bridge Creek and burned my house and barn! Let me finish him, he owes me that much!"

Paulina was not responsible for Clark's loss as he was busy knocking-off Wheeler's stagecoach at the time Clark's station was converted into Burnt Ranch, and it would soon surface that neither Maupin nor Clark had the foggiest idea as to who this Indian was.

Anyway, Maupin understood how Clark felt and readily granted his request. With a stream of invectives pouring from his lips—equally as frightening as a Shoshoni war whoop—Clark began pouring bullets into the fallen warrior. Five times he shot but Paulina never so much as flinched. After each shot dust boiled up beyond the wounded Shoshoni and Clark cussed his bad luck for overshooting. Both he and Maupin could see that Paulina had a rifle but made no attempt to fire back—for a weapon without bullets is about as useful as a toothpick in the game of war. Seeing he wasn't going to fight back, the two closed in for the kill.

His eyes never leaving the approaching white men, Paulina plunged his hunting knife deep into the earth, snapping off the blade; for it was an everlasting disgrace for a Shoshoni to be scalped with his own knife and Paulina had no doubt but that his civilized white brethren would do just that.

Clark was shocked to see that every one of his bullets had passed through the Snake's body and he had to give the devil his due . . . the old boy was plenty tough!

379

If the stage employees expected Paulina to beg for mercy, they were disappointed. He watched coldly as Maupin raised his army Colt and with Saydocarah contempt, met the .36 calibre lead ball that blotted out his face forever from the eastern Oregon frontier. Weeks later, the remains of Horse Trap were found in a depression in the rim of Paulina Basin.[4]

With the knife picked up along the trail, Maupin lifted Paulina's scalp. He then took Paulina's scalp, war bonnet, rifle and broken hunting knife back to Antelope Station where excited army officers and Warm Springs scouts identified the scalp and war bonnet. Basking in their newfound glory, Clark and Maupin paraded the streets of The Dalles waving Paulina's scalp on the end of a rifle barrel and by Monday, April 29, 1867, *The Portland Morning Oregonian* had spread the news to the waiting world.[5]

Howard Maupin and James Clark became instant heros. Headlines of the day and the following accounts were glowing in their praise of the Indian-fighters.[6] One of these articles would gush:

> "Two hardy pioneers pitted against the mighty Paulina and his trained killers! Two whites against the mongrel Paiute Chief and his warriors! The Henry rifles of Maupin and Clark went into action. Like cowards, the Indians broke and ran. One fell, his hip shattered by a bullet from the rifle of Maupin. He was clutching grass from the ground placing it on his head and shoulders, his breast. It was Chief Paulina, the terrorizer—deserted by his warriors. A bullet from Maupin's cap and ball pistol and the killer's career was ended. Not even a cairn was erected to mark the spot where Paulina fell . . . the skeleton left to bleach in the sun that daily arches across the Trout Creek country, setting early in the afternoon behind the basalt rim of the cove."

The media claimed that Maupin wasn't a cold-blooded Indian-killer but a peace-loving man. Perhaps he was, but Crook didn't give him a Henry rifle just to

---

4    U.S. Secretary of Interior Report, 1867-8, III, pp. 101-3, 40th Congress, 2d Session.

5    Allen Jacobs, a retired ballistics expert with the Oregon State Police, has done extensive research on Paulina's final days and made some startling discoveries. In late March 1996—119 years after the fatal shooting—Jacobs and Loyd Greenwade entered Paulina Basin in northern Jefferson County to search for bullets that may have killed the war chief. Backtracking a likely course of the fleeing Indians they struck pay dirt. About 60 feet south from the rocks where Horse Trap died they found a bullet deformed on the nose and one side. A micrometer measurement confirmed that the lead matched the dimensions of a .44 calibre Henry bullet. A later search turned up six more bullets, one of which was either a Spencer .56-50, which must have been fired from Clark's rifle, and another smashed bullet which was too large to be a .44 slug. Then on July 14, 1996, Jacobs and Greenwade discovered what was undoubtedly Paulina's knife. Jammed into the ground near the spent bullets they unearthed a kitchen butcher knife with the lower blade snapped off and the hilt bent over in an apparent attempt to break it. (Allen Jacob's correspondence with the author in May-July 1996.)

6    A typical version of Paulina's death, taken from *The Morning Oregonian*, April 29, 1867, was reprinted by *The Bend Bulletin* in 1925.

hunt sage rats. He also had some strange habits such as keeping Paulina's scalp, the knife and rifle that did the job and some of Paulina's bones on display in his home until the house was destroyed by fire in the early 1900s. Warm Springs Indians often visited the Maupin ranch to view the scalp. On one of these visits, they asked for a piece. Permission was granted. Instead of taking a piece from the edge of this trophy, the Indians carefully removed the scalp lock. Today, the Henry rifle is on display at the Oregon Historical Society museum in Portland.

Jim Clark, who was directly responsible for Paulina's death, has had his name thunder down through history like a quart of water down Crooked River. William Ragan, who attended the bloody finale, has had his name replaced by that of John Atterbury, (one of the earliest settlers on upper Trout Creek) who wasn't present. He was one of the Canyon City packers present at the burning of Clark's stage station in 1866 but not a participant in Paulina's last moments.

No memorial marks the place where Paulina fell. The spring around which he and his warriors were gathered feasting on a cow stolen from Maupin is now dried up. A network of fences built by homesteaders marks the encroachment of civilization on Paulina's old domain. Perhaps that is his memorial—miles of barbed wire and broken ground where once lay hundreds of miles of rolling prairie abundant in wildlife.

The Oregonians' fear of Paulina, The War Spirit, was so great that even in death his soul was not left to lie in peace. Tales kept circulating of his terrible raids. In June 1867, nearly two months after his death, it was reported that he burned out the first settlement in Mill Creek Valley. Tom Puett, a very good friend of Maupin, swore that he visited Maupin shortly after he killed Paulina . . . in 1880![7]

It was during this period that nervous settlers started a rumor that Paulina's spirit roamed the area searching for his missing scalp. Those foolhardy enough to venture into Paulina Basin swore that a ghostly apparition hovered over the land. The mystery was finally solved when a prospector discovered an outcrop of low-grade coal in the rocky cliffs overlooking Paulina's final resting place. It seems that under certain atmospheric conditions the coal was releasing methane gas which drifted across the lowland like a troubled phantom hunting for something it had lost.

Following the death of Paulina, it finally became obvious that Has No Horse was the leader of the Paviotso Confederacy. Even then, that enlightenment was treated with some skepticism. Oregon Indian Superintendent Alfred Meacham would acknowledge that "Ochoco [Has No Horse] another Snake leader assumed command and conducted the last battle fought by this band."[8]

---

7    An account of Paulina, as told by Tom Puett, February 5, 1927, put the date of death as 1880. His account was reprinted in the "Old Timer's Edition" of *The Central Oregon Shopper*, August 4, 1949.

8    Meacham, *Wigwam*, p. 215.

Has No Horse, chosen by the Snake warrior societies, had been leader of the Paviotso Confederacy since the 1850s and the loss of his number one war chief—although it would weaken his command—would by no means bring the war effort to a standstill. Backed into a corner from which there was no escape, Has No Horse would strike with renewed fury.

# CHAPTER 141

# SILENT PARTNERS

*I found a band of Indians on a little lake, almost in sight*
*of Fort Warner. These Indians had evidently been getting*
*ammunition somewhere. We killed a lot of them. . . .*

**Lt. Col. George Crook**
Summer Campaign 1867

It was claimed that Oregon residents were a zealous, optimistic breed of the opinion that great things were in store for them. With the death of Paulina, they were certain of it. An organization called the Oregon Central Railway filed articles of incorporation approved by Congress April 22, 1867, to drive a pair of iron ribbons into the heart of central Oregon. Actually, the Oregon Central was out to acquire land grants. Ben Holladay—promoter and financier—pulled the rug out from under this scheme in order to get his East Oregon Central Railroad built first.[1] By pulling strings all the way from the state legislature to Congress to win his way, Holladay kept the railroads out of the Shoshoni's hair for another two years.

At the start of this squabble, military operations were starting to liven up on The Dalles-Canyon City road. In mid-March, Steele moved more troops into Fort Watson. Covering hundreds of miles, these new raiders were picking off Shoshoni stragglers, killing as they went, destroying property and taking few prisoners.[2] By May, McKay and Darragh—seeking more action—requested to join Crook's main force at Fort C.F. Smith. Not favorably impressed with their past record of slaughter, he had them held at Warm Springs to serve as escorts for supply trains headed from The Dalles to Fort Klamath. He would finally relent and send orders for the death squad to join the main column in June.[3]

---

1   Holladay, while much disliked and described as crude and semi-literate, was noted in Oregon history as a railroad builder. Born in Kentucky, he got his start selling mules to the government during the Mexican War. Though he was born and lived a third of his life in a log cabin, at the age of 50 he had mansions in Washington, D.C., on the Hudson River and in Portland, as well as an elaborate "cottage" at Seaside, Oregon. J.V. Frederick, *Ben Holladay, The Stagecoach King*; Stuart Holbrook, *Age of the Moguls*, pp. 123-25.

2   Bancroft, *History of Oregon*, II, p. 534.

3   McKay's Journal entry for Saturday, June 22, 1867.

For the Americans, the Shoshoni war was now entering its ninth year. To celebrate the occasion, the Shoshoni defenders burned out the American settlement in the lower Mill Creek Valley. Losing everything to the flames, these unfortunate homesteaders—armed only with willow sticks in the hope they would look like rifles—beat a hasty retreat to the Willamette Valley happy to be alive.

In retaliation, the army took to the field in a spring snowstorm. It was a known fact that when Crook went out to fight Indians, he carried no luxuries but he did have his "striker" or personal servant, Andrew Peisen, a native German. Known as "Peisy" he accompanied Crook on all campaigns until the end of Crook's life, having re-enlisted in the army eight times.[4] When Crook entered the Ochoco in the spring of 1867, he was traveling exceptionally light. There wasn't a tent in his whole pack train and the men didn't even carry razors. The cavalry guidon, the only flag they possessed, was improvised by the soldiers and it would have been grotesque if it wasn't so pathetic. The red stripe was from a piece of an old flannel shirt worn by Capt. Azor Nickerson. The white stripe was a piece of canvas supplied by a packer. The blue star in the center was cut from the leg of Capt. Perry's blue trousers.

As they pushed into the southern Blues, they were living off the land and anything edible went into the pot. One day Crook "got 67 dozen eggs of the Cormorant and Coots which breed in this area." In his opinion the Coot eggs "were good eating" but the Cormorant eggs "were not healthy" being bitter and strong when cooked. His men would heartily agree.

However, Crook was well supplied with local scouts. Among them were Howard Maupin, Abraham Zell, Thomas James, James Luckey and John Luckey, all of whom would settle in Crook County. The Luckey boys, scouting out of Warm Springs and killing deer for the hides, brought word to Crook of the fate of the settlers in Mill Creek Valley.[5]

Crook was also traveling with Major Clinton Wagner, chief surgeon for the Snake campaign, and his own war correspondent. Robert E. Strahorn, reporter for the *New York Times*, the *Chicago Tribune* and the Denver *Rocky Mountain News*, was in the southern Blues to provide complete coverage of the Ochoco campaign for the folks back east.[6] Of him, Crook once said ". . . he got the news in a most reliable way and he never failed to work his rifle as well as his pen." Henry Morton Stanley, who was covering the Comanche end of the '67 campaign for the *Missouri*

---

4    Crook, *Autobiography*, p. 163, footnote 3.

5    *The Prineville News*, July 7, 1887.

6    Strahorn's wife, Carrie Adell Strahorn, would author the two volume *Fifteen Thousand Miles by Stage*, a personal history of the road west from the Missouri to the Pacific and from Alaska to Mexico, illustrated by her good friend, Charles M. Russell.

*Democrat*, was the man sent by the *New York Herald* to Africa to find Dr. David Livingston in 1870.[7]

Heading west on the Willamette Valley and Cascade Mountain Military Road, Crook—with detachments of the 1st and 8th Cavalry and the 9th and 23d Infantry—found the advance easier than anticipated for one of the greatest obstacles had been removed by sheer accident and he was never to have the satisfaction of winning a battle against the brilliant Shoshoni strategist . . . Chief Paulina. Has No Horse, smarting under the loss of his war chief, was in no mood to be pushed around by the army and was on the prowl looking for blue-coats upon which to vent his anger. Crook, forging steadily into the Ochoco was due for a setback as he turned northward on the Horse Heaven Trail. Three miles south of Gerow Butte, in a flower-carpeted meadow now drooping in a late spring snowstorm, Has No Horse and Gray Wolf (a name the Shoshoni had bestowed upon Crook) met for the second time. Lancing out of his upland retreat, Has No Horse left 12 troopers in his wake . . . seven never to rise again. Then he simply disappeared. Figuring him to head south, Crook turned back to the land of the Paiutes. Now it was Gray Wolf's turn to chase shadows in the pine—dismounted!

That evening when Crook was forced to hole-up during a raging storm, Has No Horse stampeded his herd of horses and mules setting the major portion of Crook's command on foot. A patient man, Crook stoically sent an express to Fort Dalles for a remount, and devoted the late spring and early summer of 1867 to breaking the broncos to saddle and pack. His men took to their new assignment with enthusiasm and before summer was half over Crook's main fighting forces were once again pony soldiers.[8] Meanwhile, with the few mounted men he had left, Crook continued the chase. Crook had planned to have the Snake campaign in full swing by July 1 but due to improper forts and the difficulty of remounting his troops, plus delays in obtaining supplies to subsist his command, he had lost a full two months. It appears that Lt. Col. Henry Hodges, Army quartermaster, was not doing a good job.[9] During the two month postponement, Crook traveled by night and lay in concealment during the day, covering 1,200 miles. At Fort Watson, he took over a company of cavalry and added two companies of Umatilla and Nez Perce scouts to his detachment. Like their Warm Springs counterparts, these heavily armed warriors were taking a deadly toll on the enemy. In late June, 63 Shoshoni men, women and children—including the war chiefs Buffalo Meat and No Ribs—were killed at the head of Picture Gorge on the John Day River.[10]

---

7    James Callaghon, "The Frontier War Correspondents," *Tombstone Epitaph*, Vol. IV, No. 7, July 1977.

8    Bourke, "General Crook in the Indian Country," *Century Magazine*, Vol. XLI, No. 5, March 1891, p. 4.

9    *Portland Oregonian*, August 24, 1867; Bancroft, *History of Oregon*, II, p. 536.

10   Picture Gorge lay on the main Shoshoni thoroughfare from the Columbia River to points in

Again turning south, Crook—using the old emigrant route of 1853 as a pattern—opened the Oregon Central Military Road (which was never completed by the Willamette Valley construction crew). Running from Fort Boise to Fort Klamath, it provided a connecting link between Crook's farthest eastern point of military operations to the Cascade Mountains.

In the meantime, more settlers were plowing into central Oregon. Twenty miles upstream from Burnt Ranch, Fred Sargent built a relief station at the present site of Mitchell. Following in his wake and staking claims on Bridge Creek were Al Sutton, Wick Cusick, H.C. Hal, James Marshall, William Saltman and John Moore. So many settlers were moving into the Pendleton area that Capt. Wildy with a detachment of 6th U.S. Cavalry was stationed on Willow Creek to protect the Umatilla country. More soldiers were added when the mail began coming to Portland by stage from Salt Lake City via Walla Walla instead of the long route from Sacramento. Because of the renewed Shoshoni raids prices at Canyon City were sky-rocketing. Flour sold for $62 a hundred-weight; eggs were going for three dollars a dozen; and meals, no matter what you ordered, were five dollars each.

After his clash with Has No Horse in which the bulk of his command was set afoot, Crook sent out a call for reinforcements. Near midnight June 21, Joe Delore arrived at Warm Springs with McKay's order to join Crook at Fort C.F. Smith "immediately." Darragh and McKay had been held at Warm Springs for escort duty to take Supt. Huntington to Fort Klamath. McKay was happy to get out of that detail.[11] Six days later, he arrived at Mountain House and sent his Warm Springs Cavalry out to locate cattle stolen that morning. While they searched, McKay visited Fort Watson and dined with Capt. Perry who briefed him on Has

---

Utah, Nevada and California. Its towering rock walls were covered with tribal history most likely dating from the early Spanish conquests to the dying days of the late 19th century. For writing on the overhanging bluffs, the so-called medicine men used a special compound. It was a paste made from mineral matter dissolved in a thin resin obtained from fir and pine trees and mixed with bear oil. When put on rock, this mixture would harden and glaze over, leaving a color that when shielded from the weather, would hold for thousands of years. The principal colors of red, green and brown were obtained from iron ore. Some of the pictographs were done with this coloring agent mixed with water which would oxidize and penetrate the rock. These paintings come nearer to being sign writing than anything found along the rivers of the Pacific Northwest. It has been known for years that the many Shoshoni tribes left signs along their trails which others following could read. These were not simple signs of directions and such. They really told a story. Many of these characters have been found repeated many miles apart. Much of the Snake's tribal history has been recorded in caves on Mill Creek, Paulina Valley and the Dry River Gorge.

The Shoshoni also used the tanned hides of animals to write upon, working with a vegetable dye for this purpose. Red characters meant danger and white ones stood for honor. But whether these markings were put on skin or rock, they always told of glory and happiness because the Shoshoni—somewhat like the Oregonians after them—recorded only the victories, never the sad defeats.

11    Unless otherwise noted, all information taken from McKay's *Journal* entries, June through September 1867.

No Horse's latest action. En route to Canyon City, McKay saw Snake signal fires 18 miles west of town when crossing the John Day bridge. Instead of checking them out, his troops "got drunk on liquor at the bridge."

Moving on to Fort Logan—under the command of Capt. Dudley Seward, 8th U.S. Cavalry—on July 2, McKay attacked a Snake camp and retrieved 32 of Crook's stolen cavalry horses.[12] Elated over this good luck, the Warm Springs Cavalry returned to Canyon City where the Indian troops were invited to put on a 4th of July demonstration which, according to Capt. McKay, was "quite satisfactory to all the parties concerned. Indians had a regular blow-out at McKrock's saloon." It took them a day to sober up.

A week later, Lt. Greenleaf Goodale with a detachment of 8th U.S. Cavalry out of Camp Wright, finally caught up with McKay south of Harney Lake. It was here on July 13 that Snake prisoners captured by McKay confirmed that the man killed by Maupin was "Pallina and no mistake." This was the first concrete evidence that Paulina was actually dead and it was the most gratifying news the army could have received.

On July 15, McKay's trackers picked up the trail of Wolf Dog. Capt. McKay with 35 Indian regulars and Lt. Goodale with 17 enlisted men took pursuit. Instead of running, Wolf Dog attacked on the head of the Malheur River. During the hostile charge A.J. Boyd (a packer out of Fort Watson) acting as guide for Goodale, and Squalth (McKay's scout) chased one warrior into a cave. Standing on either side of the entrance, the two waited for him to come out. Shortly after dark, the dog soldier made a break, shooting and killing Squalth but in the attempt, Boyd killed him. In a four day chase, the soldiers retrieved one U.S. mule, three horses, killed six Shoshoni, wounded one and captured two men, but made no mention of their own losses.[13]

Boyd, a braggart, was considered a good guide and "valuable in finding good camp sites and watching out for hostile Snakes."[14] In October 1867, he was wounded in action against the Snakes. The Dalles Mountaineer, January 4, 1868, states that A.J. Boyd, lately employed as guide at Camp Harney but now proprietor of the Rock Creek House on the Canyon City Road says "he is tired of hunting Indians and intends settling down, and maybe will marry." However, from April to June 1869, Boyd was again employed as an army packer at Fort Watson.

Twenty-seven days after leaving Warm Springs, McKay arrived at Fort C.F. Smith on July 19 in a snowstorm. Just before arriving, he met his brother Donald with eight Cayuse scouts. Don was working out of Camp Three Forks on the Owyhee. From Fort C.F. Smith, the McKay brothers headed into the Pueblo

---

12  Report of Secretary of War 1867, U.S. Documents, Serial 1324, Pt. 1, p. 450.

13  Report of Secretary of War 1867, U.S. Documents Serial 1324, Pt. 1, p. 82.

14  Reports of Persons and Articles Employed and Hired at Camp Watson, July 1867, Lt. George McTaylor, AAQM, National Archives, Records Group 92.

Mountains where they were joined by Archie McIntosh and 14 Snake scouts led by Six Feathers. During their 12-day push back to Fort Warner—traveling only at night—the Indian regulars were joined by Capt. Perry out of Fort Watson with three companies of cavalry. This united force now numbered 250 men. By July 27, they had killed 15 Shoshoni and taken 18 captive.

As the soldiers moved west, Pony Blanket and Fox attacked 40 Chinese laborers near the Silver City mines. Only one escaped. Then on July 27, Perry's column surprised a camp of women and children on Warner Mountain, nine miles east of Fort Warner. The Warm Springs Cavalry attacked and soon had 30 scalps. The American troopers never fired a shot. According to the newspapers: "It was rare sport for civilization this making the savages fight the savages for its benefit."[15] A few hundred miles to the north, Has No Horse wiped out a party of 25 hide-hunters in the so-called Hat Rock Massacre on the southwest slope of Powell Butte. Missing out on all the fun, Capt. Darragh was delivering beef to the various army outposts.

At the outset of the '67 campaign, Crook decided to upgrade existing forts and establish new ones. First to get a face-lift was the winter hell-hole at Fort Warner. Sgt. James Greer, an army engineer, set out with a construction crew and 40 days' provisions to build a new post on the west side of Warner Lake some 500 feet lower in elevation than the old camp. The spot he selected, in a heavy stand of timber on Honey Creek, would be accessible anytime of the year. A small sawmill was set up and quarters for officers and enlisted men were constructed of logs with siding, gables and shake roofs. There was a laundry, bakery, mess hall, offices for commissioned and non-commissioned personnel, ordinance and commissary store houses, stables, a guardhouse and hospital. There was also housing for married officers and enlisted men. The wardroom of the hospital—a room 44' x 24'—was often used for parties.

Snow stayed at the higher elevation most of the summer and ice was brought down for freezing ice cream to serve as refreshments. Officers and their ladies often danced through the summer nights, and ate ice cream with silver from Tiffany's in New York City. Gardens were planted, one for each company, and one for the hospital. Potatoes, cabbage, turnips, onions and other vegetables were grown and tended by the enlisted men. Many a brave eastern volunteer who had dreamed of fighting savage Indians on the great desert woke to find himself fighting cutworms out in the cabbage patch. Mail came in from Fort Bidwell, California, usually by horse but when snow was very deep it was brought over by men on snowshoes.[16]

---

15  *Portland Oregonian*, August 24, 1867; *Owyhee Avalanche*, August 28, 1867; *Boise Statesman*, August 31, 1867.

16  Hart, *Frontier Forts of the West; Oregon Journal, October 19, 1867.*

A general clean-up was being made of all forts in eastern Oregon, including the location of new ones in strategic areas. Crook made a complete survey of his perimeter of attack. On his push back to Fort Warner—which became command headquarters—he found Little Rattlesnake and Four Crows camped at Swamp Lake almost within sight of the fort. Crook struck but hit a different breed of leaders. Although he killed a number of braves, the chiefs held him off long enough to effect their escape into central Oregon, which was of extreme importance for they were bringing in a shipment of arms and ammunition picked up from Utah and Colorado.

It was at the battle of Swamp Lake that Crook did some serious thinking. Though the Snakes suffered many and severe losses, they always appeared to be well-armed and their number of fighting men never seemed to dwindle. Why? Being well-schooled in Indian warfare, the answer became obvious. It was not the eastern Oregon tribes alone which he was fighting . . . giving final proof that the Shoshoni nation was united in a last bloody stand against the common enemy. Gourd Rattler, by virtue of his unquestioned loyalty to the Americans, was providing a perfect screen—perhaps unknowingly—for this undercover operation.

The Plains Shoshoni who were supposedly under control on reservations in Wyoming, Idaho, Utah and Colorado were the silent partners. Men who thought nothing of traveling three or four hundred miles to steal one horse, would tell their reservation agent they were going on a hunt. Then, they would make a rapid journey into eastern Oregon, pick up stolen livestock from their red brothers and trade them hundreds of miles away where there were no hostilities for arms and ammunition. Others in turn would deliver these arms to the Oregon Shoshoni in exchange for more stolen livestock. There were always whites in the vicinity of these reservations who were willing to trade with the Indians for a huge profit. By this means a never-failing supply of men, arms and ammunition was pouring into eastern Oregon. Crook was determined to check this illicit trade.

It was his plan to isolate the Blues from all outside contact including the Modocs, whom he didn't trust. And for good reason. Captain Jack's warriors were the California gun-runners. Crook stationed his troops in a solid line around the Ochoco in a 1,200 mile circle running east from Fort Watson to Fort Boise; south to Fort C.F. Smith; then west to Fort Klamath; north to the Warm Springs Agency; and again east to connect at Fort Watson. This line was intended to block off reinforcements from any direction. Before the summer was over, the area encompassed would be designated by the War Department as the Military District of the Lakes. As an added precaution, Crook was given command of Fort Bidwell and Fort Crook in northern California and Fort McDermit in Nevada.

The summer of 1867 saw the construction of Fort Ochoco at the mouth of Mill Creek, a quarter mile from the blackened rubble that had been the first white settlement in the Ochoco Valley. Framed through the western entrance was the lonely monument of an attempt to establish a claim on the Ochoco. Stark against the bluffs stood a rock chimney that 30 days before marked the cabin of a group of men who believed they could hold out.

This outpost was nothing more than a block house—in short a siege stockade—a stone's throw from Has No Horse's hideout on the upper river; only 12 miles in a straight line from the Shoshoni inner line of defense. The blockhouse, 18 feet square at the bottom, was overlapped with a superstructure 28 feet square. To breach the walls of this log pillbox, an enemy would have to pass directly beneath the firepower of the soldiers overhead for there were rifle ports cut in the overhanging floor as well as the walls, so that defenders could shoot straight down on anyone who should get beneath the superstructure. Fort Ochoco was equipped with a mountain spring and a week's supply of provisions for 30 men.[17] It was constructed and manned by a detachment of 8th U.S. Cavalry under the command of Major George Randall.[18]

A forward observer's post in connection with the Ochoco blockhouse was established eight miles upriver. Called Camp Brown, it was located some 400 yards south of where Camp Branch Creek (possibly a misspelling of Brown) enters the Ochoco River. This outpost was named for Capt. F.H. Brown, 18th U.S. Infantry, killed in the Fetterman Massacre on December 21, 1866 in Montana, at that time Dakota Territory.

Camp Brown was burned to the ground a week after completion.[19] During its short life, one of Randall's engineers based at this camp was to map the inner Ochoco. The plan was to go up Marks Creek and across the head of the Ochoco. Traveling alone for security reasons, he never returned. A year later an unidentified body dressed in army uniform was found at a small spring in the Marks Creek watershed by William Marks and George Barnes who christened it Deadman's Spring. It was here that the remains were buried with the only marker being the pool where the man died.

By the end of July, President Johnson—acting through Congress—authorized seven peace commissioners to negotiate treaties with the Shoshoni to place them on reservations. Among others in this elite group were Gen. Sherman, Gen. Harney and Gen. Terry. The first tribesmen to be contacted were the Comanches. Meeting in Kansas with Ten Bears acting as spokesman, Lone Wolf, White Horse, Iron

---

17    The remains of the old blockhouse and the spring over which it sat, are buried under a landfill where U.S. Highway 26 and the Mill Creek Road join at the western approach to the highway bridge spanning Mill Creek at the eastern end of Ochoco Reservoir. Testimony of Earl Hereford, June 1968, whose ranch was located a few miles up Mill Creek from the old fort site.

18    During the Sioux Campaign, Major Randall—again on Crook's staff—would request Shoshoni scouts for regular army service, claiming they were "by far the most serviceable to be found on the plains." Trenholm and Corley, The Shoshoni, pp. 258-59.

19    After the destruction of the Camp Brown in eastern Oregon, Gen. Crook would have the name of the Camp Brown in Wyoming changed to Fort Washakie.

Mountain, Little Crow, Chewing Elk and Gap in the Woods signed the Treaty of Medicine Lodge, which assigned the Comanches a reservation between the Washita and Red rivers in Oklahoma Territory. To further complicate matters for the war tribes, Nevava—who would not discuss treaties and claimed that the Utes owned the Colorado Rockies and that was final—died, increasing The Arrow's (Ouray) power over the Ute tribes.[20]

While Congress was toying with the treaty idea, Capt. Darragh and Capt. Perry headed north out of Fort Warner on July 28 with two month's rations, intending to penetrate the southern Blues. Within two days, Perry returned to the fort with six prisoners and one horse. There he remained for the rest of the summer, spending his time in horse racing and awaiting the outcome of the peace negotiations. Darragh (with his unruly mob) continued northward bent on mischief. The Warm Springs Commandos would enter enemy territory to search out and destroy Shoshoni burial grounds, a disgusting act which they had been practicing since 1864 and found to be quite exhilarating.

Upon death of a member of the Shoshoni tribe, the deceased's family immediately moved the tipi from the fatal spot and the body, along with all its earthly possessions, was taken to a designated tribal cemetery. Here, the Shoshoni mourned and prayed to the dead one's guardian spirit, for they believed that each person had their own personal helper who guided them through this journey on earth and at life's end led them to the land of their fathers. The body, wrapped in skins, was placed on a high platform away from all objects so that no harm could befall it. Then all of the "sleeping one's" worldly goods were burned so that the owner, after passing through the land of shadows, could once more enjoy them in the home of the Great Spirit.

These platform burials presented intriguing targets not only for the Warm Springs allies who loved to topple them and scatter the bones to the four winds, but also to the American souvenir hunters. These grave robbers would put a stop to such foolishness as open air coffins—it was because of this that the Shoshoni were forced into ground internment from the 1860s onward.[21]

As his staff officers played and constructed new fortifications, Crook took to the battlefield in earnest. Moving with several converging columns, each

---

20    Sprague, *Massacre, The Tragedy at White River*, pp. 85, 90.

21    Some of these burial sites were located in the vicinity of Gerow Butte, Glass Butte, Coyle Butte and Mount Pisgah. Contrary to popular belief, the word "Pisgah" is not an Indian name. It is ancient Hebrew. Mount Pisgah (Phasga) sat on the east coast of the Dead Sea in the Abarin Mountains. It was from the top of Mount Pisgah on the banks of River Jordan that Moses first beheld the verdant beauty of the Promised Land. On the top of this mighty peak, Moses died at a 121 years of age and it was here that he was buried in a place "unknown to man." *The Holy Bible*, Book of Deuteronomy, Chapter 34:226. Most likely the Oregon mountain was named by some early missionary, probably Father Toussaint Mesplie, first known "Man of God" to enter the western Ochoco.

provided with an effective train of pack-mules, civilian scouts and a corp of Indian scouts, he was determined to disable Has No Horse's war machine for all time. The scouts were kept one to two days in advance of the train and covered not only the front of the column but up to 50 miles of country on each flank. All troop movement was done primarily by night and Crook was careful not to march in the same direction or to cover the same distance on any two consecutive days. Sometimes he would start at dawn and travel day and night for two days without stopping. Other times he would start after dark and stop before sunrise pausing only long enough to tighten cinches. This greatly fatigued the officers and men but it confused the dog soldiers and prevented them from calculating, with any accuracy the place and moment for an ambush.

Even so, Crook was involved in daily skirmishes with—as Lt. Waymire once put it—no signal success. During the convergence on Fort Warner, Archie McIntosh took off on his own with Six Feather's mercenaries and rode into the Sierra Nevada's where he took two Paiute women captive who were engaged in nothing more sinister than digging camas bulbs. That was a mistake. Bad Face, on his return to the Ochoco from picking up an arms shipment in northern California, rode onto the scene and McIntosh barely escaped with the loss of one man killed and one wounded.[22] He also had to give up the two women captives.

By the time Crook reached Fort Warner, the whole command was in a distressed condition. Officers and enlisted men alike were disheartened by constant but profitless clashes with an enemy who refused any inducement to be coaxed into a general engagement. Has No Horse was too battle-wise to get trapped in a no-win situation such as that. When Crook marched into Fort Warner in late August, his men were in rags, his rations exhausted, his horses and mules broken-down, and all he had to show for the torturous weeks of privation were . . . twelve dead Indians![23]

During the first week of August, Lt. Stanton—1st U.S. Cavalry—with a detachment of Perry's 14th U.S. Infantry, began construction of a camp on Rattlesnake Creek some 16 miles northeast of the present site of Burns, Oregon. By November, this outpost would be known as Fort Harney.[24] Like the rest of the army garrisons constructed in the summer of 1867, it could hardly be classified as an abode of supreme delight. Officer's quarters and enlisted men's barracks had one thing in common—they were all log cabins with the floors sunk three feet below ground level and roofed with army tents. A hole dug into one wall of each hut served as a fireplace, which was equipped with a chimney made of stakes and sealed with mud. In such palatial residences as these, Mrs. Crook, Mrs. Gilliss,

22    McKay, Journal, entry for Monday, August 26, 1867.

23    Bourke, "General Crook in the Indian Country," *The Century Magazine*, Vol. XLI, No. 5, March 1891, p. 4.

24    General Orders, Department of the Columbia, dated November 26, 1867.

Mrs. Pollock and other ladies who joined their husbands in the Snake campaign, were compelled to spend the winter of 1867-68.

Soon after construction, the little community of Harney City—now marked by a weathered sign nailed to a fence post—would spring up around the fort. With lumber furnished by the army sawmill, Harney City boasted a general store, hotel, two blacksmith shops, law office, newspaper, school, and the usual saloon.

On August 16, the same day Fort Harney was completed, army headquarters again sub-divided the Shoshoni area of operations. The eastern section, restricted to Fort Boise, Fort Lyon, Camp Three Forks and Fort C.F. Smith would continue as the Military District of Owyhee under the command of Major Joel Elliott, 1st U.S. Cavalry.[25] The western section, which Crook had cordoned off, containing Fort Klamath, Fort Watson, Fort Warner, Fort Logan, Fort Harney and the Ochoco blockhouse became the new Military District of the Lakes under the command of Brevet Major General George Crook with orders to take command of Fort Bidwell, Fort McDermit and Fort Crook if necessary. Crook's Civil War commission had been reinstated by Gen. Grant, and the promotion was received along with the sub-division order. He would now be called Three Stars by most Indian tribes but to the Snakes he remained the formidable Gray Wolf.

Meanwhile, with hostilities heating up along the Oregon-California border, Capt. James Wildy (with two companies of 6th U.S. Cavalry) was ordered out of Willow Creek to report to Fort Crook. The citizens of Umatilla County immediately circulated a petition to Gov. Woods demanding more federal troops. Wildy had no sooner left than they came under attack. In fact, Snake raids were intensifying all across eastern Oregon. Severing army supply lines, Has No Horse isolated Fort Warner and by the end of August with the outpost facing starvation, Capt. Perry was ordered to Camp McGarry, Nevada with 45 pack mules to pick up supplies.

Adding to the dreary situation, Capt. McKay would report large forest fires raging out of control in the Fremont Mountains west of Fort Warner, which were blanketing the area with smoke. Moving toward Goose Lake on a sultry afternoon, his troops would kill four members of a destitute Paiute family.[26] Capt. Darragh was also facing rough going. Iou, one of his troopers, sickened by the constant blood-letting, decided enough was enough and committed suicide.[27]

The eastern front was also facing renewed activity. On September 28, J.B. Scott—with his wife and children—was traveling the road between Rye Valley

---

25    In 1868, Major Elliott and Lt. Pepoon were assigned to Custer's 7th Cavalry. Elliott and Capt. Louis McLane Hamilton—grandson of Alexander Hamilton—were killed in the Washita Battle, November 27, 1868. Monaghan, *The Book of the American West*, pp. 230-31.

26    McKay, Journal, entries for August 24 and September 6, 1867.

27    McKay's report to Warm Springs Agent John Smith, September 26, 1867, appearing in *The Portland Oregonian*, October 7, 1867.

and Burnt River when Big Man struck. Scott, receiving two wounds at the same time, was killed instantly. His wife, although severely wounded, seized the reins as they fell from her husband's lifeless hands and escaped with the children only to die the next night from wounds received. Five days later, Big Man plundered the Howe Ranch—located almost within sight of Fort Logan—burning the barn, corrals, haystacks and running off all the livestock.[28]

A detachment of 8th cavalry under the command of Lt. William Pike was sent in pursuit.[29] Pike's scouts located Big Man's camp and he planned a dawn surprise attack. Pike, a valuable officer, was well-versed in Indian-fighting but he imprudently gave a shout which sent the Shoshoni flying, leaving a rifle behind. In a fit of rage, Pike seized the abandoned weapon by the barrel and struck it against a rock to destroy it. The rifle discharged, killing him. Lt. Kauffman took command but failed to overtake the raiders.

Bad as the Indian situation was in central and eastern Oregon, there was good reason for pulling troops to the southern border where a prelude to the infamous Modoc battle of the lava beds was about to take place.

---

28    *Umatilla Columbia Press*, October 5, 1867; *The Portland Oregonian*, Number 4, 1867.
29    Military Department of the Columbia, General Order No. 32.

# CHAPTER 142

# HELL'S CAVE

*That night we watched around the outside, in hope of killing
some, but the next morning they were gone, much to my relief.*

**Major Gen. George Crook**
Battle of the Infernal Caverns

While sporadic slaughter was taking place in the Ochoco, Sieta (the Little
Rattlesnake)—was laying siege to the Oregon-California border from Fort
Klamath to Fort Bidwell, burning ranch houses, barns, corrals, haystacks,
plundering livestock and killing settlers. This was part of Has No Horse's strategy
to keep things lively on three fronts and it was about to work very well.

Believing he was still on Has No Horse's trail, Crook pushed out of the
southern Blues into the High Desert on September 1 with three companies of U.S.
Cavalry, two companies of Warm Springs Cavalry, one company of mounted
infantry, McIntosh's Shoshoni scouts and a rag-tail following of civilian
thrill-seekers. Still marching at night and lying concealed during the day, he hoped
to surprise the enemy. After a nine day march across a treeless, grassless region,
Capt. Darragh reported a Shoshoni camp at Abert Lake. By the time Crook's large
task force arrived at Abert Lake, the Snakes had vanished. Not taking any chances
on losing them in case they doubled back, Crook divided his command. It was
Friday the 13th and his weary troops could foresee trouble ahead.

Capt. Perry, Capt. Harris, Capt. McKay, Lt. Stanton, Mike Halley (civilian
quartermaster) and Major Wagoner (company surgeon) with two companies of
U.S. Cavalry and one company of Warm Springs Cavalry headed north to scour
the country between the Deschutes, Crooked and John Day rivers on orders to
terminate their campaign at Fort Harney.[1] Two days after separation, this column
crossed the Yreka Trail southeast of Summer Lake in a blinding snowstorm on
September 15 and marched toward the South Fork of Crooked River. On the same
day, Crook, who had taken a course southwest to the California line with the
mounted infantry under Lt. Madigan, one company of cavalry under Lt. Parnell,

---

1    Bancroft, *History of Oregon*, II, p. 538.

one company of Warm Springs Cavalry under Capt. Darragh and the Shoshoni scouts was being bombarded by a violent lightning storm.

In the meantime, Bad Face with 74 mounted Paiute warriors and a few militant Modocs who had allied with the Shoshoni, joined Little Rattlesnake and his 30 Snake raiders, bringing Little Rattlesnake's force to over 100 fighting men. He was now ready to take on Crook's regulars under his own terms.

On a tip-off from Captain Jack, who had known Crook when a lieutenant of the 4th Infantry at Fort Jones, California, Crook found out that the hostiles, after scattering had turned to the southwest and would reunite somewhere on the Pit River south of the Oregon line.[2] Armed with this information, Crook's scouts discovered Little Rattlesnake's force in the mountains east of Goose Lake and the tactical game of choice of battlefield was on. Crook, knowing that Little Rattlesnake had spotted him, made no attempt at concealment but marched on the main road as if going to Fort Crook. He actually did march to within 20 miles of the post but, coming to a place where he was screened by mountains, he crossed the Pit River and encamped in a timbered canyon. The trap was now set and baited with Shoshoni women and children who would blaze the way to the waiting jaws.

On the morning of September 25, Crook's scouts found the well-marked trail of the women decoys leading toward the South Fork of Pit River. Unknown to the scouts, these tracks would lead to a point where Pit River expanded into a tule swamp six miles long, one to two miles wide, and impassable for man or beast. Taking the lure, the soldiers followed this trail for 15 miles but their horses—their hooves split from traveling over the jagged lava fields—gave out and the advance came to a halt. Around noon the next day, at the edge of the tule swamp, Crook—again pounded by a severe electrical storm—found what he had been searching for. However, as he would soon discover, it wasn't Has No Horse he'd been chasing, but the Snake war chief Little Rattlesnake.[3]

The dog soldiers, in no apparent hurry, calmly rode up a steep slope above the swamp and awaited the outcome. Crook prepared for battle, ordering Lt. Parnell to dismount half of his men and form a skirmish line to the south of Little Rattlesnake's position while Lt. Madigan formed a similar line on the north, the two uniting on the east in front of the Shoshoni's position. This maneuver took nearly an hour as the Shoshoni patiently waited for the attack. During the time Parnell and Madigan were getting into battle position, McIntosh with his Shoshoni scouts was ordered back to a bluff overlooking the valley to assess the enemy's position. Little Rattlesnake had not been caught napping and McIntosh's report was bleak.

---

2    Bourke, "General Crook in the Indian Country," *The Century Magazine*, Vol. XLI, No. 5, p. 6.

3    Crook, *Autobiography*, p. 153; Bancroft, *History of Oregon* II, p. 539.

The Indian stronghold—located on the west side of the river valley—was backed by the rim of an ancient volcanic crater some 300 feet high and nearly half a mile long. At some point in the past, massive rocks—some weighing hundreds of tons—had tumbled down and filled a depression where the Shoshoni were now taking a defensive stand. At the north end of this perpendicular basalt wall lay a ridge of boulders and at the south end, a deep canyon. In front was a low sharp ridge of lava blocks sloping into the valley. These features formed a natural fortification of great strength.

According to McIntosh, there were other characteristics of the Snake fortress which rendered it even more formidable. Running into the bluff's southeastern boundary were two rock promontories, 150 feet in length, 30 feet in height, with sheer walls parallel to each other and about 30 feet apart—making a scarped moat which could not be passed. At the north end of the eastern promontory, the Shoshoni had erected a fort of stone 20 feet in diameter, breast-high, pierced with rifle ports; and on the western promontory there were two large forts of similar construction. Between this fortress and the bluff where the scouts were stationed were huge masses of rocks of every size and contour. The only approach to the western stronghold was from the eastern slope where the first fort was located.

At Crook's command, Lt. William Parnell approached the canyon on the south. A volley was fired from the western fort and the Indians fell back under cover when Parnell, by a rapid charge, gained the shelter of a rocky rim but in reconnoitering immediately after gaining the rim, the soldiers exposed themselves to another volley from the fort which killed two infantrymen and wounded three others. It became obvious that only by siege could the foe be dislodged. Displaying his usual enthusiasm on Indian warfare, Crook commented, "Indians were found occupying, or rather ran into, some rocks. In prospecting these rocks we had some men killed and wounded."[4]

Following this setback, Lt. Eskridge—who had taken charge of the horses, herders and supplies—was ordered back into camp and preparations were made for taking care of the wounded, present and anticipated. Accompanying him was Wendolen Nus who furnished beef for Fort Klamath and Fort Warner. This move may have saved his life but not for long. Five years later in the same general area Nus was killed in the Modoc War.

The fighting now began in earnest and the afternoon was spent in an exchange of gunfire punctuated by Shoshoni war whoops and obscene curses from the troopers. A squad of Parnell's men were ordered to the bluff to join McIntosh's scouts and help them to rain bullets down into the Snake fortresses. Little Rattlesnake's warriors were entirely surrounded, yet such was the nature of the ground that they could not be approached by the infantry skirmish line and the gunfire was chiefly confined to sharpshooting. The range from the bluff above the

---

4   Crook, *Autobiography*, p. 153.

west forts was about 400 yards at an angle of 45 degrees, and during the afternoon hundreds of bullets were sent down among the defenders with little effect. From the east fort, Shoshoni marksmen could reach the bluff with long-range rifles and it was necessary for the soldiers to keep under cover. All the Indians who could be seen were clad only in a short buckskin skirts with eagle feathers in their hair. More disturbing, all weapons seen were the latest models in American-made firearms.

Near sunset, a lone dog soldier appeared on the edge of the eastern fortification in full view of the army sharpshooters; gave a triumphant war-cry as he jumped to level ground; slipped through the cordon of soldiers; and, on foot, outran his mounted pursuers. They knew he had gone for one of two things . . . either supplies or reinforcements. They were wrong on both counts. This fleet messenger was out to alert Has No Horse that Little Rattlesnake had Gray Wolf's attention and he, Has No Horse, could renew attacks on the northern front.

If it seems farfetched that an Indian could outrun a cavalry troop, consider what Col. Shields witnessed. Running Antelope, a Hunkpapa Sioux, ran down and caught an adult antelope in a straight-away race lasting five hours. The most famous runner of ancient Greece, Pheidippides, ran from Athens to Sparta, a distance of 140 miles, in 36 hours. Among the Indians such a feat would have been considered second-rate. A Hopi messenger ran 120 miles in 15 hours and in 1882, a Cree warrior ran 125 miles in 25 hours. His only comment was "a pretty good run."[5]

While horsemen pursued the Snake runner and the afternoon wore on, Crook examined Little Rattlesnake's position from every angle. There was no easy way to get at the enemy. As night approached, he stationed pickets around the stronghold to prevent any further escapes. When darkness fell, the army scouts left the bluff and crept down among the rocks between the bluff and the two lava promontories, getting within a hundred feet of the east fort. The infantrymen also infiltrated the rocks, creeping nearer to the Indians who evidently anticipated their movements and kept their arrows flying in every direction while they peppered the area with stones thrown at random. Not only were the Shoshoni conserving ammunition, but it was impossible to detect where the missiles were coming from.

As the soldiers kept up a deadly cross-fire in the darkness, one of Madigan's men was killed by Parnell's company. All night, there was the sound of rolling rocks and stone banging against stone, as if additional breastworks were being constructed. Whenever a volley was fired by the troopers in the direction of these noises, a sound of voices was heard reverberating as if in a cavern. During the early part of the night, there were frequent flashes of lightning and heavy peals of thunder to add to the confusion. As the night dragged on, no change was apparent in the position of either side.

---

5    Shields, Col. G.O., *The Blanket Indian*, New York, 1921, p. 131; Hodge, *Handbook of North American Indians*, Part II, p. 802.

Shortly before dawn, September 27, Parnell and Madigan were directed to bring in their pickets and form under the crest of the ridge facing the east fortification while the scouts were ordered to take positions on the opposite side of the ridge. Their mission was uncomplicated. The only requirement was . . . to storm the Indian fort!

According to Joe Wasson—reporter and part-owner of the *Owyhee Avalanche*—Crook talked to his men like a father, telling them that when he commanded "Forward!" they should "rise up quick, go with a yell, and keep yelling, and never think of stopping until you have crossed the ditch, scaled the wall and broken through the breastworks, and the faster the better."[6] At sunrise, the command was given.

The initial attack team—about 40 in number—sprang to their feet and rushed toward the forts. They had not gone 20 paces when a barrage from the Indians struck down Lt. Madigan, three noncommissioned officers, three privates and one civilian—eight in all. The remainder of the storming party kept on, crossing a natural moat and gaining the rock wall which seemed to present but two access points. Sgt. John Russler of the 23rd Infantry, led the way up one of these lava chutes; Sgt. Michael Meara and Pvt. Willoughby Sawyer of the 1st Cavalry, led the way up the other. Meara was the first to reach a natural parapet surrounding the east fort on two sides. He was dashing across this barrier, shouting to his men to come on, when a bullet ripped through his head with such force it hurled his dead body into the arms of his charging men. At the same moment Russler came up and, jamming his rifle through a gun port, fired. He was also shot. The next man to reach the top and live was Joe Wasson.

Wasson's news reports dealing with the various expeditions which he accompanied into the Shoshoni front indicate a remarkable education coupled with a sense of humor. His attitude toward Indians was typically frontier and he often expressed them through verses of Alexander Pope—an 18th English century poet who was sympathetic to the Indian's plight. One of Wasson's translations went like this:

> *Lo! the poor Indian, whose untutored mind*
> *Sees God (damn) in everything,*
> *And hears Him (when three sheets) in the wind!*

Wasson himself, now hearing God's summons in the wind, held a new respect for the "poor Indian" and was fighting like a demon for his life.

It was thought that the Shoshoni would be trapped in their enclosure and slaughtered but they slipped through the rocks "like lizards" and were soon attacking the soldiers now caught in their own trap. Crook had gained the east

---

6    *The Portland Oregonian*, November 12, 1867.

fortress but his men were now pinned in a cross-fire as shots were coming from the rocks beneath them. Several more soldiers were wounded or killed and the situation became critical in the extreme.

Crook would describe the dilemma with little emotion: "After we got possession of the fort, we had drawn the White Elephant prize, for the Indians were deep down in the rocks where all was darkness, and we could see nothing, whereas they, being in the dark and we in the light, they could see us. We kept up a fusillade down in the rocks in the hopes that we might hit some of them accidentally, and assuming the air of conquerors, held the fort all day. . . ." Pinned down in this trap, Crook later admitted "I never wanted dynamite so bad as I did when we first took the fort and heard the diabolical and defiant yells from down in the rocks."[7]

Fearing that Little Rattlesnake was preparing another surprise, a strange thing happened. Around noon, following sporadic rifle fire from the west fortification, a nerve-wracking lull settled over the battlefield. Though the soldiers exposed themselves to draw enemy fire and uncover their position, nothing happened. Finally a lone shot rang out. The bullet entered a rifle port, killing the soldier stationed there. Again silence. The west fort, being inaccessible, could not be stormed. There was nothing to do but wait and watch for the next movement of the Shoshoni who, so far as known, were still concealed in their western fortress where the crying of children and other signs of life could be heard through the afternoon and night of September 27.

It was later claimed that an Indian baby was suffocated to keep it from crying and exposing the hidden warriors whereabouts. One report would flatly state that the baby was "strangled by having a forked stick pressed down against its neck," which seems unlikely but whatever, a Shoshoni infant was found among the dead bodies.[8]

On the morning of the 28th, the suspense having become unbearable, Crook permitted a Shoshoni woman to pass through the picket lines. From her, he received an explanation of the mysterious silence of the defender's guns. Not one warrior was left in any of the forts. By a series of subterranean passages leading to the canyon on the south, they had all escaped and had been gone for many hours. Through these same fissures communications could and had been kept up with the outside. Having gained their objective of keeping Crook occupied while Has No Horse plundered, the dog soldiers left the women and children behind to deceive the soldiers until they were safely out of danger.

Any attempt to check the woman's story was soon determined to be foolhardy. Pvt. James Lyon, descending into one of the passageways to pick up a souvenir of the battle by scalping a dead Indian, was killed by same. His body was tossed into a deep crevasse where his comrades had much difficulty recovering it.

---

7    Crook, *Autobiography*, p. 154.

8    Bourke, "General Crook In Indian Country," *The Century Magazine*, Vol. XLI, No. 5, p. 8.

In the past two days no more than 15 Indians were killed—counting women and children—at a price of eight soldiers killed and 19 men wounded.[9] About the best that can be said for this engagement is it was now over.

The dead—except for Lt. Madigan—were buried a half mile north of the battle ground in the Pit River Valley some 50 miles south of the Oregon line.[10] Horses were picketed over the graves to obliterate all signs of disturbance. It didn't work. Later, a cavalry squadron was sent to disinter the bodies and bring the remains to Fort Warner for military burial but no bodies could be found. It was believed the Shoshoni dug them up and disposed of them. It is equally possible that the retrieval detail was not that eager to uproot their fallen comrades.

The wounded were gathered and mule litters rigged to carry them the grueling five-day march to the hospital at Fort Warner. The remains of Lt. Madigan were taken one day's march from the battlefield and burned on the north bank of Pit River, about 20 miles above the junction of the South Fork.

On learning of this latest run-in with the Snakes, the press was not kind—implying that Gen. Crook sacrificed his men in an attempt to achieve what the public expected of him. Desk reporters would accuse war correspondents attached to the expedition of releasing "laudatory and apologetic accounts" of the fight. In true armchair fashion, it was suggested that had Crook let McIntosh's Snake scouts fight their red brothers while he held his troops ready to "succor them if overpowered, the results might have been different." That opinion, based on ignorance, would have been laughable were it not so pathetic.

The only ray of sunshine so far as Crook was concerned, was a letter delivered to Fort Warner in late September from his wife. Mary Crook, born to the luxuries of plantation life, was coming to join him on the eastern Oregon frontier. Ironically, an official letter was waiting for Lt. John Madigan notifying him of his recent promotion to captain in the United States Army.

One thing above media debate, Crook was able to prove beyond all doubt that Snake warriors were well supplied with arms and ammunition which had to have been obtained by the sale of stolen property seized in eastern Oregon. Stored

---

9   The death list includes: Lt. John Madigan, Sgt. Charles Brochet (a native of Germany), Sgt. Michael Meara, Sgt. John Russler, Pvt. James Lyon, Pvt. Willoughby Sawyer, Pvt. Karl Brose, and Pvt. James Corey. The known wounded were: Cpl. McCann, Cpl. Fogarty, Cpl. Firman, Pvt. Clancy, Pvt. Fisher, Pvt. Kingston, Pvt. McGuire, Pvt. Embler, Pvt. Barbea, Pvt. Shea, Pvt. Enser, and Lawrence Traynor (a civilian packer). Seven Warm Springs troopers were also wounded. For complete details of the Battle of the Infernal Caverns see: *Portland Herald*, December 10, 1867; *Portland Oregonian*, November 12, 1867; Bancroft, *History of Oregon*, II, pp. 538-44; Crook, *Autobiography*, pp. 153-55; William R. Parnell, "Operation Against Hostile Indians With General Crook 1867-1868," *The United Service, N.S.*, Vol. I, Nos. 5 and 6 (May and June, 1889), pp. 485-91; *Owyhee Avalanche*, November 2, 1867; Hayes, *Indian Scraps*, V, p. 141; *General Order Military Department of the Columbia*, No. 32, 1867.

10  The battle site of the Infernal Caverns, northwest of Likely, California on U.S. Highway 395, is noted on California maps.

in sacks, tin cans and boxes among the rocks in Hell's Cave, was an abundant supply of powder, caps and bullets. All rifles confiscated were American made and of the latest issue. Not one breach-loading gun was found in this Shoshoni arsenal.

After this ignominious setback, Crook's blood was up. Barely taking time to care for the sick and the wounded, he was again in the saddle pushing northward toward the Ochoco in an October snowstorm and a showdown with Has No Horse.

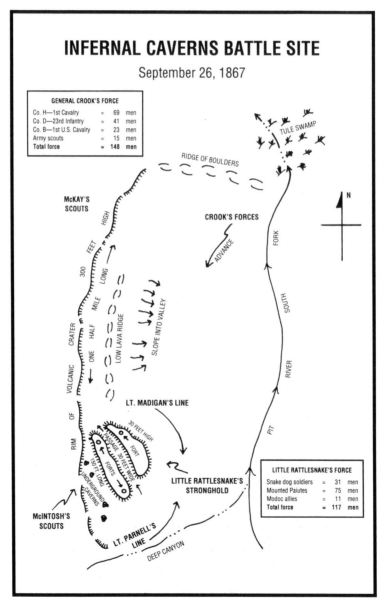

## INFERNAL CAVERNS BATTLE SITE
### September 26, 1867

**GENERAL CROOK'S FORCE**

| | | | |
|---|---|---|---|
| Co. H—1st Cavalry | = | 69 | men |
| Co. D—23rd Infantry | = | 41 | men |
| Co. B—1st U.S. Cavalry | = | 23 | men |
| Army scouts | = | 15 | men |
| **Total force** | **=** | **148** | **men** |

TULE SWAMP

RIDGE OF BOULDERS

McKAY'S SCOUTS

CROOK'S FORCES

ADVANCE

FORK

N

300 FEET HIGH

ONE HALF MILE LONG

VOLCANIC CRATER

LOW LAVA RIDGE

SLOPE INTO VALLEY

SOUTH

RIVER

LT. MADIGAN'S LINE

RIM OF

30 FEET HIGH

FORT

PASSAGE 30 FEET WIDE

FORTS

150 FT LONG

UNDERGROUND CAVERNS

LITTLE RATTLESNAKE'S STRONGHOLD

PIT

**LITTLE RATTLESNAKE'S FORCE**

| | | | |
|---|---|---|---|
| Snake dog soldiers | = | 31 | men |
| Mounted Paiutes | = | 75 | men |
| Modoc allies | = | 11 | men |
| **Total force** | **=** | **117** | **men** |

McINTOSH'S SCOUTS

LT. PARNELL'S LINE

DEEP CANYON

# CHAPTER 143

# BLOOD TRAIL

*Capt. Kelly concluded to let us all return to Camp Harney. We left at 10 o'clock . . . as the Snakes have all taken the alarm & fled.*

**Capt. William McKay**
Sunday, October 20, 1867

The expedition under Captains Perry, Harris and McKay which proceeded north from Abert Lake failed to make contact with the enemy. On September 26, in the same thunderstorm that escorted Crook into the Pit River ambush, Perry reached Crooked River a few miles west of the present site of Prineville. To date, the most ferocious thing the Long Knives had killed was a bear on Tetherow Butte north of the present day Redmond. The cavalry units then made an extensive search of the Crooked River Basin from the mouth of the Ochoco River to the South Fork of Crooked River—finding nothing. This lack of hostile sightings led Perry to the conclusions that the Snakes were defeated, thinking only of seclusion and flight.

By now, Little Rattlesnake's messenger had packed the news of his recent success into the Ochoco war camps and the valleys of the Blues were echoing with victory yells when word arrived that Crook's main force was marching toward Crooked River. In true Shoshoni fashion, Has No Horse split his forces and sent them scattering to the four winds. Their orders were to strike mining settlements, wagon roads, settler's cabins and keep on the move. In this manner, he planned to constantly harass the army without actually exposing himself until winter arrived—insuring his people comparative safety, for he believed the whites were unprepared for a winter offensive.

Three weeks before Crook's abortive clash with Little Rattlesnake, Lt. John Small with 51 8th U.S. Cavalrymen and 10 Klamath scouts (commanded by Dave Hill), rode out of Fort Klamath and were making headlines. In a 20-day march, they killed 23 Shoshoni and captured 19. According to Hill, among those killed were Big Man, Black Buffalo (who signed the Treaty of 1864) and an influential medicine man who was unnamed. To make the story more exciting, it was claimed that Hill killed Black Buffalo in hand-to-hand combat.[1] It would later be proven that this much publicized report was, for the most part, erroneous.

Neither Big Man nor Black Buffalo signed the Treaty of 1864 and it soon became obvious that Big Man was very much alive. Almost a year later, Lindsay Applegate—agent on the Klamath reservation—reported to Supt. Huntington that "a group of Snakes came onto the reservation and their chief, Chock-toot [Black Buffalo] who was reported killed by troops from Fort Klamath last summer was with them."[2]

However, Lt. Small did take many prisoners and a general council with these captives was held at the Klamath Agency on September 28, 1867—the same day Crook was under siege on Pit River. These Snake hostages assured Applegate that the war chief Pony Blanket desired to be on friendly terms with the Americans. "He has been so disposed ever since the Snake treaty but has been kept away by hostile parties." Overjoyed at this intelligence, a plan was laid to have Pony Blanket report to Fort Klamath and Applegate would insure his protection while coming.[3] This was another ploy in Has No Horse's strategy. His brother-in-law had no intention of giving himself up to the enemy.

While this hopeful council was in progress, Capt. McKay—attached to Perry's command—reached Fort Currey on Silver Creek which he described as "... a very good camp. A great deal of work done on this post and a good point to operate from, being on the divide waters of the Harney and Crooked River."[4] Nonetheless, McKay used the stockade walls and barracks for firewood—destroying another historic landmark.

On October 6, he arrived at Fort Harney and the following day made an interesting note in his journal. "This morning Capt. Gillis chief of the QM Department of this district, Capt. Perry & Capt. Harris left for Canyon City. The last two are for Camp Watson to be back in 10 days. Capt. Gillis for Portland to fetch up Mrs. Gen. Crooks & Mrs. Gillis, who are to be here in two weeks."[5] Not

---

1    Hill would identify Big Man and Black Buffalo as "Chickocclox and Chocktoot." Perhaps this was the way reporters spelled Oulux (Big Man) and Chocktote (Black Buffalo). *Jacksonville Sentinel*, September 28,m 1867; *San Francisco Alta*, September 28, 1867; *Yreka Union*, October 5, 1867; *Portland Oregonian*, November 4 and 12, 1867.

2    Voegelin, *The Northern Paiute of Central Oregon*, p. 253. An interview with Dave Chocktote in the 1930s confirmed that Black Buffalo did not die in 1867.

3    National Archives, Bureau of Indian Affairs, Oregon Superintendency, Letters Received; Lindsay Applegate to J. Perit Huntington, Ashland Mills, Oregon, October 3, 1867.

4    Quotes taken from McKay's Journals, entries dates from September 13 through October 21, 1867.

5    Capt. McKay was referring to Margaret (Mary) Dailey Crook and Julia (Julie) Stellwagen Gilliss. Traveling with them was Capt. and Julia Gilliss' infant daughter and nurse. They left the Umatilla House at The Dalles City on October 20, 1867 and arrived at Fort Watson on October 23, 1867 in an army ambulance drawn by four mules. Julia Gilliss, *So Far From Home: An Army Bride on the Western Frontier, 1865-1869*, p. 149.

exactly a safe shelter for the ladies but the General was now marching across the high desert to Fort Harney and looking forward to a reunion with his wife whom he hadn't seen since leaving Baltimore a year ago.

Following the removal of Capt. James Wildy's 6th Cavalry units from the John Day country in late August, the Snake offensive had heated up on the northern and eastern fronts as Has No Horse threw all of his remaining battle-chiefs into the fray.

On the night of October 3—the same night McKay used Fort Currey for firewood—within half a mile of Owyhee City, Joseph Colwell, a highly respected citizen, was killed, scalped and the body burned. The following night a raid was made on cattle in Jordan Valley within three miles of Silver City. Houses, barns, corrals and haystacks were set ablaze in the John Day Valley at the same time four separate raids were made into the Boise Basin.[6] Blood as well as spoils of war marked the course of the Snake invaders.

Stagecoaches running the gauntlet on The Dalles-Canyon City-Boise road, and even Snake River barges were being attacked. Letters and newspapers found in Shoshoni war camps were clotted with human gore. An organized civilian force, armed with rifles furnished by Fort Boise and aided by a squadron of cavalry, pushed deep into eastern Oregon and retook some livestock. On their return to Fort Boise, the cavalry captured two Snake warriors and executed them. The death of one would cause a severe blow to Has No Horse's eastern command. It was reported that one of the prisoners killed was branded on the face with a circle and the figures 1845.[7] Four Crows would now chase buffalo in the Spirit Land with Paulina, his boyhood friend.

While the Idaho militia was on the move, Big Man and Has No Horse were scouring the country from Antelope Valley in central Oregon to the mouth of the Payette River in Idaho Territory—taking anything of value that would produce more arms and ammunition for the final death struggle of a dying nation. In stark contrast, followers of Gourd Rattler and The Climber were being civilized and herded onto reservations. The dawn of a new era had arrived. The red brethren roaming the Eldahow were now to give up their nomadic life and settle in one place to become tillers of the soil. When told of these new arrangements, Gourd Rattler was quoted as saying "I am laughing because I am happy."[8] More likely, he was overcome with hysteria.

With bullets flying to the north and treaty papers shuffling to the east, Crook galloped into Fort Harney on October 11 to await the arrival of his wife. Twelve days after his forced march across the central Oregon desert, Mary Crook with

---

6    *Owyhee Avalanche*, October 5, 1867; *Boise Statesman*, October 22, 1867.

7    Bancroft, *History of Oregon*, II, p. 546, footnote 33.

8    Indian Office Records, Idaho Superintendency, Gen. C.C. Augur to President of Indian Peace Commission, October 4, 1868.

entourage arrived at the wilderness outpost of the Ochoco—Fort Stephen Watson—causing considerable excitement and confusion among the battle weary troops.[9] Some had not seen a white woman in over a year. She paused only long enough to pick up an escort and made the last treacherous leg of the journey on horseback, through the hostile heart of the Blues to Fort Harney. . . a four day ride during which the army wives camped at the Suplee Soda Spring.

As if his wife's safe passage wasn't enough to worry about, it became apparent that Gen. Crook had a serious problem with the Warm Springs Cavalry. The day after his arrival at Fort Harney—in a letter to Lt. Richard Strong, assistant adjutant general for the Military Department of Columbia at Portland, dated October 12, 1867—he would report: "The Indians in Capts. Darragh's and McKay's scouts (he refused to recognize them as U.S. Regulars) are very much dissatisfied and want to go back to their families, in this dissatisfied condition they will not be of any service to me." He further recommended—which within a month, Gen. Steele would make official—that the Warm Springs Cavalry be mustered out of the service and replaced with friendly Shoshoni scouts. At one point, Crook even considered training some of the younger captured hostiles for that purpose.[10] That's how desperate the situation was.

In an effort to get the Warm Springs Cavalry off the post, Crook ordered Darragh and McKay into the field along with Capt. William Kelly and Lt. McCleave with a detachment of 8th U.S. Cavalry to engage the Snakes at any cost. Darragh and McCleave headed north out of Fort Harney while McKay and Kelly pushed east. Both units were laying waste to the land as they advanced, torching grass, burning timber, polluting springs and slaughtering game. When identified, they were even trampling out camas and bitter root beds.

Spotting signal smokes, Kelly and McKay made an unproductive charge to the top of "Horse Cock Mountain" on the Malheur River—a name which may have reflected the troopers attitude toward the country.[11] Whatever the case, later historians didn't think this reference to the equine generative organ was appropriate so it was renamed Castle Rock. In a 10-day foray covering some 300 miles, McKay took one woman prisoner (who escaped the day after capture) and one army mule.

On October 20, a week before Mary Crook arrived at Fort Harney, Capt. Kelly terminated his quest for dog soldiers and turned back toward Harney Valley. That same morning, some 50 miles southeast of his position, there occurred—according to the media—"one of the most painful incidents of the

---

9    Julia Gilliss would describe Fort Watson as a comfortable outpost. "I like it here at Camp Watson very well and should be pleased if it were our destination. But I suppose Camp Harney will be equally pleasant when we arrive there." Gilliss, *So Far From Home: An Army Bride on the Western Frontier, 1865-1869,* p. 151. She would soon change her mind.

10    Military Department of the Columbia, Box 8, C18, Letters Received, Crook to AAG Dept. of Columbia, February 24, 1868.

11    McKay, Journal entry for Tuesday, October 15, 1867.

Shoshoni war." Painful, yes, to the white citizens of Oregon—but the Shoshoni could tell of many acts of equal brutality suffered by their own women and children—such as the agonizing deaths of Half Moon, Running Deer, Bright Eyes, Spotted Fawn, and Mountain Breeze.[12]

Sgt. Nickols and Sgt. Denoille—attached to the 8th U.S. Cavalry—left Fort Lyon in a four-horse ambulance en route to Fort Boise with Denoille's sick wife. Unknown to them, they were on a collision course with the Snake war chief Fox, whose wife had been brutally slain by the Warm Springs Cavalry exactly nine months to the day from this chance encounter.[13] Nine miles from the fort, while passing through a rocky canyon, Fox, with five warriors (one of whom was his father-in-law, the Snake medicine man, Left Hand) made his attack. Denoille, who was driving, was struck by the first shots. Nickols, not knowing that his comrade was hit, was giving his attention to the Indians when Denoille fell out of the ambulance dead. At this, the horses became spooked, running half a mile at full speed until one fell and arrested the flight of the others. Nickols now sprang out, followed by Mrs. Denoille, whom he urged to conceal herself before the Indians came up but in a state of shock, she insisted on returning to find her husband. Nickols, hiding among the rocks, escaped to a ranch that evening.

When a rescue party went out from Silver City to recover Sgt. Denoille's body, which was stripped and mutilated, nothing could be learned of the fate of his wife. A scouting party was immediately organized at Fort Lyon. At the Owyhee River, the cavalry came upon a camp from which the Shoshoni had fled, leaving behind two women. These women declared that Mrs. Denoille had not been harmed but was being held for ransom. One was sent to locate Fox and to inquire what ransom would be required. She failed to return. Holding the other woman hostage, the cavalrymen then returned to Fort Lyon to refit for a longer expedition.

Lt. Col. Coppinger and Capt. James Hunt immediately resumed the pursuit but Fox and Left Hand had disappeared. About mid-December, army scout Donald McKay and his Umatilla warriors attacked a Shoshoni winter camp, killing five and capturing six. Some of Mrs. Denoille's clothing was found on one of the captured women who said that the white captive had been taken south to Bad Face's camp to be held as a pawn in the game of war. The truth of the woman's fate wouldn't surface until the spring of 1868. At that time a Snake prisoner led an army scout to the place of Mrs. Denoille's death and showed him her bleaching bones. She had been taken a half mile from the road where the attack was made, dragged by the neck to a convenient rock, her head laid upon it and crushed with a war club.

---

12    The stories of these women's deaths are told in this volume as follows: Tall Man's wife (pg. 29), Half Moon (pg. 156), Running Deer (pg. 358), Bright Eyes (pg. 372), and Spotted Fawn and Mountain Breeze (pg. 429).

13    See Chapter 137, "Warm Springs Commandos," pp. 334-335.

The Indian who described the scene to a search party was riddled with bullets.[14]

The bloody account of Shoshoni terrorism is not pretty reading. But neither is it edifying to read the chronicles—bordering on genocide—of grand theft, brazen swindling and sheer brutality imposed upon the defenders of the Ochoco. True, the Snakes were not alone on this trail of broken treaties and broken hearts; but other minority groups have their vociferous defenders. Almost no one speaks for the American Indian, although the trend is beginning to become more popular and gaining momentum with each passing year.

---

14    *Boise Statesman*, October 24, 26 and December 17, 1867; *Owyhee Avalanche*, June 13, 1868.

CHAPTER 144

# SHITIKE CAVALRY IN RETREAT

*Left Canyon City and crossed the mountains to Susanville . . .
left Susanville . . . arrived at the mining camp [Granite] . . .
left the north fork of the John Day's river at the mining camp
. . . Was at Kamos Prarie [Camas Meadows] . . . Stayed all
night at Andy Sturtevants [Birch Creek] . . . left the Smith
Hotell [sic] [Pilot Rock] . . . arrived at the Reservation
[Umatilla] . . . spent about 2 hours, and went through to
Wallawalla. . . .*

**Capt. Wm. C. McKay**
Drunk and 10 days AWOL

Capt. McKay rode into Fort Harney the day of the "Denoille Massacre" and immediately dispatched a pack-mule train to Canyon City to pick up provisions for his starving Snake prisoners of war. During the army's recent purge of the Malheur country, many Paiutes had escaped into Nevada in the hope of finding safety. Among these refugees was the nine-year-old son of the Paiute visionary, Tavibo—the White Man. Born in the Ochoco at the start of Shoshoni hostilities, this boy—known to his family as Wovoka, The Cutter—had spent most of his young life along the Walker River in Nevada where his parents had fled to escape the war raging across eastern Oregon.[1] Now, he was attempting to unite with his father who was riding with Bad Face's hostiles.

In 1863, the Wilson brothers—David and George—without ceremony or permission, had taken up a large land claim in Mason Valley on Paiute hunting grounds which The Cutter now called home.[2] Instead of finding his father, The Cutter wandered onto the Wilson ranch, and being a husky lad for his age, they put him to work riding herd on their cattle. Soon everyone was calling this quiet Paiute boy, Jack Wilson—a name he didn't especially like.

---

1    James Mooney would place Wovoka's birth date at about 1856 (*Fourteenth Annual Report of the Bureau of Ethnology*, II, p. 771.) Wovoka's wooden slab grave marker, in the rocky cemetery of the little Indian town of Schurz, Nevada, states that he died September 20, 1932 at age 74 which would mean he was born in 1858.

2    Bailey, Paul, *Wovoka, The Indian Messiah*, p. 22.

This reference to a frightened Indian boy fleeing Harney Valley ahead of the U.S. Cavalry's blazing guns becomes significant when placed in its proper sequence in time. As a man, The Cutter—another displaced Ochoco Shoshoni—would fire the western tribes from the Mississippi River to the Pacific coast with a religious fervor unparalleled in the advance of American colonization.

Back at Fort Harney, fueled by increasing desertion among the Warm Springs regulars, the whole outfit was detailed to round up pack mules and horses to be taken to Washington Territory for winter pasture. This brought on more complaints. When McKay arrived back at Fort Harney from his supply run to Canyon City, he was greeted with some unwelcome news. Lt. O.W. Pollock, AAAG—on Crook's request—had issued Special Order No. 8, dated October 28, 1867 (a day before McKay's return) stating that five of Darragh's and five of McKay's Warm Springs regulars would not be allowed to go with their units to Fort Walla Walla but instead would "proceed direct to Warm Springs and be mustered out of the service." This reprimand was hand delivered to Darragh and McKay on October 29. The next morning, Gen. and Mrs. Crook, Capt. and Mrs. Gilliss, Lt. and Mrs. Pollock, Lt. George Dodge, Paymaster Johnson, and his civilian clerks, Mr. Day and Mr. Halliday, left for Fort Warner without an escort.[3]

During their brief stay at Fort Harney Julia Gilliss was not favorably impressed with the frontier citadel. "This post is destined to be a very large and busy one, but will always be disagreeable from the fact that it is situated on a flat with alkaline dust about a foot deep. I never saw such a dirty place." She would continue, "I can't complain much. I have the most aristocratic home at the fort and the only one with a floor."[4] Apparently Mary Crook was not so fortunate.

Crook's small party—traveling light and fast—made it to Fort Warner in four days and it was a good thing that they did. Snow, which had been falling intermittently since September, culminated in a furious storm on November 6, blocking the roads and trails so that supplies ordered for the various army outposts could not get in. Pack trains were dispatched to Virginia City, Nevada to obtain any subsistence stores that were available.[5] Bad as it was, the blizzard may not have been the only threat that Crook was successful in side-stepping.

The British historian, William Blackmore, had been contacting various Comanche tribes throughout the summer of 1867. On October 5, he would note that a large war party under the leadership of Silver Brooch, Little Horse and Iron Mountain had been absent from the plains for a year. This war expedition had ridden to the country west of the Rocky Mountains where "according to

---

3    Crook, *Autobiography,* p. 155.

4    Julia Gilliss would claim they were "accompanied by a whole company of 23rd Infantry with a train of pack mules with their Mexican drivers and a train of baggage wagons. Gilliss, *So Far From Home,* p. 153.

5    Bourke, "General Crook In Indian Country," *The Century Magazine,* Vol. XLI, No. 5, p. 8.

[Comanche] tradition, their ancestors had come from."[6] This information would support Crook's belief that Has No Horse was getting outside help; that, for the most part, the Shoshoni nation was solidly behind the Paviotso Confederacy; and that the Oregonians' stubborn reluctance to accept this reality was nothing short of stupidity. But ignore it, they did.

On November 1—a week before the arctic express roared across interior Oregon—Lt. James Rothermel of the 8th U.S. Cavalry, took command of the two Indian companies and placing gloomy John Darragh and budding alcoholic Billy McKay in the role of livestock herders. Pushing 403 army mules and 41 cavalry horses, Rothermel arrived at Fort Walla Walla on November 12. Hampered by wind, snow and fog, he made good time but he also had suffered a serious problem. Immediately upon arrival at Walla Walla, the lieutenant dispatched a message to Department headquarters in Portland: "I have to report to the general commanding the conduct of Wm. C. McKay, in charge of one of the Cos. of Indian Scouts. When we left Camp Harney, he was very much intoxicated and when the command reached Canyon City he became so much intoxicated that he was left behind at that place and his command marched on without him. He has not as yet joined his command, and his men are entirely without a company commander."[7] Apparently Darragh had his hands full just riding herd on his own warriors.

Six days later, Rothermel would again contact headquarters: "In my letter of the 12th inst. notifying the Department of my arrival at this post with my command, I reported William C. McKay in charge of a Co. absent. Said McKay returned and reported to me on the 14th inst. being absent from his command from the 5th November until the 14th November, 10 days."[8]

It can be suspected that Capt. William Cameron McKay—a surgeon by profession—had snapped under the strain of ordering women and children butchered in the name of progress and had decided "to hell with it!" In his erratic course to Washington Territory, the doctor hit every mining camp saloon, suttler's post and whiskey still in the middle Blues. His official journal lacked entries from Friday, November 1 through Friday, November 8, when he came back to reality. What entries were made until November 18—when again he left a gap from November 19 through November 26—were written in a shaky hand, and sometimes crosswise on the page.[9]

---

6    Blackmore, William, *The American Indians 100 Years Ago.* London, England, 1876.

7    National Archives, Record Group 393, Box 8, Roll 26027; Rothermel to Asst. Adj. Gen. Dept. of Columbia, Portland. Letter dated November 12, 1867, Fort Walla Walla, Washington Territory.

8    Ibid, Rothermel to Asst. Adj. Gen. Dept. of Columbia, Portland, Letter dated November 18, 1867, Fort Walla Walla, Washington Territory.

9    McKay's *Journal*, 1866-67: Indian Scouts, October 31, 1867 through November 29, 1867.

It would appear that Lt. Rothermel reprimanded Capt. McKay and demoted him one grade in rank for on November 15, 1867, the *Walla Walla Statesman* reported: "A detachment of Indian warriors under the command of Capt. John Darragh and *Lieut.* McKay, arrived from Harney Lake." It would then go on to extol the virtues of the Warm Springs Cavalry: "While on duty in Oregon, California, Nevada, Idaho, and Washington, they have shown themselves admirably adapted for the peculiar service in which they were engaged." However, the *Walla Walla Statesman* was quick to add a disclaimer that it didn't condone such warfare: "In a regular stand-up fight, they [the Warm Springs Cavalry] were greatly inferior to the white soldiers but when it came to scouting their services were invaluable."

During this current disruption in the Shoshoni war, Major Gen. Steele relinquished command of the Military Department of the Columbia to Brig. Gen. L.H. Rosseau on November 23, and immediately upon leaving Oregon, died of a massive stroke in San Francisco. Since Rosseau would not arrive until February 1868, this placed Major Gen. Crook in temporary command of the Columbia Department in addition to the Military District of the Lakes, and the fate of the 1st U.S. Warm Springs Cavalry was sealed.

In his report to Gen. Halleck, August 20, 1867—prior to Crook's complaint in October—Gen. Steele requested more Warm Springs Indians for regular military service. "It is my opinion that one hundred, in addition to those now employed, would exterminate the hostile bands before next spring."[10] This would never happen.

Back on the Columbia River, as Lt. Rothermel prodded his dissident red cavalry onto the sternwheeler *Owyhee*, he was joined by a portion of the '67 emigration. These transients would play a prominent role in the settlement of the Ochoco. In fact, two days after these tillers of the soil disembarked at the Port of The Dalles, seven men met at the Mall in Washington, D.C. and there, in the office of William Saunders, founded the Patrons of Husbandry; a fraternal organization to give political guidance to the flocks of farmers—commonly known as grangers—migrating west to cultivate the land wrenched from the Indians.

On December 2, the *Owyhee* docked at The Dalles and Lt. Rothermel with Lt. McKay in tow, stormed Fort Dalles. Here McKay was issued a government check for $985.22 in payment for services rendered to the United States Army and along with the rest of the 1st Warm Springs Cavalry, mustered out of the service.[11] Silently, William McKay and John Darragh thanked Gen. Crook for his decision.

---

10    U.S. Documents, Serial 1324, Report of Secretary of War 1867, p. 79.

11    Report of Secretary of War 1867; *Portland Oregonian*, December 23, 1867.

# CHAPTER 145

# SNOW SPIRIT

*For my part, I found a much worn pair of small moccasins*
*and an absurd little rag doll under a tree.*

**Tom Southerland**
Newspaper Reporter

While McKay and Darragh celebrated their early retirement, Crook re-outfitted for another frontal attack. With snow-blocked roads cutting off his line of supplies, Crook was in no better shape than Has No Horse for engaging in a bleak winter offensive. His men, weary and saddle-sore, their mounts in similar condition, were ready to call it quits. Unfortunately for them and the Snakes, this would not come to pass. But first on Crook's agenda when he arrived back at Fort Warner in November, was to get his wife settled into "comfortable quarters" as he called it.

In a nine-foot by twelve-foot log hut, the cracks plastered with mud to hold out the frigid winds moaning down from the frozen crest of the southern Blues, Mary Crook set about the wearisome task of making a home for the general. The cabin was void of windows and as an afterthought sported a tent fly for a door covering. The only light that threaded its way into this frontier mansion was through the roof and through these same openings, the snow sifted gently and formed a soft if not practical carpet for the earthen floor.[1]

By mid-winter, the garrison was running dangerously low on supplies. Fur-clad horsemen watched this growing crises with added interest from the ice-shrouded breaks of the high desert plateau. Backed by the drifting snows, Has No Horse cut off all communications to the southeastern outposts and grimly waited for the Snow Spirit to exact his deadly toll. But he too, was critically short on provisions.

Sensing the end was near for the embattled Has No Horse, Ouray—The Arrow—decided now was the time to divorce the Utes from the hostile Snakes. Encouraged by Brig. Gen. Kit Carson—in one of his last acts before dying of a hemorrhage on May 20, 1868—The Arrow, Yanko, his sub-chief and the war chief

---

1    Crook, *Autobiography*, p. 155.

Shavano, rode into Cheyenne, Wyoming and in January 1868 boarded a Union Pacific railroad car bound for Washington, D.C. Wined and dined by President Johnson, Gen. Grant, John Charles Fremont and "scads of other celebrities," The Arrow promised to stop fighting and join the white brothers' cause.[2]

Three thousand miles to the west, the eastern Oregon army posts were encased in snow and morale was hitting an all time low. At Fort Warner, the beef cattle were so near to starvation that their meat was almost impossible to eat. With temperatures hovering at 20 degrees below zero, the snow silently drifted around the isolated outpost to depths of 15 feet. George and Mary, to supplement their dwindling larder, donned great coats and faced the bitter desert to hunt for jack rabbits.

After a brief interlude with Mary, Crook was again on the prowl. Leaving a skeleton force at his Fort Warner headquarters, Crook began leading patrols through the sub-zero wasteland south of the Blues. The snow in the Blues—where Has No Horse's main fighting force was hiding out—was too deep to penetrate. The troopers stationed at Fort Watson and Fort Logan were trapped inside their stockade walls unable to do anything other than survive. Meanwhile, Crook was marching his scurvy-ridden men from 10 to 20 agonizing miles a day over unbroken fields of crusted snow from one to two feet deep. Wherever Has No Horse's warriors holed up, they were soon haunted by the drawn blue line of U.S. soldiers doggedly hounding their footsteps. They in turn were shadowing Crook's line of march like gaunt gray timber wolves and the casualties mounted on both sides. Some were unintentional.

On the headwaters of the Malheur River, Lt. James Rothermel was killed by his own men in a rabbit hunting accident on February 15. About the same time, Lt. Hayden Delaney of the 7th Infantry, on a scout out of Fort Bidwell, walked into a Shoshoni bullet. Although severely wounded, he did survive.[3] Others simply froze to death or surrendered to pneumonia. During the February death march, Gen. Rosseau issued an order that all Snakes being held prisoner at Fort Boise should be sent under guard to Fort Vancouver; those being held at Fort Harney and Fort Warner should be sent to Eugene City to be delivered to Indian Superintendent Huntington. The Boise prisoners of war took advantage of a severe storm when the guards were less vigilant than usual, and escaped.[4]

By the latter part of February, the going was really tough for soldiers and Shoshoni alike. Captains Harris and Perry of the 1st Cavalry and Capt. Kelly of the 8th,—experiencing a break in the weather—had very effective engagements in the vicinity of Malheur Lake. It was their intent to drive the enemy into the Steens Mountains and Crook's waiting guns. With this in mind, an express was

---

2    Sprague, Marshall, *Massacre; The Tragedy at White River*, pp. 91-92.

3    *The Dalles Mountaineer*, February 29, 1868; Bourke, *General Crook in Indian Country*, p. 8.

4    Bancroft, *History of Oregon*, II, p. 549.

dispatched to Crook's column alerting him of the plan. Swinging south in a blinding blizzard, Crook aimed his force toward the Blitzen River where it was reported that Bad Face and Pony Blanket were dug in for the winter. Lost in the terrible snowstorms of the northern Great Basin, it was well into March before Crook reached the Blitzen Valley. During this push, one of his more valuable scouts, John Holgate, was killed at Owyhee in a mining claim dispute.[5]

With the thermometer registering several degrees below zero, sloughs and creeks were frozen so hard that Crook's column had no difficulty in crossing the ice on horseback as they closed in on Bad Face's winter stronghold just after dusk. Although Crook was aware that the Indians were nearby, Bad Face's encampment—screened by willows and swirling snow—would present an invisible target for the oncoming cavalry. Crook was riding next to Jim Luckey, the guide, when Luckey's horse ran into the opening of a Shoshoni lodge. Dogs commenced barking and in the wild confusion of this close contact with the enemy, the soldiers panicked and Bad Face, without the loss of a man, woman or child, escaped across a deep muddy creek in the rear of the camp which for some unknown cause was not frozen.

Crook had a Shoshoni boy with him who, while prowling through the frozen willows with the rest of the command to make certain all the Snakes had fled, was shot at by a warrior lying on the ground. The bullet passed diagonally across his body, between his skin and shirt. This area had been crossed by many soldiers without detecting anything. Crook would later meditate: "I never could understand how this occurred, for certainly others of the party had passed over the same ground before, and I don't see how he [the Snake warrior] could have recognized the boy in the dark."[6]

Earlier in the day, Crook's scouts had seen the smoke of a village farther downriver and he believed Bad Face would head there to give the alarm. Hoping to out-distance him, the cavalry prepared for a night march and arrived at the village before daybreak. By now, it was so cold that frozen breath encrusted the soldiers' beards with ice. Unable to build warming fires for fear of detection, they managed to keep from freezing by dismounting, stamping their feet in the snow and pounding their bodies with their arms.

At the first hint of dawn, the cavalry attempted a charge across the frozen Blitzen River but the ice gave way and the advance turned into a rout as Snake riflemen poured round after round into their floundering ranks. In a furious exchange of gunfire in which 14 Shoshoni were killed, Bad Face outmaneuvered Crook and again escaped with a little help from the mountain spirits.[7] Charging after the fleeing Indians, the cavalry ran head-on into a new enemy. Known to the

5    *Sacramento Reporter*, April 10, 1868.
6    Crook, *Autobiography*, p. 156.
7    Bancroft, *History of Oregon*, II, p. 548.

Indians as "the Chinook," this westerly wind, tempered by blowing across the warm Japanese current in the Pacific Ocean, possessed the power to melt the hardest and deepest snowdrifts. Snow and ice which covered the surrounding country suddenly turned to mush. Within an hour, water was running everywhere two feet deep on top of the frozen ground. That too, began to thaw and horses became mired in bottomless mud.

A godsend to the Snakes, the warm Chinook winds were not regarded in the same cheerful light by Gen. Crook. Out of supplies, his troops sick and near exhaustion, he gave up the chase and floundered through the mud toward Fort Warner. Gaining high ground, Crook set up camp for the night on a soggy ridge top. Guards were posted but it was a mere formality for Crook had no fear of attack, believing the Snakes to be miles out of the territory. Bad Face and Pony Blanket had other plans. They, with a few dog soldiers, had followed Crook's line of retreat with vengeance in mind. True to Shoshoni nature, the war chiefs had no intention to engage in combat and lose more men. That was not the dog soldier's idea of intelligent warfare. They had a more unique battle plan. A man without a horse in this country was the same as dead and it was much more spectacular than shooting. That night as soldiers milled about trying to keep warm, silent shadows crept into camp under their very noses and just as silently left. The next morning, Crook was sickened to find 23 of his cavalry mounts and the pack mules dead. The animals had noiselessly passed into horse heaven by the simple process of slashing their throats.

Now, thoroughly disabled, Crook pushed on toward Fort Warner. When a short distance out from camp, he sent a detachment on the back trail to discover whether any Shoshoni had returned to salvage the horse meat. It worked. Two warriors found butchering out the horses were killed.[8] But the game of chess was to continue. Arriving at Upper Warner (Blue Joint) Lake in a starving condition, Crook and his aid-de-camp, Capt. Nickerson, decided to go hunting accompanied by a teamster, a private, and a supply wagon to haul in the game. Night approached with "a fearful rain and snow storm," so a camp was set up in inky darkness. Crook and Nickerson were sleeping in a tent next to the supply wagon. Their mounts were tied to the wagon tongue. The soldier was picketed on one side of the horses and the teamster was sleeping under the wagon right beside them. Come daybreak, the best saddle horse was missing. After searching for over an hour, they found tracks where an Indian had slipped into camp and made off with the horse. Crook would later comment: "The strange thing of his taking the pony was that on the opposite side of the wagon tongue from where the teamster was sleeping were some mules tied, and how the pony could be distinguished by the Indian in the dark is more than I have ever been able to satisfy myself about. It was not possible, owing to the lay of the country, for him to have gotten his information before dark."[9] The

8    Ibid.
9    Crook, *Autobiography*, pp. 157-8.

Wahtatkin brave who pulled this off proved that his tribe had received the name Pony Stealers for good reason.

At Upper Warner Lake, a haggard messenger brought word from Fort Harney that the garrison was riddled with scurvy. To help combat it, troopers had spent entire days gathering wild onions which they boiled into a smelly stew. The situation at Fort Warner—still buried in 10-foot snowdrifts—was no better. An express was sent to Fort Bidwell requesting any and all provisions the post could spare. On the return to Fort Warner, it took a mule supply pack train—breaking trail over crusted snow—15 days to cover less than 75 miles.

With badly needed supplies on the way, Crook again took to the field and in a raging late March snowstorm struck the mounted Paiutes a crushing blow that brought them to their knees. Before another month had passed, Bad Face—his ragged troops facing starvation—sued for peace with the terms of unconditional surrender.

However, it appears that Has No Horse, in true guerrilla warfare, was forcing the battle onto Crook's front doorstep. On March 28, 1868—two days after Crook took to the blood trail to wipe out the Paiute allies—Julia Gilliss, writing from Fort Warner headquarters would comment in a letter to her parents: "The Indians are giving great trouble killing settlers, stealing stock, etc. They do not venture near our fort in daylight, but at night they often shoot arrows into our corral and have already killed sixteen mules. Whenever the troops go after them they all hide in the stronghold of Steins [Steens] Mountains."

Then as an afterthought to the army's latest push to crush Bad Faces' mounted Paiutes before they could rejoin Has No Horse, Julia Gilliss bares her soul on the Shoshoni war.

> He [Gen. Crook] with three or four companies from here & [Fort] Harney is going out again. This persecution of the Indians goes against the grain with me. I think it is a wretched unholy warfare; the poor creatures are hunted down like wild beasts and shot down in cold blood. The same ball [rifle] went through a mother and her baby at her breast. One poor little creature just the size of my baby was shot because he would someday grow up. Ugh! It makes me sick. And all for the few grains of gold that tempt the cupidity and avarice of grasping men. The land is wretched. The fact is acknowledged that this country will never be good for anything but its mineral resources, and therefore this race of human beings which God has created and given their place on earth must be crushed to the bitter end. I do not believe such an enterprise will ever be blessed and I think the Indian depredations are a just retribution on their persecution."[10]

---

10    In this same letter, Julia would note that the troops returned from Steens Mountain "rather unsuccessful. They killed thirteen Indians, nearly all they could find." Gilliss, *So Far From Home*, pp. 166-167.

And these were the thoughts of the wife of Captain James Gilliss, a Shoshoni war veteran whose 23rd Infantry Regiment was charged with the total destruction of the Paviotso Confederacy.

# CHAPTER 146

# TWO WOLVES MEET

*Do you see any fewer soldiers than two years ago?*
*No! I see more.*
*Have you as many warriors?*
*No—not half as many.*
*Very well; that is as I mean to have it until you are all gone*[1]

**Gen. Crook to Chief Wolf Dog**
Fort Harney, Oregon, June 30, 1868

By 1868, industrial capitalism—fueled by the Civil War—was preparing to invade the West and a Republican Congress was hot to help it along with an industrial policy. That policy would include tariffs, land grants and bond issues for railroads; the Homestead Act; and the Land Grant College Act to spread scientific agriculture and other profitable knowledge to the masses. Even war was considered industrial policy when used to encourage Indians to see the virtues of western migration, and see it they would.

Crook's unrelenting counter-offensive coupled with the winter of 1867-68 had taken a devastating toll on Has No Horse's rag-tail army. With war ponies weakened from lack of forage and morale at an all time low from losses of wives and children, Has No Horse gambled that the enemy was in like straits. He was due for disappointment. Bad Face's white flag would insure that the war was lost on the southern front. As for Bad Face, he and his followers were now tasting the fruits of unconditional surrender.

During the forced removal of Indians to reserves, hundreds died of disease and starvation and the Paiutes were suffering the most heavily. In testimony before the 75th Congress, Kenneth Johnson—referring to a Paiute woman sitting near him—described a typical removal operation: "Her people were driven by soldiers and officers through the passes of the mountains without food or water, and when a woman could not carry her children, they were torn from her back and thrown under the bushes. They left their little babies behind . . . but the soldiers came along

---

1    As stated in a letter to Gov. Ballard of Idaho, appearing in *The Portland Oregonian*, July 29, 1868; *Overland Monthly*, 1869, p. 162.

and speared them, shot them and abused them."[2] It would have been more honorable for Bad Face to have fought to the death.

Re-outfitted with fresh supplies, troops and mounts, Gray Wolf followed the warming winds of spring into the Ochoco. By mid-April, he had flushed Turkey Buzzard and the young dog soldier, Cold Wind, out of the Crooked River basin. Cold Wind had just married a Big Lodge girl named Chisro—The Snow Bunting. It could be said, that the newlyweds were still on their honeymoon. Seventeen years before, when Has No Horse attacked the 1851 emigration at Hell's Gate, Cold Wind was the infant son he believed to be dying of cholera. The baby survived to ride with his father in defense of the Ochoco. On his 16th birthday, he became recognized as a war chief. Now Cold Wind and Turkey Buzzard—the Snake medical doctor who saved Lt. Fremont's life in 1843—were on the run. North of the Steens Mountains—caught between Crook's mounted 23rd Infantry and Kelly's 8th Cavalry—they and their followers were slaughtered. There were no survivors.

Adding to this loss, word drifted into the war camps that The Arrow had sold the northern Utes down the river. With nowhere to turn, Red Sand—Has No Horse's staunch ally—raised the white flag and touched pen to a treaty on March 2, 1868. The Utes were now being herded onto a reservation in Colorado. Red Sand's acceptance of defeat would slow down Has No Horse's supply of arms and ammunition, and that could be likened to severing his jugular vein.

Following the Cold Wind-Turkey Buzzard bloodbath, Crook again turned north and discovered Pony Blanket's hideout under the north rim glacier of Snow Mountain. This was a major blow, for within the past two weeks, Pony Blanket had captured two army supply trains bound for Fort Harney. In a pre-dawn attack, Crook destroyed 14 lodges, took 60 prisoners of war and retrieved most of the stolen property. Hot on Pony Blanket's trail, he was intercepted by a messenger out of Fort Watson with orders to report immediately to San Francisco and from there to Portland where he was to take command of the Military Department of the Columbia.[3] For the moment, Has No Horse would gain some breathing space.

In early May, as the soldiers jammed the Shoshoni back, young Jim Blakely—planning to make some big money—took advantage of the rapidly melting snow pack and drove 600 head of cattle over the Santiam Pass to replenish the army's dwindling supplies. The government, fast going broke fighting the Shoshoni, couldn't afford to buy them. Moving north of the war zone, Blakely summered his herd on Wild Horse Creek near Pendleton, hoping the government

---

2       Statement of Mr. Johnson, Hearings, Senate Committee on Indian Affairs, 75th Congress, 1st Session, Serial 1651.

3       U.S. Army, Military Division of the Pacific, *General Order No. 10*, April 1, 1868; *Senate Joint Resolution No. 6, Oregon House Journal 1868*, pp. 85-6; *Oregon Laws 1868*, pp. 99-100, 102-3; *Oregon Legislature Documents 1868*, "Governor's Message," pp. 4-5.

would become solvent by fall. No such luck. He ended up driving his cattle down the Columbia and up the Willamette to Brownsville firmly convinced there was no profit to be gained in cattle drives into war-torn eastern Oregon.

Stage coaching was not too successful either. Henry Wheeler, who for the past three years had run the gauntlet between The Dalles and Canyon City, was going broke. During that period, the *Blue Mountain Eagle* would toast his accomplishments with such glowing phrases as: "It seems the Indians have a reverence for Wheeler or otherwise he would certainly have been killed." Losing coaches almost weekly, Hank knew a damn sight better. Deciding his rope was getting short, Wheeler sold his stageline in the spring of '68 and went to work for Ben Holladay on the Missouri to the Pacific run.

With Crook temporarily sidetracked, Capt. Kelly took command of field operations and continued on the track of the fleeing dog soldiers. In a running battle which led to the North Fork of the Malheur, Lt. Alexander Stanton with a detachment of 37 1st Cavalry and McIntosh's Shoshoni scouts, caught up with Pony Blanket at Castle Rock on May 31. In a furious fight, Pony Blanket and four warriors were captured along with 20 stolen cavalry horses. This action would advance Stanton to the rank of captain for "gallantry in the Malheur River engagement."[4] The Climber, who had furnished McIntosh's Shoshoni scouts, would also gain undeserved recognition. In the aftermath of this engagement, he would boast to the Idaho press that "I have not the blood of a white man in my camp, nor do I intend such." In appreciation, the gullible settlers of Idaho subscribed funds toward the erection of a monument in his honor. Has No Horse marked him as a traitor.

In a last ditch stand for survival, Pony Blanket offered to bring in his remaining warriors and to contact Wolf Dog and Has No Horse in an effort to persuade them to give up. According to Pony Blanket they were as weary of conflict as he was. On this promise, Pony Blanket was released while the other captives taken at Snow Mountain and Castle Rock (including his wife and children) were imprisoned at Fort Harney.[5]

Hoping for a quick peace, a rider was dispatched to alert Crook of this new development. Unfortunately, Crook could not strike while the iron was hot. Gen. Halleck had issued an order that no treaties could be made with the Shoshoni by officers in his command without consulting him so it became necessary for Crook to continue onto San Francisco—a delay that would bring on more bloodshed. In Crook's absence, Bad Face resumed hostilities in an effort to buy Has No Horse some time to rally his demoralized troops.

---

4    Letter from Camp Harney, *The Dalles Mountaineer*, June 20, 1868.

5    Bancroft, *History of Oregon*, Vol. II, pp. 548-49. Pony Blanket's adopted children, the orphans Annette Tallman (daughter of Tall Man) and Mattie Shenkah (daughter of Broken Knife) were also imprisoned at that time.

During his march through the Crooked River country, Crook had captured or killed most of Wolf Dog's warriors. It was this purge that gained Crooked River the name of *Paga Tubic* . . . the sorrowful or weeping water. At the same time, although he had cut off all supplies from The Dalles, Has No Horse was sustaining heavy losses at the hands of Lt. Col. O'Beirne's 14th Infantry operating out of Fort Watson. Big Man was experiencing equal reverses inflicted by Lt. Col. Coppinger's cavalry units out of Fort Boise. Thirty-four of his warriors who attacked the Boise-Canyon City stage in May (killing the driver and wounding several passengers) were apprehended, mutilated and hanged.

By June, the conflict deteriorated into ruthless brutality on both sides. In a horse raid, Big Man captured Jonas Belknap, one of the horse guards. In retaliation for the mutilation of his dog soldiers, Big Man carved Belknap's body into chunks, stuck it full of pointed rods with slices of bacon on the ends, skewered the pieces on a pole like a barbecue spit, and placed the gruesome offering in plain view of the Boise-Canyon City road.[6] The Idaho militia, backed by the U.S. Cavalry, gave chase and near the Eldorado Divide some 40 miles east of Canyon City, caught up with the horse raiders. In a brief but decisive encounter, one civilian was killed and Big Man was taken captive. After securely binding him in chains, the soldiers turned Big Man over to the volunteers to be taken back to Boise City for public hanging while they continued pursuing his war party. That was a mistake. En route to Boise City, Has No Horse ambushed the Idaho militia and during the confusion, Big Man killed a guard and escaped.[7] Word of this loss was quick to reach the Willamette Valley. In early spring, a telegraph line was run from Portland to The Dalles City to speed up communications between western Oregon and the eastern Oregon front.

With rumors flying that the Snakes were willing to sue for peace, Crook cut short his departmental duties and left immediately for Fort Harney. Although he couldn't enter into formal treaty negotiations, he sent word ahead for the principal chiefs of the hostile tribes to assemble at Fort Harney for a council.[8] The army was

---

6    *Boise Statesman*, June 13, 1868.

7    *Portland Oregonian*, June 13, 1868.

8    The chiefs invited to the Fort Harney Council to be held on June 30, 1868 and the tribes they represented were:

*Has No Horse* (Otsehoe) of the White Knives (Tussawehee); *Wolf Dog* (Weahwewa) of the Bear Killers (Hunipui); *Three Coyotes* (Ponce) of the Big Lodges (Tuziyammo); *Left Hand* (Otiz) of the Juniper People (Lohim); *Black Buffalo* (Chocktote) of the Big Noses (Motsai); *Sun Hunter* (Tebechye) of the Pony Stealers (Wahtatkin); *Pony Blanket* (Egan) of the Antelope Hunters (Togwingani); *Yellow Jacket* (Paddy Cap) of the Juniper People (Lohim); and *Big Man* (Oulux) of the Wild Sage People (Pohoi).

U.S. Messages and Documents 1868-9, pp. 380-86; Haye's Scrape, Vol. V, p. 142; Portland *Oregonian*, July 13, 1868.

also making some unexpected gains to the east, thanks to Gourd Rattler. His covert action now cut off from the battle in the Blues, Gourd Rattler took to hacking away at the Sioux. One of his first hostile acts was the personal killing of Jack Red Cloud, son of the head chief of the seven Sioux war tribes. In so doing, the old dog soldier was gaining praise from government and civilian authorities alike. They believed he was killing blood enemies for their benefit.

On July 19, 1868—one month to the day before Has No Horse rode into Fort Harney—Julia Gilliss described the arrival of Wolf Dog and his followers. This historic event is best told in her own words:

They [the Snake Indians] are coming in thick and fast now to be placed on a reservation. There are nearly three hundred of them at Harney. Some of them are very fine looking men and very imposing in all their panoply of war, but there are several very old fellows who are perfectly frightful from the fact that their ancient skin is as white as parchment & the red & black paint on it makes them look as hideous as one can imagine. The day the Indians came to ratify the treaty or make terms, I don't know which, they began coming by daylight, first in twos and threes, then larger groups, 'till the Camp was swarming with them. The troops were all on keen watch, with small arms concealed on their persons, but pretended to be carelessly strolling around unarmed. Genl. Crook stood at the head of the parade, Mrs. Crook and I stood close behind him, *apparently* as unsuspicious as if we were receiving at a ball. In reality everyone was alert, and the officers behind us were keenly watchful. *Nobody* trusts a live Indian. As they moved in front of us, on their ponies, with their guns slung across, they certainly were an ugly looking party. The General with his quiet dignity told them he would have nothing to say to them until they all dismounted and laid down their arms. A turbulent spirit immediately broke forth. Scowls, shakes of the head, furious gestures and whirling around of the ponies looked for a moment pretty serious. I never before or since saw such ferocious looking beings. One single brave [most likely Pony Blanket] *seemed* to oppose the others. He rode around among the hundred screaming, gesticulating imps and with some strong influence brought them down to a sullen, muttering crowd.

In a very low voice General Crook said to us "do not look frightened, be calm and indifferent as you possibly can, and stand still right where you are." It seemed as if we stood there for hours, while those ugly braves refused to retreat unless they could retain guns and ponies. Our General stood as immovable as stone, refusing to speak unless they agreed to his first demand. Slowly, with fierce looks and ominous grunts, one after another dismounted and laid his gun at his feet. One furious chief [believed to have been Black Eagle, Wolf Dog's brother] wheeled suddenly, rode hard and fast away and was seen no more. I do not believe any man living, but General Crook could have brought these

Indians to even the semblance of yielding, and for one do not believe they will keep any treaty when they get ready to break it.[9]

The minute Crook stepped onto the Fort Harney council grounds, Wolf Dog approached and turned in the belongings of those soldiers who had been charged with desertion. Now their fate was known.[10] This peace offering was overshadowed by the glaring absence of Has No Horse. Since the leader of the Paviotso Confederacy refused to attend the council, Crook dispatched Yellow Jacket on June 30 with a message to Bad Face stating that if he didn't talk Has No Horse into surrendering immediately, Crook would hold Bad Face "personally responsible for further depredations."[11] Bad Face temporarily chose to ignore this threat but on July 18—most likely under pressure from his daughter—he, Yellow Jacket and Natchez, with some 70 warriors, surrendered to Major Jesse Walker at Fort C.F. Smith.

While waiting for Bad Face to make contact with Has No Horse, Crook met with the Snake chiefs who did show up at Fort Harney. Acting as interpreter for this occasion was Sarah Winnemucca, Bad Face's oldest daughter who later took a government job as Shoshoni advisor to Nevada Indian Agent C.A. Bateman. When Gray Wolf (in full dress uniform) and his staff officers approached from the open side of the parade ground, Wolf Dog in full war bonnet and his entourage came toward the center from the Shoshoni side. As recorded by Capt. Azor Nickerson in his report to Gen. Halleck: "The old rascal came up as smiling, childlike and bland as the proverbial heathen Chinese. He extended his dirty, bloodstained paw to shake Crook's hand. Looking him squarely in the eye, Crook refused the offer. 'Tell him' said Crook to Sarah, 'I did not come here to shake hands with him. He has murdered too many people. I came here to hear what he has to say for himself.'"[12]

Somewhat taken aback by this refusal and perhaps wondering just whose hands were the most bloodstained, Wolf Dog commented that he and his warriors were tired of fighting and wished to make peace. Running a true Indian bluff, Crook now pressed his advantage, indicating that he was sorry to hear that. "I was in hopes that you would continue the war and then, though I were to kill only one of your

---

9     Gilliss, *So Far From Home,* pp. 176-77. Although this letter to Julia's parents was written at Fort Harney, it is dated Camp Warner (Capt. Gilliss' duty station) July 19, 1968. Captain James Gilliss was promoted to colonel in 1897 and died suddenly at Governor's Island, New York on November 13, 1898 after serving in the Spanish-American War. Julia Stellwager Gilliss died in Washington D.C. on December 16, 1926 and was buried beside her husband in Arlington National Cemetery.

10   Bancroft, *History of Oregon,* II. p. 550.

11   U.S. Messages and Documents 1868-9, pp. 380-86, Message from Crook to Winnemucca, dated Camp Harney, June 30, 1868.

12   Nickerson, Azor H., *Major General George Crook and the Indians (MS); Crook, Autobiography,* pp. 307-9.

warriors while you killed a hundred of my men, you would have to wait for those little people—pointing to the Indian children—to grow to fill the place of your braves, while I can get any number of soldiers the next day to fill the place of my hundred men. [This was no exaggeration.] In this way, it would not be very long before we would have you all killed off, and then, the government would have no more trouble with you."[13]

Wolf Dog, having seen Gray Wolf in battle, knew he wasn't bluffing and insisted that he didn't want any more war, going so far as to declare the Snakes had "thrown away their ropes." This was a strong statement. To the Shoshoni, throwing away their ropes meant a great deal for by this solemn vow Wolf Dog intended to emphasize a promise that he and his warriors would steal no more horses.

After a little more parley along similar lines, the General consented to make peace although apparently reluctantly. Under the lead of Wolf Dog, the Snake headmen present accepted Crook's terms of surrender. He simply told them that he would acknowledge Wolf Dog as head chief of the Snake tribes and that Wolf Dog would be held responsible for his tribesmen's good conduct. When Crook told Wolf Dog that he would hunt down and kill every remaining Shoshoni if they didn't surrender, the old head chief knew this was no idle threat. The majority of tribesmen present at the council also knew and were terrified.

Tired of waiting for Has No Horse to appear, Crook sent word by Archie McIntosh that he was coming into the Ochoco to get him. Has No Horse's answer to this challenge was as quick as it was violent.

---

13    Ibid.

# CHAPTER 147

# THE LAND YOU LEFT ME . . . I HAVE LOST!

*The ground you steal is the blood, the flesh, the bones of my people. You will have to plow deep to find the earth . . . the upper crust is dead Shoshoni.*

**Has No Horse**
Fort Harney, August 24, 1868

In the wake of Crook's victorious spring offensive, settlers were pouring into the Ochoco like water over a ruptured beaver dam. A cocky young entrepreneur named Francis Bernard Prine nailed down a frontier saloon on the tail of Has No Horse's war bonnet. George Millican—whose son Walter would be the first white child born in the Crooked River Valley—pushed the first big cattle drive into the Crooked River Basin and was setting up headquarters on McKay Creek only two and a half miles west of Prine's saloon.[1] Fresh-peeled logs were being drug off the Ochoco Mountains to construct a schoolhouse within sight of the cavalry outpost at the mouth of Mill Creek. Farmers were grubbing out sagebrush a scant 12 miles west of the Shoshoni stronghold in the upper Ochoco Valley. William Clark—a Canyon City merchant—had obtained a government grant for the opening of a wagon road from Clarno on the lower John Day to the new railhead at Winnemucca, Nevada. Survey and roadwork, now in progress, led directly across the Ochoco Mountains, through Big Summit Prairie, to the Middle Fork of the Malheur River. Although of poor construction and with virtually no proper relief stations, it was drawing attention to the Ochoco. And 29-year-old John Devine was trail-herding thousands of head of horses into Harney Basin.

In a frenzy of hatred, Has No Horse began his ride of vengeance accompanied only by his son Red Willow, his spiritual advisor Buzzard Man and a handful of White Knife dog soldiers. The main Shoshoni encampment on the upper Ochoco River, consisting of some 120 lodges of White Knife, Big Lodge and Pony Stealer Snakes was the largest concentration of Shoshoni west of the Snake River and it would be the last ever seen in eastern Oregon. Leaving the camp under the

---

1    Carey, *History of Oregon*, Vol. II, p. 714; Southworth, *Millican Memories*, pp. 1-2.

protection of his son-in-laws, the Big Lodge war chief Woman Helper, the White Knife medicine man Wolf Jaws and the White Knife dog soldier Bloody Antler, Has No Horse had no qualms about taking off on his homicidal mission. Traveling in a murderous arc, he intended to unite with Big Man in the Owyhee country and stage a raid on the defectors now assembled at Fort Harney.

As he rode west down the Ochoco Valley surrounded by an acrid haze screening his every move, the only hope Has No Horse had of things going in his favor was a keen knowledge of the country, the element of surprise and the continued support of *Talawi Piki*—the Fire God.

After a devastating winter, the spring and summer of '68 was marked by a severe drought. Huge fires were sweeping across the country from southern Oregon to British Columbia. Smoke was so thick that sea-going vessels were unable to find their way into the Columbia River. A river boat captain would comment that "lighthouses will be needed to enable steamers to find their way up and down the Willamette River."[2] The sun disappeared for weeks, lost in a dense haze of smoke while suffocating heat filled the air. Flames roared through the Cascades, charring 225,000 acres and darkening the sky so lamps were needed to light the streets during the day in Portland. A giant inferno in the coast range burned 300,000 acres of virgin timber. Falling ashes killed most of the shellfish in Coos Bay. Other conflagrations were raging through the Blues threatening mining settlements and Oregon would in total lose an estimated one million acres of its finest timber. Newspapers demanded government action but there were no laws to protect timber. An act passed in 1864 to regulate setting of fires was designed to protect settlements, not forests.

Fire was God's blessing to the settler. Fire that could burn log piles and gnaw at the roots of stumps would kill every living plant, tree and shrub that blocked progress. Children fired the woods when looking for milk cows; hunters out after summer venison set off dry slash; at night during the spring, summer and fall, the horizon glowed a devilish red from flames that ate away the forest; while during the day the pall of raw smoke dimmed the sun. And the settlers laughed vindictively as the fire leaped at trees and young saplings and destroyed the very life of the soil they wished to cultivate.

Bearing a guilt complex, the Oregonians liked to attribute many of these fires to the Indians who, no doubt, at times were responsible. But, despite the many delinquencies of the native red man, the indisputable fact remains that the settler, in his attempt to get elbow room for a farm as he followed in the wake of the logger, caused more fires than all other sources—including dry lightning.

It was against such a backdrop of smoke and flame that Has No Horse hit the Ochoco Blockhouse on Mill Creek on July 11, 1868. During his passage down the Ochoco Valley, Has No Horse put the fear of God into two white men—Abe Zell

---

2    "Centennial Countdown," *Oregon Journal*, April 6, 1959.

(scout for Major Randall) and Thomas James—who were clearing land a few miles east of the army supply depot. They would later testify that there were a hundred Indians in the war party but the true figure is more like 20. In their rush for concealment, Zell and James never noticed a new column of smoke rising into the air until they stumbled onto the smoldering ruins that night.

The blockhouse was thought to be so impregnable that Major Randall had left only five enlisted men to guard it. The first they knew of danger was when the screen of willows along Mill Creek burst into flame. Already burning arrows dipped in pine-pitch were crackling on the tinder-dry stockade walls. Although suffering third degree burns, the soldiers escaped, but the supply depot known as Camp Ochoco was now a part of history.

When a sweaty express rider galloped into Fort Harney with the disheartening message that Major Randall had been burned out, Crook ordered his march on the upper Ochoco Valley . . . confirmed hideout of Has No Horse. With Randall's 8th Cavalry approaching from the west, Major Edward Meyer's 1st Cavalry from the south, and Lt. Col. O'Beirne's 14th Infantry from the east, they converged on their target. Although Major John Scott's 3rd Artillery was brought in, one piece of ordinance Crook had no use for was the Gatling gun. He looked upon these fire-belching weapons as a personal slur upon his reputation as an Indian fighter—but apparently his commanding officers held no such reservations.

At dawn on July 26, a brace of Gatling guns spewed a storm of molten lead across the upper Ochoco Valley tearing the heart out of the western Shoshoni nation.[3] Taken by surprise, men, women and children fought like demons . . . and they died! Warriors—in an effort to provide an escape route for women and children—made suicidal charges into the advancing blue lines. It was a self-destructive undertaking. Many women and children who found mounts galloped into the waiting guns of the infantry. Wolf Jaws—singing his death song—charged Meyer's cavalry and was literally torn from his horse. Left among the dead, he miraculously survived. Wherever the Shoshoni turned, there was no relief. Woman Helper watched in horror as his wife, Spotted Fawn, was split from shoulder to pelvis with a cavalry sabre. Gaining a pony, Woman Helper pulled his sister-in-law, Mountain Breeze—Wolf Jaws' wife—up behind him and tried to escape. The girl swayed, a .50 calibre slug shattering her back. Clutching Woman Helper's gun belt in a death-grip, she plunged from the horse dragging him with her. Like a panther, he landed on his feet as his revolver cracked hitting the pursuing

---

3    As late as 1986—118 years after the battle—Duane Mizer (a local resident) found Gatling gun casings in the upper Ochoco Valley and also on Big Summit Prairie. Over a span covering some 70 years, other articles found in abundance at the Shoshoni campsite on the upper Ochoco River included pestles, mortars, ceremonial knives, religious artifacts, stone axe heads, arrow points, spear points, awls, arrow shaft straighteners, obsidian beads (called Apache Tears), and brass cartridge shells. As late as the 1950s, curio shops in the Willamette Valley were displaying artifacts taken from this site.

cavalryman's horse in the shoulder. He fired again—his last shot—missing the mark. The trooper shot, breaking Woman Helper's left arm. Woman Helper then took two more bullets through the body. Staggering to a pine, he leaned against the trunk defiantly shaking his empty hand-gun at the charging soldiers. Abe Zell rode up, raised his .50 calibre Spencer and pulled the trigger. Woman Helper, the last survivor of the Big Lodge tribe (once the largest in the Shoshoni nation) fell . . . like an arrow in the dust.[4]

In the confusion of battle, Bloody Antler, Mourning Dove and Little Cloud (Red Willow's wife), with a few women and children made their escape up Canyon Creek into Big Summit Prairie. Hiding the survivors as best he could, Bloody Antler rode night and day to alert Has No Horse of this wholesale killing. On this ride he made contact with the Snake war chief Dead Deer—another survivor of the Ochoco River battle—who returned to Big Summit Prairie to guard the women and children.

After striking the army post on Mill Creek, Has No Horse had swung north. His 300-mile-long path of destruction from the lower John Day Valley to the Owyhee River was marked by isolated settlers' cabins burned to the ground; bodies lying in pools of blood; and slaughtered livestock polluting the land. He was within three miles of Silver City when Bloody Antler brought the staggering news of the Ochoco massacre. Already, Has No Horse had suffered the loss of his wife, youngest son and sister. Now, two daughters were dead. More heartache was to follow.

Unknown to Bloody Antler, during the grueling ride to overtake Has No Horse and just 48 hours after the upper Ochoco Valley was bathed in blood, a wagon train of homesteaders creaked into the lower valley and set up camp. The Valley of the Red Willow—Has No Horse's place of birth—would become his only memorial in death. And the war chief's planned union with Big Man would never come to pass, at least not the way he expected. On the same day Crook's blitzkrieg tore the heart out of the Snake war tribes, Big Man was leading his last raid of the Shoshoni war.

---

4    As remembered by Abraham Zell, army scout and Dave Chocktote, whose father Black Buffalo, was camped at the Fort Harney council grounds at that time.

# CHAPTER 148

# 'TIL DEATH DO US PART

*You ain't no sharpshooter, Bigfoot!*
*You best come and get me.*

**John W. Wheeler**
Bounty Hunter, July 27, 1868

On the evening of July 27, a diverse group was converging on a brush-choked depression on the Oregon-Idaho border known as Reynolds Creek Canyon. First to arrive on that fateful evening was William Andrews—a Silver City carpenter—traveling from Boise City with an empty two-horse wagon. Reaching Reynolds Creek, he pulled off the road and decided to set up camp. Andrews held no desire to enter the canyon this late in the day for in that dark corridor Snake raiders had murdered many people. The most recent slayings had been that of a man named Jarvis and a Chinese man, who were hauling a load of eggs and vegetables to the Silver City mines. The Snake war chief Big Man was blamed.[1] Just a few days before the murderous attack, the *Portland Oregonian*—on June 24, 1868—reported that Bigfoot (Big Man) had been captured on the east side of the Snake River by "a company of farmers out of Payette, Idaho." It also had to lament the fact that he had escaped. With this disturbing thought in mind, Andrews unhitched his team and turned them loose to graze.

High up on the boulder-strewn lip of the canyon, Big Man and three Snake dog soldiers dismounted and prepared for action. The old warrior One Eye would stay with the horses while Big Man, Little Foot and Biting Bear descended into the gorge on foot. With their supply-line cut off from the east and south, the Shoshoni were in desperate need of gold to purchase more arms and ammunition and Big Man intended to get it.

In a secluded glade in the canyon bottom where the road squeaked between two huge boulders, a steel-eyed lawman with robbery on his mind tethered his horse to an Aspen tree and cautiously awaited the arrival of the Silver City stage.

---

1     Ward, Porter Morgan, "Bigfoot: Man or Myth?" *Montana: The Magazine of Western History*, Vol. 7, No. 2, Spring, 1957, p. 21.

An hour before sunset, the northbound stage crested the Reynolds Creek ridge and came to a halt. Charlie Barnes was in the driver's seat and Lew Hutt was riding shotgun guard. Inside the coach, besides the usual cargo of mail and gold destined for The Dalles City, were six passengers, two of them women. Ahead lay one of the more dangerous stretches on the entire route. Anticipating trouble, Barnes laid on the whip and the stage plunged down slope at breakneck speed, bouncing wildly into the canyon. Any drunks on board were soon jarred into sobriety. As the coach careened onto the canyon floor, the crack of a rifle rent the air. Racing around the next bend, Barnes and Hutt saw a mortally wounded Indian beside the road spasmodically jerking in his death throes. Another Indian scrambled up and out of the canyon. Then for a terrifying instant before he disappeared behind a boulder, they saw a man described as "the most awesome figure that ever stalked through the old West."[2] Although neither Barnes nor Hutt had ever seen him before, they instantly recognized this Indian as the man called "Bigfoot" for on the Oregon-Idaho-Nevada frontier, Big Man was as well known and deeply feared as an active volcano.

It all began in 1863 when the Idaho Volunteers led by T.J. Sutton tangled with a band of Snake warriors and Sutton discovered and reported the seventeen and a half-inch-long footprints of a giant Indian. That's all it took. Within days, rumors were flying from the Cascades to the Rockies. Some eye witnesses claimed he was too large for a horse to carry; other reliable sources would report huge moccasin tracks as far as 60 and 70 miles apart in a single day. A woman with a buggy-load of children driving a lonely Oregon road reported that "Bigfoot" raced up to her buggy and when she put the team into a gallop, the overgrown Indian laughed, and seizing hold of the end-board, took long and springy strides to easily keep up. Finally, he relinquished his hold, and still laughing, raced off into the brush—which doesn't appear to be too life-threatening.

Some claimed that Nampuh—Bigfoot—was the figment of several pioneers' imaginations; that he was born in the fumes of numerous bottles of Redeye; and that the newspapers were only interested in creating good copy. Army and Indian affairs personnel—who knew the truth—would correctly inform the public that Big Man was a prominent member of the Shoshoni war tribes. This only inspired them to greater hysteria.

Enoch Fruit, proprietor of the Snake River ferry at Farewell Bend, who packed word of the Ward Massacre to The Dalles in 1854, had no fear of the big war chief. He was telling visitors that Big Man occasionally came to see him, traded horses and "spoke good english." Fruit was lavish in his description of the Indian,

---

2    All direct quotes, unless otherwise noted, are taken from Froman, Robert, "The Giant and the Gunslinger," *True*, Vol. 38, No. 244, September 1957; and a letter written by William T. Andrews to the Boise, Idaho *Statesman*, November 1878. Some accounts list Andrews' name as William T. Anderson.

whom he said was built more perfectly than any big man he had ever seen and was honest in his business deals.

As one historian would put it: "At this time, any 'good injun' was a 'dead injun' and Bigfoot began to gather the accumulated hatred of the white population. He was the scapegoat for unsolved crimes, the boogeyman for small children, and the recipient of obviously bent truth where the thirsty citizenry also bent its elbow along the polished bars."[3]

One thing for certain, in his present state of mind, Big Man was every bit as destructive as molten lava. His first wife Running Deer, sister to Broken Knife, had been killed in 1866 and their son taken captive by the Warm Springs Cavalry. "Since that time," Big Man once said, "I have done all the mischief I could and glad of it!"[4]

There is no doubt that Big Man—nearly seven feet tall and weighing 300 pounds—was a memorable sight to the frightened stagecoach passengers. An hour later at the Snake River ferry, Barnes would describe him as "dressed only in a breechcloth from which dangled several blobs of rotting human flesh and hair. His own straight black hair hung to his shoulders. Across his forehead, cheekbones, chest and shoulders were plastered great smears of red and yellow mud."

By means of these "smears of red and yellow mud" Big Man was telling the world of his all-consuming hatred for his fellow Americans. In Shoshoni, the red stripes signified his intent to avenge the death of brother warriors killed in battle. The yellow stripes told that his wife—in this case, his second wife, Rainbow Woman—had been recently taken captive at Fort Klamath and he was out to get her back or die in the attempt. In short, the war chief was in a mean mood.

Barnes and Hutt never realized that an odd assortment of outlaws had gathered in Reynolds Canyon to relieve them of their gold shipment. Instead of an ambush, two of these violent men locked into a fight to the death. One combatant was the Snake war chief Big Man; the other was a tall, brown-haired, gray-eyed young man named John W. Wheeler.

Slender, with a smooth, boyish face, Wheeler looked like the time-honored western hero, but his appearance was deceiving. Wheeler, whose father was a half-breed Cherokee, had grown up on the frontier. A man who never talked about his past, Wheeler arrived in Canyon City in 1864 and became friendly with Henry Plummer. Showing no visible means of support, Wheeler did his prospecting on the gaming tables of the most fashionable saloons in eastern Oregon and Idaho. Some believed he was related to the tough stage line operator, Henry Wheeler, but if so, neither man would admit it. Speculation ran high that John Wheeler was involved in stage robberies from Boise City to The Dalles but no one was going to openly accuse him for Wheeler was noted as an expert shot—a man who could

---

3    Ward, *Montana: the Magazine of Western History*, Vol. 7, No. 2, Spring 1957, p. 20.
4    Hanley, Mike, *Owyhee Trails*, p. 156.

shatter rocks tossed into the air with either pistol or rifle. "Wheeler," said a friend, "ain't afraid of anything atop the ground or under it."

In 1868, Silver City under bombardment from Shoshoni raids, was plunged into further disruption when two large mining companies—the Golden Chariot and the Ida Elmore—declared war on each other. Rival employees were being gunned down on the streets and the whole town was in an uproar demanding government intervention. Wheeler arrived in Silver City as part of a special force of lawmen dispatched by Idaho Gov. David Ballard to restore order.

By now, with rewards ranging from $1,000 to $5,000 for delivery of his scalp and feet—proof of identity—to any frontier town east of the Cascades, Big Man had a sizable fortune encased in his moccasins.[5] The thought of this untapped source of revenue intrigued Wheeler. Between keeping the peace in Silver City and gambling, he began a serious endeavor to collect one of these rewards.

The historian, Bennett Williams, would note that Wheeler was a big game trophy hunter and: "The biggest game then in the old west was Bigfoot, an armed man, a huge man, a murderous, resourceful and exclusively clever and cunning man. And Wheeler, being the kind of hunter he was, just naturally and inevitably took out after Bigfoot."[6] Perhaps it became an obsession.

On one occasion, Wheeler, Frank Johnson and Ben Cook spotted Big Man's fresh footprints on the outskirts of Malheur City and gave chase. According to newspaper reports of the day, they managed to gun-down two of his companions but Big Man—now on foot—outran their lathered horses in a 20-mile race to the Snake River. Pulling up on the bank, the bounty hunters stared at the opposite side in amazement. There stood Big Man, dripping from his swim across the river and defiantly waving his rifle. "Come over! Come over you damned cowards!"

The fatigued riders didn't accept the challenge. In fact, Wheeler ruined his saddle horse during the chase and it was said that was one of his major reasons for deciding to hunt down the Snake warrior and kill him. Wheeler later found where Big Man had camped and consumed two large salmon in one meal. From this spot, his trail doubled back to the river which he again swam while his pursuers had to ride five miles to the nearest ferry.[7] The next encounter would be accidental . . . in Reynolds Canyon. Ten years would pass before anyone—at least any white

---

5    Many eastern Oregon and northern California newspapers were printing notices of a $1,000 reward for delivery of Big Man's feet to any army post. The territory of Idaho was offering a reward—dead or alive—of $5,000. Froman, "The Giant and the Gunslinger," *True*, Vol. 38. No. 244, September 1957.

6    Bennett L. Williams did extensive research on Big Man and John W. Wheeler. In a series of articles which appeared in *Idaho Statewide* in the fall of 1948, he wrote that he did not believe in Bigfoot (Big Man) until he had done a great amount of investigation. He concluded that what he had unearthed was true.

7    Hanley, Mike, *Owhyee Trails*, p. 157.

man—learned what happened. In a death-bed confession, William Andrews revealed the true account of one of the most brutal gunfights ever fought.[8]

According to Andrews, after he arrived at Reynolds Creek Canyon and turned his team loose to graze, he thought he "might have fell asleep." At any rate, he suddenly noticed the horses had wandered far down the creek. As Andrews started after the horses, he saw three Indians lopping down the canyon in his direction and the huge warrior in the lead was Big Man. Terrified, Andrews dove into the grass and hid as the Indians passed within 60 feet of him. In the distance, he could hear the pounding hooves of the oncoming stagecoach team racing down canyon toward the advancing Shoshoni. Instantaneously, a rifle shot reverberated between the canyon walls and one of the Indians flopped to the ground. Another wheeled around and disappeared from sight. Big Man veered off toward the far side of the canyon. At that moment, the stage careened around a bend in the road and the driver, laying whip to the straining horses, continued on toward the distant Snake River crossing.

For several minutes after the dust from the stage had settled, the scene remained empty and quiet. Then Andrews saw Big Man crawling from the cover of one boulder to another while looking intently down canyon. To Andrews' dismay, the Indian was working in his direction when suddenly, and with as startling effect as the rifle shot, a voice rang out.

Why Wheeler chose to go after Big Man instead of the stage's strong box—or not wait until the Shoshoni had the gold, is anyone's guess. With his reputation for big-game hunting, Wheeler's hunter instinct must have taken over seconds before the stagecoach thundered by. Flame leaped from the muzzle of his '66 Springfield—the trusty army "long Tom"—which boasted a 40-inch barrel and mounted a triangular bayonet with an 18-inch blade which Wheeler now had tucked in his belt. Sighted in at 1,000 yards, it was a mean opponent and Biting Bear, directly behind Big Man, was literally thrown backwards and dead before he hit the ground. Unexplainably, the marksman Wheeler—perhaps misjudging the nearness of the Indians—had overshot Big Man. When the .50 calibre slug slammed into Biting Bear, Little Foot swerved quickly up slope out of sight. Big Man, knowing that he was now the prime target dove behind a large boulder on the edge of the road. Seeing this, Wheeler threw the long range Springfield aside and grabbed a Henry repeating rifle from his saddle scabbard and ducked into a screen of willows. Meanwhile, Big Man was closing in. It was then that Wheeler shouted: "Git off your knees you yellow bellied coward! You don't get no woman's scalp today. Come and git mine!"

Big Man, needing no encouragement, sprang to his feet and leveling a big double-barreled 10-gauge shotgun at the willows, cried out: "You sneakin' bastard! Come out and see how fast I take your scalp!" As Big Man spoke, Wheeler

---

8    Letter signed William T. Andrews, Fisherman's Cove, Humbolt County California, published in the Boise, Idaho *Statesman*, November 1878.

stepped out from behind an Aspen tree. Both men fired simultaneously. Big Man staggered but recovered and fired again. Throwing the empty shotgun down, he started running toward his fallen comrade. He ran only a few steps when a second shot from Wheeler's .44 Henry plowed deep into his back, stopping him as surely as if he had run into a basalt cliff. Still maintaining his balance, Big Man, in an agonizing effort, turned half around in time to catch a third bullet ripping his arm to shreds near the shoulder. He reeled but still refused to go down.

Wheeler watched in fascination as the big warrior, shaking his head like an old buffalo bull, slowly straightened to his full height and stubbornly walked on to the spot where Biting Bear lay. Methodically, he picked up the dead man's rifle, whirled and fired as Wheeler sent still another bullet crashing into his powerful frame. Blood gushing from his chest, Big Man dropped behind a screen of boulders and began crawling in Wheeler's direction.

Wheeler was still standing in the open, poised like a hunter about to flush a covey of quail. Andrews believed that it was the thrill of the hunt that placed Wheeler into this dangerous situation. As Andrews observed, Wheeler could have lain low while Big Man did the dirty work of holding up the stage and slaughtering the occupants. After Big Man departed, Wheeler could have picked off Andrews—he never did admit that he too, may have had robbery in mind—then looted the stagecoach wreckage. It was commonly known that the Shoshoni seldom took an interest in such valuables as bank notes or paper currency. One thing was clear, it was no twinge of conscience that caused Wheeler to intervene. He fired the first shot on impulse and it committed him irreversibly to this duel to death.

Wheeler was also finding out what many soldiers already knew . . . it took an awful lot of lead to bring down a Snake warrior. Col. Richard Dodge (at the time, a lieutenant in the Shoshoni campaign) had his own theory on why they were so hard to kill. According to Dodge:

> The tenacity of life of an Indian, the amount of lead he will carry off, indicates a nervous system so dull as to class him rather with brutes than man. The shock or blow of a bullet will ordinarily paralyze so many nerves and muscles of a white man as to knock him down, even though not striking a vital part. The Indian gives no heed to such wounds and to 'drop him in his tracks' the bullet must reach the brain, the heart or the spine. I have myself seen an Indian go off with two bullets through his body within an inch or two of the spine, the only effect of which was to cause him to change his gait from a run to a dignified walk.[9]

Maybe the colonel was on to something. Whatever the reason, Big Man was not going down gracefully.

---

9    Col. Richard Dodge, *Our Wild Indians*, p. 440.

It seemed that Wheeler was enjoying the game. The boulder screen curved to within 30 feet of the spot where he stood but he remained in the open, daring Big Man to come after him. As darkness approached, Big Man fired a couple of shots around the corner of a boulder. Each time, Wheeler laughed, taunting Big Man that he best learn how to shoot before he tackled him. After the second shot whizzed by his head, Wheeler tossed a fist-sized rock toward Big Man's hiding place and blasted it out of the air. "How you like the way I shoot, old hoss?" he jeered.

All this time, Andrews remained cowering on the creek bank firmly convinced that Wheeler had gone crazy and that Big Man would creep up on him and rip him apart with his bare hands. The last of the twilight was fading and only a crescent moon lit the scene. For a long time nothing happened. Andrews was trying to get up enough nerve to crawl off and find his horse. Then, with the startling effect of a bursting artillery shell, Big Man erupted from behind the boulders to Wheeler's right. He had discarded his rifle and with drawn scalp knife was making the dangerous last charge of a wounded, cornered animal.

Wheeler must have had ice-water flowing in his veins. This apparition lunging toward him, torn with bullet-holes—any one of which would have killed an ordinary man—would have caused any sensible person to blanch with fear. Not Wheeler. Cool and steady as a statue, the bounty hunter fired bullet after bullet into the charging behemoth. The sodden impact of lead against flesh was the only way of telling that he was hitting his mark for Big Man never broke stride. By now, Wheeler was firing rapidly, each bullet taking its terrible toll. Methodically, Wheeler emptied all 16 rounds into the blood-spattered war chief. As Big Man reached him, Wheeler nimbly leaped aside and the giant Indian crashed to the ground, his left leg nearly blown off at the knee. Wheeler calmly reloaded, then blasted the other leg.

"You can come out now," he called over his shoulder in Andrews' direction. Andrews never realized that Wheeler knew he was around. Ashamed, he got to his feet and saw Big Man make a sudden lunge at Wheeler's legs. Wheeler slipped aside, whipped out his revolver and shot him in the arm. When Andrews reached them, Big Man was sprawled back with mouth open, eyes closed and blood spurting from his chest and abdomen. He seemed near death but suddenly blinked open his eyes and stared at Wheeler.

"You ain't beggin' for no mercy are you?" Wheeler exclaimed admiringly. Then in a jovial tone, he asked: "How do you like the way my gun shoots?" The single feather braided into Big Man's shiny hair dipped in acknowledgment that he had heard. "I'll bet my scalp against yours, you don't scalp any more white men in this canyon." Wheeler smiled at his own joke as he levered a bullet into the chamber of his Henry rifle in preparation of cinching that bet.

"Save your ammunition, you killed me . . . give me some whiskey!"[10]

Wheeler knelt close to Big Man and, drawing an ivory-handled Colt .44, gazed at his fallen foe bleeding from 12 wounds in the body with one arm and both legs broken. He was certain the war chief was only minutes from eternity but before going after the whiskey flask in his saddle bags, he lifted the .44 and as Big Man stared back at him unflinchingly, Wheeler shattered his remaining arm. Wheeler had just witnessed one of the most unbelievable exhibitions of brute strength the old West would ever record and he was leaving nothing to chance that Big Man might possibly harm him while his back was turned.

Returning with the whiskey, he gently held Big Man's head as the Snake warrior took a long pull, jerked violently and gasped, "I don't feel so good." His eyes narrowed, "Where are you?" His body stiffened and went limp. Wheeler knew he was holding a dead man in his arms. It was during this period that Andrews claims to have measured Big Man's "corpse" and supplied his vital statistics.[11]

Lowering his body to the ground, Wheeler and Andrews turned to the topic of severing Big Man's feet and taking them to Boise City for identification and the promised reward when a weak voice called for "whiskey!" Startled, Wheeler watched with a high degree of respect as the broken hulk heaved to a sitting position. The ashen mask that was Big Man's face, cracked into a ghastly smile as he saw the stricken look on Andrews' face.

Wheeler again tipped the flask to the Indian's lips. Draining the last of the whiskey, Big Man then asked for water—not to drink—but to wash off his face so his captors could see "what a good looking man" he was. Automatically Andrews got the water and watched while Wheeler performed this last request. Both were pleasantly surprised to see a handsome face emerge from the dirt and blood. The only drawback to an otherwise pleasant countenance was his eyes—large, brown, and wicked—which were now glittering in feverish hatred although his actions belied their murderous intent.

Big Man was becoming quite talkative for he was still fighting for life and could sense help nearby. Any way to prolong death, for he had gathered from Wheeler's last remark that the whites were only stalling for time. Wheeler had asked if he knew that several thousand dollars was being offered for the delivery of his feet to any white settlement east of the Cascades. Big Man knew and offered

---

10 Dick d'Easum, veteran Idaho newspaperman and historian, claimed Wheeler gave Big Man a mixture of ammonia and alcohol "which he always carried for Snake bite." It was his opinion that Big Man, after taking a few gulps "choked to death because he couldn't stand a mixed drink." "Montana" *The Magazine of Western History*, Vol. 7, No. 2, Spring 1957, p. 22.

11 In his letter to the *Idaho Statesman*, November 1878, Andrews wrote: "Bigfoot said he weighed three hundred pounds, I had a tapeline and rule in my pocket with which I took the exact measurements of this wonderful being: Around the chest, 59 inches; height 6 feet 8 1/2 inches; length of foot, 17 1/2 inches; around the ball of the foot, 18 inches; around the widest part of the hand, 18 inches."

Wheeler a deal. If he would spare him the embarrassment of riding into the great beyond minus his feet, he could clear up many mysteries concerning lost wagon trains, the fate of their occupants and more interesting to Wheeler, the hiding places of many stolen gold shipments. Wheeler readily agreed for he planned to get the story and still collect the reward.

And so began Big Man's story . . . somberly and painfully as the life ebbed out of him. Born Starr Wilkerson, the son of a half-breed Oklahoma outlaw and a Cherokee woman, he had joined the Paviotso Confederacy in 1856 after an unpleasant love affair with a white girl.[12] Riding with the Snake dog soldiers, he soon became recognized as one of Has No Horse's ranking war chiefs—sharing honors with Paulina—and known to the Shoshoni nation as Oapiche or Oulux, The Big Man.

Andrews swore that the tale affected John Wheeler deeply because the gunman, also part Cherokee, had been betrayed by a woman. Andrews believed that it was this similar background which led Wheeler to insist on secretly burying Big Man in Reynolds Creek Canyon instead of collecting the reward.

After listening to Big Man's confession, Wheeler and Andrews went down by the creek to await his death. Two hours later, they returned to the scene of the gun fight and . . . the body was gone! Fresh moccasin tracks in the dust told the story. Little Foot and One Eye had returned and packed off the body of their fallen war chief. For some reason, they hadn't touched Biting Bear's body but later events would explain why. There was a more critical thing to attend to—keeping Big Man alive.

Now faced with a missing body—his only proof of having killed Big Man—it became obvious that Wheeler used the excuse that he had given his word to a brother Cherokee not to mutilate his corpse to account for the fact that he didn't try to claim the reward money. Andrews, having seen Wheeler in action and in fear of his own life, was not about to reveal their secret. In fact, in his deathbed confession, Andrews would stick to the story that he and Wheeler buried Big Man "under some rocks and brush, broke his rifle and buried it beside him and left his companion's body where it had fallen."

If they buried anyone—which is unlikely—it was Biting Bear. However, there is some credibility in Andrews' claim that they broke his rifle. In the fall of 1883, five years after Andrews' letter appeared in the *Idaho Statesman*, Charles Adams discovered a rusty old Mississippi Yager near Reynolds Creek where Big Man was said to have been buried. It had been broken off at the breach. Some claimed this proved the "Bigfoot" death story. Remember, Big Man had discarded his empty shotgun and retrieved Biting Bear's weapon for the final duel.

Was Big Man really dead? In a short span of time, he again surfaced—and it wasn't from the grave. At the very moment the Oregon-Idaho frontier was

---

12 For a full account of this part of Starr Wilkerson's (Big Man) life, see Ontko, *Thunder Over the Ochoco*, Vol. II, pp. 275-277.

celebrating his death, Big Man was staging a spectacular recovery in Has No Horse's camp.[13] Four weeks after the shoot-out in Reynolds Creek Canyon, Dave Hill (Wa-ua-laix), second lieutenant in the Klamath Axe and Rifle Squad, stated that Big Man was present with Has No Horse and Pony Blanket at the Fort Harney treaty council, August 24, 1868.

When John Wheeler arrived at Canyon City a few days after the gunfight, he never mentioned anything about burial nor did he give any details as to what happened, saying only that he gave his promise not to mutilate Big Man's body. Men who knew Wheeler never questioned his integrity but they also knew he was not above picking up an extra dollar for a job well done. Five thousand dollars in gold was not to be tossed aside so readily. After all, a dead man has little need for a place to hang his moccasins but that was Wheeler's business. Headlines born on the frontier press soon blazed across the far west in letters two inches high and as red as Big Man's lifeblood proclaiming the death of Bigfoot, the notorious Shoshoni renegade.

Within a few months, Wheeler would be tried and convicted of holding up the Canyon City stage on Mountain Creek in what is now Wheeler County—named for Henry not John. He was sentenced to 10 years in the Oregon Penitentiary. Released short of 10 years on good behavior, Wheeler drifted into California where he resumed his criminal career.

Andrews, also living in California, sent a detailed account of that day on Reynolds Creek to the *Idaho Statesman*. By then Andrews had lost track of Wheeler and didn't know he had been released from prison and was in California. Possibly if he had, he would not have released the story.

On May 4, 1880, Wheeler was sentenced to be hanged for the slaying of a youth during a robbery in which he participated. While the gallows was being readied, Wheeler spent his last hours putting some of his thoughts on paper. "Nine out of every ten men are ungrateful and one-half the men in the world are traitors if put to the test. That man is fortunate that he has more than one or two true friends after his mother dies . . . I never knew a bad woman unless she was made so by man . . . Dogs are true friends, but ladies and birds are the soul-inspiring companions of the world. Without these, all is gloom and darkness."[14] These were the last words of a condemned murderer.

The night before he was to be hanged, John Wheeler committed suicide by taking poison. In life, there was no profit for him in the role of giant-killer.

---

13    Information provided by elderly members of the Snake tribe. Extensive research has revealed one undeniable fact. The reward offered for Big Man's feet was never collected. In 1879, army troops chasing the Sheepkiller Snakes in Idaho's Seven Devil Mountains, reported seeing Big Man and finding his tracks. Although few people have a foot measuring 17 1/2 inches in length, it is unlikely the tracks discovered were Big Man's, because according to the Shoshoni, Big Man later committed suicide or was aided by a trusted friend to end his suffering in 1869.

14    *Montana: The Magazine of Western History*, Vol. 7, No. 2, Spring, 1957, p. 23.

Posthumously, however, he received a sort of recognition which has been given to few convicted felons. In 1940, the Sons and Daughters of Idaho Pioneers erected a plaque commemorating him as the destroyer of the man who had terrorized their ancestors at the lower end of Reynolds Creek Canyon.

Ironically, Henry Wheeler's monument—commemorating the spot where he was attacked by Paulina on Keyes Creek—was placed only a few miles west of John Wheeler's last stagecoach robbery in the state of Oregon.

CHAPTER 149

# PEACE MEDAL

*My people have suffered much for their land.*
*Do you expect me to betray them?*
*Better they die free than live half dead on a reservation.*

**Has No Horse**
Fort Harney, August 1868

Reduced to eating their horses, the final days of the Shoshoni war were marked by fear and starvation. With very little ammunition left, Has No Horse was facing the end. His mountain stronghold was destroyed, most of his family killed and most of his few remaining dog soldiers were being held as prisoners of war in eastern Oregon army stockades. Following in the wake of Bloody Antler's grim news, Has No Horse realized his only recourse was to contact Gen. Crook—whom he believed to be an honorable man—and sue for reasonable terms of surrender.

Two weeks before Has No Horse began his epic ride of destruction, President Johnson's seven man peace commission (one year after their appointment) finally arrived at Fort Bridger. Here they met with the Bannocks (Robber Snakes) and Gourd Rattler's eastern Shoshoni represented by 14 tribal chiefs. A woman claiming to be Sacajawea (which was highly unlikely[1]) persuaded Gourd Rattler it would be to his benefit to sign a treaty which he did July 3, 1868. He was soon to find out about deals made with the United States Government. On Gourd Rattler's request, the eastern Shoshoni were granted a reservation on the Wind River in western Wyoming. Then came the bad news. Gourd Rattler would share the reserve with Little Raven's Arapahos—a people whom the Shoshoni thoroughly detested, referring to them as Dog-eaters.[2]

The Fort Bridger treaty stipulated that the Bannocks, upon being placed upon a reservation on the Portneuf River in southern Idaho, should be entitled to reasonable portions of the Fort Hall and Camas Prairie countries. However, when it came to going onto the reservation, Camas Prairie—the Bannocks' main source

---

1   It was recorded that Sacajawea died at Fort Manuel in present-day South Dakota on December 20, 1812. See *Thunder Over the Ochoco,* Vol. I, pp. 210-211.

2   The Arapahos were the people known to the French as *Gros Ventres,* the Big-bellies.

443

of food supply—was excluded.[3] This omission would contribute heavily to the second Shoshoni war. In view of current proceedings, Has No Horse's chance of negotiating a fair truce was sorely limited.

With his weary braves, Has No Horse set out for Fort Harney. Enroute, he was intercepted by One Eye and Little Foot with more bad news. Big Man—with twelve .44-40 slugs imbedded in his massive frame—was strapped to a travois, more dead than alive. Buzzard Man put his medical knowledge to work and by the time Has No Horse slipped into Wolf Dog's camp on the edge of the Fort Harney parade ground some three weeks later, Big Man was on the road to recovery. He was taken to Pony Blanket's lodge where little Mattie Shenkah—Big Man and Pony Blanket were her uncles—could take care of his needs.[4] It was here, in Pony Blanket's lodge, where Big Man was seen by Dave Hill of the Klamath Axe and Rifle Squad.

Has No Horse arrived at Fort Harney in late August. Anticipating his surrender, government officials saw to it that Crook was well-supplied with trinkets to deal with the toughest war chief in the Pacific Northwest and a crowd of curious settlers had already gathered at Harney City to witness the occasion. Unfortunately, through no fault of their own, half the male population of Canyon City would miss the important event.

In its heyday the wide open frontier town of Canyon City had its share of soiled doves. The miner would refer to these nymphs as girls of the line and they took delight in their company.[5] Working the rich placers in Whiskey Gulch and the heavy-veined lode claims in Blue Canyon, the miners brought a steady flow of nuggets and dust to the purses of the appreciative and ever-so-friendly ladies.

One of these fair maidens was Mademoiselle Louise Du Puy, a lovely girl with a french accent who most likely had been no closer to Paris than the west bank of the Missouri River. It mattered little to the Canyon City boys that her oui-oui was perhaps less than natural, for they adored her. It was said that Mlle. Louise ruled their hearts—and their gold pokes—with a feminine charm that made drunkards sober and sober men mellow.

A few days before the Fort Harney cease-fire, when it was discovered that the lovely Louise was not receiving callers, nor was she even present in her small cottage, the Whiskey Gulch clientele went into a state of panic. The tale soon spread through the mines and saloons that a Spanish Gulch miner had kidnapped her during the night and spirited her away against her will.

3    Treaty with the Eastern Band Shoshoni and Bannock, July 3, 1868, Article 2; Hasley, *The History of Idaho*, pp. 223-24.

4    Mattie Shenkah would allude to this in her conversation with Gen. Howard in 1878. Howard, *Famous Indian Chiefs I have Known*, p. 242.

5    The line was a common term for the prostitution district in the mining and logging camps of eastern Oregon. The line usually consisted of a row of small houses or cabins along a narrow street at the edge of town.

On this sad note a furious posse of lovers was quickly organized, but they had no place to go as no one knew where the bedeviled miscreant had taken her. After searching randomly throughout the numerous mining districts for a week, the would-be rescuers of the fair Louise learned the awful truth. The couple had been married in the mining settlement of Dixie (now Prairie City, Oregon). The posse was dismissed, but it was too late to attend the Fort Harney surrender negotiations now in progress some 70 miles to the south.

It had become a time-honored practice when war robbed the Indian of his last acre, the American gave the Indian a medal. By 1868, quite a lot of medals were given out by the various Great White Fathers living beside the Potomac. The first so-called peace medal was handed out in 1789 by order of that original father, George Washington.

Many warriors did find them quite fascinating, even to the extent of taking them to the grave, which accounts for the scarcity of presidential medals today. And they did cost the government something to make. For instance, in 1841, to cast 260 silver medals—roughly two inches in diameter—bearing the likeness of Martin Van Buren, the federal deficit rose by an even $2,500 of which nearly half went for the purchase of raw silver. However, the government acquired over one million dollars worth of native lands to offset this expenditure.

Some Indians thought these medals possessed supernatural powers, others didn't. Red Sand in a dispute with The Arrow over the signing of the Brunot Treaty, September 13, 1873, hung his Grant medal around his neck and led his warriors into battle. In the exchange of gunfire, Red Sand was knocked off his horse by a low velocity rifle ball which hit the medal. The medal saved his life but Red Sand was angry claiming the medal should have kept the bullet away from him entirely. "Bad medicine," the old Ute grunted in disgust and promptly threw it away.

Having confiscated all Indian lands, the last of the peace medals, bearing the image of Benjamin Harrison, was struck in 1889. Has No Horse was now to be blessed with the profile of Andrew Johnson. He was not impressed.

Knowing that Has No Horse was coming in, Wolf Dog—now held responsible for all actions taken by the western Shoshoni alliance by Crook's June proclamation—and his followers were already assembled at Fort Harney. Joaquin Miller would describe the arrival of the Shoshoni in this manner: "I saw women and children chained together and marched down from their cool, healthy homes in the mountains to degradation and death on the reservation." Not a pleasant sight.

Wolf Dog had a strong incentive for arriving at Fort Harney ahead of schedule. The shackled women and children herded onto the fort parade grounds were the sole survivors of a small group of Shoshoni who were camped two miles south of Suplee Hot Springs at what is now known as Ontko Spring located in the extreme southeast corner of Crook County. On August 5, 1868 an exuberant cavalry troop out of Fort Watson had struck at daylight. When the stench of gunpowder drifted away not a warrior was left alive. Ironically, within four months, a child was born in the central European republic of Bohemia (now called Czechoslovakia) on November 30, 1868. Sixty-four years later, he too would die a tragic death at this same site . . . August 5, 1932.[6]

Two weeks after the Ontko Spring massacre, Has No Horse, Red Willow, Bloody Antler, and Dead Deer rode into Fort Harney. The day after their arrival, the newcomers, along with Wolf Dog's entourage, were ushered onto the parade ground. The headmen of the Snake war tribes—to insure a profitable meeting—were squatted in a huge semi-circle and passing the pipe of peace when Crook and his associates arrived.

The pipe, its two and a half-inch oval bowl made of translucent, green volcanic glass from Glass Butte and the stem decorated with colored feathers, was a work of art. As a mark of respect for the solemn occasion, the Shoshoni before smoking the pipe would remove their moccasins. Each smoker on receiving the pipe would make a different motion with it. One might turn the pipe around before placing it to his lips; another would describe a semi-circle; one smoked with the bowl in the air; the next would puff with the bowl on the ground; this all done with a grave and serious countenance. To the Harney Valley citizens gathered for this momentous occasion, the ceremony appeared ludicrous. Crook understood its importance to the Indians and did not intervene.

When the last man had smoked, the General in full dress uniform stepped forward with Sarah Winnemucca again acting as interpreter. Aware of the man he was now dealing with, there were no preliminaries. Crook in his blunt way told

---

6 In 1885, at the age of 17, Andrew Ontko immigrated to the United States and settled in Pennsylvania where he worked in the Pennsylvania and Illinois coal mines. Here he married Suzann Hvlmonovsky. To this union six children were born—John, Ann, Andrew Jr., Marie, Susan and Adam Thomas. A few weeks after Adam's birth, Suzann Ontko died of pneumonia. Andrew Sr., now left with six motherless children and spurred on by the glowing reports of the Oregon and Western Colonization Company, headed west to take a land claim in central Oregon accompanied by all of his children except for John, who remained in the east. John, who became a Lutheran minister educated in seven languages, also died of pneumonia at the age of 33 while tending to the sick.

By 1932, Andrew Ontko Sr. (the author's grandfather)—who had taken a homestead in the southeast corner of Crook County where Crook, Grant and Harney adjoin—was making last minute preparations to move to his son's ranch (Andrew Jr.) in the upper Ochoco Valley. Then on the morning of August 5, these plans went astray. Ontko had nearly finished haying and was mowing the last field when his team staged a runaway, throwing Ontko off the mower. The left wheel ran over him and caught his head in the machine and he was dragged about 20 feet before being released from the grass cutting machine. Pieced together later from the mute evidence, Ontko then started crawling toward the house but changed his course toward the shade of a juniper tree. Here, he bled to death. Three days later, on August 8, his body was discovered by his son, Andy. Crook County coroner George Meyer, who arrived at the scene of the accident with Sheriff Ben Groff, believed the tragedy must have occurred no later than Friday morning. Orrin Mills, Paulina rancher, was the last person to see Andrew Ontko Sr. alive. ("Runaway team takes life of A. Ontko, Sr., on ranch at Suplee," *Blue Mountain Eagle*, John Day, Oregon, August 17, 1932.)

Has No Horse the terms of the agreement. No promises were made. No apologies were given.

Crook's terms were basic and well defined. He did not offer to place the Snakes on a reservation. In his opinion, a federal reserve was only a place where they would be fed while they loafed and plotted new wars. He simply told Has No Horse that he and his tribesmen were to go back to their old hunting grounds in the Ochoco and so long as they behaved themselves honestly and properly they would not be molested. If the white people came along or interfered with them in any way, they were to come to a military post, the commander of which would be authorized to protect them to the fullest extent of his power. If at any time they were unable to secure food without stealing it from settlers, miners or emigrants, then again they were to come to the post, the commander of which would be authorized to give them food only—and this was stressed—only if he could spare it. This was to be a privilege and not a right.[7]

At no point did Crook mention confinement upon a reservation nor was there a formal touching of the pen to a piece of paper. When he finished speaking, steel gray eyes met with obsidian black and for a moment, the General and the War Chief again locked in combat.

"Well, do you agree?"

Has No Horse pointed to the pitiful Shoshoni children huddled on the alien parade ground, their stomachs swollen by malnutrition; dull eyes sunken with fear and hunger; bodies crippled by disease and festering wounds received in cavalry raids; scars no trooper cared to admit may have come from his sabre or carbine.

"Does that answer your question, Gray Wolf? Many of my warriors lie in the Ochoco. Their guardian spirit sits upon their face. My people have suffered much . . . I accept your terms."

Neither man would break that agreement as given.

One observer at the Fort Harney meeting would note: "Most of the treaty makers sent by the government would have met with Has No Horse in an effusive manner, patted him on the back, told him what a great warrior he was and concluded by making no end of promises for the Great Father to perform. Promises, the majority of which must by necessity have proved as great a myth as the Great Father himself." That was not Crook's style.

This meeting between opposing military commanders was a delicate situation as Crook well knew. The eastern Oregon delegates, grumbling in protest, were doing little to ease strained relations. Many had lost friends, relatives and property in Snake raids; most had sworn vengeance against all Indians; and none had any faith in an Indian promise. Crook explained that he had not made peace out of friendship to the Shoshoni but for the settlers' own safety so that they might

---

7    Nickerson, Azor H., *Major General George Crook and The Indians*, MS, treaty terms given at Camp Harney, August 1868.

447

be spared from further heartache and bloodshed. After much discussion, the citizens of eastern Oregon finally agreed not to throw any obstacles in the way of Crook's arbitration by committing unlawful acts against the Snakes.[8]

Crook had earlier stated that one of the problems the army faced when dealing with the Indians was: "The Indians would confide in us as friends, and we had to witness this unjust treatment of them without the power to help them. Then when they were pushed beyond endurance and would go on the warpath we had to fight when our sympathies were with the Indians." Such was the case with the embattled Shoshoni.

Crook had no faith in reservations, yet he knew that to leave Has No Horse at liberty was courting danger from the Oregonians who would be seeking revenge and which could easily provoke a renewal of hostilities but he did just that. To guard against any repercussions, he had the terms of the Fort Harney agreement published in every newspaper from the Pacific Coast to the Rocky Mountains, appealing to the reason and good judgement of the settlers by reminding them what it had cost to win the peace. He stressed that in Oregon alone, the number of persons known to be killed or wounded in Shoshoni raids was 1,394. Of these, only about 90 were killed or wounded in actual battle. And to emphasize how accurate was the savage marksman only 264 of the victims suffered wounds as opposed to 1,130 killed.[9]

Crook would further shock the citizens of Oregon. No sooner had Has No Horse agreed to the terms of surrender than he invited him and Wolf Dog with a select group of Snake dog soldiers to accompany him to northern California to punish Little Rattlesnake's band of Pit River raiders. Has No Horse, who had ridden so many years side-by-side with Little Rattlesnake, declined the invitation but he gave a nod of consent and immediately 12 of the toughest Snake warriors stepped forward. They were dressed in cavalry uniforms, armed and mounted amidst gasps of dismay from the assembled white settlers. The next morning, the Snake Cavalry left with the last expedition led by Major Gen. Crook in eastern Oregon. The clash with Little Rattlesnake—called the Battle of Devil's Garden—broke Shoshoni power in eastern Oregon.

Although Crook's newfound Snake allies were branded as "heathen wild men" by the Oregon press, army field officers said they proved as loyal and were much more useful than either the Warm Springs or Klamath scouts. Lt. John Bourke, one of Crook's staff officers, on seeing them in action, remarked with admiration: "Only one thought occupied my mind, and that thought was what fools we were not to incorporate these nomads—the finest light cavalry in the world—into our permanent military force."[10]

---

8     Crook, *Autobiography*, p. 159; *Oregon Laws*, 1868, pp. 99-100, 102-103.

9     Bancroft, *History of Oregon*, II, pp. 550-51.

10    Bourke, *On the Border With Crook*, p. 338; Nickerson, *Major Gen. Crook and the Indians*, MS.

In later years Capt. Bourke, in his praise of Gen. Crook as winter Indian fighter on the Great Plains, would tell how Crook gained his experience in the eastern Oregon campaign against the Snakes. During the winter of 1867-68, "his pack trains had been obliged to break their way through snow girth deep and his whole command had been able to make but 33 miles in 12 days—a campaign of which little has been written but which deserves a glorious page in American history as resulting in the complete subjugation of a fierce and crafty tribe." And he would remind the American public that the Snake campaign secured safety for Oregon, Idaho and Nevada miners while "they developed ledges which soon afterwards poured into the national treasury four hundred millions of dollars." Bourke would also note that wonderful as Crook's success had been in defeating Has No Horse's Paviotso Confederacy, had it not have been for General—and soon to be President—Grant, "in all likelihood the outside world would never have heard of it."[11]

For whatever reason—if any—Oregon's seemingly dedicated effort to shield its less desirable characteristics from national scrutiny would also apply to Has No Horse. Had the initial Shoshoni rebellion occurred anywhere else, or even at a different period in time, Has No Horse would have gained the recognition given to Crazy Horse, Joseph and Geronimo.

Has No Horse and Little Rattlesnake were not alone in defeat. Other freedom fighters were also suffering heavy setbacks. Lone Wolf and White Bear, the Kiowa chiefs, had been captured and imprisoned in Texas. Less than a month after Has No Horse's surrender, the great Cheyenne leader The Bat—known to the Americans as Roman Nose—was killed at Beecher's Island by Lt. Col. James Forsyth's Colorado Cavalry.[12] Within six weeks of The Bat's death, Black Kettle was killed on the Washita by Custer's 7th Cavalry in his first engagement against hostile Indians. Little Robe, head chief of the Cheyennes, had lost his two most valuable war chiefs. However, this victory was not purchased without sacrifice. Two cavalry officers and 19 enlisted men were killed on the Washita and one officer and 13 enlisted men severely wounded.

With Has No Horse's surrender a mighty weight seemed to have been lifted off the Pacific states. In September, 1868, Crook—now in full command of the Department of Columbia—moved to Portland where he remained until relieved by Gen. Edward Canby in 1870. In typical understatement, Crook would reflect: "Nothing of note occurred during these two years." Actually, the moment he left the eastern Oregon battlefield, things began to go astray.

---

11    Bourke, *On the Border With Crook*, pp. 253-54; Bourke, *General Crook in the Indian Country*, p. 10.

12    Within 10 years, Forsyth, now a Brig. Gen. in the 1st Cavalry, would march to the North Fork of the John Day River in eastern Oregon and on July 20, 1878, take charge of the final fight in the Bannock War. He was also in command of the 7th Cavalry at the Battle of Wounded Knee, December 29, 1890. Monaghan, ed., *The Book of the American West*, pp.245-257.

Soon after Crook arrived in Portland, he was invited to Salem to attend the seating of the legislative assembly and receive the thanks of that body on behalf of the grateful citizens of Oregon.[13] Had the Indian Department acted at that time, things may have gone more smoothly in its negotiations with the Snakes. As it was, three months would pass before Superintendent Huntington reacted. Finally, on December 10, 1868, he "dashed to Fort Harney" and attempted to draw up a treaty with Wolf Dog, Storm Cloud, Pony Blanket, Dead Deer, Left Hand, and Sweet Root. It was a wasted effort.

One article of this proposed treaty—which was never ratified by Congress—stated that "In case wrong has been done or committed by whites, redress is guaranteed." This provision could not or would not be honored. The only clause stipulated by Crook was omitted. It stated that "all chiefs who turn themselves in voluntarily at this time will not be tried for crimes committed." The assembled chiefs were not rushing forward to sign Huntington's latest covenant. They remembered the terms of surrender.

In essence, Crook had told them, "You are free as air so long as you keep the peace." Now Huntington was arguing that, "You signed a treaty in 1865 which Congress has since ratified and you must go where you agreed to go, or forfeit the benefits of the treaty and we have the power to use the power of the military against you if you don't." Has No Horse and Wolf Dog indicated that they might go to the Klamath Reservation but they refused to stay there. During this debate, Huntington died and was succeeded by Alfred Meacham, who operated a stage station in the Blue Mountains. And Gen. Crook, who could have talked Has No Horse into staying on the reservation, declined to do so.[14]

Crook made few promises, and none that he could not keep. The peace concluded at Fort Harney August 24, 1868 would last for a period of 10 years.[15] When it was broken in 1878, it was caused by the citizens of Idaho, and the settlers of central and eastern Oregon would reap the bitter harvest.

---

13   Oregon Legislative Documents 1868, Governor's Message, p. 4-5; Oregon House Journal 1868, Senate Joint Resolution, No. 6, pp. 85-86.

14   Military Correspondence, Department of the Columbia, December 7, 1869.

15   General Halleck, in his report of September 22, 1868 states: "The Indian war which has been waged for many years in southern Oregon and Idaho and the northern parts of California and Nevada, had been conducted with great energy and success by General Crook since he took command in that section of country. On the twenty-second of August he reported that about eight hundred hostile Inidans had surrendered and that the war was virtually closed." *Message and Documents,* 40th Congress, 2nd session, abridgement, op. cit, p. 367; see also *Crook's Report,* p. 383.

# Appendices

LIST OF SHOSHONI NAMES
BIBLIOGRAPHY
TREATY REPRODUCTIONS
INDEX

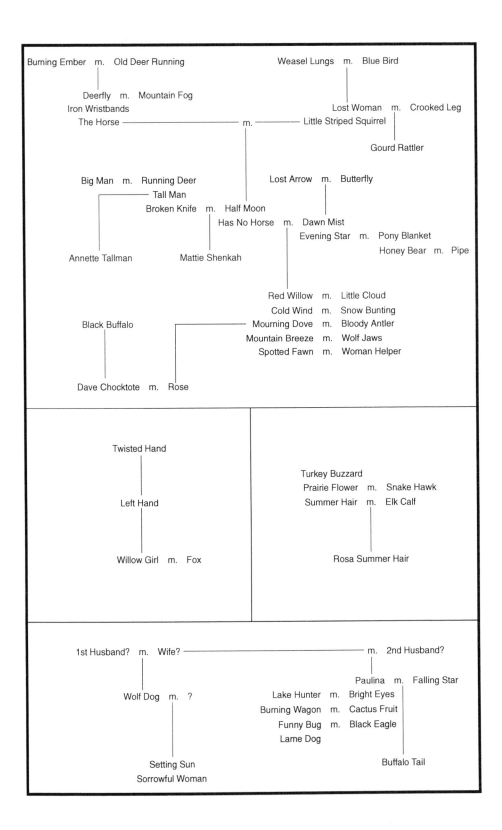

# LIST OF SHOSHONI NAMES

## The following is a list of the known Shoshoni who fought to protect the Ochoco from American invasion

| TRANSLATION | NAME | OTHER INFORMATION |
|---|---|---|
| Always Ready | | Signed Bruneau Treaty 1866. |
| Annette Tallman | Odukeoi | Daughter of Tall Man, resident of Prineville, born 1859; mother killed by Warm Springs scouts along the John Day River in 1859. |
| Arrow | Ouray | Head chief Northern Utes 1859. Part Apache. |
| Bad Face | Wobitsawahkah; Winnemucca the Younger; Mubetawaka, Poito | Son-in-law to old Winnemucca (One Moccasin), The Giver of Spiritual Gifts; wife Tuboitonie; surrendered June 1868; poisoned 1882. |
| Beads | | War chief Bannock War; shot 1878. |
| Bear Claw | Honaunamp | Hung at The Dalles 1855. |
| Bear Hunter | Honauka | Chief; shot 1863. |
| Bear Skin | | Medicine chief killed by the Arapaho in 1824. Father of Little Bearskin Dick. |
| Big Man | Oapiche; Oulux; Oualuck; Youluk; Howlock; Howlark; Nampa; Bigfoot; Chickocclox; Starr Wilkerson | Married Running Deer 1864; married Rainbow Woman 1867; shot 16 times in 1868 and survived; disappeared in 1869. |
| Big Porcupine | Muinyan | Red Wolf's war chief. |
| Big Rumbling Belly | Kwohitsauq | Medicine chief; father of White Man; grandfather of Wovoka (The Cutter). |
| Big Water | Pahwuko, Yahuskin (Water Belly) | Head chief; died in 1816. |
| Biting Bear | Haune Shastook; Annoyed Bear; Irritated Bear | Signed 1865 treaty; shot 1868; Always Ready's war chief. |
| Black Beard | Toomontso | Man Lost's war chief. |
| Black Buffalo | Chocktote; Chewhatney; Chatchatchuck; Chewhatne; Chokkosi; Sahtootoowe; Chocktoot; Tchaktot; Chowwatnanee; Chacchackchuck; Tchatchaktchaksn | War chief during the Sheepeater War of 1879; father of Dave Chocktote. |
| Black Coal | Tovuveh | Twisted Hand's war chief. |
| Black Eagle | Wahweveh; Weahshau; Kwahu (Eagle Eye) | Often confused with Weahwewa (Wolf Dog) his half brother; brother to Paulina, Bright Eyes and Cactus Fruit. Head war chief in Sheepeater War of 1879. |
| Black Gun | Cameahwait; Tooitecoon | Brother to Sacajawea; died of smallpox 1847. |

| TRANSLATION | NAME | OTHER INFORMATION |
|---|---|---|
| Black Spirit | Tamanmo; War Jack | Spiritual leader in Sheepeater War of 1879; killed by firing squad 1879. |
| Bloody Antler | Alatuvu | Married Mourning Dove; son-in-law to Has No Horse; daughter Rose married Dave Chocktote; shot in 1898. |
| Blue Bird | Chosro | Wife of Weasel Lungs; mother of Little Striped Squirrel; died of typhoid in 1838. |
| Boy | Natchez | Son of Bad Face; brother to Sarah Winnemucca. |
| Bright Eyes | | Sister to Paulina and Black Eagle; married Lake Hunter; died in 1867. |
| Broken Knife | Shenkah; Shezhe; Shaka | Brother to Tall Man and Running Deer (sister). Brother-in-law to Has No Horse and Pony Blanket. Married to Half Moon. Shot in 1866. Signed treaties of 1855 and 1865. |
| Buffalo Horn | Kotsotiala | War chief; shot in 1878. |
| Buffalo Meat | Ahtootoowe; Amaroko; Buffalo Meat Under the Shoulder | Signed 1865 treaty; shot in 1867. |
| Buffalo Tail | Peter Pahnina | Paulina's son; taken captive by Oregon Volunteers 1865; served as Warm Springs scout during Modoc War in 1873. |
| Burning Ember | Kooyahtovu | Wife of Old Deer Running; grandmother of Has No Horse; died of cholera 1832. |
| Burning Wagon | Enkaltoik; Enkaltoak; Tovucoona | Brother-in-law to Paulina, Black Eagle and Wolf Dog; shot in 1864. |
| Butterfly | Buli | Wife of Lost His Arrow; mother of Dawn Mist and Evening Star. |
| Buzzard Man | Urie-wishi | Has No Horse's medicine man. Picture in *Handbook of American Indians*, p. 556. |
| Cactus Fruit | Puna | Sister to Paulina, Black Eagle, and Bright Eyes; married Burning Wagon. |
| Cold Wind | Kinauni; Kinauney | Ochoco's son; married Snow Bunting; killed in 1868; 17 years old at the time of death. |
| Cougar Tail | Tahretoonah; Tonouh | War chief; shot 1867. |
| Cow Lick | Nowweepacowick; Nowhoopacowick | Warrior; signed 1865 treaty; shot in 1868. |
| Coyote Hair | Ishauya | Warrior; signed treaty of 1855 (No. 88). |
| Crooked Leg | Paseego | Married Lost Woman; Washakie's father; killed by Blackfeet in 1824. |
| Cut Hair | Wiskin | Medicine chief; succeeded by White Cloud (a white man named James Kimball). |
| Dancer | Genega Taniwah; Tauwadah; Tanwahda; Tanwah | Spiritual leader; shot in 1878. |

| TRANSLATION | NAME | OTHER INFORMATION |
|---|---|---|
| Dawn Mist | | Daughter of Lost Arrow; wife of Has No Horse; mother of Mourning Dove, Mountain Breeze, Red Willow, Cold Wind and Spotted Fawn; shot in 1866. |
| Dead Deer | Masiduedeeheah; Mike Daggett; Shoshoni Mike | Shot by the Nevada State Police in 1911. |
| Death Rattle | Tamowins | Paulina's medicine man; shot in 1864. |
| Deer Fly | Mohwoomkah; Mouche De Daim (Fly of the Deer) | Son of Old Deer Running; brother to The Horse and Iron Wristbands; shot in 1856. |
| Elk Calf | Chaizralelio | War chief; married to Summer Hair; shot in 1865. |
| Elk Tongue | | War chief; shot in 1787. |
| Evening Star | Ashohu | Sister to Dawn Mist; married to Pony Blanket; shot in 1878. |
| Falling Star | Shohu | Wife of Paulina; spiritual leader; sometimes called Wild Wind. |
| Fish Man | Numaga | Minor Paiute head man who signed the 1863 Ruby Valley Treaty. |
| Four Crows | Watsequeorda | Clan chief; face branded in 1845 by members of Lost Wagon Train; shot as a prisoner of war in Oct. 1867. |
| Fox | Wahi | Surger, son-in-law to Left Hand; married Willow Girl; shot in 1878. |
| Funny Bug | Leliotu | Sister of Lame Dog; wife of Black Eagle; sister-in-law to Paulina. |
| Good Man | Teyuwit, Tasowitz | Clan chief. |
| Gourd Rattler | Washakie; Washaki; Washano; Washekeek; The Rattler; Pinaquanah (Smells of Sugar); Rawhide Rattle; Shoots Straight; Sure Shot; Shoots-On-The-Fly; Shoots Buffalo Running; Gambler's Gourd; Buffalo Killer | Son of Crooked Leg and Lost Woman; head chief eastern Shoshoni nation; died February 23, 1900 of old age. |
| Grass Woman | Boinaiv; Porivo; Sacajawea | Sister to Black Gun; died December 20, 1812 at Fort Manuel. |
| Gray Head | Tosarke | Spiritual leader; shot in 1866. |
| Great Rogue | Tasokwainberakt; Le Grand Coquin | Weighed 275 pounds; head chief. |
| Ground Owl | Tecolote | War chief; shot in 1866. |
| Hairy Man | Poemacheoh | Clan chief; shot in 1864. |
| Half Horse | Peeyeam | War chief; shot in 1879. |
| Half Moon | | Sister to Has No Horse; wife of Broken Knife; mother of Mattie Shenkah; prophet; murdered in April 1864. |

| TRANSLATION | NAME | OTHER INFORMATION |
|---|---|---|
| Has No Horse......... | Cho-cho-co; .................. Chocho-co-i; Shosho-ko; Chok-ko-si; Ochoco; Ocheko; Ocheo; Otsehoe; Ochoho; Ochiko; The Man Who Has No Horse; Albert Ochiho | Son of The Horse and Little Striped Squirrel; grandson of Old Deer Running; married Dawn Mist; children—Red Willow, Cold Wind, Mourning Dove, Mountain Breeze and Spotted Fawn; granddaughter Agnes Banning Philips; grandsons Tom, Dick, and Harry Ochiho; great grandson Burdette Ochiho. Signed 1869 treaty; shot in 1898 but survived. He was serving a two year prison sentence in Reno, Nevada when he died in 1914. |
| Hawk .............. | Walkara .................... (Hawk of the Mountains) | Head chief of the southern Utes. |
| High Head .......... | Kalama; Kalim............... | Clan chief; signed treaty of 1855. |
| Honey Bear.......... | Penointi .................... | Sister to Pony Blanket; married Pipe; shot, 1878. |
| Horn .............. | Ala;........................ Mopeah | Sometimes called Horned Chief or Horn of Hair on Forehead; war chief in Bannock War; shot in 1878. |
| Horse Trap .......... | Hadsapoke ................... | War chief; shot in 1867. |
| Iron Crow............................... | | Gourd Rattler's war chief. |
| Iron Wristbands ....... | Pahdasherwahundah............ Hiding Bear | Brother to The Horse and Deer Fly; Has No Horse's uncle; succeeded Yellow Hand in 1842; died in 1842 of natural causes. |
| Jerk Meat............................... | | Married Grass Woman's (Sacajawea) imposter; had five children; warrior with Gourd Rattler's eastern Shoshoni. |
| Lake Hunter ......... | Pagorits; Lapakugit ............ | Warrior; imprisoned at Fort Klamath in 1866; killed in 1867. |
| Lame Dog........... | Shirriitze; .................... Sheapchis; Shezhe | Brother to Funny Bug; brother-in-law to Black Eagle; executed in 1867. |
| Laughing Hawk ....... | Tambiago; .................. Laughing Jack | War chief; hung in 1878. |
| Lean Man ........... | Torepe ..................... | Warrior; married Sorrowful Woman; shot in 1864. |
| Left Hand ........... | Otiz; Owitze; Oete; ........... Oits; Awiteitse; Owits; Oytes; Oitis; Oites; Puhiawatse | Prophet; grandson of Twisted Hand; father of Willow Girl; father-in-law to Fox. |
| Leggins............. | Cheegibah .................. | Son of Natchez; grandson of Bad Face; associated with Yellow Jacket. |
| Little Bearskin Dick .... | Honalelo.................... | Medicine chief; shot under a flag of truce in 1878. Son of Bear Skin. |
| Little Cloud ......... | Okuwa ..................... | Married Red Willow. |
| Little Foot........... | Walsac ..................... | Associated with Big Man. |
| Little Lizard ......... | Nana; Nawi;.................. Nuni; Nooey | Signed 1865 treaty at Fort Klamath. |
| Little Rattlesnake ...... | Sieta; ...................... Chihiki | Pit River war chief; surrendered in 1868; shot in 1878. |
| Little Shadow ........ | Siwiin...................... | Wife of Tall Man and mother of Annette Tallman; shot in 1866. |

| TRANSLATION | NAME | OTHER INFORMATION |
|---|---|---|
| Little Striped Squirel | Nanawu | Daughter of Weasel Lungs; wife of The Horse; mother of Has No Horse (Ochoco). |
| Lost Arrow | Paiakoni | Father of Dawn Mist and Evening Star; married Butterfly; father-in-law to Has No Horse; clan chief. |
| Lost Woman | | Daughter of Weasel Lungs and Blue Bird; wife of Crooked Leg; Gourd Rattler's mother. |
| Magpie Man | Uriposiwu | Sheep Killer chief; shot in 1864. |
| Man Lost | Pocatello; Pikatello; Pocatellah; Bokatellah; Paughatello; Man-Who-Strayed-From-The-Trail | Head chief; sons were Tom and John Pocatello. |
| Mattie Shenkah | | Daughter of Broken Knife and Half Moon; died on death march to Fort Simcoe, Washington Territory, in 1879. |
| Moses Brown | Motcunkasket; Moshunkoskkit; Moshenkosket; Moskosket; Moskosket; Moghenkaskit; (Modoc name: Pomoaks) | Head chief; listed in historical records as a Yahooskin Snake, but there was no such tribe. |
| Mountain Breeze | | Has No Horse's daughter; married Wolf Jaws; shot in 1868. |
| Mountain Fog | Pogonip | Deer Fly's son; cousin to Has No Horse; shot in 1868. |
| Mountain Lamb | Umentucken | Red Wolf's daughter; married Joe Meek; killed by a Banattee arrow in 1836. |
| Mourning Dove | Huwitubic | Has No Horse's daughter; married Bloody Antler. |
| No Ribs | Kewatsana; Kepoweetka | Sub-chief; signed 1865 treaty; shot in 1867. |
| Old Bull | Teverewera | Warrior in Bannock War; escaped to Canada in 1878. |
| Old Deer Running | | Father of The Horse, Iron Wristbands, and Deer Fly; married Burning Ember; died of cholera in 1836. |
| Old Woman | Lamneya | Taken prisoner on Lookout Mountain, June 1864. |
| One Eye | Giltewa | Warrior blind in one eye; prisoner at Fort Klamath in 1866. |
| One Moccasin | Wunamuca; Winnemucca; Onennemucca; Captain Truckee; The Giver of Spiritual Gifts | Medicine chief; prophet; father-in-law of Bad Face; died in 1859 of natural causes. |
| Otter Bear | Pansookamotse; Pahagiveto; Otter Beard | Clan chief; killed in May 1864 during a raid on Fort Maury. |
| Pigeon Hawk | Kela; Kele | War chief; first Shoshoni to sign 1855 treaty; beheaded in 1860. |
| Pipe | Chongyo (Charlie) | Medicine man; war chief; brother-in-law to Pony Blanket; shot in 1878. |

| TRANSLATION | NAME | OTHER INFORMATION |
|---|---|---|
| Pit Viper | Chukai; Chumi; Chua (Mud Lizzard) | Warrior in the Bannock War. |
| Pony Blanket | Egan; Eegan; Ehe-gant; Ezichquegah; E.E. Gantt; Weegant; Enkaltoik | Son-in-law to Lost Arrow; married Evening Star; Has No Horse's brother-in-law; succeeded Buffalo Horn as war chief in Bannock War; beheaded in 1878. |
| Prairie Flower | Olsombunwas | Sister to Turkey Buzzard; threatened to kill Kit Carson; married Snake Hawk. |
| Race Horse | Pohave; Parvekee; Pahvissign | War chief in 1878. |
| Rainbow Woman | Tahaka | Second wife of Big Man; taken captive in 1868. |
| Red Sand | Tuwa; Tabby; Taiwe; Tabbi; also known as White Eye | War chief; ally to Has No Horse; signed treaty March 2, 1868. |
| Red Willow | Ochiho | Son of Has No Horse and Dawn Mist; married Little Cloud; natural death. |
| Red Wolf | Gotia; Roux Loup; Rougeatre Loup | Head chief Shoshoni nation; often confused with Twisted Hand; father of Mountain Lamb; father-in-law to Milton Sublette and Joe Meek; died of cholera in 1852. |
| Rippling Voice | | Daughter of Sits-Under-The-Pine; married Wolf Tail. |
| Rock Way | Oraibi | Sub-chief; shot in 1845. |
| Running Deer | | Sister to Broken Knife; called "Little Dear Legs" by soldiers; married Big Man; killed in 1866. |
| Runs Behind | | Warrior in Bannock War; friend of Laughing Hawk. |
| Setting Sun | Tawasi; Tawash | Wolf Dog's son; Paulina's nephew; signed treaty of 1855 at age 17. |
| Shell Flower | Tocmetone; Sarah Winnemucca; Sally | Daughter of Bad Face; Paiute activist; U.S. Army scout and interpreter. |
| Six Feathers | | Warrior; leader of Snake scouts; killed by Gourd Rattler in 1867. |
| Snake Hawk | Wakachau | War chief; married Prairie Flower; signed 1865 treaty; shot in 1865. |
| Snow Bunting | Chisro | Daughter-in-law to Has No Horse; married Cold Wind; killed in April 1868. |
| Snow Spider | Kokyou | War chief; shot in 1868. |
| Sorrowful Woman | | Wolf Dog's daughter; married Lean Man. |
| Speaking Spring | Chakpahu | Medicine chief; died in 1854. |
| Spotted Elk | Chaizra; Boss; Medicine John | Spiritual leader; shot in 1878. |
| Spotted Fawn | Sowinwalelio | Has No Horse's daughter; married Woman Helper; shot in 1868. |

| TRANSLATION | NAME | OTHER INFORMATION |
|---|---|---|
| Spotted Rabbit ........ | Sowiette .................... | Sometime friend of Gourd Rattler; peaceful chief 1840-1860; Snakes wanted his scalp for being a traitor. |
| Starving Dog ......... | Goship ..................... | Clan chief; bullet removed all of his teeth. |
| Stiff Finger .......... | Taghee ..................... | War chief; died in 1871; signed the Treaty of Peace and Friendship in 1863. |
| Storm Cloud .......... | Gshaneepatki; ................ Shaw-nee | War chief; shot in 1878. |
| Summer Hair ................................... | | Sister to Turkey Buzzard; married Elk Calf; their daughter, Rosa Summer Hair, was placed on the Umatilla Reservation where her picture was taken by Major Lee Moorehouse. |
| Sun Hunter .......... | Tebechya; ................... Tebachne | Warrior; member of treaty council of 1868. |
| Swamp Man .......... | Pahragodsohd ................ | Warrior; shot in 1866 on Dry Creek. |
| Sweet Root .......... | Tashego; ................... Jageon; Pasego; Passequah; Pashego; Petego; Pasheco | Snake prophet who caused much religious unrest among the Pacific Northwest tribes in the 1860s and 70s. |
| Swooping Eagle ....... | Tobe ...................... | Guide for Lewis and Clark; died of typhoid in 1838. |
| Tall Man ............. | Odukeo; .................... Tokio; Injun Charley | Father of Annette Tallman; warrior; brother to Broken Knife; shot in 1866. |
| The Climber ......... | Tendoy ..................... | Chief of the Lemhi Snakes; defector. |
| The Cutter........... | Wovoka; .................... Jack Wilson | Son of White Man; founder of the Ghost Dance religion; died September 20, 1932. |
| The Horse............................... | | Father of Has No Horse; son of Old Deer Running; brother of Iron Wristbands (Hiding Bear) and Deer Fly; shot by the Blackfeet in 1833. |
| Three Coyotes ....... | Ponce; ..................... Shoshoni Jack; Bannock Jack; Snake John; Big John; Paiute John; Ishaui; Big Bill; Bannock Bill | With the Mormon John D. Lee in the Mt. Meadow massacre in southwest Utah September 11, 1857. Mother was Apache; tracked down Cochise for the army. |
| Tiny Ant ............. | Leliotu .................... | Married Sun Hunter; captured and imprisoned at Fort Vancouver in 1864. |
| Tobacco Root ......... | Kooyah; .................... Chemma; Cheonma | Warrior; signed 1865 treaty. |
| Turkey Buzzard ....... | Wishoko; ................... Wiskaka | Brother to Prairie Flower and Summer Hair; brother-in-law to Snake Hawk and Elk Calf; doctor who treated Lt. Fremont; signed treaty of 1855; shot in 1868. |
| Twisted Hair........................... | | Clan chief; shot in 1838. |
| Twisted Hand ......... | Owitze; .................... Bad Left Hand; Mauvais Gauche | Took control of Shoshoni nation in 1785; grandfather of Left Hand; shot in 1837. |

459

| TRANSLATION | NAME | OTHER INFORMATION |
|---|---|---|
| Walking Rock | Oderie; Omrshee | Chief of Nevada Snakes; ally to Has No Horse. |
| War Hoop | Weerahoop | Warrior. |
| War Spirit | Paulina; Paluna; Pushican; Paninee; Panaina; Poloni; Paulini; Paunina; Pichkan; Pelinis; Pannina; Purchican; The Brutal Devastator; | Has No Horse's number one war chief; had a scar on his forehead from Gourd Rattler's war axe; signed treaty of 1855; married Falling Star; brother to Black Eagle, Bright Eyes, and Cactus Fruit; half-brother to Wolf Dog; father of Buffalo Tail shot in May 1867. |
| Water Lizard | Momobic; Monoa | Medicine man; at Council Ruby Valley, Nevada, October 1, 1863. |
| White Cloud | James P. Kimball | Succeeded Cut Hair as Wolf Dog's medicine chief; a native American born in New York state in 1829; taken captive by Bear Killer Snakes in 1848; escaped in 1859. |
| White Man | Tavibo; Taviwunshear; Taysoba | Married into Walking Rock's band; father of Wovoka (The Cutter); spiritual leader; died 1870. |
| Willow Girl | Ohoctume | Daughter of Left Hand; married to Fox; shot in 1867. |
| Winter Frost | Oyike | Prophet. |
| Wolf Dog | Weahwewa; Weahweah; Kwewa; Wasenwas; Wewawewa; Weyouwewa; Yewhowewa | Succeeded Red Wolf as head chief of the western Shoshoni nation; half-brother to Paulina, Black Eagle, Bright Eyes and Cactus Fruit; signed treaty of 1855; shot in 1878. |
| Wolf Jaws | Kwewu | Son-in-law to Has No Horse; married Mountain Breeze; in 1880s was Has No Horse's medicine man. Shot by IZ sheep shooters, 1898. |
| Wolf Tail | Kwewatia | War chief. |
| Woman Helper | Tonnat; Tonoyiet | Head game driver, son-in-law to Has No Horse; married Spotted Fawn; shot in 1868. |
| Yellow Badger | Sikamonani; Skytiattitk | War chief; shot in 1865. |
| Yellow Hand | Ohamagwaya; Amaquiem; Yellow Wrist | Commanche prophet; often confused with Twisted Hand; associated with Shoshoni by 1820; succeeded by Iron Wristbands (Hiding Bear) in 1842; died natural death, 1841. |
| Yellow Jacket | Potoptuah; Paddy Cap; Paddy; Whitka; Padé Kape | Head chief; army scout; served as a double agent; signed treaty of 1855; placed on the Duck Valley reservation on the Oregon-Nevada border in 1878; listed as a "mounted Paiute." |

*Note:*
All historical documents and newspaper articles refer to Big Man as Oulux,
which in Chinook Jargon means The Snake.

# THE SNAKE WAR TRIBES
## Which Comprised the Paviotso Confederacy

| ENGLISH TRANSLATION | SHOSHONI TRIBE |
| --- | --- |
| Antelope Hunter | Togwingani, Pit River |
| Bear Killer | Hunipui, Hoonebooey |
| Big Lodge | Tuziyammo |
| Big Nose | Motsai, Gwinidba |
| Bird People | Kuyuidika, Giditika, Gidutikadu |
| Buffalo Killer | Saidyuka |
| Dog Ribs | Shirrydika |
| Juniper People | Lohim |
| Mountain People | Walpapi (a minor offshoot of the Hunipui) |
| Pony Stealer | Wahtatkin, Wadihtchi |
| Robber | Banattee, Bannock |
| Rye Grass People | Waradicka, Wadatika |
| Sheep Killer | Tukaricka, Tukuarika, Tukaduka |
| Sun Hunter | Tebeckya |
| White Knife | Tussawehee, Tosawi |
| Wild Sage People | Pohoi, Pohogwe |

The northern Utes were also involved in the Confederacy.

**NOTE:** Such terms as "Kutshundika" (Buffalo Eaters) or "Agoitika" (Salmon Eaters), etc. were not tribal names. The same people could call themselves both depending on what they were hunting or eating at the time. Dr. Sven Liljeblad who did extensive research on the Shoshoni and their culture has this to say: "To interpret them as tribes as has frequently been done in literature is utterly wrong." Anyone who has interviewed the old-time Shoshoni will find this to be a true statement.

.

# BIBLIOGRAPHY

## Books, Manuscripts and Pamphlets

- Adams, James Truslow, *The Epic of America*, Washington, D.C., 1931.
- Amundson, John, "History of the Willamette Valley and Cascade Mountain Wagon Road Company," University of Oregon Thesis Series #17, 1928.
- Angel, Myron, *History of Nevada with Illustrations and Biographical Sketches of its Prominent Men and Pioneers*, Oakland, 1881.
- Applegate, Lindsay, *Applegate Collection*, Oregon Historical Society, MS.
- Armstrong, David A., *Bullets and Bureaucrats: The Machine Gun and the United States Army, 1861-1916*, Westport, New York, 1982.
- Arnold, R. Ross, *Indian Wars of Idaho*, Caldwell, 1932.
- Ascherman, Butch, *Fort Bidwell*, Private 1981.
- Bailey, Paul, *Wovoka, The Indian Messiah*, Los Angeles, 1957.
- Bancroft, H.H., *History of Oregon*, II (2 Vols.), San Francisco, 1886-1888.
- Bernard, Kenneth A., *Lincoln and the News of the Civil War,* Caldwell, Idaho, 1966.
- Bledsoe, Anthony Jennings, *The Indian Wars of the Northwest*, San Francisco, 1885.
- Bourke, Captain John G., *On the Border With Crook*, New York, 1891.
- Brace, Charles Loring, *The New West: or California in 1867-1868,* New York, 1869.
- Brackett, Albert G., *History of the United States Cavalry,* New York, 1865.
- Brady, Cyrus Townsend, *Northwestern Fights and Fighters*, New York, 1907.
- Brandon, William, *The American Heritage Book of Indians*, New York, 1961.
- Brown, J. Henry, *Autobiography; Military Information*, MS, N.D.
- Brown, J. Henry, *Political History of Oregon From 1865-1876*, San Francisco, 1885.
- Bullfinch, Thomas, *Oregon and Eldorado*, Boston, 1866.
- Butler, _____, *Life and Times of the 1860's*, MS, Bancroft Library, Berkeley, California.
- Capps, Benjamin, *The Great Chiefs*, Time-Life Books, New York, 1975.
- Capps, Benjamin, *The Indians*, Time-Life Books, New York, 1973.
- Carey, Charles Henry, *A General History of Oregon*, Vols. II and III (6 vols.), Portland, 1922.
- Carrington, Margaret, *Ab-So-Ra-Ka, Home of the Crows*, Philadelphia, 1868.
- Catton, Bruce, *Mr. Lincoln's Army*, New York, 1958.
- Clark, Don E., *The West in American History*, N.D.
- Cole, Henry E., *Stage Coach and Tavern Tales*, Cleveland, 1930.
- Corning, Howard McKinley, (ed.), *Dictionary of Oregon History*, Portland, 1956.
- Dimsdale, Thomas J., *The Vigilantes of Montana*, Virginia City, Montana, 1866.
- Dodge, Richard Irving, *The Plains of the Great West and Their Inhabitants*, New York, 1877.
- Douglas, C.L., *The Gentlemen in White,* Dallas, Texas, 1934.
- Downey, Fairfax, *Indian Fighting Army*, New York, 1941.

- Drake, Capt. John M., *Expedition from Fort Dalles, Oregon into the Indian Country 1864-65*, Oregon Historical Quarterly, Portland, Oregon, Vol. LXV, March 1964.

- Drannon, Capt. William F. *35 Years on the Plains and the Mountains: Or the Last Voice from the Plains*, Chicago 1904.

- Drawson, Maynard C., *Treasures of the Oregon Country*, Salem, 1973.

- Drew, Charles S., *Official Report of the Owyhee Reconnaissance 1864*, Jacksonville, Oregon, 1865.

- Dunn, J.P. Jr., *Massacre of the Mountains: A History of the Indian Wars of the Far West*, New York, 1886.

- Ebey, (Mrs.) Winfield S., *Journal*, MS, Vol. II (12 vols.), Bancroft Library, Berkeley.

- Forsyth, George A., *The Story of the Soldiers*, New York, 1955.

- Foster-Harris, *The Look of the Old West*, New York, 1955.

- Gaston, Joseph, *Portland, Its History and Builders* (3 vols.), Chicago, 1911.

- Gatschet, Albert S., *The Klamath Indians of Southwest Oregon*, Washington, D.C., 1890.

- Ghent, W.J., *The Road to Oregon*, New York, 1929.

- Gibbs, Addison C., *Collection*, Oregon Historical Society, Scrapbook 5.

- Gilliss, Julia, *So Far From Home: An Army Bride on the Western Frontier, 1865-1869*, Oregon Historical Society Press, Portland 1962.

- Glassley, Ray H. *Pacific Northwest Indian Wars*, Portland, Oregon, 1953.

- Gluckman, Arcadi, *United States Martial Pistols and Revolvers*, New York, 1944.

- Gluckman, Arcadi, *United States Muskets, Rifles and Carbines,* New York, 1948.

- Grant, Ulysses S., *Personal Memoirs of U.S. Grant*, New York, 1894.

- Hailey, John, *The History of Idaho*, Boise, 1910.

- Haines, Francis, *Nez Perce and Shoshoni Influences*, Greater American Series, Berkeley, 1945.

- Hamersley, T.H.S., *Complete Army and Navy Register of the United States of America*, N.D.

- Hanely, Mike, *Owyhee Trails: the West's Forgotten Corner*, Caldwell, Idaho, 1974.

- Hart, Herbert M., *Old Forts of the Northwest*, Seattle, 1963.

- Hart, Herbert M., *Pioneer Forts of the West*, New York, 1967.

- Hasley, John, *The History of Idaho*, Caldwell, Idaho, 1961.

- Haven, Charles T. & Frank A. Belden, *A History of the Colt Revolver and Other Arms Made by Colt's Patent Fire Arms Manufacturing Company From 1836 to 1940*, New York, 1940.

- Hayes, Benjamin, *Scrapbooks, 1850-1874*, Vol. V (129 vols.), Bancroft Library, Berkeley.

- Heline, Theodore, *The American Indian*, Los Angeles, 1952.

- Hodge, Frederick Webb (ed.), *Handbook of North American Indians North of Mexico*, Bureau of American Ethnology, Smithsonian Institution Bulletin 30, 2 vols., Washington, D.C., 1907.

- Hopkins, Sarah Winnemucca, *Life Among the Paiutes: Their Wrongs and Claims*, privately printed in 1883.

- Howard, Maj. Gen. O.O., *Famous Indian Chiefs I have Known*, New York, 1908.

- Howard, Maj. Gen. O.O., *My Life and Experiences Among Our Hostile Indians*, Hartford, 1907.

- Howe, Carrol B., *Ancient Tribes of the Klamath Country*, Portland, 1968.

- Howe, Carrol B., *Unconquered, Uncontrolled: the Klamath Reservation*, Bend 1992.
- Hull, William, *Autobiography*, Daughters of the Utah Pioneers, N.D.
- Hungerford, Edward, *Wells Fargo: Advancing the American Frontier*, New York, 1949.
- Hunter, George, *Reminiscences of An Old Timer: A Recital of the Actual Events, Hardships and Escapes of a Pioneer, Hunter, Miner and Scout of the Pacific Northwest*, San Francisco, 1887.
- Jackson, Helen Hunt, *A Century of Dishonor*, Boston, 1909.
- Jacobs, Allen F., "The Last Days of Chief Paulina," *Metal Detection Publication,* 1996.
- Johnson, Lonnie, *An Historic Conservation Program: Silver City, Idaho*, BLM Publication, 1975.
- Josephy, Alvin M. (ed.), *The Great West*, New York, 1965.
- Karolevitz, Robert F., *Newspapering in the Old West*, New York, 1965.
- Kean, Roger H., "Dr. William Cameron McKay," *Pacific Northwest Collection*, University of Oregon Medical School Library, Portland, 1933.
- Kimball, James, *Eleven Years a Captive Among the Snake Indians*, Cleveland, Ohio, 1861.
- Kip, Lawrence, *Army Life on the Pacific*, Redfield, 1859.
- Knight, Oliver, *Following the Indian Wars; The Story of the Newspaper Correspondents Among the Indian Campaigners*, University of Oklahoma, 1960.
- Knuth, Priscilla (ed.), "Cavalry in the Indian Country," *Oregon Historical Quarterly*, Vol. LXV, No. 1, March 1964.
- Langford, Nathaniel Pitt, *Vigilante Days and Ways: The Pioneers of the Rockies, the Makers and Making of Montana, Idaho, Oregon, Washington and Wyoming*, Missoula, 1957.
- Lord, Elizabeth, *Reminiscences of Eastern Oregon*, Portland, 1903.
- Lyon, Juana Fraser, "Archie McIntosh, the Scottish Indian Scout," *Journal of Arizona History*, VII, Autumn 1966.
- Mack, Effie Mona, *Nevada: A History of the State from the Earliest Times Through the Civil War*, Glendale, 1936.
- Madsen, Brigham D., *The Northern Shoshoni*, Caldwell, Idaho, 1980.
- McArthur, Lewis A., *Oregon Geographic Names*, Portland, 1974.
- McConnell, W.J., *Early History of Idaho*, Caldwell, Idaho, 1913.
- McCoy, Keith, *Melodic Whistles in the Columbia River Gorge*, Pahto Publications, White Salmon, Washington, 1995.
- McCroskey, William B., *An Architectural Survey of Silver City, Idaho*, BLM Publication, 1977.
- McKay, William, *Journal 1866-67*, Oregon Historical Society, 1978.
- McKay, William, *Papers*, Umatilla County Library, Pendleton, Oregon.
- McLeod, William C., *The American Indian Frontier*, N.D.
- McLoughlin, Denis, *Wild and Wooly: An Encyclopedia of the Old West*, New York, 1975.
- McNeal, William H., *The History of Wasco County*, The Dalles, Oregon, 1953.
- Meade, Irene Kimnear, *Some Early Day School Events in the Wind River Valley*, MS, Crowheart, Wyoming.
- Meier, Gary and Gloria, *Those Naughty Ladies of the Old Northwest*, Bend, Oregon, 1990.

- Miller, C.H., Report, Senate Executive Document No. 36, 36th Congress, 2d Session, Series 984.
- Monaghan, Jay (ed.), *The Book of the American West*, New York, 1963.
- Nevin, David, *The Expressmen*, Time-Life Books, New York, 1974.
- Nickerson, Azor H., *Major Gen. Crook and the Indians*, MS, Army War College Library, Washington, D.C., 1869.
- Noble, Lt. John F., *Diary of 1st Oregon Cavalry 1864* (4 notebooks), State Archives, Salem, Oregon.
- Oliver, Herman, *Gold and Cattle Country*, Portland, 1962.
- Ontko, Andrew Gale, *Thunder Over the Ochoco*, Vol. II (4 vols.), Maverick Publications, Bend, Oregon, 1994.
- Palmer, William R., *Pahuite Indian Legends*, Portland, 1946.
- Peterson, Ethel M., *Oregon Indian and Indian Policy*, Salem, 1939.
- Peterson, Martin S., *Joaquin Miller, Literary Frontiersman*, Palo Alto, California, 1937.
- Powers, Alfred, *History of Oregon Literature*, Portland, 1936.
- Reck, Franklin M., *The Romance of American Transportation*, New York, 1938.
- Reese, John Major, *The Indian Problems in Utah 1849-1868*, Undated University of Utah Master of Science Thesis.
- Reiter, Joan Swallow, *The Women*, Time-Life Books, New York, 1978.
- Rinehart, Maj. W.V., 1st O.V.C., *Campaign Against Chief Paulina, June 1862 to December 1863*, MS, Oregon State Archives, Salem.
- Ruby, Robert H. & John A. Brown, *A Guide to the Indian Tribes of the Pacific Northwest*, University of Oklahoma Press, 1986.
- Schmitt, Martin F. (ed.), *General George Crook, His Autobiography*, University of Oklahoma Press, 1946.
- Schmitt, Martin F. & Dee Brown, *Fighting Indians of the West*, New York, 1968.
- Scott, H.W., *History of Oregon Country*, Vol. V (6 vols.), Cambridge, 1924.
- Scott, R.N., *War of the Rebellion: A compilation of the Official Records of the Union and Confederate Armies*, Vols. XIII and L (130 vols.), Washington, D.C., 1880-1901.
- Seton, Ernest Thompson, *Gospel of the Redman*, Los Angeles, 1948.
- Shane, Ralph M., *Early Exploration Through Warm Springs Reservation*, Portland, 1950.
- Shaver, Fred (ed.), *The Illustrated History of Central Oregon*, Spokane, 1905.
- Sherman, Stuart P. (ed.), *The Poetical Works of Joaquin Miller*, London, 1923.
- Skovlin, Jon M. & Donna McDaniel, *Hank Vaughan (1849-1893), A Hell-Raising Horse Trader of the Bunchgrass Territory.* Reflections Publishing Co., Cove, Oregon, 1996.
- Smith, John E., *Bethel, Polk County Oregon*, Portland, 1941.
- Spencer, William V., *Spencer Collection*, Oregon Historical Society, Portland.
- Spier, Leslie, Klamath Ethnography, Berkeley, 1930.
- Starr, _____, *Idaho*, MS, Boise Library.
- Stern, Theodore, *The Klamath Tribe*, University of Washington Press, Seattle, 1967.

- Stone, Irving, *Men to Match My Mountains: The Opening of the West 1840-1900,* Garden City, New York, 1956.
- Stoutenburgh, John L., *Dictionary of the American Indian,* New York, 1960.
- Strahorn, Carrie Adell, *Fifteen Thousand Miles By Stage: A Woman's Unique Experience During Thirty Years of Path Finding and Pioneering From the Missouri to the Pacific and From Alaska to Mexico,* Vol. I (2 vols.), New York, 1911.
- Talbot, Ethelbert, *My People of the Plains,* New York, 1906.
- Thompson, Col. William, *Reminiscences of a Pioneer,* San Francisco, 1912.
- Trenhold, Virginia Cole & Maurine Carley, *The Shoshonis: Sentinels of the Rockies,* University of Oklahoma Press, 1964.
- Voegelin, Erminie Wheeler, "The Northern Paiute of Central Oregon: A Chapter in Treaty Making", *Ethnohistory,* No. 2, Indiana University, Spring 1955.
- Waymire, Lt. James (Co. D, 1st O.V.C.), "Historical Correspondence," *San Francisco Evening Post,* October 28, 1882.
- Wheat, Margaret M., *Survival Arts of the Primitive Paiutes,* Reno, Nevada, 1967.
- Wheat, Margaret M., *Notes on Paviotso Material Culture,* No. 1, Carson City, Nevada, 1959.
- Whiting, Beatrice Blyth, *Paiute Sorcery,* Anthropology Publication No. 15, New York, 1950.
- Winther, Oscar Osburn, *The Great Northwest,* New York, 1947.

# State and U.S. Government Documents and Legislative Reports

- Annual Reports 1859-1869, U.S. Superintendent of Indian Affairs
- Annual Reports 1860-1869, Adjutant General of Oregon
- Annual Reports 1860-1869, U.S. Commissioner of Indian Affairs
- Annual Reports 1863-1869, U.S. Secretary of War
- Bureau of Indian Affairs, Idaho Superintendency, Field Papers, Letters Received and Annual Reports 1865-1869
- Bureau of Indian Affairs, Oregon Superintendency, Field Papers, Letters Received and Annual Reports 1859-1869
- Congressional Document Series 1220
- Congressional Globe 1860-1861, Major Steen's Military Road Report
- Congressional Globe 1865-1866, Military Records, Paulina's Attack on Fort Klamath, Pt. V
- Crawford, Medorem, Journal of the Expedition Organized for the Protection of Emigrants to Oregon, January 9, 1863, Senate Executive Document 17, 37th Congress, 3rd Session.
- Grant County Mining Records 1864-1865
- Lane County, Oregon, Luckey Family Records No. 12133
- Military Correspondence, Department of the Columbia 1868-1869
- Military Correspondence, Department of the Pacific 1858-1868
- Military Correspondence, First Oregon Cavalry 1863-1865
- Military District of Oregon, General Orders 1863-1865

- Official Army Register 1866-1867
- Oregon Code 1862
- Oregon General Laws 1845-1864
- Oregon House Journals 1860-1868
- Oregon Legislative Documents 1860-69
- Oregon Senate Journals 1860-1866
- Pacific Railroad Report 1857
- Political History of Oregon from 1864-1869
- Senate Miscellaneous Documents 1860-1869
- Statutes at Large and Treaties of the United States 1851-1875
- U.S. Adjutant General Office, General Orders, Special Orders and Circulars 1859-1869
- U.S. Army Division of the Pacific, General Orders, General Court Martial Orders, Special Orders and Circulars, 1852-1879
- U.S. Census for 1860 and 1870
- U.S. House and Senate Executive Documents 1859-1869
- U.S. Inspector Generals Department, Outline Descriptions of the Posts and Stations of Troops in the Geographical Divisions and Departments of the United States, Washington, D.C., 1872
- U.S. Messages and documents 1859-1869
- U.S. Secretary of Interior Report for the Years 1867-1868, Vol. III, Part II, 40th Congress, 2nd Session, Gov. Woods' order to kill Shoshoni regardless of age, sex or condition
- U.S. Senate Miscellaneous Document No. 59, Lt. Col. Charles Drew's account of the origin and early prosecution of the Indian War in Oregon
- U.S. Statutes at Large, Indian Treaties, Vols. 13, 15, 16, 18, Washington D.C.
- U.S. War Department Annual Reports 1859-1869
- Wasco County, Oregon, Marriage Records 1855-1865

# Miscellaneous Material

- *American Heritage Magazine*, Vol. VII, No. 6; Vol. VIII, No. 6.
- Baker County Sketch Book, N.D.
- Biographical Directory of the American Congress, 1774-1949.
- Bourke, Capt. John G., "General Crook in Indian Country," *Century Magazine*, Vol. XLI, No. 5, March 1891.
- Bowman, Hank, "Ten Guns That Built America," *Cavalier*, Vol. 7, No. 68, February 1959.
- "General Crook in Indian Country," *Century Magazine*, Vol. XLI, No. 5, March 1891.
- *Grit Magazine*, December 24, 1972.
- *Harper's Weekly,* February 12, 1859.
- *Historical Register and Directory of the U.S. Army 1789-1903*, 2 Vols., Washington D.C., 1903.
- *Idaho*, Idaho's Writer's Project, Oxford University Press 1950.

- Kappler, Charles J. (complier), Indian Affairs, Laws and Treaties, Senate Doc. No. 452, Serial No. 4254, Vol. II, 57th Congress, 1st Session, Washington D.C., 1904.
- McKay, Donald, Captain 1st Warm Springs Scouts, *Official Report to Oregon Headquarters, Salem from Fort Steele*, Ochoco Country, January 10, 1867.
- *Military Map of Eastern Oregon Indian Battles 1863-1865*, Western Guide Publications, Corvallis, Oregon 1972.
- *Montana: The Magazine of Western History*, Vol. 7, No. 2, Spring 1957.
- *Oregon Argus*, 1860, 1862, 1863.
- *Oregon Historic Landmarks*, Eastern Oregon Society D.A.R., 1959.
- *Oregon Historical Quarterly*, Vols. IX, XVII, XXI, LV, LXXIX, XLVII.
- *Overland Monthly*, Vol. II, 1869.
- *Pacific Northwest Quarterly*, October 1870.
- Parnell, Lt. William R., "Operations Against Hostile Indians with General Crook, 1866-1868," (Battle of Infernal Caverns) *The United Service*, Vol. I, Nos. 5-6, May-June 1889.
- Pony Express and Overland Mail," *True West*, December 1956.
- *Prospector, Cowhand and Sodbuster*, Department of Interior Publication, 1967.
- *Real West*, Vol. 5, No. 24, July 1962.
- Reed, Cyrus A., Report to the Adjutant General of the State of Oregon for the Years 1865-1866.
- *Silver City Final Environmental Statement*, USDI-BLM, 1978.
- Small, Capt. Henry C., Report to the Commanding General, Department of the Columbia, November 1864.
- *The Idaho World*, November 24, 1866.
- *The Oregon Herald*, Washington Territory, September 16, 1859.
- *The Wind River Rendezvous*, Vol. XXI, St. Stephens Indian Mission Foundation.
- Truby, J. David, "Hailstorm of Death," *VFW Magazine*, February 1972.
- *True West*, "Pony Express and Overland Mail," Vols. 2-3, 1955, 1956.
- *Washington Historical Quarterly*, No. 22.
- Welty, Raymond Leo, "The Indian Policy of the Army 1860-1870," *Cavalry Journal*, Vol. 36, No. 148, Washington, D.C., 1927.

# Newspapers

- *Ashland Tidings* (Ashland, Oregon)
- *Blue Mountain Eagle* (John Day, Oregon)
- *Boise City Statesman* (Boise, Idaho)
- *Central Oregon Shopper,* "Old Timers Edition," August 4, 1949 (Prineville, Oregon)
- *Central Oregonian* (Prineville, Oregon)
- *Daily News* (Alta, California)
- *Daily Oregonian* (Portland, Oregon)

- *Desert News* (Salt Lake City, Utah)
- *Eugene Register Guard* (Eugene, Oregon)
- *Evening Post* (San Francisco, California)
- *Idaho State Journal* (Pocatello, Idaho)
- *Idaho Statesman* (Boise, Idaho)
- *Jacksonville Reporter* (Jacksonville, Oregon)
- *Morning Oregonian* (Portland, Oregon)
- *Olympia Herald* (Olympia, Washington Territory)
- *Olympia Pioneer and Democrat* (Olympia, Washington Territory)
- *Olympia Standard* (Olympia, Washington Territory)
- *Oregon Journal* (Portland, Oregon)
- *Oregon Spectator* (Oregon City, Oregon)
- *Oregon Statesman* (Salem, Oregon)
- *Oregonian* (Portland, Oregon)
- *Owyhee Avalanche* (Silver City, Idaho)
- *Owyhee News* (Silver City, Idaho)
- *Placer Herald* (Auburn, California)
- *Portland Daily Herald* (Portland, Oregon)
- *Puget Sound Herald* (Seattle, Washington Territory)
- *Reese River Reveille* (Austin, Nevada)
- *Sacramento Union* (Sacramento, California)
- *San Francisco Alta* (San Francisco, California)
- *The Bulletin* (Bend, Oregon)
- *The Dalles Mountaineer* (The Dalles, Oregon)
- *Whitcom Reveille* (Kalispell, Montana)
- *Yreka Union* (Yreka, California)

# 1864 TREATY

# 1865 TREATY

TREATY

BETWEEN

## THE UNITED STATES OF AMERICA

AND THE

### WOLL-PAH-PE TRIBE OF SNAKE INDIANS.

CONCLUDED AUGUST 12, 1865.
RATIFICATION ADVISED JULY 5, 1866.
PROCLAIMED JULY 10, 1866.

Articles of Agreement and Convention, made and concluded, at Sprague River Valley, the twelfth day of August in the year one thousand eight hundred and sixty five by J. W. P. Huntington, Superintendent of Indian Affairs in Oregon, on the part of the United States, and the undersigned Chiefs and Headmen of the Woll-pah-pe tribe of Snake Indians, acting in behalf of said tribe, being duly authorized so to do.

Article I. Peace is declared henceforth between the United States and the Woll-pah-pe tribe of Snake Indians, and as between said tribe and all other tribes in amity with the United States. All prisoners and slaves held by the Woll-pah-pe tribe, whether the same are white persons or members of Indian tribes in amity with the United States shall be released, and all persons belonging to the said Woll-pah-pe tribe now held as prisoners or slaves by other Indian Tribes, shall be given up.

Article II. The said tribe hereby cedes and relinquishes to the United States all their right, title and interest to the country occupied by them, described as follows, to wit: Beginning at the point that is the Summit of the Blue Mountain Range near the heads of the Canon Grande River and the North Fork of John Day's River, thence down said North Fork of John Day's River to its junction with the South Fork, thence due south to Crooked River, thence up Crooked River and the South Fork thereof to its source, thence South Easterly to Harney Lake, thence Southerly to the Heads of Malheur and Burnt Rivers, thence continuing northerly to the place of beginning.

Article III. The said tribe agree to remove forthwith to the Reservation designated by the Treaty concluded on the 15th of October 1864, with the Klamath Moadoc and Yahoo-skin Snake Indians there to remain under the authority and protection of such Indian Agent or other officer as the Government of the United States may assign to such duty, and no member of said tribe shall leave said Reservation for any purpose, without the written consent of the Agent or Superintendent having jurisdiction over said tribe.

Article IV. The said Woll-pah-pe tribe promise to be friendly with the people of the United States, to submit to the authority thereof, and to commit no depredations upon the persons or property of Citizens thereof or of other Indian tribes, and should any member of said tribe commit any such depredations he shall

Article IX  The Tribe are desirous of preventing the use of ardent spirits among themselves, and it is therefore provided that any Indian who brings liquor on to the reservation or who has it in his possession may in addition to the penalties affixed by law, have his or her proportion of the annuities withheld for such time as the President may determine.

Article X  This treaty shall be obligatory upon the contracting parties as soon as the same shall be ratified by the Senate of the United States.

In testimony whereof the said J. W. Perit Huntington, Superintendent of Indian Affairs, and the Undersigned Chiefs and Headmen of the Tribe aforesaid, have hereunto set their Signatures and seals at the place and on the day and year above written.

# INDEX

# THUNDER
## OVER THE OCHOCO

### VOLUME I: *The Gathering Storm*

Covering hundreds of years from pre-Columbian times to the collapse of the world fur trade in 1840, Volume I meets the Shoshoni Indians before the arrival of the Europeans and tracks their rise from peaceful eastern Oregon agriculturists to the aggressive Snake war tribes, rulers of the Pacific Northwest. By 1812, they had clashed with every major world power in their jealous guardianship of a land they called Oyerungun. Their undisputed hunting grounds beyond the setting sun would soon become coveted by white foreigners searching first for precious metals and later for valuable fur-bearing animals. The gathering storms of hatred would hover ominously on the distant horizons. Volume I chronicles the events which inevitably would lead to war.

### VOLUME II: *Distant Thunder*

The twenty-year period between 1840 and 1860 would see overland migration across the land known to the Shoshoni as the Ochoco—Land of the Red Willow. The Americans would call it eastern Oregon. Never on friendly terms with the white invaders, the Shoshoni tolerated passage across their ancestral hunting grounds only so long as the American homesteaders stayed strictly on the dusty thoroughfare called the Oregon Trail. When they transgressed, the distant thunder of gunfire reverberated across interior Oregon like the tolling of a death knell. Volume II narrates the suffering, heartache and death of those unfortunate souls who dared to venture into the Ochoco; and it covers the first brutal Indian wars fought west of the Mississippi River.

### VOLUME III: *Lightning Strikes!*

Between 1860 and 1869 rich deposits of gold were discovered in eastern Oregon, and the citizens of the Willamette Valley were out to claim their share at any cost. Shoshoni dog soldiers were equally determined that they keep to their side of the Cascade barrier. War was officially declared. The opposing forces went for each other's throats locked in a death struggle that seemed endless. The crashing crescendo of thunder was accompanied by lightning strikes of destruction which ricocheted into four western states—and the military campaign they thought would last but a few weeks stretched into years. In flashing raids, Shoshoni dog soldiers humiliated the Oregon Cavalry, taking a deadly toll on mining settlements, homesteads, stagecoaches and wagon trains. It would take a battle-hardened army baptized in the carnage of the Civil War four years to bring the Shoshoni to their knees: an aggressor with unlimited resources pitted against a foe that was undermanned, undernourished and outgunned—but desperately fighting for survival. Volume III is the story of the first violent Shoshoni outbreak, which would again erupt in the 1870s.

## VOLUME IV: *Rain of Tears*

The thirteen year interval between 1866 and 1879 would witness monumental changes in the Ochoco. With the surrender of Has No Horse's battered army, western Oregon had free rein to exploit the Ochoco as it saw fit. In a blind daze, the Shoshoni would witness frontier towns springing up where their lodges had once stood. As thousands upon thousands of bawling cattle and sheep trampled their ancestral hunting grounds to dust, the proud warriors of a by-gone year again rebelled. And, for a fleeting moment, shook the state of Oregon to its very foundations. Then it was over. Stripped even of reservation rights, the few survivors drifted between the four winds on their final journey into the bitter rain of tears.

## VOLUME V: *And the Juniper Trees Bore Fruit*

Between 1880 and 1916, the birth of industry would give vent to new bloodshed in the Ochoco. Six-shooters roared in the night, ranchers disappeared never to be seen again ... and the Juniper trees bore fruit: the dangling bullet-ridden bodies of men whose only crime was to oppose the land barons who ruled old Crook County with a Winchester rifle and a rawhide rope. As the 19th century staggered to a close, a Shoshoni visionary born in the Ochoco foretold the rebirth of Indian supremacy. His wondrous dream was buried in a common grave at Wounded Knee, South Dakota. By the time the 20th century blundered onto the scene, saddle-blanket blazes hacked into the Ochoco pines marked the deadlines between sheep and cattle range and woe unto him who crossed these barriers. Rifle shots echoed the length and breadth of the Deschutes canyon as the Hill-Harriman railroad giants battled to link central Oregon to the outside world. Ironically, the last Indian war fought in the United States would explode on the Oregon-Nevada border in 1911 when a Shoshoni chief led his followers, armed only with bows and arrows, in a suicidal charge against a group of stockmen. Thus ended the *Thunder Over the Ochoco*. Would the new owners do a better job of managing the land they had wrenched from the Shoshoni? I leave that to other writers to decide.